TAROT MAJORS

G.O. Mebes

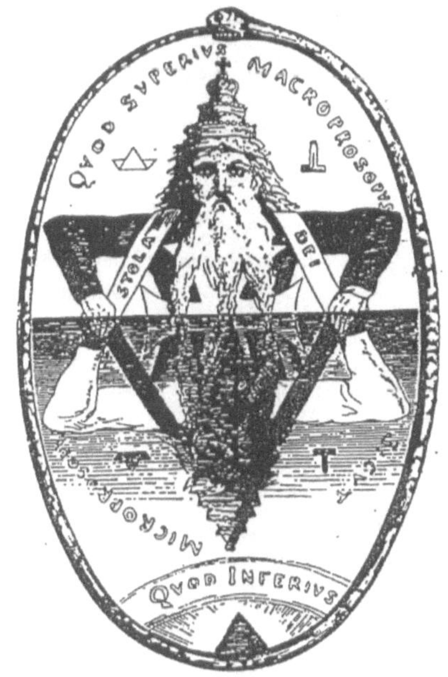

As Above, So Below[1]

with companion notes

Tarot Majors

G.O. Mebes

(Gregory Ottonovich Mebes)

With companion notes

English Translation of text, copyright © 2020 Shin Publications

First Edition

Published 2020 by Shin Publications, England

ISBN: 978-1-9163365-3-7

http://alchemical-weddings.com/

The image on the preceding page Illustration was first published in Eliphas Levi's *Dogme et Rituel de la Haute Magie*. Lévi was inspired by Johannes Trithemius (1462 –1516), who devised a symbol composed of a white triangle joined at the base with a black triangle. The base of the white is inscribed with the Tetragrammaton and the black contains a fool peering at his own reflection. Lévi set much store by this, saying that "By meditating on the pentacle, one will find "the last word of Kabbalism and the unspeakable formula of the Great Arcanum."

Dedicated to Our Lady of Guadalupe and St Francis of Assisi

Stella Maris, ora pro nobis

Contents

In Memoriam

At St. Petersburg in Russia, around fifty years ago, there was a group of esotericists who composed the flower of the capital's "intelligentsia".

At the head of the whole school was the professor of special mathematics from the Pages College in St. Petersburg, Professor Gregory Ottonovitch Mebes.

Now, it was after the Bolshevik revolution (which, it goes without saying, put an end to this group and its work) that the one who is writing these lines met some members of this dispersed group and became friends with them. The friendship being true, i.e. based on unreserved mutual confidence, they (who belonged to the so-called "Rosicrucian" elite of the group) transmitted all that they knew and recounted everything concerning the work of their group, including the crises and painful experiences that they had undergone.

This was in 1920. It was then that the one who is writing these lines - although he had already studied the masterly work by the engineer Schmakov, Velikiye Arkany Taro ("The Major Arcana of the Tarot") and the book on the Tarot by P.D. Ouspensky in 1917 - was struck to learn to what degree collective work on the Tarot can be fruitful for study, research, training and advancement in the esoteric domain. For the whole work of the Martinist-Templar-Rosicrucian group was founded on the Tarot.

Although the teaching and experiences of this group of St Petersburg esotericists lives now in the soul of the author of these letters only as a general impulse received in his youth to penetrate the symbolism of the tarot more deeply.

It is a matter, therefore...of putting a 'memorial wreath' on the non-existent tomb (ie, non-existent here below) of the group of St Petersburg esotericists from the beginning of this century.

Meditations on the Tarot, Letter XXI, The Fool

About the Author

The collegiate adviser Baron Gregory Ottonovich Mebes was born in Riga in 1868. After graduating in 1891 from the Physics and Mathematics Faculty of St. Petersburg University, Mebes gave up his career and devoted himself entirely to the study of "secret knowledge". In the 1904-1905 school year he taught physics and mathematics at the Czarskoye Selo real school and the Nikolaev gymnasium, as well as physics at the women's school of the Ministry of Public Education; in 1906-1917 he taught mathematics in the Page Corps and Nikolaevsk Cadet Corps. His first wife was Olga Yevgrafovna Nagornova, with whom he broke in 1912, which did not prevent her from subsequently playing a prominent role in Martinism.

The Martinist Lodge, which was a branch of the French Order of the same name (the Kabbalistic Order of the Rose and the Cross), was founded in Russia by the French occultist Gerard Encausse, known under the pseudonym Papus. At the end of 1910, Mebes became the Inspector General (Secretary) of the St. Petersburg branch of the Order, and in 1911-1912 he read in St. Petersburg a lecture course on the Encyclopedia of the Occult, which followed Papus' theory in almost everything. These lectures, published under the pseudonym of G.O.M., were very popular, as evidenced by dozens of memories and reviews.

In August 1912, Mebes tried to be free from the tutelage of the Paris leaders, announcing the proclamation of the independence of the Russian Martinists. The Apollonia lodge, headed by Mebes, (with the initiatory name of Butator[1]) was declared a great lodge (Grand Council of Russia). The situation was cleared up by the end of 1912, after the official report by Mebes, Papus's report about his break with him and the establishment in Russia of an independent order called "Autonomous discharge of Martinism of Russian obedience" led by the "Invisible Master".

In 1913, St. Petersburg Martinists, led by Mebes, formed a special autonomous chain of O.M.O.R. with a pronounced Templar colour. In 1916, it was transformed into the "Order of Martinist Eastern Obedience". It was ruled by the Order of the "Invisible Master" or the Father (G.O.M.). His official representative was the student of Mebes, Inspector-General I.K. Antoshevsky (the initiatory name Hyacinthus). In the summer of 1917, when I.K. Antoshevsky was killed, he was replaced in this position by another student of Mebes – V.V. Bogdanov. The

---

[1] The Guardian Angel Butator is the regent of calculations, who serves in the third hour of the day and is invoked during ritual magic

Chapter of the Order consisted of seven persons and the official print organ of the Russian Martinists was the occult magazine, Isis.

In 1918-1921 Mebes gave lectures on the Book of Zohar in Petrograd, and his second wife Maria Nesterova lectured on the history of religion. The declarative goal that the Russian Martinists had set for themselves was, on the one hand, to prepare the one going for the Highest Initiation (maximum programme), and on the other, to expand the esoteric secondary education of those who were not recognised as capable of the Highest Initiation. In addition to purely theoretical studies, practical work was carried out in the "school" to develop its capabilities for telepathy and psychometry among its members.

Aleksandr M Aseev[2], the publisher of the book "Occultism and Yoga", owns the version according to which all three main branches of the Russian initiating movement – Freemasonry, Martinism and Rosicrucianism – existed in the form of separate and independent organisations. However, they were led by the same person – G.O. Mebes. Needless to say, all three orders worked in close contact with each other and often included the same persons. Martinist and Rosicrucian lodges were located, according to A.M. Aseev, in the apartment of Mebes in the Sands and were beautifully furnished. The text commentator on A.M. Aseev, N. A. Bogomolov, notes, however, that in fact, Mebes' apartment was not in Sand, but at the corner of Greek Avenue and 5th Rozhdestvenskaya Street. This is in fact the case, but Bogomolov does not take into account the fact that in 1917 – early 1918, Mebes really lived for some time in Peski, where he was a teacher. All this indicates that A.M. Aseev was very, very well informed, and his information can, therefore, be trusted, although his conclusion that Mebes was supposedly the unofficial leader of the initiating movement in Russia, not only at the beginning of the century, but also in the 1920s, is a clear exaggeration. Another thing is that the Masons, the Martinists, and the Rosicrucians, in essence, are links of one chain – they have always worked and work in close contact with each other. Their secretive activity in Russia, and then in the USSR, continued until 1925, when the OGPU became seriously interested in their groups and work. In the middle of 1928, the Leningradskaya Pravda and Krasnaya Zvezda newspapers reported that "an investigation into the Great Lodge Astraea, led by 70-year-old Black Occultist Mebes, was opened by KGB agents".

---

[2] Aleksandr M. Aseev (1902-1993) was a medical doctor by profession who founded the annual publication, Occultism and Yoga. Fascinated by Agni Yoga, AM Aseev struck up a correspondence with Nicholas Roerich in 1931 and went onto launch the publication, Occultism and Yoga, in Belgrade, guided by Helene Roerich, wife of Nicholas. The published correspondence between Aseev and Roerich was the highlight of the journal.

The investigation, as claimed by the newspaper, soon showed that Leningrad had "quite serious Masonic lodges with several dozen members, with Masters, with dedication, oaths signed by blood, statute, foreign correspondence and membership fees."
According to AM Aseev, Grigori Ottonovich Mebes died in Ust-Sysolsk in 1930[3].

Notes

In his book, The History of Esotericism in Soviet Russia in the 1920s and 1930s, Konstantin Burmistrov examines the hazardous trajectory of the underground current of occultism and the influence of Maria Nesterova, who in 1916 founded the Society for the Revival of Pure Knowledge and the Martinezist Order.

Another society, the Promethean Group, was established with the purpose of forming an inner circle of G.O.M.'s initiates within the Society, to whom lectures were delivered in secret during the Civil War years (1919-1922). G.O.M. focused on Kabbalah, Nesterova on the history of religion[4] and Boris Astromov[5] led courses on the history of Freemasonry.

Astromov was appointed Inspector General of the Martinist Order by G.O.M. but the two fell into conflict and Astromov founded rival groups, Autonomous Russian Freemasons and the Grand Lodge Astreia. In 1925 he offered his services as an informant to the OGPU – the secret police of the Bolshevik regime - and proceeded to betray his old friends. The swathe of arrests which followed in 1926 became known as the Case of the Leningrad Freemasons.

G.O.M. himself was arrested, accused of being a 'Black Magician' and sent to a gulag on the White Sea islands where he is believed to have

---

[3] Sources:

Aseev A.M. Ordinary orders: Freemasonry, Martinism and Rosicrucianism. Publ. N.A.BoG.O.M.olova // Literary Review. M., 1998, №2.
Brachev V.S. Masons in Russia: from Peter I to the present day. SPb., 2000.
Magee against Stalin. Interfax Time, 08.26.1999.
Serkov A.I. History of Russian Freemasonry. 1845-1945 SPb., 1997.
Finkelstein K., a teacher of mathematics, physics, and French, GO Möbes (kfinkelshteyn.narod.ru).

[4] One wonders if Nesterova was the source of the fascinating treatise on ancient religions given in the Eleventh Arcanum of the present publication.

[5] 1893 – 1941?

died four years later[6]. With the bulk of his work destroyed by the OGPU in the purges of those revolutionary years, the teachings of the great Magus seemed destined to be all but lost in the mists of time[7].
Thankfully, all was not really lost, for in the 1920s Russian esotericist, Catarina Sreznewska-Zelenzeff, was making ready to leave Europe for Brazil when her friend, Nina Rudnikoff – a disciple of G.O.M. who had also escaped Russia – gave Catarina the notes she had written on the Minor Arcana of the Tarot, as taught by G.O.M. to the Promethean Group. Nina asked Catarina to transfer the legacy to someone 'dignified' and capable of preserving the lessons for humanity.
Years later, while she was living in Brazil, Catarina met Nadia Iellatchitch, widow of Gabriel, who had also been a great friend and disciple of G.O.M. The ladies decided to live together and invited Nadia's brother, Alexandre Nikitin-Nevelskoy – another follower of the White Russian mage – to stay with them. With his profound knowledge of esotericism, Alexandre proved to be the 'someone dignified' who would translate the Minor Arcana into Portuguese.
In later years copies of the Encyclopedia of Occultism found their way to Brazil where they were translated by Marta Pecher, who with help translated them into Portuguese under the title Os arcanos Maiores do Tarô. This book was edited by Editora Pensamento, in Brazil.

---

[6] This date might possibly be disputed, as other sources have claimed that G.O.M. died four years later.
[7] The notes of his lectures on the Sefer ha-Zohar given to his closest disciples were amongst those confiscated. Only the text of twelve lectures he gave in 1921 appears to have survived and these were published recently in Russian.

About this book

We have included at the start of each Arcanum an illustration created by Papus (*Gérard Analect Vincent Encausse, 1865 - 1916*) of the relevant Tarot Trumps. These were first published in Paris, 1909, in his book, Le Tarot Divinatoire, Le Livre des Mystères et les Mystères du Livre (The Divinatory Tarot, The Book of the Mysteries and the Mysteries of the Book). These images have been made available to the public domain and can also be found online at: http://insightfulvision.com
Sketched variations of these images were included in the original Russian edition of G.O.M.'s Tarot Majors course. The High Priestess of these images, all of which are coloured with a distinctive blue tone, has been enhanced to make the cover of this book, whilst the fourteenth Arcanum, Temperance, is depicted on the back in honour of our Guardian Angel. We have also found space within the text to include each of these sketches somewhere alongside their relevant Arcana. Following each illustration page are reflections on the Arcana as they have been given by the occult teachers Eliphas Lévi (Alphonse Louis Constant, 1810 - 1875), Paul Christian (Jean-Baptiste Pitois, 1811-1877) and P.D. Ouspensky (Pyotr Demianovich Ouspenskii, 1878 – 1947). These were not part of GOM's original book. We have included them in an attempt to help synthesise and draw closer together various threads of the tradition, and to provide material for reflection which we hope will complement the core work of G.O.M.
This is not an arbitrary whim, for the attainment of 'Transcendental Synthesis' is a key hermetic task and readers will see many instances of G.O.M. using the term 'synthetic' in his own lecture material. This urge to 'synthesise' is partly inspired by the idea that there is a 'Perennial Philosophy', wherein all of the world's religious traditions are seen as tapping a single fountain of metaphysical truth from which all knowledge – both esoteric and exoteric – originates and has sprung from. This idea of a unified font of wisdom was inspired by the neo-Platonism of the Renaissance and its concept of the 'One' source of divinity. The integration of Hermeticism with Hellenistic and Judeo-Christian thought was carried out in the 15th Century by Marsilio Ficino (1433-1499), amongst others.
Alongside the symbolic representations of Papus, gems of insight from Lévi have been included to acknowledge his status as a founding father of the Western Mystery tradition. Based upon the 16th century treatise, Christian Cabala, by Athanasius Kircher, Lévi's Dogme et Rituel de la Haute Magie (Dogma and Ritual of Transcendental Magic, 1856) became the gold standard of European esoteric studies. Lévi associated

each Tarot Trump with a letter of the Hebrew alphabet and integrated all
78 cards into the Kabbalistic Tree of Life. He emphasised the mysteries
of the Tetragrammaton, the four Hebrew letters which denote the name
of God spelled, ה ו ה י (typically pronounced as 'Adonay' to shield the
sacred name from taint or abuse). Almost half a century later, Papus
also focused on this holy name as a word of power and used it as the
foundation for his system of Tarot correspondences. As readers shall see,
the hero of the present book, G.O.M, fully embraced this system and
used the same correspondences in his own course on the Tarot Majors.
Paul Christian was an almost exact contemporary of Lévi and their lives
show certain parallels. They both undertook serious monastic training
and were a hair's breadth away from joining the priesthood before
becoming more fully absorbed in the occult studies which fascinated
them. Christian encountered Lévi in 1852 and became rising star
amongst other pupils and seekers, emerging as a leader of the occultists
who followed in the master's wake. His survey of occult history and
practice, Historie de la Magie, du monde Surnaturel et de la fatalité à
travers les Temps et les Peuples (1870) (trs: History of Magic, the
Supernatural World and Fate, through Times and Peoples), was a
popular success in Paris society, which by this time was enthralled by
the occult. Christian gained some renown as an astrologer – a rare art at
that time in Paris - and developed his own system of Kabbalistic
Astrology, an area of study which was also of great interest to G.O.M.
In his excellent publication, Eliphas Lévi and the French Occult Revival,
Christopher McIntosh cites from Le Petit Homme rouge des Tuileries by
the clairvoyant Mlle Le Normand: "Only two men in Paris read the
future like an open book". By these two she meant Lévi and Christian,
who she described respectively as a "solitary magus" and an "eagle in
his eyrie".
As for the relevance of tarot symbolism to occultists, this is summed up
rather well in a little book published in 1913 by Ouspensky, who might
possibly have encountered G.O.M. during his time in St Petersburg:

*The history of the Tarot is a great puzzle. During the Middle Ages, when
it first appeared historically, there existed a tendency to build up
synthetic symbolical or logical systems of the same sort as Ars Magna
by Raymond Lully[8]. But productions similar to the Tarot exist in India
and China, so that we cannot possibly think it one of those systems
created during the Middle Ages in Europe; it is also evidently connected
with the Ancient Mysteries and the Egyptian Initiations. Although its
origin is in oblivion and the aim of its author or authors quite unknown,*

---

[8] Ramon Llull, Third Order of St Francis (c.1232, Palma, Majorca – c.1315, Palma, Majorca)

there is no doubt whatever that it is the most complete code of Hermetic symbolism we possess[9].

There is no sound evidence that Ouspensky was an initiate of G.O.M., but he was clearly inspired by the same esoteric ferment which brewed in St Petersburg at that time. By including some of his visions we have hoped to 'build a bridge' and to keep the magic circle open, so to speak, whilst encouraging readers to awaken into their own personal reflections on the Arcana. Let nothing here be set in stone, rather let it be blown by the wind, for:

The wind blows where it wills, and you hear the sound of it, but you do not know whence it comes or whither it goes (John iii, 8).

Mouni Sadhu (Mieczyslaw Demetriusz Sudowski, 1897 – 1971), who reproduced much of G.O.M's work in the book, The Tarot - A Contemporary Course on the Quintessence of Hermetic Occultism (1962), claimed that Ouspensky's early occult master was G.O.M., but we cannot be sure of Mouni Sadhu's reliability as a source. Ouspensky's Symbolism of the Tarot is in concord with the teachings of Eliphas Lévi, Papus and G.O.M. in many respects, especially in its emphasis on associations between the first four Arcana and the letters of the Tetragrammaton. On the other hand, Ouspensky's numerical ordering of the Tarot Majors does not precisely match that of the others, which is a significant difference. Would a close disciple of G.O.M. have got this wrong or dared to contradict his numbering?
The companion notes we have included at the end of each Arcana are primarily based upon the work of Valentin Tomberg (February 27, 1900 – February 24, 1973), whose Meditations on the Tarot (MotT) is considered a masterwork of Christian Hermeticism. Indeed, it was more than two decades of studying this sublime opus which inspired us to learn more about the equally enigmatic schoolmaster, G.O.M. For more about this, please see our Afterword, from page 470.

---

[9] The Symbolism of the Tarot, 1913, St Petersburg.

Foreword

Over the course of the past few years we have been working on this original translation of G.O.M.'s masterwork, with the invaluable help of Russian, Portuguese and Dutch friends and a lot of time spent with online translation programmes.

Lacking the advanced polyglot skills of the masters whose titanic footsteps we have attempted to faithfully follow, we have done the best we can in accordance with our knowledge and abilities. Our sincere hope with this work is that we shall both honour the memory of the Master G.O.M. and answer the call made by Valentin Tomberg in the twentieth Arcanum of Meditations on the Tarot, The Judgement, where he requests the reader to become an unreserved "trustee of the task in question", should they consent to do so:

"If you consent, do all that you judge to be proper"

The task in question is to continue the theurgical work of this spiritual stream and to develop 'The Book' which rests upon the lap of The High Priestess.

At the time of writing it is almost exactly 100 years since the most advanced teachings of G.O.M. were shared with Valentin Tomberg and we have strongly sensed that the time has come for the rich threads of the tradition they represent to be woven together.

We do not flatter ourselves that we are able to complete this monumental task alone, especially given that such work involves 'administering' the fruit of intellectual and spiritual attainment far superior to our own. We can but try to make the way forward a little bit easier for anyone else who is willing and able to take up this mantle in future.

We have spent over two decades studying the works of Tomberg and he is more familiar to us than G.O.M., though both men are mysterious, as esoteric masters are wont to be. Whilst there are significant differences between their work, the bonds of history, culture and fraternal affection which unite them are a joy to behold for those of us who love them.

By reinforcing the connection between these two occult masters we hope to fortify the structure of the road that is to be walked by Christian Hermeticists of the future, to smooth over points along the way where much became unclear, either lost in time or confused by the dividing roads taken by later path walkers.

Drinking afresh from the fountain of wisdom that is Meditations on the Tarot, in the light of our later study of G.O.M., we were delighted to see countless indicators of Tomberg's early education in the secret schoolrooms of St Petersburg and later in Estonia with G.O.M.'s intimate disciples. A turn of phrase here and a specific point of teaching there make clear the indelible impression left upon him by his teacher, though they are subtle tributes, the product of a well-formed magical memory and touching proof that we cannot help but *remember* who and what we love.

It is with the help of Meditations on the Tarot that we came to understand what many intuitively know, which is that memory is integral to higher supernatural realms: *We remember, we awaken, we live, or we forget, we sleep and we die.* Let us, then, be awakened to our memories of the divine, that we may live in the House of the Lord; in the green pastures and beside the still waters.

In addition to such sentiments, there is another important reason for our recourse to Tomberg for assistance with the commentary on G.O.M.'s Tarot Majors course. The latter was in some definite sense preparing his students for one of the most tragic periods of history, in and around the two World Wars, and his work is uncompromising. Such rigour also reflects the requirements of masonic degrees, of which he was the grand Master, and underscores the peculiar qualities of the Russian mind, which is, we shall wager, intrinsically more psychic and suited to occultism than most.

The inner sanctum of G.O.M.'s threefold study group was strictly limited to carefully selected pupils who were deemed capable of a high degree of initiation. This is strong meat, and it was brought into the world during terrible – some might say apocalyptic - times in one of the most dangerous possible environments on Earth, especially for a practising magician.

With Tomberg's later text, written from a place of comparative safety (albeit following a long, hard journey) and with the benefit of much wisdom, hindsight and Christian piety, we are given a highly refined resolution to the 22 Major Arcana. These are introduced with a potent reminder that is to be impressed upon the minds of all readers, that the yoke should be easy and the burden light, as offered by the Master Jesus via St Matthew's Gospel, ch. 11 (28-30).

It is worth bearing in mind that not all those who digested the teachings of G.O.M. went on to become dazzling luminaries of the universal faith, as in the case of Tomberg, or devoted followers who were able to safeguard their Master's work for posterity, as in the case of Nina Rudnikoff and Catarina Sreznewska-Zelenzeff. Certain members of the G.O.M. circle went onto form occult groups of their own where some of the practices they engaged in did, in our opinion, quite clearly cross the line into black magical sorcery. You will read in the present volume what the teacher had to say about black and white magic, dark and light initiations.

In desperate times people are pushed to desperate measures, and there is another, more somber reason, for the sense of urgency we feel towards our present mission, as humanity is haunted once again by the dark egrégore of communism and other forms of political extremism. In his foreword to Russian Spirituality and other Essays, Mysteries of our Time seen through the eyes of a Russian Esotericist, by Valentin Tomberg, Robert Powell writes:

"Even though Soviet communism has died, its spirit lives on in a variety of contemporary manifestations – for example in a draconian apparatus for control over the populace on a scale now undreamt of in the Soviet Union. Aided by modern technology, it is more possible than ever for 'big brother' to keep a large portion of humanity under constant surveillance."

Readers can decide for themselves how prescient these words - published for the first time in 2010 – have turned out to be.
By reinforcing and helping to advance the most powerful means of neutralising the radical communist egrégore, which is the collective force of the Western Mystery Tradition and universal Christian devotion, we might hold the balance of this egregious entity in check.
How does one render impotent a monstrous egrégore, the product of millions of minds and souls, generated over the past 100 years, and how might the two extreme poles of contending powers be neutralised?

For the answers, please read on.

Preface to the Russian language book

This book is just a sketch of the panorama of the greatest wisdom
unfolding before us in the evenings that Master has dedicated to us.
We have conveyed the essence of the lectures correctly and accurately,
but, inevitably, I had to greatly reduce the live oral presentation and not
to cite examples from life that so vividly and witty illustrated the
thoughts and positions expressed. Therefore, it is necessary to meditate
upon the text very much in order to extract from it everything that was
transmitted at the lectures.
We have also included here all the elementary instructions regarding the
development of intuition and the power of realisation.
Whoever, having studied this encyclopedia, applies the instructions
contained within it, can fearlessly take up the special branches of those
stages of the Initiation into Occultism, which can be briefly
characterised by the terms "Kabbalistic, Magical and Hermetic cycles".
Perhaps next year it will be possible to print the contents of these special
initiation courses, since this does not contradict the duty of the Secret of
the Initiates [vow of secrecy]. In the meantime, the appearance of this
information would be premature and even harmful.
For the convenience of readers, it was possible to attach an article by
B.M. Pryamina-Morozova, referred to by the lecturer in the presentation
of the fourth Arcanum.
The course of the Encyclopedia that I publish is based upon the Tarot
Major Arcana. According to tradition, the Memphis priests, predicting
the fall of Egyptian civilization, concealed their knowledge in the form
of a deck that is now known by name and bequeathed to the profane,
knowing that through repetition such knowledge would achieve
posterity.
The most important factors in the life of an intelligent person are the
degree of consciousness of life and the degree of realisation power
granted to this person. The desire for the so-called "dedication" is the
pursuit of one or another element, and most often - both.
Initiation is based on the so-called. "Arcanum" and here it will be
appropriate to find out the difference in the meanings of the three terms:
secretum, arcanum, mysterium[10].
Secretum is something that several people, on a whim, fantasy or for
some everyday reason, agreed to hide from others.

---

[10] In MotT the same distinctions are set out and explained in detail towards the start of Letter I,
The Magician.

Arcanum is a mystery whose knowledge is indispensable for understanding a certain group of facts, laws or principles. Without the knowledge of the "Arcanum", nothing can be done in the moment the need for such understanding arises. "Arcanum" is a mystery accessible to a sufficiently diligent intelligence in this sphere. In its broad sense, the term "Arcanum" includes all theoretical science, referring to any practical activity in a given field.

Mysterium is a harmonious system of arcana and secrets, synthesised by a certain school, as the basis of its worldview and the measure of its activity.

Today, the term Arcanum is important to us. An arcanum can be expressed orally, by writing a common language, or even, symbolised. The ancient initiatory centres used the third form of arcana transmission and recorded them symbolically. We can distinguish three types of symbolism:

1. The symbolism of flowers and colours
2. The symbolism of geometric figures and paintings
3. The symbolism of numbers[11]

There has come to us the grandiose monument of the symbolism of the Egyptian schools[12] in which the three types of symbolic presentations come together in a deck, better known as the Gypsy Tarot, or Tarot of the Bohemians, and is composed of 78 cards/letters (22 + 56). These letters represent the so-called Archangels and they consist of 22 Major Arcana and 56 Minor Arcana.

So we will consider tarot as a scheme of the metaphysical worldview of the ancient initiates. But each nation has its own worldview, namely, the language of this nation. If, moreover, the people have a written language, then the elements of the language are represented by its alphabet.

---

[11] The author of the Preface assigns these three symbolic systems to what he terms the 'black race', 'red race' and 'white race', respectively.

[12] The French theologian who was known as Court de Gebelin, was an early proponent of the idea that tarot symbolism was derived from the Egyptian school, which he wrote about in his book Le Monde Primitif (1773). According to Christopher McIntosh in Eliphas Lévi and the French Occult Revival, Court de Geblin's "subsequent career is interesting, for in about 1776 he became a freemason and president of a Paris lodge". This Egyptian-Tarot thesis was picked up by one, 'Alliette, who became another prominent exponent of Tarot under an anagram of this name by which he is better known: Etteilla. To the Egyptian idea he added the idea that 171 years after the flood, "seventeen magi had collaborated for four years to produce" this symbolic system, originally conceived by Hermes Trismegistus, "which was therefore called the Book of Thoth." (ibid). McIntosh asserts that Etteilla is also significant in this field of study for synthesising popular kabbala into the work.

Thus, our tarot will be a kind of initiatory alphabet. The general outline of the illustration will be the outline of the language(s) of this alphabet; details of the illustrations, their shades and colours, with our comments on these signs. We will associate the 22 major arcana of tarot with the hieroglyphs of the. Hebrew alphabet

The signs of this alphabet are assigned certain numerical values, in the order in which we will consider them, bearing in mind the motto of the White Race "all by number, measure, weight."

One way or another, a numerical representation is associated with each card. These images, according to legend, were placed on the walls of subterranean galleries, which the neophyte penetrated only after a series of tests. Each letter, in one way or another, corresponds to a numerical value. According to tradition. The Tarot is considered a scheme of the worldview of Initiates of antiquity.

It is true that people have their own vision of the world expressed by their language. If an individual makes use of writing, language elements are also presented in the alphabet. Consequently, the Tarot can be considered as an initiatory alphabet. The [trump] cards represent the letters of this alphabet. The details of the cards and the shades of their colours constitute symbolic details about those letters."

We proceed to the Arcana.

Arcanum 1

א

THE MAGICIAN

Pathway from Keter to Tiphareth

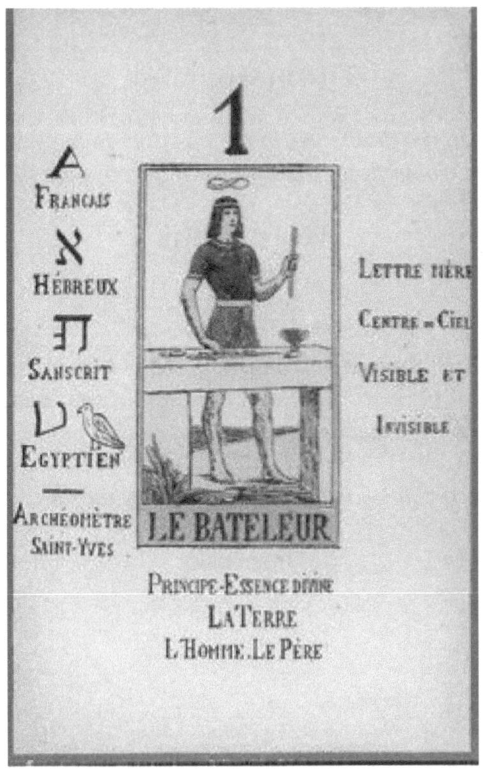

The Magician has *Discipline*

A prayer is a perfected act of will, it is a link connecting human words with the divine Will. All ceremonies, consecrations, ablutions, and sacrifices are prayers in action, and are symbolic formulas; and they are the most potent prayers because they are translations of word into action.

Levi

THE MAGUS: Will

A--1 expresses in the divine world the absolute Being who contains and from whom flows the infinity of all possible things

Paul Christian

His face was luminous and serene, and, when his eyes met mine, I felt that he saw most intimate recesses of my soul. I saw myself reflected in him as in a mirror and in his eyes I seemed to look upon myself.

And I heard a voice saying: --"Look, this is the Great Magician!

Ouspensky

The sign of the Hebrew alphabet corresponding to this Arcanum is א (Aleph) and its numbers is 1. On this card is depicted a man standing, holding a wand in his right hand, which is raised up; with his left hand, the man points to the earth, so that, in general, his figure resembles the aleph symbol itself. The sign of Infinity is inscribed above his head; the head is crowned with a golden hoop; he is belted with a golden belt; in front of him is a table of cubic form; at the disposal of a man, in addition to the wand (or baton) in his hand, are three more objects lying on the table — a bowl, a sword, and a coin. Thus, the picture, in addition to a hint of the trinity (a human body that neutralises oppositely directed hands), still speaks of some mysterious four objects.

Let us first deal with the interpretation of the dual position of the arms/hands.

In all areas of knowledge there are so-called. "biners" or "binaries," that is, the totality of two polar opposite regions. Metaphysicians speak of essence and substance - two goals to be studied - opposing each other. Scientists speak of principles, opposing facts. Another frequently mentioned binary is spirit-matter. In everyday life we find binaries: Life – death, good - bad and consciousness – very low power of realisation are two examples. The more specialised fields of science offer us various binaries such as light-shadow, heat-cold, etc.

In special subjects, in most cases, it is easy to find the neutralisation of the binaries, that is, the third term, the medium, which constitutes the passage from one of the extreme elements to the other, thus establishing a threefold scale, formed by three degrees of the same manifestation. Consequently, the two, through the third form are united. Between light and shadow is the penumbra, revealing degrees of illumination or, if you prefer, degrees of darkening. Between hot and cold are intermediate temperatures.

Between high and low we find the average and between positive and negative currents the neutral state. The sexual antagonism of husband-wife is neutralised by the birth of the child, which unites them all in a family unit. And so on.

Let us pay attention to the fact that the neutralising middle (third) term possesses, as it were, duality in the construction – by its characteristics it is akin to both extreme terms.

Not all binaries can be neutralised equally easily.

In philosophy, the binary "essence - substance" is satisfactorily neutralised by the term nature, but try to neutralise the binaries:

Spirit – Matter
Life – Death

Good - Evil
Consciousness – Power of Realisation

This task does not seem particularly easy and we will define the term, 'initiation' as being the power to neutralise these two last binaries. This science was part of the ancient Great Mysteries.
The Lesser Mysteries encompassed the cycles of knowledge included in what we now call general education subjects. The neutralisation of the spirit – matter binary is the subject of the so-called. theoretical dedication. The remaining three great binaries will be subjects of practical dedication.
Now we know what we are striving for, we can note general ideas concerning the unitary scale in the form of three steps.
Note the hierarchical principle governing the construction of ternary scaling. The upper step, being the higher hierarchy, *but identical in essence* to the other steps is as if it were simply reflected in these steps, but gradually diminished in intensity.
It is deduced that subaltern power (below) is distinguished from the superior power only by the breadth and intensity of competence, and not by its character. Consequently, an ordinary chief of some subordinates, responsible for different tasks, must have in himself a summary of the competences of these various specialisations. Note also the idea of continuity of passage between one step and another step. We have outlined only three, but in most of the examples cited, passing from one step to another is smooth and continuous.
From the consideration of unitary turners, the possibility of their dual genesis follows. You can proceed from extreme terms, as we did, and get the average.
From the study of the unitary ternaries we deduce that their genesis can be dual. We can proceed from the extreme terms, as we did, and reach the average. We will call this genesis a general kind of ternary (figure 1).

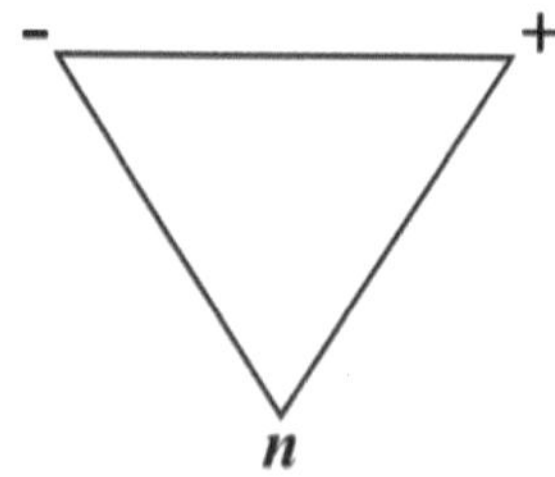

Figure 1

The sign "+" corresponds to the positive pole, that is, to that principle of what we consider expansive, masculine. The "-" sign corresponds to the negative, attractive, feminine pole of the binary. The letter "N" represents the middle term, neutral, androgynous term.

In many examples, no one forbids us to proceed from the middle term and by defining it to define the poles.

Neutral electricity, by the process of surface friction, separates into electrical positivity "+" and negativity "-". Nothing prevents us from considering a partial shade as a shadow space, partially illuminated by a light source, as in twilight.

The child, on the one hand, is attractive to us; he in his growth and nutrition attracts a number of elements; on the other hand, he discovers activity, expansiveness that extends to external objects: both properties are connected in it, and they can be mentally divided in it.

In such cases we will have another type of ternary, to which we will give the name of "Ternary of the Great Arcanum". (figure 2).

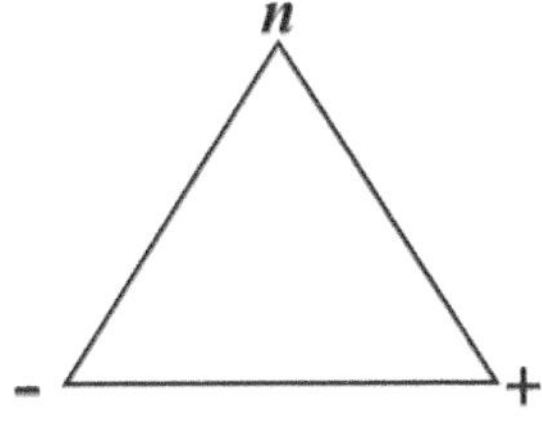

Figure 2

We will leave the ideas for the moment and move on to the method of obtaining them.

Today, using some analogies, we approach the so-called Symbolism. But what is symbolism? It is a method of analogy applied to a particular case.

Let's look at the ternary: Light - Penumbra - Shadow. Under these elements we place other ternaries, and also under the other extreme elements Un-neutralised binaries.

Example:

Light	Penumbra	Shadow
High	Medium	Low
Essence	Nature	Substance
Spirit	-	Matter
Life	-	Death

If I compare all the lines with the first, then I symbolise the elements of all the lines with the elements of the first line; perhaps in one of the lines I neutralised the extreme poles only because the top line prompted me to do this.

Then this will be an example of the realisation power of a symbol in the metaphysical-logical world.

As we can see, in the fourth line we cannot neutralise the "spirit-matter" binary, because the realisation power of the symbol has not yet been found here, but only the possibility of a conditional comparison: "if you liken spirit to light and matter to shadow, then the term I'm searching for corresponds to penumbra. " This is already something.

Let us return to the study of the card of the first Major Arcanum. The figure represents a man, that is, an individual being, which means that the Arcanum of Oneness is, at the same time, the Arcanum of Individuality.

If some elements come to be unified, the group will then live an individual life. Every cell is alive. If several cells come together in a group and form an organ, that organ will become to live an individual life. The organs, grouping together, form an organism, which, in turn, lives an individual life. All the organic kingdoms of the planet, including the mineral, together, form an individual and living manifestation called the planet. A group of planets constitutes a planetary system, and so on to infinity.

In general, a cell considers itself free and struggles for itself with other cells, ignoring the life of the organ and organism and considering such only the environment of its small life; there is no need that an academic scientist, resembling this cell, is equally irreverent towards the Earth and the Solar System, denying them individual life and believing that they are just like the inanimate environment in which his useful activity takes place; the Earth, in turn, faces the life of the wise with the same contempt that he manifests in relation to his renewing cells. Arcanum I reveals to us that these individualisations exist, that not only a group of atoms was individualised into a molecule in the name of life, but that even an artificial group of people united in a collegium individualises and lives a collegial life, treating with contempt the small private interests of each one of its members.

This universal idea is best formulated by Christ in the text: "*... for where two or three are gathered in My name, there I am in the midst of them*" (Matthew, chap. XVIII, art. 20). Outside of the Logos there is no realised life, therefore, "in My name" means - "in the name of life." Returning to the illustration, let us pay attention to the fact that it depicts a man, and, moreover, a man who is standing, a posture that corresponds to the positive, active element. This will serve as an indication for the title of the first Arcanum. This Arcanum is called "Magus" by esotericists, and in common parlance it is called "Le bateleur", that is, a popular juggler who performs in circuses and fairs. For us it represents an active individual being.

If, in the universe, we admit three basic elements: Archetype, Man and Nature, we can establish a theosophical ternary and give the Arcanum a title in each of these three planes:

1. In the plane of the Archetype (active aspect) - "Divine Essentia"
2. On the plane of Humanity (active aspect) - "Vir", the Man
3. In the plane of Nature (active aspect) - "Natura Naturans" (in Spinoza's terminology).

In this brief course, we will study what the Man of our Arcanum means and his individual characteristics, manifested through their activity.
In the activity of Man we perceive, first and foremost, the great binary:

Spirit – Matter

Man, spiritually, lives on the plane of ideas. On the other hand, he expresses himself on the physical plane - material, that is - in the region where the perceptions are realised by the reaction of the senses to concrete or material objects.

Our first effort on the path to self-initiation will be to neutralise the above binary Spirit-Matter we have just mentioned. What asks to link the spirit with matter? What might be the passing from the plane of ideas to the plane of concrete objects?

We will reply: The plan with which Energy determines the Forms. Here is the outline of our stepped ternary:

Spirit - Energy - Matter
Ideas - Forms - Material Objects

We will call this intermediate plane "Astral" and to extremes we will give the names, "Mental" and "Physical".

The transition from the Mental plane to the Astral is accomplished by the process of grouping, juxtaposing, summing up, or, expressing ourselves more exactly, the process of progressive condensation of ideas, governed by the great Law of the Individualisation of the Collectivities, shown above.

If, for a general idea of a polygon, we add the idea of equality of length of its lines, we will devise a new, more condensed, more precise idea of a regular polygon. Compare this idea with the idea of number four. This will produce the idea of a square, which you are already inclined to attribute to the plane of Forms.

Similarly, we can move from the Astral plane to the Physical.

A metal disk fixed on an axis will not scratch a diamond, but if upon the same disk we impose a rapid circular movement or, in other words, increase the amount of its kinetic energy, or even, concentrate on it new astral properties - then it will scratch the diamond.

Thus, by the condensation of the astral can be modified the purely physical properties, in this case the hardness of the periphery of the disc. The passage from the astral to the physical took place, although only partially.

If one concentrates on the desire for a person in another room to perform a certain action, this concentration will consist in a condensation of ideas into images, that is, forms. Holding these forms in the imagination, or, in other words, condensing the desired movement is performed. There will be a demonstration accessible to the senses, thus belonging to the physical plane. Here we have a direct analogy with our first example.

It may be objected that in the first example the immobile disk already possessed a certain degree of hardness - a physical property - and that, by the condensation of the astral, this degree of hardness was only increased; that in the second example the magnetiser not only used his imagination, but, also controlled your breathing according to defined rules and perhaps even performed one or another movement with the body, momentary or continuous, rhythmic or not.

To these objections we can answer with the alchemical aphorism: "To make gold, you must have gold."

This is the law which governs most of the processes taking place in the field of manifestations. We are not required to recreate the Universe, nor do we know how long it would take to do that. It is sufficient that we take a foothold in the achievements already made. We are similar to the man who throws small crystals into a saturated solution to cause a rapid crystallisation of the same solution. Most of the magical operations carried out have the same characteristic: an appropriate choice of points of support.

We do not have an understanding of the coagulation mechanism. We only know how to use the "machine" that already exists. We can, by the intense and persevering effort of the intellect and the will, choose from between machines the most simple and effective, but, the construction of the same, is not our subject.

For this, as we will learn later, there are special entities, known under the name of Angels (within the limits of the mental plane), Spiritus Directors (in the astral plane) and Elementals (on the physical plane). Each has a function.

Thus, we will try to distinguish throughout the Universe and in each of the elements that compose it, even if it is approximately, the spheres of the three planes: mental, astral and physical. They interpenetrate each other but can be studied separately.

In man, consequently, we discern three component elements: "Mens" or spirit, "Anima" or soul, also called astral body or astrosome and, finally, "Corpus" or the physical body.

If the man engages in intellectual work, we will say that Mens and Anima in him are more active than Corpus. If the passionate life or the work of the pure imagination prevails, active or passive, the preponderance belongs to Anima and so on.

We will assume that the Mens of Man, coagulating, determined his soul, or anima; that this Soul, coagulating and taking the materialised (though quite subtly) elements delivered by the parents as a reference point in the physical plane, manages to create a physical body for itself, both for uterine and external life. According to the already planned form, the soul sustains the functions of the physical body, repairing its damage.

To speak of how the Mens directs the functions of the soul, and how it also seeks, eventually, to repair it, it would be too soon.

That is what I wanted to dwell on in this lecture.

I will add only one thing: nothing prevents us from replacing our rough ternary division of the Universe and of Man, on the other, more detailed, in which the planes already enumerated will be divided into sub-planes. We will soon be forced to do this.

Notes on the first Arcanum

The Magician occupies the great catalytic point of the Great Work, the scintillating, activating force which sets the Wheel – the Work - in motion. It is here that we learn there is a direct correlation between personal effort and spiritual reality, with a formula given by the Master Jesus and written in the Gospel of Matthew 11:30:

"My yoke is easy and my burden light"

This formula is picked up very early in MotT, where it is written:

Learn at first concentration without effort; transform work into play; make every yoke that you have accepted easy and every burden that you carry light!

Here The Magician is the "Arcanum of the Arcana", who "reveals that which it is necessary to know and to will in order to enter the school of spiritual exercises whose totality comprises the game of Tarot".
Whilst this first Arcanum is associated with Aleph as the first letter in the Hebrew alphabet, The Magician also occupies a fundamental position as representative of the first letter of the Tetragrammaton – the potent spark of ' – which is further revealed through and completed by the subsequent three Arcana of High Priestess (the He in this equation), Empress (the Vau) and Emperor (final He).
This association of Magician with Aleph is not accepted by all other occultist schools such as The Builders of the Adyton, founded by Paul Foster Case (PFC), who places Aleph with The Fool and numbers this '0'. Eliphas Lévi, G.O.M. and MotT firmly associate The Fool with Shin in the 21st position, acknowledging that this Arcanum is mobile and can also occupy the zero point (See Notes the Twenty-First Arcanum)
One thing all agree on is that "The master-key to the Hebrew wisdom is the "name" pronounced Adonay in Hebrew, translated "Lord" in the Authorised Version of the Bible, and "Jehovah" in the revised versions. It is not really a name at all, but rather a verbal, numerical and geometrical formula. In Roman letters corresponding to Hebrew it is spelt IHVH. This is a noun form derived from a Hebrew verb meaning "to be". Correctly translated, it means

That which was, That which is, That which shall be[13].

The unfolding mysteries of the 22 Arcana are not necessarily presented in the same order by G.O.M. as they are in MotT. For example, it is in Letter IX, The Hermit, of MotT, that the author presents his magisterial denouement of the key hermetic task of neutralising binaries/resolving antinomies, which – as we have already seen –is introduced by G.O.M. from the outset via The Magician.
MotT sets out to deepen our spiritual understanding of the seemingly endless task of neutralising binaries – which G.O.M. describes in largely practical terms - by explaining that it is achieved via a form of transcendental synthesis - resolution above the horizontal plane of the two opposite poles, as in the uppermost point of an ascending triangle. The successful attainment of the ability to resolve antinomies is to be known as the 'Gift of Black Perfection', or 'Gift of Perfect Night' and is equivalent to drawing light from darkness, from the depths of one's self.

---

[13] PFC, Introduction to The Tarot, A Key to the Wisdom of the Ages, p3.

We have already seen the first ascending triangle, presented above by
G.O.M. in The Magician, which is also where the method of analogy is
introduced as the primary means by which to resolve binaries.
It seems this method was well known to students of magic, for as
Ouspensky writes in Chapter VI of Tertium Organum: "A series of
analogies and comparisons are used for the definition of that which can
be, and that which cannot be, in the region of the higher dimension…Let
us try to investigate everything that this method of analogy can yield".
There are further resonances with G.O.M. in his Symbolism of the Tarot,
where he agrees that:

*The basic idea of the Kabala consists in the study of the Name of God in
its manifestation. Jehovah in Hebrew is spelt by four letters, Iod, He,
Vau and He--I. H. V. H. To these four letters is given the deepest
symbolical meaning. The first letter expresses the active principle, the
beginning or first cause, motion, energy, "I"; the second letter expresses
the passive element, inertia, quietude, "not I;" the third, the balance of
opposites, "form"; and the fourth, the result or latent energy.
The Kabbalists affirm that every phenomenon and every object consists
of these four principles, i.e., that every object and every phenomenon
consists of the Name of God (The Word),--Logos.
The study of this Name and the finding of it in everything constitutes the
main problem of Kabalistic philosophy....There is a complete
correspondence between the Kabbala and Alchemy and Magic. In
Alchemy the four elements which constitute the real world are called
fire, water, air and earth; these fully correspond in significance with the
four kabbalistic letters. In Magic they are expressed as the four classes
of spirits: elves (or salamanders), undines, sylphs and gnomes.*

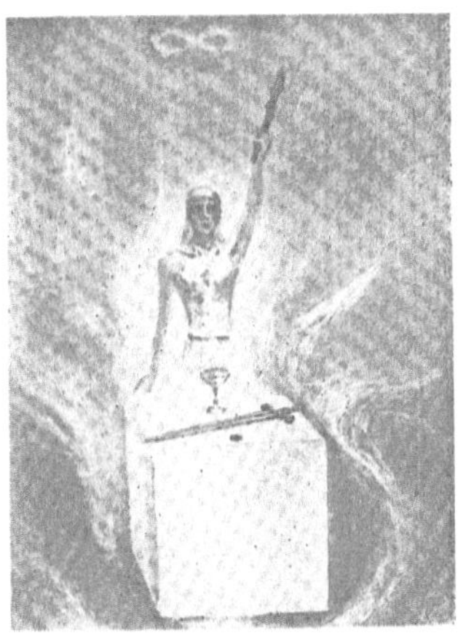

Arcanum II

THE HIGH PRIESTESS

Pathway from Keter to Chokmah

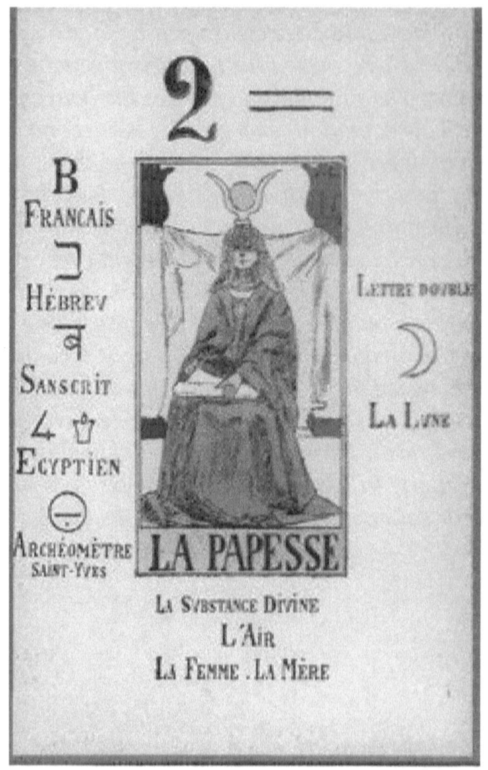

The High Priestess accomplishes *Magical Equilibrium*

Depth is equal to height, darkness is contrasted with light, matter is but the garment of the spirt

Levi

THE DOOR OF THE OCCULT SANCTUARY: Knowledge

B--2 expresses, in the divine world, the consciousness of the absolute Being who embraces the three periods of all manifestations: the past, the present and the future.

Paul Christian

This is the Hall of Wisdom. No one can reveal it, no one can hide it. Like a flower it must grow and bloom in thy soul. If thou wouldst plant the seed of this flower in thy soul--learn to discern the real from the false. Listen only to the Voice that is soundless... Look only on that which is invisible, and remember that in thee thyself, is the Temple and the gate to it, and the mystery, and the initiation."

Ouspensky

The highest manifestations of man in his earthly life are intelligence and will. If this binary is neutralised in a person, then its existence proceeds under favorable conditions.

Let us return to the ternary: spirit - astral - matter.

A person needs a healthy mind, a healthy astrosome and a healthy body. The mental monad of a person is in itself healthy due to its high origin, which will be discussed later. It is only necessary that it be active in a person, and then consciousness is ensured in life, which can be identified with the presence of spiritual aspirations.

A healthy astrosome will give an element called mental harmony (this is the third term of the binary: consciousness – low realisation power). This harmony will ensure the productivity of the totality of passions in man, and this totality is what is colloquially called personality. If someone tells us how and what he wants, his I will become familiar to us.

A healthy body will ensure the correct transmission of volitional impulses in a person; it will balance the world of physical needs and bring into life an element of power realisation.

What do we study first of all - the physical body, the astral or the spirit? The body and its functions are occupied by other specialists. Manifestations of the spirit, its aspirations, are also not alien to people who are thoughtful and inclined to engage in philosophy. Our role at the present moment is the study of the astrosome, and therefore the astral world, as the medium in which it circulates. So - if, firstly, we needed to ask ourselves - what is a person as an active unit, then secondly - the next step should be to seek to *know the astral world.*

The mark of the second Arcanum in the Hebrew alphabet is ב (Beth); the numerical value of this sign = 2.

If the hieroglyph Man was assigned to the first sign, then the hieroglyph of the mouth of the Man will refer to the second sign. The scientific name of the corresponding tarot picture is Gnosis (cognition). Occultists often refer to it as la Porte du Sanctuaire (The Door of the Sanctuary). Its vulgar name is la Papesse.

The image shows two columns in the background: The red pillar, usually with the sign of the sun, is called Jaquim; the other, dark blue (sometimes black), decorated with the sign of the moon, has the name of Boaz. The half-moon between the columns corresponds to the middle Masonic language. On the card, this space is hidden by a curtain. In the foreground we see a woman sitting upon a cubic seat. The symbol of infinity, above the head of the preceding card, is replaced here by the adornment - horns and full moon - on the head of the woman. Her face is covered by a semitransparent veil and the whole figure is shrouded in wide clothing. In her lap, she holds a roll of papyrus (sometimes a book)

half hidden by folds of clothing. On the chest, a cross, whose arms are of equal length.
The names of Arcanum II, in the planes of: Archetype, Man and Nature are respectively: "Divina Substantia", "Femina" and "Natura Naturata". We will try to study this Arcanum.

1. Its numerical value indicates that the Unit should be divided in two and polarised as often as necessary to participate in the process of life.
2. The very figure of the letter Beth, as well as the two columns, clearly shows the method that prevails in the deductions of occult science. Let us remember the great Law of Analogy, whose formula, in verses of the Emerald Tablet, is, in its Latin translation, expressed as follows:

"Quod est inferius est sicut quod est superius, Et quod est superius est sicut quod est inferius Ad perpetuanda miracula rei unius "

That is:

"What is below is similar (analogous - not equal) to that which is above and that which is above is like unto that which is below, to accomplish the wonders of the one thing".

Note that the upper part of the letter Beth is only similar to the lower one, and that the right column is only similar to the left column, but they are not the same. This indication of the method for acquiring the knowledge, together with the representation of the "Gate of the Sanctuary" on the card, is why the name "Gnosis" is given to Arcanum II.
3. The horns indicate the binary principle. The columns also show the binary principle, but, among them, a woman is sitting - an individual being - who must neutralise this binary. The woman is the symbol of passivity and even more so when she is seated. This posture demonstrates a state of expectation, of meditation and receptivity that the one desirous of studying must possess.
In addition, the card tells us that the secrets of science are accessible only to a penetrating intelligence - they are half hidden by a veil. The results of the scientific investigations of sages are recorded in the writings; the laws of Nature - in his living book. But to assimilate the knowledge contained therein is only possible within the folds of clothing or the mantle, which isolates us from worldly agitation, conditioning and other harmful influences. The Hieroglyph of the Arcanum - the Human Mouth - symbolises a refuge, a place where it is possible to shelter, a

building or temple dedicated to study. The two jaws that are similar, but not equal, illustrating the Law of the Analogy given above.

4. The Arcanum shows the importance of in-depth study of the binary: masculine principle - feminine principle.

In Arcanum I, we note above the head of man the unitary symbol of infinity: ∞

In Arcanum II, we find the horns, that is, a more tangible element. The mother number is more materialised than the father. The passive is always more concrete than the active. The subtle element, active, the fruitful element passive, more tangible. However, the passive must be condensed to the exact measure of the active, and it should suit you. What is the purpose of the coexistence of these elements? This goal is the very act of fertilisation. Here it is symbolised by a cross on the woman's chest. The vertical part of the cross is a phallus, the horizontal is a cteis.

This solar cross is absolutely equivalent to the so-called. - stauros of Gnostic symbolism (figure 3), or Lingam of Indu symbolism (figure 4).

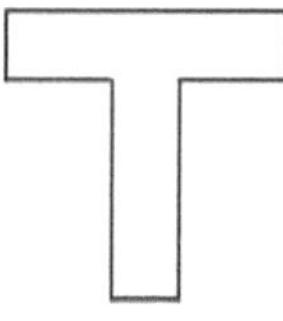

Figure 3

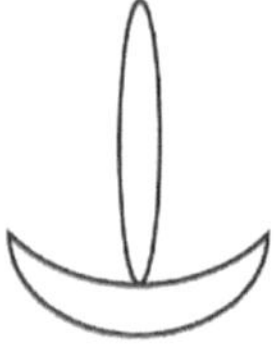

Figure 4

So, the 2nd Arcanum suggests the idea of a binary and, moreover, clearly indicates its productivity.

Another configuration of these principles (more philosophical, as we shall see later) is given by the Arcanum X of the tarot (' sign), as a masculine principle, and the fifth (He sign), as a feminine one.

Arcanum II belongs to the feminine principle. The moon, appearing on the Arcanum, indicates the principle of motherhood (the Moon is the world uterus). Astrologically, the Arcanum belongs to the moon, which also indicates the principle of motherhood. The corresponding astrological character of this Lunar Arcanum - is the Universal Mother. Thus, Arcanum II reminds us of the binary and indicates clearly its fecundity.

Let us look briefly at the basic phases of this fecundity. Let's take the example of two equal forces, but of opposing directions which, applied to a material point, condition the equilibrium of that point.

This rough scheme of a binary will help us to understand that, in general, manifestations are productive due to the existence of an opposition; without it they remain unproductive.

Is it worth preaching virtue in a society of absolutely virtuous people? Does it make sense to tease someone in whom this will not cause the slightest reaction? Is it possible to lean on an object that goes out of hand without showing the slightest resistance?

Keep this circuit in mind every time you have to balance, i.e. modus vivendi in any field, that is, an equilibrium, whatever the field of its application.

The line delimiting the positive and negative fields in the binary and balancing them can be displaced, according to the circumstances, but the balance of the moment is always governed by the above scheme.

An act or behaviour that neutralises the great binary of good and evil can, after a short time, fall into the region of good or evil, and at this new moment the binary is neutralised by a completely different act or behaviour.

Under certain conditions it may be appropriate to limit ourselves simply not to help a person, but we may, five minutes later, feel that our conscience compels us to help them through a certain beneficial and elevated action. The dividing line is in the balance but the principle of neuralisation has not changed.

But let's move on to another phase of using the binary. This other phase can be called dynamic if the first is conditionally assigned the name static.

Again, I will give a rough mechanical diagram. The same forces, parallel and equal to each other, are applied in opposite directions to two different points of the solid. This gives us an idea of rotational motion. This is exactly what we wanted to get, but we want to obtain yet more. The idea of a stormy movement, of a whirlwind.

Next, let's imagine this movement applied to the astral matter: The impetuous astral vortices provoked by the powerful effort of will and imagination, forming swirls that spread and grow like spouts and are governed by the same laws. It is not permissable to reveal the secret of the general formation of these trunks, but we can allude to a particular case in which man, instinctively, creates such eddies, which form individualised coagulates of matter and can be clearly perceived, proving thus its realising power; this work is linked to the matter of the neutralisation of the Life – Death binary.

We have touched another initiation binary: spirit - matter, neutralised by the astral plane, as a secondary plane. It is therefore appropriate here to give a general outline of the knowledge of this plan, which for the first time will be limited to acquaintance with its inhabitants. Indeed, generally speaking, this familiarisation can be carried out either inductively, by means of relations with the mentioned inhabitants and recording the results of these relations; or deductively, based on the definition of the astral plane. At your stage of occult development, only the second is available to you. Apply it.

The astral plane, by definition, is adjacent to the mental and physical. This means that imprints and reflections of those elements of these planes that are close to its area should be visible in it.

The very condensed and typically grouped collectivities of ideas are reflected in the astral plane of the so-called. Astro-ideas, i.e. ideas already requested by the form. These astro-ideas are caught by metaphysicians and other scientists at those moments of their mental work, when the question is about choosing forms for already chosen ideas.

Often the same astro-idea is caught by different scientists in closely related sub planes, and then we see the simultaneous emergence of two or more systems, very similar, but not identical in form. Recall the generation of the infinitesimal calculus, on the one hand, by Leibniz (differential calculus), and on the other, by Newton (fluxia method). Acts and phenomena realised in the physical plane through the subtle (higher) subplanes of the physical plane are reflected in the astral plane, as if in a mirror, and, with these reflections, are firmly fixed in this plane, giving the so-called. astral clichés of events of the physical plane. The astral sphere is not subject to the limited laws of three-dimensional space, nor of the time of a dimension. There you will find clichés of not only past, but also future events. You will say that future events are somewhat dependent on the volitional impulses of free individuals.

I will answer you: 1) - yes, it is, but each of our desires, every measure we take in the physical plane partially alters the cliché of future events and may even erase them; 2) - the higher this astral sub plane in which one takes the cliché of the future event, the less that cliché changes and the better it predicts the event. There is a great secret - this is the secret of free will, identical with the secret of the production of astral tourbillons in the most general form; hence some nebula and apparent contradiction in the presentation of this paragraph.

If astronomers are sought after by scientists, then the astral clichés are hunted by the lucidity (imagination) of clairvoyants, fortune tellers and diviners of every kind. These clichés open to them in a trance, in a dream, etc. states of prevalence of the astral activity of the human essence.

The clichés of any anomalies or events of a grandiose nature are easier to catch than others. Hence the opportunity to see the cliché of great crimes, disasters, as well as encouraging events of grandiose world significance. In the case of the person having a certain degree of sensitivity, these clichés may even be perceived in the waking state.

Let us now suppose the case of someone conceiving a bad desire in a very common way. That person has not yet realised that desire on the physical plane, but has already sketched the astral intention. By this, he gave birth to an entity (by coagulating the astral plane and using the great law of individualisation of coagulates).

The generated entity does not have a physical body, but there is an astrosome - typically expressed, and also a semblance of a mental monad - the idea of evil desire. Such an entity, by the property of its monad, can act, influence, only in accordance with this idea.

To whom does its influence extend?

First of all, on the father himself, or the artist who painted the astral picture of something evil. This essence, or larva, encourages him not to forget this evil desire, to repeat his volitional impulse and thereby strengthen the larva itself. It can act on another person, inclined to desire the same things in a similar form.

So they say that the larva of such and such a person sticks to such and such another. How to get rid of these larvae, friends or strangers? Three means can be recommended for this:

1) a conscious volitional effort in the form of a desire not to obey the larva, to defeat it, to drive it away from itself, to act like an artist who scornfully looks at the pornography of his own work;

2) focus on thought and imagination on another subject or other desire. A strong absorption in this second object will deprive us of the opportunity to correspond with the first. Prayer is the most desirable form of application of this second method. Indeed, strictly speaking, every prayer is an act of concentration, and vice versa - every act of concentration can be defined as a prayer to God, to oneself, or even to the devil, depending on the nature of concentration.

By the devil, we mean here a picture of the scheme of the Higher Elements, distorted to extremes, brought to the synthesis of all anarchies by incorrect reflections and refractions.

This method of concentration can be likened to the method of turning away from a harmful picture for contemplating another, better one.

3) the use of realisation power, based on the physical plane - the destruction of larvae with a magic sword, i.e. a metal tip mounted on an insulating handle (wood, hard rubber, etc.) or separated from the operator's hand with an insulating glove (silk, wool, fur).

The action of the magic sword is based on the fact that astral tourbillons change their character near the metal tip so sharply that getting it into the ganglionic node of the astrosome larva causes its complete decay.

Larva in this case should be sought in the so-called. aura (atmosphere of astral emanations) of the affected larva subject. This atmosphere borders his body. This technique is similar to the destruction of a painting by the complete destruction of the canvas on which it is written[14].

Imagine that a rational, able to concentrate person thinks a good idea, wrapping it in a certain form. He finds like-minded people, agrees with them regarding the form of the idea, and thus creates the collectivity of people who think the general idea in the same form.

These people seem to draw a pencil line around the contours of the same figure, thickening these contours and making them more visible. The general idea of these people is clothed in an astrosome, called the egrégore of collectivity.

This egrégore, like any astrosome, stores, restores and encourages the physical body of collectivity to activity and self-preservation, i.e. the totality of the physical resources of its members that are used in the implementation of its ideas. For example, the egrégore of a charity will encourage its members to donate and work, help increase the contingent of the members themselves, replace those who have left with new ones, etc. The egrégores of collectivities that are hostile to each other in the physical plane are fighting in the astral plane.

If, in the physical plane, the enemies of collectivity destroy the physical bodies of its members, the astrosomes of the latter strengthen the egrégore in the astral plane.

Let us remember the case of the persecution of the adherents of primitive Christendom by the Jews and pagans, which ended with the triumph of the Christian egrégore.

---

[14] During a discussion about these methods cited by G.O.M, a colleague and companion of the English translator suggested that there may be a fourth way, through the art and science of Alchemical transmutation.

More detailed information about the egrégores and their life is related by me in the study of Arcanum XI.

Man has ended physical existence in one of his incarnations. His body disintegrates. According to the unchanging laws of nature, all the elements of this body, up to the vitality of the blood and even to the energy of nerve manifestations, slowly or more gradually come at the disposal of nature and come in handy on other formations. Man remains in the spiritual monad and astrosome. The lowest of the planes in which it can evolve is the astral plane. At this stage he is called elemental. For him, manifestations in the physical plane are possible, but here they are caused by the mediumship of certain subjects from which he borrowed for a while the elements of the lower, transitional subplanes of the astral plane and the highest subtlest elements of the physical plane. To facilitate this process of borrowing, we also need temporary passivity of the medium, or the individual will of the magician, or the collective will of the magic chain (at the sessions), or the administrative directive power of some egrégore, or something like that. But this is all a coincidence. The normal life of the elementary takes place in the contemplation of astral clichés and in communication with astral beings. These are his comrades in science, in suffering in the field of mob law, in preparation for further incarnations.

Among the temporary meetings in the astral plane, meetings with the so-called exteriorised astrosomes of living people are very interesting for the elementary.

For a living person, a strong arbitrary or involuntary concentration of his activity on the sphere of astral manifestations is possible. In this state, the physical activity of a person is reduced to an extreme minimum. It must be said that the astrosome not only forms the human body in the womb, not only controls its development, but also maintains its shape, manages the exchange of cells, repairs damage, and when the body comes to decay, it also controls the decay process. The elemental is at first busy with the process of destruction of its material body and the phantom of its nerve fluids.

In a word - an astrosome is Brahma, and Vishnu, and Shiva of the material body. The activity of the astrosome in relation to the physical body is especially intense during a person's sleep, when mens almost does not use the services of the astrosome as a transfer authority, and the astrosome has time to do 'maintenance' work, i.e. nutrition, health, etc. If the astrosome is asked to do only insignificant work on these questions, if, for example. the body is in a state of lethargy, catalepsy, the so-called. trance, etc., then the astrosome is almost free and can manifest itself quite vigorously on the field of external objects, on the functions of a foreign body (treatment of a stranger by exteriorisation of his astral body to him); maybe, having stocked up the fluid energy of some medium or even having taken it from your own physical body, manifest yourself at a far distance by mechanical phenomena (knocking, moving objects, touching), light effects (the appearance of the figure of a person in a place far from the location of his physical body) etc.

This is a manifestation of the astral energy of a person far from his physical body and is called his exit in the astral body or the exteriorisation of the astral. It unconsciously occurs in persons severely affected by fear, grief, etc. (after all, emotional affects relate to astral activity) or to persons who have plunged into certain types of sleep - lethargy or catalepsy.

Mages and sorcerers deliberately cause the same state in themselves when they need to show their activity at a distance. But every י (Iod) has its own ה (He). And the state of manifestation of energy at a distance is associated with the presence of perception (perception) at a distance in the corresponding subplanes of the astral plane. They are exteriorised to look out for the astral cliché of earthly being, to catch the astroid, to solve a complicated theoretical question, to experimentally familiarise myself with what I am presenting to you theoretically.

Mental man at this time does not work particularly hard; his activities are forked. On the one hand, he accompanies the astral body, supplying him with a certain presence of volitional impulses in his wandering; on the other hand, some participation of mens in the guard service over the physical body is recognised, which is exposed to a number of significant dangers during the exteriorisation of the astrosome, which will be discussed later. This guard service to some extent guarantees the rapid return of the astrosome to the physical body in case of extreme danger.

Regarding the role of the astral body in a person, it is interesting to note two circumstances: 1st - the absence (i.e. the so-called state of exteriorisation) of the astral body while the physical body is damaged, there is a favourable factor for correcting this damage in the future, and even for the realm of pain. If, being subjected to an injection, wound, etc., you managed to at least partially exteriorise, then the damage was transferred to the tourbillons of your astral system a little, and the latter, returning to the body, fixes everything better, the less it was affected by the corrupting influences. This thesis finds its application in the practice of fakirs, piercing themselves various parts of the body and quickly healing them with the energetic activity of the returning astrosome.

If, on the contrary, the tourbillons of the astrosome were damaged (well, at least with the tip of the magic sword) while this astrosome was exteriorised, that is, it used the physical body as a reference point only to a small extent, then this damage is dangerous for the astral body in the sphere of its lower manifestations, and therefore, in particular, in the sphere of the process of protecting and maintaining the physical body. If an externalised astrosome has at least a secondary ganglionic node damaged, then upon returning the astrosome to the physical body, damage to the astrosome causes a wound in those parts of the physical body that were protected by the activity of the system of this node. The lower the sub-plane in which you exteriorised, the more sensitive this damage.

It remains to say a few words about the elementals, usually attributed by textbooks to the number of inhabitants of the astral plane. These are not astral entities. The elementals have a mental monad, directed towards specially involutive activity, an astrosome that forms this activity, and a physical body that is invisible under ordinary conditions by the very uniformity of its structure with the environment in which these elementals operate. Elementals are dominated by chemical and physical phenomena, many physiological processes, etc.

If their body is predominantly gaseous, they are called bellows. If liquid - with undines. If it's solid - dwarves. If their body is more subtle and in structure approaches what we call the world ether, then - salamanders. There are beings that possess only a mental monad and an astral body and operate involutively in the astral medium, just as elementals operate in the elements. These entities are given the name Spiritus directors astral. There are purely mental beings engaged in involutional processes, their name is Angels.

Notes on the second Arcanum

In the second Arcanum of MotT, The High Priestess is presented as the symbol of Gnosis, receptive to the influx of light and catalytic force of The Magician, which she reflects. She occupies the place where 'wisdom builds her house' and is to The Magician as Gnosis is to Wisdom and Aleph is to Beth. The High Priestess is the personification of Sophia in the Tarot.

It is also in the second Arcanum that the "problem of the number two, the problem of legitimate twofoldness and illegitimate twofoldness" are examined.

G.O.M. introduces another very important concept in this letter – that of egrégores – to which he returns many times in the course of this study. MotT introduces the same concept later in his book, in Arcanum VI, The Lovers, with his description of the anti-Christ, which he says is: "an egrégore, an artificial being who owes his existence to collective generation from below", that is, from the minds and emotions of human beings.

A definition of egrégores given by Robert Ambelain in La Kabbala pratique is quoted with approval:

One gives the name egrégore to a force generated by a powerful spiritual current and then nourished at regular intervals, according to a rhythm in harmony with the universal life of the cosmos, or to a union of entities united by a common characteristic nature.

We are told that this definition is inherently complete and there is no need for Ambelain to have expanded upon and - in Tomberg's view - muddled it in the next paragraph, where he writes:

In the invisible, beyond the physical perception of man, exist artificial beings – generated by devotion, enthusiasm and fanaticism – that one names egrégores. These are the souls of great spiritual currents, good and evil. The Mystical Church, Heavenly Jerusalem, the Body of Christ and all these synonymous names are the epithets that one commonly gives to the egrégore of Catholicism. Freemasonry, Protestantism, Islam, Buddhism are other egrégores.

We might naturally expect the devout Tomberg to mount a strenuous rebuttal of the idea that the Mystical Church and Body of Christ are nothing more than artificially generated egrégores, which he goes on to do at length. With this regrettable addition, Ambelain presented, he says, "a singular mixture of truth and falsehood".

The truth of the statement is that "artificial collectively-engendered beings exist, ie, that egrégores are real; but what is false is the confusion of things which are of an entirely different nature (the "Body of Christ" and "political ideologies"!).

The error deepens when we consider that if the Mystical Church, Body of Christ, Buddhism and so on are to be classified as egrégores, the logical next step is to conclude that God is also an egrégore. No, it is asserted, "there are superhuman spiritual entities which are not artificially engendered, but which manifest themselves and reveal themselves" and this essential point is one that we must always bear in mind when studying the immense and complex matter of egrégores, to which G.O.M. will turn our attention frequently.

We are also warned not to get confused about the difference between phantoms and souls, lest we fall into a serious error, and nor must we confuse revelations with inventions – "of spiritual beings who reveal themselves from above and egrégores engendered artificially from below." egrégores may be exceedingly powerful but their existence is entirely ephemeral and dependent upon continual nourishment given by human beings. Humans are themselves nourished by the souls and spirits who are above.

Notwithstanding his robust defence of the independent reality of spiritual entities, MotT does acknowledge that there is an egrégore *of* the Church – of every church – in the form of a shadow side, or "double". Every human being and every nation has such a double. We must take care when looking at a being, group or nation to see the true form and not the double, to look rightly in order to see rightly.

to look rightly means to see through the mists of the phantoms of things.

The antichrist, we are told

is the phantom of the whole of mankind...he is the "superman" who haunts the consciousness of all those who seek to elevate themselves through their own effort, without grace.

It is worth pointing out that on several occasions in MotT the dangers of a Nietzschean philosophy or warned of, for its focus focuses on the double instead of true and sacred forms.

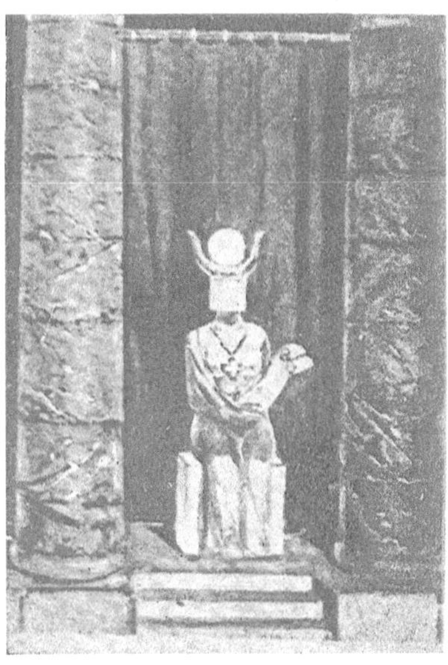

Arcanum III

ג

THE EMPRESS

Pathway from Keter to Binah

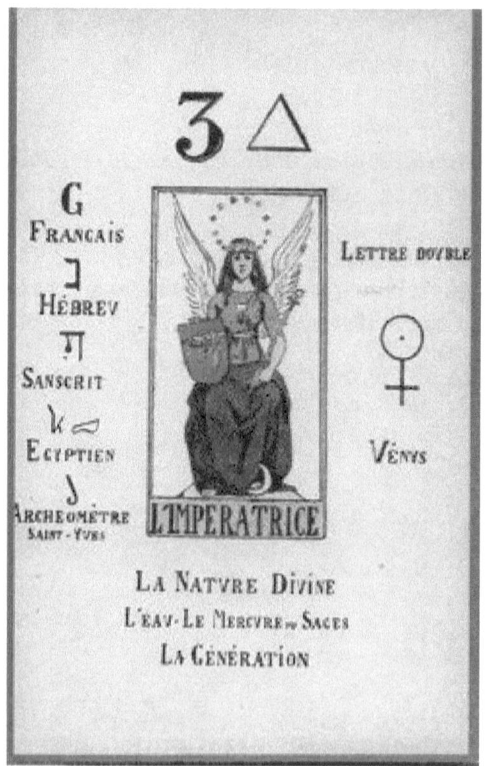

The Empress expresses *Perfection of Speech*

ISIS-URANIA: Action

G--3 expresses, in the divine world, the supreme Power balanced by the eternally active Mind and by absolute Wisdom

Paul Christian

How can you smile so joyfully on the opening flowers, when everything is destined to death, even that which has not yet been born?"

For answer the Empress looked on me still smiling and, under the influence of that smile, I suddenly felt a flower of some clear understanding open in my heart.

Ouspensky

The sign of the Hebrew alphabet that corresponds to this Arcanum is Gimel and its number is three. The hieroglyph is a hand that grabs, arranged in such a way that it forms a narrow channel that can hold something.

From the idea of a narrow channel, they move on to the idea of the vagina, which serves as the last stage in the process of birth, and from this to the very idea of birth. Hence come the three names of the Arcanum, according to the hypostases of the theosophical ternary: "Divine Natura," "Partus," "Generatio."

The idea of creation is closely linked to the element of love or, in the broadest sense, to the element of love and attraction. Universal gravitation, common love, compassion, impersonal love - all these manifestations are particular expressions of this general principle.

The goddess of attraction is Venus, and one of the erudite names of this Arcanum is "Venus Urania", that is, Venus of the Universe, Cosmic Venus.

Another erudite name is "Physis" - the Nature. The common name is "Empress."

Arcanum III, which by its number and geometric symbol evokes the idea of the ternary, has for its geometric symbol a triangle that, according to the character of the ternary, will be ascending or descending.

The card shows a seated woman, crowned with 12 stars, which symbolise the 12 zodiacal signs. There is a close link between birth on the physical plane and the 12 phases of solar energy received by the Earth. These phases correspond to the progressive presence of the Sun in the 12 zodiacal signs. It is for this reason that in the occult the term "zodiac" alludes to the physical plane, to physical characteristics.

The woman of the card "is wrapped in the sun and writhes in the pangs of childbirth."

The meaning of Arcanum III is revealed by the presentation of the birth process. the soaring rays, involving the woman, remind us that the sun - the centre of gravitation - is the example of the planetary love of our system. He is the centre emanating from life and therefore from creation. In her right hand, the woman holds a sceptre topped with the Venus symbol. This means that she reigns permanently for love, for everything that was born and what will be born.

The Astrological partner of Arcanum III is Venus, whose symbol presents a synthesis of two others:

The Sun – creative emanation, positivity; and the world of the elements, that is, all the influences of the environment - as we will learn later, the world of elements, or elements, i.e. set of environmental influences. The symbol of Venus can be interpreted as follows: the constructive emanations, thanks to love, overcome the difficulties of the environment.

In her left hand, the woman holds a shield where there is an eagle; this means that the principle of creation embraces the highest spheres. The eagle holds in its beak a cross of equal arms, indication that birth is a natural consequence of the union of the active principle with the principle (see Arcanum II).

The woman again appears seated on a cubic stone placed on a globe (we will explain this later) and under her feet is the moon, which symbolises here the matter of the sub-lunar world, as the lower sphere of creation. Sometimes we find a change in this picture: instead of being surrounded by the sun, the woman has wings. The wings show that the "Isis Terrestris "comes from" Isis Celestis ".

What is the meaning of this Arcanum?

First of all, it is given by the Gnostic formula: "Nothing is created, everything is born". That is, there is always a י (Iod) which fertilises a ה (He), and thereby determines the birth of the third element, ו (Vau, see Arcanum VI). The father, the mother and the son; the active and the passive neutralised by the androgyne. Arcanum III proclaims the Law of the Ternary to be general and universal. In addition, for better understanding, we will briefly review some typical ternaries. We begin with the theosophical ternary:

Archetype - Man - Nature.

We can see here the theological scheme of the Divine Trinity: God in God, or God the Father; God manifesting himself in Humanity, or God the Son and God manifesting Himself in Nature, or God the Holy Spirit. Speaking of this triple manifestation of the One God, in which a third term neutralises the two extremes - because Humanity connects Nature with the Archetype - we will take advantage of the opportunity to mention God's three ways of seeking souls. There are souls who seek God the Father for metaphysical paths; there are souls who seek God the Son within their heart and human groups are formed in the name of this search; finally, there are souls who seek God for the contemplation of Nature and acceptance of its immutable laws, those who seek the Holy Spirit. You will learn more about this in the Secrets of Kabbalah.

Now, let's look at an example of a ternary of the type of the Rising Triangle like ternaries of the Great Arcana.

Let us now take the same ternary: Archetype - Man - Nature, in its sense of the life of the Universe.

Imagine the Archetype as something totally harmonious, androgynous, omniscient, well blessed, possessing the total capacity of action and consequently, being able to limit the sphere of activity. This Higher

Principle, using the common expression, is divided into active and passive manifestations, thus giving the scheme of the ascending triangle. Parallel to this conception of the Archetype, we will conceive of Humanity as a single organism, formed by cells that in the earth are called "men", and perhaps they have a different name on other planets. Admitting the existence of such cells in various cosmic worlds, suns, planets, etc., to which they belong, we will obtain the general idea of the Universal Man, living the life of a collective entity and owning its own will, in accordance with the Individualisation.

We can also talk about Nature, as a result of the grouping of all elements, both individualised by one's worldview and non-individualised, and think of this totality as dynamised by the basic patterns of regular manifestations, i.e. - the principle of causality.

These two poles - Humanity and Nature - will be manifestations of the Archetype: the first - active, the second - passive according to the scheme of our triangle (here the terms "active" and "passive" are taken in relative rather than absolute meaning).

Now let's deal with the ternary, clearly suitable for the same type of ternary of the Great Arcana, namely the "past - present - future" ternary. After all, the present, as a moment, determines by its location the area of what we call the past and the future. Without indicating the moment that we call "the present", we are not able to distinguish between these areas. The "present" emanates the "past" and "future", and in the past it is affected by its relatively passive, inert side (it cannot be altered), and the future corresponds to the active aspect.

Having brought our two ternaries closer together, we will say that the Archetype owns the law of analogies of the present, that the future belongs to Humanity similarly, and Nature bases its manifestations on the analogy of the Past. We go further: Humanity owns the future by the right of human freedom with the help of an instrument called the collective will of humanity. Nature is based on the past in the form of so-called. Fate, the instrument of which is Rock (blind, inexorable, and therefore inert, as if relatively passive).

The archetype has the properties of an androgyne; this property is reflected by the law of Pleasure and Higher Harmony in that great world Lamp, which is called Providence. Providence, accordingly, is neutral, androgynous, and plays the role of Light, illuminating the field of activity of the other two elements.

I draw your attention to the fact that in our language the term "present" has two meanings: one - relating to the reality of the object, the other - placing the object at a certain point in time.

Any method of birth, emanation of anything should be real for the childbearing, emanating, in order to be real in the plane of life manifestations corresponding to it. The formula of the suggestion should be read: "You do this", and not "you do" or "you did."

An immutable metaphysical or scientific thesis is also formulated in the present tense. The feeling that you will characterise as the past or the future will not be recognised as real by anyone. It will at best be called vague terms like "reflex," "hallucination," etc.

Approaching the two ternaries, we will say that the present, by analogy, corresponds to the Archetype; future - to Humanity and the past - to Nature.

Returning to our ternary, we will argue with Fabre d'Olivet that world history is based on a mystical triangle (Fig. 5).

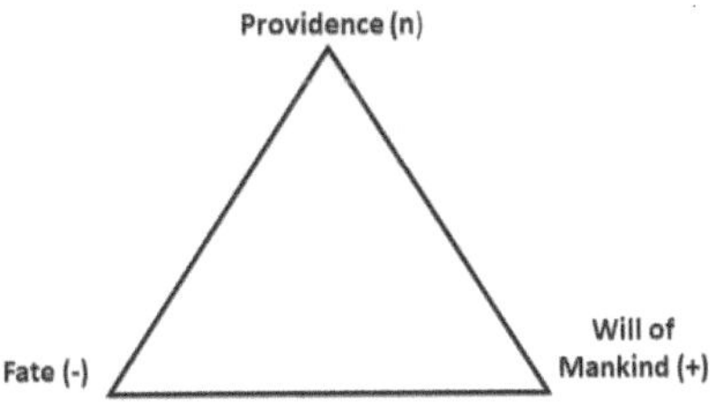

Figure 5

Providence illuminates the Present with its light; The will of Mankind rushes to build the Future, but at the same time it is limited in its manifestations by Fate, which nails it to the Past. If the Will of Humanity unites, enters into an alliance with the enlightening influence of Providence, then it is stronger than Fate: at this time the history of Humanity is evolutionary.

If Mankind turns a blind eye to this influence of Providence and engages in martial arts with Fate, then a general thesis on the course of its history cannot be expressed: it all depends on the relationship of the forces of Will and Fate, which is stronger.

If Humanity consciously fights with its Will with Fate, backed up by the instructions of Providence, then this Will shall be defeated: nothing will come of it. If, finally, Mankind attaches its Will to the influences of Fate, unfavourably assessed by Providence, then the implementations turn out to be very powerful, very sensitive, but the course of history moves the world away from the principle of Harmony and will need subsequent corrections to solve the Great Problem of the ultimate goals of the existence of the Universe. World history at this time is involutive.

Let us now try to apply the mystical triangle of Fabre d'Olivet[15] to the life of a particular soul during one of his incarnations. In this case, the triangle will be that of figure 6:

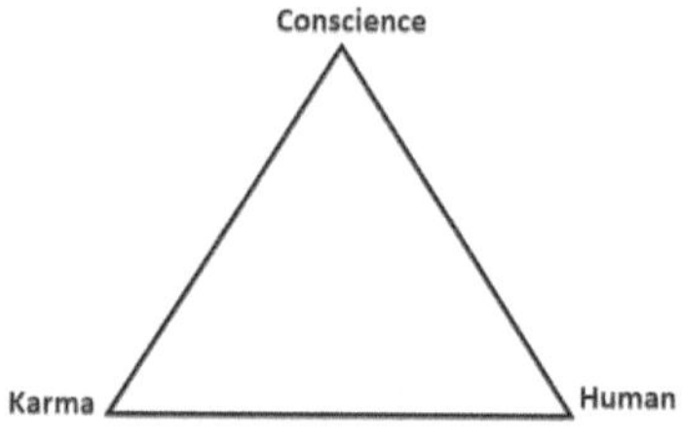

Figure 6.

Providence in a separate human instance has the representative of a so-called conscience that is absolutely neutral, does not push or hold back, but only illuminates the path, indicating how to neutralise in the present moment the good-evil binary.

The human will determines future events, but is limited in their choice of the so-called. karma. This karma is, as it were, the general form of all previous incarnations of the soul of our person. He was born for the first time in conditions favourable to the acquisition of wisdom, as they say - with pure karma; sinned; in the second incarnation, in addition to the task of acquiring wisdom, he still has to clear karma, which will not do without struggle and suffering. Of course, with this second birth, karma puts him in less favourable living conditions. Further incarnations follow the law of alternatives to aggravation and correction of karma until it is finally cleansed. Very aggravated karma, which could not be corrected by conscious efforts of the will alone, is partly corrected by the very element of suffering in the incarnation corresponding to it: the sufferings that a person is doomed to karma can be so strong that they partially redeem karma, even in the case of complete passivity and conscious maliciousness subject during incarnation.

Here are some combinations of vertices possible for this particular scheme of the Mystical Triangle, applied to the life of a being human being:

---

[15] Fabre D'Olivet (1767 – 1825) is a particularly important figure in this school, having mastered a number of ancient languages, upon the basis of which he claimed to have discovered the true Hebrew language and grammatical structure. Using this knowledge he translated the first ten chapters of Genesis in what he claimed was their spiritual interpretation and published it in La langue hébraïquerestituée et le véritable sensdes mots hébreux rétabli etprouvé par leur analyseradicale (1816).

1. The will in harmony with the conscience and fighting against karma.
Result: purification of karma.
2. The will agreeing with karma but opposing the indications of
consciousness. This is selfish opportunism and results in visible
successes in life, but with a karmic charge.
3. The struggle of the will against karma, without consulting the
conscience. The overall result cannot be determined as it will depend on
the respective forces in action.
4. The will against karma and consciousness gathered together.
Outcome: failure in life and increase in karma.

The staggered ternaries, similar to those analysed in this Arcanum, that
is, those which present the three basic degrees of the same manifestation,
we will call absolute ternaries. These will resemble other ternaries -
conditionals - that we will call analogous ternaries, binding each
conditionally or symbolically to a given absolute ternary.
Let us take two examples of such ternaries: the first, belonging to the
field of Nature, and the second according to that of ritual symbolism.
Let us analyse the human body, dividing it into the head, thoracic region
and abdominal region. Per analogy, the head will correspond to the
mental plane, for the mental manifestations of man incarnate has a
certain connection with the functions of the brain; the thorax will
correspond to the astral plane, even considering only the main role
attributed to respiratory exercises in the physical treatment of astral
labours; the abdomen will correspond to the physical plane, since the
alimentary organs are naturally linked to the renewal of the cells of the
body.
This will be an analogous ternary. We can also give it a slightly different
shape: the activity of the head governs the distribution of nerve fluids;
that of the chest governs the renewal of the blood; and activity of the
abdomen, the restoration of tissues (lymph circulation).
Wanting to verify this artificial construction practically, we will analyse
separately the head - the analogy of the mental plane - looking at the
three sub-planes of the mental plane: the eyes represent the mentality;
according to the survey, we conclude superficially about the activity
of the individual.
The nose will represent the astral part of the head; according to the
formation of the same, superficial conclusions are often drawn regarding
the pathology of the thoracic legion of the person.
The mouth will represent the physical plane; it will be an envoy of the
abdominal region, whose disturbances can be perceived through the
observation of the lips, the tongue, etc.

This subdivision confirms the fact that our ternary is not entirely arbitrary but has a natural symbolic basis.

We will now give an example of an artificial-symbolic ternary, explaining the scheme of the famous Trident of Parcelsus (Tridens Paracelsis), presented in figure 7.

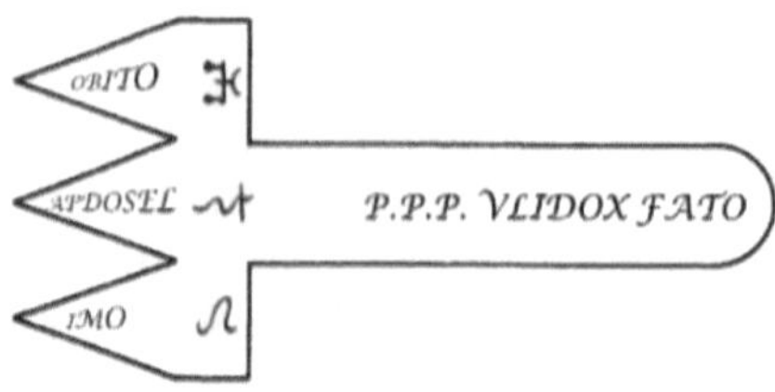

Figure 7 - Trident of Paracelsus

Metal teeth (iron, sheet metal or steel); cylindrical handle - wooden or hard rubber, i.e. in any case - insulating. The device, from a practical point of view, is a magic sword with three points.

Let us analyse the inscriptions on the teeth, signs drawn near the base of the teeth, and the golden inscription on the handle. Let's start with the prongs.

On the upper, **OBITO** is engraved (obey, give in, be obedient, heed); this inscription outlines the sphere of passive manifestations of Man in the field of life of the physical plane (or rather, in the field of three planes in the presence of incarnation in the physical).

On the lower prong we read: **IMO** (Immo would be more accurate, which means: - on the contrary, contrary to, in the sense of - resist, show yourself actively).

The middle tooth concludes the inscription: **APDOSEL**, which must be decomposed as follows: ap + do + sel.

"Ap" must be replaced by Greek αρ, the initial letters of the word αρχη (arche) = beginning = higher element = mens.

The syllable "do" should be read from right to left - od; this is the name of a positively polarised astral. Therefore, it is an astrosome in the sphere of male manifestations. "Sel" (Latin sal) means salt = roamed the physical plane - symbolises the very physical plane.

So we see that three prongs dictate the phrase with their inscriptions.

The three-component active Man (mens + anima + corpus) must balance the binary of obedience and resistance; he must manoeuvre between these tricks. This ternary outlines the scope of human activity.

In the second ternary of signs, the first sign, similar to cancer, is set instead of the sign of Cancer. This zodiac sign is astrologically the house of the moon, the planetary influence of which leads the passive beginning to the passive upper tooth.

The serpent bearing the sign of Jupiter with its head is a symbol of the astral tourbillon, by which the authority (sign of Jupiter) of Man is carried into the world astral.

The third sign is the spoiled sign Leo of the zodiacal Leo, which serves as the home of the active Sun, which conducts its influence in the lower, active prong. As you can see - the second ternary belongs to the field of forms that conduct the influence of the handle into the teeth. The handle is decorated with a gold inscription

P.P.P. VLIDOXFATO

where the triple P should be overturned to obtain the triple lingam - fertilization in three plans. V is the Latin numeral 5, - an indication of the pentagram, - a symbol of human Will; LI - the initial letters of the word libertate - (freedom); VLI = pentagrammatica libertate = freedom of human Will. DOX means doxa (awareness), i.e. that gives us an element of conscience. FATO means Rock, Fate, Karma. This means that the hilt tells us about the Human right to attempt to produce in three planes and because of the existence of what we placed at the tops of the Mystical Triangle Fabre d'Olivet.

This ternary concerns the sphere of the mental, even metaphysical, nature of our absolute rights to the three planes.

The whole trident will symbolise Man in general in two higher planes (hilt, chart of astrological signs) and differentiate him as a Man in the physical plane (the middle tooth contains a hint of activity).

In practice, the device serves as a magic sword in a man's hand, and in a greatly reduced format is used in hermetic medicine in the treatment of male impotence. Here is an example of a system of three ternaries in the field of symbolism.

Notes on the third Arcanum

MotT distinguishes between three distinct fields of magic: Sacred Magic, which is embodied by the Christian Sacraments, Personal Magic (the grey zone); and Sorcery, which is Black Magic. The Empress is the Arcanum of Sacred Magic, which Papus defined so memorably as:
The science of love

Sacred magic is accomplished by the union of divine and human will, through which is made possible the work of Redemption. "The mystery of the God-Man is the key of divine magic", we are told, as an essential condition of the redemptive work on a par with the Creation of the World. The performance of miracles therefore depends upon this union of wills, which gives birth to a new power. Miracles and magic are part and parcel of the same phenomena, for the will of a magus is "essential for the realisation of a miracle".

Gnosis derived from Mystical experience must precede the operation of Sacred Magic, just as The Empress follows sequentially from The Magician and The High Priestess. Thus, sacred or divine magic is no less than the putting into practice of mystical revelation.

Just as MotT extols the miracle of divine magic, so does he stridently warn against the dangers of personal magic and sorcery. This stance might put him at some odds with other mages less concerned with such distinctions and not above engaging in what we might term 'practical kabbalah'.

The eagle on the shield of the Empress - which inspires us with the aim of 'liberation in order to ascend' - indicates that we must throw the eagles of our desire to the winds. The authority and legitimacy of The Empress are signified by the crown she wears, which is conferred from above, whilst the sceptre is emblematic of magical power. The task of magic, as shown by the crown, is the sublimation of nature, just as the tiara of the High Priestess denotes that she has the task of carrying revelation through three planes, right down to 'the book', or tradition

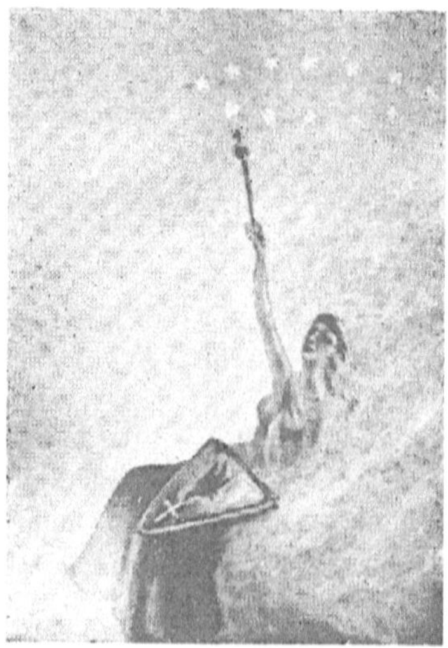

Arcanum IV

ד

THE EMPEROR

Pathway between Chokmah and Binah

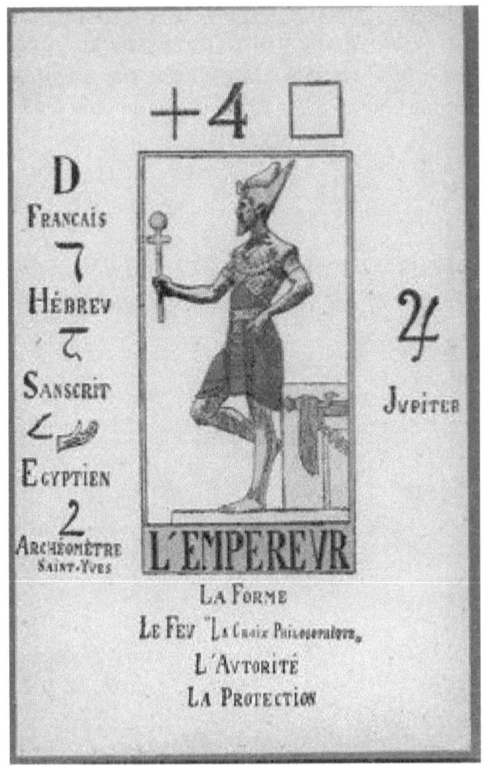

The Emperor exudes *Majesty*

This is the first formula of the mystical explanation of the enigma of the Sphynx.

Levi

THE CUBIC STONE: Realisation

D--4 expresses, in the divine world, the perpetual and hierarchical realisation of the virtues contained in the absolute Being

Paul Christian

"I am The Great Law," the Emperor said. "I am the name of God. The four letters of his name are in me and I am in all.

Ouspensky

The sign of the Hebrew alphabet that corresponds to Arcanum IV is ד
(Daleth). Its numerical value: 4. The Hieroglyph of the Arcanum is the
Breast; hence the idea of feeding and being fed. Food strengthens the
creature and enables it to act and acquire authority in its environment.
The card of the Arcanum features a man crowned with a triple tiara. This
means that the principle exists in all three planes and that this authority,
to be real in any field, must extend to the three planes of this field.
In the left hand, the man holds a sceptre, surmounted by the sign of
Venus, or the sign of Jupiter. the former means that it is indispensable to
know how to create complex, individualised and finished entities. The
second simply indicates the astrological correspondence of the Arcanum
- the planet Jupiter - with all the characteristics of the god Jupiter of
Mythology.
The position of the man's arms and shoulders should form an ascending
triangle. In many decks of the Tarot this particularity was omitted. The
left leg is crossed with the right so as to form a cross with equal arms.
Behind the figure there is a cubic stone in which is represented an eagle,
carrying around its neck the emblem called "Cross of the Great
Hierophant" (figure 8). The man rests his right hand on the upper cube.

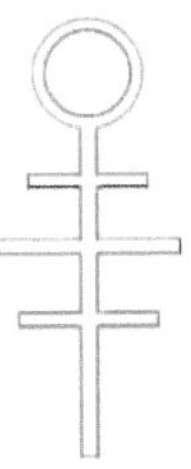

Figure 8

Let's look at the explanation of these symbols: A cubic stone, evenly cut
and smooth, is the symbol of all that has been worked and finished,
receiving a definitive form. It indicates that authority manifests itself
through the forms, previously well elaborated. Each side of the cube, of
course, has a square - one of geometric symbols of this Arcanum.
The image of the eagle on the stone demonstrates the necessity of a great
elevation of thought for one who intends to give things a finished form.
It must be, say, an engineer and not just a labourer at work. This idea is
confirmed by the presence, in the Arcanum, of the Cross of the Great
Hierophant. The line of the cross symbolises a channel leading to the
lower end, the influence of the three planes of the Universe, represented

by three horizontal sleepers. To complete the shape, to polish the stone, it is necessary not only to grasp the idea of the thing in the highest, but also to pass it through the mental, astral and physical phases and aspects of its realisation.

It is still necessary to explain the cross formed by the legs of the man. This cross with equal arms will be the second symbol of this Arcanum, the first being a cubic stone, one of the names ("Petra Cubica") of the Arcanum. In common language the name of the Arcanum is the "Emperor" because of the sceptre and the crown. In the sphere of the theosophical ternary, the titles of the Arcanum will be the following:

"Form" - in the plane of the Archetype
"Auctoritas" (authority) - in the plane of Man
"Adaptatio (adaptation) - in the nature plane.

Let us now turn to the interpretation of the quaternary, represented by the four arms of the cross. This one quaternary symbolises, first and foremost, a general scheme of every complete dynamic process in the Universe.

The active, masculine, expansive principle – י (Iod) - fecundates the passive, feminine, attractive, principle, ה (He). From this union is born the neutral androgynous principle, ו (Vau), which transmits to the lower plane all it has received from the superior. As soon as this scheme is realised, the idea of the family appears, that is, the idea of a completed cycle of manifestation. A statement of the fact of the existence of this idea is, as it were, to trace a contour line around the internal life of that family and to note that in external life, this familiar nucleus, although composed, acts as an independent composite unit.

When we simply state the presence of the completed י ה ו (Iod He Vau cycle), we put the fourth letter ה (He) after the three letters, recognising the cycle as expired, the family formed, completed; hence the designation of it with the passive letter ה (He) (it was made, it turned out). In this form, the quaternary of the elementary cycle will be symbolised by the Third Great Name of God י ה ו ה.

The Kabbalah attributes to this name a miraculous force when correctly pronounced.

Most likely, the High Priest pronounced it, on especially solemn occasions, three times. The first time he spelled it - י ה ו ה; the second time - dividing into two parts and reading the first name of the letter י Iod (masculine), and the second etymologically - Heva (feminine); it turned out Iodheva or Iodhava. The third time the whole word was read etymologically. In all likelihood, his pronunciation was Jove or Jave, but in any case not Jehovah, as some authors of the XVIII century thought, based on conditional punctuation of the Hebrew text, referring not to this name, but to another, replacing it during loud reading.

In this way the Hierophant first pointed out the complete scheme of the elementary cycle; then the androgyny of humanity, and finally, oneness and the Unitarian Law in general. So that the profane could not hear the sacred name, the words of the Hierophant were muffled by the sound of some percussion musical instruments.

The cycle ה ו ה י is distributed in the cross of the quaternary according to figure 9, being read the same one in both directions of the rotating movement. Arrows indicate the right direction. The reading of the third Divine Name, but in reverse, results in the word "Havaioth", considered as symbol of anarchy (the kingdom of the devil). This word is obtained when the rotary movement starts at one end of the horizontal line, rather than at the top of the vertical line.

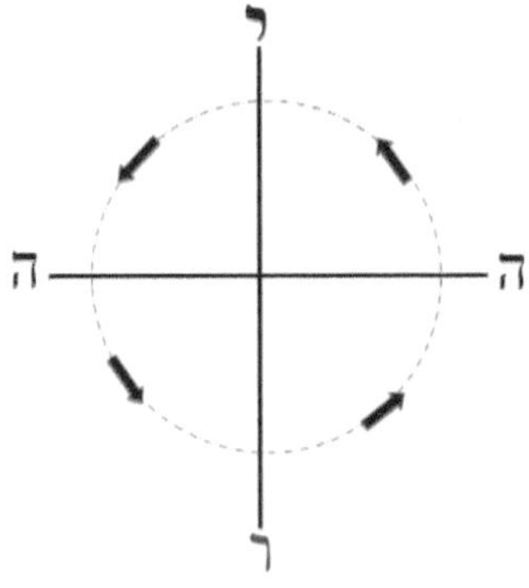

Figure 9

Imagine now that our component unit, our family, featured in the second He of the Holy Name, actively exerts and influence on some element of the external world, that is, simply that our elementary cycle, by its completion, determines the beginning of a new cycle. Then the passive symbol He is no longer suitable for the fourth element; This ה (He), in a mysterious, but natural process passes into the י (Iod) of the next cycle. Our cross, as it were, turns 90 degrees, becomes a circle; the so-called. Quaternary rotation in the hermetic circle.

This is not the place to describe the essence of this process. We restrict ourselves to stating the fact of the transition of the second ה (He) to the new י (Iod). This new י (Iod) seeks or forms for itself a suitable ה (He), fertilises it; ו (Vau) is born, which leads to a second cycle. The fact of the existence of the second cycle, outlined either by the symbol ה (He), if this second cycle is final, or by the sign of י (Iod) if it goes into activity, is ascertained. etc. to infinity.

If we compare the series of elements obtained in the successive cyclic processes to a series of natural numbers, we can verify that in this last series, all multiples of three will correspond to ו (Vau); numbers which, according to the scheme of three, take the place of the number one will correspond to י (Iod), and all who occupy the place of two will correspond to ה (He).

Thus, for example, the 58th element of the series will be an י (Iod), the 62nd a ה (He), and the 75th a ו (Vau). If the series ended on the 58th element, then we would call this element the second ה (He).

Examples of such series: the first element is the father, the second is the mother, the third is the child, the fourth is the influence of the whole family, well, at least on another selected family, which will be the fifth element; this influence will give rise to the common interests of the two families (6th element); the group of two families connected by these interests (the 7th element) acts well, at least on another group of families (the 8th element), creating solidarity between both groups (the 9th element).

We get a diagram of the formations of groups in general and states in particular.

Let's move on to another example: A genius (1) fecundates the mind of a sage (2) who lives in a world of abstractions. The wise man generating and transmitting the idea, creates the possibility of formation of the androgynous element (3), or a human being. This, on the one hand, receives passively the food provided by the wise and, on the other hand, acts in the world according to the teaching received. If your behaviour is more passive ה (He), the whole cycle will be characterised as passive intelligence. If it is active and becomes an י (Iod) of the next cycle (4), fertilising the environment capable of assimilating the new cultural impulse (5), this cycle will be called active intelligence.

Here, then, we have the scheme of the process of cultural transmission, from the point of scientific and philosophical intuition. We can apply the same scheme to the field of aesthetics.

Third example: Morning (1) prepares and schedules the activity of the day (2); the fruit of this activity appears at night (3) and, through the mysterious passage through the night, becomes the starting point for the plans and the next morning (4).

The sowing of spring (1) incubated by the summer conditions (2), provides the autumnal harvest (3) and the winter period determines the degree of activity in the following spring (4).

Applying all this to the scheme of the quaternary spin within the circle, we will have the following data: the trajectory of the displacement of the first quadrant ׳(1-Iod); the trajectory of the second quadrant ה (2-first He); the trajectory of the third quadrant ו (3-Vau) and the determination of the centre. With this, we will have the determination of the circumference, without which we could not be sure that the fourth element ה (the second He), after having turned 90 °, would fall into the place of the ׳ (Iod) of the next cycle.

Each cycle of Initiation has three stages, corresponding to the three quadrants of the hermetic circle.

In the three symbolic degrees of the legitimate ethical Masonry of Ashmole and Fludd, the ׳ (Iod) element is represented by the degree of apprentice. In this degree, the Freemason strives to know as much as possible and for perfection, and only then does he realise the darkness of ethical ignorance in which lives the common man. This degree, being active, requires hard and tiring work. The very ritual of the Apprentice degree is rich in symbolic allusions to errors, deviations from conduct and painful trials of life.

The ה (He) element in the Masonic initiation corresponds to the second degree, the Companion, whose field of application is expanded. The Companion enjoys the pleasant aspects of relationships with his "brother-in-arms" who, like himself, overcame the painful stage of Apprentice. The ritual of degree symbolises the pleasure of knowledge in general, and in particular all friendship, mutual help and protection from experienced instructors.

The ו (Vau) element corresponds to the third degree, that of Master, already familiar with life in the Masonic environment, and [requires the initiate] to become familiar with the idea of death with all its implications. The Lodge of the Masters represents a synthesis of the entire Masonic family. If we consider a closed unit, it will correspond to the second ה (He). If we consider it from the point of view of influence upon its environment, it will correspond to a new ׳ (Iod).

For a detailed acquaintance with the etiology of Freemasonry, I recommend the article by B. M. Pryamin-Morozov (journal "Isis", December No. 1910 and January No. 1911) "Essay on the etiology and general history of Freemasonry", which briefly outlines the dogma and ritual the symbolism of the degrees of the Disciple, Comrade and Master, and to the more detailed work of Papus "Genesis and the development of Masonic symbols" ("Ce que doit savoir un maitre-macon") in the Russian translation of Wojciechowski, which contains, in addition to the analysis of the Hiram Legend, a brief history of the most important Masonic currents due to the origin of 33 degrees Otlandskoy systems.

Returning to the numbering of the elements of the dynamic cycle, we draw attention to the possibility of analysing cycles of nine elements and not three as we did before.

The place of an element in the cycle of nine is determined by the smallest positive subtraction, according to the nine modules. Thus the 58° element of the series will be the 4th element of its cycle of nine, ie the ' (Iod) of the second family of that cycle of nine; the 78th element of the series will be the sixth element of its cycle of nine, ie the second family of the same cycle. We can get these results in a faster way, adding the figures of the number, according to a well-known arithmetical method:

$$58: 5 + 8 = 13;\ 1 + 3 = 4$$
$$78: 7 + 8 = 15;\ 1 + 5 = 6$$

This calculation, which is called "extracting the Theosophical root from number," will be very useful in the future. To complete our presentation, we will add that if we apply to any number of the cycle of three the theosophical addition, that is, the addition of all natural numbers, including the number itself, we will obtain the following results:

1. If the number corresponded to 0 (or to 3, which is the same), in the module of 3, the theosophic sum will also correspond to 0 in module 3. The agenda will remain ternary.

2. if the number corresponded to 1, in the module of 3, its theosophical sum corresponded to 1, according to the module of 3. the unit remains a unity.

3. If the number corresponds to 2, in the module of 3, its theosophical sum will correspond to 3 (or 0, which is the same), according to the module of 3. The binary, after synthesis, no longer remains binary, but it neutralises itself in ternary.

These theorems can be easily demonstrated in general. Here, we will limit ourselves to three particular examples, according to the formula Sn = (al + an)? n ' 2

About the sum of the terms of an arithmetic progression.

$$1.\ 1 + 2 \ .. \ + \ 6 = \frac{7 \times 6}{2} = 21 \rightarrow 3 \qquad (\text{mod. } 3)$$

$$2.\ 1 + 2 \ .. \ + \ 16 = \frac{17 \times 16}{2} = 136 \rightarrow 10 \rightarrow 1 \ (\text{mod. } 3)$$

$$3.\ 1 + 2 \ .. \ + \ 20 = \frac{21 \times 20}{2} = 210 \rightarrow 3 \qquad (\text{mod. } 3)$$

The 6 is Ternary, the 16, Monad and the 20, Binary.
Having analysed the Quaternary as a general scheme of elementary dynamic processes, we will now turn to the symbolism of the cross with equal arms, as a scheme of active manifestation and passive of man on the astral plane.
The vertical bar of the cross, which connects the י (Iod) and the ו (Vau), is divided into two parts by the central point. The from above - י (Iod) - predominates over the below - ו (Vau) - therefore the י (Iod) is more active than the ו (Vau).
The upper part is considered as the field of positive actions of the human being - the field of the good - and the lower part, as the field of negative actions, the region of evil. An Initiate, in every moment of life, must discern between these two fields, remaining always at the neutral point. This is knowing the good and the evil of actions.
The horizontal bar of the cross is also divided into two parts, both corresponding to the receptivity, to the passive sphere of man. The right arm belongs to the second ה (He) which can transform into י (Iod); this is therefore more active, dominates the left arm and corresponds to the sphere of favourable reception. The left arm represents the sphere of unfavourable receptivity. An initiate has the ability to delimit, at any moment of life, clearly, these two regions, that is, has the knowledge of the neutral point.
In summary, on the basis of this new analysis of the cross, we can say that in order to control the authority, man must not only consider the good and evil of his actions, but also know how to use all external influences, both good and bad. He will know how to use both anger as well as a feeling of gratitude, as stimuli of action; both tenderness and disappointment, as means of quenching.
The basis of man's authority is his ability to remain at the centre of the hermetic cross, in tune with all its elements, but remaining master of its spheres.
From this analysis we turn now to the traditional analogies of the Quaternary elements:
We associate the י (Iod) element with what tradition calls Air; the first He is with the Earth; ו (Vau) - with Water; the second ה (He) is with Fire. In ancient times, these four terms were called "Elements of the Quaternary".
In a metaphysical plane, air means time, water - space, earth - the principle of inertness, inertness of matter, fire - the kinetic state of matter. Here we are in the field of theoretical mechanics.
Morally, air indicates the need to dare (oser) for any initiate; water - the need to know (savoir); earth, the duty to remain silent (setaire); fire - to know how to desire (vouloir).

The notion of symbolic animals in the quaternary is associated with these designations: The Eagle is bold; the Man is knowing; the Bull is silent; the Lion is ardent in his desires.

The contemporary Hermeticists symbolise these four manifestations by the shaped emblems of crosses formed by gutters, in which the horizontal correspond to the receptivity in the given and the vertical ones to the momentum of the act.

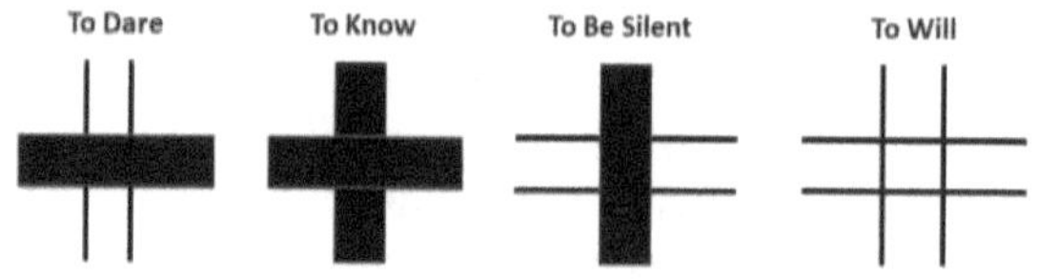

Figure 10

He who dares, drowns in himself the consciousness of danger (dark horizontal gutter) and wakes up activity (light vertical gutter).

He who is satisfied with his knowledge does not study and does not show activity (two dark gutters).

He who is silent does not show himself (dark vertical gutter), but takes everything into account (light horizontal).

He who desires is active and receptive - you need to know what you want (both gutters are light).

Going down into the physical plane, we will interpret the elements as four states of matter: earth - solid; water is liquid; air is gaseous; fire is radiation.

Bringing this explanation closer to the analysis of the quaternary of human actions and perceptions, we clearly understand the following formulation of the theses of the occult classics about the so-called. elementals: Man has a body made up of all four elements; it is synthetic; he knows the four sides of the cross.

The elementals are subordinate to the authority of a balanced person; they do not know good and evil; they do not stand in the centre of the cross, but only live on its sides: the sylphs are in the air; undines - in water; gnomes - in the earth; the salamanders are on fire. Their bodies are composed of each of the materials of the element in which he/she lives; they merge with the elements themselves and therefore they are not visible with the physical eye, are not heard with physical hearing, etc., until they are manifested by a mediumistic loan of the elements of other elements; then they can be contacted by physical organs.

These elementals control the details of what we call physical and chemical phenomena.

It may be useful to give brief instructions on the distribution of the so-called. alchemical elements in terms of the Quaternary י ה ו ה.

The term Air corresponds in alchemy to the universal solvent Azoth, the sign of which is a triple caduceus crowned by the wings of an eagle.

The term Water corresponds to metallogenic Mercury, which can be extracted from mercury and therefore the sign of it is Mercury. Azoth is often called the Mercury of the Sages or the Mercury of the Philosophers, but it must be firmly remembered that it cannot be extracted from metallic Mercury.

The term Earth corresponds to the element of Salt and its sign is of salt.

The term Fire is an element of Sulphur with the sign of Sulphur.

Sulphur and alchemical salt should not be confused with substances of the same name used in chemistry. In alchemy these names indicate two attributive principles of bodies that can be neutralised by either the metalogenic mercury (in the involutionary process) or by the mercury of sages (in the evolutionary process).

In Ethical Hermeticism, which is the analogy of alchemy in the astral plane, to the element "Salt" corresponds perseverance in the pursuit of improvement; to the element "Sulphur", the ardour of prayer or other modes of concentration; to the element "Mercury", the state of being aware; to the element "Azoth," the subtle sensibility and innate understanding of working conditions.

Ethical Hermeticism and alchemy are particular aspects of a general work, known as the "Great Work" and symbolised by the Arcanum XIX. This enterprise can be defined as being a process of transmutation of a given environment or matter, its state the most subtle it can achieve, without, however, exceeding the limits of its own medium, that is, retaining the same general qualifications of the plan to which it belongs. Alchemy deals with the great work of transmuting common metals or even any material dross into nobler metal; the gold. The purpose of Ethical Hermeticism is to transform ethically inferior man into another, different, perfected being that, keeping the general characteristics of an incarnate human being, realises in himself the synthesis of the qualities of an evolved soul.

It is evident that each transmutation of this type is based on the principle of the basic Substance in which transmutation is carried out. In other words, if any dross can be transformed into gold, it is because all material bodies present different modes of coagulation of the single basic substance. In the transformation of an inferior man into a higher man, the basic composition remains the same, the difference is only in the grouping of its astral elements, which in each one is different and varies to infinity. That which is in disorder in an inferior man, is perfectly ordered in the higher man.

We also have the important question of the distribution of the cardinal points between the elements of יהוה. The east corresponds to י (Iod); south to the second ה (He); west to ו (Vau) and north to the first ה (He).

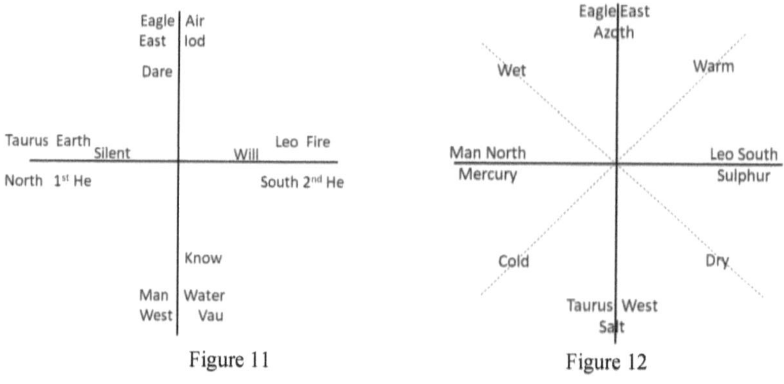

Figure 11	Figure 12
Quarternary of Ezekiel	**Quarternary of St John**

East; Air; Time; Dare, Eagle
South; Fire; Kinetic state of matter; Will, Lion
West, Water, Space, To know, Human
North, Earth, Inertia, Silence, Bull

This scheme is based on the apparent 24-hour solar movement, which takes place in the sense that we call it "contrary". If we arrange the sacred animals as we have done so far, that is:

Eagle - East - Air
Bull - North-Ground
Man - West - Water
Lion - South - Fire

We will have, as it were in a mirror, the reflection of the scheme given in the first and tenth chapters of the book of the prophet Ezekiel. The applications of Ezekiel's quaternary (Figure 11) play an important role in the operations of invocation (a spinning movement called by us "straight", that is, in counter-clockwise) and conjuration (clockwise). Another scheme given by the Apostle John (Figure 12) in the fourth chapter of the Apocalypse presents the reflection of a similar image which, however, differs from the first by the inversion in place of two elements. In it, the Bull - Earth, corresponds to the West; and Man - Water, to the North.

This second scheme makes it possible to introduce certain foreign terms relating to qualifications and attributions: "Wet", "Dry", "Hot" and "Cold". Thus the air would be moist and hot; Water, damp and cold; the earth, cold and dry; Fire, dry and hot. These qualifications are widely used in astrology and alchemy.

About the great Arcanum of Magic

A magic operation is any application of Human Will (single or collective) to the solution of a task, the fulfilment of which depends on the activity of individualised Entities, operating in two or three planes.

Examples of such tasks:

1. A self-suggestion of something sharply determined. In this case, the process acts on the magician (a being living in the three planes) or on a part of its cells.
2. Any suggestion to another human being: influence is again exercised on all three planes.
3. The acceleration or deceleration of any process in the elements: influence acts on the elementals; therefore, also in the three planes.
4. The evocation of an elemental (bipolar being) who, with the aid of a mediumistic loan, can manifest itself in the third plane.
5. The search or attraction of an astral cliché (influence encompasses two planes) or exteriorisation of the elemental of the magician himself, that is, the influence on his own elemental, which can be also considered as action on two planes, etc.

If the magic operation is directed at three-tier entities, its effectiveness will depend on the preponderance of the capabilities of the operator over those of the entities to which the operation is directed.

If the operation acts on entities of two planes, such as egrégores, larvae, etc., then, even if the forces on both sides are equal in both planes, the desired result can be achieved simply because the operator has the reinforcement of the third plane - the physical.

In this case we say that, to carry out the operation, the operator leaned on the physical plane. The point of physical support may be the operator's own body, the body of other beings or material objects outside.

From our definition of magical operation we can conclude that it must be composed, obligatorily, of three elements:

1. The mental, that is, the idea of the operation, supported by an act of the will.
2. The astral, which is the form, that is, the internal structure of the operation.
3. The physical, constituted by the aforementioned operation support points, that is, the symbols used, the resources of the operator's own body, the body of the entities of three planes that help in the operation, etc.

According to what we have learned about the oneness of the basic substance, all elements of mental, astral, or physical aspects of magical performance must be considered as individual manifestations, that is, as forming part of, respectively, a single mental element (the axiom metaphysical), of a single astral element (the universal whirlwind), or of a single physical element (the point of support in the physical plane). Moreover, the mental principle must give birth to the astral form astral, to this, by its condensation, will inevitably determine physical manifestation.

This action, in its totality, that is, the metaphysical axiom, the astral swirl and the physical manifestation, constitutes the Great Arcanum of Magic. The Great Arcanum, being the key to the greatest human power, is never revealed to the disciple by the instructor, for the following reasons:

1. If the disciple, by himself, did not attain the Great Arcanum in all its fullness, it is because in one of the planes, his/her development is incomplete. It cannot therefore be guaranteed that revelation of the Arcanum will not constitute a danger to the Initiator himself.
2. The character of the Great Arcanum is subjective in its understanding and its application. As we will learn later, the spiritual Monads of human beings already have the specific characteristics in their quality as Universal Collective Man cells. We can say they have different colourations and shades. The astrosomes are also different and subjected to different planetary influences. Not even bodies are the same. Thus, a schematic transmission of the Great Arcanum, though accompanied by instructor, will not exempt the disciple from strenuous and prolonged work to adapt the scheme given by the instructor to his individual particularities and the conditions of his own life in the three planes. Consequently, what we say about the Great Arcanum will only be a development of their definition.

The Great Arcanum, like all magical operations, must have in its composition the mental part. The operator should understand and determine the most complete operation. In other words, should be oriented perfectly about the character of each entity, should know its origin, he must know his parents "mentally," that is, he must understand "matrimony" of each ׳ (Iod) with each ה (He) on the mental plane. The key to this understanding is hidden in a static in the Great Law of the Ternary. This Law is symbolised by the ascending triangle (figure 13) which constitutes the upper part of the scheme that alludes to the construction of the Great Arcanum of Magic.

The mental part of the Arcanum, that is, the "marriage" of the determined ׳ (Iod) and ה (He), will give rise to his astral part - the mystery of the basic whirlwind, the ו (Vau), the "son" of "matrimony." As we already explained in Arcanum II, this whirlwind is bipolarised. In addition, it determines the passage of the mental to the physical and vice versa. In it lies the general mystery of involution and evolution. Graphically, it is shown in figure 14, and the number corresponding to it is 2, while the metaphysical part number is 3.

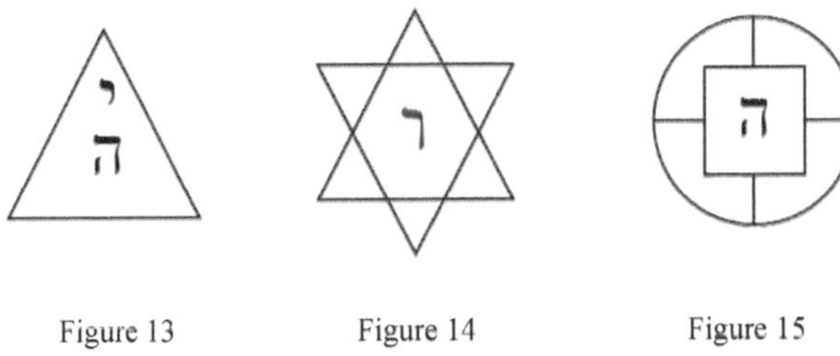

| Figure 13 | Figure 14 | Figure 15 |

The astral swirls of the general type, when condensed, should lead smoothly to the sphere of elements, that is, to the physical world, mysteriously connected with the understanding of Arcanum IV.

The realisation of power over the elements corresponds to the second ה (He) of the dynamic process of the Great Arcanum of Magic. In the physical plane he is represented by the valet, that is, the activity of our ׳ ה ו ה (Iod-He-Vau) family. In this part, synthesised and symbolised by figure 15, we have the domain over the elements (the cross with equal arms, with the mystery of its rotation within the hermetic circle) and the result of the application of this domain - one of the faces of the cubic stone, the square. To this figure corresponds the number 4.

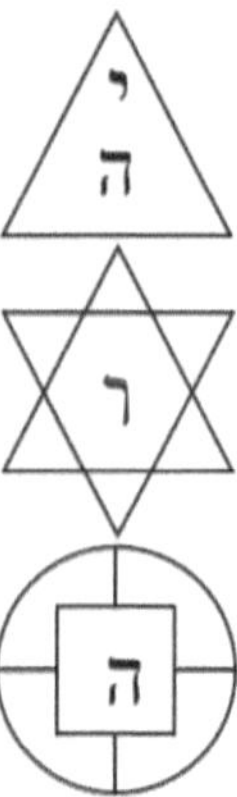

Figure 16

The general scheme of the Great Arcanum is presented graphically by the set of three symbols (figure 16).
We repeat: At the top is the Metaphysical Great Arcanum Ternary. The central part is the binary of the astral "Rota" (the swirl). The lower part, the quaternary of the elemental "Route", or the mystery of achievement, the mystery of the point of support. The attainment of the higher part depends on the degree of the incarnation in the human being of his/her Spiritual Monad, which has always had the knowledge of the mystical marriage ה י (Iod-He).
For the realisation of the intermediate part, man must create in himself, astrally, the androgynous ו (Vau).
To perform the lower part, the physical, it is necessary, besides the creation of the astral androgyne, to know which instrument will serve as the physical support point of the operation and know the passage from this point in support of the astral swirl. A purely logical method can help us to find this instrument. Let us try to make a part of the universe disappear mentally, giving what remains the attributive qualities of the totality. Let us apply to this new universe, this new macrocosm, the Great Arcanum. We will see that the instrument of this application will not change. Continuing to diminish thus the Universe, we will contract it until it is limited to the operator itself. This is a replica of the world – the microcosm - and to him we can also apply the Great Arcanum. Now, the only instrument that the operator can use to act on his own microcosm, is his physical body. This will be, therefore, the great "Athanor" of the Arcanum of Magic.

The knowledge of the operation, however, is not enough. This is just walking on the ground floor of the building. We have a good example of this in the history of King Oedipus. On his path he finds the Sphinx, asking him who in the morning walks with four feet, during the day with two and at night with three feet. The enigma symbolises the director of the Great Arcanum. Let us look at the subject:

The Sphinx represents a synthesis of the four sacred animals. Has the human face, the paws and claws of a lion, eagle's wings and bull's hips. These creatures, by their attributes, condition the access to the astral world, through the four elements they represent. The sphinx is the astral. She is a watchful watcher of the pyramid. The base of the pyramid consists of the square of the elements; however, its triangular sides, delimited by the edges, symbolise the mental triangles, evolutionary processes which at their apex merge into oneness. The mental plane is protected, guarded by the astral.

What was Oedipus's response? He answered that it is the human body, which in childhood walks with four legs, in youth and adulthood, with two feet, and in old age adds a third – the stick on which it is based. Oedipus only guessed the physical part of the enigma, and thereby acquired power only over the body of the sphinx, which he later destroyed, proclaiming himself its conqueror.

The future proved that he had not solved the astral binary of the Arcanum. The downside polarised from the whirlwind dragged him to the horrors of parricide and incest. The dominion over the physical plane only was not enough to prevent what happened. The initiation of the astral plane was given to him by suffering, and on the mental plane he attained peace through the mystery of Universal Love, the self-denial and dedication of his daughter Antigone. It is very significant that astral Initiation reaches maturity, and mental as well, in old age.

Returning to the graphic representation of the Great Arcanum, it is customary to complete it with three words per or by its initials:

חΩZא

TARO ou ROTA

INRI

The first word – Azoth - is composed by the first ideogram of the three alphabets: the Hebrew (Aleph), Greek (Alpha) and Latin (A), which resemble each other phonetically, and the last letters of the same alphabets, namely: Z (from Latin), Omega (from Greek) and Tau (from

Hebrew). That word symbolises the Universal Synthesis and is the motto of the Alchemical School.

The second word - Tarot - is the name of the Bohemian deck, composed of 78 arcana, and is equivalent to the words Rota, Tora (or Torah), Otar, Arot (or Aroth). It represents the tradition that, due to a misunderstanding, was called "oriental."

The fourth word - INRI - on the mental plane is read: "Iesus Nazarenus Rex Iudeorum", the Latin inscription on the cross of the Saviour. In the astral plane, it is read: "Igne Natura Renovatur Integra" (The whole of Nature is renewed by fire). Here, the term "fire" is understood according to the explanations given in this Arcanum. The word INRI was the motto of the Rosicrucian School.

The simultaneous presence of these words in the graphic representation of the Great Arcanum, the Divine Name י ה ו ה, which is the key to Hebrew Kabbalah, indicates that for both Kabbalists (ה ו ה י), as with the Alchemists (Azoth), both the tradition of the Bohemians (Tarot) and the Christian Enlightenment (INRI), seek the same achievement, have the same and unique aspiration, a single target. All these ways are included in the Great Arcanum.

Notes on the fourth Arcanum

French Martinist, Papus (Gerard Encausse), author of The Tarot of the Bohemians, is referenced as a key source by both G.O.M. and in MoTT and also taught the cyclical progression of the י ה ו ה cycle:

India and Egypt are still strewn with valuable remains, which reveal to archaeologists the existence of this ancient science.

We are now in a position to affirm that the dominant character of this teaching was synthesis, which condenses in a few very simple laws the whole of the acquired knowledge.

*

The whole Tarot is based on this word ROTA, arranged as a wheel.

INRI! is the word which indicates the Unity of your origin, Freemasons and Catholics!

Igne Natura Renovatur Integra - Iesus Nazareus Rex Iudeorum are the opposite poles, scientific and religious, physical and metaphysical, of the same doctrine.

ה ו ה י is the word which indicates to you both, Freemasons and Kabbalists, the Unity of your origin. TAROT, THORA, ROTA are the words which point out to you all, Easterners and Westerners, the unity of your requirements and of your aspirations in the eternal הוה - אדם (Adam-Eve), the source of all our knowledge and of all our creeds.

All honour, therefore, the Gypsy Nomad.

In Chapter 2 Papus further explains:

the second He is described as the "synthesis of the Sacred Word.

The י (Iod): The active principle pre-eminent; The Ego = 10
The ה (He): The passive principle pre-eminent; The Non-Ego = 5
The ו (Vau): The Median letter, the link, which unites the active to the passive. The affinity between the Ego and the Non-Ego = 6.

These three letters express the Trinitarian law of the Absolute.

The second ה: The second ה marks the passage from one world to another. The Transition....it serves as a means of ascension from one scale to another.

From the above we see how closely G.O.M. agrees with Papus on certain fundamental keys to the Arcana.

In MotT, The Emperor appears as the Arcanum of Authority. As the fourth sign we can also see in him the completion of the quarternary and – as detailed in G.O.M.'s teaching – the final He of the divine name – the 'means of ascension' – and potential starting point of a second cycle (as Iod). As the author says:

To be something, to know something and to be capable of something is what endows a person with authority.

It is natural to see in the image of The Emperor a symbolic representation of mages such as G.O.M., and indeed we are told that whomsoever is endowed with the characteristics mentioned above has sufficient authority to found a 'school', whilst those in possession of yet higher authority are able to 'law down the law'. The source of this authority comes solely from the divine name of the Tetragrammaton – YHVH – and the legitimacy of the law itself derives from this.

Authority is the completely manifested divine name.

The right to rule of The Emperor is signified by his sceptre. His standing position indicates that he also functions as a sentry and has renounced any sense of personal mission in order to serve as guardian of the throne of power, of law and order, of freedom itself. It is also in this letter that MotT explores the kabbalistic concept of tsimtsum – the 'withdrawal of God' – that is analogous to the Christian idea of creation ex nihilo. It seems likely that some of this content was inspired by the inner kabbalistic circle of G.O.M. As for the post of Emperor – the spectre of which MotT sees as haunting Europe – it is to be considered an occult matter, a spiritual appointment, which cannot be filled by the likes of Napoleon or anyone else who aspires to the idea of the superman.

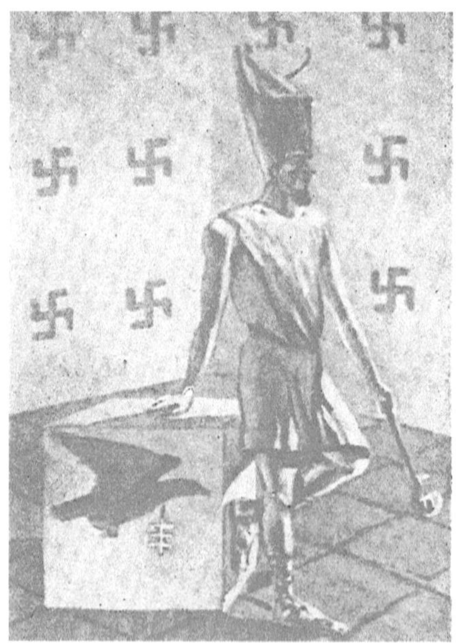

Arcanum V

THE POPE

Pathway from Tiphareth to Chokmah

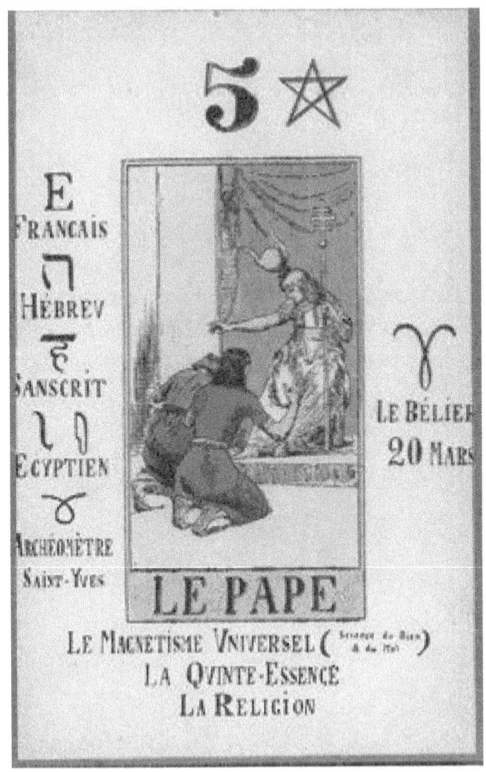

The Pope *Beholds*

Great marvels can be shown by the pentagram

Levi

THE MASTER OF THE ARCANA: Occult Inspiration

E--5 expresses, in the divine world, the universal Law, regulating the infinite manifestations of the Being in the unity of substance

Paul Christian

"Seek the Path, do not seek attainment, Seek for the Path within yourself.

"Do not expect to hear the truth from others, nor to see it, or read it in books. Look for the truth in yourself, not without yourself.
"Aspire only after the impossible and inaccessible. Expect only that which shall not be.

Ouspensky

Arcanum V corresponds to the letter ה (He) of the Hebrew alphabet. The numerical value of this letter is five. The Hieroglyphic correspondence is breath. Breathing is the basis of the vital processes of the organism. Hence its interpretation as "the life," which is in accordance with the astrological correspondence of the Arcanum, Aries, the zodiacal sign of the Ram. The presence of the Sun in the sign of Aries determines the first spring month, and spring is the י (Iod) element of the annual solar cycle. This period prepares the life of the year, it is the first breathing. Two questions immediately arise:

1. If in the י ה ו ה scheme, the ה (He) corresponds to the Feminine Principle, what is there in common between the Feminine Principle and life?
2. The Arcanum II - ב - is interpreted as the Feminine Principle, so because the same interpretation is applied to Arcanum V, what is the nuanced difference between the two?

We will answer the first question by making a small foray into the field of Christian theosophy, both in the most modern (16th, 17th and 18th centuries), as well as in the oldest (14th and 15th centuries).
If each dynamic cycle of the י ה ו ה type succeeds a similar cycle, whose י is a transformation of the second ה of the preceding cycle, then reversing the direction, we can consider that the י of our initial cycle is a transformation according to the ה of a previous cycle. The search for the elements of this cycle will be an ascent in the chain of causality, leading us to the knowledge of the new י of the higher order and to asking the same question about the previous cycle. We can then retreat several times.
The very initial cycle in a series of causations, or, figuratively speaking, the First Family of the quaternary type, of course cannot be considered absolutely independent, that is, as not having predecessors in a number of elements of dynamic processes. After all, the Beginning of all Beginnings cannot have the name י (Iod), for the active element is animated by the desire, the need to fertilise and the Beginning of all Beginnings must have the attribute of Pleasure. This principle must be neutral, androgynous, embodying all the elements of those dynamic processes that it is able to generate. To symbolise this beginning, we will put an end to י (Iod) by writing the scheme of the First Quaternary transcendental region in the form of י ה ו ה (He-Vau-He-Iod).
This point will remind us of the Great, Incomprehensible, Infinitely Homogeneous, Ideally Bright, Radiant Beginning of Ain Soph (Hebrew), of Great Nirvana (Indus).

This Incomprehensible Principle, unable to constitute the object of logical speculation, was manifested by the masculine element ׳ (Iod), the impregnating, expansive, radiant element, which can be given the name of Universal Love.

This Universal Love delimited in itself Passivity, Attractivity - the Feminine Principle – that has a certain quality of a shadow nature, the so-called Restriction, whose name is Universal Life, and impregnated this. From the Union of these Elements, the Higher ׳ (Iod) and the Higher ה (He), the element of the ו (Vau) of the First Family is born. His name is Logos. The Primary Emanations of this Element will be the Second ה (He) of the First Family and will transfer us already to the transcendental world of Olam ha Aziluth of the Second Family.

That is why Life has turned out to be a feminine element.

In the writings of the abbot Trithemus (1462-1516) are transmitted the modern Rosicrucian theories of the time, wherein the element Iod of the First Family is called the Super-Essential Fire, the Element He is called the Super-Essential Air, and the Logos is called the Super-Essential Light. As we see - Air, Breath, was identified with the feminine element.

It is easy to notice that the Rosicrucians considered this terminology an interpretation of the Dogma of the Christian Trinity, with Fire being its First Person, Air the Third and Light the Second.

The Kabbalistic World of Aziluth in Trithemus appears under the name Spiritus Mundi (Spirit of the Universe).

It seems to us that the above help gives an answer to the first question, and we move on to the second.

The Arcanum ב (Beth), points to the feminine, as something existing in the form of correspondence to the masculine, something to be studied (Gnosis - cognition), something fundamentally necessary in the progression of the arcana.

The Arcanum of ה (He) is already the form in which the Arcanum ב (Beth) is clothed. Not more specifically than Beth. Beth outlines the feminine realm. He fills this sphere with something formally existing. In general, the higher the number, the more specific its value. ב (Beth) had a hieroglyphic mouth. ה (He) is the breath emanating from this mouth. Having given these explanations, we pass to the arithmological analysis of the Arcanum.

$5 = 1 + 4$ or $5 = 4 + 1$ and $5 = 3 + 2$ or $5 = 2 + 3$: The first two decompositions of the five will give us headlines for the contents of the Arcanum in the three areas of the Theosophical Ternary. For the Archetype, 1 means the Essence of the Divine, 4 - the fundamental necessity of form. The element of Radiance in the Divine Essence indicates the choice of a positive pole in the matter of evaluating the forms of mental manifestations.

Forms that are not distorted by incorrect reflection and refraction will become synonymous with Good; distorted forms - synonymous with the realm of evil. The Arcana in terms of the Archetype will interpret the Tree of Knowledge of Good and Evil, with a conscious preference for Good over Evil.

The title is Universal Magnetism (Scientia Boni et Mali).

In terms of Man, 1 is interpreted as Vir - an active, fertilising element, and 4 - as elements whose synthesis forms the human body, or as Auctoritas - the secret of ethical dominance in the centre of the Cross (Quaternary). In both cases, the fifth principle that controls their transmutation mysteriously adds to the four principles that exist in the outside world, which makes it possible to realise the Great Work.

In alchemy, this fifth principle is called Quintessence. This word will be the second heading.

We will find the heading of the arcanum in the natural world if, through the external manifestations of the four elements of the fourth Arcanum, we can see the Natura Naturans element of the first arcanum summed with the fourth. He who, through the contemplation of Nature and deep meditation, perceives the Unity behind the veil of the four external influences, will attain the Natural Religion. Thus, the title of Arcanum V in the nature plane will be "Religion".

If in the deconstruction 5 = 1 + 4, under the number 4, we understand the world of the elements, and under the number 1, the Superior Principle, conscious, as explained, then the sum 1 + 4 will symbolise the man, dominator of the elements, who has under control the impulses of his elemental nature.

Putting 4 in first and 1 in second place, we will have the opposite, that is, the formula of an impulsive man whose manifestations depend on external influences on his physical nature.

Let us now turn to the second scheme of division of the number 5 into its components.

5 = 3 + 2 means that Arcanum V is composed of upper and middle principles of the Great Arcanum of Magic, that is, of the metaphysical ternary (3) and the astral binary (2). Thus presented, the Arcanum symbolises the manifestation in the two higher planes of some entity whose metaphysical knowledge rules the astral mechanism. The following beings are capable of this action in two planes:

1. A white magician while doing work on the astral plane, even taking a point of support on the physical plane.

2. An elemental of the positive type (eg the "mens" and the human soul, united, studying with evolutionary purpose the clichés, during the interval between two incarnations).

3. The egrégores of the positive (evolutionary) type.
4. The "Spiritus Directors" who form a superior "policing" in the astral plane, etc.
The opposite deconstruction - 5 = 2 + 3 - symbolises the cover-up of the Absolute Truth of the Trinitarian Law by the mirages of false astral clichés, driven by involutive whirlpools. This deconstruction corresponds to the manifestations of tenebrous entities, such as:

1. A slim dark man, working in the astral.
2. An elemental of the negative kind, for example the "mens" and the human soul, united, seeking misrepresented clichés, during the interval between two incarnations, in order to reincarnate, not to repair his karma, but to be able to return to physical enjoyment again. These entities are content to satisfy their desires in any other way, even if it is through mediums.
3. egrégores of the negative type (involutive).
4. The larvae, etc.

The two deconstructions studied (3 + 2) and (2 + 3) are respectively illustrated by the positions: evolutionary (figure 17) and involutive or inverted (figure 18) of a geometric symbol of a huge theoretical meaning and realising value: The Pentagram.

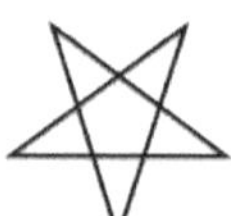

Figure 17   figure 18

In the evolutionary pentagram (3 + 2), it is customary to insert the human figure, whose head, arms and legs form the pentagram. In the inverted pentagram (2 + 3), it is easy to insert a goat head, putting horns, ears and beard on the tips. This goat symbolises the devil, the "father of lies", thus embodying the clichés of true manifestations but deformed to the point of being no longer recognisable.
Before proceeding with the pentagram, we will study the card of Arcanum V. His erudite name is "Magister Arcanorum" (Master of the Arcana), that is, the Great Hierophant. His common name is "The Pope". The image shows a man sitting. Upon his head we see the horns of Isis, and between them the full moon. The binary of the horns is dominated

by the ternary of the Cross of the Great Hierophant (see Arcanum IV), fixed on the end of the staff that the man holds in his right hand. The staff is quite long so that the cross stands well above the head slightly inclined toward the Hierophant. The Hierophant's left hand extends over the heads of two figures kneeling before him. In some pictures, the gesture of the hand is a blessing, in others it is a gesture of silence. In both cases, the gesture expresses a manifestation of the will. Of the two kneeling figures, one is lighter, one darker.

The Hierophant is seated, like the woman of Arcanum II, between the columns of Jaquim and Boaz, with the traditional curtain between the two. Here as there, the torque of the columns is neutralised by a personality, but in Arcanum V the figure is masculine. The man is seated, which expresses the passive state, receptive to the teaching of binaries, but it is a male being, that is, an active being who is adapting this teaching to life. In addition, his gesture expresses the will.

This element of the will enlightened by knowledge, this element of active (not inert) power, is the main characteristic of the Arcanum V and its graphic symbol: The Pentagram. The whole environment suggests Initiation.

The kneeling figures suggest that the pentagram – the Magician - along with the forces of Light is triumphing over the forces of darkness, forcing them to serve higher purposes. He knows the great temporary ignorance of these elements and, consequently, their weakness. This allows one to use them for good, thus facilitating the future atonement of their errors.

The following questions now apply: How will the man whose astrosome is vivified by the "mens" have the ability to perform the functions of the pentagram? How should one create this pentagram?

A succinct enumeration of the trials, to which those who seek Initiation are subjected, will answer the first question. The second we can reply by sketching a general plan of the physical, astral and mental training of the Mage. We will soon. The Initiation is of two basic types: that of white magic and that of black magic, according to what it serves. That is, to create a human being:

1. Aspiring to the good by the dedication to the good and despising one's own comforts or annoyances;
2. Enjoying evil by its own attraction to evil, even if it brings harm; enjoying the lie, because of the attraction to the lie and the darkness, because of the attraction to the darkness.

In the two types of initiation, the first stages are similar. The neophyte must prove his/her 1 + 4, that is, demonstrate that he/she is not disturbed by dangers and surprises coming from the elements; prove that he is not a coward on the physical plane, that he does not lose his head. In this stage is the traditional proofing of the fire that he/she must cross boldly, without fear of burns; [in the trial] of the water one needs to swim through without being intimidated, even if the current is very violent; [in the trial] of the air, one is required to hang on, without fear and without dizziness; [in the trial] of the earth, its depths must be penetrated without fear of being crushed by the dark vaults of the underground.

The evidence from the second stage of trials is again similar in both types of Initiation. They are astral trials concerning fear, passion, and consciousness. The neophyte is proven through the fear that can be felt before horrible and even aggressive astral clichés that are presented. At the same time the neophyte's sensitivity is artificial and temporarily increased.

The second ordeal - that of passion - seeks to verify whether the neophyte is able to control his/her sexual desire, even if the conditions are the most conducive to their satisfaction. This ordeal is generally divided into two parts:

1. To be able to oppose an approaching temptation;
2. To know not to take advantage of a victory, obtained by the very effort in overcoming the indifference of the person of the opposite sex.

The third ordeal - that of consciousness - is to demonstrate their ability to perform a particular job, fulfil a mission, keep a secret or simply not give up despite enormous temptations and the full guarantee of impunity.

Although these trials are equal in form, in both types of schools - those of white magic and those of black magic - they are not the same in their essence and purpose. The white magician must not fear the most horrible clichés, for you will have to cross the world of them to reach the Luminous Principles; the black magician should not fear them either, for you will have to stay in touch permanently with horrible and repugnant manifestations.

The white magician must be able to be firm in his chastity to be sure that he will not succumb when temptation appears; the black magician must only understand that self-control, even in certain moments of life, gives him advantages over those who do not possess such control. The white magician must always fulfil his accepted duties and obligations to become firmly in the service of the good. The black magician must only understand that, having trained his firmness in the execution of a determined plan, he could do much more harm than acting at random and when opportunity arises.

Black magicians sometimes go through additional proof of dedication to evil, which we will not describe here.

Let us now speak of the artificial pentagram - the symbolic figure - or the great Sign of the Microcosm.

The word "microcosm" literally means "the world in miniature". It is the name given to being in which, according to the Law of Analogy, there is a full synthesis of the correspondences of the elements which make up the external world or (of the Greek) "Macrocosm".

The pentagram is one of the so-called magical symbols that were already mentioned at the beginning of our course.

If, for example, we take two corresponding series of letters of the alphabet, beginning the first series with the letter A, and the second with the letter M:

1. A, B, C, D, ...
2. M, N, O, P, ...

The M can then serve as a symbol of A and vice versa: A as a symbol of M; or N as symbol of B and vice versa: B as symbol of N, etc.

We have already had the opportunity to affirm that the symbols, on the mental plane, have a power. Therefore, acting on this plane consists in the creation of ideas and the analogy is a powerful inventive method, as are induction and deduction. As an example, let us take the algebra, in which the manipulations of the symbols greatly facilitate the deduction of ideas.

To clearly understand the influence of a symbol on astral entities, we need to notice how much our emotions sometimes change under the influence of an association one way or another - to a certain emotional manifestation. An exclamation, an image or an object associated with the emotion of fear, lived in the past, can in itself provoke fear. A threatening cry from a completely weak and harmless creature can scare away the enemy, if it has already heard a similar cry coming from another strong and dangerous creature.

The emotions belong in their totality to the astral world, and it is because of this that the symbols employed by magical schools or of common use among the members of a determined egrégore, have acquired a great power in the astral world.

Those who know the importance of the symbol of the Cross in the relations between Christians, would certainly not be surprised to hear that this symbol exerts an influence on the elementals. However, for the elementals, the emotional association is different: The Cross represents for them man's synthetic composition, his external activity, and reminds them that Man reigns over the elements, and therefore also themselves.

Just as on Earth, in the course of time, various organisations lose their popularity, so too, in the astral world, the symbols, as well as the forms associated with certain emotions, go through a slow but continuous evolution. It would be very naïve to think that all the symbols of the ancient Egyptians, keep until our time, the same force of magic, and invariably provoke the same manifestations. Of course, they have not entirely lost their power, but unless they are completed and adapted, shall not have the same effect as in antiquity. The phalanx of Philip of Macedon would not be capable of frightening a battalion of Marines today, but could well disperse a group of marginal people in the streets, even when armed with knives and clubs.

There are symbols that are qualified as simple, that is, that cannot or will not usually decompose. For example: the point, as a symbol of oneness; the circle, as a symbol of something complete or unified, and even the triangle as a symbol of the ternary of a given type, etc.

In contrast, compound symbols are formed by several simple symbols. A syllable will be a simple symbol. Several syllables, pronounced next, will constitute a compound symbol.

A graphic symbol, composed of simple symbols, forming a harmonious association of emotional manifestations, an association linked by analogy to a metaphysical synthetic conception - such a symbol will be called PANTACULO[16].

In the symbolism of sound, the pantaculo corresponds to a set of syllables united in a word or even in a whole sentence.

Take the pentagram as an example of a pantaculo. It is, of course, a synthesis, for it can be deconstructed into 2 + 3 or 1 + 4.

In the mental plane - plane of ideas - to this pantaculo corresponds the idea of Free Will. At the physical plane, among beings endowed with this privilege, the most outstanding manifestation is to be human. The astrosome of the human being and bearer of the *pentagram* and its "mens" expresses, characteristically, the will.

We have already had another good example: that of three pantaculos united in one, that is, the figure examined and representing the graphic scheme of the Great Arcanum. The name ה ו ה י, as we write it, must also be considered as a sign symbolising a dynamic cyclical process.

In the field of sound manifestations, both simple and compound formulas are divided into two types: the *Mantrans and the Setrans*. The

---

[16] We have maintained the Portuguese version of this word throughout the text. A Pantaculos is a magical symbol or object that, either by similarities or confusions in the uses and names, has been considered synonymous with pentacle, pantaclo, pentaclo, pentalfa and pentagram. For G.O.M it seems to have denoted any kind of star with any number of points.

mantric formulas are those that are intended to act on the astrosome of an entity other than the operator himself, even if that entity is a part of the operator's collective self. Thus, a formula destined to act on another human being, on an elemental, etc., will be a *MANTRAM*. A formula that the operator will use to act on, for example, *his own liver*, to improve its operation, will have the same name.

The *Setrans*, unlike the mantrans, are intended to strengthen the entire astrosome to regulate the functions of the entire ganglion node system of this astrosome, in order to facilitate the process of transmission of the manifestations of *the Will*, the mental plane to the physical. The setrans, using the common language, give the operator the *security* to perform a magical operation successfully.

Let's go back to the *pentagram* once more. We postpone until Arcanum VII the subject of the materials that should be used to make an artificial pentagram, to be used during magical operations, and also the explanations of the complementary signs and symbols sometimes placed in it.

Now, we want to draw attention to a very important fact that gives the pentagram prominence over the other pantaculos. It is necessary to emphasise that the astral entities, being biplanic, possess only astral bodies and, therefore, they know only the astrosomes and not the physical manifestations of the beings or objects with which they come into contact. An astral entity can enter into relation with the physical world only temporarily and with the help of the mediumistic fluids, that is, through a temporary appropriation of the life force of the subtle material principles of people called mediums. The same can also be achieved with the help of some organic matter or the components of living organisms on the physical plane, such as the sap of plants, saliva, blood, semen, milk, sweat, etc. In certain cases, this loan may be made until the evaporation of water or burning of organic products, such as resin, dried herbs, etc.

In the case of mediumistic loan of fluids, the astral entity temporarily manufactures for itself physical organs, and during this time is able to see, hear, smell, etc. as we do. Without the aid of mediumistic principles, an astral entity cannot see, for example, a table; nevertheless, it perceives the astrosome of this table, that is, its formal principle, which forms the physical appearance of the table; she cannot hear the spoken words, but realises the formal principle that built the phrase, etc. We can say that this entity:

1. Is aware of the amount of energy expended in giving the table a shape, or that a certain sentence was pronounced.

2. It records all the energy transformations that arose during these processes, their order and their exact scheme.

These are the principles of the so-called purely astral view which, to be more exact, should be called astral receptivity.
Let us now try to imagine an astral entity, looking with its purely astral sight, for a human being. This entity will perceive only a certain scheme of manifested energy sources. The magic says this scheme is very similar to the scheme of energetic manifestations, emanated by a pentagram made with seven metals, and the latter differs little from the scheme of the manifestations emanated by a pentagram made with pure gold. Some authors advise the use of a pentagram of light, produced by electrical equipment.
Considering all this, one arrives at the conclusion that the pentagram has the power not only to evoke the idea of Free Will, but also to create the illusion of the presence of an active human being. Besides being a symbol, the pentagram can also serve as a scarecrow.
The more man is active, the more his will is firm and determined, the more the scheme of his energetic manifestations resembles that of a pentagram, ritually consecrated by a magician, that is, properly magnetised by his fluids.
Taking into account all that has been exposed, we take the liberty of calling *pentagrams* all entities that belong to our categories of 3 + 2 and 2 + 3.
Thus, when we speak, for example, of an astral struggle between two men, or between a man and an elemental or even an egrégore, we will call it a struggle between two pentagrams. It would be appropriate to mention here the advantages that determine the victory of one or the other party.
If two entities struggle in the astral, it is necessary to consider astral force, that is, the sum of the activity and receptivity of each. If the two forces are equal, that part which has a point of stronger support in the third plane - the physical - will be favoured. Thus, a magician whose astral power is equal to that of an elemental, will undoubtedly be the Victor, because he possesses a physical body. If, at that moment, the mage will die, he will lose his advantage and the forces will remain the same.
A Planetary Spirit, who finds himself away from his planet, could be defeated. However, this is not possible when the astrosome has support in the physical body of the planet. The influence of the Spirit of Saturn or the Spirit of Jupiter on the Earth can be overcome by an earthly ceremony, but no magical ceremony on the earth's surface can overcome the Spirit of the Earth.

A magician, in his physical body, that is, when his astrosome is supported by this body, is more powerful than during an astral output, when the astrosome maintains only a weak link with the physical body. If the astral force of two incarnate mages is equal, the Victor will be the one whose nervous system is stronger. If they also match at that point, the one with the most vital force in the blood wins. The latter being also equal, victorious shall be the one whose physical organs find themselves in better conditions.

All that we have just said explains the frequent use of the pentagram in magical symbolism and the importance given to this symbol by the magicians.

The Flaming Star with which we became acquainted in the Masonic Lodge of Companions is a pentagram with the letter "G" in the centre. For a master, this letter means "God". For the intermediate degrees it means "Gnosis" (Greek word, synonym of knowledge). For the higher degrees Hermetic degrees it means "Generatio" (generation, production, a Latin word).

Studying the use of the pentagram in Freemasonry, where we find it in the symbolism of several degrees, we should not rush to draw conclusions or be suspicious when we see inverted (2 + 3). In this case, this presentation does not correspond to black magic, since it has a purely metaphysical sense and alludes to the transformations that take place in the course of time. We can explain it thus: in the beginning, there are the binaries (2), but, with time, meditation and study, the binaries are neutralised by the terms of the medium, and there are the ternaries.

Even in the interpretation of the deconstruction 1 + 4, there are several points of view.

The "4" does not always symbolise the material and the "1" the spiritual-astral. In The Great Astral Cliché of the Redeemer, יהשוה (Iod-He-Shin-Vau-He, Iehoshua or Ieshua) the letters יהוה symbolise the Divine Will, the Word, the Logos, as the organ of this Will. The symbol ש (Shin) (numerical value 300, see Arcanum XXI) symbolises the mechanism of involution, of materialisation, that is, the Incarnation of the Word. In this case, the top tip of the staff symbolises the Material Instrument with which the Divine Will operates on the physical plane. This is the cliché of the most powerful of the pentagrams throughout the astral plane. On the mental plane it corresponds to the dogmas of the Incarnation and the Redemption, professed by the Rosicrucian Schools of the XVI to XVIII centuries.

If the יהוה, in the same symbol, does not represent the Divine Will, but appends its weak reflex, that is, the will of a particular human being, the symbol ה ו ש ה י (Iod-He-Shin-Vau-He) will correspond to a simple human pentagram (figure 19).

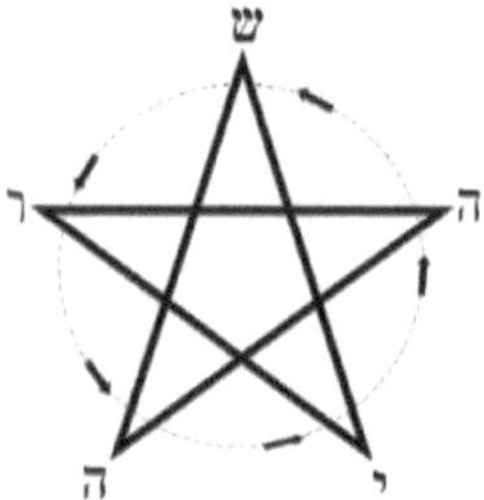

Figure 19

Let us now turn to the second question: how to create in ourselves this human pentagram, this astral nucleus?
For this, a rigorous mental work, an astral and physical training, is indispensable. When someone decides to build the pentagram in himself, there are always several difficulties, since the person will have to create in himself, not only new manifestations, but also correct the consequences of their inadequate education, education, both received from others and as a result of their own efforts. The task of re-creating a personality can be divided into two parts:

1. To form within yourself a volitional, conscious being.
2. Re-educate the impulsive being, the being who acts in all fields, under the influence of reflexes and responds to the external impacts of these or that banal manifestations: who shouts when he feels pain, who escapes when there is danger, who responds to a blow by another blow, and by a smile to adulation. This impulsive being must become an adequate instrument for the realisation of the conscious will of man. Certain reflexes should be reinforced, others suppressed.

Let us now deal in more detail with the task of creating in oneself a man of will. Let us suppose that within a pentagram from top to bottom we enter a human figure; The upper tip of the pentagram, by the law of analogy, will correspond to the central part of the forehead, and this, in turn, will correspond to the region of thought.
First of all, let us try to understand a little the process of meditation which is the act of thinking consciously and voluntarily. They are part of meditation:

1. The filtration of sensory receptions by the corresponding organs.
2. The fixation of ideas (by memory).
3. The confrontation of ideas.

Accordingly, we can indicate the following general rules to facilitate meditation:

1. Avoid giving answers to questions, automatic responses, dictated solely by memory, without participation of other elements that are part of meditation.
2. Avoid discussions that usually lead to confrontation of forms only (dialectic), not of ideas. The vast majority of discussions have:
a) A different understanding of the terms used; in this case, the discussion revolves around an evil understood.
b) A basic difference of the dogmas of the worldview; in this case, the discussion is useless.
3. Exercise in perceiving the invisible in the visible: The astrosome and the "mens" in the physical envelope. To see the contours of the human body, is not enough. It is necessary to penetrate the astral correspondences in the dynamics of the manifestations of the astrosome (the aura), and even in the characteristics of the mental monad of the person. To analyse a work of art it is not enough to limit oneself to its appearance; it is necessary to penetrate the essence of its form and even the idea that created it.
4. Look everywhere for natural analogies, as we have done with respect to the human body, studying Arcanum III and interpreting these analogies as broadly as possible.
5. Seize opportunities to penetrate the laws governing harmony and perfection of form in works of art; visiting the museums, listening to good music and, in general, not departing from the world of art.
These indications for the development of the ability to meditate are only very general. It would also be useful to understand the mechanism of meditation a little more. We'll start with the analysis of the so-called concentration of thought.
Let us imagine that we voluntarily limit the field of our attention to a certain number of objects - this will be concentration of thought on these objects. Let's take as an example a man who is writing an article. Your thoughts will address three issues: the idea of the article, the way of expressing itself and the sharpness of its handwritten handwriting. He firmly decided not to allow access to other thoughts, not listening to external noises, not paying attention to the state of the organism, the environment, the passage of time.

Another example would be to focus on a particular person just like in the picture or thought that person wants to convey to us. Our thoughts would then be confined to these two ideas exclusively.

A third example: focus on the presumed age of a person.

A fourth example: try to focus on the total absence of any subject in our mind. This will be called passive concentration, which is the opposite of the concentration practiced in the three examples above: the active concentration.

Let us briefly indicate some ways of exercising in active and passive concentrations. Let's focus our thoughts on an organ or some place in our body, imagining its harmonious state. This is not only a good exercise in concentration, but also, the possibility of healing the disharmony or the weakening of the functions of this body. If by otherwise, we focus on the image or desire for disharmony of the same organ, we will obtain the opposite result. Here we have the explanation of the appearance of the "stigmas" in the people who concentrate on the idea of wounds in one or another part of the body, such as the ecstatic mystics, which during Holy Week focus on the wounds of the Crucified Christ.

For very impulsive people it is advisable to focus on any object, even insignificant, but taking the decision to control during this time the muscular movements reflexive type, such as turning your head when you hear a noise, etc. These types of exercises are preparatory in nature.

A third type of concentration exercise, quite important and recommended in appropriate literature, is the realisation of an imaginary journey. To do it, we can, or try to remember with all the details of a trip actually made in the past or to invent it in its whole or in part, living almost concretely the smallest details, the movements executed, received impressions, and completely forgetting the real environment. The exercise could be accomplished in 20 or 30 minutes with the help of the alarm clock.

A fourth type of exercise will be concentration on an object that belongs to us, seeking to penetrate with our mind in its basic form, its construction, its origin and the idea of its goal. The exercise can take up to 30 minutes.

A fifth type is to imagine clearly and meticulously an object that we do not see and compare it then with the reality. Exercise 30 minutes.

After practicing the exercises mentioned above, we can move on to the sixth type.

Let us try to create in our imagination the general form of a non-existent object or something never seen by us and, in that general way, go to the details. From there, in the opposite direction - details to the general and the initial idea - to verify the logical construction and the correctness of our creation. Exercise up to 40 minutes.

After this stage, it is good to exercise in passing quickly and clearly from an active concentration on a subject, to an active concentration on another chosen subject. If we can, it will be a proof of considerable concentration. It's evident that the less comfortable the conditions in which the concentration is practiced, the more value the result will have. Let us now turn to the types of passive concentration exercises. Many find it more difficult than the active one. As conditions that can facilitate it in the first experiences we can list the following: darkness, the absence of everything that attracts attention, the lying position, the weakening of the respiratory process, the closing of the eyes, the covering of the ears, etc. In these conditions the person seeks to actively focus on a symmetrical form, such as by example a circle or a disk of a certain dimension, motionless or rotating on a background of infinity. The colours of the disc and the background can be chosen at will. Then, the dimensions of the figure will gradually decrease until they are reduced to one point. Finally, for an act of the will, make it disappear to the point, remaining only the idea of the bottom. This is called conditionally achieving a passive concentration in the field of astral receptivity. Then, in later exercises, we will try to suppress the fund, too, that is, achieve a total absence of voluntary imagination in any field. In this state of passivity and void, an external cause (for example, a will of others) may introduce something to the student such as a geometric figure, an acoustic, tactile, gustatory or olfactory [stimulant]. In such a case, the person must know that the received is from an active source and not from the own imagination.

The modes of preparatory exercises may vary to infinity and the schemes given above are just examples.

Passive concentration exercises should not take more than ten minutes and, in the first times, no more than three to five minutes.

Active and passive concentrations are typical forms of meditation for an occultist. They can be used in various ways.

The most characteristic way of concentrating for a practical purpose is an active concentration on an issue and then a passive concentration. This passive concentration is to receive the answer on the subject of active concentration. Here, we must distinguish three cases:

1. The question is formulated in such a way that the answer relates only to the mental plane. Example: we cannot establish a stream of logical deductions that leads to the solution of a philosophical, mathematical or other problem, that is, in this current we are missing some links, be that due to a memory failure, or due to uncertainty about the chosen method.

In this case, the active concentration will allow us to see clearly the links of the chain that we already have, encouraging in us a keen desire to discover those that are lacking. The passive concentration will be made soon after, like a simple rest. However, after this rest, we will find that the gaps are suddenly filled in very clearly. This process, which can hardly be explained, is called intellectual vision.

2. The question is of astral character, that is, a question that can be answered through a visual or acoustic form. This response is generally received during the merger process, passive, appearing the form on the background mentioned previously, or by perception of sound.

3. The question has a physical character. We note that this terminology is only conditional. We can consider a question as being of a physical nature when it can be answered through a tactile, olfactory or gustatory perception. Generally, this response arises when one is still in active concentration or at the passive threshold, making it unnecessary to stay in this last. Example: we want to remember the perfume corresponding to a given name; the taste of some food product, or the tactile impression of the surface of a fabric, etc. All these cases are physical issues.

We can see that the interpretation of the "mental," "astral," and "physical" terminologies we use is quite free and was introduced exclusively by the custom of creating analogous ternaries.

Among other specific concentration applications, we will mention psychometrics in the state of vigilance (there is also psychic medium or somnambulic psychometry). Contemporary occult science characterises this type of exercise as a manifestation of the sixth sense, the odic or astral. We have already given the name of "astral receptivity" to this manifestation. The authorities in the field are unanimous in recommending that persons trained for psychometry minimise, during the sessions, the receptivity of the organs of the five physical senses. For us, this recommendation simply stresses the importance to a psychometrist, of knowing passive concentration.

The process itself proceeds as follows: the psychometrist, before the session, concentrates actively on the desire that its astrosome contacts the astrosomes of certain objects. Soon after, he takes these objects one after another and touches them with his forehead (the location of the centres) the heart or the solar plexus (the choice of place depends on the temperament of the subject and empirical data). In doing so, the psychometrist increasingly enters passive concentration, during which it receives a visual image (in colour or not), less frequently an acoustic perception and, more rarely, a tactile perception, linked to the history or formation of the object, to people or other objects that are in astral connection with the psychometrised object, etc. The psychometrist will see, for example, the manufacture where the envelope that squeezed was made the subject of the letter contained therein, or you will see the face of the person writing, or even the events of that person's life. You can also see the breakdown of mail where the letter was sealed, or other related images. If the object is an old currency, you may see an interesting historical cliché. A fragment of mineral, a shell, an object petrified, can provide geological clichés.

The duration of the passive concentration on each object should be, in general, about 5 minutes; however, if the object begins to provide more than a single cliché, it can be extended by 20 or even 30 minutes, especially when clichés have a scientific or other. Clichés often appear in an inverted chronological order.

The first exercises of a person who is not sensitive by nature, but wishes to develop psychometric abilities, can be chosen according to the preferences of that person; however, we recommend starting with exercises in which the person should answer a question formulated above; for example: "We have seven sealed cards and we know they were written, each one by a different person. Who is the author of each of these letters? "Or, "We have four sachets each containing a different, odourless mineral?".

The diagnosis of internal diseases, made by people very sensitive and provided with an acoustic channel to the external dimension, also belongs to the field of psychometry.

Generally, these people act in the following way: the sensitive person asks the patient to insert his little finger in the ear of the sensitive himself; after a few minutes, it provides detailed information regarding the state of the patient's internal organs.

To examine the auras, the astral emanations of persons or objects, their colours, the dimensions of the colour layers, etc., a short active concentration is applied first - the desire to see the aura - and then a passive, more prolonged concentration during which the aura becomes visible. Many people can see the aura without closing their eyes. The ability to discern its denser layer is probably due to the improvement of the physical vision and the ability to concentrate on the observation of a given region. However, the aura is observed more frequently with closed eyes, that is, perceived by the sixth sense.

However, for an occultist, the most important application of concentration is conscious prayer. At the process of prayer, active concentration is directed to the entities of various plans and sub-planes, according to the evolutionary level of the person who prays and the reason for his prayer. This active concentration is followed by a passive one, which determines the degree of satisfaction that the person experiences as consequence of his prayer, as well as the character and intensity of the Superior Influxes by him received.

There are still some brief indications regarding the processes of self-suggestion and the creation of thoughts-strength or ideas-strength.

We will describe the self-suggestion process in its simplest scheme, accepted by several German schools, reserving for the Arcanum X, its wider study.

When practicing self-suggestion, one must choose naturally calm moments, such as, for example, at night, after the day's chores, lying down, but in full wakefulness, or at the time of falling asleep, when we lose the notion of the environment, but we still have the control about our thoughts and gestures. Under these conditions, we need to elaborate our self-suggestion according to the ternary scheme: "mens", astral and physical plane.

Let us suppose that it is a matter of suggesting to ourselves the ease and the absence of distraction during the next day's exam. This idea already constitutes the "mens" of self-suggestion. Next, this "mens" should be clothed with astral matter; for example: we formulate an appropriate phrase, such as "I am diligent, I feel free, I am perfectly willing to reflect on the examiner's questions and to respond without shyness or nervousness. "Having formed this phrase we repeated it two or three times in a low voice, without opening his eyes; then four times whispering it just, and two more times, again in a low voice. During this exercise we clearly imagine the exam scene, the environment (real or imaginary), the room, the examiners, and our laid-back attitude towards them. In addition to imagining the scene, we must come to live it, to feel the state we want in the meet. We must bring forth in us that inner joy and satisfaction that conditions the self-affirmation and propitiate success. In this way, we will have all the astral elements of the self-suggestion and even a small loan taken from the physical plane - the sound vibrations of the half-voice. However, we will try to imagine the physical plane more intensely by the pronunciation of the sentence aloud (a couple of times) with eyes open and accompanying it with the gestures that they may be customary to us when we are confident and joyful. With this, the suggestion cycle will be complete.

We will also mention two important conditions for the success of the suggestion:

1. All phrases, images, etc. should refer to present tense (see Arcanum III).

2. In self-suggestion, the faith of the operator is not indispensable for the success of the operation as in another any kind of suggestion. When we try to suggest something to another person, it is very important there is

no doubt about success. In self-suggestion, by doing everything consciously, we can get a good result even doubting it. This is explained by the fact that our will harmonises more easily with our own astral than with the astral of an alien entity. Using this self-suggestion method, we can achieve many good results, such as, for example, cures, victory over bad habits, general strengthening of the organism, memory, etc.

Let us now turn to the creation of ideas-force. The scheme is as follows: we want to create an entity (astral) that must act on us or about another person in a certain sense, even if it's just "I want my uncle to be less nervous." This idea, even words, will constitute the "mens" of the entity. To create your astral body, we will stand and, without moving, we will try to forcefully retract all the muscles of the extremities. Then we will focus on the thought of transmitting to the entity that we create all the energy of our muscles, simultaneously relaxing them to the state of sagging. The energy that was stored (but not used) for a mechanical work, will become created entity, that is, it will form its astrosome. We can facilitate the formation of a thin layer physics of this entity, placing in the vicinity a glass of milk taken at the time, of honey or fresh blood. The vital force of these products will play the role of the mediumistic principle.

The gaze, with its emanations (fluidic, odic, magnetic), corresponds to the upper tip of the human pentagram We will deal with this briefly, since in Arcanum X we will have to return to all the subjects mentioned here and concerning the acting through the eyes, the hands and the legs. The elemental form of action through the eyes is called the central gaze. It is the fixation with the two eyes in the central part of the forehead, above the base of the nose, the individual with whom we experience. Such a fixation, accompanied by an active concentration on what we want and an image of the movements that the individual must perform, the emotions that must feel or of the thoughts that must have, can lead you to carry out our intent; this if it is not actively concentrated in another direction. In addition to the central gaze on the forehead, the central gaze is also used on the nape of the neck and the shoulder blades. The place on which the central gaze is placed may not be covered by any insulating material, such as silk, wool, furs, etc.

The best distance to obtain a good result with a man of medium sensitivity will be: to the forehead - up to 50 steps; for back and neck - up to four or five steps.

Besides being able to apply the central look, it is indispensable to know how to dominate with our eyes in the case where it is necessary to combat the central gaze of an alien pentagram.

In the struggle of two pentagrams, in the mutual fixation of the eyes, the following factors, in the order of their importance, determine victory: the mystical power, the astral power, the nervous force, the vital force of the blood and the functional and organic health of the body.

When there is no need to fight with the central outlook of others, and if we want to submit to it, then we lower our eyes and passively focus. The central gaze has greater influence on a person asleep or hypnotised. In the technique of the central gaze, we must, first of all, determine exactly the point of encounter of the optical axes; then, to maintain the firmness of the eyes, without blinking, without tearing, without causing congestion of the eyelids etc. To strengthen the eyelids and outer shells of the vision, eye doctors recommend ocular baths, showers, compresses with infusions of different herbs, etc. For those who do not possess, by nature, a penetrating look, exercises are recommended: Fixation of a black point the size of a small coin, placed on the wall, at the height of person's eyes and a distance of 3 to 4 meters. In the beginning it is necessary to fix the perpendicular to the surface on which this point is drawn. Having mastered this exercise, one can pass to the second, which will be done by moving away and looking at the point from a different angle and, in the next stage, walking through the room, without however looking away from that same point. It is also expedient to exercise a rapid eye-catching look - without diminishing its intensity - point to point.

After these exercises, occult literature recommends the practice of fixing the central gaze on one's own image in a mirror, and the exercise of fixing the gaze, also in a mirror, on their own eyes. The duration for the exercises of the central gaze is not delimited, depending on the abilities natural or acquired of the subject.

In the central gaze directed at the forehead of someone, the observer must fix, in his visual field, all the details of the person's face without any movement of the visual focus. The concentration during the central gaze should, if possible, be added to the conviction - without any restlessness or doubt - that desire will come true.

Let us now turn to the magnetism of the hands. The classical literature on magnetism, confirmed by the findings of the sensitive psychics, states that the fluidic emanations of the extremities of the body, when observed in the dark, take the form of plant shoots. It also states that, from the right hand of a man whose fluids are normally polarised, a positive magnetism emanates, that is, an energy capable, via the short distance between the hand and the compass, to repel the magnetic needle we call boreal and which indicates approximately the north. Consequently, if we consider boreal magnetism positive, we can say that, from the right hand of a man emanates this magnetism (the positive +), considering, however, several limitations. Similarly, from the left hand of a man, generally emits negative (-) magnetism. For a woman the polarisation of

the magnetism of your hands is inverted, that is, positive for the left
hand and negative for the right hand.

To check these laws and measure the intensity and regularity of
polarisations in people, there is an instrument called a magnetometer. A
static needle is hung like a galvanoscope; the tip of the needle,
oscillating, indicates the degree of intensity of magnetism.

In this Arcanum we will not speak of the use of the magnetism of the
extremities for the cure and other purposes; we will add only that the
normal polarisation of the left foot is similar to the right hand and vice
versa, and also that the magnetic force of the feet is used in different
from that of the hands. If, by an act of the will, we suppose, for example,
the emanations of the right foot, this force will be available and can be
transferred, for example, by the left hand, thereby increasing its
magnetism, which will be indicated by the magnetometer.

The normal magnetism of a male pentagram can be presented, as it is in
reality (figure 20) or as seen in a mirror (FIG. 21), the latter system
being often used in occultism.

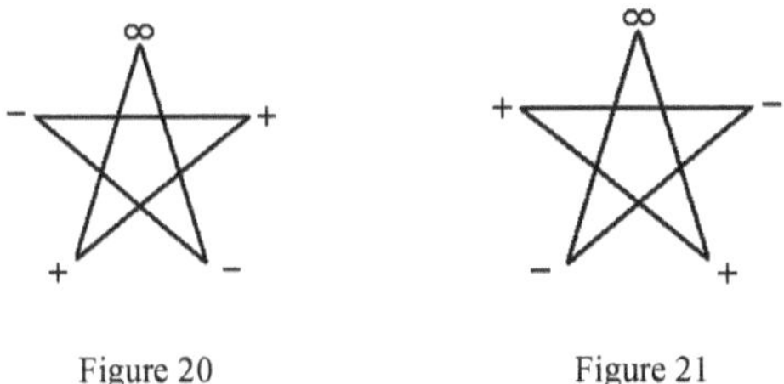

Figure 20   Figure 21

The normal female pentagram corresponds, therefore, to Figure 21.
However, both men as well as women may have an opposite polarisation
of their gender. The changes in the polarisation can be constant or
temporary, caused by the states of the soul, physical states and even by a
conscious volitional effort. A weak pentagram, also changes your
magnetisation under the influence of proximity or contact (passing,
laying on of hands, etc.) of a strong pentagram, in the same way that a
weak magnet modifies its magnetisation when it enters in an induction
field of another, stronger.

We would like to add, regarding the training of a conscious man, that if
the meditation can be compared to a means of receiving spiritual food,
there is also a powerful "stimulant" to facilitate this reception: it is
LOVE, in all its forms of manifestation.

Physical love expands the circle of selfishness of a primitive man,
transforming personal selfishness into family egoism. The bonds of
friendship between the neighbouring families transform the family
egoism into tribal and, later, national, called patriotism. The mental or

artistic affinities, metaphysical, or astral themes, mutually attract people grouping together in circles or schools. The highest, Universal Love for all that lives, that manifests itself via Archetype, Humanity, and Nature, is the most powerful of the stimuli in the process of creative meditation, evolutionary and redemptive, which is the main instrument of realisation of the Hermeticist.

An incarnate human being can be studied as consisting of:

1. The conscious, volitional man, able to meditate and, in general, capable of what we call creativity.
2. The impulsive man, governed by a reflex behaviour, not chiselled, manifesting himself in a stereotyped and almost automatic mode.
3. The physical being - the human body - which can be considered as the instrument at its disposal of the first two.

The task of studying the physical being belongs to the field of anatomy and physiology with its numerous subdivisions. From our side, we will only remember the analogous ternary: head - breast - abdomen, stressing that the quality and quantity of nerve fluids depends on the quality and quantity of quantity of the vital force of the blood, and this force, in turn, is under the direct dependence of the nutritious juices, elaborated by the digestive process.

We will now deal briefly with the impulsive man and his relationship with conscious man.

The impulsive man, by the essence of his definition, is passive. Reacts only to external impacts, and this, according to definite and immutable laws. According to the basic Arcana, he is also triple, since it is composed of:

a) of the lower, sensory Man, who lives through his physical instincts and needs.
b) the average, emotional Man who has passions and lives expressing his desires, which should not be confused with conscious will.
c) The impulsive-intellectual man, reasoning and calculating.

The work of the conscious man consists in balancing the reflexive attitudes of the impulsive, and at turn them into their opposites. Let's look at behavioural examples of these three types of impulsive man:

The sensory man will withdraw his hand from an object that burns, reflectively and abruptly; A conscious mind can control this reflex and even, if necessary, play the role of Múcio Scevola.

The emotional man will ordinarily respond with a smile to an adulation; the conscious man can repress the smile and even turn it into a grimace.

The impulsive-intellectual man, responding to a legal question, will automatically quote a law and its usual application; the conscious man, along with this law, will analyse the particular case and whether or not to apply the law in question.

The impulsive-intellectual man is a very dangerous phase of human development, is a supporter of routine, an enemy of new hypotheses; is the patron of these intellectualised people which automatically apply methods and formulas to cases to which they need not apply.

Each of these three phases of impulsive man can lead him to specific excesses and vices, if the conscious element does not oppose it in due time. The lower phase can lead to addictions of a material nature, the most common being alcoholism. The middle phase can lead to another series of vices, among which the most typical is debauchery; we understand the astral debauchery, multiplying by the imagination the forms of passionate manifestations.

Finally, the impulsive-intellectual man is subject to the vices promoted by his mind calculator. Such a prototype is the game.

In order to avoid digressions in the subsequent study of the Arcana, we will respond immediately to possible questions:

Question 1: Can a conscious man lose, in a passing way, the control of his physical body?

Answer: You may, in the following cases:

a) absence of the functions of the conscious man and presence of impulsive man (sleep, lethargy, etc.)

b) deterioration of the nerve cell of a sensory organ or of a motor centre, and also in the case of rupture of a nerve;

c) disturbance of the circulation or production of nervous fluid (what medicine calls functional disorder of the nervous system).

All these circumstances can mean an impediment to the conscious man, to exercise control over the impulsive, and this may manifest itself: in the instinctive field, by the lack of good sense; in the psychic field, by the lack of harmony; and, in the intellectual field, by the lack of insight.

Question 2: What are the abnormalities of the human imagination that can manifest?

Answer: To answer this question we must consider the fact that the forms created by our imagination, as well as depending on our astrosome, still depend on two other factors:

a) The perceptions of our senses

b) The regulatory logic of our "mens" if the mens does not participate adequately in the process of creation of forms, then the imagination will become the so-called "fantasy."

If the nervous transmitters of the sense organs react abnormally to the impact of external actions or if, mistakenly, reactions appear without the intervention of any external impact, then we will have the "hallucination".

Question 3: What is the action of alcohol on the human being in the various stages of drunkenness?
Answer: We can discern three phases resulting from the ingestion of a high amount of alcohol:
1. The man is only just drunk, the alcohol absorbed increases the dynamism of the blood. The nerve plexus ganglia, which constitute a reserve of the nervous force, are more intensely spent. This causes an increase in mental activity and activity in the physical body.
2. The body absorbs more nerve fluids than the mens. Impulses are no longer controlled by the conscious part of man; inappropriate gestures and words appear, the person staggers, etc.
3. The reserve of the nervous force that has been expended must be restored by the astrosome that is dedicated totally to the organism, being unable to supply any more of its astral energy to consciousness. There follows, then, deep sleep, characteristic of heavily intoxicated man.

Question 4: What is hypnosis in relation to our division of the human being?
Answer: In the hypnotic process, the hypnotist irritates or exhausts the nervous system governing the sense organs, and thereby separates the impulsive part from the conscious part of the person. By replacing the latter with his own consciousness and will, the hypnotist can direct the impulsive personality of the hypnotised. We are only considering mechanical methods for hypnotic results, without any magnetic action (which we'll talk about later). The mechanical methods are to irritate or tire the view with shiny objects placed on a dark background, or with rotating mirrors. Hearing is irritated by the beating of a gong or tired by the repetition of monotonous sounds; the result can also be obtained by a scare. Being the action of a conscious man over the impulsive, extending not only to the present time, but also to the future, the hypnotist may suggest future actions and perceptions.

Question 5: How to understand madness?
Answer: We must differentiate two types of madness:
1. For physical reasons
2. For astral reasons
Madness, by its manifestations, may resemble the permanent state of intoxication, in its second level. In the madman, the impulses

predominate and, in addition, each madman, according to the disturbance of certain nerve centres, presents manifestations of a specific type. The cases of madness, of course, can be caused by an organic or functional disturbance of the nervous system. However, it is also possible that due to purely astral cause, the activity of certain centres has been over-accelerated, harming others. Let us not forget that the human body was performed by the astrosome that continues to rule it. The "mens" is manifested by middle of the astrosome. Imagine the fact that an alien astral entity has joined an astrosome, seeking to interfere in the regency of the body. We will have abnormalities in the manifestations of the astral and physical planes. There may be an impediment or impossibility of a normal manifestation of the partially paralysed the astrosome functions.

It may also happen that to the astrosome is added a larva, own or alien. This results in a reluctant larval incarnation, causing in the patient the predominance of a typical habit of that larva. In such cases, the larva, in the beginning, predisposes the victim to a certain vice; later, having exhausted all the resources of the body, in that field, and wanting to in most cases seek to destroy the body to which it was strongly linked by the long stay in him. The death of the body will release it, giving it the possibility of separating from the astrosome and entering in another body to, again, suck your resources. It is also possible that in a human body incarnates a depraved elemental which fights the astrosome of the patient, causing the alternations of the periods of madness and lucidity. But when and how can all this happen? When the man is too passive and does not sufficiently protect his body against the aggression of a "strange astrality". A larva can easily enter not only a sleeping man, but also, in a man discouraged by the failures of life in which he sees no purpose, and even in a more active man, however, who is enslaved by the characteristic vice of this larva. Also, an elemental can incarnate relatively easily in a man's body during conscious or unconscious exteriorisation of its astrosome. The unconscious exteriorisation is more frequent than is usually thought. A fright, an unforeseen misfortune, a situation with no way out, anything that causes us to momentarily postpone life on the physical plane, facilitates the process of exteriorisation. A great sudden joy can have the same effect, although different. The human soul, in the moment in which it experiences great happiness, stays as such imbued by gratitude to the astral principles that caused such an event that, attracted unconsciously by these principles can reach the outside to pray. Sometimes the astrosome externalised, upon returning to the body, is able to expel the undesirable visitor who took hold of his body (temporary madness); other times, the astrosome does not reintegrate and, within his body acts the entity that has seized it (permanent madness or, in best of all, personality change of character; in these cases, the presence of a strange and therefore not suitable astrosome, harms and destroys the body). Finally, one can give the case of the astrosome which returns to the body without, however, being able to expel the other astrosome; there will then be the coexistence of two astrosomes in one body and, consequently, a constant struggle between them (intermittent madness).

Having answered these five questions, we can now turn to the subject of the impulsive man in his three stages of development.
Let us study the most adequate norms of life in order to achieve the subordination of the impulsive being to be conscious, and to the realisation of the evolutionary goals of the latter. These norms of life are naturally distinct for the three phases. Let's start with the rules instinctive-impulsive (sensory) being, where the greatest importance must be given to the diet.
First of all, we must understand the normal effects of abstaining from food. A temporary abstention from food makes it possible for the organs of digestion to rest and, because of this, higher levels of nerve fluids to the upper organs, more intense spiritual activity. Overeating produces the opposite effect - predisposes the man to spiritual stagnation. Of course, a too long abstention from food weakens the body. The frequency and time of feeding must be adapted to the individual conditions.
As for the way of eating, we can say that the constant vegetarian regime is only for those in tropical and subtropical countries. Wizards of temperate regions only adopt this diet in preparation for an action that requires a certain appeasement of the mental centres, without a pronounced diminution of the functions of the instinctive centres. A diet composed solely of vegetables maintains instincts, and animal foods - the animic. In tropical countries, the animal is sufficiently nourished astrally by the intensity of the solar emanations.
The vegetarian diet that the magicians adopt before a performance, usually extends for 40 days, and strict vegetarian regime (fruits and vegetables cooked without salt) - no more than 7 days. In animal foods caution is advised. Meat is often attached to bad astral fluid, that is, to the phantom (the lower part of the astrosome) that governs, after physical death of the animal, the functions of deconstruction and reintegration into the nature of the physical body. The slaughtered animal dies frightened, nervous, angry. To avoid incarnation in us of this bad astral, it is necessary, before ingesting the meat, to pronounce mentally some "setram" to strengthen our self-defence, or a "mantra," to drive out the evil astral entities.

The reasons for so-called "sentimental vegetarianism" are not real. Vampirism is a basic law of the subsistence of beings, because not only in food, but also in the process of breathing, we annihilate other lives. As for the efforts to achieve self-improvement through asceticism, in any field that, based on the fact that the Great Teachers were ascetics, we will respond to the man who has reached a high level of perfection, dedicating himself almost entirely to the spiritual work, you may not need more than a handful of rice a day for your survival. However, the process cannot be reversed because by the restriction of food, unaccompanied by the necessary immersion in spirituality, no profit will come.

An anchorite who leads a contemplative life, does not need phosphates to nourish the brain, but an intellectual, a professor who teaches his or her knowledge, a student or a writer, does need them. To complete the subject of the regime of an instinctive man, it must be pointed out that, in addition to feeding, it may sometimes need stimulants. To those who lead a methodical life, the feeding alone is sufficient, but those in whose lives are inevitable heavy expenditures, nervous periods may, from time to time, employ stimulants that cause an additional absorption of the energy stored in the plexuses and ganglia.

The material stimulants are coffee, tea, alcohol, hashish, opium, morphine, etc.

Coffee and tea have a typical binary. The coffee corresponds to the negative pole of this binary, since it especially increases receptivity. The coffee action phases are as follows: initially, facilitates digestion, seizing fluids to speed up the process; after two or three hours, facilitates a secondary loan for the benefit of intellectual receptivity; the reaction after the coffee effect - that is, the drop in receptivity - takes place around 5 hours after being ingested.

Tea is the positive pole of the binary; makes digestion slower and during this reduction of the rate digestive activity, favours intellectual activity, due to the non-use of nervous energy for digestion. The post-tea reaction is a prolonged withdrawal of fluids from the intellectual sphere to the digestive organs in order to repair the effects of the delay. Insomnia, due to strong tea, is not a reaction, but a phase of its action; the person does not want to sleep but think. The reaction occurs later.

The mentioned binary can be neutralised by alcohol, whose short but strong action raises both the receptivity and the activity. Alcohol can be used before moments when we need quickness of wit and wit in the responses. Apart from these cases, we should not make a habit of ingesting it, because of the reaction to alcohol we talked about earlier. All that has been said refers exclusively to the man not yet accustomed to using the stimulants mentioned.

Opium and morphine decrease the sensitivity of nerve fluids, thereby giving the illusion of indefatigability; the same can be said of cocaine. The action of hashish is less studied; under its effect the connection of the astral with the physical body is less felt and can give the illusion of exteriorisation of the astrosome, while opium and morphine facilitate a real exteriorisation. We shall return to these matters later, as well as to the action of the sulphuric ether.

Let us now turn to the standards of life of the soul-man. Analogy of food, and aromas - the analogy of stimulants. The breathing exercises of the occultists aim at three targets:

1. The regularisation of the acidification process (oxygenation of the blood, which renews the provision of vital force).
2. The control of the respiratory rhythm through the will, resulting from this control of the functions of the heart.
3. A reduction of unnecessary wear of carbonic acid.

The first is carried out by gentle deep inspiration and sufficient retention of the breath; the third - partly by retention and partly by slow expiration; the second - the proper distribution of all the phases of the respiratory process. We will give a brief general outline of the initial breathing exercises:

Taking care not to be with a loaded stomach, the person lies in almost horizontal position, leaving the head and shoulders a little taller than the rest of the body, legs outstretched, the arms also extended along the body and the muscles relaxed. The place should be well ventilated but not cold. The absence of any concern or concern and that nothing will interrupt the practitioner in the exercise are very important factors. The transgression of the last rule may have an adverse influence on the fate of persons who interrupt the exercise and on the subject itself.

When these conditions are fulfilled, the person closes the mouth and breathes in the air through both nostrils, the slowly, but without forcing the natural rhythm, and even lifting the thorax and abdomen; all this without causing any pain. The inspiration phase is followed by the retention phase, and this, by the slow expulsion of the air by the two nostrils. When all the air has been blown out, a small pause between the end of the last exhalation and the beginning of a new inspiration. This will be the respiratory activity.

Theoretically, it would be desirable for the first three phases to be of equal length if possible. In practice, the result is somewhat different, as the comparative duration of the phase of inspiration corresponds to the individual's ability to draw [vampirize] from the environment; the phase of retention - the ability to properly use the energies acquired, and the phase of interruption - passive concentration. The latter, for a magician, should not be prolonged too much.

These are the reasons why the following is recommended: focus during inspiration on the appropriation of some energy or capacity; during retention - about their assimilation, or its adaptation to our own person; during expiration - about its proper use. The final pause is dedicated to a passive concentration.

The absolute and relative durations of the phases, as already mentioned, are determined by the individual characteristics of the astrosome of the subject. We can, however, indicate an approximate duration for an average subject: at the beginning of the exercises - 10 seconds for each active phase and about 2 seconds for the passive phase, the fourth; after a few months of exercise - 25 seconds for each active phase and approximately 3 seconds for the passive, the last.

We recommend practicing the exercises two or three times a day. At first, it will be 5 minutes; over time - up to 25 minutes at a time.

The above method is often called Western. Many consider it dangerous because if it is not used together with an active meditation and the evolutionary type, can cause the assimilation of negative principles and effects from the environment, that is, elements that enliven thoughts or selfish feelings. For this reason, many occultists replace it with the so-called oriental method, proposing, in the breathing exercises in the following way: air is inspired first by the left nostril only, tightening the right nostril with the thumb of the right hand. Then, during retention, the two nostrils are tightened with the two thumbs. It exhales through the right nostril, the left remaining tight; after a short break, it is breathed in by the right nostril, again it retains the air with the two nostrils tightened, it expires through from the left; is inspired by the left, following successively the previous process. This method is very useful, even for people who practice the former, as it can be applied temporarily in a case of coryza, when the first method cannot be used.

Once started, the course of breathing exercises should not be interrupted due to coryza or laryngitis, or even mild bronchitis. In febrile states, the exercises become and in cases of acute bronchitis or pulmonary congestion. Do not even think about it.

In the case of respiratory exercises, we will also mention the exercise of the solar plexus called, sometimes "plexus massage". This exercise alternates pressures on the diaphragm, pushing it down and up. It should be done very carefully, meticulously, without any precipitation, completely ignoring it when unwell or in a state of emotional distress. It consists of the following:

In the same position indicated for breathing exercises, we breathe in the air, obligatorily through the two nostrils, filling only the thorax and holding the abdomen tight. Then, only by the effort of the thoracic muscles, that is, without expiring, we obtain a gentle thoracic volume and, simultaneously, elevation of the abdomen. Then, making only the abdominal muscles, contracting the abdomen, causing the chest to rise; then, we take the chest again, etc. After 5 or 6 of these double phases - elevation of the thorax and abdomen - we finish the exercise in the phase of elevation of the thorax and let the air leave slowly through the nostrils. All these items constitute a single cycle of plexus exercises. It is necessary to run about five cycles.

Then we can give the exercise over. It is not advisable to do more than one exercise daily, nor start them before having acquired a certain practice of exercises because the expansion and retraction of the chest or abdomen takes about 8 seconds and therefore a cycle of exercises lasts more than half a minute, which presupposes a certain practice in holding the air during this time. The full exercise will have a duration of three and a half or four minutes.

At first we can limit ourselves to 2 or 3 cycles, and even take breaks of 1 to 2 minutes between each cycle, filling them with usual breathing exercises. If, a few hours after exercise of the plexus, the person experiences nervous pains in the stomach, it should be advised that there may have been some irregularity in the "exercise" technique, or it may even still be premature.

The exercises of the plexus, or more exactly of the whole region neighbouring the diaphragm, have as a purpose to attract the blood flow to the solar plexus to nourish it more intensely and also fortify the muscles of the region. All these requirements constitute important points of support for the human will in its lower astral realisations.

If breathing exercises in the training of a mood-impulsive man include the role of food, the aromas, as has already been said, will play the role of stimulants. We will not enumerate here all the scents used in magic; we will mention only three of the most typical that form a ternary analogous to the ternary of the planes of the human being:

1. Incense - positive pole of the ternary - causes mystical states (facilitates prayer, etc.)
2. Musk - the middle term of the ternary - acts in the soul sphere (love, etc.)
3. Tobacco smoke - the negative pole of the ternary - causes, in unaccustomed persons, a a very short period of excitement, followed by a reaction of a purely instinctive nature – the sleep.

When tobacco is constantly used, it is important to be aware of its side influences, determined by the method of smoking and the qualities of the

tobacco. To people who work intellectually, Papus recommends mild and aromatic tobacco cigarettes; people who lead an animated life, such as the follies - cigars; to manual workers, workers, etc. - the pipe.
Let us now briefly indicate the standards of life of an intellectual man. To the role of environmental influences. The recommendations are as follows:

1. Surround yourself, as far as possible, with an environment that does not create tensions and does not reduce normal, impulsive reactions to aesthetics. Avoid the company of people who are very ugly, as well as unpleasantly asymmetrical forms and disharmonious colours; Surround yourself, on the contrary, with aesthetic objects.
2. Exercise and automatically maintain self-control in times of danger and restlessness, and even develop a purely instinctive ability to do so.
3. Do not emphasise, with impulsive-intellectual reaction, dislikes in terms of touch, taste or smell. If one does not like, for example, the smell of garlic, limit the corresponding astral reaction, without expressing it with gestures or words, just by hearing the word "garlic".
For the intellectual-impulsive man, the role of the stimulant will also be played by music. In this case, we will also have a similar ternary, since each type of music acts as a stimulant in one of the sub-planes.
During a military campaign, a vigorous military march can influence the physical courage of soldiers, through impulsive-intellectual reactions. A psychic man will be stimulated, also, by impulsive-intellectual reaction, by the sounds of a waltz, or perhaps by opera music. A purely intellectual nature will need, as a stimulant, chamber music.
Finishing the subject of the impulsive man's training, we once again draw attention to how much of it is relative to the sub-division of the human in ternary, used by us. I allow to adopt this division only as an example of how to use analogous ternaries that facilitate the construction of any scheme.

Notes on the fifth Arcanum

In contemplating this card, first we shall invoke the ultimate high priest, Melchizedek and will also note the ongoing significance throughout the history of occult movements of the letter M[17] as a prominent initial letter of initiatory group leaders.

With the emphasis on breath there is much resonance between G.O.M.'s teaching on the fifth Arcanum and that of MotT, where spiritual respiration is a key theme. As the bearer of five wounds in the image of Jesus Christ and guardian of the fifth Arcanum, The Pope of MotT would also seem to correspond perfectly to the upright Pentagram within a human being, as contemplated by G.O.M.

We see the underlying congruence between G.O.M. and Eliphas Lévi's teaching emerge very clearly in MotT, where the emphasis in the fifth Arcanum on Eliphas Lévi's pentagram teaching is highly reminiscent of G.O.M.'s own focus on the same.

From Eliphas Lévi, Dogme et rituel de la Haute Magie; trsl. A.E. Waite, Transcendental Magic. Its Doctrine and Ritual, 1968:

The Pentagram signifies the domination of the mind over the (four) elements; and the demons of air the spirits of fire, the phantoms of water and ghosts of earth are enchained by this sign. Equipped therewith, and suitably disposed, you may behold the infinite through the medium of that faculty which is like the soul's eye, and you will be ministered unto by legions of angels and hosts of fiends. The empire of will over the Astral Light, which is the physical soul of the four elements, is represented in Magic by the Pentagram, placed at the head of this chapter. (trsl. p. 67)

*

We must remark, however, that the use of the Pentagram is most dangerous for operators who are not in possession of its complete and perfect understanding. The direction of the points of the star is in no sense arbitrary, and may change the entire character of an operation, as we shall explain in the Ritual (trsl. p69).

Tomberg also wrote detailed notes on the elemental trials of fire, air, water and earth, all of them arduous spiritual tests with the power to drive the neophyte to the brink of despair.

---

[17] There is also a "Mem Key"

In chapter five of Transcendental Magic. Its Doctrine and Ritual, we find the following summary of Eliphas Lévi's doctrine concerning the pentagram:

The Pentagram, which in Gnostic schools is called the Blazing Star, is the sign of intellectual omnipotence and autocracy. (ibid, trsl. p.237)

And then, in The Key of the Mysteries:

The quinary (or quinternary) is the number of religion, for it is the number of God united to that of woman. (Eliphas Lévi, The Key of the Mysteries; trsl. A. Crowley, London, 1969, p.30).

Summing up one of the great problems not just of occultism but human affairs, comes further into Letter V of MotT: "We have arrived at a very serious problem: that of the pentagram of the evil quinternary and that of the Pentagram or good quinternary". Here he touches on a matter expounded upon at length by G.O.M. – of the upright vs the involutive Pentagram. A solution to the problem is given by Louis Claude Saint-Martin:

"...the quinternary is good "as long as it is united and bound to the decad" and it is "absolutely evil" when it is separated and isolated from it. In other words, the pentagram, as the sign of intellectual autocracy, ie, the emancipated human personality, is good when it is the expression of the personality whose will is united and bound to the fullness of the manifestation of Unity (the decad); and it is evil when it expresses the will of the personality separated from this Unity. Or, in other words again, the sign is good when it expresses the formula: Fiat voluntas tua ("Thy will be done"); and it is evil when the formula of the underlying will is: Fiat voluntas mea ("my will be done"). Here is the moral and practical meaning of Saint-Martin's statement".

Here, again, do we see the practice of sacred magic epitomised by the five wounds and fifth element of the quinternary contrasted with personal magic or sorcery, the difference being in "Thy will" over "My will". The difference between "personal sacred magic" and "personal arbitrary magic".
The fundamental role of Prayer is emphasised throughout MotT, especially in the Fifth Arcanum, where the author describes how "The prayers of humanity rise towards God and, after having been divinely "oxidised", are transformed into benedictions which descend below from above." The columns of Jachim and Boaz, seen clearly on traditional

depictions of The Pope on Tarot cards, are channels for this rising and falling of prayer and benediction. It is the pillar of Severity which motivates the upward channel of prayer, whilst Mercy delivers the blessings. This process is likened to spiritual respiration.
There is agreement that "the letter He, the fifth letter of the Hebrew alphabet, has breath as its primitive hieroglyph".

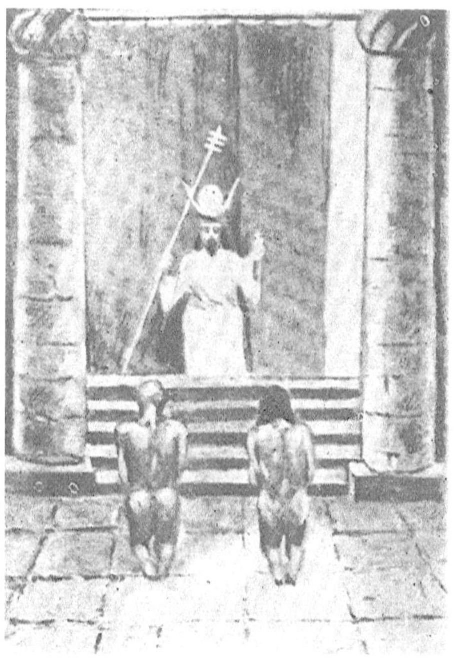

Arcanum VI

ו

THE LOVERS

Pathway from Binah to Tiphareth

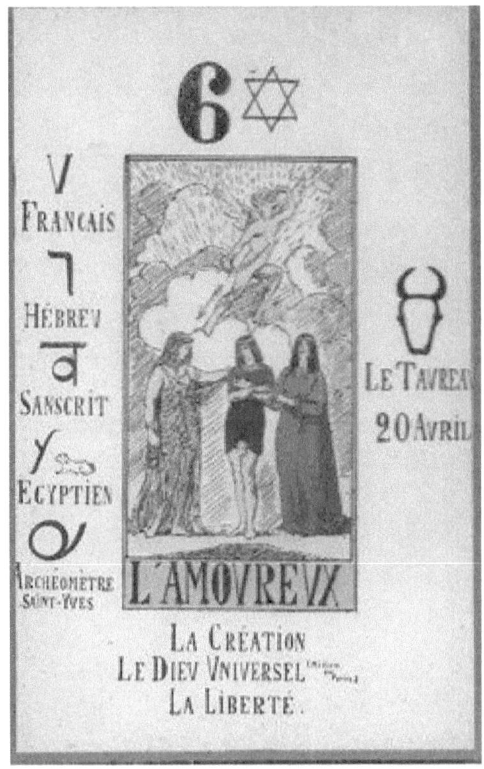

The Lovers are *beautiful*

Ever bear in mind that Equilibrium results only from the opposition of forces and affirmation can only triumph over negation

Levi

THE Two ROADS: The Ordeal

U, V--6 expresses in the divine world the knowledge of Good and Evil

Paul Christian

That wisdom, which crawls on earth, advises belief in the earth and in the present. This is the Temptation. And the man and woman yielded to it.

They dropped from the eternal realms and submitted to time and death. The balance was disturbed. The fairyland was closed upon them. The elves, undines, sylphs and gnomes became invisible. The Face of God ceased to reveal Itself to them, and all things appeared upside down.

Ouspensky

The sign ו (Vau) of the sixth Arcanum is already known to you through the word יהוה. The hieroglyphs of this Arcanum are: the eye and the ear, that is, the two most important organs that facilitate contact with the external world. What are the consequences of this contact?

It is evident that external concepts will correspond to certain subjective concepts. What is internal has the receptive capacity for what is external. The macrocosm corresponds, in each of us, to the microcosm, our miniature universe. Here again we have the law of analogies, the law of reflected images.

The pantaculo of Arcanum VI is formed by two interlaced triangles, one being the image reflected from the other. The names given to this pantaculo are: Star of Solomon, Seal of Solomon, Right face of the great pantaculo of Solomon, Mystic hexagram, Sign of the macrocosm.

At the centre of the figure is the "Stauros" symbolising the process of fertilisation: The vertical line (activity) fecundates the horizontal line (passivity). This means that the rising triangle should be regarded as the original, and the descendant, as the reflection of the first. This pantaculo (figure 22), despite its simplicity - and perhaps because of its simplicity - contains almost the whole significance of Arcanum VI, and allows so many different interpretations, that the knowledge of only part of them, already proves a solid degree of initiation.

Figure 22

Let us try to indicate some of his interpretations:

1. The ascending triangle can be considered as the triangle of Jesus, symbolising the evolutionary process of our redemption. Consequently, the descending triangle will be considered as the triangle of Mary, the element that participated in the involutionary process of the Incarnation. The "Stauros" points to Redemption as a target, and the Incarnation as a means.

2. Analysing the pantáculo as a sign of the Macrocosm, that is, as the general scheme of the unrolling of phenomena in Nature, we will call the ascending triangle - Triangle of Fire, symbol of evolutionary processes,

subtlisers, renovators, purifiers. The descending triangle is the Triangle of water, which symbolises the involutive processes, multiplying and complicating the manifestations, creating the stagnant routine. The "Stauros" indicates to us that the existence of all that is dense, inert and complicated, is only a reflection of all that is radiant, subtle and simple, because matter exists thanks to the Spirit, not the inverse.

3. Draw an ascending triangle so that the figure of the Radiant Elder is woven into it. Within the descending triangle, we will delineate another human figure, no longer radiant, but more dense and with a black beard. Thus we will have the representation of the great scheme of the two Universally powerful androgynes: the Macroprosopus or God of the white beard and its reflection, the Microprosopus, or God of the black beard.

In the literal translation of the Greek, Macroprosopo means "long face, "and Microprosopus," short face "or" narrow face. The "Stauros" shows us that the figure of white beard fecundates that of black beard, pouring into it the bliss of grace.

What is the theoretical the role of these Androgynes in the general scheme of the dynamic process? Let us search through the ascending scale of the process.

We have already learned that each י (Iod) is a transformation of the second ה (He) of the previous tetragrammatic cycle. Let us therefore seek to go back to the first י (Iod). This י (Iod) cannot be the Root Cause of the dynamic cycles, that is, it cannot be the Initial Link of the World of Emanations, for this Initial Link must be capable of generating the inferior links in itself, and, therefore, possesses the attribute of the Androgyne.

We will try to symbolise this Primordial Bipolar Link via the point over the first י (Iod); thus the first tetragrammatic cycle will be written: י ה ו ה. The starting point will correspond to the Superior Androgyne, the Ancient of Days, the Macroprosopus, from whom the Father י (Iod) and the Mother ה (He) who completes the Father emanate. The union of the two generates the Microprosopo - ו Vau. The latter creates for itself, in the wife or Bride (Spouse) a second ה (He), in which will manifest the activity of the Entire family. Man's path to Macroprosopo is through ecstasy, while the path to the Microprosopo can be found through the heart of each of us.

Astrologically, Arcanum VI corresponds to the zodiacal sign of the Taurus, simply because the sign of the Bull follows that of the Ram. The titles of the Arcanum in the plans of the Theosophical Ternary are the following:

In the plane of the manifestations of the Archetype, the Seal of Solomon indicates the great Law of Analogy - "Methodus Analogiae".

In the realm of human activity this pantaculo represents the concept of what we call the Free Will - "Pentagrammatica Libertas".
On the plane of the life of nature, we associate the analogies with the environment in which they manifest and which unites or separates them, as we prefer. In this plan, the title of the Arcanum is "Medium" (medium - environment).
Let us consider separately the meaning of these three names:
The first title - "Methodus Analogiae" - corresponds to the arithmetic division of its number "6" in two identical numerals, that is, $6 = 3 + 3$, and means that a manifestation (Arcanum III) requires another analogous manifestation, another "3". This is the essence of Arcanum VI. That the first title of the Arcanum is best illustrated by the "Words of the Mysteries of Hermes" (Verba Secretorum Hermetis) which constitute the first of the so-called "Emerald Verses" of the Hermetic code of the ancient Egyptians. The Latin text of these verses is as follows:

"Verum sine mendacio, certum et verissimum: quod est inferius est sicut quod est superius, et quod est superius est sicut quod est inferius, ad perpetranda miracula rei unius."

And the English translation:

"True and not false (that is, absolutely true in the mental plane), accurate (that is, correctly transmitted in form without distorting the astral clichés) and absolutely true (that is, so convincing that it can be verified by the senses in the physical plan - St. Thomas's system): the lower is similar to the upper and the upper is similar to the lower to complete the miracles of the whole (or, even better, to penetrate the miracles of the whole)."

This text needs almost no comment. It begins with the proclamation of the law of the three planes and ends with the classical formula of the law of analogy. What cannot be extracted from it!
By the organisation of our body, we can judge the organisation of the solar system, by the Theosophical Ternary - the turner of the parts of the trunk of our body, etc.
We have already talked about the division of the body into three parts.
The second title - "Libertas" - covers the following deconstructions:
$6 = 4 + 2$ and $6 = 2 + 4$: The sixth Arcanum is the result of the summation of the second (Gnosis = knowledge of the nature of the paths provided for free choice) and the fourth (authority determining the right of free choice). The result is a complete picture of the dilemma of good and evil, subtle and gross, true and false, temporary and eternal, active

and inert, etc., so often, it can be said every minute, which appears in human life.

The choice is free (both triangles are available), but the Stauros reminds us that the impetus for choosing an evolutionary triangle is given by the impulse of the Higher Activity, fertilising our inertia. This thesis is beautifully illustrated by the picture of the sixth Arcanum of Tarot. The subject who is to apply human freedom is depicted on the card as a young man (youth is a hint of the need for an element of timeliness in choosing).

The evolutionary triangle in the picture corresponds to a modestly dressed, seemingly plain-looking girl, who is inviting a young man to take the right path of a crossroads of two roads. This is a virtue.

The image is presented as the reflection in a mirror; the right path is the path to the right of the one looking at the card.

An involutive triangle corresponds to a woman, luxuriously dressed up with a very attractive beauty, attracting a young man to the left path.

The role of Stauros is interpreted by the Justice Genius soaring in the clouds by directing the punishing arrow in the direction of the left woman personifying vice.

The scientific name for the Arcanum picture is Bifurcatio (crossroads); the vulgar name - l'Amoureux - is due to the awkward pose of the young man and his confusion.

It remains to consider the issue of a visible indicator of systematic correctness in a person's choice of a road at a crossroads. This indicator is called spiritual harmony. It serves as a reward to those who generally seek to choose the right path and realise this desire.

The harmony of the soul is manifested by the balance and equanimity of the human being, as by the equal and parallel development of their activity and their receptivity.

A person who perceives clichés well in any field and is not gifted with realising power in the amount of his understanding of this field will be inharmonious and unhappy in this field.

And vice versa - if you are powerful in something that you cannot navigate in, which you are not sufficiently aware of, then again you cannot have harmony.

We can consider harmony as a neutralisation of the binary הוה - אדם (Adam-Eve), or Activity-Receptivity, within astral Man himself. This polarity of the torque is neutralised by the synthesis of the extremes.

We also note the question of free will in its essence (in the sense of quantifying this freedom in various planes and sub-planes of being). Slightly initiated man is aware that, generally speaking, there is no smoke without fire. Therefore, if on the one hand there are ardent determinists, and on the other hand, there are fanatical champions of the

idea of absolute freedom of will, then, generally speaking, in a certain subplane of our being there is a certain portion of karmic slavery (the laws of nature are the karma of the Universe) and a certain portion of human freedom the choice between evolutive and involutive.
Let us imagine the entire surface of the descending triangle of Figure 23, as the exclusive field of involutive paths that appear before us, and the surface of the ascending triangle - the field of evolutionary paths. We interweave the two triangles, forming the Seal of Solomon, and we fill the figure with horizontal and parallel lines which, symbolically, correspond to the various sub-planes of the existence of the human being.

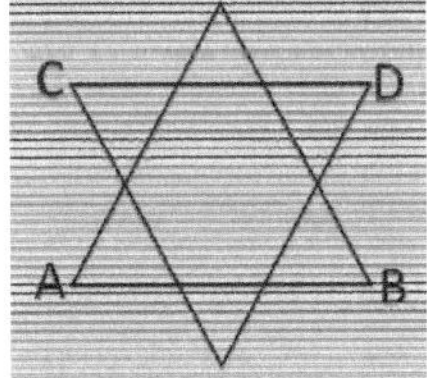

Figure 23

We see that in the lower layers there will be only involutive paths. At this stage, our body holds us as a lathe to our instinctive manifestations. As we go through the lower sub-planes, the possibility of choosing between the involutive paths becomes bigger. Attaining the AB level, we suddenly find [the possibility] to choose, the evolutionary paths.
In the middle part of the pantaculo, the possibilities for the two types of paths become equals. This part corresponds to the central ethical regions of the great binary of Good and Evil. The influence of the Higher Principles, represented by the sign of the "Stauros", becomes decisive. From the CD level, which already corresponds to the mental plane, the possibilities change again and suddenly we find ourselves in the dilemma of choosing only among evolutionary paths. Besides the line CD, the field of choice between evolutionary paths becomes increasingly limited and, finally, passing to the higher spiritual sub-planes, already near the vertex, the possibility of choice disappears, for the current which leads us necessarily to the Primordial Principle excludes any alternative. To those who dedicate themselves to a deep meditation on this scheme, there can be unravelled the great mysteries of Binary.
Let us now consider the third title: "Medium", which corresponds to the deconstructions:

6 = 5 + 1 and 6 = 1 + 5: The deconstruction 5 + 1 (life + will) corresponds to the influence of life, modulating the individual, which, in the future, will express his will. This deconstruction gives us the scheme of Macroprosopo in Nature.

The deconstruction 1 + 5 (will + life) emphasises that the will of the One is enough to create the life at all stages and at all levels. It is the scheme of the emanations, the Macroprosopo creating Nature. In the continuation of the already mentioned text of the Emerald Verses, and we quote below, we find the best general picture of the processes of Nature:

"Et sicut omnes res fuerunt ab uno, meditatione unius, sic omnes res natae fuerunt ab hac una re, adaptatione."

In the literal translation this would be:

"And just as all things came from the one principle through the One, so also all things born have come from the adaptation of the one substance"

In free translation it would be:

"Just as all principles were emanated by the one principle, by its very nature, so that everything that was born was formed of the unique substance by means of adaptation (coagulation or rarefaction) thereof ".

In the foregoing, we have the synthesis of the principles of emanating and governing forms, through two processes whose names are written along the muscles of the arms of Heinrich Khunrath's "Androgyne" (Amphitheatrum, 1602), and which is one of the ten most edifying pancaculos left by this great hermeticist.

The pantaculo in question symbolises the astral substance, with its resources, and the fields where these possibilities can be applied. In the raised arm of the Androgyne we see the word "Solve" (dissolve); on the lower arm - "Coagulate" (coagulate). It is a catechism left by wisdom and his art of exercising mastery over the astral.

Finishing our analysis of the Seal of Solomon, we will add that the colours normally used in the pantaculo are: blue for the background, golden (fire) for the ascending triangle, silver (water) for the descending triangle; golden (activity) for the vertical bar of the Stauros, and silvery (passivity) for the horizontal bar. In the latest pantaculos, which symbolise something more and in which the Seal of Solomon is included, we find certain divergences from this colour scheme, which will be explained in due course.

In the case of Adaptatio, that is, adaptations and preparations, we shall say a few words about homeopathy, as an adaptation of the VI Arcanum. The remedies can act in three ways: mechanical, chemical and dynamic. As an example of mechanical action, we will mention the use of liquid mercury in case of anastrophy (bowel reversal); of "ferrum oxidatum" to increase the peristaltic movement of the intestines; of lubricants, such as castor oil, etc.

A chemical action is expected from most allopathic medicines, disinfectants, products that restore a weakened chemical reaction of the organism, etc.

A dynamic action is expected of homeopathic products, such as belladonna, aconite, arsenic, strychnine, etc. which are not disdained by general therapists either. The explanation of the dynamic action was given somewhat nebulously to the profane, but very clearly for the initiated, by Paracelsus[18] in his "Hidden Philosophy".

The deductions of Paracelsus are characterised by their "a priori". They are based on the planetary and zodiacal [schema].

Later, Dr. Hahnemann, called "the father of homeopathy" researched the same subject "the Hahnemann's conclusions "can be found in his works: "Organon", "Fragmenta de viribus" (1805) and "Reine Arzneimittellehre" (1811).

Homeopathic treatment is based on three concepts:

1. Subjectively, the disease is perceived through the synthesis of its symptoms.

2. A product which, under certain conditions, causes a particular organism to be symptomatic of disease, may, under different conditions, help to eliminate the same symptoms in a sick body (the law of resemblance).

3. The doses that eliminate the symptom of a diseased organism, are much weaker than the doses which cause the same symptom in a healthy organism (the law of small doses).

The first topic sparked strong opposition from medical authorities who accused homeopaths of eliminating symptoms instead of fighting the disease. After everything we've said on the physical plane and the illusory character of its manifestations, we find it unnecessary to explain to the concealment of this accusation.

The second law formulated by Hahnemann "*similia sumilibus curantur*" (the similar is cured by its similarity) clearly shows us that the dynamic

---

[18]Philippus Theophrastus Bombast Paracelsus - dictus 1491 - 1541

action of the remedy on the organism is based on the establishment of a correspondence between the astral of the remedy and the astrosome of the patient. The action of the remedy, as the case may be, is different. This is not surprising if we take into account that even on the mental plane, the same food - the study, for example - acts differently, according to the doses used and according to the particular mental state, of the person. Let us remember the well-known sentence, perhaps unilateral, but not less certain:

"A little science drives us away from God, a deep science brings us back to Him."

The law of small doses in homeopathy recalls the principle of the point of support in magic. We must add that Hahnemann recommends choosing among all products the "*simillimum*" (the most similar), that is, the one corresponding to the greatest number of the main symptoms of disease. We must also consider the fact that the general symptomatic picture of the disease is always only approximate.
From the hidden point of view it is remarkable that homeopaths attach great importance to the prolonged process of stirring the solutions and crushing the powders, in order to prepare the "dynamisations" of the medicines. This proves that they consider the energy state (electric, caloric, etc.) of the product as a sound that must be introduced in the basic scale of the homeopathic product, to create the harmony.

Notes on the sixth Arcanum

We learn in MotT that whilst the fourth arcanum is associated with the vow of obedience and the fifth with poverty, the sixth Arcanum is concerned with the practice of the vow of chastity and is "at the same time the summary of the two preceding Arcana – chastity being the fruit of obedience and poverty." It is here that these three sacred vows and methods of spiritual discipline are contrasted directly with the trials and temptations of power, richness and debauchery which are set in opposition to these vows.
Chastity is possible only when "one loves with the totality of one's being", a love which is "strong as death and whose flashes are flashes of fire, the flame of the Eternal".
This living unity is threefold, incorporating spirit, soul and body as one. From two individuals united in spirit, soul and body is derived the six-pointed Seal of Solomon, the number and symbol of the Arcanum, The Lovers. Herein are Father, Son and Holy Spirit united with Mother,

Daughter and Holy Soul, as fire and water combine in the alchemical mystery of fiery water in a sublime union of opposites. This six-pointed bliss is the formula of אדם - הוה (Adam and Eve), in whom lives on the eternal memory of Paradise.

"If human souls come into the world with the imprint of this memory, and also with the impression of knowing that the meeting with the other will not take place for them in this life here below, they will then live this life as if widowed, in so far as they remember, and as if engaged, in so far as they hope….yes, dear Unknown Friend, "life is profound and its profundity is like an abyss of fathomless depth." (MotT, p126)

The Tetragrammaton, the sacred name of God – (יהוה) - signifies Yahweh, pronounced in Hebrew as Adomai, in English became Jehovah. The root of יהוה is הוה, which means being, life or woman, once interchangeable concepts. In Latin הוה is spelled EVE and the esoteric meaning of the יהוה is, therefore, Eve, Mother of all living.

A second version of the Tetragrammaton is spelled EHYH and is derived from Hayya, another name of Eve that expresses her connection to women in childbirth

A central tenet of philosophical kabbalah is that God the Father has lost the Great Mother, his feminine aspect, also called the Shekinah. For universal peace and harmony the Holy Mother, the Shekinah must be restored to God the Father. We can support this cosmic mission – this generation of 'fiery water' as the supreme resolution of elemental binaries.

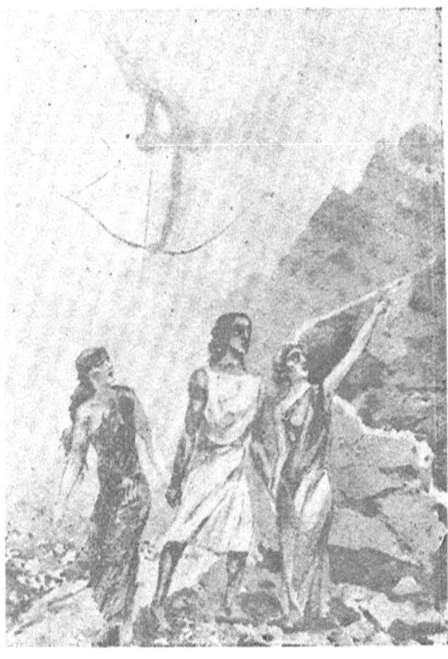

Arcanum VII

ז

THE CHARIOT

Pathway from Binah to Geburah

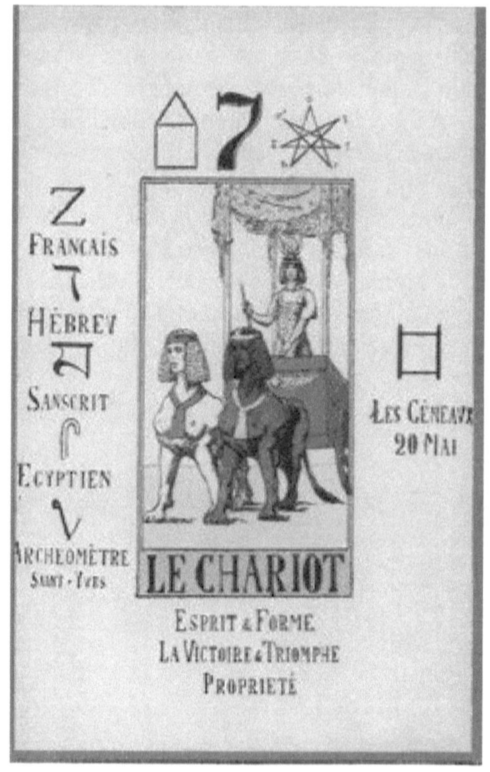

The Charioteer is *Victorious*

Hermes, seated in the Chariot, touches the Black Sphinx with the point of a sword of steel, but the White Sphynx with a sceptre of gold

Levi

THE CHARIOT OF OSIRIS: Victory

Z--7 expresses in the divine world the Septenary, the domination of Spirit over Nature

Paul Christian

He controls the sphinxes by the power of a magic word, but the tension of his Will may fail and then the magic word will lose its power and he may be devoured by the sphinxes.

Ouspensky

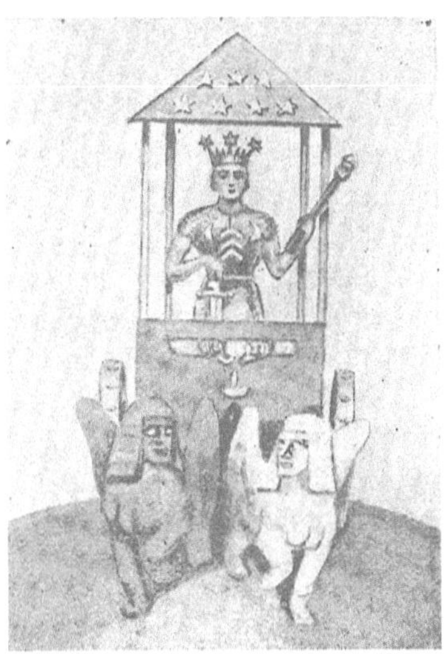

Before proceeding to the analysis of the seventh Arcanum, we will be aware of the constructive scheme of the first six Arcana, which determines the existence of the seventh as the final link in the chain of six.

All authors who dealt with this issue propose the following construction (Fig. 24), i.e. wish to recognise the role of the elements of the main series of the dynamic process for the Arcanum.

We will draw this point of view for one row of headlines of the Arcanum, leaving the listener to repeat the exercise for the other two rows.

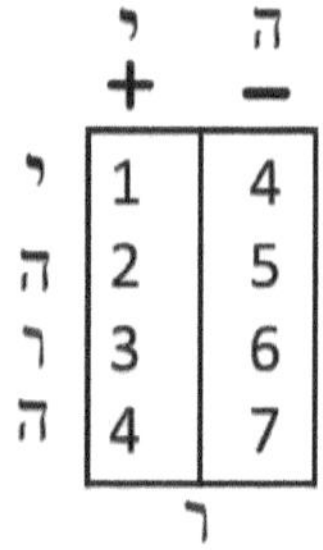

Figure 24

As an example, let's apply this system to a series of Arcanum titles in the field of Man and their manifestations, letting students repeat the same exercise with the sets of the other two fields.

A husband (1) fertilises his wife (2), thereby determining the birth (3) of a child who, physically and astrally nourished (4), acquires authority (4), sufficient to manifest himself on behalf of the whole family in the astral plane, i.e. in the field of quintessential manipulations (5), but here it meets the dilemma of good and evil (6), chooses good and celebrates victory (7).

I draw your attention to the fact that, firstly, in some way, each subsequent element of a series of arcana is passive with respect to the previous one and active with respect to the next, and secondly, each element of the second column is passive with respect to the element of the first column placed in the same line. Authority (4) is an area (passive) that can be exploited by a person - father (active); life (5) is an element that the mother can cultivate (2); the choice of paths (6) is an element in which (passive) will have to turn to the element of generation (3 active); victory (7) is a manifestation (passive), accessible to authority (4, active).

This all makes possible the construction of another scheme, equivalent to the first and proposed by Papus (Figure 25) where the vertices of the dotted triangle constitute a reflection of the vertices of the triangle of full lines; are its negative poles, its "wives" so to speak. This scheme of two triangles will become clearer as we study other manifestations of Arcanum VII, whose number we will place in the middle of the figure.

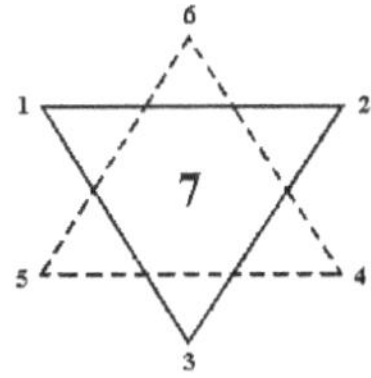

Figure 25

Let us pass to the Arcanum itself:
To Arcanum VII corresponds the Hebrew letter ז (Zain) and the zodiacal sign of Gemini. The hieroglyph is an arrow, thrown with certain aim and that, following a straight line, will hit the target. The titles of the Arcanum are provided by three arithmetical deconstructions of evolutionary order.
The deconstruction: $7 = 3 + 4$, that is, the predominance of the Spirit (3, "Divine Natura", Arcanum III) on the form (4, Arcanum IV) determines the title "Spiritus dominat formam", in the field of manifestations of the Archetype. The same deconstruction, but in the reverse order: $7 = 4 + 3$, will give us the opposite of the above currency and will correspond to obscurantism and the artifices of black magic.
In the human plane, we will be guided by the deconstruction $7 = 1 + 6$, that is: Will + Probation, by the bifurcation of the roads, lead us to Victory. The title of the Arcanum, in this plane, will therefore be "Victory". Formula $7 = 6 + 1$ expressed by contrary, the failure of the ordeal is tantamount to defeat.
In the plane of Nature, the title is given by a very interesting deconstruction: $7 = 5 + 2$, which expresses the predominance of pentagrammatic principles (tradition, customs, "religio") on "Natura Naturata "(Arcanum II), that is, on the creation of Nature. This predominance translates into law of property, hence the title "Jus Proprietatis" (right of ownership).
The arithmetical divisive possibilities of the Arcanum do not exhaust themselves with those who gave us their titles in the fields of Theosophical Ternary. We can also deconstruct it into $7 = 3 + 1 + 3$,

where the element of the will (1) oscillates between the two triangles: that of the Archetype and that of Nature. Another deconstruction is 7 = 2 + 3 + 2, in which the central ternary - World of Emanations – rules the two binaries-Lingans, that of Man and that of Nature, which, by fertilisation, resemble. The analysis of these secondary deconstructions is less frequent than that of the others mentioned.

Let us pass to the card of Arcanum VII. The scholarly title is "Curriculum Hermetis" (The Hermes) and the common is "The Chariot", a title suggested by the image.

On the blade, we see on top a blue canopy, all interspersed with massive gold staves, symbolising the higher sub-planes of the astral, with its inhabitants - the Pentagrams – whose power is superior to that of man and sometimes protects him.

The canopy is supported by four columns, symbolising the hermetic virtues: daring, silence, knowledge and love. Among these columns are the activities of the Wizard -Victor, which is under the baldachin. On his head - a golden crown with three pentagrams signifying penetration, conscious and volitional, in the mysteries of the three planes of the Universe. His robe is a breastplate of the Knowledge and Victory, protecting it against the dangers that for the profane can be destroyers. On the left shoulder of the Victor we see a white moon crescent, which symbolises the power

"Solve", that is, the power of evolutionary and subtle achievements. On the right shoulder - a growing darkness, or the power "coagulates" - the possibility of dense forms and realising them in the lower sub-planes. The three right angles in the armour indicate the methods by which the Victor knows how to protect himself against aggression. They are: the accuracy of logical thinking, the proper form and the circumspection and infallibility in the achievements of the physical plane.

The Victor's left hand wields a cane surmounted by a sphere on which is a square, which, in turn, supports an equilateral triangle, that is, the Spirit-dominates the form which, in turn, rests on the terrestrial sphere (the physical plane). In his right hand we see the Victory, that is:

a) a weapon in the physical plane,
b) a convincing word in the intermediate sub-planes,
c) a figurative presentation of that word in the astral plane,
d) a penetration of thought on the mental plane.

And where was the Victor to celebrate his Victory?
In a cubic-shaped chariot (his own accomplishment, Arcanum IV). And what was the method used to build that carriage? We found the answer in the two symbols, at the front of the carriage. The first is an Egyptian

ornament: a sphere ׳ (Iod) from which split two serpentine-shaped extensions (the two ה) and which is supported by two open wings ו (Vau). This is, of course, the dynamic cycle י ה ו ה. Further down, we see another symbol - the Lingam - alluding to the second way to read the Great Name - Iodheva or Iodhava - (male principle + female principle). The carriage is drawn by two sphinxes: the symbolic pair of astral torque, which corresponds to the medium term of the Great Arcanum scheme. The sphinx on the left is black, the one on the right is white. The sphinxes look at each other, but pull in opposite directions (the two polarities of an astral swirl). They run over the surface of a large globe - the quaternary of the Elementary Route of the Great Arcanum. The wheels of the chariot are trimmed with gold hoops, and the nail heads replaced by eyes. The wheels symbolise the astral vortices that carry the whirlwind; the eyes mean that the cells of these astral formations have their own individuality and concepts.

"These wheels were so high that they were afraid, and the four had their chests full of eyes all around" (Ezekiel I, 18).

As we can see, the image of the card is very synthetic, as is the synthetic character of that Arcanum ending the first septenary of the Tarot Majors. From the picture of the Arcanum, let us move on to the pantaculo of Arcanum VII. Occultists of antiquity and the Middle Ages correlated Arcanum VII with the seven-pointed star (figure 26).

Figure 26

Modern occultists frequently use the pantaculo of figure 27.

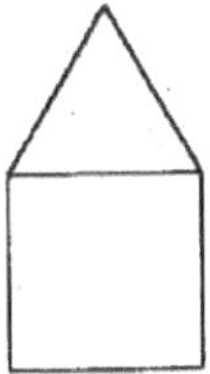

Figure 27

Neither of the two is considered a fulfilling force, they are just symbols. Both can be reversed, symbolising black magic and corresponding to the deconstruction 7 = 4 + 3, that is, "seeking to subjugate the ternary of spiritual manifestations, creating the confusion and complication of forms, difficulty understanding the essence of the Universe, and thereby dominating the victims of the widespread obscurantism ".

In initiation ceremonies, when testing a neophyte for fear of astral manifestations, astral clichés, true or simulated, the path of the neophyte is [along] carpets representing the seven-pointed star, for white magicians in the upright position, for black in the opposite, inverted direction.

Let us talk about the Septenary pantaculo, which will be useful to us in the future, let us set out to study the most important Septenaries, placing them in similar tables.

I want to start with the Great Septenary of Secondary Reasons.

In Arcanum III we discuss the various ternaries that belong to the ascending triangle type, and which can be encompassed in a general concept of ternary of primary causes. An adept of the unitarianism, imbued with occult theories and who proposes to study from a purely scientific point of view manifestations of the Primordial Principle that outline the World of Emanation, the existence of "Tres Causae Primae" (Three Primary Causes):

1. The Neutral element
2. The element to Be (+)
3. The element to Know (-)

Thus, the concept of the World of Emanation, in its higher plane, will be expressed as an idea of Manifestation, bipolarised in the idea of what is capable of acquiring knowledge, and of what may be known. The last idea (-), of course, will limit the field of manifestation of preceding (+). If we are to achieve a spatial and symbolic representation of the World of Emanation, we must clothe the idea of the Manifestation with the totality of the manifested, embracing both ourselves, as to the Universe with its countless solar systems. This totality will divide symbolically, on the one hand, in our eagerness for astronomical (+) knowledge, and, on the other hand, in all that is yet to be known (-).

The three Primordial Causes manifest in the soul plane by a series of reflexes that the Old schools sought to order in a sevenfold system of so-called Secondary Causes ("Septem Causae Secundae").

Symbolically, these Causes can easily be identified with what the ancients called planetary manifestations of our solar system. The observations of many centuries, and perhaps many millennia, have added to the essence of this symbolism, establishing correlations between angular positions of the planets in the celestial vault and the quality of their influence on the field of terrestrial life.

We will now explain what we mean by "planet" and "planetary life." The study of the seven coagulates we call the body of Saturn, Jupiter, Mars, Sun, Venus, Mercury and Moon, is part of the astronomy and astrophysics sciences. Many fields of knowledge study the eighth object - the body of the Earth.

We will associate with the idea of each of these coagulates, which we attribute to the physical plane, another 2 pairs of representations, one of which will lie in the astral plane, and the other in the mental one.

For example, on the Earth we, in addition to the body in the physical plane, will seek the Genius and the Astrosome in the astral plane, the Spirit and the Angel in the mental plane.

The Spirit of the Earth is the synthesis of the spiritual impulses of terrestrial Humanity in relation to the Earth. In the present moment, the Spirit of the Earth corresponds to the synthesis of our aspirations for the development and improvement of the Earth.

The angel of the earth is the ideological part of the opposition that earthly karma exerts on these aspirations. The spirit is evolutionary, the angel is involutive.

When the binary "Spirit - Angel of the Earth" will be neutralised by the agreement of its elements, the task of evolution of the Earth will be solved in principle. The genius of the Earth is a synthesis of the forms in which the Spirit carries out its evolving ideas. These are the forms and formal methods that Mankind pursues in the system of cultivating the planet by it, adapting it to its goals.

Earth's astrosome - this is the synthetic astral tourbillon that is struggling in its plan with Genius, trying to defend the goals of the Angel.

The neutralisation of the "Genius - Earth Astrosome" binary provides a formal solution to the Earth's evolution problem, without creating a real solution to this problem, which should be attributed to the neutralisation of the "Earthly Humanity's Body - Earth's" binary.

If the neutralisation of the Highest Binary is called the Kingdom of God (on Earth) in principle, then the second binary is neutralised by the Kingdom of God in forms, and the third in realities.

On each of the seven so-called. planets something similar happens. Each of the seven planets has a Spirit with an Angel, a Genius with an Astrosome, and a kind of Humanity (in the animal, vegetable or mineral world - depending on the degree of development of the planet).

For us, the general, even if understandable, planetary life could not be expressed through normal terrestrial schemes, for only those elements of general planetary life which are reflected in the forms of terrestrial life 'are accessible to us. Astrology, Kabbalah, magic, etc. cover only the influence of the Spirit, the Genius, and so on. from this planet or another planet, as manifested on Earth, but do not penetrate, neither in its essence nor in its nature. The same happens in our daily lives: we form an opinion about the people we know as they manifest in relation to us; little do we know about their intimate lives.

It is these incomplete characteristics that we correlate, by analogy, with Secondary Causes, giving the latter the planetary names.

We must remember that the main Mythological egrégores nowadays called "Divinities of the Antiquity" were in close astral connection with planetary entities, and in accordance with their manifestations at certain times. This strengthened the deities. However, the Planetary entities evolved, and deities were more stationary. The link that existed between both gradually weakened. When the great ascetic and occultist, known in history as Julian the Apostate made an evocation of the Mythological egrégores, they were so that they presented themselves before the great magician as "pale, thin and sickly gods of the antique".

After this preparation, let us turn to planetary influences and their correspondences. We will distribute the Seven Secondary Causes (which, as explained above, are reflections of the three Primary Causes), in a three-column scheme (Figure 28).

To the planets of the right column (+) we will give the qualifier "good"; to the planets of the (-) the term "bad". We will say that the sun is "synthetic"; that Mercury "fits"; that the Moon is "passive." The Sun in relation to the Moon will be a masculine element, fecundating it with the help of Mercury.

-		+
♂ Mars	☉ Sun	♀ Venus
	☿ Mercury	
♄ Saturn	☾ Moon	♃ Jupiter

Figure 28

Mars and Venus "approach" through the synthetic Sun, because in this there are the elements of the two planets; in the same way "Saturn and Jupiter" approach. From Mars, Apollo (Sun), Saturn and Jupiter, we will say that they are masculine planets; Venus and Moon - female (according to a purely mythological presentation). Mercury is attributed to androgyne, which agrees with its role as mediator in fertilisation.

We will now distribute the seven Secondary Causes with their main analogies within a general framework (Table 1). This explanation needs further commentary, which we will give, column by column.

Planets	Angels	Nos. & Symbols	Colours	Fragrance	Metals	Stones
Saturn	Oriphiei Jehudiel Zaphkiel	3 Cobra	Black	Sulphur	Lead	Chalcedony
Jupiter	Zadkiel Sealtiel	4	Blue	Saffron	Tin	Sapphire Beryl
Mars	Samael Barrachiel	5	Red	Peppermint Ginger Pepper	Iron	Amethyst Diamond Jasper
Sun	Michael	6 Whirlwind	Yellow	Red Sandalwood	Gold	Chrysolite Solar Stone
Venus	Anael Uriel	Regular geometric figures	Green	Verbena Musk	Copper	Lazurite
Mercury	Raphael	8 Caduceus	Rainbow	Mastic	Mercury	Emerald Agate
Moon	Gabriel	9	White	White Sandalwood Amphor	Silver	Pearl Crystal White Coral

Planets	Sacrament	Life Period	Front Talisman	Reverse Talisman	Days of the Week	Attribute
Saturn	Extreme Unction	Old Age	Sythe	Head of a Bull or Goat	Saturday	Cold & Dry
Jupiter	Eucharist	Maturity	Crown	Head of an Eagle	Thursday	Hot & Humid
Mars	Penitence Confession	Youth	Sword	Head of a Lion	Tuesday	Hot & Dry
Sun	Sacerdotal	Childhood	Circle	Man	Sunday	Hot & Dry
Venus	Matrimony	Youth	G	Dove	Friday	Hot & Humid
Mercury	Chrism	Metanoia	Winged Caduceus	Head of a Dog	Wednesday	Adaptable
Moon	Baptism	Adolescence	Lunar Sigil	Cup	Monday	Cold & Humid

Column 1. The planetary symbols are composed, in their initial form, of the following basic figures:

- a) The sign of the Sun, symbolising the emanations of vital energy, nutritious fluids;
- b) the sign of the Moon, symbol of receptivity, of intuition, of the capacity to reflect the received;
- c) + sign of the elements and their influences.

Let us analyse the composition of planetary signs in the order in which they are found in the first column.

In the symbol of Saturn, the sign of the elements is placed above that of the Moon which means that, under the influence of Saturn, the elements, that is, the environment predominates over the Intuition.

In the symbol of Jupiter we have the same basic symbols, but in the reverse order, that is, the predominance of intuition in relation to the influence of the environment. In the symbol of Mars beyond symbol of the Sun, there is an arrow indicating the increase in vital fluids and giving them a characteristic Martian impetuosity. The arrow, in general, indicates the element of fire in the zodiacal signs.

The symbol of Venus shows that, under its influence, vital forces predominate over the environment.

The symbol of Mercury indicates the influence of this planet, in the first place, on the receptivity of the subject, then on the vital element, and finally on the environment. If we apply this influence on the educational system, the greatest importance will be given to the student's abilities, quality of the school, and finally, the conditions under which the teaching is transmitted.

Some authors introduce the symbol as being that of the Earth. It is a sad symbol because it shows that in terrestrial life, the influence of conditions prevails over vital, astral principles.

Column 2. We will list only the most common names of angels. The diversity of terms to designate the angel of the same planet is due, in part, to the parallelism of the nomenclature of Hebrew, Chaldean and Syrian languages and partly to the introduction of a later nomenclature of the Gnostic. In this column, by the term "angel" we mean what corresponds to the whole aspect and mental state of a planet (ie, its Spirit + its Angel), felt in the manifestations of terrestrial life.

For a better understanding of the picture we will give the characteristics of each planetary influence in the mental and astral field of terrestrial life. We will also give their influence on the manifestations on the physical plane. The latter result from the encounter and interpenetration of mental influences and planetary astral, with the corresponding terrestrial manifestations, being able to be called, with restrictions, of influences of the planet in the physical plane. We will follow the same order as the planets.

The influence of Saturn on the mental teaches the immutability of logical laws; in the astral, this influence oppresses, for it recalls the severity of karma; on the physical plane, it provides the experiences of life, provokes melancholic states and accentuates the caution that sometimes leads to avarice.

The influence of Jupiter, in the mental, teaches that in everything there is need of system and method; at the astral - creates and upholds the principle of authority; in the physical - develops the administrative talents, justice, friendliness and the tendency to protect the weak.

Mars, in the mental, activates and accelerates all processes; in the astral - increases courage and decision, which on the physical plane is expressed as impulsive (often anger) and violent actions.

The influence of the Sun, in the mental, transmits abundantly all the active influences which, in the astral, create the desire to give them form and share this creativity with others. In the physical, the Sun is the giver of artistic tendencies, generosity, contempt for everything that is vulgar, that is, why it lacks original manifestation.

Venus, on all planes, represents the principle of attraction. In the astral, this principle manifests itself in the various forms of love, and in the physical plane - as productivity in the most diverse fields.

Mercury, in the mental, confers adaptability to ideas; in the astral - the flexibility in the desires, facilitates all transformations; on the physical plane, it sponsors the changes and any kind of speculation.

Moon, "the mother of the world", gives receptivity to mental flows; in the astral, grants intuition. At the physical plane, its influence is manifested by the susceptibility to the various influences; for the most varied moods, by the ability of clairvoyance.

Column 3. The column of figures was introduced to complete the table. The symbols and figures are sometimes used in modern schools to conceal planetary symbols. The explanation is that the 3 resembles the symbol of Saturn and a serpent undulating, symbol of this planet; 4 recalls the symbol of Jupiter; 5 - the symbol of Mars, evil written; the 6, written with fantasy resembles a whirlwind, in which the sun is so generous. The beautiful, regular geometric figures, can be consecrated to Venus; the 8 remembers the Caduceus of Mercury; and the 9 - the poorly designed crescent of the Moon.

Column 4. The colours of the planets, in addition to their conditional value, in the preparation of a planetary ritual, also allow to hit the planet that governs a certain manifestation, since the auric emanations, subtle, partially materialised planetary entities, have this basic colour.

Column 5. The column of the aromas indicates which scent should preferably be used during a planetary magical ceremony. As for incense, your perfume is a synthesis that can replace any of the listed aromas. Under the influence of incense, the internal operator takes on a more mystical character (because of this, incense is not used in planetary system ceremonies of black magic). The odoriferous substances used during the ceremonies are burned directly or set to burn in braziers. Vegetable flavours, both can be used in form of alcoholic extract, as in the form of dehydrated plants; the latter is preferable.

Column 6. Planetary metals are indicated not only as material for the preparation used during the ritual, but also for the preparation of talismans and planetary systems.

Let's point out the difference between a pantaculo and a talisman. Both one and the other, if the dimensions allow it, can be worn next to the body. A talisman is a condenser of planetary energy that already exists in the person. If, for example, a person lacks the energy of Jupiter, it is not appropriate for it to use a talisman consecrated to this planet. The pantaculo, unlike the talisman, by the power of his consecration, attracts the fluids of the determined planet and thus, in an artificial way, it creates a connection with the egrégore elements of this planet. With our example, because there is no natural bond with Jupiter, the person can use a pantaculo of this planet, so to receive its influence, if it is wanted.

It will be useful to briefly indicate how to prepare a pentagram to be used by the magician during the performance. The quality inherent in the pentagram is its synthetic character. This is why, on the physical plane, this must be composed of an alloy of the seven planetary metals. In the astral plane, the ceremony of his consecration must establish contact with all seven planetary influences. A pentagram is therefore consecrated through six minor and one major magical ceremonies. The latter is made under the influence of the predominant planet in the astral of its future bearer. Six smaller ceremonies, which precede the greater, are dedicated, one by one, to the six planets remaining. On the pentagram, in addition to the sum of planetary influences, the polarities of both human nature and those of the evolutionary path neutralised by the person of the magician. They are therefore placed on the pentagram:

1. The signs י ה (Iod and He), symbolising the human androgyne;
2. The signs Alpha and Omega, corresponding to the knowledge both of the Primordial Source of the man, that is, of its origin, as of its goal - Reintegration;

3. The signs א ת (Aleph and Tau), as they respectively correspond to the first and last of the Major Arcana of the Tarot, a set that encloses all occult philosophy.

4. The designations חסד (Chesed) and פחד (Pachad), ie, Mercy and Severity, that is, two elements which, neutralised, create harmony in the field of the ethical evolution of the human being.

The last ceremony - the greatest - of the consecration of the pentagram must have a synthetic character also in relation to so-called hermetic elements. In this ceremony the magician occupies the central position of the cross of the elements. The pentagram should receive the breath (Air), be sprinkled with consecrated Water, dried by the Fire in which the aromatic substances burn and placed on the Earth. Each of these manipulations is performed five times, together with the enunciation of the letters: י (Iod, East), ה (He, North), ו (Vau, West), ה (He, South) and ש (Shin, centre of the cross). An element indispensable in the final consecration of the pentagram is the low voice of the great traditional synthetic word - Azoth (see Arcanum IV).

If it is not possible to make the pentagram with the alloy of the seven metals, we can limit ourselves to the androgyny, that is, to the two noble metals: gold and silver, or even gold alone. We can, also, paint in gold a pentagram drawn on a virgin parchment and to use it as if it were made of metal.

Column 7. The stones listed in this column were used in the past to prepare the Gnostic talismans, known under the name of "Abraxas." In these talismans it was engraved: for Saturn - a lame old man, or a serpent wrapped around a sunstone; for Jupiter – an eagle, holding a pentagram in the beak or claws; for Mars - a dragon biting the wrist of a sword; to the Sun - a serpent with a lion's head; for Venus - the lingam; for Mercury - an airtight Caduceus with three convolutions (symbol of Azoth) or a cinéfalo (man with dog's head); for the Moon - a dove cut by two lunar crescents.

Column 8. The column of sacramental correspondences accepted by most representatives of the Episcopal Christian Egrégore, is a direct consequence of the knowledge of certain esoteric influences by certain Fathers of the Church[19].

The Extreme Unction that transmits Grace so that the astrosome can be purified from the clichés of transgressions which - for some reason -

---

[19] The Christian Sacraments are cited as supreme examples of Sacred Magic by by Tomberg in Letter III, The Empress.

subsisted in the sacrament of penance, is consecrated to Saturn, for these clichés relate to karmic factors.

The Eucharist is the sacrament which, received for the first time by a baptised being, grants it the authority in the field of evolutionary Christian principles, renewing it every time; this sacrament, naturally, corresponds to Jupiter.

Penance, which demands of the one who does it, a great internal effort, is related to Mars.

The Priesthood, which confers on its possessor the gift of spreading the rays of light of Christendom, relates to the Sun.

Marriage, the result of a mutual attraction of the spouses, belongs to Venus.

The Chrism, which confers the capacity to reason in the field of Christian dogma and morality, preparing the person to follow the Christian ideals - belongs to Mercury.

Baptism, ritually linked to the element of water, represents naturally the lunar influence. It is necessary that the ritual of baptism, as it is practiced in the Orthodox Church, symbolises in an exact way the first exit in the astral of the person being initiated. This output is effected under protection, or even in the company of the initiating Instructor and future companions. Penetrating the sphere of the terrestrial astrosome, the initiator finds and must overcome the involutive reactions of their clichés, to reach the pure astral, and to return to the body, to begin a new life of. The flow of the circular current of the terrestrial astrosome is symbolised by the water of which the christening emerges renovated. During the ritual, the role of the instructor is performed by the baptism, and the role of future companions in the astral plane - by the godparents.

Column 9. Periods of life are easy to relate to planetary influences.

Childhood, the period in which the most important is the regular reception of vital forces - relates to the sun.

Puberty, when the environment is more receptive to the environment - with the Moon.

Youth, the greater the power of attraction and the tendency to impulsive actions - with Venus and Mars.

The transition from youth to maturity, characterised by adaptability – with Mercury.

Adulthood, which introduces in life methods and systems - with Jupiter.

Old age, ruled by logic and prudence - with Saturn.

Column 10. On the right side of the usual magical planetary talismans must appear the image symbolic of the microcosm (the pentagram) and below it - one of the attributes listed in column 10.

Column 11. The reverse of the talisman must present the sign of the macrocosm (the Seal of Solomon) below, one of the attributes of column

11. The metal used to make the talisman must correspond to the planet to which the talisman will be consecrated. For Mercury the amalgam is used with some other metal that is not in opposition to the planetary configuration, under which the future bearer of the talisman.

Column 12. To find the planets that govern the days of the week, we adopt the next system. We place the planets in this order: Saturn - Jupiter - Mars - Sun - Venus - Mercury - Then from the Sun, to which Sunday is consecrated, we omit two planets, which will give - for Monday - the Moon. Continuing the same method from the Moon and starting over the line again, we will have Mars for Tuesday, Mercury for Wednesday and so on.

We can also illustrate this scheme by placing the planets at the vertices of a star of seven tips - symbol of the septenary (figure 29). The circular order in the direction of the arrows corresponds to the sequence of planets, shown above. Accompanying the straight lines at each end of the star, in the direction of the arrows, and beginning with the Sun (Sunday), we will have, at each vertex of the star, the consecutive day of the week and the planet that governs it.

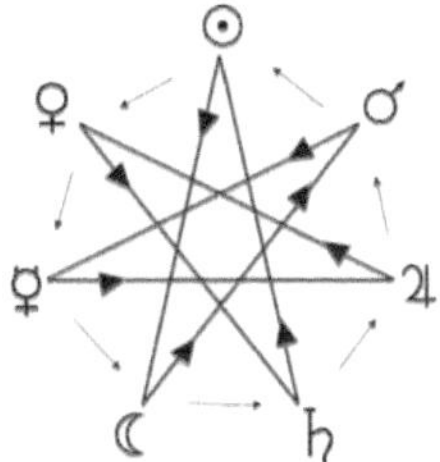

Figure 29

These correspondences between the planets and the days are justified mainly by the claims of all medieval schools, which gave them considerable strength in the astral. For every planetary magical ceremony, it is recommended to choose the day of the week ruled by the planet at which ceremony is consecrated. In some Latin languages, the names of the days of the week etymologically confirm the planetary correspondences of the above picture.

Column 13. In the column entitled "attributes of the planets", we give the characteristics of the astral of each planet, serving us in this way of conditional language.

We will not explain the reasons for this terminology here, we will give only the attributes of the four hermetic elements. The attribute corresponding to the degree of humidity has two poles: wet and dry; the attribute corresponding to the degree of heat also has two poles: hot and cold. Qualities attributed to the elements are as follows: hot and humid; water - humid and cold; earth - cold and dry; fire - dry and hot. This allows the conjugation of the quaternary of the elements with that of the attributes of these elements, as it is the case in the quaternary of the Apostle John (figure 30).

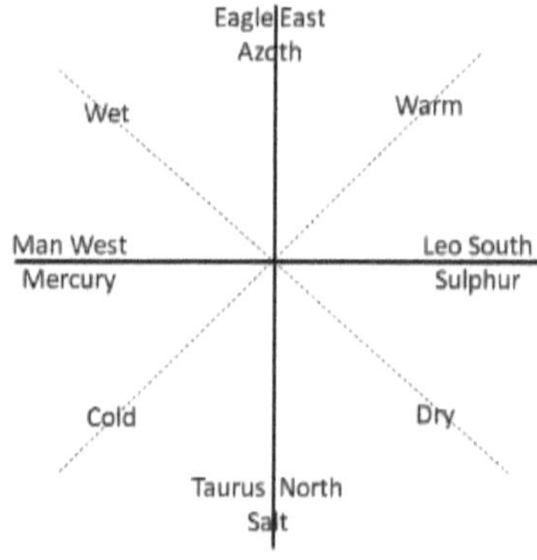

Figure 30:

It remains for us to speak a few words about the so-called "friendships" and "enmities" of the planets and also explain the method of calculating planetary hours for the days of the week.

In astrology, when we talk about "friendship" between one planet and another, it is understood the strengthening of good influences or the influence of one planet on the other. In magic, the concept of friendships is somewhat different, since each strengthening of influence, whether good or bad, of a planet over another, is considered "friendship," and every weakening of influence - "enmity."

Leaving the analysis of astrological friendships and enmities for later, let's just list the magical friendships and enmities among the seven planets, according to the scheme accepted by the modern schools.

Saturn is in friendship with Mars and in enmity with all other planets. The impetuosity and Martian violence accentuate the fatal, Saturnian events; they are deferred or softened by the active influences of other planets.

Mars is in friendship with Venus and in enmity with all other planets; in fact, the force (Venus) admits the violence and the Martian impetus, but the Saturnian logic, the Jupiterian affability, solar generosity, Mercurian expansiveness and adaptability and lunar passivity, do not combine with the violence of Mars.

Beneficial solar radiation is accentuated by the Jupiterian affability and Venusian attraction, but it is certainly hampered by the coldness of Saturn and the rapture of Mars.

The emanations of Venus are benefited by the richness of vital fluids (Sol), by the sincerity of the (Mercury) and receptivity (Moon), but they do not support the cold logic of Saturn. As for the experienced administrator - Jupiter – it cannot be said that it does not combine with Venus, but we must admit that it always seeks to introduce its methods and regulations, and because of this gained neither its sympathy nor its antipathy.

Mercury adapts to all influences, and the Moon receives them passively. Let us now calculate the planetary hours. It is indispensable that the magical planetary ceremonies be performed not only on the day consecrated to the planet, but also at the right time.

The magic 24 hours begin with the moment of the local sunrise and divides in two the "magic day" (until sunset) and the "magic night" (from sunset to sunrise the next day). Both "day" and "night", depending on location and season, have a variable duration. We divide the "magic day" into twelve equal parts, thus obtaining 12 "magical hours of day", the same division of" magic night" will give us 12 magical night hours." On Sunday, the first "daily magic hour" belongs to the Sun, on Monday - the Moon; on Tuesday - to Mars, etc. In other words, the first "hour" is always devoted to the planet that governs the day. The hours" are each consecrated to one of the seven planets that follow in the established order in frame 1, that is: Sun - Venus - Mercury - Moon - Saturn - Jupiter - Mars. Thus, in the Sunday, the second hour will be from Venus, the third - from Mercury, the fourth - from the Moon, the fifth - of Saturn, the sixth - of Jupiter, the seventh - of Mars and the eighth again of the Sun, etc. to the twelfth "hour" which, on Sundays, belongs to Saturn, and ends the "magic day." The "next hour", that is, the first "night time" (following the same order of the planets) will belong to Jupiter, etc. The 12 "night hours" (from Sunday to Monday) end with the hour of Mercury, and at the time of Monday's sunrise, the hour of the Moon begins.

Notes on the seventh Arcanum

We see clearly why the author of MotT said an entire volume could be devoted to the seventh Arcanum and the subject still wouldn't be satisfactorily concluded, so with this in mind we shall keep our notes brief.

One of the key lessons we can take away from the seventh letter is that whilst the charioteer, on the one hand, represents victory over the three temptations and is faithful to the vows of obedience, poverty and chastity, he also faces the greater danger of the fourth temptation. A synthesis of the preceding three temptations, this is "the spiritual temptation of the victorious through his victory itself. It is the temptation to act "in one's own name", to act as master instead of servant. Mastery over this temptation is a necessary attainment within the seventh Arcanum if we are to avoid falling into the spiritual temptation represented by the 'superman', or 'Nietzschean Übermensch'.

In the life of Valentin Tomberg we might see a certain conscious devotion to the planetary influences which oversee the life of man, or natural inclination towards the same. In the later years of his life Tomberg wrote masterworks of Jurisprudence – corresponding to the Saturnian old age spoken of above by G.O.M, and the whole of his life might be said to correspond to a classic initiatory path.

This being the Seventh Arcanum we are also put in mind of the Kybalion, where it is written:

The Principles of Truth are Seven; he who knows these, understandingly, possesses the Magic Key before whose touch all the Doors of the Temple fly open

The Seven Hermetic Principles cited are: Mentalism, Correspondence, Vibration, Polarity, Rhythm, Cause and Effect and The Principle of Gender.

Arcanum VIII

JUSTICE

Pathway from Chesed to Chokmah

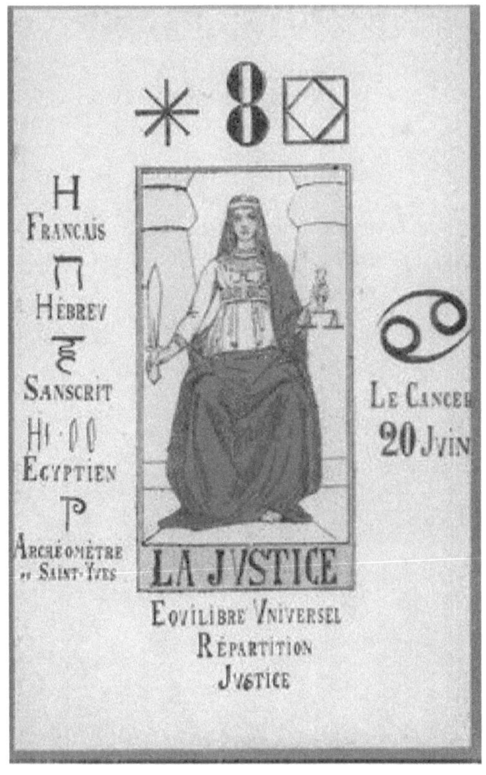

Justice is *realised*

The science of life is written in the Book of Nature, but man alone can read it.

Levi

THEMIS: Equilibrium

H--8 expresses in the divine world absolute Justice

Paul Christian

"You wished to see Truth and now you behold it! But remember what happens to the mortal who beholds a Goddess!"

Ouspensky

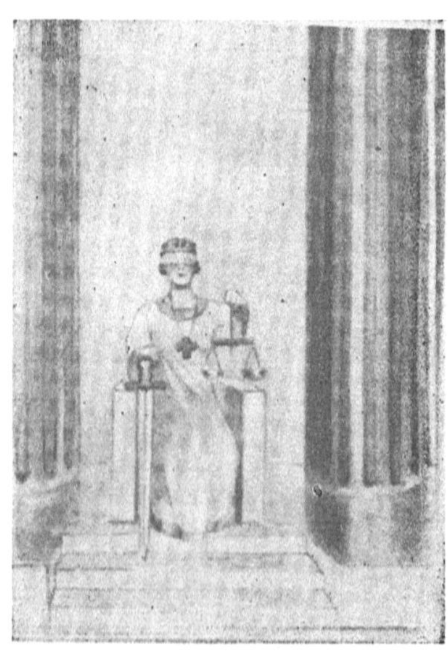

The Hebrew letter corresponding to Arcanum VIII is ח (Cheth), whose numerical value is 8. The Astrological correspondence is the zodiacal sign of Cancer.

The hieroglyph from this Arcanum is a field, symbolising all which can be subjected to cultivation. And it is the passive region to which the activity of the Victor of Arcanum VII should be directed.

The Card of Arcanum VIII has, at the bottom, two columns; between them, further on, a seated feminine figure: Themis. The forehead of the figure is girded with a ribbon of gold; the eyes are blindfolded. On her chest, attached to a chain, there is a solar cross. In her left hand Thémis holds a scale; in her right hand, a sword. It is assumed that the figure is sitting on a cubic stone, although the folds of her garment cover and conceal it. We will try to interpret the picture.

The figure is female; the Arcanum therefore represents something already existing, already materialised. On the card we see the binary three times, always balanced by a third element. The first the columns (such as those of Arcanum II) neutralised by Themis, sitting in the middle. The interpretation of this binary is somewhat different from that of Arcanum II. It would succinctly be the following: seeing Jachim, and there being Themis in the middle, we can deduce that, on the other side, is Boaz. In other words: if we perceive what is symbolically called by us one of the two forces that compose the pair and recognise the existence of an astral vortex (whirlwind), whose system includes the force that we see, then we must also recognise the existence of a second force that complements the first pairs, and therefore equal to it, parallel to it, but directed in the opposite direction.

If we are aware that we have an imagination depicting images in the present for us, and at the same time imagine some clichés as past ones, then we should know about the possibility of presenting other clichés in the future.

If we believe in the Higher Androgynous Manifestation of the Divine and see in any emanations its characteristic feature of activity, expansiveness, that which knows, then we must be convinced of the existence of other emanations of a passive, attractive nature that coincide with the field of what to know can.

If there is justice (-) and there is the possibility of spiritual harmony (n), then, probably, there is mercy (+).

If there is an idea of ascent (+) and if the idea of level (n) is allowed, then there must be an idea of descent (-).

These formulas explain the title of the Arcanum VIII in the plane of the Archetype "Libratio", that is, the law of the equilibrium of the Great Metaphysical Scale in which one of the dishes is charged with the positive value of the Great Arcanum, and the other, with its negative value. The pointer symbolises the androgynous apex of the Ascending Triangle.

The sword in the hand of Themis explains to us the Arcanum in the Human field of the Theosophical ternary. The sword reminds us that there is the law of Themis, even when conditioned by the times, places and environments and that the transgression of this "Lex" (-)[20], will bring a punishment (+), due to the action of the equilibrium principle (n). The word "Lex" is the name given to conditional rules, which are evolutionary within time and space, but inevitable at every given moment. Thus, "Lex" will be the second title of the Arcanum.

In the other hand Themis holds a balance - another binary - with its neutralising element: the pointer. Let us bring this symbol to the field of Nature. If someone breaks the balance of balance, it will necessarily provoke a reaction aimed at restoring equilibrium. If someone put a five-kilogram weight on the left plate, you should, in order to balance the scale, load the right plate with another five kilos.

If someone stained his Karma by a process inconsistent with the laws of equilibrium, in the individual accounts within the chain of their incarnations, then s/he will have to erase this spot and restore balance when s/he repeatedly stumbles upon the page which has been stained. The third name of the Arcanum will therefore be "Karma." The card itself is called "Themis" or "Justice".

Let us turn to the evaluation of arithmetic deconstructions of the Arcanum.

Let's start with two-digit deconstructions.

8 = 1 + 7 - The 1, or the first Arcanum, represents the conscious manifestations and the application of the balanced androgynous principles. The 7th Arcanum is that of victory. Therefore, 1 + 7 means the application of victory. In fact, the first duty, the first concern of the victor should consist in establishing the order, justice and legality on the ground conquered. Justice is the "wife" of victory; the Arcanum VIII is the "wife" of the Arcanum VII.

But where does the magician apply the fruit of mental victory? Naturally, on the astral plane, during the astral performance. Here you must remember the law of "Libratio" into account the opposing mood influences.

We have decided, for example, to suggest to a patient a certain action; with this the momentum given is mental. However, if we ourselves ardently desire that the patient performs what is suggested, that is, if we are astrally interested in this, we create a hindrance to the formation of

---

[20] By 'Lex' we can read 'system of law'

the second indispensable force to provoke a whirlwind, which should serve as an instrument for the suggestion. In addition, to this second force, other volitional flows may join, complicating and forcing us to reinforce our suggestion. For all this to be avoided, counterbalance our desire with an absence of desire, equivalent in strength; and it is indispensable to convince us that the realisation of the suggestion is indifferent to us, while at the same time remaining mentally convinced that it should take place. So, in fact, the suggestion will be made in an impressive way. In general, we better achieve what our personal animistic interests do not interfere with. It is the reason for which we get more easily to something other than ourselves.

The same rules apply to punishment. In order for someone to punish fairly and promptly, [they must] be imbued with mercy. In general, an ignorant and weak being throws himself into the fight, when emotionally involved, thus diminishing their chances of winning; a strong being is controlled, knows how to wait and choose for the fight, the most favourable moment.

Since we speak of justice, it is natural to know to what extent and in what way an occultist can allow himself to punish his fellow man. The astral cliché of punishment is formed automatically and according to the Arcanum VIII, therefore, can only be the mental evaluation of the offense of his fellow man. This will form the axis of a whirlwind. The rest will fit the astral. However, we should not forget that the law of karma - the negative pole of Fabre d'Olivet's triangle - was established once for all and will act even without any participation on our part. Therefore, an enlightened occultist knows that he has a right to a mental censorship of the actions of his fellow man only to the extent that he himself participates in the work of the Emanations of the Primordial Principle. In other words, only a Theurgist has the right to censor and, even so, only to the exact extent where he really is a Theurgist.

Theurgy, even of temporary nature, requires a very clear worldview and a great internal purity. Therefore, it is rare that participation in a punishment is in accordance with the Law.

Magical punishments allowed by Christian Illuminism for their adherents are collectively called Reprobatio (literally, condemnation). There are three degrees of Reprobations: disapproval, sorrow for the act of one's neighbour, and censure.

Disapproval is formulated as follows: "although you are my brother, I would not want to share with you the clichés of your actions. We are not together."

Christ allowed this degree of punishment to his disciples in the most extreme cases. Its symbolic formula is: *"Shake off the dust from our feet."*

Christ himself, in rare cases, applied the second degree, the degree of sorrow for the act of one's neighbour: *"it would have been better if this man had not been born"* ...

The third degree - rebuke - impresses with the violence and inexorability of its consequences. The cases of the application of the latter can be seen in the story of Moses, who widely used theurgical methods. It will not be too much to remember the episodes of Koré, Dathan, and Aviron (Numbers, 16).

In closer times, we can quote the famous censure made by the Grand Master of the Templar Order Jacobus Burgundus Molay from the flame of a fire at the address of Pope Clement V and King Philip the Beautiful, who destroyed him, calling them to the Court of God, the first - no later than 50 days, and the second - no later than a year. Both predictions of death came true even before the time specified.

From all that has been said, the danger of the punishment that we have called the "curse" follows.

The degree of strength is not always the same If, say, a father curses his son, then he often relies only on his authority (4th Arcana), without any further arcana. But the right of reprobation, as related to the 8th Arcanum, undoubtedly requires passing through of the 6th and 7th by the operator, that is, the prior internal realisation of the hermetic victory. Another decomposition of the eight into the same terms, $8 = 7 + 1$, I provide to the audience themselves to analyse how the superiority of personal victory over the manifestation of balanced will, i.e. as a conscious and voluntary inertness of the Victor.

I pass to the decomposition $8 = 2 + 6$. $2 =$ Gnosis $=$ Knowledge; 6 - the law of reactions in the world; therefore, in general, the work of an enlightened operator in the field of static and dynamic binaries.

But how does the law of reaction expand the world outlook of a learned operator?

- It will inspire him with caution, warning him of the existence of return strikes.

Imagine someone operating magically, that is, creating and directing an astral whirlwind to a person for a particular purpose. The scheme of this magic operation is as follows: a whirlwind is created by the operator in the most efficient way possible and directed to a specific person. Reaching its target, the whirlwind causes a physical manifestation, whose cliché will join the operator's karma, in the positive or negative direction. Sometimes, though, the whirlwind, despite its existence, has no effect. This can happen in three cases:

1. When the patient consciously protected himself from the attack by concentrating on generating the astral counter-vortex with the lowest

subplane, equivalent to the subplane of the approaching vortex or even more compact. This is the so-called active reflection of the attack.

.2. When the patient at the moment of energetic contact with the vortex was shielded from the action by conscious and powerful concentration on another object of realisation, which is part of a cycle of more powerful projects better than the attack plan than the plan of attack. For example, when the patient whom you are involving to death is busy with a grandiose plan of creating or destroying collectivities, in comparison with which personal hatred is something very small, insignificant in all astral subplanes.

3. When, at the moment of contact with the attacking vortex, the most active part of the patient's pentagram is floating in subplanes much higher than the most active regions of the vortex. For example, you want to ruin a person who lives, as they say, outside the sphere of material interests; or wish failure in the service of a person exclusively immersed in scientific aspirations and neglecting all the elements of careerism; or send larvae of hatred to a person praying for his enemies, etc.

In all three cases the whirlwind will not hit the target person. However, the formation of this whirlwind will have entailed a certain, though limited, imbalance in the astral world and the equilibrium will have to be re-established again by creating a corresponding cliché. If the astral aggression has failed to reach the person to whom it was destined, it will inevitably affect another entity whose astrosome resembles more the essence of the created astral swirl. One such entity, first, will be the operator, himself, since he used his own fluids in the formation of the whirlwind. Thus, he will receive what is called, in magic, "the return stroke."

Let us suppose You magically tried to inspire love; the whirlwind reflected, and you yourself fell in love. You have been spoiling; failed - and you yourself fell ill, etc.

To avoid these bad consequences, representatives of black magic always insure themselves against return blows by choosing a second, dummy patient, directing the whirlwind for two, but including the first patient in a more prominent way in the ceremony of magic operation.

For example, they direct the disease at you with a turn, in case of failure, at a familiar horse or dog, or at some very passive person who cannot be expected to repulse the blow.

The inverse deconstruction, that is, $8 = 6 + 2$ corresponds to the case in which knowledge (2) is subordinate to the choice of path (6). In other words, it is the awareness of the danger that knowledge can be put both in service of evolution as well as involution.

Let's pass to the deconstruction $8 = 3 + 5$. Here, metaphysics, that is, the high world of the ternaries (3) is introduced into daily life and dominates the field of impulses of the personal will (5). We can ask ourselves how metaphysics is introduced into life. Transforming mature ideas into forms and, by analogy, realising the concrete plane, as mature forms.
A man who desires to be called "righteous" (8) and has broadly constructed his conception of the world, has no right not to elaborate it in an ordered philosophical system. If he does not, it will create a damaging mental strain. And in exactly the same way, it would be embarrassing, having drawn up a plan of a grandiose, well-adapted building or mechanism, not to make attempts to implement it.
The same deconstruction can greatly confuse the so-called supporters of Platonic love, thinking of confining themselves to astral manifestations of the mental field and forgetting that they have come true for nothing and, moreover, are obliged not to shy away from the consequences of existence in the third (physical) plane. After all, this plane provides a reference point for the astral process of purification of Karma. If, on the physical plane, a human being meets the temptation of two roads, it is not for them to remain undecided, postponing the choice for a future incarnation, but rather to choose consciously and decisievely the right way. We can say that these people, having pronounced ׳ (Iod) and after that ה (He), are afraid to pronounce ו (Vau) so as not to see the second ה (He), the beauty of which they fear.
The conduct of such persons is typically indecisive and cowardly when there are some divergences of opinion in parties or groups. If we offer something our sympathy, this should be offered in all three planes. If we hate it, then it is preferable to hate on all three planes.
People who, on the mental plane, have a determined conviction, and on the astral plane the well-formed cliché of this conviction and, nevertheless, maintain the "neutrality" on the physical plane, are called by Christ "warm," to differentiate them from the "hot" and "cold". There can easily be a mutual inversion of a "hot" and a cold "but nothing can be done with a being always amorphous, always fearful, "lukewarm".
This was well understood by the Masons of the last three centuries (XVII, XVIII, XIX). Upon initiation into the 30th Scottish degree, the highest of hermetic degrees, the future Chevalier Kadosh, before taking the oath, was called to simulate the murder of the traitor Freemasonry in order to test how much he hates his enemies. The Initiation candidate did not know what was striking in the heart of a ram with its side shaved cleanly, and sincerely imagined himself to be the executor of Areopagus's orders to punish the traitor brother.
The simulation of murder under these conditions, of course, stained the collective Karma of the Masonic chain and overshadowed its egrégore,

but this inconvenience was put up for the sake of urgent recognition of the "hot" from the "warm".

The opposite deconstruction - 8 = 5 + 3 - can be well illustrated by the way of proceeding of the people who adapt their logic and their metaphysics to personal manifestations. "*I like him, therefore, he serves this or that*" - this is the reasoning of a man of type 8 = 5 + 3. Other comments are unnecessary.

Let's go to deconstruction 8 = 4 + 4 - the most typical of the Arcanum we are studying. 4 opposes 4, that is, form to form; authority to authority; adaptation (adaptatio) to adaptation. Offending someone (a form) we'll have to apologise (otherwise); a revolutionary government (an authority) was created, a dictatorship opposes it (another authority); someone prepared a ruse to circumvention or breach of the law (an adaptation), the police will act in an appropriate way to the culprit (another adaptation). It is a general formula of karma and also of relative human justice.

The contrast of forms prevails in magic, the contrast of authorities in politics, and the opposition of adaptations (supply and demand) in the economic field.

Having finished the arithmetic survey of the arcanum, we turn to its most popular pantaculos. There are two of them. The first is called the "Wheel of Ezekiel" or the "Wheel of Pythagoras" depending on the kind of symbolic styles; the second is known as the "Pantaculo of Realisation." The wheel of Ezekiel in the interpretation of the Rosicrucian Schools is featured in figure 31.

The "Wheel of Ezekiel", as it is used in the Rosicrucian Schools, is shown in figure 31. The solid cross gives the ה ו ה י quaternary scheme, that is, one of the cycle's dynamics. The cross of dotted lines or the INRI quaternary represents the anagram of one of the three following propositions:

Igne Natura Renovatur Integra
Iesus Nazarenus Rex Iudaeorum
In Nobis Regnat Iesus.

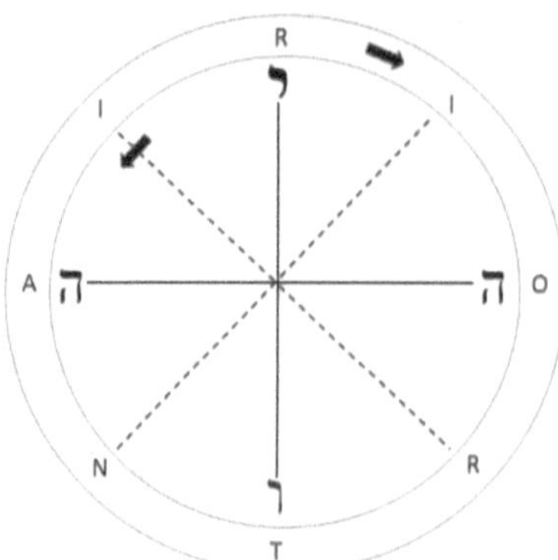

Figure 31

We have already found the first proposition, which clarifies the role of "Fire" as a purifying and renewing element, indicating the means of moving the "Wheel" and passing from one cycle to another, in the creative processes. The second proposition points out the importance of Christ's redemptive sacrifice in the evolution of the "Wheel".
The third proposition - the motto of the first Rosicrucians - literally translates as "in Jesus we reign" and, of course, should not be understood in the sense of proud isolation of the initiated in relation to the profane, but as an indication of the duty of each to seek the Christ within his heart and, through this search, to move the quaternary of the elements in the evolutionary direction.
The circular inscription ROTA indicates the direction of rotation of the י ה ו ה quaternary: from R to O, i.e. so that י goes into the second ה - in other words - in the direction of seeking causation.
The figure is presented in the form of beams from eight straight lines and suggests the idea of a spinning wheel within another wheel (see Ezekiel, chapter I and X). According to Ezekiel, "*the colour of the wheel is like unto topaz colour* ".
The "Wheel of Pythagoras" (figure 32) differs from the previous one by the following:

1. In place of the letters י ה ו ה and INRI are five-pointed stars.
2. There is no indication of the direction of movement.
3. Within the wheel are complementary signs that symbolise the seven secondary causes (the planets), as well as two Greek letters (alpha and omega), the meaning of which is identical to that of Lingam, that is, the fertilisation of the passive principle by the active.

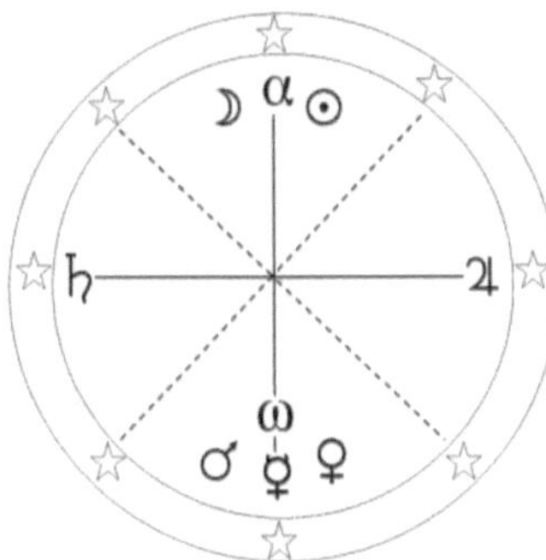

Figure 32

The figure formed by the intersection of solid lines in the centre of the physical plane, which presents itself as a small island surrounded by the waters of the astral (inner circle) which, in turn, are insignificant compared to the immensity of the mental (outer circle). A more concrete analysis of the pantaculo will lead us to the field of astronomy. The outer circle would symbolise the stellar universe; the inner circle, our solar system, and the beam central continuum, the elemental life on our little planet.

The "Pantaculo of Realisation" (outline, figure 33) appears like this: the background is black (the lower astral); The outer square is silver and represents a frame already prepared beforehand, passively, inside which something should be done. The inner square is golden (active lead to achievement). Letters that eight times repeat the Great Name must be of the colour of fire, because they correspond to the assertion "Igne Natura Renovatur Integra"[21].

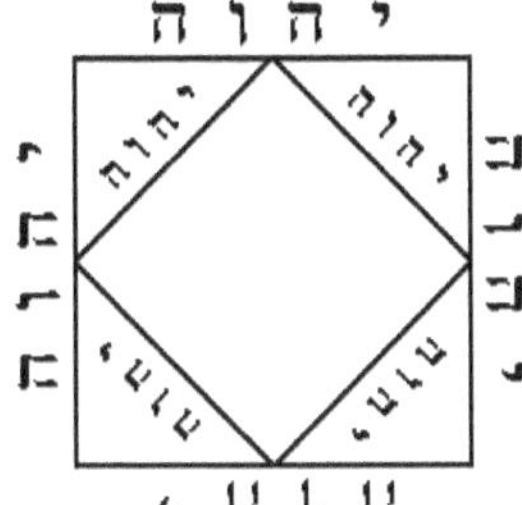

Figure 33

---

[21] Through Fire Nature is Reborn Whole

This pantáculo is used when there is need to concentrate on the realisation of a project, of a task, of an association, or even of a more abstract subject, but always of relevant importance.

The force generated by the eight-fold repetition of יהוה will be analysed in Arcanum X.

Notes on the eighth Arcanum

This being the eighth Arcanum, we are moved to remark upon the sacred qualities associated with the number eight in both Eastern and Western mystery traditions.

In the Pythagorean Tarot of John Opsopaus, which we found particularly useful for learning the numerical meanings of the Minor Arcana, the eights appear as gateways separating the lower levels from the upper degrees of attainment represented by nine and (especially) ten.

In this system it is taught that the four Eighth Gates are barred by Rivalry (Wands), Memory (Swords), Delusion (Cups) and Inertia (Pentacles/Coins) and herein we may see a form of justice: One cannot pass the threshold of the upper levels without the proper attainments and degree of mastery learned from the preceding Arcana.

In MotT (p174), we are told that the Arcanum of Justice shows us how to maintain our inner equilibrium, as indicated by the balance held by the woman of the image. We are also reminded of the first commandment, Thou shalt have no other Gods before me (Exodus XX, 3), which indicates that we are not to "substitute an intellectual abstraction of God for the spiritual reality of God".

We are reminded that in order to judge properly and fairly we must be conscious of the extent of our own knowledge and ignorance relative to the matter at hand. As we cannot know the soul of another, our human judgement does not impress upon the souls of others.

Let he who is without sin cast the first stone.

It is also natural for us to consider the Tree of Life in the context of this card, where Justice holds the balance between the dual pillars of Mercy and Severity and ensures that karma is overcome by the "justice of grace". (MotT, Letter VIII, p 178).

Arcanum IX

THE HERMIT

Pathway between Geburah and Chesed

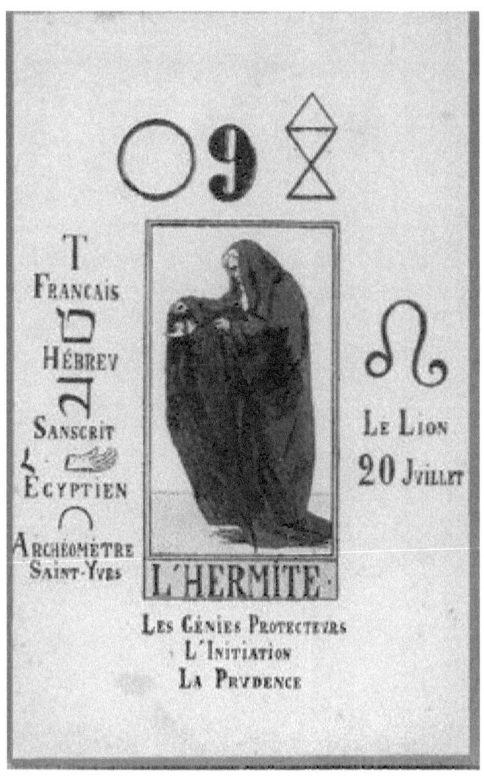

The Hermit is an *initiate*

The light of this Magical Lamp should work marvels, it should illuminate the consciences of men and women so that you may read them and should enable you to recognise each type of spiritual being.

Levi

THE VEILED LAMP: Prudence

TH--9 expresses in the divine world absolute Wisdom

Paul Christian

"Initiation unites the human mind with the higher mind by a chain of analogies. This chain is the ladder leading to heaven, dreamed of by the patriarch."

Ouspensky

The sign of Arcanum IX is ט (Teth), its numerical value 9; the astrological correspondence is the zodiacal sign of the Lion. The hieroglyph of the Arcanum is a roof, as a symbol of protection, shelter and isolation from harmful influences.

The card represents an old man walking, holding in his right hand a lamp, with three wicks lit. A broad hooded garment surrounds the old man, forming three folds that cover the lamp. With the left hand, the old man rests on a stick in which are visible three nodules.

The three flames of the lantern obviously indicate the initiation on all three planes. The mantle with its folds in the same way clearly indicates insulation on the same three planes. The baton, with its three knots, symbolises triple support.

The pilgrim's age is an indication that only the man who has overcome the storms of passions, the pursuit of personal happiness and the ambitions of earthly life, can devote [himself to] aspects of life as symbolised in the card. Walking indicates that the presence of the elements presented in the card prevents any stationery state.

The common name of the Arcanum is "The Hermit." The erudite name, "Lux Occulta" or "Lux in Occulto".

Let us turn to arithmetic analysis. In 2-digit deconstruction, we first have $9 = 1 + 8$: That is, an individualised, balanced unit (1) that seeks to manifest itself in the environment, according to Law (8). If the plane of this manifestation is that of the Archetype, then the human being finds there the idea and the image of the Protective Genii, who help him discover in himself his own Higher Being. Here comes the first title of the Arcanum: "Protector".

If manifestation is sought in the plane of man, it will entail understanding of himself, his own astral knowledge and the harmonisation of the soul. This process of evolutionary work is called Initiation or Self Initiation. In the latter case, the "Protector" is found within itself. Thus, the second Arcanum title will be "Initiate".

Finally, if the plane of manifestation desired is that of Nature, that is, the physical plane, then the being learns to face the god of materialists, called "Chance" and to orient oneself in life through theory of probability that often dictates various degrees of prudence. Hence the third title: "Prudence."

The inversion of the first deconstruction will give us $9 = 8 + 1$. Here, the legality (8) of the environment weighs on a crystallised but healthy personality (1) and limits it. That personality is unable to circumvent prudently the demands of his environment, through internal isolation, and rise beyond the dictates of that environment. This is the formula of talented personalities, but drowned out by their environment or their time, and therefore not influencing the process of the evolution of Humanity.

The second two-digit deconstruction gives $9 = 2 + 7$ that is, the sum of science (2) and the victor (7). Who is the Victor? The one who passed through the stages of the first seven metaphysical Arcana. And what will this science be?

The Science of the Victor has two aspects: Female, passive, receptive, called - "Divinatio", i.e. the ability to "see" in the Archetype, Man and Nature.

Prophetic ecstasy, sudden consecration by Grace, which gives inspiration for the creation of a religious cult and its morality, will be good examples of divination in the Archetypal plane.

Divination according to Man will be reduced to sensitivity in the field of astral manifestations of others (watching auras, quick judgments about the nature, development and degree of moral evolution, assessment of the ability of odic emanation, etc.), as well as to those systems that bear the well-known names of palmistry, phrenology , physiognomy, etc., and with which we will have to deal in the seventeenth Arcanum.

Divination by Nature spills over into forms known under the names of astrology, geomancy and its subdivisions — cartomancy, hydromancy, pyromancy, etc. fortune telling by the elements (again the seventeenth Arcanum).

The Science of the Victor also has a male, active side - the ability to own the astral, i.e. direct and apply the energy of his personality in the forms of magnetisation, telepathy (transmission of forms at a distance) and even the exteriorisation of the astrosome, as well as the ability to formulate ceremonial magic to forcibly enter into communication with various astral beings.

Many people are attracted to these Victor Sciences, a field that captivates many with the depth and breadth of its applications, often dangerous, often fatal for its owner.

We may ask whether the "Victor" (7) might voluntarily renounce his activity and receptivity in its field, cherishing the safety of his victorious personality (7), putting this personality ahead of the interests of science (2)? - Maybe. This will be a decomposition of $9 = 7 + 2$.

We pass to the decomposition $9 = 3 + 6$. Metaphysics (3) is ahead of the choice of the path (6); metaphysics, so to speak, determines the choice of path.

But what, they say to me, in addition to the metaphysical worldview, can affect this choice?

Impulsiveness. We will not speak of the instincts (the physically impulsive man), nor of the passions (the astral impulsive man); this subject has already been discussed and presents no problems. We will speak of an impulsive intellectual man, with his superstitions, prejudices and conditioning. Superstitions are the greater impediment to Initiation. Let's deal with them.

What are superstitions? They are the vestiges, impulsively admitted in a way that, once, when the person in question created astral clichés and volitional entities, were necessary and useful but, due to the progress of this person, have become a great burden to hinder or even prevent authentic manifestations, proper and appropriate to its actual (current) evolutionary stage.

We can deduce from what has been said that all superstitions belong to the astral plane; however, according to the field to which they refer, they can be subdivided into mystical, precisely astral, and physical ones.

If a person faces conditions of life where there is no possibility of maintaining hygiene, and yet strictly clings to some acquired hygienic habit, it can be considered superstitious on the physical plane.

The same can be said of a man who, sufficiently evolved to create, through meditation, propitious conditions to be able to pray outside a temple made of masonry, complains that the absence of it makes it impossible for him to pray.

Let an example of astral superstition be the conviction of a magician who has reached in his power the stage at which his ideas themselves are clothed with astrosomes, of the inability to operate without pronouncing one or another formula, without observing one or another symbolism.

Another example, somewhat comic and very commonplace, is a person who recognises Monday as a difficult day, or that the thirteenth day is unlucky, without any empirical data in his autobiography.

There are many examples of mystical superstition.

We see people firmly convinced that there is no salvation outside the totality of the smallest details of a particular religious dogma.

At the same time, we see people who are indifferent to the differentiation of religions, if only they recognise a certain, dear to them dogmatic element, for example, the dogma of the Atonement by the Incarnation.

We also meet people who demand from religion only recognition of the possibility of the Reintegration of Mankind through evolution.

Of course, a man belonging to the third category will find superstitious another who is culturally similar, but belongs to the second, and a man of the second category will qualify as superstitious someone who belongs to the former.

We can thus deduce that no superstition can be qualified as absolute. To evaluate the superstition, it is indispensable to have an understanding of the mentality, the astral and the physical state of the same. The lack of such understanding has always provoked persecution of the Initiatic

Centres, for they were accused of propagating different dogmas, maintaining various ethical codes and different duties, which, in fact, were in accordance with the initiatory degree of members.

To conclude, we suggest a very important subject to be meditated upon: if we acquire an ascendancy over a person who is our mental, astral and physical equivalent, this is almost always due to their superstitions, prejudices or conditioning.

Prejudice in the field of citizenship and conventionality in the field of everyday life play the same role as superstition in the field of dogmatic outlook.

The inverse deconstruction, that is, $9 = 6 + 3$ means, of course, that the choice of the path (6) determines the later metaphysics (3).

This formulation will cause an associative idea of the behaviour of people who have chosen (often without being conscious enough) a certain path, a certain course of action, and thereby are forced to look for metaphysical data in the future for the benefit and in justification of their activities, prompted to this partly by the need to maintain self-esteem, partly the desire to defend their dignity over others.

The fourth deconstruction: $9 = 4 + 5$ is interpreted as the fact that it rises from the plane of the elements (4) to the astral plane (5).

The magician is proud of his astral science, but he prudently compares the manifestations of his will not only with astral influences, but also with the conditions, the knowledge of which he owes to physics, chemistry, astronomy, physiology, etc.

Do not hesitate to delay a magical ceremony, if it can be performed later with greater success. Do not act when you feel sick. Consciously apply to your life the hygienic measures of physical purity (bathing, feeding with fresh produce, abstaining from all artificial food and drink). You know perfectly well that excessive fatigue caused by work is as harmful as laziness. If you are sensitive to climatic conditions, carefully choose the right place to live and, lastly, always and everywhere, behave according to the theory of probability (what we call "being prudent in the physical plane").

There are cases of individual implementations playing the role of rivets or nails in the general mechanism of systematic work. It is important to hammer these nails at a certain moment, regardless of physical difficulties and from the seemingly untimely work in terms of the elements. This is necessary - and we are launching the active Mars of our astrality, even if the achievement of the goal was worth the loss of enormous quantities of vitality or material means.

The inverse deconstruction: $9 = 5 + 4$ gives us the formula intelligently applicable only in exceptional, isolated cases, and that usually bring short-term results. This formula means that, at the individual will (5) the influence of the elements (4), and sometimes, in opposition to them, is given primacy. It can be applied in cases where, in order to proceed with the planned work, we need, a given strength. It is important that this commitment be made at that very moment, despite physical difficulties and unfavourable conditions at the element level. Being necessary, we activate the Mars of our astral, although this operation costs us great loss of vital forces or material resources.

In the ninth Arcanum, despite the importance of double decompositions, the central place should be left behind the symmetric triple decomposition $9 = 3 + 3 + 3$.

If double decompositions have given us the definition of initiation and indications of the means to achieve it, then this triple decomposition will determine the hierarchical steps of the initiation itself.

In the initiatory scale we discern three cycles, and in each of them three sub-divisions, that is, three degrees.

To the lower cycle, under certain conditions, we will call physical because, in general, the initiate (candidate for initiation) appears in his physical body at the ceremony of initiation, and the ceremony itself is made in a particular place and of three dimensions, being led by an incarnated initiator.

In the composition of physical initiation three elements come into play: the mental (content of so-called "Initiation notebooks" or the initiation formula, orally transmitted); the astral (fluidic, magnetic influences, transmitted by the initiator to the initiate and the initiation symbolism) and the physical (all the manipulations that accompany the act of initiation). Finally, the physical is the totality of manipulations in the physical plane that accompanies the act of Initiation. The dogmatic content of the youngest of the physical Degrees is the Synthesis of Theogonic, Androhonic and Cosmogonic views of the School, toned up by the normal scheme of the Great Drama of the human Fall and the methodology of Human Rehabilitation.

The second Degree will familiarise the initiate with the astral plane, give him the opportunity to make correct judgments about it (theory) and teach him how to influence this plan without leaving his own physical body (part of Psychurgy and all Ceremonial Magic).

The cycle called by us "physical" contains three degrees:

The third physical Degree will introduce the initiate into the field of Universal Love through Ethical Hermeticism.

All these three degrees can be achieved without the participation of the incarnate Initiator. To do this, it is enough to have a certain intellectual and ethical development (which partly depends on the number of previous incarnations of the subject) and, moreover, have a certain astral protectorate. Of course, I do not mention the need for a steady, well-established desire for Initiation.

Thus, under certain conditions, in the initiation of this cycle, the presence of another human being outside the self-initiating, is not mandatory. In other words, the intelligent contemplation of Nature, accompanied by meditation, and in parallel, of a progressive self-knowledge, are sufficient. Because of this, it is sometimes said that the physical cycle of initiation is given to us by Nature - the third link of the Theosophical ternary.

The element of the astral, fluid influence of the Initiator on the initiate is reduced to the process of the effect of the will of the Initiator on the astral body of the student in the forms of such arrangement for self-processing in the initiatory direction, i.e. to the acquisition of certain degrees of intuitiveness and activity, neutralised by spiritual harmony.

I don't have to speak about the symbolism and ritual features of the Initiation - these are elements determined by the spirit of one or another School, the trends of one or another era; and sometimes personal tastes of the Initiates.

We can now turn to the second cycle of initiation which I will allow myself to call astral, because its characteristic is the need for the Initiate to exteriorise in the astrosome and in this form enter into communication with the Teacher (or Teachers).

The Teacher-Initiator, with whom the neophyte comes into purely energetic contact, already essentially independent of the gross idea of time and unable to coordinate in the space of three dimensions, can either be an exteriorised person, or a two-plane elementary of the human essence. In any case, the Teacher here will be a certain Personality, which will give me the right to say that the second initiation cycle is given to us by the Universal Astral Man.

Of course, one should not speak here of the nature of this initiation or of its ritual. We cannot. We note, however, one very important circumstance: the student's traditional Rosicrucian astral trial accompanied by "Those who went there before him", the exit so gracefully symbolised in physical terms by the initiation ceremony in the 18th Scottish degree of Freemasonry (for its ceremonial), and by Christian Baptism (for ideological significance), should take place in one form or another no later than the gap between the third (highest) degree of the physical cycle and the first (youngest) degree of the astral.

Turning to the degrees of the higher cycle, which I allow myself to call mental, I will characterise it as a simple attachment of a human being to that stream of ideas, the affinity for which is naturally determined by the type of its monad.

There is no more here the astral personality of the instructor, performing the act of initiation: Here, simply the Collective Universal Man accepts into his body a cell that belonged to him right from the beginning of the eternity, cleansed of the contamination of the fall and returning to its place with a reserve of acquired Wisdom.

Of course, the question of the content and ritual of the Initiation also disappears, we can say, however, that it is made possible by the existence of the process of the emanations of the Archetype, a process that caused the principle of the existence of the Universal Collective Man in its primordial purity.

It is customary to say that at this Initiation a person is exteriorised in the so-called "mental body", i.e. in that thinly astralised shell of the spiritual monad, which is inherent in it even at the stage of its organic communication, as cells of the Collective Man, with its other cells.

If the process of the Rosicrucian "Astral Baptism" was placed between the lower degree of the astral cycle and the highest physical level, then the phase of the so-called Rosicrucian Reintegration should be placed between the higher degree of the astral cycle and the lower mental level.

"Reintegrated Brothers of the Cross-Rose" refers to the elementaries, although they may have retained the middle astral shell, but they can separate from it just like embodied people can exteriorise in the astral body.

The Reintegrated Rosicrucian seems to temporarily lull the middle astrosome, i.e. voluntarily renounces energetic manifestations, limiting his or her activity to mental manifestations peculiar to the אדם (Adam) cell before the fall, just as during exteriorisation we voluntarily renounce sensory perceptions in order to cast off slavery from time and space of three dimensions.

But we use exteriorisation for operations in the physical plane on the basis of mediumistic manifestations, simultaneously vampirising the lower astral of other organisms and their physical bodies.

The reintegrated Brother of the Cross-Rose can take advantage of mental exteriorisation for borrowing forms of the middle astral to create evolutionary astral clichés outside the scope of his usual activities in the middle astral, for example, to complement the dedication of the astral nature of some chain other than his own mid-astral egrégorean Mercury.

You might ask: Can an embodied person be mentally initiated?

Yes, it is possible, because exteriorisation in the mental body is possible with catalepsy of the physical body and most of the astrosome. This is Ecstasy; but how short it is for an embodied person, and how difficult it is to carry the minced crumbs of a reintegrating mentality into our physical world that are not distorted in essence!

People who achieve this are called Masters. Both ignoramuses and Initiates inevitably distinguish them from the crowd, considering them as Messengers of the Higher Plane, i.e. recognising the obligation for them to live not for themselves, but for us and thereby mentally, figuratively taking away their physical body and all lower astral subplanes, unnecessary to the Reintegrated Brother of the Cross-Rose. This is how we treat the Prophets, so we relate to many Teachers of the Initiative Schools, correcting our requirements with the anomaly created by the high impulses of the Mentally Baptised non-corporeal Brothers. One more observation: the mental cycle of initiation takes place by itself within the human being. Here there can be no question of wanting or accepting something, because, in the process of Reintegration, the Pentagram loses its personal character. Desires and passions disappear, yielding the work of one of the cells of the Universal Collective Man, consciously participating in their volitional impulses, in a particular field of their organism.

In the astral Initiation, the initiate of the Pentagram has the right not only to want, but also to demand the Initiation, just as a rhombus has the right to be credited to parallelograms by the process of accessing the definition of such.

Here the will of the Initiator must submit to the logic of the Initiate. Another thing in the physical cycle. There, the teacher's knowledge of the degree of development of the student is complicated by the complexity of the divination processes and the dependence of the teacher's intuition on the moment at which he operates, and on the degree of interest that causes him to meditate on objects that are outside the question of Initiation of this person.

Here, acquaintance with the student takes place gradually, not by order, and it is important that the invitation to the Initiation comes from the Teacher. The consent or disagreement of the student serves as a good control apparatus of the Master's intuition. When the latter is mistaken and risks harming the Initiation, the student often relieves himself of danger by refusal, and the Master eliminates the spot on Karma, but again I repeat - it is possible and desirable to initiate without a Master, whose role is mainly to state the fact of Initiation.

I will say a few words about the meaning of the physical cycle of Initiation. Of course, astral initiation is more important than physical, because its cultivation prepares the process of Reintegration. But it is possible to imagine a period of time, even an entire era, during which, due to the unpopularity of occult teachings or the presence of a worldly, so to speak, anti-sanctuary character, no one will have hermetic virtues to achieve at least the lower astral degrees.

You will say: it does not matter! This era will pass, and the Initiates will appear again.

This is so, the Initiates will appear, but the abandonment of Occultism for a whole era, the oblivion of symbols and the methods of initial preparation will greatly complicate these Initiates' influence on their modern society and, at best, will force them to develop again methods of preparing students, elementary symbolism that allows a multi-stage interpretation elementary techniques of training, the mechanism of application of initiatory discipline, etc.

If, on the contrary, the "Great Chain of Traditions" does not break off, existing continuously, even if only within the physical cycle of Initiation, there will always be a group of "Guardians of Tradition", so to speak, archival watchmen and faithful chroniclers of the history of Esotericism, who are not always deeply versed in the occult, but continuously observing the system of connections between the external Masonic and deeply esoteric manifestations of Mankind.

It is for this reason that all historians and supporters of esotericism have always given great value to the physical cycle of the initiation, to the specific characteristics of their respective degrees and to the transmission system of initiation, by succession.

In the second half of the 18th century (1760), a current arose which, by the name of its founder Martines de Pasqually (or Pasqualis), should be called Martinezism, but is better known under the name of Martinism, thanks to the works of the philosopher-theurgist Claude de St. Martin. The school of Martinez Pascalis was presented in the form of a powerful magic chain of a somewhat modernised Rosicrucianism, and therefore I will postpone a more detailed mention of it until the 11th arcanum. As for Louis Claude de St. Martin, he allowed the then-unusual (and somewhat contrary to the views of his Teacher Pascalis) institution of the "free Initiation" (Initiation libre), which makes it possible to continuously transmit the three elements (mental, astral, physical) of the cycle of physical Initiation, regardless of the existence of sororities, fraternities , circles and other types of Masonic confraternities.

At the initiation of Louis Claude de St. Martin there was only one degree: S ...I ("Supérieur Inconnu ", or Unknown Superior), conferred to the highly evolved and prominent intellectual type called "Men of Aspiration". The two later innovations of the Martinist Order, the degrees A ::: (Associate) and I ::: (Initiate) were only preparatory sub-grades, sub-grades of disciples, facilitating a careful and well-considered choice of future Superiors. Louis Claude de St. Martin divided humanity into four categories:

1. Men of the Torrent seemed to him in that category of weak-willed, poorly individualised people, following the fashion of this moment and the spirit of this era, which so tormented by its existence every thinker-philosopher and every conscious progressive figure

2. Men of Desire or those who seek the Absolute Truth and work consciously and perseveringly for their self-improvement, through the contemplation of Nature, the penetration into their own heart and study of sources of Tradition.

3. New Men or those who, having reached a certain degree of astral development, no longer, therefore, subject to the same mistakes as a Man of Aspiration, even the most sincere, not to judge himself or his neighbour.

4. Spirit Men or those who have totally gone beyond the attraction of the physical plane and who are liberated, with this, from the slavery of the soul sphere, reaching the full awareness of its high origin in the Sphere of Emanations.

It is easy to see that the "Man of Desire" corresponds, in our terminology, to the initiate of the degree of the physical cycle, since he already knows where he came from and where he goes, that is, he has understanding of the Fall and Human Reintegration.

The "New Man", already knowing the astral, enters the second degree of the same physical cycle, and the "Man Spirit", who underwent an elemental Hermetic transformation, in the third.

Let us return to the arithmetic deconstruction of our Arcanum and analyse another formula: $9 = 3 + 2 + 4$. It is not difficult to read it: initiation (9) leads to the Great Arcanum, that is: its mental part (3), astral (2) and elemental (4). It is interesting to note that a minor change in this distribution gives the general method of training in the process of self-initiation.

We write $9 = 2 + 3 + 4$, putting the component figures in their order of magnitude. The number 2 is the number of the polarity; the idea of polarity is closely linked to the idea of attraction, magnetisation, and so on. We will have in it the first recipe: by the powerful aspiration of a true Man of Desire, for his ardent prayer magnetises the environment, and from this, he will attract to himself the individualised elements which may facilitate his initiation.

Among the elements thus attracted, those who are superior, make his protectors will be made, and the inferiors will be accessible to his vampirism, that is, they may be for him assimilated. The number 3, which symbolises the balanced ternary, androgynous by its composition, but which can be manifested both in the active field and in the passive field, indicates the need for the condensation, within us, of everything that has already been attracted and assimilated. This process is carried out by means of increasing or decreasing, alternately and as the case may be, the activity or passivity potential of the subject, or rather, its astrosome, for the purpose of establishing a state which will be the third element in the aforementioned binary of potentialities.

After this, comes number 4. This is the symbol of the elementary ROTA, the symbol of the applications in the dense plane. It is the outline of the constructive work of the adept who knew how to evolve sufficiently by the process to deepen in oneself and by the training of his personality. This corresponds to what the masons, in the ritual of the master's degree, so appropriately called the "journey to spread the Light," resembling the master in the rising sun, culminates, sets and continues his way down the next day, a new cycle of movement, a new quadruple phase of the 24-hour daily Route. This "4" is an allusion to the emanation-phase of magical development of the future Instructor.

Let us return to the card of our Arcanum, to meditate on its elements. The elder's lantern is usually called the Light of Hermes Trismegistus. Hermes is the personification of the harmonious system, uniting metaphysical wisdom, knowledge of the astral and science on the physical plane, a system that flourished in the shrines of ancient Egypt. This lantern is indispensable to the initiate and she expresses the thesis: "Do not despise the profane physical world, study the astral plane with assiduity, and elevate oneself by the mental to the transcendent level. You are a tri-plane, study all three planes."

The mantle that isolates the old man is called the mantle of Apollonius of Tyana, the famous Teacher of the School of Alexandria. It is the symbol of the self-determination of the Monad on the mental plane, the self-knowledge on the astral plane and solitude on the physical plane. Determining yourself on the mental plane means becoming clearly aware of one's role as the cell of the mental organism of the Universal Collective Man, and of all the colourful nuances of that paper. Astral self-knowledge – a path typical of the development of Apollonius - is to delve into the astrosome itself, to make its analysis, a scrupulous classification of its resources, a re-orientation so we can say - of their molecular magnets and, finally, carry out a general synthesis as well assimilated. Apollonius' biographers present this work quite well, of a great Magician, wrapped in a fleece of wool, concentrated on contemplating his own navel.

Let us consider the meaning of solitude. What does it mean to be lonely? It is the capacity of work, to meditate without allowing the intrusion of energetic influences from other pentagrams. One can be lonely in the midst of a crowd. However, in the early stages of development, many need an anchorite life, an effective isolation, on the physical plane. This procedure has its good and bad aspects. The good side of the life of a hermit consists of the following: on the mental plane, prayer becomes easier; in the astral plane, there is the possibility of purification by the prolonged silence, one of the recommendations of the Pythagorean School; on the physical plane, there is no loss of time with the concerns of everyday life.

The negative aspects of hermit's life are these: on the mental plane, the inability to observe the progress of his fellows in the metaphysical field; in the astral plane, a certain absence of support of the chain of people united by the same evolutionary tonic. This increases the danger, in moments of passivity, of falling temporarily under the influence of the lower astral. This influence on the physical plane often takes the form of sexual manifestations, called incubi and succubi. Elementals and even wizards externalised, having made a mediumistic loan from the hermit or the organic realm surrounding them, can materialise in a sufficiently condensed state, to perform "coitus" with the hermit (the succubus of the astral entity) or the hermit (the incubus of the astral entity). Incubuses and succubus naturally cause great damage by the physical weakening they cause in their victim, and also because they prepare conditions that, in the future, may facilitate to the hermit the creation, by their own will, and under various pretexts, of any kind of larvae.

There is an alternative that, removing the evil aspects of the life of a hermit at the same time preserves the good. In other words, an alternative that seeks to neutralise the bi-nary: life of hermit - life in society. Attempts have been made, still in term: the monastic coexistence. The success of the work in these institutions varied and depending on the season, the environment, the members and the leaders of the communities, discipline and other conditions.

The elder's staff, as a symbol of prudence, almost dispenses with comment; the essential has already been said previously.

Concluding the analysis of Arcanum IX, we will outline a short program of efforts that facilitate the self-initiation and prepare the initiation itself. We will list nine phases of these efforts, emphasising that they are usually carried out in parallel and non-consecutively.

1. Overcoming physical cowardice itself.
2. Overcoming physical indecision itself.
3. Overcome regrets about what has been done and cannot be changed.
4. Fight as much as possible against superstitions.
5. Fight as much as possible against prejudice.
6. Fight, to the maximum, with the conditions.
7. Maintain health and the external environment in good order.

8. To realise, also, the astral order, both in itself (harmony of the soul) and outside of itself, that is, to acquire the empirical knowledge of the entities of the astral plane and its manifestations, classifying them properly.

9. Perform a mental order, that is, achieve purity, clarity and certainty in your worldview, but also the full awareness of its emanation from the Archetype.

The pentacle of the ninth Arcanum is realized according to the scheme 9 = 3 + 6, i.e. it can simply boil down to depicting the upper two parts of what we called the Great Arcanum (figure 16).

There are, however, attempts to introduce another configuration - a set of nine points (Fig. 34), of which the first three are located as the vertices of an evolutionary triangle, giving two reflections of an involutive type (i.e., 6 more points).

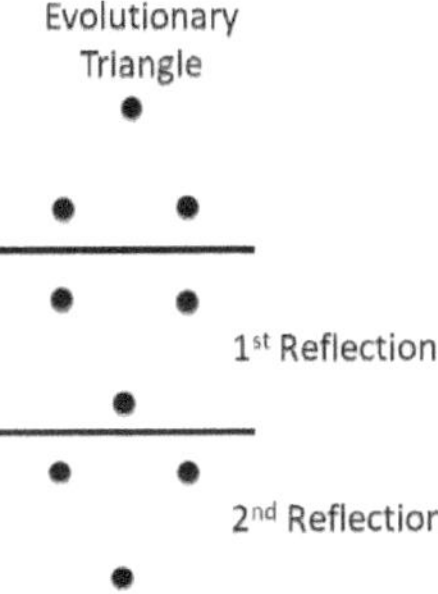

Figure 34

Notes on the ninth Arcanum

In Letter IX, The Hermit, MotT presents a masterly denouement of the key hermetic task of neutralising binaries/resolving antimonies, which – as shown in the present volume – constitutes for G.O.M. the major ongoing exercise and duty of the Great Work, starting with The Magician.

With respect to more subtle divergences between the teachings of Eliphas Lévi, G.O.M. and in MotT, we acknowledge that The Devil, as they say, is in the details. One such detail may be found in MotT's meditation upon the ninth arcanum, where it is recalled that Eliphas Lévi believed the inverted Tetragrammaton HVHY (Hava-jot) to be of great import in black magical rituals and evocations. Whilst Eliphas Lévi saw chaos and irrationality in this inversion of the name, MotT presents it as the essence of empirical science, which puts the principle of matter above and beyond all other principles. Rather than being the formula of irrationality, it is seen as the "formula of cunning ("ruse"), ie, of reflected intelligence, which is that of the serpent of Genesis:

It is precisely the inverted tetragrammaton which is the arcanum of empirical science....In the name, ה ו ה י, if י is the active principle (effective cause), the first ה is the passive principle (material cause), ו is the neutral principle (final cause) and the second He is the whole phenomenon which results from it, then the inverse name, HE-VAU-HE-YOD would be the series "passive principle-neutral principle - passive principle - active principle" or "matter, reason, evolution, scientific method".
The series HVHY means to say that nothing precedes matter; that nothing moves it; that it moves from itself - that mind is the child of matter; that evolution is matter which engenders mind; and that, lastly, mind, once born, is the activity of matter in evolution, which becomes conscious of itself and takes evolution in its hands. (MotT, p216)

It is in this Arcanum of MotT that we learn initiation can only be conferred by the Holy Spirit, not by human beings upon each other.

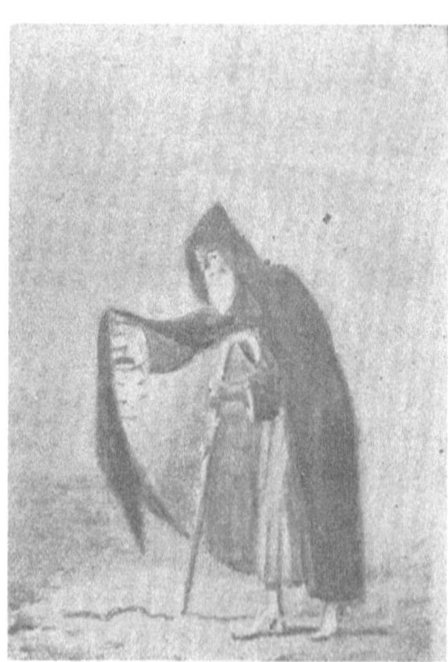

Arcanum X

י

THE WHEEL OF FORTUNE

Pathway from Tiphareth to Chesed

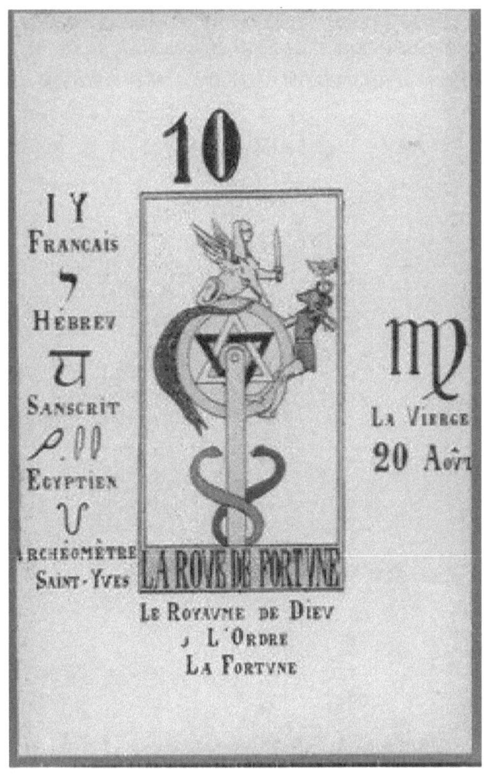

The Wheel of Fortune is the *Key of Occultism*

THE SPHINX: Fortune

I, J, Y--10 expresses in the divine world the active principle that animates all beings.

Paul Christian

"Existence begins at every moment. Round each "here" rolls "there". The middle is everywhere. The way of eternity is a curve".

Ouspensky

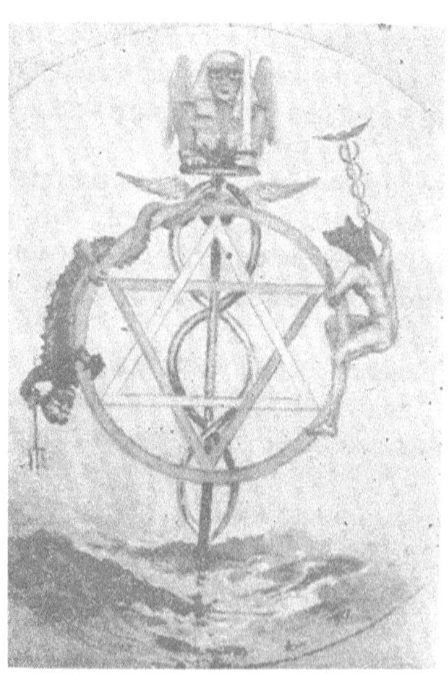

The sign of Arcanum X, in the Hebrew alphabet is ׳ (Iod); its numerical value, 10, and the astrological correspondence, the zodiacal sign of Virgo. The hieroglyph of the Arcanum is the index finger of a person. The indicator serves for the imperative gesture of a human being. If the latter is identified with Microcosm by being considered as a closed system, the imperative gesture of the index finger will correspond to a manifestation from the inside out of this closed system.

This meaning of Arcanum X is even more clearly characterised by the phallic form of ׳ (Iod). The Phallus, even more than the index finger, symbolises the mentioned manifestation of the outwardly closed Microcosm system.

The card of the Arcanum is called Sphinx or Rota Fortunae (Wheel of Fortune). In its upper part it displays the image of the Sphinx, armed with a sword and resting on a motionlessly fortified platform. A little lower we see the Solomon Hexagram (the sign of the Macrocosm), rotating with the wheel that outlines it with its rim. The cage, on which the wheel axis rests, in its lower part (under the wheel) passes into a double caduceus. The wheel itself on the right side (mirror-like) with its rotation carries up (to the Sphinx) the Hermanubis - a cinecéfalo[22] - cinema with a triple caduceus in its right hand. On the left, the same wheel carries down the crocodile to the body of Typhon, with a human head and a two-pronged (sometimes trident) in the left hand, pointing down.

What, broadly speaking, does this representation mean?

Some kind of closed system, gifted with processes of internal transformations. This system is crowned with the invariable, always uniformly valid, uniformly productive Sphinx method - to dare, to will, to know, to be silent - which means to reach the creative activity and the perfection of the astrosome.

The mill of life, dominated by the square of these four guidelines, rotates uninterruptedly, taking some up and causing others to fall. Those who rise (like Hermanubis), bearers of the sign of the Great Solvent "Azoth" (the Caduceus), still keep the dog head, symbol of its anterior and inferior state, traces of uncontrolled impulsivity and evil instincts.

Those that fall from the heights, like Typhon, are still slaves of the non-neutralised binaries, nevertheless keep traces of former greatness, discovering in an unexpected way a human head - remnants of nobility, justice, fidelity in the field of dark combinations that have little application to these principles, coexisting with the degradation (the crocodile body), caused by the degradation of the human principle.

Here is a straightforward picture of the tenth major Arcanum of Tarot.

---

[22] A dog-headed creature

The "Mill of Transformations" grinds and leads, all of us, relentlessly and yet in this general process there is a clear and methodical higher motivation. It is sanctified by something Higher.

It does not matter that only the astral region is outlined in the picture: our imagination will supplement it with spectacles of mental currents and the elementary (physical) Wheel of Fortune.

With the Archetype and his high influences we are connected by what is commonly called the "Testament." May the first headline of our Arcanum therefore be Testamentum. Mental principles flow through the area of this Testament.

In the midst of Mankind itself, so to speak, in the sphere of its manifestations, we have the "Great Wheel of Tarot" leading to what the human race calls - Qabbalah - Kabbalah; that which serves as a verification tool for the construction of astral forms by us. This word "Kabbalah" will be the second title of the Arcanum.

In terms of Nature, we are dealing with the merciless Wheel of Fortune, otherwise called the "World Mill". This wheel grinds everything, assimilates everything, adjusts everything, lifting one, lowering the other and, like any Rota, leaving nothing motionless, stationary, except for its axis, the name of which is: the possibility of the existence of an illusion called "Matter". And so let there be a third heading - Fortuna.

This is what nature gives us in the tenth Arcanum.

In everyday courses of Occultism, we often see this Arcanum presented with other headings: Regnum Dei, Ordo, Fortuna. These names correspond roughly to the same ideas in a less defined form. The conception "Regnum Dei", that is, "Kingdom of God", whether it is the plane of its manifestation, the period of maximum bliss, harmony and functional adaptation. The kingdom of God for a planet will be the time of its greatest prosperity in the aforementioned sense.

The Kingdom of God for a human being will be the time of greater harmony for the totality of their receptivity and activity. Of course, it must be remembered that the "Kingdom of God" for an entire organism may not coincide with the same epoch of the "Kingdom" to one or other of their particular organs. The moment of this "Kingdom" for our whole solar system, for example, may not coincide with the analogous "Kingdom" moment for the planet Mars.

I am inclined to consider faith in the Kingdom of God as a reflection of the Testamentum in the mirror of Hope.

Ordo means order. But Kabbalah is the highest synthesis of the orders of all astral manifestations that are accessible to us. As you can see, our headlines are no different from the generally accepted ones. Let us turn to the arithmetic analysis of the Arcanum.

10 = 9 + 1: A single manifestation is not by itself, but by nine clichés, so to speak, by nine reflections or refractions characterising it as its totality. Speaking scholastically: we perceive an object through nine attributions. 10 = 9 + 1: These nine attributions are realised in one synthetic tenth manifestation, playing the role of a seed or grain of a particular object. Together, these two theses can be expressed by the following formulation: the essence of the subject is hidden behind the veil of its properties, and the properties are not felt on their own, but on something concrete. We will develop this thesis in the scheme conveyed to us by a certain Tradition.

Sephirotic System

The essence of each object, according to the Law of Triplicity, manifests itself first and foremost by the ternary type of the Great Arcanum.
The first manifestation has, like the object itself, that we imagine integrated, the character neutral, androgynous. This finding is sufficient to be able to determine the type of triangle formed by the three initial manifestations. In it, the second manifestation has an active character; the third, passive, according to the scheme: הי (Point-Iod-He).
This superior ternary is twice reflected in the form of ternary of the type of descending triangle.
The whole system is synthesised in a concrete way in the tenth manifestation of the mentioned essence of the object. According to the law of synthesis, this manifestation will naturally have the androgyne.
In general, we will have the scheme shown in figure 35. The ten manifestations marked on it called the Sephiroth of the object.
"Sephiroth" is the plural of "Sephira". The meaning of the word Sephira corresponds to "number", the "radiation" and "visible".
From this it follows that in each object we can discover ten manifestations or, in other words, that each object has ten visible aspects. To illustrate this, let us take the example of a flashlight which, having ten differently coloured glass sides, would present ten different aspects of the same light. The ten Sephira of the object constitute a kind of family.

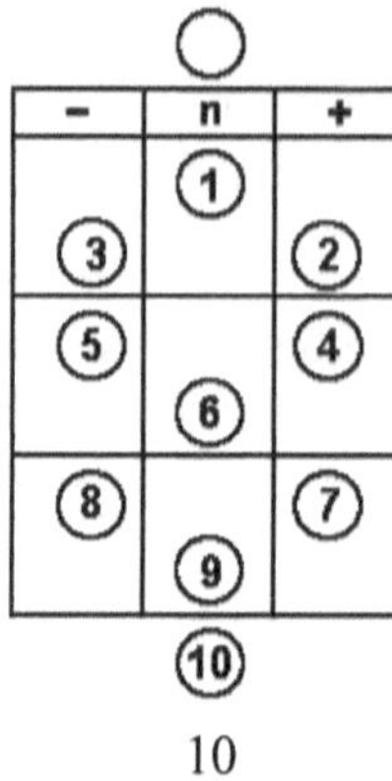

Figure 35

Ten Sephiroth objects make up a family, as it were. In this family, Jewish Kabbalah distinguishes between: I) Supreme Androgyne (1), or Macroprosopus (Greek term; translated Heb. Word "long-faced"); II) Father (2); III) Mother (3); IV) their Child, represented by a combination of six Sephira (4, 5, 6, 7, 8, 9), possessing androgyne features and bearing the name Microprosop ("small-faced"). The centre of the functional activity of Microprosopus will be the sixth Sephira, and the ninth is the organ of its activity. V) Spouse or Bride of Microprosopus, i.e. tenth Sephira.

But after all, any closed family in the chain of causality will be preceded by some other family, etc., up to the Primary Source.

Jewish Kabbalists ascended only to the family of the Primordial Sephirotic System of the Universe, considering this System as a manifestation of some Incomprehensible Essence, which we call Ain-Soph, or Ain-Soph (literally – without end). They did not allow the analysis of Ain-Soph itself.

The Rosicrucians allowed themselves to name not only the first Sephira of the Universe, but also the Members of the Family placed between Ain-Soph and these Sephira. So, in the Rosicrucian scheme, the Incomprehensible, Infinitely Homogeneous, Infinitely Harmonious, Almighty Beginning expresses itself actively, so to speak - it wants to manifest itself by some Iod, namely, what we will call Transcendental Love. This manifestation will be the Father of the First Family of the Rosicrucian Scheme.

This Father, by his own aspiration (bearing the character of radiance), will determine the existence of some Passivity, strictly proportionate to his activity. This passivity will be the first ה of the First Family, what we will call the Transcendental Life.

This element, in contrast to the Radiant Iod, should have a shadow character. This is something darkened, ready to receive the Radiant Influx of the Unknowable. Hence its Latin name - Restrictio - Shadow Restriction in the environment of Infinite Light.

So, in our tradition, Transcendental Love (First Father) impregnates Transcendental Life (First Mother).

These Rosicrucian Mystic Entities give birth to the Logos, the Transcendental Word, the Great Architect of the Universe, "without Whom there is nothing."

The Logos emanates the second ה of the First Family, manifested by the ten Sephira of the Second (Fig. 35) through the first of them, i.e. Macroprosopus of the universe, called the Sephira of the Crown (Kether). Next are the remaining nine Sephira of the Second Family in the so-called scheme. Four Worlds. (figure 36)

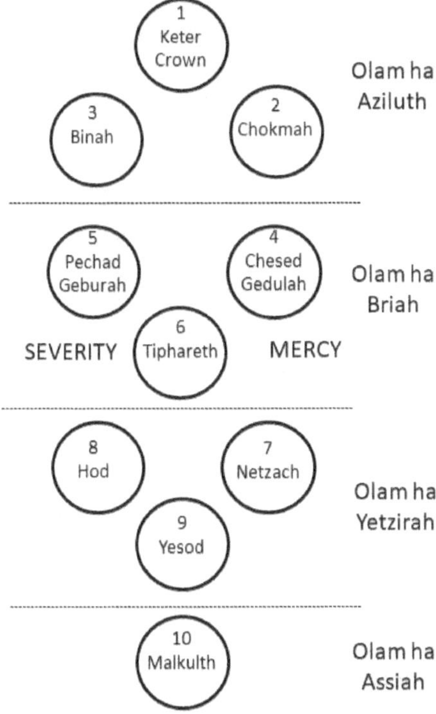

Figure 36

The World of Emanations - Olam ha Aziluth - contains, as we see in this figure, the Androgynous Crown Sephira, Keter (Macroprosopa), manifesting itself, as befits a balanced Mentality, on the one hand - the totality of what aspires to knowledge (Sephira of Wisdom - Chokmah), on the other hand - the totality of That which be known, which is the object of knowledge (Sephira of Mind - Binah, naturally limiting the previous one).

In the World of Creativity - Olam ha Briah, - we meet with the active Sephira of Mercy (Chesed, 4), which is a reflection of the thirst for knowledge, i.e. the expansiveness of the Second Sephira (Wisdom), and with the passive Sephira of Severity (Pechad or Geburah), limiting Mercy due to the finiteness of the field of objects of knowledge, the Sephira of Reason, Binah.

These Sephira are neutralised by the magnificence of the radiance of the Sephira Tiphereth - World Harmony, Universal Beauty.

And what could be more radiant in ethics than the exact balancing of Charity with Severity, Goodness with respect for Law? Is not the excess of mercy burning with the intolerable fire of the sinner, forcing him to pray for justice? Cannot an excess of severity deprive of hope for the salvation of a lost member of the Family of Souls?

Mercy, commensurate with rigour, solves any ethical problem.

Let us now turn to the World of Formation: Olam ha Yezirah.

In it we see the Victory of Good over evil, Spiritual over material, Light over dark, Active over inert - the active seventh Sephira Netzach, in which the Initiate resides, faultlessly choosing the right path in the sixth Arcanum.

But an active desire to choose the right paths does not exclude the need for calm movement along the path already chosen, without feverish thirst, to rest in the conquered position in order to see the fruits of what has been well sown

Yes, you need to limit this powerful Sephira to the passive Sephira of Glory or Peace (Hod).

This mysterious Sephira gives us a seemingly paradoxical combination of lack of movement with the presence of life. After all, to move means to meet new crossroads, and to live means to move, at least within the limits of our understanding of the material plane. The Sephira Hod puts us as if the thesis of life without movement. This is the Great Mystery, comprehended only in an ecstatic state.

Victory and Glory are neutralised by the androgynous, completed Form, the Foundation (Yesod) of any specificity (Fundamentum omnium rerum).

Indeed, in order for a form to exist, it is necessary to single it out, choose it (Victory is the choice of a path) so as to stop at it (Peace, Glory).

Here is the process of creating the ninth Sephira Yesod projecting into the World of Realities (Olam ha Assiah) by the Sephira of the Kingdom (Malchuth or Malkuthh), i.e. the embryonic state of the concrete world we inhabit.

So we have the following distribution of the Members of the Second Mystical Family: Keter - Macroprosopus - Crown; Chokmah – Father – Wisdom; Binah - Mother – Reason; Microprosopus is the Sephira of Mercy, Severity, Beauty, Victory, Glory and Form. (Chesed, Geburah, Tiphareth, Netzach, Hod, Yesod; The wife of Microprosopus is the kingdom, Malkulth.

We draw attention to the system of projections of the Sephira on the three vertical pillars, which can help our understanding.

On the middle, neutral column (n) the Blow of the Logos - the Great Crown - is projected from the Name of the Archetype by the principle of Beauty. Beauty is reflected by Form, and Form by Concreteness.

In the right, male column (+) Wisdom teaches Mercy and prepares Victory. In the left, female column (-) the Mind of things teaches Justice and gives Peace.

Each of the second family Sephira can be considered in itself as a closed system and therefore has its own sephirotic manifestations; these manifestations, again, lend themselves to analysis according to a sephirotic scheme, etc., and therefore we can say that these schemes will serve us as a general template for analysing elements that are included in our course of Esotericism.

Before giving examples of such studies, I allow myself to acquaint you with what Kabbalists call the "channels of the sephirotic system", i.e. possible ways to go from sephira to sephira. There are 22 channels (according to the number of characters in the Hebrew alphabet), and they are distributed according to one of the following two schemes. (Figures 37 and 38):

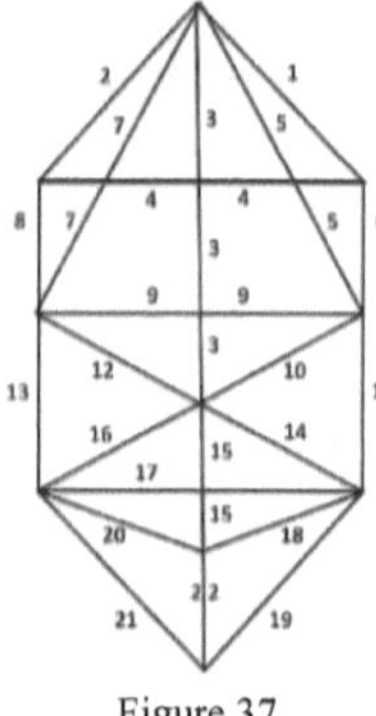

Figure 37

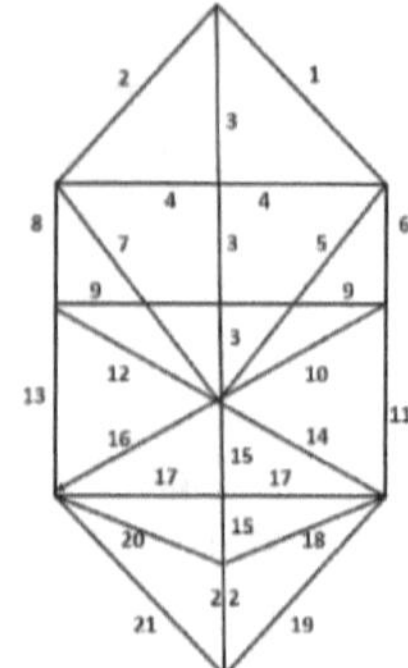

Figure 38

These channels will allow us to conveniently map out the so-called "diabetic processes"[23]., i.e. the operation of a complex transition from one Sephira to another through some intermediate sephira. Diabatic processes can be upward or downward. We give examples of processes of both kinds[24].

First example: Normal downward diabetic process, or the process of creating the world:

The idea of knowledge (Crown) naturally separates into the Sephira of the thirst for knowledge (Wisdom) and the Sephira of the domain of objects of knowledge (by the way - which is closed, limited for this universe). This is the so-called Mind of things. In this phase, the distance traveled is determined by channels 1, 4.

Returning through channel 4 to the Sephira of Wisdom, we, through channel 6, reflect it in the form of Mercy and are immediately forced to balance it with the Sephira of Justice, using channel 9 for this.

Then we can give rise (channel 12) to the Harmony (Beauty) of formal manifestations; a taste for absolute beauty will easily lead us (on channel 14) to permanent Victories by a good choice of forms; there will be a desire (with the help of channel 17) to taste the Glory - the fruit of Victory, i.e. simply stop, calm down on certain Forms, which, as it were, will be delivered to us by further movement forward (on channel 20). and will lead us to Sephira Yesod. We complete the process, involving the forms, that is, making them concrete, which will correspond the descent (by way 22) to Sephira Malkuthh.

Second Example: A normal, ascending diabetic process.

---

[23] A diabatic process is one in which heat (energy) transfer occurs, that is, it is the opposite of an adiabatic process.

[24] Other schemes have also been proposed, e.g. by Patrick Mulcahy in Sefer Yetzirah Magic

Studying the concrete world (the Kingdom), man attains the Sephira of Forms (Yesod), that is, he no longer need manipulate the dense, as he begins to manipulate, in the imagination, the intrinsic forms. Thus, he travels the path 22.

However, he must revive these forms, keeping them in an exalted environment, illuminating them by the light of Glory. He passes, thus (by way 20), to the Sephira Hod. The illumination of these Forms will allow you to distinguish in them the polarities of good and evil, light and dark, subtle and dense, and so on. By doing so, it will follow path 17 and will prepare the Victory of Sephira Netzach.

This Victory, that is, the correct evaluation of the Forms, their polarities and their relationship will lead you (along path 14) to the aspiration to create Harmony (Sephira Tiphareth) between said polarities, that is, to neutralise the binaries. A clear understanding of the latter, will direct the man (through path 12) to the Sephira of Severity (or Justice). The primacy given to the positive poles, which characterises a Victor, will allow one to balance Justice with Mercy (way 9). However, one will have to take into account both the elements: Justice and Mercy. This will force you to go back (on Route 9) to Justice and understand it fully, as being a severe respect for the Law.

Meditating on the Law, one shall discover that the edification of the schemes of the Universe, ordered strictly according to the Law, determines the finiteness of the materialised spheres. This will transport you (on path 8) to Sephira Reason (Binah). Meditation on what is possible to be known will make you compare the subjective world with the objective world, leading it, without realising (on the path 4), the Sephira Chokmah: search for knowledge. Hence, led by his aspiration to Wisdom in general, he will enter with ease on path 1, rising to Sephira Keter, the Crown of Mental Power. Besides the Crown there may be only attempts to capture a ray of Eternal Light from the First Family.

Third Example. Climbing along the central paths.

A scientist, studying in the dense plane, gradually rises (through path 2) to the study of Shapes. The full knowledge of these, even in the absence of the element of inspiration, can lead you to understand the principle of Beauty (Sephira Tiphareth). This difficult but possible passage becoming the path of astral power. Further on, comes the ascent to the Crown of the World of Ideas - Keter - by the path 3, that could be called the bed by which flows the fountain of the breeding astral activity. In this way, man, constantly dealing with the Laws, can sometimes grasp the Principles.

We think that these examples are enough so that each one can try to outline other means of passages by the ways. This occupation is one of the most useful meditations. The rabbis of the Middle Ages consecrated themselves to her with great assiduity.

Let us now turn to examples of the division of closed systems into their sephirotic attributes.

Example of the Theurgy field: Mental Plane.

We call theurgic action a very serious, planned and rational attempt to act on the plane of the Archetype on the mental flows of the Universe, with the purpose of producing or accelerating certain astral formations or physical manifestations. In other words, the "mens" of the theurgist he comes in contact with the Archetype, to carry through him something astral or concrete.

The most elemental type of a theurgic operation is what we call prayer. The prayers are more or less complicated, according to the worldview of the one who prays and the purpose of prayer. The prayer that does not contain a particular request, because it seeks only a contact with the Archetype in order to be able to receive Superior Influences for all the planes of the vital manifestations, reflects the worldview of the person praying. We could say that, in this case, it presents a theurgical photography of the operative Microcosm.

It follows that the prayer of the Kabbalist will be a closed system, decomposable according to the Sephirotic scheme of the Universe. Such is the Lord's Prayer:

Pater noster qui es in coelis

The invocation in the Lord's Prayer will likewise correspond to that which is higher than all the Sephira of the Second Family, i.e. simply to the Persons of the First Family. The very term in coelis (in heaven) indicates the presence of the One who is addressed, above the so-called Horizon Aeternitatis (Horizon of Eternity).

At the same time, we see in this invocation the observance of the basic thesis of Theurgy, which states that all prayer is to Ain-Soph, and not to any Sephira or organ of a Sephira. Prayer ascends through all the Sephira of the Universe; sometimes it can be supported by an appeal to the Intercessors, but this appeal only plays the role of merging a small stream of prayer of a private monad with a huge river of Theurgic operations, and yet the water of this small brook rushes into the Immense Ocean of Ain-Soph.

Sanctificetur Nomen Tuum (Hallowed be Thy Name): The first petition, which means: hallowed be Thy Crown (Keter), that is, the Great Arcanum of Thy Emanational Manifestation in the metaphysical plane. "Hallowed be it" means that the mystics, in their search, do not lose sight of the apex of the Evolutionary Triangle.

Adveniat Regnum Tuum (Thy Kingdom come): The second petition is about the generation of the Kingdom of Harmony of Forms (Sephira Tiphereth) in the soul of the worshiper and in the astrosome of the entire outer Universe.

Fiat Voluntas Tua sicut in coelo (Thy will be done): The third petition means: "I bow to the Great Law יהוה of the metaphysical world, my mental aspiring to participate in the application of this Law (the sphere of Sephira Binah which contains in itself Reason of things, governed by the Law mentioned).

... et in terra (as on Earth): The fourth petition means in translation: "*and the astral generation of the regular ethical manifestations of the Sephira of Justice (Geburah).*"

Panem nostrum quotidianum da nobis hodie (Give us today our daily bread): What is "daily bread" of the fifth petition? The "bread" is the possibility of knowing life through the form, of the experiences "of each day". "Today", that is, since the last choice of the path (from Arcanum VI) and up to the next choice. The request, as we can see, refers to life in the Sephira Hod, the period of rest that follows the temptations and the Victory.

Et dimitte nobis debita nostra (and pardon our debts): The sixth petition means: apply to our personalities the Expansive Wisdom Principle (Sephira Chokmah) ...

... sicut et nos dimittimus debitoribus nostris (as we forgive our debtors): The seventh petition is reflected in our astrosomes by the Laws of Mercy to the neighbour." (Sephira Chesed).

Et ne nos inducas in tentationem (and lead us not into temptation) The eighth petition means asks that we are saved from the unbearably frequent encounters with the 6th arcana, so dangerous for the result of the incarnation of the tempted. (Sephira Netzach).

... sed libera nos a malo (but deliver us from evil): In the ninth petition we add, "*and even save us, if possible, from frequent contact and closer proximity to cliché systems that could attract us to the negative path of vice (evil) in the mentioned applications of the 6th arcana*". (Sephira of Forms and clichés, that is, Yesod). The "evil" in this petition is simply an artificial attempt to personify the desire to endlessly seek the display of the Absolute. The esoteric trait is simply "the father of lies" or "an occasion to complicate and improve the false to infinity." We shall learn later that such an "improvement" of the lie cannot be taken to the

infinite, that it is possible to incur the lie, the evil, the depravity, only until certain limits; that the process of progressive immersion in lying must lead to a return to Truth.

However, the illusory character of the "devil" does not prevent him from owning servants. This fact is illustrated by the mythologies of all races, in which we find several personifications of the opposite pole of Truth and Absolute Good.

In this analysis we see that the Lord's Prayer is a passage through the nine Sephira; scheme (figure 38) is based on the first system (figure 36) of the sephirotic paths.

The Orthodox Church concludes the Prayer for a formula of glorification, most likely given, by the Apostle John, and which symbolises the manifestation of the Crown (Keter) in the tenth Sephira (Malkuth), thus completing a magical achievement of the Great Metaphysical Arcanum. The text of this formula, translated from Greek into Portuguese, says:

"For Thine are the Kingdom, the Power, and the Glory for Aeons. Amen".

The term "Aeons" is found in the teachings of the Gnostics. It refers to certain cycles, separated and personified, of a basic and dynamic series, constituting the schema of the creation of everything that exists. It is a series of individualised, closed systems, each pair having positive and negative polarisation, and multiplying according to the י ה ו ה law or, to be more exact, י ה י ה (Iod-He-Iod-He). The totality of all the Aeons, in the sense explained above, is equivalent to all of which populate the Universe in all its planes

These considerations lead us to the following interpretation of the formula of glorification:

"For You are the Primordial Source of the manifestations of the Great Arcanum in all the Creative Cycles of the three planes of the universe".

In the scheme presented by us from the Great Arcanum of Magic, the term "Kingdom" corresponds to the Wheel Elementary (4), the term "Power" - to the Astral Wheel (2), and the term "Glory" to the Metaphysical Triangle. A Kabbalist, therefore, will be inclined to read the formula as follows: "Quoniam Tibi sunt Malkuth, et Tiphareth, et Keter, pereone. Amen

In practice, another way of reading it is accepted, in which the "Kingdom" is Malkuth; the "Power" - Geburah and the "Glory" - Chesed.

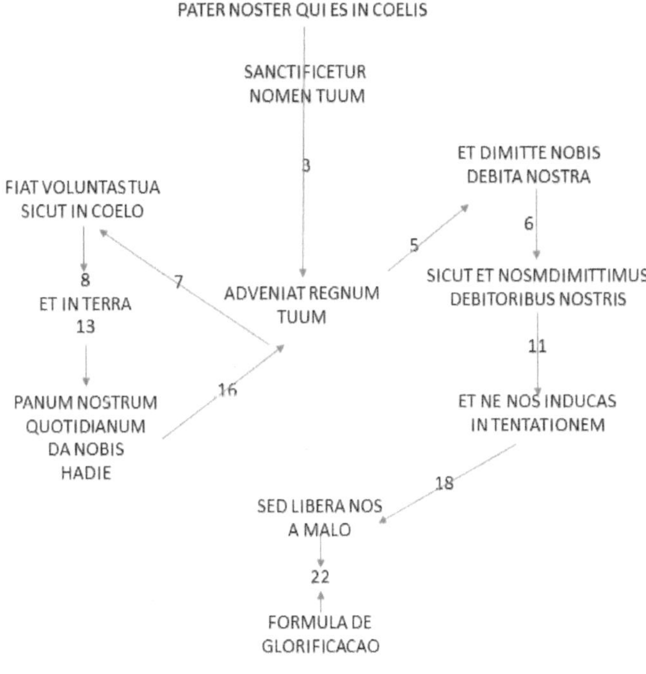

Figure 39

In the general sephirotic scheme, these three Sephira form a descending type triangle. If we take into account the presence of the term "Tibi" (Teu), whose region is above all Sephira, then "Tibi", together with the Sephira Geburah and Chesed, will form a new triangle, of the ascending type. We will have the configuration shown in figure 40.

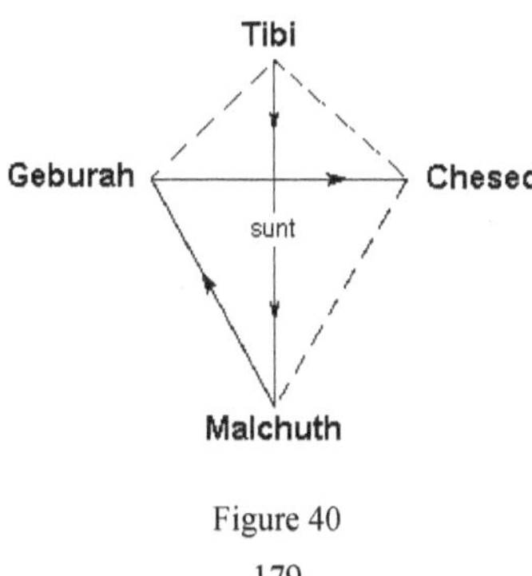

Figure 40

179

The four terms of this figure form a cross, whose projection onto a person who prays is made in the following way: The vertex (Tibi) is projected on the forehead; Malkuth - on the solar plexus; the third tip of the cross (Geburah) on the shoulder, on the left; and the fourth tip (Chesed) on the shoulder, on the right. We can also delineate the sign of the cross in ourselves, formula of glorification. Arriving at the words "per aeonas. Amen" it is customary to join hands in a gesture expressing concentration.

Example of the Magic field; Astral plane.

We had a chance to speak in the fifth Arcanum about auto-suggestion according to the German method, and moreover, we mentioned the abbreviation of our proposed scheme, which played the role of a sketch of the process, and not its complete picture.

Now, as an example of the sephirotic analysis of closed systems, we will apply it to the process of suggestion, whether directed to the operator's own astrosome, to the astrosomes of his or her particular organs and their cells, or the astrosomes of other people.

The Pentagrammatic Freedom of Will of the operator will play the role of the First Family in relation to the system of Sephira and of suggestion that will arise.

The very idea of suggestion will correspond to Keter's schema. This idea, containing in itself the conception of the manifestation that we want to obtain, will be the Chokmah of the process, and the field to which the suggestion is directed, that is, to whom or to which the suggestion is made - the Binah of the operation. These three Sephira, together, will constitute the mental part of the volitional process that is operating. The content of the suggestion will act upon the emotional aspect of the astral plane of suggestion, creating an emotion which, due to the very power of suggestion, will be transmitted to the patient. This will correspond to Chesed.

However, an emotion, in general, as a consequence of a suggestion, unfolds differently in different patients, and may differ not only in emotional sub-tones but also in their composition. What will make one angry will only surprise another and, in a third, it will provoke an affable meditative disposition. This subjective emotional reaction, along with the laws that govern it, will be the Geburah of the analysed process.

The two Sephira - Chesed and Geburah - must be naturally neutralised by their Tiphareth, that is, by the general image of the emotional totality of the process, perceptible by the operator's "mens" as unfolding in the present rather than in the future (let us remember what was said in Arcanum V).

Let us now turn aside from the suggestion concerning form. The Netzach of the operation will be all that constitutes an impediment in the transmission of the suggestion, and which should be overcome, either in the nature of the patient, or in their environment.

The Sephira Hod will correspond to the degree of Victory obtained in the preceding Sephira or, in other words, it will correspond to what we will be content with in the realisation of our suggestion. An example will explain better: suggesting to a patient that he can move the foot, hitherto immobilised, we must imagine with what demonstration of mobility we will be content, with which result we will finish the session or the healing cycle.

According to the Law of Ternary we must neutralise the last two manifestations - that of the Sephira Netzach and that of Sephira Hod - for a geometric image, clear and accurate, of the suggested. This will correspond to Sephira Yesod. This image is repeated again, it must refer to the present, the actual, and not to the future.

We still lack the presence of concrete Malkuth. We know, from what was said earlier, that this last part of the process is constituted by elements of vocal manifestation, loud voice or whispering, gestures, or movements (eg, swapping) made by the operator. The synthesis of these manifestations, accessible to the sense organs, will be the tenth Sephira - the Malkuth of our suggestion process.

Example of conducting character

The lower astral plane is adjacent to the physical and, with respect to manifestations, inseparable from it.

Imagine an incarnated pentagram, acting through the emanation and receptivity of its magnetic, odic centres. These centres are inseparably connected to certain physical centres of the human body.

The middle point, between the eyebrows, corresponds to the magnetic Keter. The process of meditation, in its physical part, is connected to the passive aspect. When we actively use the central gaze, we operate through two fixation axes: that of our Chokmah (right eye) and that of our Binah (left eye), joined by Keter's mental activity.

If we want, we can, with our central look, attack only our opponent's Chokmah, paralysing the activity of his Keter; or just Binah, paralysing his receptivity. We can also, defend us against the central look of others with a look in the eyes of the adversary, subjugating Binah strangers with our Chokmah and voluntarily submitting our Binah to the Chokmah, thus leaving the victory to the more powerful of the two Keter, his or ours, who act through their polarised organs (Chokmah and Binah). If we wish, in the sphere of the three magical centres, to receive a suggestion from others, lower our eyes and concentrate passively, subjecting our Keter to the operator's performance.

The above refers to the male polarisation of fluids, and in these cases the magnetism of the right hand corresponds to Sephira Chesed; the magnetism of the left hand - the Geburah. The reservoir solar plexus will be the Tiphareth. From this reservoir of positive and negative fluids. We can use it whenever we want. Sephira Netzach will respond to the action of wear of the right (negative) radiations in order to otherwise use the energies so spared. The reverse operation on the left (positive) foot will be the Sephira Hod. The role played by the reservoir of the odic energy of the sexual organs will correspond to Sephira Yesod. As for Sephira Malkuth, his correspondence will be the magnetic receptivity of the neck and back toward which the operator's central eye is odic emanations from his hands.

It is also necessary to mention the navel which, in our scheme, corresponds to the central region of the channel that links Yesod to Tiphareth. The navel is not a centre emanating, but it is extraordinarily vampiric, both in relation to the positive emanations, and to the negatives of an odic emanator that with it (eg, a finger). This characteristic of the navel is used to therapeutic purposes.

A point emanating from the healer is brought into contact with the region of the patient's navel, and another point of the healer, but of opposite polarisation, is also brought into contact with another sephirotic centre of the patient, thus establishing a current. The choice of the second point, as the direction of the chain, depends on the evil being combated. This choice is made according to the cabalistic indications. Application gives sephirotic analysis a complicated manifestation of general ethical character.

We have already mentioned that sephirotic analysis is applicable to organs of closed systems, if only these organs could be considered as closed systems from one or another point of view.

Let's say more: every sphere, every region can decompose sephirotically insofar as it is considered by us as a closed system, even if we did not have time or failed to present this sphere in the complex that we call the Essence.

Let us give an example of the sephirotic decomposition of what is called the domain of Virtue in ordinary language. We often call such areas distractions, abstract concepts, etc. This is how the great hermeticist Heinrich Kunrath interprets this area in sephirotic decay.

According to him, Keter of the manifestation "Virtue" would be the Purity which naturally possesses a synthetic character. The positive pole - Chokmah - of this Keter will be Goodness. Goodness will be limited by the negative pole of Keter (Binah) and will be Prudence.

In the next world of the Sephira Tree - the world Olam has Briah - Goodness will be reflected as the element Mercy (Chesed), and Prudence - as the element of Courage (Geburah). The binary of these last elements will give birth to the average term - Tiphareth of the system, which will be Patience. Thus, we will have all the Olam ha Briah system, ie Chesed, Geburah and Tiphareth.

For kindness to be reflected as Mercy in Kunrath's scheme, is not surprising. For Purity to manifest as Goodness in its positive pole and in its negative pole as Prudence is also not difficult to understand.

Goodness can be seen as a desire to protect another being from the danger of falling, and Prudence - as an idea of protecting himself.

If Prudence has the source of Purity, then self-protection can go on until it manifests as courage in self-defense. The composition of Patience is easy to understand.

Let's move on to the next world - Olam ha Yezirah - from the system. The Sephira Hod will be constituted by the reflection of Courage in the astral planes, that is, plans of the Shapes. According to Kunrath, it will manifest as Humility (Humilitas). Sephira Netzach, according to him, will manifest itself as Justice (naturally in the sense of assigning to each one that fits him). The role of the neutralizing element Yesod will be played by Temperance, which well deserves to be called the daughter of the Justice - Humility couple. The concrete Malkuth of this scheme, Kunrath sees it as the Fear of God.

We will end our series of examples with the statement that in this course, as far as our capacities and possibilities, we will seek to analyse sephirotically the subjects covered by our studies. We will do so much because of the real advantages of this system, our desire to give this teaching a kabbalistic character.

We will leave for the moment the deconstruction $10 = 1 + 9$, which has already given us such abundant materials, to direct our attention to other arithmetic interpretations of the Great Arcanum X.

$10 = 2 + 8$: Gnosis (2), that is, our study of the Absolute, can and must influence the formal side and legal (8) of our Kabbalah. This will be clearly seen when we study the general scheme of the Tarot.

$10 = 8 + 2$: The established environment (or legality) (8), be it general, or particular, influences, not only on the forms of the study, but also on its essence. In other words, schools or teachings belonging to a particular environment often general, the conceptions formed in the most limited sphere of their own environment. In case of Kabbalistic studies, this deconstruction can be interpreted as the use of a particular system of cabalistic calculations, within the general initiatory system we are studying. For example, let us cite the omnipotence or kabbalistic applications to the alphabets whose number of letters differs from Hebrew.

10 = 3 + 7. This is the motto of the Theosophical Schools that seek to develop, first, in its adherents, the mental intuition in relation to the primordial causes (3) so that it automatically enables them to orient themselves further within the field of secondary causes (7).

10 = 7 + 3: Motto of the Magic Schools which recommend, first, to know the sphere of secondary causes (7), as a basis for the subsequent passage to the primary causes (3).

10 = 4 + 6: This arithmetic formula expresses the following thesis: the four Sephira of the central column have primacy over the six polarised Sephira. In fact, to characterise briefly the process of the Universe, it is enough to enumerate the four Sephira of the middle: The Crown, the Harmony, the Form, and the germ of the Concrete World. The remaining six Sephira do not allow us to understand the interrelationship of the elements of the Universe, as long as we do not take into account, for each par, the middle Sephira.

10 = 6 + 4: This means that, in Kabbalah, the Hexagram of Solomon (6) is superior to the Rota (4) or, in other words, that the essence of the subject is not in the realisation of the symbols, but rather in their astral interdependence. No matter if someone owns the 22 blades of the Tarot, another person - the 22 letters of the Hebrew alphabet, and yet another - the 22 hieroglyphics; the important thing is that, by determined and similar methods, either one or the other person, can relate these signs to one another, with the full understanding of their essence.

10 = 5 + 5: This means: 5 opposite to 5, and expresses a certain connection, a certain relationship between two parts of a totality. The Ten Sephira of the Second Family, as we know, group together in five Mystical Persons: Macroprosopo, Father, Mother, Microprosopus and his Spouse.

These, in turn, reflect their influences or, we might say, have their plenipotentiaries, in all the closed systems of the Universe, and for this reason, also in each individuality of the present humanity, that is, fallen humanity, that is, its initial purity.

When we come to the story of this fall, we will see that in the primordial state we were looking for a point of suspension in the radiant heights, and not, as it happens now, a point of support in the more dense, in matter, this cluster of illusions. So we should not be surprised by the fact that in the traditional kabbalistic diagram, which shows how Superior mystics are reflected in the composition of the individual man, these reflections are in an inverted hierarchical order.

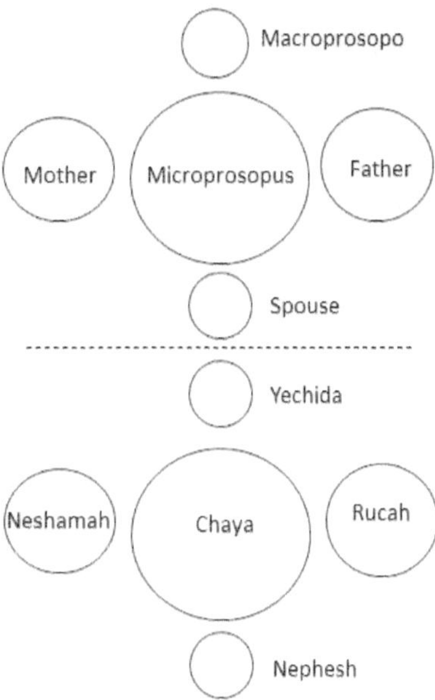

Figure 41

When we get to the story of the fall of such, you will clearly see that if we now take the fulcrum in matter, in this final storehouse of confused illusions, then earlier, in the primeval state, we did not chase the fulcrum below, but behind the gain point in the Radiant Top. And therefore, may it not surprise you that in the proposed traditional Kabbalistic table — the process of reflection of the Highest Mystical Persons as part of the current individual person — the reflections of the Principles are arranged in the reverse hierarchical order.

In the composition of man (figure 41), Macroprosop is reflected in the Nephesh element - the border region between the nervous system (physical plane) and the lower astral perception (astral plane).

The Father is reflected by the element Ruach - the soul in the proper sense, i.e. a complex of passions, desires, the ability to generate forms and the ability to perceive and classify those.

The Mother is reflected by the element of Neshamah - what we colloquially call reason, intelligence, ideological humanism, etc.

The Microprosopus is reflected by the element of Chayah[25] - that part of a person which enables him know spiritual bliss.

---

[25] Derived from the Hebrew word 'Chavah', meaning 'Life' or 'Breath'

The spouse is reflected in the element of Yechidah - the one in the person who unites him with the Divine.

We see that the list of elements of the composition of man did not include purely material elements: his body, the life force of blood, etc. Only that which determines the nature of the circulation of the nerve fluid has entered. This element is called Nephesh, and this "animal soul" is placed below all elements.

So, Kabbalah is imbued with the idea that a person, even a fallen one, is nevertheless more closely connected with Heaven by the Yechidah element than with the Earth by the Nephesh element. For brevity and convenience, the characteristics of these elements I will combine them into a table containing three explanatory columns.

Element	Polar Opposite	Sphere of Knowledge	Human Manifestations
Nephesh	Passive in relation to external world	Facts, observations, what is registered	Species
Ruach	Androgynous in relation to external world	Laws and their formulation	Personality
Neshamah	Active in relation to external world	The principles and their bases	Mindset
Chaiah	Androgynous coalition of Neshamah with Yehidah	Upper influx, Intuition of Truth	Emanation of Divine Principles
Yechidah	Passive in relation to the Archetype	Fusion with Absolute Truth	Archetypal Manifestation

Notes on the Table

Nephesh is passive in relation to the external world; it's just a kind of auto-registration of the facts, transmitting them to the soul; he does it in the same routine way, same for all units of the same species.

Ruach evaluates facts recorded by Nephesh according to the personal psychological characteristics of the perceiver. A person, of course, also influences the formulation of laws derived from facts.

Laws are combined into fundamental judgments that already belong to the human Neshamah, which determines uniformly universal human logic up to (including) what we call the transcendental realm. In the transcendental area, the influence of the higher Influx of the Spirit of Chajah, which can lead a person to the consciousness of the Yechidah element in himself, is already taking place.

In one species, the Nephesh is similar to all its individuals. In those to whom we call "like people" the Ruach is similar. Logical argumentation becomes possible. only thanks to the presence of the Neshamah common to all mankind. Mutual understanding and fraternal solidarity of the blessed is due to the resemblance in them of the Chaiah element. The Final re-integration is possible thanks to Yechidah.

In Kabbalah, the Neshamah (in its limited sense) Chaiah and Yechidah - the three together - are often called simply "Neshamah," in the broad sense of this term. This one Neshamah broad corresponds in the terminology adopted by us, the "Mens" or the mental. The Ruach corresponds to what we call "astrosome" and Nephesh - the "ghost." Having completed the arithmetic deconstructions of the Arcanum, let us return to its symbolic image: the card.

Its central part is occupied by a wheel. This wheel synthesises several representations, the most typical of which, for the profane, is the representation of what we call "the mill of the world." This one on the physical plane, the elements of the various lives so that, from the same, other lives can grow; sometimes it all flushes; sometimes, on the contrary, it elevates a being or a country, in detriment of another It is a ruthless wheel acting strictly according to the Law, however, regretfully illusory; as illusory as any plane in which it operates.

 true Hermetist watches the wheel spin with a smile of disdain. He makes use of it if it is necessary, in order to perform Alchemical work, considering it as the "Elemental Route" of Azoth, Sulphur, Salt and Mercury.

However, in the wheel of the Arcanum X also conceals the Astral Wheel. Your movement can be perceived and observed only by a person whose sensitivity has already been refined both in metaphysical speculation and Ethical Hermeticism. This wheel, by its turn, causes all visible and subtle changes and transformations of the complex giant of life in the world.

As we have already said, so that the teachings of Kabbalah could be preserved and transmitted to generations, they were synthesised and, in the form of a deck, entrusted to both initiates and to the profane. This deck contains 78 cards and is called Tarot or Tarot of the Bohemians. With this we are occupied now.

Among these letters, 56 are part of the so-called "Minor Arcana" and the remaining 22 are "Major Arcana". The Minor Arcana, in its totality, unrolls the ה ו ה י scheme in the world of creation of forms, of Humanity not yet fallen. For this humanity, the realisation of the Great Work was a natural task, a normal and customary labour; a job conscientiously accomplished in all its phases.

The Major Arcana, on the other hand, are reports and show the fallen man's path that only with the sweat of his forehead, purifying his conception of the world and transforming himself, can return to the י ה ו ה Law, which to him it had become obscure. The present humanity has to separate the tares from the wheat and, paying for its errors, arrive at relative truths. Only via the thorny path of these relativities can it laboriously move toward the Absolute, taking the narrow passage between the Scylla of pride and the Charibda of discouragement. Thus, we can see that only by a misunderstanding the term "Minors" was given to the series of 56 Arcana.

The Minor Arcana, metaphysically, are purer than the Greater. In addition, they can easily be divided in the metaphysical sense. The scheme of its construction is very clear. A mathematician would say that these variables are in strict functional interdependence.

In the Major Arcana, on the contrary, everything seems confusing. They give birth to one another, following some obscure laws. They are comparable to notes on a piano that can be tuned in a scale of thirds, fifths or octaves, while taking into account that the tuner uses, to check the quality of their work, imperfect human ear.

In short, we could say that in the Lesser Arcana the cliché י ה ו ה unfolds correctly and that, in the Major, this unfolding presents a confused, deformed, adapted to the world of illusions and limited understanding. Let us first deal with the Minor Arcana. The 56 Tarot cards are divided into four suits, each containing 14 cards:

Wands/Clubs symbolises י.
Cups/Hearts symbolises the first ה.
Swords/Spades symbolise the ו.
Coins/Diamonds symbolises the second ה.

Where and in what Family can we find these elements?
Establishing a relationship between the four suits and the four persons of the First Family (the Transcendental), we will find that:
Wands correspond to the influence of the Higher י - Transcendental Love. This influence is reflected in all the Sephira of the Second Family. We will study the reflection of this, as well as other influences, only in the Sephira Chokmah, where, before the fall, our souls remained, forming the synthesis of humanity - the Universal Man. Wands, therefore, are the accounts of what, in souls, corresponds to this י, that is, to Active Love, descending, which fecundates with its radiation. This Love is the first impulse for any beginning, within any individualised, closed system. In Sephira Chokmah, it will be the initial impulse of souls in any direction.

Cups corresponds to the reflection of the first ה - the Transcendental Life, the Superior Love, upward, attractive - occupying second place in the deck.

Swords, the reflection of ו, the influence of the Logos, brings back the element Love, but Love Androgynous, Love that creates the new life, according to the similarity of its own birth. The ו, thus manifesting himself as Architect of the Universe. It comes from the union of the. Active Love with Passive Love, emanating from the Point on the י, by its polarisation. Moved by your love to what is above and acting in the likeness of the Point on י, decided to love the what is below, thus becoming the Architect of the Universe. Swords, therefore, symbolises the transmission, by the Logos, of the Life of the Mother, by the power of Love, Love is similar to that of the Father.

Coins represent the influence of the second ה on souls. The second ה of the First Family is characterised by the emanation of the ten Sephira of the Second Family. The emanation was the first stage of that which, on the physical plane, we call "realisation." Let us not forget, however, that the "physical" realisation is only a stark analogy of Primordial Emanation. The Transcendental manifested Himself by the Transcendent; the Transcendent made Himself known by Form; the shape it condensed, giving rise to dense. For our convenience, we will use the term "achievement", referring to Coins.

In each of the four suits we have, firstly, four figures. They symbolise active people, conveying the idea of the suit. In addition to the figures, each suit includes ten other cards with values, from the one - the ace - to the ten. These letters correspond to the ten Sephira of influence of this suit.

Let us first deal with the figures of the four suits. Each suit has its King (the י), then his Lady (the first ה), his Knight (the ו) and his Jack (second ה). The latter is the server that conveys the influence of the suit. In modern decks, the Knights were suppressed; there is only the King, the Lady and the Jack.

Each of these figures acts in the field of each of the ten Sephira of his suit, which results in 4 x 10 = 40 combinations of influences. Therefore, the number of combinations for the deck of the Tarot will be 160, if, as was proposed, we limit ourselves to the analysis of the reflexes of the influence of the First Family, exclusively at Sephira Chokmah. If we analyse these reflections in all ten Sephira, we would have 1600 kinds of influence.

In the present study we will give only a brief explanation of the role of the 16 figures, as well as the "titles" of the sephirotic charts of numerical values of all four suits.

Analysis of the 16 figures of the Cards

Wands

1. The King receives the title of Father, therefore, he is the hierarchical leader, the starting point of manifestation of Power.
2. The Queen is the wife of the Father, indispensable to give birth to the Knight.
3. The Knight is the active agent who transmits power and operates through Jack.
4. The Jack (or Page) is the POWER server.

Cups

2.The Queen is the main card of this suit, as it represents the beginning of Attraction
1. The King is only the husband of the Lady, indispensable to give birth to the Knight.
3. The Knight is the intermediary that attracts to the work the external elements. Operates with the help of Good luck.
4. The Jack is the Duration of the server.

Swords

3. The Knight is the main card of this suit; is the agent who actively transmits Life.
1. The King is only the Knight's Father.
2. The Queen is just the Knight's Mother.
4. The Jack is the server in Vida transmission.

Coins

4. The Jack or "Server of the Children" is the main card of your suit.
Let's not forget that the achievement is evaluated according to the results it brings.
1. The King, or the Father Director and
2. The Queen, or "The Donor of the Children", together, gave birth to the Knight.
3. The Knight, an active agent, unifies the individuals that make up the complex organisms. The last three figures remain in the background, giving prominence to the Jack, the "handyman":

	י of Wands	ה of Cups	ו of Swords	2nd ה of Coins
י	**King of Wands & Ace of Wands**	King of Cups	King of Swords	King of Coins
ה	Queen of Wands	**Queen of Cups**	Queen of Swords	Queen of Coins
ו	Knight of Wands	Knight of Cups	**Knight of Swords**	Knight of Coins
ה	Jack of Wands	Jack of Cups	Jack of Swords	**Jack of Coins**

Analysis of number value charts

Wands

1. The Ace- represents Keter of the suit of Wands. and the metaphysical synthesis of Active love, radiating down. This idea can be illustrated by the Tarot Wheel, which does not set in motion without the First Impulse of Active Love. Without this there would be no Universe, there would be no Tarot or, to be more exact, the Wheel of the Arcanum would exist only potentially, but without turning, and there would be no one to be touched by it.

2. The Two - the Chokmah of the suit of Wands - corresponds to the Wisdom of the First Impulse and its expansion, as reflected in the Sephira of Human Souls. According to Eliphas Lévi, this represents the "help of the Savior." He refers, no doubt, to the great cliché י ה ש ו ה (Iod-He-Shin-Vau-He), of which we have already spoken.

3. The Three - Binah of the suit of Wands - is The Reason of Things, limiting the wisdom of the First Impulse. In other words it is the total of what we expect from the י ה ש ו ה Redeemer Cliché, that is, Reintegration.

4. The Four - Chesed of the suit of Wands - corresponds to the Mercy of the First Impulse. It is the reflex of the cliché י ה ש ו ה in the field of ethics, in the field of Egrégores and of astral purposes. And the influence י ה ש ו ה, expressing itself as the centre of the Egrégore, as Father of the Church.

5. The Five - Pechad of the Wands suit - is the aspect Severity, compliance with Law of the First Impulse, limiting his mercy. We can ask what will limit, for and also the mystical expansion, the savior of a Church or a community of believers. Are the reasons ethical character, perhaps the desire to strengthen his Egrégora, perhaps an effort to raise the moral level of its members, which, at certain times could be realised.

6. The Six -Tiphareth in the suit of Wands - is the Harmony, the Beauty of the First Impulse is the son born of the unified totality of the believers who make up a Church and of the ethical value of
it. This is expressed as support and comfort that an Egrégore provides to its supporters. Taking, as an example, the Christian Church, we find in it many impressive episodes its beauty, and proving the harmony that reigned in the hearts of its martyrs and other selfless followers. These episodes brought a greater number of conversions than metaphysics, since the man is more attracted to Tiphareth than to Keter of an Egrégore.
7. The Seven - Netzach of the suit of Wands - is the Victory of the First Impulse, that is, the victory Hierarchical Law, the introduction of the Hierarchy in everything and everywhere, that is, the recognition of the single measure of magnitude.
8. The Eight - Hod of the suit of Wands - Peace, the Glory of the First Impulse corresponds to what can be rested after establishing the hierarchical principle. To realise this peace, is equivalent to admitting the role of the vertex in the triangle of Fabre d'Olivet, that is, to admit the existence of the Providence in the Universe. Providence, in every human being, is expressed by the voice of conscience. Having admitted the hierarchical power, we must attend to the voice of conscience; we cannot ignore it.
9. The Nine - Yesod of the Wands suit - is the Form of the First Impulse, the result of the coherence between the admission of the Hierarchy, and Peace, given by consciousness. Yesod is manifested by Orientation we acquire in life, when we attend to the voice of conscience, considering it as divine direction to guide us through beings in the various degrees of the hierarchical scale.
10. The Ten-Malkuth of the suit of Wands - is the concretisation of the First Impulse, the incarnation of the synthesis of the elements contained in all the Sephira; the synthesis that enables us to rise
from the dense world to the Idea of the Primordial Impulse.

Cups

1. The Ace - Keter of the Cups suit - is the metaphysical synthesis of everything that introduces Transcendental Life in Sephira Chokmah of the Second Family; is the Vitality, attracting and
capturing the First Impulse.
2. The Two - Chokmah of the Cups suit - is the Wisdom of Attractive Love; through Vitality, the Higher Influx or, in other words, the yearning to save.

3. The Three – Binah of the cups suit limits this aspiration; and the Divine Goodness express by the elements of Salvation, given by Him to us.

4. The Four-Chesed of the cups suit - is the reflection of the yearning to be saved. This reflex is expansive and expresses itself as a desire to do good.

5. The Five - Pechad of the Cups suit - restricts the above-mentioned expansion; gives the continuity in doing good, however, without enlarging it; gives the notion of duty, leading not to abandon the already benefited. It accurately evaluates our affections and knows clearly that it is the that, and to whom and to what, we would sacrifice ourselves in case of necessity.

6. The Six -Tiphareth of the Cups suit-is patience in altruistic work which, in turn, is the fruit of the union of the two preceding Sephiras.

7. The Seven - Netzach of the Cups suit - is the Victory, in the field of altruism, of the subtle on the dense and the idealism in love.

8. The Eight-Hod of the Cups suit - is the firmness and constancy of idealism in love.

9. The Nine - Yesod of the Hearts suit - is the Form, already shaped, for Attractive Love.

10. The Ten-Malkuth of the Hearts suit - is the concretised synthesis of all the Sephira of this suit; is the accomplishment of the attractive action.

Swords

1. The Ace - Keter of the Swords suit - is the starting point of the Transmission process of Life, of fertilisation with the vital elements received.

2. The Two - Chokmah of the Swords suit - is the full awareness of the purposes with which transmits life.

3. The Three - Binah of the Swords suit - is the clear knowledge of the closed system (of the mill) to which life is transmitted.

4. The Four - Chesed of the Swords suit - is the equanimity in the manifestations of transmission of Life. This equanimity is the reflection of the consciousness of the purpose of this transmission.

5. The Five - Pechad of the Swords suit - is the planning of the effects of Life; this is the reflection of the clear knowledge of the closed system to which Life is transmitted.

6. The Six -Tiphareth of the Swords suit-is the beauty of transmitted Life.

7. The Seven - Netzach of the Swords suit - is the victory of the transmitting impulse of Life on the inertia of the environment in which it is implanted.

8. The Eight- Hod of the Swords suit - is the adaptation of the victory results to the characteristics of the environment.
9. The Nine - Yesod of the Swords suit - are the forms of the development of Life transmitted.
10. The Ten-Malkuth of the Swords suit - is the incarnation of the transmitted Life.

Coins

1. The Ace - Keter the suit of Coins - is the point of match for the realisation. And the Matter Primordial (in the alchemical field); the Primordial Astrosome (in the field of Ethical Hermeticism)
2. The Two - Chokmah of the suit of Coins - is the polarisation of matter (in the alchemical field); The great binary of Destiny and Will (in the field of Ethical Hermeticism).
3. The Three – Binah of the suit of Coins - is the principle of neutralisation of the poles in the alchemical field); the Triangle of Fabre d'Olivet (in the field of Ethical Hermeticism).
4. The Four – Chesed of the suit of Coins and the condensation according to law of Dynamics (in the alchemy); the Hermetic Quaternary, symbolised by the Cross (in Ethical Hermeticism).
5. The Five - Pechad of the Coins suit - is the predominance of the energetic principle (the quintessence) on the four elements (in alchemy); the birth of the Pentagram (in the Ethical Hermeticism).
6. The Six -Tiphareth the suit of Coins - is the establishment of two currents: an evolutionary and the involutionary (in alchemy); the problem of the two paths (in Ethical Hermeticism).
7. The Seven - Netzach of Suits of Coins - is the penetration of the subtle in the dense (in alchemy); The victory of the Three on the Four, that is, of the Spirit on the Form (in the Ethical Hermeticism).
8. The Eight - Hod of the suit of Coins - is to establish the periods of formation, that is, phases of Appearance of the Philosopher's Stone (at alchemy); The conditional law and natural Karma (in the Ethical Hermeticism).
9. The Nine - Yesod of the suit of Coins - is the general scheme of the evolution of matter (in alchemy) that is revealed during the process called sublimation; the general framework of Initiation, revealed by the successive transmission of the Higher Influx (in Ethical Hermeticism).
10. The Ten-Malkuth of the suit of Coins - is the concrete transmutation of matter (in alchemy), that is, the use of the Red Powder, already prepared, in the transmutation of the alloy; the return of the Initiate to the world, to dedicate itself to the ethical transmutation of human society (in Ethical Hermeticism).

All, of course, have already realised that the numerical values of the suit of Coins very much resemble, by their titles, the first ten major Arcana of the Tarot, already studied by us. The explanation for this is that the suit of Coins is the refraction of the Knave of the First Family and "organ" creator of the Major Arcana, like the Minor Arcana.

It could be said that the Minor Arcana of the suit of Coins corresponds to the scheme of the world as it stood before Humanity before its fall, while the first ten Major Arcana correspond to the understanding of our truths by the already fallen Humanity.

If we could purify the first ten Major Arcana by taking from them the envelope that formed around them, we would obtain the Arcana numerical values of the suit of Coins in its natural succession.

Let us return, once again, to the Major Arcana, enumerating them according to the natural order of letters of the Hebrew alphabet and indicating, at the same time, the numerical value and the hieroglyph that each of them was attributed by the former Initiatory Schools. These hieroglyphics will allow us, even if it be done in a brief and incomplete way, to unroll the system of titles of the Arcana, which have not yet been studied in the fields of the Theosophical Ternary. Titles are indispensable for understanding the general picture of kabbalistic speculation. We will also present some examples of such speculation. The titles of the first ten Major Arcana have already been given. We will therefore seek to understand the meaning of the remaining hieroglyphs, so that they can deduce the corresponding titles:

Number	Name of Sign	Numerical Value	Hieroglyph
1	Aleph	1	Human being
2	Beth	2	Human mouth
3	Gimel	3	Clasping hand
4	Daleth	4	Breast feeding
5	He	5	Respiration
6	Vau	6	Eye, Ear
7	Zain	7	Arrow in straight motion
8	Cheth	8	Field of cultivation
9	Teth	9	Protective roof
10	Iod	10	Index finger
11	Kaph	20	Squeezing hand
12	Lamed	30	Open had
13	Mem	40	A woman
14	Nun	50	Fruit
15	Samekh	60	Arrow in circular motion
16	Ayin	70	A material bond
17	Peh	80	Mouth with tongue
18	Tzadik	90	Oppressive cover
19	Qoph	100	Axe

20	Resh	200	Human head
21	Shin	300	Swinging arrow
22	Tau	400	Cozy chest

The Arcanum XI has, like hieroglyph, the palm of the hand tightening something with force. It is a clear indication of the Force. This force, in the field of the Theosophical Ternary gives the titles "Vis Divina", "Vis Human "and" Vis Naturalis "(Divine Force, Human Force and that of Nature), which dispenses comments.

The Arcanum XII has for its hieroglyph an open hand that, along with the slightly folded arm is similar to the letter Lamed, and expresses the desire for expansion, perhaps even at the expense of figure that extends the hand. This gives rise in us to the idea of sacrifice, to offer something, even contrary to their own interests, to give up their own life force. The sacrifice of the Archetype gives the title "Messiah"; human sacrifice is expressed by charity - "Caritas"; the sacrifice of Nature - by the energy offered to us by the sun, hence the title: "Zodiacus".

The hieroglyph of Arcanum XIII - the woman - evokes, by association, the idea of death and Rebirth. The woman is the means in which the process of the uterine life of the child is effected, dying for this uterine life, is born into a life in the atmosphere. The idea of death and Renaissance, in the Archetype's plan, gives us the title "Immortalites" or "Permanentia in Essentia". At the plane of Man, brings forth the image "Mors et Reincarnatio" (Death and Reincarnation). On the plane of Nature, which, through the power of energy and its multiple transformations, is eternally renewed in forms, the title will be "Transmutatio Virum" (or the 'Transformed Man' using the Helmholtz terminology).

The Arcanum XIV has as its hieroglyph fruit, or that which is obtained through the woman and with her help, and what is the result of the Arcanum XIII. The immutability of basic metaphysical theses brings the possibility of establishing deductive systems; hence the title "Deductio". The fruit of sequence of the incarnations of the human being is the hermetic modeling of souls, that is, their harmonization, giving, in the human plane, the title "Harmonia Mixtorum". The laws of transformation and conservation of energy in Nature are closely linked to the question of reversibility of processes; hence the title "Reversibilitas".

In Arcanum XV, his hieroglyph - an arrow moving around a circle – logo evokes the idea that every time we try to go beyond this circumscription, we will find the inexorable arrow. Such arrows, for a human being, are inevitable in the three planes of the Ternary Theosophical. The Archetype does not want to let us leave the enchanted circle of our system's metaphysical logic; hence the title "Logica". The human astrosome contains elements of passions and tendencies, on which he himself stumbles in his efforts of expansion and subtilization. This one Enchanted circle is the biblical serpent "Nahash" (the second title), the traditional tempter. Nature surrounds us with a ring of predestined manifestations that sometimes constitute impediments unsurpassed during a whole incarnation. It's the "Fatum" - the third title of our Arcanum.

We note that Arcanum XV results in a natural way from the XIV: logic is based on deduction; Ethical Hermeticism cannot ignore the technique of fighting the passions; the laws governing the reversibility are closely linked to the manifestations of fate.

The hieroglyph of Arcanum XVI is a material connection or even, using the language of mechanics, a bond in a state of tension, characterised by the existence of a certain reaction in it. The previous Arcanum had, as its main purpose, the establishment of such links. Let's go to explanation of the titles. By logical reasoning, we can definitely eliminate one or the other hypothesis; this is "Logical Eliminatio"; the formation of certain eddies, requires a particular astrosome to manifest itself in an already fixed form; that is, "Constrictio Astralis," the basis of all Ceremonial Magic. Relentless fatality can destroy works, the most solid in the concrete world; this is "Destructio Physica," the third title.

The hieroglyph of Arcanum XVII is a mouth with a tongue, a mouth that speaks. And one simply needs to know how to listen to it. We know the language of the Archetype well, coming to us in the form of hope - "Spes" (1st title) - even when everything around us is silent or prognosticates the misfortune. If we will also hear the voice of human intuition, which van prevent, protect and save; hence the second title - "Intuitio". The peoples of antiquity, leading a simple life and in contact with Nature understood better the language of this and, to understand it, they did not have to resort to the complicated methods we nowadays call astrology, physiognomy, chiromancy, phrenology, etc. Hence, the third title: "Divinatio Naturalis". The Arcanum XVII is a passive, natural complement to the active Arcanum XVI. It is not enough to have logic, to have a conviction; Hope is often necessary too. Astral has not enough force; one must also have the tact and intuition to know if such action is useful and that should be given. It is not enough to know that fatality is inexorable on the physical plane, it is what I must also be able to determine, through divinatory methods, in what form this fatality will manifest itself.

The hieroglyph of Arcanum XVIII is again (as in Arcanum VIII) a roof, but no more as a symbol of protection, but of something that limits, oppresses, crushes and impedes vision of the world. We can see that the

Arcana, becoming progressively ever more concretised and dense, have reached a degree in which compression is felt by the very weight of the material. We have already studied in the previous Arcana the language of the Theosophical Ternary and we know that in this Ternary there are elements that limit us. Hope is needed, but we should understand that "expecting something," we can only of the one who is higher on the hierarchical scale; hence the title "Occult Hierarchy". Intuition provides us with great services, but it also makes us understand that we have hidden enemies - "Host Occulti". The divination that, at sometimes gives us a clear indication of a particular danger, more often our general vigilance, warning us of some threat: "Pericula Occulta".

Arcanum XIX, by the symbol of the axe, gives us the possibilities of opening a passage in allowing the arrival of light, that is, it shows us the possibility of improvement and reintegration into the world of the Minor Arcana. We can ask what this symbolises "Axe"? It's the Hierarchical law that we allow to overcome the "roof of the dialectic" and raise ourselves to Light of Truth fruitful, "Veritas Fecunda." The desire to have no enemies will make us all facets of altruism that can so beautifully reflect what is called "Human Virtus" (Human Virtue). The danger of the waste of the noble matter which we possess, danger of premature destruction of the body, etc., will compel us to think of the Philosopher's Stone and the Elixir of life. Thus, the third title of the Arcanum will be "Aurum Philosophale" (Gold of the Philosophers).

Arcanum XX has for its hieroglyph a human head, a head that must appropriate the Light that arrives through the opening on the roof, made by the ax of the preceding Arcanum. The influence of the Archetype, by its attractive power, impels us towards evolution; hence the first title "Attractio Divina". By our own hermetic effort we reach the astral rebirth that allows us to use human gifts well. This rebirth or inner transformation is called "Transformatio Astralis. "The Nature which, according to the Law, accompanies our internal efforts, causing changes in the physical plane, helps us in the direction of improvement, which explains the third title: "Mutationes in Tempore".

Arcanum XXI is called, by many people, the "Arcanum Zero" because of its exceptional content and because it is completely different from all others. It has as its hieroglyph an arrow, progressing in a certain direction, but by means of an oscillating movement. The Arcana have shown the possibility of elevating us to the Light. However, when we are surrounded by a wall and covered by a roof, just knowing that we can break free is not enough. We should also know how to practice opening on the roof so we will not be crushed by wreckage that will fall and leave intact the part that does not need to be demolished. For this, we should know the secrets of roof construction. In other words, knowing the mystery of action, and protection. The phase of human evolution presented in the Arcanum XXI is not as dangerous as that of a closed ring, like the Arcanum XV. It is the field in which we will walk sooner or later. The "arrows" move there in both directions. Happy is he who knows how to take advantage of the movement of the arrow that moves away from him; bitter will be the experience of him who is found in the way of an arrow to meet him.

The Arcanum ש (Shin) belongs to the primordial mysteries and has its origin in the emanation, by the Archetype, of the world Olam ha Aziluth; therefore, the first title of this Arcanum will be "Radiatio" (in relation to the Knave of the First Family). In the field of Man, the Arcanum ש is realised when the human astrosome connects with a sign, egregorically generated by a chain of pentagrams and, therefore, possessing a realising power. Thus, the second title will be "Signum", in the sense of a stable astral symbol. The Arcanum ש is no stranger to the activity of Nature; it realises it when it "materialises the forms". The third title of the Arcanum will therefore be "Matter".

The Arcanum XXII presents the synthesis of the results of the application of the knowledge of the Arcanum above. It is the Arcanum of the "Great Work", to allow the passage of the Minor Arcana. His hieroglyph is a breast, in the sense of something that encompasses everything. Its meaning is so clear you do not need comments. We note only that our passage from the Minor to Major Arcana was done by the suit of Diamonds. The passage from the Greatest to the Minor is done through the last four Major Arcana that synthesise the fruits of life's wisdom. The titles of Arcanum XXII, in all three planes, are easy to understand. In the Archetype world, the Arcanum corresponds to the upper triangle in the scheme of the Great Arcanum (fig 16), that is, the Absolute Mystic - "Absolutum". In the world of Man, it corresponds to the middle hexagram, of the same scheme, representing the bipolar action on the astral, that is, what could be called the application of the Great Work to the astral, or "Adaptatio Operis Magni". In the world of Nature, the Arcanum expresses the natural omnipotence of the Elementary Route - "Omnipotentia Naturalis".

We want to emphasise the fact that several Arcana have similar hieroglyphics. This, in the case of an abbreviated study, allows us to limit the examination to 16 Arcana only. This reduction is not desirable in the initiatory work, but it is quite enlightening from the philological point of view. The Arcana corresponding to the signs of the alphabet whose pronunciation is:

"b" or "ph" have, as hieroglyphic, the mouth
"g" or "kh" have, as a hieroglyph, the palm of the hand

"d" or "th" have, as hieroglyphic, the breast (sinus)
"z" or "s" have as an hieroglyph an arrow
"t" or "tz" have, as a hieroglyph, a roof.

This similarity between the hieroglyphs of the Arcana suggests that there was a time when the hieroglyphic "mouth" corresponded to the two similar lip sounds; the hieroglyph "palm of the hand" to the two guttural sounds; the hieroglyphs "chest" (sinus) and "roof" - to the two types of dental sounds; The "arrow" was always the preferred symbol of the whispering and hissing sounds.

Kabbalah divides the signs of the Hebrew alphabet into three essential groups: the three mother-letters, the seven double letters and twelve simple letters.

The mother-letters - א מ ש (Aleph, Mem, Shin) - symbolise the basic, metaphysical aspects of the Ternary. א (Aleph) corresponds to the neutral term (n); מ (Mem), to the negative pole (-); ש (Shin) to the positive (+) pole. The triangle of the Great Arcanum, in this notation system, is presented as in figure 42.

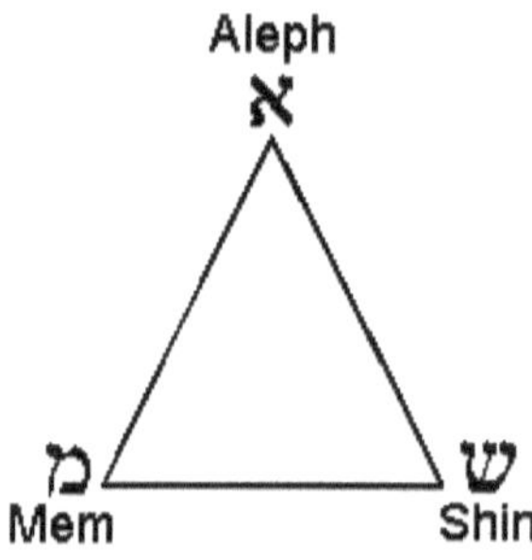

Figure 42

Any combination of these three letters can be interpreted in terms of the Ternary. Assigning to these letters correspondences in the field of the elements and writing: א ש מ (Mem, Shin, Aleph), א means conditionally "Air", ש, "Fire" and מ, "Water". We thus get the phrase:

The water, placed on the fire, evaporates, assuming a gaseous state, similar to the air.

By using the hermetic terms but metaphysically, the same combination of letters can be read:

If in space (מ) we observe phenomena, that is, modifications of energy (ש), we will also notice the passage of time (א).

In the mystical interpretation, the מ ש א combination can be read as:

The inert element, i.e. the profane (מ), encouraged by the energy (ש) elaborated in him or transferred to him - becomes a magician and an androgynous being (א).

The second group is the seven double letters ת ר פ כ ד ג ב (Tau, Resh, Peh, Kaph, Dalet, Gimel, Beth), which correspond symbolically to the seven Secondary Causes. If the mother-letters can be called metaphysical, the seven double letters can be called planetary or astral. Their correspondence is as follows:

ב - Beth   Moon
ג - Gimel   Venus
ד - Daleth   Jupiter
כ - Kaph   Mars
פ - Peh   Mercury
ר - Resh   Saturn
ת - Tau   Sun

These letters were called "double" for the following reasons:

1. From the etymological point of view, they initially had two modes of pronunciation: B and BH, G and GH, D and DH, K and KH, P and PH, R soft and R hard, TH and S.
2. From the esoteric point of view, we know that each of the planetary influences has both a good side as bad. The good aspect of Jupiter, for example, is expressed by the affability, ability to deal with the people, etc. and its bad aspect, is in Jupiter's pride, etc.
The twelve simple letters - ק צ צ נ ס ע ל י ט ח ז ו ה - correspond astrologically to the twelve zodiacal signs:

ה - He   Aries
ו - Vau   Taurus
ז - Zain   Gemini
ח - Cheth   Cancer
ט - Teth   Leo
י - Iod   Virgo
ל - Lamed   Libra

נ - Nun   Scorpio
ס - Samekh   Sagittarius
ע - Ain   Capricorn
צ - Tzadikk   Aquarius
ק - Qoph   Pisces

As you know, the twelve zodiacal signs, in the plane of Nature, symbolise the twelve phases of a complete solar cycle, that is, a cycle of the sacrifice that in our planetary system is made by the Sun, on behalf of the Earth, sending her astral fluids.

In the ethical field, the Arcanum XII – ל (Lamed) – symbolises the sacrifice of man to man, to the Nature or the Divine. This sacrifice can only be done by an incarnated pentagram. At the plane of the archetype, the Twelfth Arcanum is the Arcanum of the Messiah. This brings up again the idea of incarnation, therefore, of the physical plane, showing it as a plane of sacrifice. We can also, reversing, regard sacrifice as something closely related to the physical plane.

	י		ה		ו		ה ח
	+	−	+	−	+	−	
ל	1	4	7	10	13	16	19
ה	2	5	8	11	14	17	20
ו	3	6	9	12	15	18	21(0)
ה	4	7	10	13	16	19	22

Figure 43

Figure 43 presents the scheme of the Major Arcana as an outline of the י ה ו ה Law.

Notice that the system of the Minor Arcana is interpreted in the same way. The difference is that the Minor Arcana's numerical value cards exactly and totally perform this interpretation. Minor Arcana could be compared to a perfect musical instrument, while the Major Arcana would correspond to an imperfectly tuned instrument, and at only approximately similar intervals. One of the instruments - the exact one –

was destined to undiminished Humanity; the other - the imperfect - to the confused worldview of fallen humanity.

From the distribution of the Arcana of the ׳ column we already speak in Arcanum VII. In the columns ה and ו a distribution is the same. As for the column of the second He, his androgynous Arcana constitute, in its totality, the passage from the system of the Greater to the Minor. They could be considered as the "organism" that gives birth to the Minor Arcana. Let us remember that, speaking of the reverse direction, we call the Minor Arcana of the suit of Diamonds, also an "organism" that gave birth to the Major Arcana.

Let us briefly review the phases of the development of an incarnate man according to the table of the Major Arcana.

A man who seeks self-knowledge (1) creates science (2), takes it as his wife, and thanks to it becomes productive (3), thereby gaining authority (4). This authority (4) births, in him, the human pentagram (5). Once this is formed, he must face the problem of the two paths (6). He chooses the right path, thus becoming Winner (7).

With this Arcanum the first phase ends, that of ׳, that is, the formation of the personality in the field of ideas.

The Winner begins the second cycle, that of self-education in the field of forms, instituting legality (8) in the environment in which it should work. The establishment of such legality ensures a certain ethical level that will serve as a stepping-stone, so that man can give a leap into the higher planes of ethics, in the field of form. His aspiration and perfection will be crowned by Initiation (9). After initiation, there is a deepening of some "closed system" (10). This "closed system" may be the external world to which the Initiate will return periodically to influence their peers. This "system" may also be the Kabbalah, into which the Initiate goes deeper for rational improvement of the complex of clichés of those around him; finally, the system can be reduced to the area of meditation of what we call the "Testamentum". The deepening in a "closed system" (10) will lead the Initiated to form a Current of Force (11). Here, the need for sacrifice (12), both internal (to strengthen the current), as external (in favor of Humanity). The consummation of the sacrifice will lead to the change of plane (13).

The development in the field of forms is followed by an effective contact with the elements of all three planes. Each death (13) is at the same time a birth to a new life, bringing the understanding of the reversibility of certain energetic manifestations (14). If our change of plane was achieved by an exteriorisation, we will bring with us, from the astral plane, the reversibility clichés of this process. Each change of plan has a certain power over the astral whirlwinds (15) or, similarly, the logical power (in the mental plane), or, the capacity to take advantage of the manifestations of destiny (on the physical plane) (15). The Arcanum XV will manifest itself enveloping itself in one of the forms belonging to the Arcanum XVI. Manifest, therefore, either by the power of logic, by the progressive exclusion of other hypotheses, by the power to constrain certain astral entities or, finally, by the ability to physically beings of three planes by a skillful use of the conditions provided by destiny. The Arcanum XVI completes the first cycle of the ו column of our scheme.

With the same Arcanum XVI begins a new half cycle, that of the active application of one or the other power (16). For this, the Arcanum XVI needs a "wife", which will be found in the form of use of some divinatory capacity (17). This will allow man to guide his activity. Knowledge of your own power and experience in this field will lead you to discover other entities, not only friendly but also hostile. You will know that there are enemies in all planes (18). Distraught and persecuted, he will seek a means of uniting himself to the Light. This will be put before him as the necessity of realising in himself the Great Work of the Hermetic transformation (19).

This completes the ו cycle. The remaining four and last four Arcana are Hermetic transformations. Those who pass through these stages are already in the path of Reintegration.

The cycle of the second ה begins with the consideration of this Hermetic task (still 19). The first will be the deep conviction that you can contribute, both to your own the rebirth, as you can to that of other beings (20). The absolute necessity of internal transformation will lead the human being to penetrate the mysteries of Arcanum ש (21), the realising Arcanum, in the strict sense of this word.

In order to subtilise the dense, that is, the coagulate, it is necessary first to know how it was formed; it is necessary [for one] to coagulate to some extent. The mastery of all this will allow the human being to realise the Great Work (22), and for this very reason, move directly to the suit of Wands of the Minor Arcana.

Addition and Decomposition of the Arcana

If we do not take into account the inequality of the intervals between two Arcana in the entire range of the Major Arcana, we may take any of them, as the starting point from the count, according to a scale of our convenience. In other words, if we admit that Arcanum III, for example, derives from Arcanum II, just as II Arcanum I, and V of the IV, then we can give any Arcanum a number corresponding to that which the Arcanum possesses in the normal cycle, that is, the cycle that begins with Arcanum I. Such operations are called "addition of the Arcana".

Adding Arcanum "a" to Arcanum "b", means progressing in circular order to Arcana corresponding to "a + b", or, if it does not exist, to one of the Arcana whose number corresponds to the number "a + b", according to module 9. Thus, the sum of Arcana VII and XVIII will be Arcanum VII or XVI, then, 7 + 18 = 25 = 7, and also 16, since the sum of 1 and 6 is 7.

For a more clear explanation of this technique, I allow myself to arrange the number of Arcana around the circle, closing the system with the border along which the first and eighteenth lanes are in contact. I take only 18 Arcana for the full major cycle, considering the last four Arcanum additional, assigned only to go to minor. I consider the nineteenth Arcanum only the development of the first or tenth ($19 \equiv 10 \equiv 1$); twentieth - by the development of the second ($20 \equiv 2$); the twenty-first is the development of the third ($21 \equiv 3$) and the twenty-second is the development of the fourth. Figure 44 gives a diagram of our transitions.

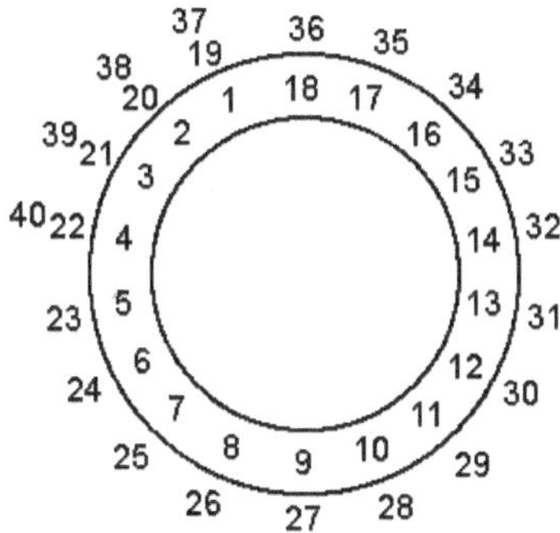

Figure 44

We will add, as an example, the Arcanum V to the X, taking for both its titles in the plane of the Man, that is: "Pentagram" and "Kabbalah". Our starting point will be the Arcanum V, and from this we will continue around the circumference, counting 10 intervals, that is, we will look for the tenth Arcanum, but from the ה and not from the א as usual. The "Pentagram", together with the "Kabbalah" and expressing itself through it, will give us the Arcanum XV: "Nahash", that is, an astral whirlwind cabbalistically created by the Pentagram. Of course, the conscious human will, along with the knowledge of the astral plane, bring this result.

We can, of course, obtain the same sum - 15 - by adding "Kabbalah" and "Pentagram" in the reverse order, that is, 10 + 5 = 15. In this case we start counting Arcanum X and, adding 5 intervals, we will look for its manifestation as Pentagram (5). We will see that the laws of Kabbalah, expressing themselves through a conscious, volitional entity, will manifest themselves as the Nahash Serpent, all-powerful in the astral, that is, again the Arcanum XV.

Let us try to add Arcanum XIII to VII, that is, to look for Victory in the Arcanum of Death. We will get the sum of 20, the Arcanum of the Renaissance. We would find the same result by adding the Arcana in the reverse order (7 + 13); in other words, trying to find out what Victory, inevitably linked to Death, that is, the change of plane. We will find the Rebirth.

If we add the Arcanum XIX to the XI, that is, we confer strength (11) to the one who seeks the Light Superior (19), will we get 30 = 3, the Arcanum of Productivity (Creativity). Comments are unnecessary.

Other examples would be superfluous, since we have had similar cases studying the arithmetical deconstruction of the numerical values of the Arcana.

Multiplication of the Arcana

An approximately correct thesis clearly follows from a comparison of the series of the first ten major arcana cards with the complex of the suit of diamonds: "Just like cards in the suit of diamonds are the Sephirotic manifestations of her Keter - Ace of Diamonds, the first ten major arcana can be considered the Sephiroth of the First Arcanum, taken for Keter. "

The Sephiroth of the first Arcanum are obtained from it sequentially by transitions in one interval according to the numbers of our circle.

If we assume that the Sephiroth of the second Arcanum, as more complex, more complicated, can be found in a row of the same numbers in irregular intervals over two intervals, then it turns out that if Kether = 2, then Chokmah = 4, Binah = 6, Gedulah = 8, etc.

Applying the same system to the third Arcanum as Keter, we will follow the numbers of the circumference, jumping each time three intervals.

The ten Sephira would then correspond to the numbers 3, 6, 9, 12, 15, 18, 21, 24, 27 and 30.

In general, we apply "interval" jumps to find the Sephira of the Arcanum "a". We can thus establish the following rule: The Sephira "b" of Arcanum "a" will be represented by the Arcana whose numbers correspond to the result "ab", according to module 9.

Here are some examples:

1. Let us look for the 7th Sephira of the Arcanum II: 2 x 7 = 14, or in other words, let us try to find in which consists of the Victory (7th Sephira) of the subtle on the dense, in the field of science (Gnosis, Arcanum II). We will obtain the Arcanum XIV, that of the reversibility of the processes and the internal harmony of the astrosome. This is clear. It may be said that 14 = 5. Well then! The formation of the Pentagram cannot do without Arcanum XIV, which of course will be the Pentagram whose three tips are directed upwards.

2. Let us look for the 8th Sephira of the Arcanum XV, that is, the Glory, the Peace of the Nahash element. We will have 15 x 8 = 120 = 12 = 3. We will first obtain the Arcanum of Sacrifice (12) which, at the same time, is the Arcanum of the Zodiac (12), that is of the physical plane. Indeed, on the one hand, the victory of the animated element of the astral vortices in its refinement cannot go beyond the astral work for the victim; this is the pcak of the refinement of the motives of astral work, on which one must calm down. On the other hand, in the field of applications of this work, it is impossible to go below the physical plane (12). More complete realisations do not exist. But what does the number 3 say? The glory of the astral vortex is the Arcanum of Productivity (3). This Arcanum must be satisfied (8th sephira).

3. Let us look for Severity (Sephira V) in the divinatory elements in the field of Nature (Arcanum XVII). We will have: 17 x 5 = 85 = 13 = 4. Severity, the ruthless justice of fate first, to the Arcanum of death or transformation of energy (13). It is not difficult realise that nothing will be done without it. However, in our equation we also have 4. This number corresponds to the Form or the presence of the four elements or four states of matter. Of course, without form and without presence of the elements, there would be no manifestation in Nature.

These examples are sufficient to understand the following: numerical operations on Arcana and Sephiroth do not give an exact answer to our question, but rather an indication that makes it easier to find the answer. The great hermeticist Raymond Lull, in one of his works, "Ars Magna" (The Great Art), proposed that readers convince themselves of the usefulness of operations on the Major Arcana and the Sephiroth, if they exercised in finding, by this means, arguments and answers to subjects little discussed in a meeting.

If it is necessary, we can look for the answer to our question in the row of the supplementary circle, as shown in figure 44. Sometimes also, for example, instead of the plane of Man, we must take the plan of the Archetype or Nature or vice versa. Associations will usually be easy to establish.

In our study "Archetype - Man - Nature", a special interest should be given to traditional privileges of Humanity, since this, in the Theosophical Ternary, occupies the place of the middle.

Before the fall, as we have already explained, man's natural task was the Great Work, which he performed without difficulty. The titles of the Arcanum X we are studying provide a clue of certain privileges that fallen mankind still holds.

The mental privilege of humanity is "Testamentum" (The Testament) given to it by the Archetype and is equivalent to His promise to always remain the "vertical bar of the Stake". The "horizontal bar" corresponds to the inertia of man, in his present state.

Language, an exclusively human attribute, is considered by Tradition as a privilege in the astral plane.

This requires some explanation. The confused worldview of the present Man can be encompassed and expressed by 22 synthetic theses of the 22 Major Arcana. These, in their totality, also resemble the horizontal bar of the Stake. The role of the vertical bar, in this representation, would be played by the simplified alphabet י ה ו ה that, participating in the constructive scheme, continually fecundated, one could say, the inert and confused world of the Major Arcana, with the principle of activity, clarity and accuracy of the Minor Arcana. In this sense, the term "language" is equivalent to the term "Kabbalah". Let us develop this idea.

If language is not just a random set of conventional signals, laws, then all the roots of this language will correspond to something existing in the Universe. The totality of the roots, used in the language, will express the total conception of the world of the speaker. Laws that link roots to one another and determine their complexities, will present an analogy of the laws that a given microcosm has the possibility of formula regarding the components of the Universe. For this microcosm, the role of Universe is played by the Major Arcana. The elements of language will be the s lyrics initiatory alphabet. For our current study we use those of the Hebrew alphabet.

Each act and event in the Universe, when registered, requires, compulsorily, the use of corresponding (analogous to this action or event) of words, roots and, finally, the very signs of the alphabet. Thus, Kabbalah or, to be more exact, the passive side of the Kabbalah, can be defined as "the reflecting mirror of all that happens in the universe". However, we must not forget that, according to the Law of Analogy, for each process to be exercised the influence is reversible. All influences are reciprocal. If the activity of the brain reverberates in peripheral branches of the nervous system, the activity of the branches also brain centres. If the government exerts its influence on society, it will also influence government decisions. If a teacher, in teaching, transmits his influence to the students, these, in turn, lead the teacher to adapt to the needs of the students. This leads us to the conclusion that if we change the position of the letters by alternating the roots and the words, these changes will be reflected in a certain way in the field of world events. This is the active aspect of kabbalah.

It is evident that, for this to correspond to reality, the kabbalistic operation must have the vitality needed and be carried out with full awareness of the operative microcosm. In the same way, as regards the passive aspect of Kabbalah, it is certain that only the manifestation of vitality, unconditioned in their relationship, will be reflected in the mirror. If one receives a fictitious title, corresponding to no real degree of power, or if you win a little by playing cards, it is doubtful whether this event can be kabbalistically predicted or recorded. However, if one, possessing power and knowledge, acts on the signs and formulas, this action reflects in the events of the plane Changes in the astral clichés and may even influence mental flows. This is the manifestation of the active part of the Kabbalah and the reason for its widespread use in magic and theurgy.

There is an old adage: "the letter kills, but one can also kill the letter". The "letter kills" expresses the power of a kabbalistic operation. "To kill the letter" means that one can overcome, overpower or destroy a kabbalistic performance of others, acting directly on the plane of ideas, or in the physical world, totally disregarding the world of forms (the astral). Let's not forget ever that the Son of Man is the "Lord of the Sabbath." The symbol that, according to tradition, corresponds to the two privileges of humanity on the physical plane, which we are quoted, is the ritual of circumcision. This ritual, as something obligatory, imposed by tradition, can be symbolised by the Stave.

The vertical line, fecundates and represents the tradition. The horizontal element of the figure represents the human passivity, his tendency to remain as he is born. However, the ritual of circumcision is also interesting from another point of view and also gives rise to comparison with the Stave. In the physical execution of the ceremony, explained as being a purely hygienic, we can also see the symbol of the sacrifice of a portion of the flesh (corresponding to the inertia) in order to achieve a certain liberation, that is, active capacity. So we have again the symbol of the Stave or Lingam, as triumph of activity over inertia, and also the allusion to the physical plane as the plane of sacrifice.

Let us now look at the construction of the old initiatic language, whose distorted and materialised form is called, today, the Hebrew language and that would be more precisely called Aramaic. The roots of this language have, in general, two consonants or, for occultists, are constituted of two Arcana. The vocal sounds, which corresponded to the pronunciation of the words, changed with the and differed according to the different localities.

The roots composed of three letters are explained by the joining of two roots of two letters, when the same letter ends the first root and starts the second. The character of prefixes and suffixes is determined by the consonant (or consonants), that is, again by the Major Arcana which compose them.

The totality of the Major Arcana is 22; therefore, the number of all possible combinations of two Arcana would be: $22 \times 21 / 2 = 231$

Taking into account the possibility of reversing the order of two signs, the maximum number of combinations will be 462. If we add to this number yet the 22 cases in which the same Arcanum is opposed to itself, but in two different fields, we will have: $462 + 22 = 484$,

the total number of roots. These 484 combinations, in their totality, the chaotic and approximate worldview of fallen humanity. Joining these roots into more complex, we only form combinations of by doing the same when we put the words together to form a sentence. The subjective understanding of the world of a being human, in particular, does not, in general, encompass all of these 484 complexes. This is the progressive reduction of the roots in use.

Of course, the same set of Arcana can be interpreted differently in different planes of the Theosophical Ternary. However, the roots tend to materialise. In the initiatory language, in their beginnings, they corresponded to certain metaphysical conceptions; over time, the roots were applied to analogous conceptions, but already in the field of forms and, finally, have been used in relation to the manifestations of the concrete world. For this reason, the comprehension and literal interpretation of ancient texts, based on the contemporary significance of Hebrew words, leads to great perplexities and disagreements. Here are some examples:

1. The combination Aleph-Beth (אב), second initiatory system of interpretation of the Arcana is read as: a complete and balanced three-plane entity (א) wishes to be manifested by division or polarisation (ב). By making this combination a little more accessible to our understanding, we will easily come to the following two interpretations, especially if we replace the general by an individual:

(a) An entity of three planes, complete and balanced, manifests itself giving birth to another entity.

b) A complete human being gives birth to another, by a similar process to that of separating, from itself, a part. The last sense of the אב set is interpreted, in contemporary language as "father."

2. The Aleph-Mem (אמ) combination (AM, AME or AMA) also allows the following interpretations:
a) The world of the three planes, integral (א), is manifested through the Arcanum of Death and Rebirth (מ).
b) In a balanced environment (א) something is formed, to die in that environment and to be reborn anew (מ).
c) A human being - woman - bears the child, who dies for the intro-uterine life, being born for the external life. The common translation of this combination is the word "mother."

3. The Ain-Tzadik (עצ) combination (AATZ or ETZ) gives the interpretations:
a) The restriction (ע) of the functions of the organism, results in a very limited life full of hazards (צ).
b) Vegetative life.
c) Tree (going from the general sense to the particular).

4. The Ghimel-Nun combination (גנ) means:
a) A birth (ג) associated with reversibility, moderation or proportions (נ).
b) A geometric solid.
c) A fence.
d) Garden (in the Bible).

5. The Resh-Mem combination (רמ) corresponds to:
a) Rebirth (ר) through Death (מ).
b) Rebirth for the environment due to death of the personality.
c) Formation of a homogeneous environment through the assimilation by him of external elements.
d) Formation of a nourishing environment by the absorption of external material.
e) Blood.

6. The Lamed-Lamed combination (לל) means:
a) Sacrifice as opposed to sacrifice.
b) Expansivity as opposed to expansivity.
When the letter י is added to the לל combination in the centre, that is to say a "system
closed ", the word means" night ", which is interpreted as follows: the closed space (י) is surrounded on all sides by the "sacrifice of light," as by visors. Thus the darkness is completely obtained, that is, the night.

7. The Resh-Teth combination (רט) gives:
a) Rebirth (ר) under the direction of the restrictive element (ט).

b) A new flow directed by something.
c) Water flow through a pipe.
d) Canal, tube or avenue, or a walk (whose path is delimited as in the case of a Valley).

Methods of Kabbalistic Calculations

Kabbalistic analysis and synthesis consist of various methods and manipulations of the Arcana and its numerical values. We will speak only of the most usual.

1. Notarikon is a system based on the acrostic principle. Various modalities are used, for example:
a) Develop each letter, which comes in the composition of a word, in an independent word and which begins with the letter in question;
b) Form a new word, composed of the first letters of the words that enter the composition of a sentence;
c) Replace the letters by their name, used in the alphabet or other particular methods.

Take examples of some of these methods.

a) Development of a word in complex of words. Example: the word MELECH (King, מל) can be enlarged in three words: Mov (ומ - brain), Leb (לב - heart) and Kaban (כב - liver), which form a kind of "analogous ternary," similar to that studied by us - Head, Thorax, and Abdomen. The central place of the letter Lamed, in the word Melech, confirms the theses we have studied and of the medium term of the Ternary, and the very word underlines the importance of mentioned in the three parts of the human body.
b) Formation of a new word with the initial letters of the words of a sentence.

In the first book of Kings (II, 8) David says that Simel cursed him with a terrible curse: NIMERTZETH (נמרצת). Kabbalists seek to explain this word as being composed of initial letters of various other curses:

(נאפ) Noeph - Adulterer
(מואב) Mobai - Moabite
Rotzeach (רצח) - Assassin
(צורס) Tzores - Violent
(תאב) Thoeb - Cruel

c) Substitution of the letter by its name, used in the alphabet; for example:

The letter א (Aleph) is replaced by letters אלף. Thus, to the very meaning of the letter Aleph is added the idea of surrender to the sacrifice (Lamed), of hope, of intuition and of divination (Phe).
ב (Beth), developed in בית, adds to the Arcanum of knowledge, the idea of a closed system (Iod) and the idea of the Great Work (Tau).
י (Iod), developed in יוד, to the idea of ca closed system preparing for a manifestation, adds the idea of the choice of ways (ו) and the idea of authority (Daleth).
ה (He), developed in הא, adds to the idea of life the idea of his three planes (Aleph).
The procedure of dividing a word into its components is also one of the methods of Notarikon. Thus, for example, the word that initiates Genesis בראשית - Bereshith (in the beginning) - is deconstructed into "ברא, BARA" (created) and "שית, SHITH" (six) and interpreted as creation in six symbolic days.
The Notarikon system, despite its apparent naivety, is structured on cabalistic principles so that the meaning of the word is based on the significance of the Major Arcana of which it is composed.

2. Gematria (corruption of the word geometry) is a method of comparing the meaning of words that have the same numerical sum of their letters. In this way the word סבא (Samekh-Beth-Aleph, old), for example, is approximated by the word נביא - Nun-Beth-Iod-Aleph, because the numerical value of the first one is $60 + 2 + 1 = 63$ and the second one is $50 + 2 + 10 + 1 = 63$. אחד (Aleph-Cheth-Daleth, union) with the word אהבה (Aleph-He-Beth-He, love), because the value of the first is $1 + 8 + 4 = 13$ and that of the second, $1 + 5 + 2 + 5 = 13$.
The Gematria method approximates not only the words of the same numerical value, but also the words whose values are corresponding, according to module 9. Still some examples:

a) Take, on the one hand, the great name יהוה ($10 + 5 + 6 + 5 = 26 = 8$); and, on the other side, the static of the Ascending Triangle, symbolised by the אמש (Aleph-Mem-Shin) configuration, where א represents the term neutral (n); מ, the negative pole (-) and ש, the positive pole (+). That configuration "EMESH" has the numeric value $1 + 40 + 300 = 341 = 8$. Hence the Kabbalistic deduction of the equivalence of the static systems אמש, with the יהוה dynamic cycles. Statics originate from dynamics, and also vice versa. As we can see, the thesis is very deep.

b) The word אדם (ADAM) corresponds to the numerical value $1 + 4 + 40$ = 45, that is, the ninth element, according to module 9. On the other hand, the scheme of the Mystical Cross of Superior Initiations of metaphysical character, contains the signs י ה ו ה and א, which, added, give the value 279. Hence the approach of the pantáculo of the name אדם (ADAM) with the referred scheme of the Cross.

Gematria is widely used as a means of aid for a definitive assessment of a word, previously analysed by the deconstruction in Major Arcana. The numerical value of the determines its definitive explanation. Generally, the lowest sum is used, but times, the other sums are also as an auxiliary indication. Thus, the אמש (Aleph-Mem-Shin) clichés (8) and י ה ו ה (8) correspond to the Arcanum of Legality (8); the cliché אדמ (Aleph-Daleth-Mem (9) to the Arcanum of Initiation (9); the cliché שט (Shin-Teth), the biblical name, Seth, whose value is $300 + 400 = 700 = 7$ - to the Arcanum of Victory (7); the אנוש (Aleph-Nun-Vau-Shin) cliché (Enosh, son of Seth), that is, $1 + 50 + 6 + 300 = 357 = 15 = 6$, Arcana XV and VI, etc.

Without Gematria you cannot take a step in the Kabbalah. This method is most accepted by the White Race for his metaphysical speculations. It is advisable to study your adaptations so you might later be able to deal with the original texts of the Initiative language.

For the initial exercises of Notarikon and Gematria, the ten Hebrew names of the Sephiroth and the ten Holy Names (Divine Nomina) corresponding to them, and of which we will still speak in this Arcanum. Let us now apply Gematria to the three groups of letters in our initiatory alphabet.

Mother Letters (The Metaphysical World of the Primordial Causes)

א - Aleph, which in the ternaries corresponds to the term "n" = 1
מ - Mem, which in the ternaries corresponds to the term "n" = 40
ש - Shin, which in the ternaries corresponds to the term "+" = 300

Total $341 = 8$

The Law, therefore, characterises this world.

Double Letters (The Astral World of Secondary Causes)

ב - Beth (Moon)   2
ג - Gimel (Venus)   3
ד - Daleth (Jupiter)   4
כ - Kaph (Mars)   20

פ - Phe (Mercury)   80
ר - Resh (Saturn)   200
ת - Tau (Sun)   400

Total $709 = 16 = 7$

The world of Secondary Causes is therefore characterised by the Arcanum XVI (the force which compels) and Arcanum VII (the Victory). In other words, planetary influences are used both to act upon another (Magic) and show how to overcome oneself (Ethical Hermeticism).

Simple Letters (The Zodiacal Concrete World)

ה - He (Sheep)   5
ו - Vau (Taurus)   6
ז - Zain (Gemini)   7
ח - Cheth (Crab)   8
ט - Teth (Lion)   9
י - Iod (Virgo)   10
ל - Lamed (Libra)   30
נ - Nun (Scorpio)   50
ס - Samekh (Sagittarius)   60
ע Ain (Capricorn)   70
צ - Tzadik (Aquarius)   90
ק- Qoph (Fish)   100

Total $445 = 13 = 4$

As we see, the physical plane is characterised by the Arcana:

a) of Death (13); it is certain that on the physical plane everything is transient;
b) Elements or Adaptation (4); on the physical plane you have to adapt to everything, to the influences from the zodiacal stages, to the states of matter, etc. The physical plane, also called "the third plane," it is a TIME plane and it is important that time is not wasted on it.

3. תמורה (Temurah[26]): this method consists in the exchange of place and substitution of letters for their correspondences and the study of the relationship between the words thus formed. The main Themurah, are:
a) גילגול (Gilgul), in which a complete picture of all possible combinations of the order of letters in a given word. Applying, for example, Gilgul to the name י ה ו ה we will have:

1. Iod-He-Vau-He	7. Vau-He-Iod-He
2. Iod-He-He-Vau	8. Vau-He-He-Iod
3. Iod-Vau-He-He	9. Vau-Iod-He-He
4. He-Vau-He-Iod	10. He-Iod-He-Vau
5. He-Vau-Iod-He	11. He-Iod-Vau-He
6. He-He-Iod-Vau	12. He-He-Vau-Iod

The elements of this framework established for the name י ה ו ה, are called הויו (HAVIOTH). We will find them later in the Twelfth Arcanum.

b) TZIRUPH: is a systematic substitution of letters for others, according to rules and changing the order of letters in the alphabet. The number of such systems is very large; we will mention only the most used ones.

1. The alphabet אתבש (ATBASH): The alphabet is written in two lines, in the first letters are written right to left; in the second, left to right.

אבגדהוזחטי כ | למנסעפצקרשת
תשרקצפעסנמל | כ יטחזוהדגבא

To analyse a word, according to this system, we look for each of its letters in the line of and replace it with the letter that corresponds to it on the bottom line. Thus, א will be changed in ת, ב , ש, etc. Hence, comes the very name of the alphabet: "Athbash" (אתבש). To simplify the work we can, of course, limit ourselves to writing half of each line, looking for the letter in one of the half-lines and replacing it with the his correspondent from the other half-line. Applying the Athbash to the name י ה ו ה, we will obtain the word מצפצ (Matzpatz, Mem-Tzadik-Peh-Tzadik) whose numerical value is 40 + 90 + 80 + 90 = 300 = 3, clearly indicating the metaphysical plane. The word EMESH (אמש), by the same method, will become חיב (Tau, Yod, Beth, 400 + 10 + 2 = 412 = 7), indicating that the Upper Ternary - Emesh - has in itself the ability to

---

[26] Temurah is one of the three ancient methods used by Kabbalists to rearrange words and sentences in the Bible, in the belief that by this method they can derive the esoteric substratum and deeper spiritual meaning of the words. (The others are Gematria and Notarikon.)

produce the Septenary of Secondary Causes. The word בנ (BEN - Son), composed of Beth-Nun (2 + 50 = 52 = 7) related, therefore, to the Septenary, will transform into שט (Shin-Teth), whose value is 300 + 9 = 309 = 12 corresponding to the duodenary, that is, to the zodiac or physical plane.

2. The alphabet ALBATH (אלבת) is given by the lines:

אבגדהוזחטיכ
לתשרקצפעסנמ

The letters of the word analyzed are searched on one of the lines and replaced with the letters from the other line. Thus, י ה ו ה will move to נקצק having the value 50 + 100 + 90 + 100 = 340? 7. This is interpreted: the Septenary is the product of the Law of Dynamics.

3. The alphabet ALBAM (אלבמ). The scheme of substitution is given by the lines following:

אבגדהוזחטי כ
למנסעפצקרשת

The procedure is the same as in the preceding alphabet. The name י ה ו ה became שעפע Shin-Ayin-Peh-Ayin, receiving the numerical value 300 + 70 + 80 + 70 = 520 = 7. This gives again the Septenary of Secondary Causes. We can invent as many alphabets as we like similar to those that have been presented.

The Value of the Kabbalah for an Occultist

We may ask ourselves, what is the purpose of all this Kabbalistic cogitation? It would, perhaps, only be to exercise intellectual acumen? Certainly, the target is not this, and the intellect is only a help in the acquisition of wisdom. The purpose of the study of Kabbalah is twofold: 1. This study allows us to deepen the meaning of the writings in hieroglyphic-initiatory language, revealing not only everything in them that was closed by its authors, but also everything that can be deduced from the theses that these writings present. This can be done by speculation of the work of the mercurial elements of the human personality.

2. It allows us, through the use of the word, to create, by our inventive power, outlining our volitional impulses with a form. From the pronunciation of the words used in them, mantras and, what is important, mantras real to us, that is, mantras whose composition we understand and which are in harmony with us, having been created by ourselves or received from the Egrégorean currents with which we are in contact.

The Kabbalah, in general, enables the study of Tradition, clarifies the Theogonic, Androgonic and Cosmogonic systems and indicates to its followers the means of realisation.

The name כבלה - QABALAH (100 + 2 + 30 + 5 = 137 = 11 = 2) corresponds to the Arcanum of the Force (11) And to Science (2) which in itself can serve as a summary of all that has just been said. Etymologically, the word כבלה is translated by tradition.

Kabbalistic code of the Occidental School

The codex of the Western School is composed of the following monumental works of undoubtedly Kabbalistic content:

1. The book SEPHER YEZIRAH - ספריצירה (Shin-Peh-Resh-Iod-Tzadik-Iod-Resh-He), attributed to containing the complete code of the static part of Kabbalistic metaphysics, that is, the relationship between the Three Primordial Causes, the Seven Second Causes and the zodiacal world of the physical plane, encompassed in a unitary system.

2. The book of LIFE: SEPHER BERESHITH - ספרבראשית (Shin-Peh-Resh-Beth-Resh-Aleph-Shin-Iod-Tau) and the other remaining books of the Pentateuch of Moses containing the code of the basic theses of the theogony, cosmogony androgyny and a part of the history of the transmission, by succession, of the Tradition of the White Race.

3. Other books of the Old Testament in which, alongside exclusively exoteric texts, there are purely kabbalistic chapters, such as chapters I and X of Ezekiel, some chapters of the prophet Daniel and others.

4. The book SEPHER HA ZOHAR - ספרהזוהר (Shin-Peh-Resh-He-Zain-Vau-He-Resh or He-Zain-He-Resh), which consists of a wide set of comments by several authors, whose names, in the majority are unknown. The Zohar, in addition to the commentaries on the Bible and Sepher Yezirah, contains a near-complete code of the dynamic part of Kabbalistic metaphysics. We found applications of various kabbalistic methods to sacred texts, as well as treatises on the PNEUMATIC, which is the teaching about souls, the methods of acting on astrosomes, the conditions under which life plans are changed, theurgical operations, etc. The Zohar was first printed in Mantua in the year 1559. As for the time

when it was compound, there has always been controversy. With this, we will not occupy ourselves.

5. The books of the Talmud, name familiar to all. Many of them have no kabbalistic data, however, its structure, the scheme of division of its material, the way of synthesising, have, without doubt, a kabbalistic character. Because of this, the books of the Talmud should not be omitted in this enumeration of kabbalistic writings inherited from the past.

6. The so-called "Clavicles of Solomon," which came to us in a Latin translation of the Rabbi Abognazar, and which consist of a collection of talismans, pantalons, conjurations and prayers used in ceremonial magic. We also find a series of astrological-kabbalistic indications. The preface consists of a text entitled "Recommendations of the King Solomon to his son Roboan. "One could say that the" Clavicles "present a collection of kabbalistic recipes.

7. The whole New Testament, and especially the books of the Apostle John, are rich in texts which, in part or in full, allow a Kabbalistic interpretation. In the Apocalypse we find satirical descriptions of several Tarot Major Arcana. The Gospel of St. John contains 21 chapters that correspond to the Major Arcana, from the א (Aleph) to the ש (Shin) inclusive.

This whole Kabbalistic codex was interpreted during the Middle Ages by numerous Kabbalistic classics of different Schools and nationalities and that, in turn, left us much material susceptible to meditation and to which we can apply this "Mercury of Esotericism" which is called kabbalistic speculation.

The Names of Sephira the Corresponding Sacred Names

The shorter exposition of Kabbalah would be very incomplete if, even at an elementary level as this, the ten Divine Names were not mentioned. These Names, as well as the names of the Sephira, may serve as material for the first exercises of Notarikon and Gematria.

As an example, we will look in general terms at the first three Divine Names, as well as the names of the Sephira that correspond to them.

1. The name "EHIEH" (אהיה - Aleph-He-Iod-He) by the Notarikon method, decomposes in two "Marriages": Aleph-He and Iod-He, which allows us the following interpretation: Just as a tri-plane, balanced individuality (א) fecundates the passive elements (ה) of the same. In this way, an active closed system (י) can fecundate a passive system (ה) that suits it.

The numerical value of this name (1 + 5 + 10 + 5 = 21 = 3) indicates the metaphysical plane (3) and, at the same 'time, the mysterious process of the passage to the lower planes (21).
The name of the Sephira that corresponds to it - Keter - (כתר - Kaph-Tau-Resh) decomposes in the Arcanum of Force (כ-11), in the Arcanum of the application of the Great Work (Tau-22) and in the Arcanum of the Renaissance (ר-200). The numerical value of the sum (11 + 22 + 200 = 233 = 8) allows us to add: "such is the Law of the world. "As we see, the analysis of Sephira-Keter's name has characterised the way in which the process determined by the Divine Name "Ehieh" unfolds.

2. The Divine Name "IAH" (יה) is the formula of a normal, Gnostic union of two polarities of the same level. Its numerical value 15 = 6 indicates the role played in this union by the astral whirlwind (15) and warns against the dangers of Arcanum VI, since union can have both an evolving as well as an involutive character.
The name of Sephira Chokmah (חכמה) can be interpreted as (ח-8), cultivating the Force (כ-11) which, after the change of plane (מ-40), determines the elements of a new life (ה-5). The numeric value of the sum (10) indicates a cycle of transformations, closed, independent and active. Again, the Divine Name indicates the process, and the name of Sephira - the conditions in which it unfolds.

3. The name י ה ו ה is the formula of a normal family, of a normal dynamic cycle. Its numerical value is 8, which underlines the legality of the cycle.
The Sephira Binah (בינה) that is, 2 + 10 + 50 + 5 = 67 = 13 = 4) tells us that Knowledge (ב) leads to a closed, complete system (י), in which Life (ה) is possible in the conditions of reversion of the processes (ו) or also, under conditions of moderation (נ). This environment is fully suited to the manifestation of the Dynamic Law. The numerical value (13) makes us remember the principle of the transformation of energy, and the "4" - the indispensability of applying it to the world of the elements, to carry out the י ה ו ה cycle.
Students are advised to apply the same rapid analysis to all ten Sephira. By doing so, they will convince themselves that the Divine Names corresponding to the Sephira of the column (the left one - in the Sephirotic scheme) contains limiting elements and determiners in relation to the processes caused by the Divine Names corresponding to the Sephira of the male column (the right one) - of the same sub-planes. Thus, for example, the name "IAH" (יה) corresponding to the Sephira of the male column, Chokmah, evokes the process from UNION and the name י ה ו ה, Corresponding to the Sephira Binah, from the feminine

column (both belonging to the same world Aziluth), is a family formula, which delimits and determines the quality of the union, structuring it in the form of a family.

In addition to the ten Holy Names, the Sephirotic names and the Hebrew term AIN-SOPH, given to the Unattainable, superior to all Sephira, it would be useful to "kabbalise" in various ways the words "AB" (father) and "AGLA" (אגלא) which have a wide application in Ceremonial Magic and in Theurgy.

The word "AGLA" is composed of א which means the balance in the three planes, reached by the full metaphysical understanding of existence; ג, corresponding to the creativity of Universal Love, reunifying everything that, at any time, has been separated; ל, symbolising the limitless expansiveness of readiness for sacrifice; the three signs, together, lead again to the principle of oneness - א. This is the reason for translating "AGLA" as "TRI-UNO" and the reason that this word is attributed to a mantric power, even when pronounced by a profane.

We think that now the role of the ten names in Theurgy and Magic can now be perceived. These Names correspond to the separate cycles of the Great Diabetic Process of Universal Life. The totality of the Names embraces all that has been manifested and all that can be manifested. It is the complete reflex, one might say, of the subjective understanding of the Mysteries of the Universe by Collective Man; understanding expressed through the signs of the Initiative Alphabet and the sounds of the Language Initiative of this Collective Man.

All Theurgical and many Magical ceremonies are accompanied by the ritualistic pronunciation of some or of all these Names, according to the Sephira who participate in the scheme of the ascension of the prayer or invocation.

A good knowledge of the Divine Names and Sephira is indispensable even for a student beginner. This domain allows him to obtain kabbalistic, mental indications regarding one or another branch of the universal diabetic process, regardless of any written work, and brings possibility of affirming his volitional impulses by the formulas that bind him to the Immortal Egrégore. Great Chain of the Carriers and Guardians of the White Race Kabbalah.

Notes on the tenth Arcanum

Tomberg's reflection upon the tenth Arcanum is less exhaustive than G.O.M.'s but no less powerful. In the evocative image of the Wheel of Fortune he sees a visual expression of *"the nostalgia of fallen and fragmented beings for the lost state of fullness and integration*" (p235), stating that this is the Arcanum which "*teaches, through its actual context, an organism of ideas relating to the Fall and Reintegration.*" It does so via a full circle which encompasses the ascent as well as descent. He acknowledges such a circle of involution and evolution is "*generally a platitude in occult literature, but it is not so when it is a matter of involution understood as the Fall and evolution understood as salvation.*"

Further into this Arcanum of MotT the idea of a closed circle of captivity is contrasted with that of an open circle or living spiral. This is analogous to the world before the Fall and represents the opportunity offered by Christ – the Door - to escape the closed prison. The hazard of closed circles is an important theme the author returns to from various perspectives, at one point urging students about the danger of closed magical groups – secret occult circles - and earnestly requesting that they never form any such group in his name.

The good news of religion, on the other hand, is that it is not a closed circle but has an exit and an entrance, offering a way out of the endless cycles of recurrence, the "cosmic hell" of Nietzsche. Indeed for MotT "*the idea of hell can be understood as eternal existence in a closed circle*", and "*the Fall is a cosmic event, a whirlwind[27] set in motion by the closed circle of the serpent biting his tail and sweeping down part of the created world.*" The act of Redemption involves no less than leading humanity out of this circle via a safe path of exit and into the living spiral and "*transforming the fallen world from within by the radiation of the incarnated Word (Jesus Christ)*".

A very important phase of Valentin Tomberg's spiritual work, especially during the period he spent in Holland during WWII helping the Dutch resistance, was teaching what has come to be known as 'The Lord's Prayer Course'. This aspect of his work has been picked up and developed by subsequent schools and teachers, including that of Robert Powell's Sophia Foundation and the late Willi Seiss, whose student, Sebastian Niklaus, has published a volume in several parts on the course with commentary from Seiss. Powell has gone even deeper into this field of study with a series of teachings and eurythmy exercises based on the 'Our Mother' prayer.

---

[27] In the use of the term 'whirlwind' we naturally see a strong impression made by G.O.M. upon Tomberg.

Arcanum XI

FORCE

Pathway from Geburah to Tiphareth

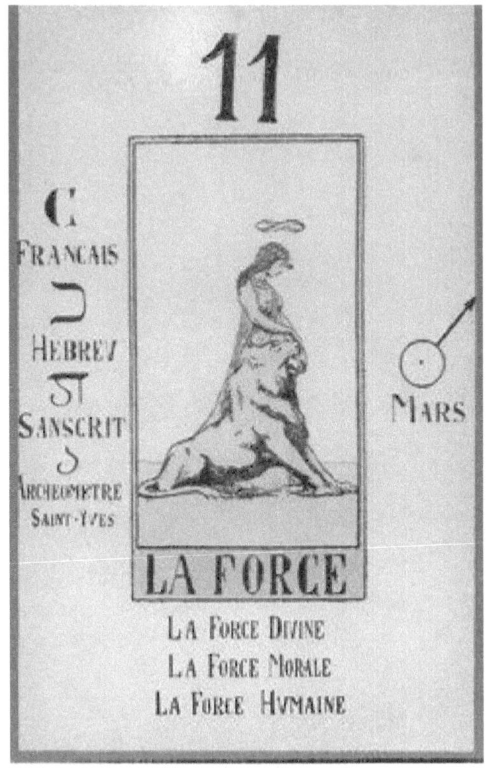

Force is a *Magical Chain*

THE TAMED LION: Strength

*C, K--20 expresses in the divine world the Principle of all strength,
spiritual or material*

Paul Christian

*"This is a picture of power", said the voice. "It has different meanings.
First it shows the power of love. Love alone can conquer wrath.*

Ouspensky

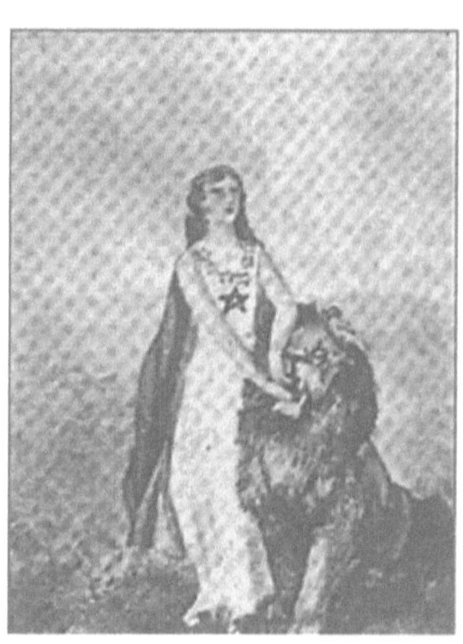

As already stated, the sign of Arcanum XI - כ - has numerical value 11= 2, meaning that the force can be used in two ways. The astrological correspondence of the Arcanum is the planet Mars.

The titles of the Arcanum, in the field of the Theosophical Ternary, are: "Divine Vis", "Human Vis" and "Vis Naturalis" or, in other words, three modes of manifestation of force.

The title of the card is "Leo Dominatus" (Dominated Lion) I "Force". The card depicts a girl who, without effort and with a complete aplomb, opens (or closes) the mouth of a lion; the maiden has a ∞ sign of Astral Light above her head.

It is easy to understand the picture's content. She presents the necessary conditions for the emergence and use of evolutionary forces. Such conditions are: knowledge of the astral (∞), purity of intentions (a girl is a symbol of innocence) and self-confidence (a laid-back pose of a girl). The arithmetic analysis of the Arcanum gives us certain indications as to the creation of force and the mechanism of application.

11 = 1 + 10 and 11 = 10 + 1: In the first deconstruction, the monad (1) governs a closed system (10). Translating it to the common language, we say that only a will must govern a current, formed by individual links. This is the formula of the collective entities governed by the Hierarchy. The second deconstruction tells us that a current (10) composed of individual entities must manifest externally as a single unit (1). That is, for a community to exist it must, at all levels, be in line with the aims of its members.

11 = 2 + 9 and 11 = 9 + 2: The first formula tells us that the human inability to neutralise the binaries (2) leads the Initiates (9) to work and manifest their strength (11). The second formula will be read as follows: the force (11) of the Initiates (9) consists in the use, for the inability of others to neutralise the binaries (2).

11 = 3 + 8 and 11 = 8 + 3: The first version is: the force (11) consists in being productive (3), within the established Law (8). The second version gives: force (11) is in the preservation of Law (8), within productivity (3) already existing.

11 = 4 + 7 and 11 = 7 + 4: The dependence of elements (4), regardless of the interpretation of this term, arises in man to the action of secondary causes (7) and thereby makes him strong (11). Or: the causes (7) govern the elements (4) and this results in force (11). This last interpretation indicates, clearly, the necessity of participation, in the magical current, beyond the pentagrams, also of the elementals (4) who, knowing the mysteries of the mechanism of involution, help in the purposes of the chain. These elementals, however, must be submitted to pentagrammatic elements of the chain, which, in turn, are supported by influences (7).

11 = 5 + 6 or 11 = 6 + 5: The first decomposition gives the normal formula for activity in Ceremonial Magic: "The microcosm (5) operates on the macrocosm (6)."

The second decomposition will give the normal formula for divination in the astral plane - a purely passive operation: "The macrocosm (6) gives directions to the contemplating Microcosm (5)."

And in fact, and in other combinations lies part of the secrets of the Force.

Now I will try to briefly convey the etiology and general history of the implementation of the Force on our planet by the method of formation of Magic Circuits controlled by certain egrégores.

The most typical form of such chains is collectivities professing one religion or another. And therefore, to some extent, I have the right to say that I am giving you at the moment a sketch of the emergence and development of religious teachings.

But this itself obliges me to outline with brief strokes, in as pure and primitive a form as possible, the view of the Initiates on the question of the Fall and Reintegration of Man.

I begin by reminding you of the composition of the First Family, standing as a Transcendental Group above the Sephira of metaphysical, ethical and concrete content.

The members of this Family — Transcendental Love, Transcendental Life, the Logos (or Adam Kadmon) and the Jack of the Logos (or Logos Server) emanating from the Crown of the Second Family — are already known to you. The latter emanates the Crown of the Second family.

The Second Family itself is generated by the said Jack in the following complex of Mystical Persons:

1. The Sephira Keter in which the Macroprosopo of the Family remains.
2. The Sephira Chokmah in which the Father of the Family should remain and where, in primordial state, was the Androgynous Complex of Human Souls, forming only one organism called ADAM PROTOPLASTA (Adam Protoplast).
3. The Sephira Binah is the natural position of the Mother of the Family and the primordial place of the permanence of the Complex of Angels. The Souls were to perform the evolutionary work of the Triangle of Fire: all subtle, all to raise, keeping uninterrupted the ascending current of the great Closed System of the ten Sephira of the Universe. The activity of the Angels, limiting the sphere Gives activity of Souls, corresponding to the involutive work of the Triangle from water. The angels concretise the subtle, coagulate it, governing the totality of the descending flow of the Closed System of the Second Family.

4. The 6 Sephira: Chesed, Geburah, Tiphareth, Netzach, Hod, and Yesod serve in their entirety as the place of residence of the Family Microprosopo. Microprosopo is androgynous. The centre of your body is the Sephira Tiphareth. And the organs through which he acts upon the Bride constitute the Sephira Yesod. The right side of the Microprosopus contains two positively polarised organs: Chesed (the Mercy) and Netzach (the Victory). These two organs of the Microprosopo are constituted by Souls and used for evolutionary purposes. The left side of the Microprosopus contains negatively polarised organs: Geburah (Severity) and Hod (Peace), both created by the influence of the Angels, and destined for involutionary ends. Thus, from the Father, the Microposopo received evolutionary possibilities that the Mother limited to the involutive ones. The personality of the Microprosopo determined at Central Sephira - Tiphareth. Its activity, downward, into the Sephira Yesod.

Now the purpose of Microprosopus is clear: the whole field of (in Latin "COGNITIO", in Hebrew דעת (DAATH) will be the Sephira of his activity. This sphere is neutralised by Harmony and should be considered androgynous. It is very complex in composition, and therein lies the danger of a possible violation of its functions. A purely active individuality, or a purely passive complex, never needs such keen protection and such proper nutrition as androgynous complexes. We find something similar to this in all double-acting mechanisms: they work well, as long as all the rules for dealing with them are met to the finer point; the slightest violation of these rules entails grandiose changes in their action and violates the harmony of their composition.

5. Sephira Malkuth - the natural abode of the Spouse of Microprosopus, i.e. the scope of elementary implementations, which is closely dependent on the performance of Microprosop and is always calculated in its composition according to its state.

Figure 45 gives a diagram of the initial distribution of the elements of the universe in the Sephira of the First Family. This scheme is called - Institutio.

Later the falls occurred. The Daath sphere (the Sephira of Microprosopo), in its quality of an androgynous complex, reflected in a similar way, both what he received from the Logos and his Serivdor (the Jack), and what came from a still higher level, that of the Perfect Androgyne.

from the Upper Point above the First Iod. The difference between the manifestations of these Three Androgynous Units consists in this:

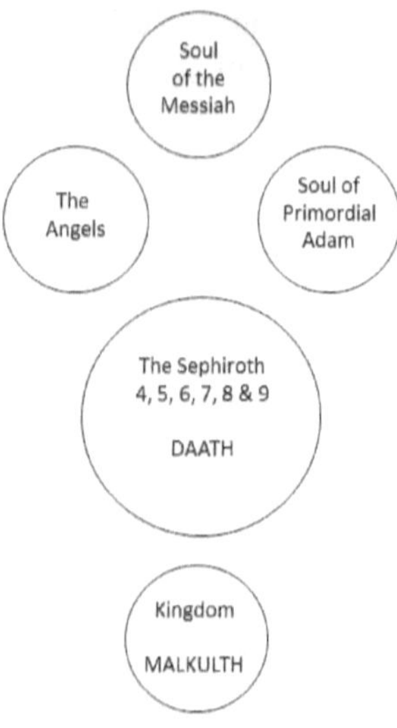

Figure 45

Institutional Scheme

a) The Upper Point receives nothing; only sends a Transcendental Flow;
b) The Logos nourishes itself with the Transcendental Influx and, in turn, sends the Transcendent Flow [onward];
c) The Sephira of the Microprosopus receive the Transcendent Influx, already enveloped in a slightly nebulous form, and transmits it, even more condensed, to the sphere of definite forms, that is,
to the world of the formation of seminal principles ("Formae Seminales").
The Highest Point is self-existing; the Logos is independent; Daath is only harmonic; and Malkuth only dense.
The Sephira Daath intended to create an illusion of independence for itself; for this it needed Freedom, without which there can be no independent life. But the desire for freedom was tantamount to a refusal of food transmitted by the Higher Influx. This refusal was processed and what happened is called the fall of the Six Sephira — and is what led these Sephira to the Kabbalistic Death.
Not fed by Higher Currents, the very subtle shell of these Sephira coagulated into what we now call the lower astral.
The sephirotic organism is fragmented, its polarities appear as unresolved binaries. The Sephira Tiphereth has ceased to emanate its Light. The differentiation of the cells that made up Daath went to extremes, and its name became legion.

Here is the so-called Fall of the Angels, which revealed to the Universe the Mystery of Death. (Figure 46)

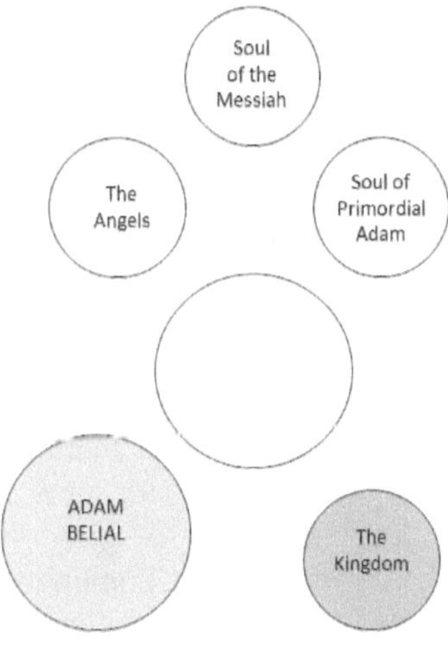

Figure 46

Scheme of the first phase of the Destitute Epoch, connected with the fall of the middle Sephira

The contents of the Sephira Malkuth, that is, of the Bride of Daath, also coagulated correspondingly, nevertheless continuing to serve as the field of manifestation of the fallen "legion" Daath. In other words, Malkuth has become the field of the densest manifestations of non-neutralised binaries. It can be said symbolically that during this period, the Tree of the Knowledge of Good and Evil is grown in Malkuth.

Although the contents of the six Sephira of the Microprosopo declined, the principles governing sephirotic construction remained immutable, just as a code of laws remains in force even if it is transgressed by all citizens, without exception.

Souls and Angels were faced with the task of re-filling empty spaces with formal manifestations, in order to save Malkuth, which these manifestations would begin to impregnate. And through Malkuth, her Spouse, the fallen Daath, could be saved.

Daath, however, did not want to lose the acquired Freedom by the process of restoring the Tree of Life, that is, the Astral Light Tiphereth. Therefore, Daath seduces the passive side of the Sephira of Souls (הוה - Heva) leading him to experiment with the binaries of the Sephira

Malkuth (the most coagulated elements of the Universe) as convenient reference points for applying personal power. הוה (Heva), letting herself by seduced, formally grasps this thought, that is, tastes the fruit of the Tree of the Knowledge of Good and Evil. Having mastered the system of binaries, הוה (Heva, the passive side) conducts it into the active practice of Souls, which bears the name מ of the final אדם (Adam). Thus, the wife gives her husband the same fruit.

The active side of Souls, above all, applies the binary basis to the content of the Sephira Chokmah itself: אדם and הוה (Adam and Heva) recognise themselves as poles of a non-neutralised binary, that is, no more a couple, but a couple of opposites. Hence: shame and the subsequent need to cover themselves with clothes, that is, new shells or coagulations.

But the principle of binary perceptions is carried out further, and the whole Adam-Protoplast crumbles into cells that become both more compact and surrounded by shell bodies, the more differentiation advances.

The power and the authority of Sephira Chokmah and the subtlety of its content - the souls -cell-souls – are not the inferior astral, such as the elements of the Daath legion, but of what we now call Matter.

These cells become subject to time and space and this is their bondage. They broke away from the Higher Current, but became slaves of Space and Time. Due to these changes, the sephirotic scheme of the Universe, transforms itself from "Institutio" (Figure 45) into "Destitutio" (Figure 47), disorganisation, disaggregation.

What could the upper Sephiroth do, whose harmony was affected by the fall of the Souls?

The collectivity of the Angels, generating entities called "Spiritus Directors" spreads through its influence on all the astral sub-planes. Imbued with its involving task, it generates elementals, thus penetrating into Malkuth, since the elementals have material bodies that constitute the physical basis of the Universe.

There is a popular expression stating that Angels materialise the Kingdom (Malkuth) so that the astral devils cannot rejoice there.

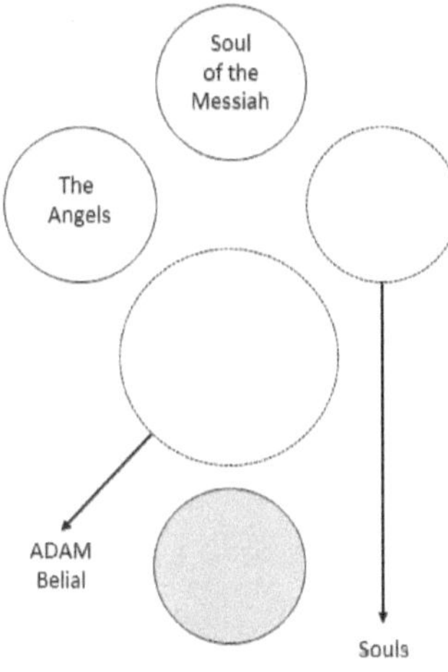

Figure 47

Scheme of the second and final phase of the Destitute Epoch. Here, Keter is called the "Soul of the Messiah".

The content of Keter, the "Soul of the Messiah," being androgynous, spreads throughout the region of Microprosopo, recreating the Sephira, in order to later fertilise Malkuth through a redemptive Atonement Incarnation. This is the plan represented by the scheme called "CONSTITUTIO" (Figure 48).

Below "Adam Belial" in Figure 48 are indicated angels and souls in the Scheme of the Constituted Epoch

So - the Influx of the Incarnation of the Messiah should give an impetus to the Souls, awaken them from sleep within matter, cause them to evolutionary effort, fully armed with their three-planes, giving them magical superiority over the fallen Daath (the latter can manifest itself in the physical world only with the possibility of mediumistic loans).

Souls, striving for Reintegration into the Sephira Chokmah, will progressively thin not only their shells, but also the whole Sephira Malkuthh, in which they work. And, following the Wife (Malkuth), the Husband - fallen Daath - rises as well. In this way, the Souls work, in order to realise the ideal, the so-called "RESTITUTIO", or restoration of the primordial state of the sephirotic system of the Second Family.

Now let's take a look at the history of fallen Humanity.

The fall did not happen instantly; the compaction and thickening of the shells of fallen Humanity also occurred gradually being accompanied by the progressive oblivion of past perfection and the slow adaptation to the new deplorable condition. Obviously, it should be assumed that different individuals, i.e. in different Adam Protoplast cells, this forgetting and adaptation came at different speeds.

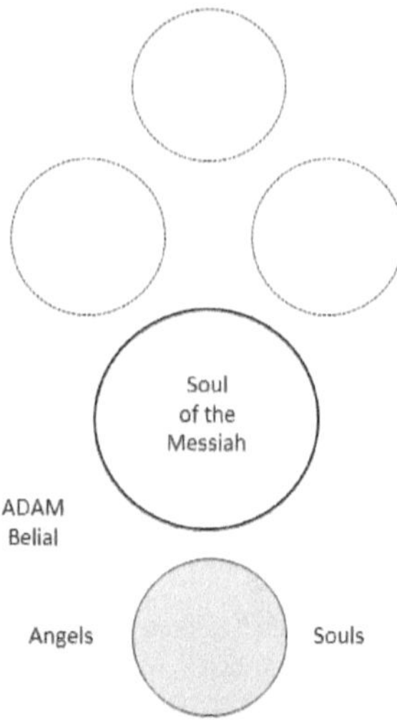

Figure 48

Constituted Epoch

We now need to consider what can be forgotten and what cannot be forgotten from past greatness.

Imagine the period when fallen humanity visibly lost the ability to receive the influence of the ' of the First Family, but still retained the receptivity to the less transcendental reflexes. At that time, the memory of the past - religion - was expressed by the worship and abstract veneration of the first ה of the First Family, that is, the cult of the Great Principle of One Life. Naturally, the adherents of this religion occupied an incomparably higher position than those of the adherents of the various practical philosophies, modern, such as the struggle for life, etc. But nevertheless the religion of the One Life is shadowed in comparison with the religion of Transcendental Love, illuminating the Protoplast before His fall.

We will not deal here with the continent where the relatively happy adherents of the One Life are, nor will we make chronological assumptions about the corresponding epoch. For us, this is not the essential. However, it is necessary to make a slight outline of what constituted the ethical-natural code of the followers of this religion.

They respected the One Life in all its manifestations. For them, the same Life flowed with its powerful force both through the mineral, a blade of grass, the smallest specimen of the animal kingdom, as through the human being. They had not yet lost their understanding of the evolutionary power of Life (after all, Souls originally from Sephira Chokmah) and therefore very much loved and appreciated it, considering as good everything that collaborated with the flow of Life, and as evil, everything that would contradict it.

Here is the form in which the Tradition gives us their practical Commandments:

1. To confess the metaphysical principle of One Life.
2. Do not fractionate this Life metaphysically, that is, do not multiply it in mental principles.
3. Do not fractionate it astrally, that is, do not apply the mystery of the dynamic cycle in the direction diverging from the usual hierarchical direction.
4. Do not obscure it, destroying in physical terms the memory of the emmanational origin of all life.
5. Respect those who gave you Life (including the parents on the physical plane).
6. Pass life yourself chastely and consciously.
7. Do not attempt an individual life on the physical plane.
8. Do not encroach on property related to the life of an individual in the physical plane.
9 and 10. Do not encroach on the astral plane against what is connected with some individual Life, neither passively (9) by lying, nor actively (10) with envy.

Let us now turn to the second period of human fall and the second possible religion.

Although humanity at that time had already lost its clear understanding of Transcendental Life, it had not yet abandoned the idea of the Logos, the Great Architect of the Universe. At this stage of the fall there was no longer an intuition of the unity of Life, but the understanding of the unity of the Sources of Ideals had still been maintained. Since all ideals are generated by the Logos, there could be no opposition between them. At the moment of difficulties, at the moment of choosing decisions, at the moment of possible disappointments, an adherent of the religion of the Logos calls for help to Him, asks for alms in the form of an ideal that could save him.

In the next stage of the fall, the image of the Logos is erased from human hearts, but remains still the image of the second ה (Knave) of the

First Family, that is, the ideals themselves. There is no one to turn to for ideals; but if you are ready, you can try to escape. Belief in the second ה of the First Family smoothly descends to the level of the Macroprosopo Religion of the Second Family (its Top Point over the י).
And then?
And then the Transcendental religion of the Father of the Second Family will come down, which boils down to the memory of the Sephira Chokmah, about the presence and permanence in her of all Souls - cells of a single unique being, the Adam Protoplast.
This religion will be a clear understanding of the principle of human Brotherhood with the loss of consciousness of the Brotherhood of Man with entities of involutive types (Angels). After all, at this stage Keter is forgotten, and therefore forgotten that Chokmah and Binah are its two manifestations, which must carry out the circular cycle of Life of the Second Family in fraternal and friendly work, the work of the Life Cycle of the Second Family.
And if you lose the understanding of the Brotherhood? Then the situation becomes dangerous; sometimes egoism begins to reign, leading to anarchist manifestations, up to veneration of the legion of dark forces, up to the struggle with the normal formula of dynamic evolutionary processes, up to the exchange of one's personality with a legion of passions, strictly analogous to the legion of demons of the lower astral. Humanity as a whole, as well as for individual races and nationalities, has experienced, is and will continue to experience the listed types of religions and, unfortunately, even the phase of anarchic fractionation of individuals described at the very end of the list.
Of course, the task of Reintegration seemed most clearly and conveniently fulfilled in that era when the simple, but deeply wise Primitive Religion of One Life did not manage to get lost or distorted. Whatever the temptations that have torn off most of Humanity from it, it is certain that the loss of the majority was immediately followed by the reaction of attempts to return Humanity to ancient wisdom by preaching. The reactionaries - champions of a return to the old worldview - quite rightly called themselves Initiates, and those who fell from the cult of One Life - profane. The first, in fact, had preserved, a certain contact with the pure reflex of the first ה while the second had obscured and distorted it, or in other words profaned it. The former were not saints; they also fell as Protoplastic cells, but, nevertheless, remained indirectly touched by holiness, as if preserving its reflection.
Their attempts to return Humanity to the true path resulted in more or less complex schemes, depending on the degree of decline in their environment, and subsequently on the living conditions of the ethnic

groups that made up this environment. These attempts can be called by a common name: "Foundation of Religions".
Frequently, the Teachers who instituted the religions, dealt with an environment where most people were on the verge of losing even the conception of the Human Fraternity, this is, to lose the memory of Sephira Chokmah. Therefore, the Instructors should:

1. Remind men of the Brotherhood of Souls.
2. Reestablish the understanding of the great involutive-evolutionary flow, that is, of Jacob's Ladder, in which, on the left side descend the Angels (Binah), by the right ascend the Souls (Chokmah) whilst the Radiant Macroprosopus (Sephira Keter) always remains on his throne.
3. Establish respect for Teachers, whose role is analogous to the second ה of the first family, which, mysteriously and by emanation, transmits the higher influx via emanations to the second family.
4. To lead men to lose their proud pretension of wanting to transform the Universe according to their personal comfort and convince them of the necessity of the contrary, that is, from the hermetic transformation of one's own personality, shaping it to resemble - albeit quite remotely - the Logos' androgynous-harmonic image.
5. Seek to purify the characters, in the name of the first ה of the first family, that is, try to get human beings to understand and apply the One Life guidelines outlined above.
6. To work so that humanity, purified by the True Religion, may again become able to receive the Influx of the י to subtilise its shells and, having raised the Sephira Malkuth and his Spouse (the Micropospo), to recreate for himself the Collective Oneness, that is, the Adam Protoplast, inside the Sephira Chokmah. This would constitute the full reintegration of Humanity, restoring the Oneness of Adam Protoplast in the Sephira In order for these goals to be achieved, the Initiates realised and performed the Arcanum of Force, joining in currents controlled by egrégoric principles.
The mental nuclei of these egrégores, in essence, have always been reduced and are reduced to the principles of the Unified Primordial Religion, carried out in their entirety or in private groups. The astral part of the egrégore is born when the mental principles, mentioned, are involved with a form. The physical body of the egrégore corresponds to the manifestation of worship on the physical plane. Of course, the "physical body" of the egrégore depends strictly on its astrosome and on the environment in which religion is founded and on which nourishes the same egrégore, manifesting itself in different countries, can give birth to many different cults.

Based on these data, we will deduce that the foundation of a religion can be compared to the formation of a collective whirlwind. The activity of this whirlwind will depend on the dynamics of its י ה ו ה cycles. Of these cycles, the most important for us is the first, the one that begins in the Point above the י. However, it should not be forgotten that religion, so to speak, "embodies" with the purpose of finding, for itself, adepts; because of this, it must have, in addition to elements of the dynamic cycle י ה ו ה, some kind of "magnet" (ש), capable of winning followers or, in other words, facilitating the penetration and dissemination on the physical plane. This one "magnet", besides attracting to egrégore those who are in tune with it, should also serve as a "bond" to retain those whose pentagram would be tempted to break the link already established and move away from the egrégore.

Thus the first cycle of a religious whirlwind can be expressed by the formula יהשוה (Point-Iod-He-Shin-Vau-He) and defined as materialisation of the total or partial aspect of the teaching of the One Source of Truth, in order to spiritualise a given environment.

The symbolism of the terms of the first cycle of a religious whirlwind can be explained by the following scheme, which could also be called the "plan" of a religion:

1. The Point above the י corresponds to the purposes of the creation of an egrégore. These must be selfless, in the broadest sense of the word.

2. The י corresponds to the metaphysical content, which is a general or particular reflection of the One Philosophy.

3. The first ה is constituted by the state and the conditions of the environment in which the religion is founded.

4. The ש is the aspect of the egrégore capable of attracting and retaining adepts.

5. The ו and the cult itself - the child of the environment - fertilised by the principle of Esoteric Oneness.

6. The second ה represents the final link of the first cycle, linking the preceding elements in a family and determines the influence of this family, that is, the influence of the whole current on the external world. This link can be called the "politics" of a religion. Let us now ask ourselves what elements are needed to form a living, egregious current. These elements are:

1. Point above י, that is, the existence of a scheme of egrégoric ideas and forms.

2. י - the person of the Instructor, possessing a mystical and astral power.

3. First ה - a prepared environment.

4. שׁ - the possession, by the chain, of a certain contingent of concrete facts or astral clichés to ensure proselytism and provide a guarantee against a schism or away from his followers.
5. ו - a set of valuable disciples around the Instructor.
6. According to ה - a community of good believers.

We will not go into details about the astral birth of the egrégore. We will discuss this in Arcanum XV. The conditions necessary for the "life" of an egrégore, the causes of its "illness" or "death" have already been mentioned in broad outlines. Now let's just say a few words about the need to introduce, in the egrégoric current, beyond the energy of the pentagrammatic entities of an evolutionary type (living and disembodied human beings) also the energy of the elementals (Spirits, Directors and even Angels), since it should not be forgotten that egrégore uses the current involution to transmit the teaching to the Earth; only later does it help the evolution of your adepts. In popular parlance it is said that a magical current is formed of living men, dead men and elementals of various kinds.

Regarding what the personality of the Instructor-Director should look like, we can find sufficient information by studying the history of religions and their founders.

The preparedness of the environment is most often determined by its ethical (less often - material) adversities, which led it to the awareness of the need for improvement. Nations and peoples have epochs in which their own perversity or their own ignorance becomes intolerable. Then they crave religious renewal and willingly go to meet their Master.

The שׁ element most often comes down to fulfilled prophecies or so-called miracles of the Teacher and the Disciples. However, sometimes in a certain environment these elements are successfully replaced by features of the form in which religion teaches Unitary Philosophy, or even the content of philosophy itself. These rare cases require a high ethical and cultural level and, generally, guarantee the egrégore a long period of life.

The disciples fall into two categories:

1. Main Disciples, what could be called "Apostles of the Doctrine" and in its totality, should represent the four hermetic types: that of the Eagle or bold thinkers; the Lion or ardent natures; that of Man, or clear, logical and provident minds; the Bull or persevering workers.

2. Secondary Disciples who, as a whole, should be carriers of the active element (י) - love of metaphysics right up to paradox; the passive element (ה) – manifesting as intuition and extreme, almost hysterical sensitivity; the androgynous element (ו) that is, the ability to convey to others their sympathy and interest in the teaching; the ability to infuse it

and spread it by personal methods going to the point of exaggeration; the element of service (second ה) - discipline and applicability to the ethical requirements of the doctrine, up to the desire for complete self-sacrifice. As for believers, the possibility of observing and evaluating their abilities and psyche should be determined so as to be able, among them, to choose as disciples those who stand out from the general level and can actively serve the egrégore. It is very dangerous to not to bring closer to the Initiation Centre those cells of the body of the Chain whose energy is manifested consciously and with due intensity. It is as dangerous as artificially inhibiting the flow of healthy blood to nourish the noblest organs of any individual.

In conclusion, we will speak about the dangers that threaten religion and the nature of the machinations of these enemies. A finished or emerging religion can be undermined in three ways.

Mentally, religion is ruined by a mixture of scholastics[28] in its theology. This is an involution of the ideological part of religion.

In the astral plane, religion is undermined by an admixture of aesthetic principles in its formal ritual. The pursuit of the beauty of symbols undermines their purity. This is an involution of forms of ritual use.

In physical terms, religion is undermined by an admixture of sensory (emotional) manifestations authorised by its code. Remember the historically confirmed fragility of cults that encouraged sensual manifestations at religious festivals – they did not have a long life.

Now I begin to review the most important Teachings in chronological order, and dealing mainly with their etiology, only occasionally resorting to historical references to facts.

Krishna (3150 B.C.)

Analysing the egrégore of Krishna's religion according to our scheme, we have:

י - Metaphysical decomposition of the Unit into a Ternary and the construction of a descending triangle, similar to the ascending one. In general - the scheme of the Solomon Star.

First ה is a people, tired of the sensual nature of the cult of the goddess Kali, longing for a renewal of morals, praying for ideals.

ש - a guarantee of the fencing of the acquired degree of humanity and comfort by the Great Thesis, so far dear to all Hindus: "matter is an

---

[28] Tomberg is keen to defend scholasticism, urging in Letter XIX, The Sun: "Do not scorn Medieval scholasticism…to it we owe a number of masterpieces of thought – thought in the light of faith." It is through scholastic study, he says, in reference to St Thomas Aquinas, that "The believing thinker thus became a seeing mystic."

illusion; suffering and misfortune in the physical plane is also an illusion; enjoyment in the same plane is three times an illusion; reality is higher; look for them in the astral and in mental plane. "

ו - the cult is reduced to admiration of Krishna, to perpetuation of his memory, to outpourings thankful to him.

The second ה is the policy of centralisation, strict hierarchy, caste divisions.

The strongest elements are ש and partly the second ה.

The weak point is the first ה, for when the people rested from the cult of Kali, their gratitude to Krishna became less intense. The second ה partly also showed its negative aspects - caste isolation caused a number of abuses, tormented the people, and ultimately caused a reaction in the form of the emergence of Buddhism.

Fo-Hi (China 2950 BC)

י is the same as with Krishna, only with the Chinese names for the vertices of the triangle.

First ה - the Chinese, who knew how to suffer, endure hardship, full of submission to fate and love of work.

ש - the charm of the Mystery surrounding the past and present of the highest adherents of the school, their lifestyle and the cult itself.

ו - the cult of the Ancestors and the Past, vividly illustrating the thesis: "the grandfather was the Initiate of the father, the father - the Initiation of the son; the century before last was wiser than the past, the past - wiser than the present."

The second ה is a hierarchy, built, so to speak, as a pyramid. A complex system of scientists and initiatives, representatives of which had the opportunity everywhere and in everything to use their prerogatives.

The Egrégore's positive element was ו.

The danger was represented by both ה in their interdependence.

Hermes Trismegistus (Egypt)

The names of Hermes, Thoth, Enoch personify the harmoniously synthetic three-plane system of metaphysics, developed by Egyptian adepts in the depths of the Sanctuaries of the Temples of Memphis and Thebes.

This system served as an element of the י religion, whose egrégore managed to maintain its manifestations in the physical plane for about thirty centuries in a row.

The environment that he had to fertilise, in other words - the first ה scheme of religion, consisted of cowardly slaves who inhabited the Nile valley and were mainly interested in the issue of the crop, on which the whole structure of their life depended.

Such a composition of believers, of course, forced the priests to support the prestige of religion to discover their realisation power in the form of what the profane call "miracles." Less developed elements took these miracles into account as a sure sign of the friendship of priests with the Divine, and more intelligent and thoughtful believers - as evidence of Shkola's understanding of the laws of Nature and the ability to apply them. In both cases, the need for egrégore's confession and humility to the priests, who somehow influenced the country's food conditions, was clearly outlined. The miracles of the priests, in all probability, boiled down, first, to showing tricks based on knowledge of physics, chemistry, personal and ceremonial magic, psychurgy, etc.; secondly - to manipulations with atmospheric electricity - from a simple indication of particular effects to managing its overall distribution over a very large space. There is almost no doubt that, in electrostatics, the ancient Initiates stood far above current experts. Much in history makes us believe that the knowledge of the priests in this area made it possible for them to actively intervene in meteorological phenomena. But what could be more important than this for the agricultural people?

So, it is clear that ש religion was precisely in these miracles.

ו egregoric scheme, i.e. the cult itself varied by epoch and locality, but in general it came down to showing the individual facets of the doctrine and hiding its overall picture. Not only were the people limited in their right to possess the meaning of one or another myth, but Initiates of various degrees received strictly defined portions of revelation and were greatly constrained in the subplanes of the interpretation of the latter. The distant prehistoric moments of the life of Egypt more clearly formulated the unitary theory by the cult of the god "Ptah" and the memory of King Menes, who was reborn in the "Osiris-Hammon". Then the centre of Initiation was Memphis. But we know little about these times. For us, the era of the establishment of the Mysteries of Isis (2703 BC) with the transfer of the centre to Thebes is unfolding more typically. Isis instead of Osiris, the female pole instead of the male or, more precisely, instead of the Great Androgyne (Ptah). This fact alone indicates a fear of the invasion of neighbouring cults, mainly the rude-sensual cult of Astarte. The cult of Isis exoterically had to resemble other female cults and thereby insure the people from their invasion. On the other hand, the mythological part of the Isis cult carefully and skillfully symbolised and interpreted the Unitarian turner in the form of a descending triangle.

Osiris is killed by an evil genius (Typhon Set), cut into twelve parts and scattered across the four countries of the horizon (the birth of a duodener from a quaternary, the Sun because of our sins, because of our immersion in matter cannot fatherly accept us into its fold; it only can pour its vibes on us from afar in stages of the twelve zodiac Signs). Faithful Isis tries to collect the remains of her husband to restore their unitarity; but she can only create an astral cliché of this unitarity - a plan for possible reintegration into the Solar Centre; this plan will not be implemented by her, but by her son Horus, [the generation of] this ו marriage of Osiris and Isis. The old order of things cannot be restored. His idea must be embodied in the form of a new life and reworked it in an evolutionary sense. Horus, wiping his mother's tears, tells her: "Father Osiris is the Sun of the dead, I am already the Rising New Sun." You easily interpret hermetically this parable. Influx (Osiris), reaching unhindered to the Perfect Protoplast, was exchanged when it fell on the illusory vague interests of the material plane (12). Intuition (Isis) prompts us to collect the scattered, lost pieces of Osiris: we will have to collect them in the directions of the four winds, four hermetic virtues - *oser, se taire, savoir, vouloir* - but we will collect them only in the astral. To bring about real evolution on earth, we will have to embody the collected remains in Horus's Masonic chain, which will lead Humanity along the path of Reintegration.

Isis was not given in the open form that I quote. No, in front of her was a veil impenetrable to the layman, hiding her evolutionary significance from any evil person. Isis-Moon, at first glance, seemed like an ordinary mother-patroness of a roughly materialised moon, and only past trials could benefit from the beneficial revelations of her Mysteries.

Without dwelling on the external symbolism of the cult, well known to you, I pass to the second ה of the system, i.e. to the politics of religion. This policy came down to the justification of a strictly theocratic regime, which subsequently brought the priests to the exploitation of the people in favour of a small circle of Initiates. The discipline that guaranteed the stability of this regime was so categorical and merciless in its demands that not only neophytes were indignant in the depths of Egyptian temples but even representatives of the middle degrees of Initiation. Persistent natures fell victim to their inconsistency, their liberalism. The more flexible types humbled themselves, submitted to power, and then, in old age, with the rank of adepts of the highest degrees, they themselves confidently supported the theocratic regime and smashed its opponents. The strong points of the egrégore Thoth-Hermes were the elements of ו and י. The powerful synthesis of Unitarianism, the property of the highest Initiative Degrees, amazed and attracted with its harmony, reinforcing the core of adherents. Careful concealment of certain secrets of learning from the younger ones eliminated the possibility of abuse of consciousness or exercising power.

The weaknesses of the Egyptian theocratic system were: 1) a certain duality in the management of churches: the High Priest possessed administrative power, the Great Hierophant had mystical power; skilful balancing of these polarities ensured balance; but as soon as one of these poles took an advantage - and the machine began to act incorrectly, with strong friction, with a useless expenditure of energy; 2) the absence of the element of self-sacrifice in the members of the Initiative Brotherhood, inculcated by him with the desire for the vampirisation of the profane and for the exercise of power, promising earthly benefits. These negative aspects, together with the change in the composition of the first He, expressed in the awakening in the masses of higher needs than the desire to provide themselves with physical nutrition, led to the death of the egrégore.

We must give justice to the Egyptian School in the persistence of its efforts to support the egrégore; Egyptian theocracy was able to artificially maintain its existence in the most adverse conditions and, dying, gave herself the trouble to attend to the salvation of the element י. She passed on to posterity what we call the Tarot, or Genesis of Enoch, or the Holy Book. We will be grateful to her for this.

Zoroaster (Iran 2450 B.C.)

The י here is the astral meaning of the solar system in its active manifestations.

First ה - people provided with the nature and climatic conditions of the region but tormented by their passions and thus deeply unhappy; a lot of selfishness and what the French call veulerie[29].

ש - the bait of the passive side of the Solar Astral - a division in all its forms, as it facilitates the passage of the hardships of earthly life and guides fortune tellers in choosing paths.

ו is the cult of Mithra, the central part of which is the preaching of altruism, so vividly outlined in the traditional addresses of the Initiate to the Initiate in the Great Mysteries. The Master Magician served the neophyte with bread and said: "*Break it, eat it yourself and feed all the hungry!*" Then the neophyte was given a cup of wine, and the Master exclaimed: "*Drink yourself and give thirst to thirst!*"

The second ה came down to a liberal, but strictly Masonic policy of reviving the crowd ethically, with guarantees of the triumph of the initiative of the more Initiates.

Strengths were the first ה and ש; weak - the incompleteness of the coverage of the meanings of the mean term (Miter) of the Great Turner

---

[29] spinelessness

of the Light Scale "Hormuzd - Mithra - Ahriman" and the resulting apparent binary (Manichaean) course of religion. Only the priests owned the Turner School; the people were fond of the antagonism of the poles of Good (Ormuzd) and Evil (Ahriman), which subsequently allowed unscrupulous Mage people to terrorise the people in the name of the dark pole and allow themselves abuses, which ultimately undermined the egrégore in the physical plane.

Orpheus (1580 B.C.)

The main phase of the revelations of the Thracian Orpheus is the story of the birth of Zeus-Androgynus son of Dionysus - the god of One Life. The development of this thesis led to what we would now characterise as the birth of Art by father-Love and mother-Mind. That is why I define the term ׳ of the Orpheus religion as the ideal of life in the Tiphereth Sephira with the aim of perceiving its beauties (I note the passive nature of this aspiration).
The first ה turned out to be the environment of people who loved the body and therefore transferred to its forms the astral knowledge it taught from the passive side.
The ש element was the promotion of the grand aesthetic.
The cult of ו resulted mainly in religious festivals full of fun and aesthetics.
Second ה, i.e. deliberate politics, this religion just didn't get enough and the garden died just because they forgot to fence it off. The cult materialised, the sensual mixed in with the aesthetic side, the symbolism degenerated into androlatry, and the mental core of the egrégore made itself inaccessible to his later formal followers.

Moses

(Actually, Hosarsiph, son of Ramses II's sister; the pseudonym "Moses" means "taken from the water", which is symbolically equivalent to "received astral baptism"; the origin of the Teaching of Moses dates back to about 1560 BC).
Raised at the Egyptian Court, Moses, of course, had the opportunity to initiate in the Mystery of Isis. An exceptional circumstance in his life, namely, murder in passion, put him in a position truly tragic for the initiate. He had a choice between the death penalty, suicide or, finally, removal to the desert, the only surviving repository of the Initiation of the Black Race - the Temple of Amon-Ra. The high priest of this temple, Jethar, was famous for the cruelty of the trials to which he subjected the graduate students of Initiation.

Simply put, in Egypt it was known that no one passed the test; and since those who could not stand them were put to death, the removal to Jethar (or, as we call him in Russian, to Iophor) was considered tantamount to suicide. But then Moses was lucky: a prophetic dream, opening to him the prospect of a victorious exit from Egypt at the head of an entire nation of which he was supposed to be the guardian of Tradition, of course prompted him to choose the third of three evils, as leaving at least a weak hope for the possibility of remaining alive and justifying the cliché of the prophetic sleep.

And here is Moses at Jethro. There, he liked the daughter of the terrible Lord of the Sanctuary, the damsel Sephorah. She set out to have him as her husband and rescued him with the most dangerous of trials - an alternative to choosing one of two identical-looking goblets of wine. Hiding behind the curtain, she managed to point the neophyte to one of the goblets in which the wine had not been poisoned. The saved Moses successfully passed the rest of the trials and, having successfully completed the school of the Initiative Degrees of the Black Race, he married Sephora and became an employee of her father. Returning subsequently to Egypt on a legal basis, he already felt a sufficient supply of knowledge, astral and mystical power and self-confidence in himself to fulfil the mission that was once announced to him in a dream.

Around 1560, he launched all his theurgical and magical resources to influence the pharaoh and the Egyptian priests, on the one hand, and to unite the Jews with an element of trust, on the other hand.

The application of our scheme to the egrégore of Moses gives the following table.

The point above ' is the idea of transmitting the synthesis of two Traditions (Egyptian and Black Race) in their metaphysical part.

' is the true Religion of Unitarianism, revealed boldly in full by the metaphysics of the Teachings of Hermes Trismegistus. I want to say by this that Moses, through his Initiation Books and oral Kabbalistic comments, opened to the Priests and other Levites the full possibility of a wide Initiation in the mentioned area.

Moreover, he was not afraid to proclaim Monotheism to the profane; everything he said to the people was truthful and frank. Not everything was revealed to everyone from the Dogma of the Doctrine of יהוה אלהים, (Adonay Elohim) but that which was revealed was absolutely true. I repeat that this remark applies only to the metaphysics of Egyptian Hermeticism: magic realisation secrets, of course, were masked by the widespread use of symbolism, and sometimes, perhaps, were hushed up. It was important for Moses to guarantee the transmission of the Tradition in the possibly undistorted form.

The first ה egrégore, that is, the medium into which Moses had to plant this Doctrine turned out to be a people with a typical inclination towards a materialistic worldview, exploitation of both near and distant, to some cowardice, as a direct consequence of this materialism and, to all this, with extreme variability in moods, depending from successes and failures in the physical plane.

The element of ש in the egrégore, accordingly, was the widespread use of all sorts of realisation effects of Theurgic and magical origin, which made up the glory of Moses. Due to the need for the presence of these effects, many elementals and elementaries of various subplanes entered the egregoric chain. These principles greatly complicated the management of the chain, but guaranteed the impression of fear and respect for the power of egrégore, on the one hand, gratitude and hope for egregoric power, on the other. Not only did the Master master techniques for controlling the elements and population of the astral, but his closest assistants were also dedicated to the secrets of Kabirov. I recommend that you read Stadelmann's article "Die Elektrotechnik in der Bibel", which tries to justify this remark, at least in relation to Kabir electricity.

The ו element of the egregorical scheme is naturally the Cult of the One God with the consequent moral necessity of the veneration of the Principle of One Life (this is best seen from the text of the Ten Commandments of the Law). Of course, the properties of the environment — typical features of the Jewish people — necessitated the prevalence of the Geburah principle in the formulations of ethical theses. It was too early for a people like the Jews of Moses to talk about the Kingdom of Universal Love, the triumph of Mercy, non-malignancy, etc. It was important to draw a framework restricting for the common good the freedom of manifestation of the pentagram will of individuals and groups; and restrictive activity in this direction, as you know, is the destiny of the left Sephira. In them, mainly, the life of adherents of the Moses Doctrine proceeded.

The second ה of the egrégore was a policy of isolation of the race for the sake of carrying and transmitting Tradition. This policy of isolation was carried out by the leaders of the people, sometimes even with a donation of the interests of the latter. It must be remembered that the motto of Moses was the preservation of Tradition, and not the preservation of the integrity and inviolability of the tribe; the second was an official beginning in relation to the first.

I will say a few words about the fate of the Pentateuch of Moses, as the basis of his Teaching. I do not set myself the goal of expounding all the phases of the history of this great monument: expounding it in the first part of the Rosicrucian Initiative cycle. I set out only a brief encyclopedia of Western Tradition, and therefore it is permissible for me, having jumped for many centuries, to reveal to you a panorama of the phase that the emerging Christianity has found.

In the first century before Christ, the Pentateuch of Moses, and partly the rest of the books of the Old Testament, were not even understood by the Levites, due to the loss of the last Elements of oral Initiation. This era coincides with the very question of the interpretation of the Bible, which gave rise to two warring camps. For a literal understanding of the text, many Jews have long stood; their opinions were best held by the Sadducee sect. The opposite pole was well-called the so-called. The Pharisees, who stood exclusively for the allegorical interpretation of the Law and, in their attempts to interpret this, reached widespread manifestations of arbitrariness of the personal imagination of the interpreters.

These two opposing currents have long been harmoniously neutralised by the existence of the sect of Essenes, who recognised the literal meaning of the Bible as a veil, covering from the eyes of the profane the true esoteric meaning of Scripture, accessible only to persons Initiated in the Arcana of Tarot, i.e., in that same Initiation language, which Moses transferred from the Egyptian Sanctuaries to his School. Allegorical interpretations were recognised by the Essenes as a natural transition from the literal meaning to the Initiative-hieroglyphic. You can see that the Essenes, by neutralising a certain binary, were thereby approaching the true Initiation. But I will say more - they were initiated in the full sense of the word and not only guessed the true meaning of the Bible, but also possessed its interpretation in the symbolism of the Tarot.

When Demetrius from Thaler, at the command of Ptolemy, obtained a translation of the Bible into Greek, he turned to the Essenes, as experts in the Law. They did not reveal the Initiation Secrets, but very skillfully conveyed the literal meaning, leaving behind it the role of the veil of the esoteric.

I repeat that the Apostles of Christianity found the three streams I have enumerated and, of course, were forced to reckon with their influences in various spheres.

Returning to the study of the egrégores in their chronological order, I will say a few words about Buddhism.

Buddha (Gautama-Savarthasiddh-Siddartha, 700 BC)

In the so-called Buddhist ' element is the content of the mechanism of the Ascending Triangle, conducted through the chain of all incarnations of the human person. If you like, just bear in mind the motto - "use your incarnations for self-improvement; they are not without reason given to you."

The first ה was originally an environment of Indian nationalities, exhausted by the oppression of the caste privileges of the minority, which became a source of abuse.

The powerful-comforting ש Element of this religion was the thesis of the illusory nature of matter. "Is it difficult for you in the material plane? So know that matter is an illusion and it is therefore very easy to save oneself from harm: it is worth stopping to cherish matter, become indifferent to the sufferings of the physical plane and more and more separate from it. Also dispose of it on the astral plane: free yourself from the astral personality, how you freed yourself from the physical body; get into the general mental current that will ultimately immerse you in Nirvana; this is the general task of your incarnations."

The corresponding ו cult, of course, will be, in addition to the ritual of expressing gratitude to the Delivered Teachers, that the broadest practice of the Brotherhood is a natural consequence of the desire to get rid of selfishness.

The second ה of the egrégore, of course, is the policy of the World Brotherhood, which excludes any possibility of religious wars. This is just one of the positive aspects of the egrégore, which sharply distinguishes it from many religious products of the population of the mainland of Asia, preaching the so-called holy wars. You will tell me that one of the branches of Buddhism - Lamaism - is not alien to too wide a preaching of religious self-defense and that this contradicts the general theses of Buddhist ethics. I will answer that I consider Lamaism to be a distortion of Buddhism, not suitable for the above scheme.

I pass to other egrégores.

The Templars

At the beginning of the Crusades, the marked influence of the Gnostic current in the schools of Arabia and of Palestine, served as inspiration to several Crusader expeditionaries, leading them to form one of the most powerful egrégores - the Templar Egrégore.

The point above the י of the Templar scheme was the grand ideal of creating a universal empire, perfect and balanced on all planes, and which would introduce, everywhere, the penetration of the subtle in the dense. In this empire, the Higher Influx, coming from the plane of the Mystical Power,

should give life to the Astral Power and, by instructing and governing the Director Power, to create prosperity, happiness and the possibility of evolutionary work, that is, to facilitate salvation for all classes regardless of the nationalities to which they belonged. However, they should be local customs and the conditions of national environments. This formidable The scheme included all dreams: to curb abuses of papal power, to raise and perfect all classes of human society, to develop industry and commerce worldwide and to end the loss of energy, spent on struggles between nationalities, social classes or individual struggles caused by ill will or mutual incomprehension. In short, it was the dream of realisation of the Kingdom of God on earth, cherished by conscious and intelligent men, by souls minted in chivalry and who, to do so, relied on the support of their healthy bodies and their honestly acquired wealth. The element "י", in the scheme of the Templars, consisted of the teaching of Hermes Trismegistos, breathed by the sound influence of gnosticism.

The first ה, as we have said, was constituted by the environment of the Crusaders, providing the new egrégore with its elements more capable, stronger, pure and spiritualised.

The ש element of the new chain formed from the beauty of the ideal, from the attractive perspective of the future power, at all levels, of its supporters and the possibility that they would have to use this power, in a general or particular way, in the realisation of the ideals that were dear to them.

The element ו of the Templars was constituted by what today is called "Cult of Baphomet ". The word "Baphomet", read, kabbalistically, from right to left, is the result of a particular way of adapting Notarikon (see Arcanum X) to the phrase: "*templi omnium hominum pacis abbas*" which, translated, means: "*the father of the temple of peace for all men.*" This name corresponds to a personification of the manner in which the Templars realised their ideals, and which consisted of creating, with the volitional impulses of the Current, a powerful astral swirl. Because of this, in the secret ceremonies of the Templars, an important role was played by a statue representing Baphomet, symbol of the astral swirl Nahash, of which we shall speak in the Arcanum XV.

The second ה of the Templars corresponded to the policy of theocratic character, with the preservation of hierarchical law and the principle of complete centralization. Groups of "Comendadorias" of the Templars formed "Priories"; the latter rallied to the "Great Priory"; groups of Great Priories constituted "Languages", that is, groups that used the same language. Above all Languages was the Grand Master. This, in the application of his pentagrammatic power, it was based solely on the broad Templar motto: "Mercy and Knowledge".

On these bases, in the year 1118, the Order of the Temple was formed. We have already mentioned its dissolution later, in the year 1312, by papal bull, and, prior to this, on October 13, 1307, the tragic end of the

Grand Master of the Templars, Jacques de Molay and his closest collaborators.

The powerful י and "He" elements of the Templar egrégore, along with its magnetic ש led the Order to the summit of flowering on all planes. Its enemies, envious of this success and coveting the riches of the Order - vast territories belonging to the Temple - sought ways to destroy it. Pulling back from the current's magical power, they chose a hidden weapon - the slander - attacking the " ו " of the egrégore and accusing the Templars of practicing black magic, organising orgies and worshiping Baphomet.

Tracing a real network of intrigues, they finally achieved their goal: the destruction of the Order (on the physical plane).

Can we ask what happened to the knights of the Temple who did not perish? Who risked welcoming them, being fraternal to them?

In response to this question, we must remember that, in parallel with the emergence of Templars, two other currents were created and strengthened in Europe: The Hermetic, which aspired to the "Great Work," and that of the builders of the Gothic cathedrals, called Freemasons, who professed the cult of their work, preserving traditional symbolism in architecture. These two currents approached, creating associations composed of two types of elements: workers on the mental plane and workers on the physical plane. The link that bound them was the astral world, the world of traditional initiatory symbols, enlivened by the work of Hermetists and coagulated and expressed in accessible form to the senses, by the work of the Masons.

It was these Free Masons, officially recognised by Rome in the year 1277, that decided to accept as brothers the Knights Templar, saved from the destruction of their Order, who thus became "Accepted Maçons". This refers to the physical plane, but what happened to the astrosome chain, its powerful egrégore?

The great egrégores do not dissolve because of a disaster on the physical plane. Even though by a point of support on Earth, they have the possibility of purification and perfection in the astral plane.

It could be said that the shells of these egrégores, shells that formed from the mistakes of their adepts on the physical plane, dissolve or subtlise, allowing the inner Light to appear with higher intensity. The possibility of such an improvement is a privilege only of the egrégores who, speaking in terms adopted by us, have a very pure point above י and the closed system of a powerful י very clearly determined.

The egrégore of the Templars was cleansed in the astral plane for a little more than seventy or eighty years and then gave rise to a collectivity on Earth, to which we will give the code name "Rosicrucianism of the primary type."

I do not impose on you faith in the existence of the Brotherhood, allegedly founded by Christian Rosenkreuz (1378-1484), composed of a small number of mystic virgins; I just want to defend the thesis of the fact of a distinct formation in the astral of the formal side of those ideals and those ways of perfection, about which the famous Fama Fraternitatis Rosae + Crucis interprets.

Since these ideals are registered in the form of a specific code, I have the right to state the very fact of Egregor's awakening in a much earlier era. But in what form should the egrégore of the primary Rosicrucianism be presented to us according to the mentioned composition, as well as according to Confessio Fidei R + C? - It is clearly seen that this powerful egrégore attracted the vibes of three broad, rich flows of Truth: Gnosticism, Kabbalah and Hermeticism of the Alchemical School.

The highest point of the modification of the Templar Egrégore (The Upper Point above the ʼ) was the ideal of the Theurgical Work of the Kingdom of Elias Artista, together with a firm belief in the coming of such a Kingdom in the future.

What does it mean? Who is "Artist Elias"? Where did "Elias" come from and why "Artist"?

In the Bible, Elias and Enoch are symbols of something that is brought alive into heaven. However, the direct path to the Empyrean of metaphysics is open only to the streams of Absolute Truth. The Minor Arcana of the Book of Enoch are part of such flows. Elias, in turn, is like the more concrete image of Enoch, is closer to us. Therefore, Elias and not Enoch. But what is Elijah; in what ways will he lead us to the Minor Arcana, to the Rosicrucian reintegration? Is it really by blissful, by artless hearts, by unenlightened, but infinitely simple believers "Christ for the sake" of holy fools?

No, the egrégore was not engaged in this happy, but rarely encountered category of people. He had in mind the salvation of those who had time to taste the refined taste of knowledge, of sciences and who cannot refuse the high pleasures bestowed by it. The Rosicrucian Elias leads his followers to the Minor Arcana by painstaking, skillful analysis of the Major; he tricks, he combines; he deserves the name Artist.

The powerful ʼ with which he impregnates his followers is displayed as an immortal symbol of the Rose-Cross. In whatever frame you put this symbol, whatever overtones you provide to its main melody, it was, is and will be the same in its central part. The cross, a symbol of the path of selflessness, limitless altruism, unlimited obedience to the laws of the Highest, represents one of its poles. The rose of Hermes, the seductively fragrant symbol of Science, proud of its three-pronged completeness, wraps around this Cross. Those who are familiar with it can wear the Cross but are not able to tear the Rose from it. Let her thorns prick scientists, they will not cease to enjoy its aroma. Rose is the second pole of the binary.

The task of the Rosicrucian is to neutralise this binary. An adherent of Rosicrucianism should neutralise Self-Renunciation and Science in person; combine them in the self and be in service of one ideal, become like the third symbol placed in the considered pantaculo at the foot of the Cross + Rose: There is a Pelican with wide wings, feeding its own meat and blood to its chicks in a fit of parental sacrifice. In the emblem, the chicks of the Pelican are of different colours.

In the primitive emblems there were only three chicks, symbolising the three Primordial Causes; in the later emblems there are seven, symbolising the seven Secondary Causes, each of the chicks being of a different planetary colour. This indicates that the sacrifice must be made according to the science of colours, that is, each one of the chicks needs a specific treatment.

Here is the true Rosicrucian י meditation.

The first ה of this Rosicrucianism, of course, was the environment of a very few selected natures, inclined to combine mysticism with subtle intellectual aspirations.

The ש of the Rosicrucian scheme took on a certain self-appreciation, even self-worship, as a consequence of being considered as chosen instruments. There were so few people, capable of satisfying these demands, that the conviction of superiority introduced itself. It was accentuated further by the severe rules of Rosicrucian lifestyle ethics, which the elect introduced into the life.

The worship - the element ו - was expressed by meditation on symbols, especially on the great pantaculo of the Rose + Cross and partly by the mystical ceremonies during the meetings of the Rosicrucians.

The second ה School was the policy of secrecy of the personalities of the Rosicrucians themselves, striving to anonymously realise all that the conscience of adherents considered to be conducive to the progress of Mankind, both in the field of ethics and in the field of intellect. In this second ה we see the shells of the Templars, which did not have time to dissolve in the pure astral plane. One can see the hatred of the Roman Church, reaching the formal generation of the elements of Protestantism (in the Fama Fraternitatis and Confessio, the Pope is equated with the Antichrist; only two Sacraments are recognised, etc). Of course, sharp manifestations against Rome should be recognised as a reflection of the astral revenge on Clement V.

The primary Rosicrucianism could not naturally count in its ranks many adherents: too many had to combine opposite traits in order to go to its ideals without breaking away from its developed form. Later, in the sixteenth century, from the initial School, gradually emerges what could be called "Secondary Rosicrucianism". If the first was only accessible to a very few chosen ones, the second could be followed by all conscious men. while the former tyrannically imposed certain forms of self-improvement on its adherents, the latter was distinguished by extreme tolerance in all areas accessible to the mind and heart.

The highest point over the ׳ and the ׳ element itself remain the same. The first ה has noticeably changed. The environment, fertilised by the Rosicrucian ideas in the 16th, 17th and partly in the 18th centuries, was an aggregate of encyclopedists in the broadest and best sense of the word. It required only the versatility in intellectual aspirations, the ability to scientifically speculate, the breadth of views and devotion to the idea of good. This included highly mystical natures, and inveterate pantheists, and people of practical aspirations. But, I repeat, only people who were remarkable in their intelligence and erudition, who had personal will and certainty in their views on the coming Humanity, were taken. *

THE PUBLICATION OF THE SHIN ELEMENT WAS NOT AUTHORISED BY MASTER G.O. MEBES[30].

The element of ו was the ritual of Initiation of the members of the Chain in the degree of Rosicrucianism, defined in general terms, but with differences between different schools, the ritual formalities of the general meetings of the Supreme Teacher Councils of one or another branch of the egrégore; if you want, this includes the methods of astral processing and training of the personality, which have joined the main process of meditation and are borrowed for the most part from different Eastern schools.

---

[30] We have naturally mused long and hard on the possible essence of the Shin teaching which G.O.M. prohibited as far as publication of his book was concerned, but which he must have revealed to his inner circle. As the aspect of Shin described in the preceding section on the original Rosicrucian organisation related to the character of involved individuals, it seems possible that the same rule applies in this second part. Could it be related to the emergence of an individual who embodied the Shin force with either positive or negative (good or bad) results? Names which spring to mind in this context include Sabbatai Zevi (or those of his school) and Rasputin, though clearly there is a significant time difference between these two. Perhaps it is connected with a branch of black magic which G.O.M. does not wish to strengthen by revealing one of its entrances or touched dangerously on the contemporaneous political situation in Russia. We are only speculating here, and have also considered that Shin was repressed in this section of the Arcana because of its proximity to the Holy of Holies and united relationship between the Divine and enlivened Human Wills, which may be signified by the four-pronged Shin, wherein the fourth prong of the 'fork' represents the human being connected with the 'three pronged' fire of the Holy Trinity. In fact this was our initial thinking on the matter, which would make a good subject for further advanced study of the Arcana.

The second ה of the system under study became a special policy of influencing society, firstly of a purely ethical nature, and later on, of a strongly implementing one. The divisions and subdivisions of the Second Rosicrucianism had different political mottos in different eras. These mottos dealt with the next major political or religious reform. But the Templar Egrégore, the bearer of the edifying cliché of the fall of the Jacques de Molay chain in the physical plane, vibrated to caution every time the Rosicrucianism was about to take one or another decisive step, and inspired it to the adherents of the scheme of the surest and safest way to influence society. The result of one of these vibrations was the foundation of the so-called "Masonic Order".

The thin astral of the Rosicrucianism, very suitable for Teaching, could get confused in solving practical issues, could show a lack of tact in the field of juggling with everyday conditions, could suffer essentially from a direct encounter with the trifles of everyday life. And so, a corporeal shell has been created, the soul of which is Rosicrucianism, but which is hardened in everyday affairs and is not afraid of hard work. This shell is Freemasonry - I mean the Orthodox Freemasonry of the Scottish ritual with an ethical-hermetic interpretation of Traditional Symbolism. It will preserve the very symbols, maintain in its midst and in public respect for the symbols themselves and their interpreters - the Rosicrucians, and, based on this respect, inspire everyone and everyone that a good example of the relative purity of Masonic manners has as its starting point the very content of the Initiation Teachings.

Freemasonry carried out the reforms decided by the Rosicrucians, protecting them, with their own people, against possible hostility and human persecution on the physical plane.

The founders of Freemasonry, among which Elias Ashmole (1617-1692) occupies a prominent place, with great skill adapted for its use, the system of the Masons Free degrees, making it the basis of his own first three degrees, the "symbolism", of Initiation Freemasonry. This work began in 1646, and in 1717 there was already a fully organised system of Chapters of the Scottish Masonry.

Thus Freemasonry has become an indispensable tool in the work of the Rosicrucian Enlightenment, whose "politics" (the "Second He") received the name "Mason", a name that it kept so far. The effects of Rosicrucian policy, achieved by Freemasons in the external world, were called "cannon shots". Among other such "cannon shots" were considered the religious reforms of Luther and Calvin, as well as the liberation of the United States of North America from the British dependence (Lafayette and its official Masons). The Rosicrucian used the Masons, especially since among them they chose those who deserved to be initiated into Christian Enlightenment.

However, each medal has its reverse. While Freemasonry was an organisation submitted to Rosicrucianism, while practicing the principle of Hierarchical Succession by transmission, it did its job and there were no problems. Unfortunately, several very strong branches resolved to introduce the method of electing its leaders, thus rejecting the traditional hierarchical principle. As a result, the Masonic work began to change its character and, from evolutionary, it became almost revolutionary. An important moment in this new direction was the dissent of Lacorne and his followers (in 1773) who, in a split, separated themselves from legitimate Masonry and founded a new association that became known under the name of "Grand Orient of France".

With this we will conclude our brief sketch on Freemasonry and move on to the end of the XVII century, to analyse one of the currents, still existing, of the old Christian Enlightenment.

Around the year 1760, the famous Martinez de Pasqualis (or Pasqually) founded a fraternity of "Servants of the Sacred," the "Elus Cohen," with nine hierarchical degrees. The three degrees were Rosicrucian.

The School of Martinez was a magician-theurgist, with a strong predominance of purely magical methods. After the death of Martinez, his two favorite disciples, J. B. Willermoz and Louis Claude de Saint Martin, altered the character of this Chain.

Willermoz gave him Masonic colouring and Claude de St. Martin, a writer known under the pseudonym "Le Phil. Inc." sent the Chain to the mystical-theurgical side. Contrary to Willermoz, he favored a liberal initiation and not the rules of the Masonic lodges.

The Influence of Saint-Martin predominated and gave rise to a movement called "Martinism." The egrégore of the original Martinism, which had its own Freemasonry and was firmly incarnated in all European countries (for Martinism in Russia, see Longinov's book Novikov and Moscow Martinists, Moscow, 1867), was composed approximately according to the following scheme:

The highest point over ׳ is reconciliation with oneself in the ethical field. ׳ is a spiritualistic philosophy of the works of de Saint-Martin, which varied somewhat during different periods of his life.

The first ה consisted of a set of very pure and disinterested people, possessing more or less pronounced mystical aspirations, people ready for any philanthropic work.

The ש element, in fact, was not, probably depending on the nature of the first ה. Pure idealists do not need magnets to bait fans, since they aspire to an internal reconciliation with conscience.

The ו element boiled down to a very simple ritual of prayer and the initiation ceremony, distinguished by its extreme simplicity. Among the Freemasons of the Martinists were some who gave more importance to the ritual and this, in certain lodges, became even imposing by its magnificence; however, we now emphasise pure, independent Martinism of any Masonic addition. In Martinism all value was given to meditation, to formation of the "Man of Aspiration" and not to the magical environment, as was the case in "Martinism" or "Willermozism."

The second ה of old Martinism was the philanthropic impulses of its members, the inexpressible help of the poor and dejected, the lack of desire to cheat when confronted with external influences and the kind of steady modesty that greatly impressed all layers of modern Martinism of society. The Martinist Initiation during the period of the First Empire and subsequent eras until the 80s of the 19th century, whilst transmitted by a very tenuous link, on the other hand, counts in its ranks very respectable persons (Chaptal, Delage, Constant). In the 80s, the well-known Stanislav de Guaita (Stanislas de Guaita) started an attempt to update the esoteric movement and created the "The Kabbalistic Order of the Cross + Rose" (Ordre Kabbalistique de la Rose + Croix) according to the following scheme:

The point over י is the reconciliation of the Academic Official Science with the Complex of esoteric teachings available to our time, with the aim of fruitful joint work of representatives of both movements.

י is a synthesis of all the Traditions available to our research plus a set of experimental techniques that have arisen in recent times and is greatly facilitating many ways of research.

Unfortunately, the first ה again turned out to be the environment of encyclopedists, but of unsuccessful encyclopedists In our era, capable people move quickly in their specialty and often do not have time to develop diversely in others; people who are disappointed in their special careers sometimes push themselves into encyclopedia with this very disappointment, which allows them to scatter in class and appear to the superficial observer as multifaceted intellectuals, thus resembling the really exceptional people as were the members of early Rosicrucianism. The Shin element of the new egrégore was a seductive prospect for equal rights with the recognised leaders of academic science by virtue of their Rosicrucian privileges.

The element of ו was the work of reprinting, translating and commenting on classical works of occultism, which by that time had become bibliographic rarities, almost unaffordable for the price of even a wealthy man in the street. In this regard, the Paris Rosicrucians brought many benefits to lovers of the occult and deserve the greatest gratitude from all who honor the great monuments of the Traditions.

The worst element of the system was the "Second He", manifested as a political opportunist, in order to attract the university world. The traditional theses, in their explanation, were altered to make them agree with the latest scientific works, thus losing their value. The commitment of certain Rosicrucians to obtain the approval of representatives of official science, naturally impaired the prestige of the School. On the other hand, attempts by a part of the membership, to mitigate the Rosicrucian theses in order not to run counter to the Roman Church, led to a split within the School itself (the removal of Péledan[31]). In general, still in the time of Stanislas de Guaita, the situation became precarious. Therefore, an attempt was made to approach Freemasonry, which, misrepresenting the purposes of the Order, precipitated its fall. It still exists, but rather weakened.

In parallel with the formation of the Kabbalistic Order of the Cross + Rosa, Guaita made an attempt to revive the initiatory movement on a large scale, which we examined under the name of Martinism. The "Neo-Martinism" of S. de Guaita, became quite different from the initial stream; however, Neo-Martinism adopted the Martinist ritual of Initiation to the degree of S - I ... and in this ritual he based his symbolism. The ideals of Louis Claude de St. Martin and the internal formation of the "Man of Desire" could not satisfy the energetic Guaita, who was too drawn to the visible results. He did not voluntarily Interrupt external activity, even when necessary to magnetise the environment. In the works of Stanislas de Guaita there are often ironic words about such interruptions.

So that the almost reborn egrégore of Martinez de Pasqually could bring to the new Order of the Cross + Rose adepts chosen from the most capable S::I:: of the new Martinism, it was necessary to introduce in the scheme of it a great tolerance in the dogmatic field.

The point above י of the new scheme is still the formal motto of the ethical reconciliation of man with himself.

The choice of the element י was left to the free will of each member of the Neo Martinist stream. Of course, the works of St. Martin retained their leading role.

Due to the choice of י, the ה element turned out to be the most diverse and multi-colored circles. Here, weary and tired of religious pursuit, and disappointed in academic science, and simply curious and longing for the likeness of Freemasonry, but unable to get into other associations, and ambitious in the field of seeking external signs of mystical power, and lovers of conversations on occult topics in crowded circles, and hysterics (the Order also allows women), always inclined to join associations, surrounding themselves with an element of mystery, and, finally, firmly aware that an uneven student chain is better for them than

---

[31] In Eliphas Levi and the French Occult Revival, Christopher McIntosh expands on the split between de Guaita and Péledan in Chapter 15, The Wars of the Roses

a complete lack of egregorical support. Since the Cross + Rosa put in their chain (and are) setting the candidates to pass the three degrees of neo-Martinism, the representatives of the latter always included several people who deserved to become teachers of the uneven Martinist chain of Hommes de desir and properly direct the development of their abilities, which should be considered the basis of the survivability of the Order, after Guaita has noticeably grown and still has a large number of adherents. At the head of the Supreme Martinist Council is now a very prominent figure in the promotion of occultism through the press, Dr. Gerard Encausse (esoteric pseudonym - Papus).

Due to the diversity in tendencies and the degree of ethical development of the members of the Martinist Chain, the Shin element is a variety of different lures. One is attracted by the ritual, the other is solidarity with the links of the Chain, the third is the possibility of expanding esoteric development, the fourth is the purity of the continuity of power in the chain of Martines de Pasqualis, etc.

The ו element, in addition to the mystical ceremonies uniting the Martinists, consisted of meditation and, facilitating these meditations, instructor's lectures addressing initiatory issues.

The second ה is a rather passive policy of waiting for the phases of ethical improvement of society and the impact on such good examples of life in good faith. Of course, it cannot be categorically affirmed that not a single Martinist circle attaches to this policy a more active element of a philanthropic or other nature. But these, I repeat, are particular phenomena, and I do not dare to introduce them into the framework of the analysis of egrégorean principles.

I will save the listeners from a detailed analysis of other current trends, but I will allow myself to cite the names of secret societies with which my venerable listeners may meet with members under certain circumstances. Without listing the Masonic rituals, except the Orthodox Scottish (33 degrees), Memphis (97 degrees), Misraim (96 degrees), French (7 degrees), I will draw your attention to the Order of the German Illuminati (philanthropy and national politics), which is close in design to the Masonic scheme, to the Asian Rosicrucians (solid acquaintance with esotericism and bold international politics), to the English Rosa Crux Esoterica (the study of esotericism and the very strictly conducted Rosicrucian ritual), and, finally, the existence of many circles of a more or less Rosicrucian type, of which some are not worth mentioning by their insignificance, while others are not allowed to be listed, due to their categorically expressed desire not to be mentioned in the press and not to remove the curtain of Strict Secret. Brotherhoods of this type call themselves in correspondence nothing more than initials, and do not reveal the names of their leaders to anyone.

Notes on the eleventh Arcanum

Tomberg also looks deeply into the mystery of fallen nature in his reflection upon the Arcanum of Force with its "waters" and its "creatures", as he reads in the Revelation of St John the origin of this "sea":

The Serpent poured water like a river out of his mouth after the woman, to sweep her away with the flood. But the earth came to the help of the woman, and the earth opened its mouth and swallowed the river which the dragon had poured from his mouth. (Revelation xii, 15-16).

Such strange waters are presented in stark contrast to the serene and stable "sea of glass" that is before the throne of God, just as one in the world might either be held in peaceful contemplation of the divine or *"swept away by an electrifying flood of passionate arguments aiming at a desired end."* Illuminated faith – as that of true Christians and true humanists - is tolerant, patient, calm and steadfast – "like crystal" – whilst *"the faith of those who are swept away is, in contrast, fanatical, agitated and aggressive."*…Nazis and communists are of this faith. The notion of being swept away with the crowd and participating in mass movements is needless to say anathema to the Christian hermetic sensibilities of the author of MotT.

The Arcanum of Force epitomises the serene illumination of the crystal sea as it resists being swept away by the flood, just as the gentle Virgin is depicted holding safe the jaws of the Lion. The Virgin is the woman clothed with the sun, with the moon at her feet who is crowned with 12 stars, she is the Virgin Sophia, who was "present in Mary and it is thus that the soul of non-fallen Nature gave birth to the divine Word" and Nature accomplished her task. As the mother of the Logos, Christ the Messiah:

She has surpassed herself, and since then the epoch of the supernatural – the epoch of divine magic – has begun. Natural religion is now flooded in the radiance ("glory") of supernatural religion, and non-fallen Nature has become a dispensator and cooperator in the miracles of the new evolution, ie, the evolution of the Second Birth. (MotT, p274)

The Force upon which he reflects is that of natural religion, of non-fallen Nature, which in turn awakens the pure virgin nature of the Lion and enables it to lie down with the lamb again. We are warned not to be caught up in polemical opposition, but to continually strive to resolve antimonies as we were taught in the ninth Arcanum. Religious and

political tolerance is called for, so agreements might be reached and conflicts averted. Militancy in all its forms is to be shunned as the electrifying – and stultifying – work of the serpent, whilst a transcendental synthesis of ideas is sought above all poles and polemics, for "it is through the fusion of opinions that truth lights up".
In the Virgin Sophia we see the Shekinah of the Zohar, the ultimate Force by which that of the serpent might be neutralised and calmed. Much is made of electricity as a manifestation of serpentine energy, a power which is "due to the antagonism of opposites, whilst life is the fusion of polarities." In her obedience to the divine will, the Virgin is the soul of life – the life force itself, which in turn wins the cooperation of the lion in his obedience to the force of his own life.
It hardly needs emphasising that a powerful devotion to the Virgin is evident not only in this reflection upon the Arcanum Force, but throughout MotT, which is dedicated to Our Lady of Chartres. An interesting biographical detail features in the eleventh Arcanum, however, in reference to the visions of Our Lady of all Nations in Amsterdam, where Tomberg lived for some time and formed a prayer group to fortify resistance during the war. It is only by donning the Mantle of the Blessed Virgin that we are able to safely traverse the 'Belt of Lies' or 'Zone of Delusion' as the Master Peter Deunov described it, otherwise known as the realm of Maya.

It is therefore the protection of this "mantle" which is absolutely necessary in order to be able to traverse the "sphere of mirages" without falling prey to the influence of its illusions. (MotT, p281).

In the blindfold of the Fool, the twenty-first Arcanum, we see an echo of this mantle, the hallmarks of which are purity and innocence deriving from Love, no less, the power by which even an enemy might not so much be made impotent, but fully transformed into a friend. As a witness to the union of Christ and Sophia, the Fool who falls – but falls in love – is given the occult name of AMOR, as we shall see in time.

Tomberg may also had in mind the split between the authoritarian de Guaita and the devoutly Catholic, artistically-inclined Péladan, briefly referred to by G.O.M in this Arcanum, when he wrote in his first Letter, Arcanum I that Christian Hermeticists:

do not have the pretension of elevating themselves above the holy faith of the faithful, or above the fruits of the admirable efforts of workers in science, or above the creations of artistic genius.

Arcanum XII

THE HANGED MAN

Pathway from Netzach to Chesed

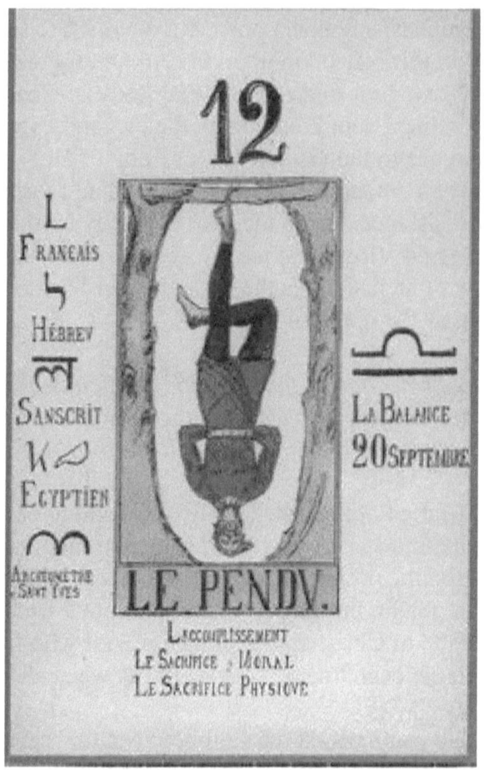

The Hanged Man has accomplished *The Great Work*

The true aim of the Great Work is to volatise the fixed after having accomplished the fixation of the volatile.

Levi

THE SACRIFICE: Violent Death

L--30 expresses in the divine world the revelation of the Law.

Paul Christian

"He chose this way himself.

"For this he went over a long road from trial to trial, from initiation to initiation, through failures and falls.

"And now he has found Truth and knows himself.

Ouspensky

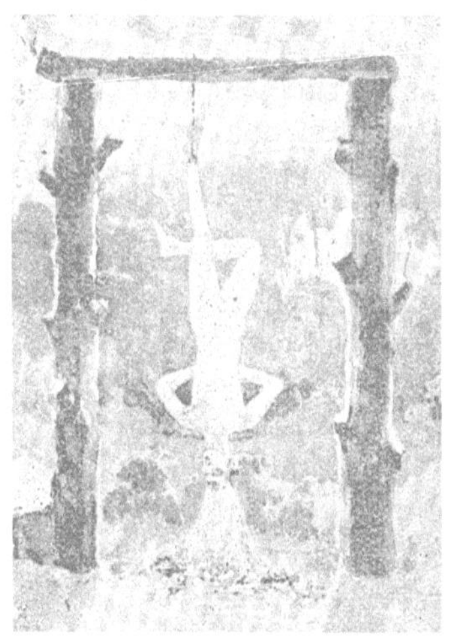

The sign of the Twelfth Arcana is Lamed; its numerical value = 30; astrological correspondence is the Sign of Libra in the Zodiac. The hieroglyph of the Arcanum is a hand in a wide sweep that sets all its joints in motion. This is the powerful scope of a person who has acquired rights personally and wants to use them; it's like the new Aleph, not only balanced in three directions, but already rich in the wisdom of life!

Let's see what the arithmetic deconstruction of the number of the Arcanum can give us.

12 = 1 + 11: The master of the twelfth Arcanum placed his poise and his essential being (1) ahead of the Arcanum of the Chain (11). This is the Head of the School plus the School itself. The three-planed א honored the world with the process of generating the egregoric Chain. He descended from higher subplanes and did not disdain implementation; he incarnated, in the literal or figurative sense of the word.
But where do we look for this three-plane א?
The above deconstruction gives us the titles of the Arcanum in the fields of the Theosophical Ternary.
If the Archetype is embodied, then the term assigned to this incarnation by the School of Jewish Scriptural Interpreters will be Messiah.
In the case of a lesser א, belonging to the plane of Man, a balanced and harmonious being that by his own will created in his astrosome the desire to help his neighbour, then the act of such a person will be named Caritas (Mercy in the realisation plan is love for the neighbor, as Christians understand it). This is also a kind of embodiment of a harmonious person, immersed in serious issues and voluntarily agreeing to do other things that he himself would never need to engage with.
How, however, to find the analogy of this in the plane of Nature? What will be the example of manifestation of the subtle in the dense, of the dispersion of the one in differentiation, an example of the centre nourishing the periphery?
For such an example, walk close. We will not be original and dwell on the long-known to mankind, which is found in all mythological systems, a description of the nutrition of the planets of the Solar system by its radiant centre - the Sun. The visible movement of this Centre in the ecliptic creates an idea of the Zodiac and its division into the so-called 12 Signs. Zodiacus will be the third name of the Arcanum. Look for the mechanism of the twelfth Arcanum not only in the objects of the first two headers, but also in the mysterious transition of subtle solar emanations, as if committed in themselves, into those crude attributions

of the worlds of fauna, flora and mineral formations that they are determined.

12 = 11 + 1: Eleven was before the unit; eleven encircled the unit, eleven seemed to temporarily assimilate the unit, and this is the mystery of the number twelve.

But the unit spawned our eleven. It turns out that she sacrifices herself to her own offspring. It turns out that if the Chain - eleven - was created by the great principle of the Covenant, then the appearance of the Messiah is in itself the character of the Sacrifice of the Archetype, manifested for the salvation of Mankind; if a person has actively shown mercy to his neighbour, then in this mercy lies the law of the voluntary sacrifice of the interests of the benefactor to the interests of the beneficent; if the Sun gives our planet life-giving emanations, then in this process you can see an element of the sacrifice of the vitality of the Sun to the interests of the life of the Earth.

The picture of the twelfth Arcanum illustrates precisely this side of its interpretation. On it we see the figure of a man hanged with his left leg upside down. The right leg of the hanged man is bent at the knee and laid behind the left so that the figure of a four-pointed cross is obtained. The hands are connected behind his back, so that the arms and head of the figure form a descending triangle. The crossbar, to which the figure is suspended, rests on two tree trunks with chopped branches; the number of remaining branches is 12 (6 on each side).

Who is this hanged man, what does he do or what did he do? His legs and feet are facing up, his head is facing the ground. This means that his best resources serve the earth, his attention is focused on the earth. At the top, he takes only the gain point. He is the messenger of the upper in the lower, the Higher in the lower, the mentality in the physical plane. It carries within itself the completeness of the process of the involutive triangle; it involves into the matter a higher principle for the revival and refinement of matter itself. But his involutive triangle is crowned with a cross of hermetic virtues, which indicated the path to this involution, to this sacrifice, and regulated its implementation. The hanged man is outlined by the shape of trunks and crossbars, strongly reminiscent of the sign of the synthetic Arcanum ת (Tau); the idea of sacrifice mysteriously contains the idea of completeness. The sheer number of branches - twelve, a symbol of the physical plane - again brings up the idea of completeness of an involutive process.

Summarising the impression delivered by the picture I'll say: everything breathes here with the idea of serving the Higher to the lower for the salvation of the lower and with the exact plan of completeness of the involutive half-cycle. It symbolises the sacrifice of the Superior to save the inferior.

12 = 2 + 10: An attempt at cognition (2), prevails over the system of the Universal Mill (10).
Where is the victim? This is a formula for those brave minds who, during one or several incarnations, consciously sacrifice the joys of their personal lives, the pleasures of the physical plane, maybe even part of their mystical urges for work in classrooms and laboratories, for dry searches of imperfect, relative, sometimes illusory secular science, for the future of humanity. They believe that the wise neutralisation of terrestrial binaries - by the scientific and altruistic effort - will overcome the involutive tendency of the astral of our planet. All these people's lives are an act of sacrifice.
12 = 10 + 2: No, say others, our idealisation of the future is better. Science is an enemy of humanity. The Universal Mill is your best friend. The only useful science (2) is that whose conclusions fit the Wheel of the Sphinx. May this Wheel teach us! So that weak cells of our planet do not fight against the powerful astral flow of the whole organism; that they are general transformations of the whole system and rest is satisfied during static epochs. Down with civilising ideals! Down with the pentagram effort, overwhelming the natural impulses! Life in conformity with Nature is the key to salvation. The traditions that glorify the struggle for culture, the victory over the elements, must be sacrificed. Then the gesture of the Lamed's extended arm will be integrated into the figure overall; it is not about being able to move this arm, but to move with him.
12 = 3 + 9: The metaphysical development (3) determines the degree of power over the work of Trismegistus, the cloak of Apollonius and the staff of human prudence; summarising: -determines the Initiation (9) and the application of initiatory elements to life. That is, this development leads to a modification of initiatory systems and the sacrifice of their antiquated methods, when the triangle that governs us - אמש (Aleph-Mem-Shin) - appeared to us in a different light, that is, when our absolute logic has been perfected.
12= 9 +3: It is best - say others – to follow the established tradition streaming in a chain of teaching; It is better to use the wise prescriptions of old, until, in time, the metaphysical-creator element (3) is perfected through the method and routine of the old and proven. It is the formula of the established Schools (9) that prepare generation after generation, so that each person, with time and the natural growth of the creative element, can become productive (3). In this formula the possibilities offered by the time are sacrificed to the routine Principles.
12= 4 +8: And the primacy of authority: formula on which authority (4) creates the laws (8); in which the legality of the demonstrations is sacrificed to the hierarchical principle.

12 = 8 + 4: Here, on the contrary, there is the primacy of law (8) logically deduced from the conditions of life of a given time. To this law, individual authorities are sacrificed, even more firmly established.
12 = 5 + 7: Let the inner work on the personality (5) lead to the victory of the subtle over the dense (7). However, the "7" (the immediate victory of the subtle (3) over the dense (4)) must be sacrificed to the process of formation of the pentagrammatic principle (5).
12 = 7 + 5: No, say others, on the contrary: the victory of the spirit over form (7) must be the starting point of the formation of the pentagram (5). That work on the individual principle (5) is sacrificed to the principle symbolised by Sephira Netzach (7).
12 = 6 + 6: This formula is the synthesis of the desperate polemics of all deconstruction precedents; polemics whose negative aspects are so well presented by Stanislas de Guaita, in the V chapter of his work "La Clef de la Magie Noire" (The Key of Black Magic). "6" versus "6" - is the friction arising from different understandings of the Arcanum VI by two individuals. And the struggle of two consciences, not illuminated by the superior principle of unitary philosophy and, therefore, not being able to manifest totally in its carriers; fight of two intelligences nourished with various relative truths; of two wisdoms acquired partially in fields other than the life experience; of two intuitions reflecting in a different way the same cliché, etc. In effect, this formula corresponds to a confusing image that gives meditation. It is not easy to find in it the sacrifices that must and can be made; however, each of us should seek to discover and understand them.

After this analysis by division into two components, let's deploy the number 12 in more elements. These developments will reveal to us the Zodiacal Plane, which can be called the "physical plane" and, more wisely, "plane of sacrifice."

Every accomplishment or work, be it the transmutation of common metals into noble metals, or the effort to teach abstract science to a lazy and staid student, belongs to the involutive hemicycle. It is a descent, a sacrifice of the subtle to the dense, an affirmation to establish in this density the fulcrum for the future ascent, for the beginning of the evolutionary hemicycle; is the basis for the work that will ennoble and make subtle the dense. This is why, in hermetic symbolism, the final phase of The Great Work is represented by the Descending Triangle which, all the more, is still oppressed by the Quaternary Cross. This symbol is the "guiding star" of all incarnations of the Logos principle, even if the manifestation seems insignificant to us.

We cannot explain here all the possible deconstructions of the number twelve. We will analyse only the following:

$$12 = 4 + 4 + 4$$
$$12 = 3 + 3 + 3 + 3$$
$$12 = 2 + 2 + 2 + 2 + 2$$

The first of these figures is interpreted as being a ternary of quaternaries; the second, a quaternary of ternary; the third, a set of six binaries, forming a double polarised duodenary. Let us analyze these deconstructions one by one.

$12 = 4 + 4 + 4$: It is a ternary, let us apply it to the Superior Liberation scheme אמש and look at each of the points of this triangle the 4 elements: Fire, Earth, Air and water. This will give us the full interpretation of this deconstruction. Applying it to the case of a human incarnation, we will have the following three phases:

1. א phase: the general picture of the resources that man has in his incarnation. This phase is subdivided, according to astrology, in the following four elements:
a) Health, that is, the general provision of vital forces (Vita);
b) Material resources (Lucrum);
c) Environment and composition of the family in which the human being is born (Fratres);
d) The father and his "status" (Genitor).

It should be noted that the first item corresponds to the subtle, active element - the Fire; the second - to the passive and dense - the Earth; the third - to the Air that stirs and activates as the י and the fourth - to the transmitting element of tradition, the ו, which corresponds to Water.

2. מ phase: the evolutionary human achievements during the incarnation. This phase can be subdivided into the following four elements:
a) Generation of children (Nati);
b) The support provided by the state of health (Valetudo), by the servers, friends and other auxiliaries;
c) Marriage (Uxor) - Wife;
d) Everything related to death itself (Mors) and the death of its ancestors.

3. ש phase: the evolutionary transformation of your life, transformation that can be achieved by own effort and depends on:
a) Religious conceptions (Pietas) - devotion;
b) Individual, social or political activity (Regnum);
c) All the aspects that the person knows how to create to support the activity above (Benefacta);

d) All obstacles that hamper his achievements, that is: enemies, dangers, limitations of the freedom, etc. (Prison).

We advise students to meditate, particularly on the "Mem" and "Shin" phases, relating them to the hermetic elements - Fire, Earth, Air and Water – that correspond.

12 = 3 + 3 + 3 + 3: Here we deal with a quaternary, whose elements can be studied one by one, either as a static ternary, or as a dynamic, gnostic cycle: יהו (Iod-He-Vau).

Among many examples, we can take the quaternary of spring, summer, fall and winter, dividing each of these stations in three months. It is, however, preferable to re-examine the example of the human incarnation, grouping the titles already enumerated, this time in a quaternary.

1. The first element of the quaternary shall consist of the following conditions:
a) "Vita" - life (י);
(b) "Lucrum" means the material conditions (ה);
c) "Fratres" - brothers (ו);

Note that the first factor already exists within ourselves; the second, can be created by us or "fertilised"; the third is given to us by fate, but we can influence it and, in turn, suffer their influence as well.

2. The second element - the Gnostic transformation of life - is subdivided into the following factors:
a) "Genitor" - the father - who, again, due to the laws of heredity, lives partially in we ourselves;
b) "Nati" - the children - whose existence depends partly on our desire to have them;
c) "Valetudo" - health (and in the figurative sense, the servants and helpers) - we are given partially by destination.

3. The third element - "Fratres" - naturally and inevitably influences us and for us is influenced. In it we find the following factors:
a) "Uxor" - the wife - who merges with us;
b) "Mors" - death - which depends partly on our way of expending vital forces;
c) "Pietas" - devotion - which is to some extent the expression of gratitude of human nature for its existence.

4. The fourth element allows us to evaluate the breadth of the and achievements during incarnation. On here there are also three factors:

a) "Regnum" - kingdom - which potentially hides within ourselves;
B) "Benefacta - everything that is acquired;
c) "Carcer" - the prison - the impediments and limitations imposed by destiny. It is certain that we can fight them, but they restrict us.

It would be good to memorise these titles, useful in the study of astrology. They can be easily remembered in the form of traditional hexameters of the medieval schools:
Vita, lucrum, fratres, genitor, nati, valetudo
Uxor, mors, pietas, regnum, benefactaque, carcer.

$12 = 2 + 2 + 2 + 2 + 2 + 2$: This decomposition gives a scheme of six pairs of the ʼ-He type connected by a common cyclic routine. To be consistent, we apply the scheme again to the previous example.
The first pair will consist of the elements "Vita" and "Lucrum"[32]. The reserve of the vital forces of the individual vivifies and "fecundates" his material environment. A human being, to develop his activity, needs material means, just as a husband needs his wife. According to the individual's needs, his reserve of vital forces creates an appropriate material environment, just as an "ʼ" forms a corresponding "He".
However, one must not forget that the material environment without its ruler would be completely sterile.
The second pair consists of "fratres" and "genitor"[33]. The term "fratres", by its meaning, obliges us to go back to the term "parent", as the conditional "ʼ" which creates the corresponding "He".
Often, the "fratres" we encounter, awaken in us the interest in the "parent" of the family.
The third pair - "Nati" and "Valetudo"[34] - has, as element "ʼ", the process of family, and as an element "He" - the environment that helps to achieve this, continuation and the preservation of the entities generated. They are, therefore, the servers that help in creating and protecting of children.
The fourth pair "Uxor" and "Mors"[35] - puts the wife (or spouse) as the positive pole of the binary, whose field is limited by the element of death. In other words, marriage guarantees work and solidarity throughout the incarnation, but is the Arcanum of the change of plane: death.

---

[32] Life, Gain
[33] brothers, father
[34] Son, Wellbeing
[35] Wife, Death

The next pair ("Pietas" and "Regnum")[36] is very edifying. Religiousness serves as a measure for the ability to receive higher inflows, and human practical activity ("Regnum") – measure for the transmission of these inflows downwards. The general picture of human achievement (" ו") is outlined by the intertwining of these two processes.

The last pair - "Benefacta" and "Carcer"[37] - gives us the picture of the limitations of success in life, by what we call karmic impediments.

This does not deplete the interpretation of the bi-polarisation scheme of the duodenum. We can distribute its elements in a different way and obtain, once again, six "marriages" or, if in these the union was not performed, then their binaries.

Putting together the first element with the seventh, that is, "Vita" with "Uxor", we will have, on the one, the life of a separate individuality; on the other, the union with another individuality. With two units which retain their independence, we will have the binary Adam (+) and Eve (-), that is, the antagonism of the sexes; if the spouses merge, forming a single unit, the binary referred to becomes realised and then, instead of the opposition of the poles, we will have a powerful unity, indivisible and androgynous: JODHEVA.

Adding the second element "Lucrum" to the eighth - "Mors" - we will get the mysterious and depressing binary of terrestrial wealth (+) and the inevitable law of death (-) that mocks the rich and confirms that the power of terrestrial wealth is only an illusion. This binary can be neutralised if terrestrial wealth is used, not for selfish purposes but creating, on the material plane - with the aspiration and conscious effort - support points for the work of future generations for humanity. This is an indispensable condition.

Let's confront the elements "Fratres" and "Pietas". On the one hand we will have the environment and the state evolution of our own generation; on the other, tradition, the hierarchical transmission of Superior Influences. Again, the neutralisation of these elements will depend on ourselves.

The next binary, "Genitor" - "Regnum" makes us understand that we are, in a certain manifestation of Arcanum III (we have a father - "Genitor"), but also, we are the "י" in the field of our own activity ("Regnum").

Then comes the binary "Nati" - "Benefacta", that is, on the one hand the transmission of life, in the sense of transmitting something of itself, a part of its own vital forces, and on the other hand, the reception of fluids, the condensation of forces, the attainment of successes in life.

---

[36] Compassion, Kingdom
[37] Acquisitions, Prison

The duodenary ends with the binary that is perhaps the most difficult to neutralise: the binary "Valetudo" - "Carcer", that is, wellbeing - prison.

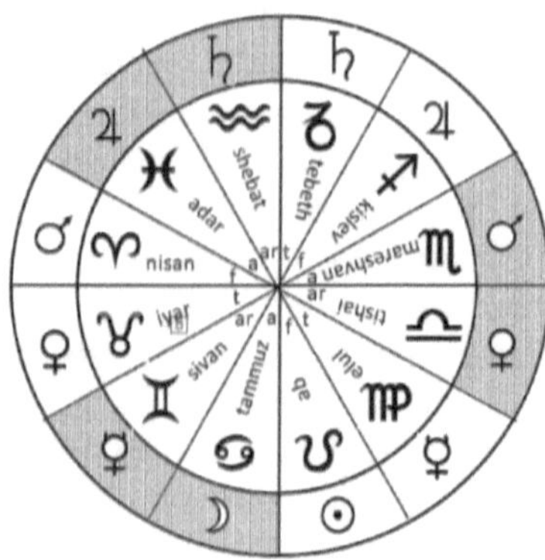

Figure 49

All of these deconstructions, in our analysis, were applied to a human incarnation. For what the student can metaphysically generalise the schema of the duodenary, we will take the example of classical configuration of the zodiacal signs. Figure 49, in its central part indicates the polarity (positive or negative) of the sign. The astrological symbols of the signs are placed on the cusps, that is, at the initial points of the corresponding ecliptic arcs. In the sectors of signs, are indicated the hermetic elements to which the sign belongs (Fire, Earth, Water or Air). In Latin letters are written the Hebrew names of the magical 12-month solar calendar. The beginning of the magical year, as it has been said, corresponds to the vernal equinox, that is, of spring, in the Northern hemisphere. Thus, for example, the month of Nisan begins approximately on 21 March and ends around April 21, etc. The figure, besides the indications on the composition of the duodenary, also presents the scheme of the planetary regencies. At the moment, we are interested only in the outer part of the figure, that is, the distribution of the planets in the signs that govern.

The Sun and the Moon are placed, respectively, on the signs of Leo and Cancer. The Sun occupies the right, and the moon to the left of the figure. Of the two sides, that is, both on the side of the Sun and that of the Moon, the planets are distributed as follows: the signs adjacent to the Sun or Moon, belong to Mercury, the planet closest to the sun, in our solar system. The two signs following belong to Venus, the second planet in the order of its distance from the sun. Then, we have two signs belonging to Mars, then to Jupiter, and finally two contiguous signs - Saturn, thus obeying the order of the distance of the planets from the Sun. The figures in the shaded parts are called nocturnal domiciles of the planets, and the white parts - daytime households. The Sun has only one sign - diurnal, and the Moon also has one sign - nocturnal. All planets have two domiciles: one diurnal and one nocturnal. The sequence of signs and shades of white, divides the circle into six pairs or binaries of the duodenary, of which three binaries are relatively positive, (diurnal domiciles of the planets) and three relatively negative (night-time households).

As a practical exercise, we advise students, in the duodenary of human life we have analysed, to interpret the binaries "Vita" - "Lucrum", "Nati" - "Vale-tudo" and "Pietas" -"Regnum" as positive, in relation to the three remaining: "Fratres" - "Genitor", "Uxor" - "Mors" and "Benefacta" - "Carcer". By doing so, you will clearly see the light sectors (day domiciles). Meditation on the duodenum scheme is so important to the process of self-initiation of the incarnated individuality, that this scheme started one of the most well-known pantaculo, the "Mystic Cross".

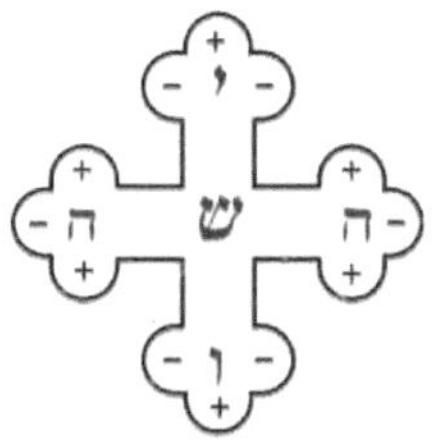

Figure 50

The instructor places the image of this cross on the forehead of the disciple who initiates or has already begun, as symbol of the blessing to the prickly path of the 12 stages of the earthly incarnation. The protrusions which end the arms of the cross symbolise these steps. The path starts at the centre of the upper arm. Let's look at the picture closely: the central protrusions of both vertical arms of the cross are marked with the positive sign, active (+), i.e. י and ו. However, י is totally positive, while ו, although it has the active element, is androgynous. The central protrusions of the horizontal arms are marked with the negative sign (-), because they correspond to the passive sign ה however, the right arm, which corresponds to the second ה, is more active than the left, since the second ה becomes the י of the next cycle; It has, therefore, in itself the germ of future activity, while the first ה, in his capacity as mother, can give only an androgynous fruit ו. We can deduce from all this that the Mystical Cross is a Kabbalistic cross, in which the upper and the right predominate over the lower and the left, and the vertical on the horizontal. This cross confirms the hierarchical superiority of the asset over the passive, subtle over the dense, and confirms it through the elements of the י ה ו ה cycle.

However, this is only the explanation of the astral scheme of the Mystical Cross. It remains for us to explain kabbalistically the symbolism of the 12 protrusions. To do so, we put the letter Shin in the centre of the cross. Thus, he is transformed into the Redeemer Cliché יהשוה. It is the scheme of hermetic force (ש) acting in the world (י ה ו ה) with the intention of realising in him what is symbolised by the ש, that is, that which is inevitably linked to the Law of Sacrifice. The sacrifice can be made on the plane of the "Testament," in the field of human mercy, or even in the physical plane, such as, for example, the sacrifice of the vitality of the Sun for the benefit of the Earth.

In the centre of the Cross could be placed the sign Aleph, instead of Shin. In this case, the Cross would assume a different meaning: it would become a synthetic schema of the three plans of the Universe; we would say more: in a scheme of the full understanding of these plans, according to the law of Hermes Trismegistus. The Aleph, in the centre, represents a balanced mentality; the four arms - the great law (י ה ו ה) of the astral creations, and the protrusions that end the arms – the twelve arcs of the zodiac on the physical plane. In other words, it is a scheme of the complication and multiplication that govern each passage to dense. The sum of the numerical values of the Aleph sign is 9 ($10 + 5 + 6 + 5 + 1 = 27$-9), corresponding to the Arcanum of Initiation.

Meditation on the Mystical Cross, in any of its kabbalistic interpretations, always helps fertile ideas emerge in the respective sub-plane.

We repeat that, in order to penetrate the meaning of Arcanum XII, we must convince ourselves of the necessity of sacrifice on the physical plane, or the limitation of this plane in which, in the progressive descent to the denser layers, one inevitably comes to a wall, which is the limit of the "coagulation" of the illusory. This wall serves as a foothold in the opposite direction, the ascent, to cross all sub-planes in the opposite direction.

The first of these possibilities is more understandable to those who deeply feel the Gospel; the second, those who are closest to Buddhism. In the context of the Twelfth Arcanum, the complex called "human individuality" is like a strange visitor on the earth plane, someone who is outside his home. The visitor, of course, should be courteous, must be ready to give way to any other guest; should neither criticise nor refuse food being served, nor any of the accommodation of the house. However, you should never forget that he owns his own home or neglect the interests of that home. You must remember that any gossip or misconduct in another's home, will have negative consequences for his or her own and that every misuse of their talents, in the social field, will pay with the privations in their own home. Parties and receptions may have a certain value as a point of support for constructive work, but in themselves they are pure illusion and have nothing of real value. We can, our perishable physical shell distracting us into futile social pastimes, coagulate the Malkuth, but if we are sufficiently developed we must not forget the inevitable and beneficial hour to return home, the hour of death, so well symbolised by the attributes of the Lodge of the Masters in Masonic Initiation.

As for that hour, in which the human being takes up his rights to a purely astral life and how much to the various transient states between the two modes of existence and the post-incarnation stage, of which we will speak in the next Arcanum (XIII).

Notes on the twelfth Arcanum

This Arcanum is thought to conceal momentous secrets and hold the key to great mysteries. A clue is to be found in the sign of the Hebrew letter, Lamed, which is the only letter in that alphabet which reaches above the baseline. (In Hebrew letters are written below the line, in contrast with most modern languages, which are based above the line). This indicates the exalted position of the Lamed as it extends towards the divine, like a ו upon the Kaph.

The Hanged Man of this Arcanum is an adept who has been able to put into practice the teachings of his Master. He has accomplished the spiritual exercises of the preceding Arcana and is 'resting' – as if suspended in his 'solution' – in the powerful twelfth position. The upper part of the letter he represents is seen as a mysterious Tower in the Air which evokes powers of ascension and/or levitation. It is a very important letter for those who want to learn more about the Divine. The full spelling of the letter lamed – lamed – mem - daleth - is a shortened version of phrase: *"a heart that understands knowledge"*.

The ו inherent in the upper section of Lamed represents the Spiritual self which reaches for Godliness and channels this spiritual energy from above into the human being signified by the Kaph which it rests upon. In this way does the lamed merge spiritual and physical qualities via a powerful teaching impulse.

Through this Arcanum we discover that our spiritual roots are in heaven and from this celestial foundation do we reach down to Earth.

In MotT, the powerful image of Jesus walking on the water is evoked to explain the individual whose gravitation is entirely towards heaven, and yet without shunning the domain of Earth, which constitutes the usual force of gravitation for the majority of human beings.

Gravitation being the pertinent force in question with respect to this Arcanum, our attention is also drawn to the contrasting image of Simon Magus, who we are told was able to levitate. Here we must make the distinction between an individual who 'levitates' through the power of celestial attraction (gravitation towards the heavens) and one who is lifted from below by an electrified force of repulsion via the root chakra and through the kundalini.

An even more sinister analogy can be found for this unholy form of levitation in the broomsticks of witches, which is very far from being similar to the celestial 'rising' of Saints.

We are told that the Nephilim, sons of God, changed their celestial gravitational orientation in order to be enfolded by Earthly gravitational influences received through the daughters of men. Thus were heroes and supermen – the giants – born, whilst celestial radiation gives birth to the tsaddik or righteous men. "The world is divided" says Tomberg, between those who worship the strong men and those who revere the righteous. (MotT, Letter XII, p315).

We cannot serve two masters and are thereby asked to align ourselves with the righteous and ensure our orientation is towards heavenly radiation, lest we risk being enfolded or even swallowed by the Earth. The will of the spiritual man is connected with and aligned with the divine will – the 'zodiacalised will' - which emanates from the heavens above and leads us towards the 'solarisation' of thought.

Such spiritual alignment is dependent upon faith and requires effort and application, especially in the realms of thought, memory and imagination. Meditating upon this Arcanum helps to educate our minds in the proper direction of spiritual orientation.

Arcanum XIII

נ

DEATH

Pathway from Hod to Geburah

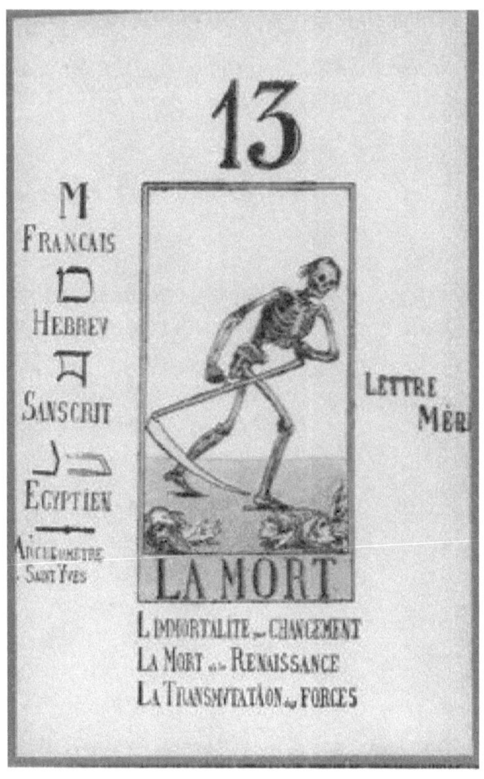

Death is the field of *Necromancy*

An effort must now be made to learn the truth concerning the greatest and most consoling, yet also the most formidable of the Minor Arcana - concerning Death

Levi

THE SCYTHE: Transformation

M--40 expresses in the divine world the perpetual movement of creation, destruction and renewal

Paul Christian

An illumination entered me, and, looking at the receding rider and the descending sun, I understood that the Path of Life consists of the steps of the horse of Death.

Ouspensky

The Sign of the Thirteenth Arcanum is מ (Mem); its numerical value = 40; there is no astrological correspondence to it. The hieroglyph of the Arcanum is the figure of a woman, as a mediator in the transformation of the plan of life: for a woman, for her fetus, makes the transition from uterine life to life in the earth's atmosphere.

The picture of the Arcanum gives us the figure of Death in the form of a traditional skeleton with a scythe. It emphasises the importance of Death as the transformer of the One Life in the field of the diversity of its forms. The skeleton mows crowned and uncrowned heads, but under its scythe new arms and legs grow out of the ground. Death only seems to pay off something in a certain plane: in fact, it only transforms the values of this plane. It cannot be put in analogy with the process of burning credit papers without issuing new ones; rather, it could be likened to the process of smelting some coins into others. In the picture of the thirteenth Arcanum, Death is depicted unilaterally, partially, but certainly analytically completed.

I draw your attention to two more details in the disassembled picture. Death is depicted as an operating skeleton. But what is a skeleton from a symbolic point of view? This is what we consider the most coagulated and least changeable in our body; it is, so to speak, the derivative of the body in its hardness; this is what the other elements of the body build on. Therefore, the principle of death is inextricably linked with the beginning of the so-called strong coagulation, and moreover, it is connected by a chain of causality. We died in a past time because we must coagulate, and this conclusion is an immutable truth of a mathematical nature. This truth is under the auspices of Saturn, like all the inexorably logical consequences of the chosen premise. That is why the skeleton with a scythe appears on the mascots of Saturn; that is why in everyday life the skull and cross-bones are so eagerly chosen by us as the hieroglyph of the motto *Memento mori*. The need to decompose our bodies in a mocking way reminds us of exactly what in other people's bodies did not have time to decompose, but which is undoubtedly also condemned to decomposition and weathering. A completed picture of death would turn into a picture of a new life, and an unfinished picture emphasises the transition that we call death. Crisscrossed bones, this gloomy quaternary, serves as the last challenge of coagulating gnomes to a thinning salamander, the last threat to constrain the astrosome with the physical body through the destruction of the latter, which is mandatory for the phantom connecting them. The bone shouts to the Personality: "You had a reference point and thanks to it you operated magically; so now, in punishment, be connected with this reference point until you give the elements coagulated by you to nature. You will not have complete freedom of the astral life, you will have a little earthly "Caring.

You will not instantly move from a three-pronged life to a two-pronged life; you will know the transitional stage and give it the name Death." This is what the picture says; it will not be harmful to think about it. When analysing the arcanum, we will try to take all these points into consideration and begin with a simple description of the process of death of a human individual as it is understood in everyday life.

Let's take as an example the body of an individual person that has become incapable of maintaining the vital functions of the physical plane, either because of his own will (suicide), or by the will of another pentagram (violent death), or for mixed reasons (laws of nature, collisions with other people's volitional impulses, his own negligence, his own legal impulses, leading to an increase in the expenditure of vitality, etc. etc., etc.), has become unsuitable for fulfilling the vital functions of the physical plane. The astrosome fights against the failure of physical functions, clings to the slightest pretexts to prolong the life of the body as a whole in the physical plane (agony), but in the end is forced to leave the body as an unsuitable mechanism and begin a new two-planed activity, called the gap between incarnations.

The passage to the other plane contains several phases. In this elementary course we will not delve into the theoretical and practical meaning that each one of these stages possesses for an initiate who naturally wishes both to prepare himself for death, how to facilitate this passage to their fellow men, by a specific, magical act. These subjects belong to a special course of magic, and for the most part they cannot be revealed.

In our present course, we would just like to answer three possible questions:

1. What means do we have to study the death process?
2. What should be, in general, a good preparation of oneself for the passage to the other plane?
3. What are the means of helping people who are dying if we understand this expression according to the initiatory teachings?

Let us begin by answering the first question. First of all we have the testimony of sensitive people by nature, or whose sensitivity was artificially stimulated by suggestion or self-suggestion, so that they could observe by the 6th sense of the death process. We also have the Law of Analogy, which we allow, by studying a less subtle process and therefore more accessible to the organs of the physical senses, that is (i.e., the passage from the fetus of intrauterine life to the life of a child in the world) to establish the analogies in the two processes. Studying these analogies makes it easier to formulate the questions that one puts to the sensitive or, the sensitive himself - to himself. It is important, not only observe the process of death, but also, know what to focus our attention on, that which to keep in memory and what differentiations to establish. In addition to these resources, we have kabbalistic methods of a priori study, with the help of the alphabet, which in turn leads us to ask certain questions and differentiate several unobserved death process.

Subjects tuned for sensitivity indicate that the process of death, strictly speaking, from the occult point of view begins at the very moment when doctors say that the subject is dead. The cessation of the heartbeat and the beginning of the cooling of the body coincide with the first phase of the final exteriorisation of the astrosome. First, the senses can see the astral branch of the limbs (mainly lower). Then comes the separation of the astral elements that control the parts of the body. Finally, the exteriorisation of the head parts of the astrosome begins. The observer notes the separation of the astral figure, its removal from the body, with which it remains connected as if by an umbilical cord, the entry point of which is the so-called "Brahma's hole" at the back of the head.

Following the umbilical cord, what can be called the "astral body" slowly emerges, if we adhere to obstetric terminology, which is fully justified by the above reference to the law of the analogy of the process of death with the process of birth in terms of atmospheric perception. The entire process of "childbirth in the astral" continues on average for an adult about 48 hours. But during this time, and the next 10-40 days, the dying person has to adapt to a lot and experience multiphase impressions.

At first, that is, in the period immediately following the agony, the deceased experiences the difficulties of separating his astral. These difficulties are all the greater the less he learned during his incarnation to separate, through meditation, his inner self from the envelope that contained it. The suffering experienced by him in this phase is in the nature of a difficult parting with what he used to consider the most essential reality. During the mentioned period, the complicated edifice of illusions that were dear to him collapses. When there is familiarity with this collapse and acceptance of the inevitability of the passage into the world of new experiences, the "deceased" begins to feel the discomfort of this change. First of all, you have to face the astral forms of the elementals. Here comes the division of activity of the astrosome, the activity the "Ruach" (the soul) and the activity of the "Nephesh" (the ghost). The latter has as its task the return of components of the old physical body to the elements of Nature or, in other words, the task of progressive deconstruction of this body. The "Ruach" should analyse the clichés created, both by received (element "-"), as well as by active pulses ("+" element) of the personality, during the newly completed incarnation. When this analysis is completed, the soul (Ruach) goes on to study the clichés of planetary currents which could, in future incarnations, correct the mistakes of their past incarnations and contribute to the formation of a more perfect.

As we can see, the tasks of the ghost (Nephesh) and the soul (Ruach) form a binary which must be neutralised through meditation in the bipolar field of the astral world. In the first times, this meditation is greatly hampered by the astral environment itself.

When the elemental (the deceased) frees himself from the Nephesh and goes beyond the layer of elemental forms which now seem very ugly to him and only evoke in him the composition of his old body and his slavery to the elements, enters the sphere where the lower elementals (animals, plants, minerals) united in egregorial currents, work on perfecting their future physical organs. For them, hastened to be able to incarnate again, this work is very important.

The human elemental must prepare to pass quickly through this region, for it can learn only how to perfect the organs of the physical senses of the future incarnation. This, for him, is not the main thing. The main task is one's hermetic improvement. At first sight this does not seem to be a difficult task, because the Ruach, separating from Nephesh, purified his ability of objective self-criticism. However, the Ruach must now pass through the vortex of temptations, the vortex of darkness, and has to face the involutive flow of the Earth Astral. It is a chain that serves the involutive purposes of the Planet and that has, as a point of support, the very body of the Earth. The Ruach who has just lost his pentagrammatic foothold - the physical body – must now face the involutive current of the Earth itself.

It may be objected that the Ruach, being of the highest essence, should prevail and that the encounter with the terrestrial involutionary flow could not harm it. This is truth about a highly evolved pentagram, but if it is a being that has not time, the field of your desires and your receptivity, in cases where the astral level does not progress beyond that of the planet, that flow will avenge itself cruelly of the participation of the "deceased" in the evolutionary activities. It is as if the planet told him: "As a link of the great evolutionary current of the men of the Earth, you fought with me, but as an individual you were not always pure and faithful, professed ideals and sometimes you took advantage of the solidarity of the chain to promote your selfish ends. Now, therefore, that you are in the field of my influence, and without support on the physical plane, you will be subject to the Law of the attraction of the like. By the lower desires that still exist in you, you will be drawn to the vortex where they are condensed, you will be defiled, so that you become my temporary ally in involutive work. Perhaps these desires will lead you to create for yourself a new ghost, worse than the previous one; perhaps you will abandon your aspirations to the higher spheres; maybe you'll give in to temptation, and you'll join my school where you'll learn new ways to perform selfish enjoyments. I hope you will conclude a pact with me and incarnate to promote my involutive purposes ".

Unhappy is the one who does not know how to overcome the temptation of the Great Serpent of the Planet. He will incarnate but to serve involution.

If, on the contrary, the human elemental wins the proof of the involutive flow, then, ascertaining in the astral his abilities, he could become a worthy student of that World University in which they draw up the plans for redemptive work and the ascension to the Absolute Truth.

These are the experiences the dying and the dead go through in a relatively short time.

Soon the question might arise if all this data was captured exclusively through the sixth sense. No. This means would not be sufficient to state the above. This research is helped greatly by Kabbalah, which allows us to penetrate the mysteries of the beyond when we know how to apply its methods.

In this course we cannot go into the study of the so-called "Pneumatics", which addresses these issues. We can say, however, that a wise kabbalisation of the book Sepher Yetzirah and the in-depth study of Zohar's extensive original commentary gives us much insight into the subject of death.

In addition to the aforementioned means of knowledge, there is another, of which we shall speak in later chapters and which are our own frequent exteriorisations in the middle astral plane. The way and the experiences during such externalisations differ only in details of the common process of death.

Let us now turn to our second question: how can a supporter of esotericism prepare for the death?

First, he must not forget that it is inevitable; you should not close your eyes to the continuous spectacle of the impermanence of life.

In Freemasonry, a mason receives the recommendation to remember death. If we look for the whole human incarnation as a preparation for death, we will understand the importance of this initiatory training which, whilst not having a practical use in the three-dimensional world, is an important preparation for the existence of two planes in the world. To arrive, through meditation, to differentiate what constitutes the true human being from that which is only its physical envelope, is the ABC of preparation for death and existence in the astral, since it allows us to know that real human life takes place in the astral and not in the plane of what is his physical enclosure. By the word "to know" we do not have in mind only a simple intellectual admission of life in the astral, nor a logical conviction of the independence of our inner self from its physical enclosure; we have in mind something else: the constant awareness of the difference between the body and the internal. The latter can manifest itself strongly even in a weak and suffering body. One's own weakness and suffering can even increase awareness of the diversity between the two. Physical weakness is an impediment only in the field of achievement, but never in the field of ethics or self-knowledge. The true homeland of the human being are those currents of planetary systems to which it aspires, and never the environment in which the physical body is. The soul does not feel "at home" inside the body. By its very nature, it is foreign to the coagulates which imperfectly correspond to the most perfect forms of the astrosome. These, although subtle, are much more durable and intense in their manifestations.

In life, one has to get accustomed to giving preference to the more subtle states, for example: liquid to dense; to the gaseous, rather than the liquid, to the radiant rather than the gaseous. We must learn to feel that the intrinsic form - the internal structure – we are more like the dense matter that surrounds and fills this form.

Having become accustomed to meditate on these subjects and helped by the reading of the classic works with regard to Kabbalah and Magic, and mental exchange with people who work in it sense, we can begin a systematic preparation for the process of externalisation of our astrosome.

All exercises that lead to overcoming the normal reactions of one or another organ, one or another group of organs, or overcoming the normal exchange between body and external nature, are preparation for further exteriorisation.

For example, such training includes breathing retention, heartbeat, numbness of any part of the body, sleep or, on the contrary, to fall asleep at will, to hear without seeing or feeling tactile impressions, of receiving only visual perceptions, being insensitive to acoustic, of perceiving by the sense organs only certain colours or certain sounds, to hear exclusively the voice of a certain person, to see only objects of a certain shape or colour, etc.

The role of such exercises will perhaps be more understandable if we add that externalisation - voluntary or involuntary - in general, occurs only in states of lethargy or catharsis.

Naturally, provoke in yourself or another person a state of cathepsis by will effort or by narcotics is insufficient to reach the exteriorisation of the astrosome. For exteriorisation, not the external influences but the will and the capacity of the person himself to leave the body, that is, of already knowing his inner self and having learned to separate it from all the elements belonging to the physical plane [are decisive]. At the moment of exteriorisation, a simple thought about an object of everyday use, reminiscent of a flavor or a perfume, the awareness of the physical well-being, etc. can easily compromise their success.

In any case we will indicate a scheme of exercises that can lead to astral output, considering it as the best method to become familiar with death and to know the first phase of its process, and sometimes, also, its more advanced phases.These exercises can be divided into several groups. We never advocate a rigid system that is identical for all. Each serious and prepared student will be able to modify and complete the general system, according to the achievements he has already achieved, the difficulties he encountered and also, as the physical state of your body and the individual characteristics of the interrelationship between your body and the astrosome

First group of exercises:

1. Get to the super-tiredness of the physical organs without giving in to their reactions.
2. Know how to counter your physical tastes and even your normal needs.
3. Knowing how to be voluntarily disappointed with physical enjoyment at the exact moment when experiencing it.
4. To be able to evoke the sensation of such joys without actually experiencing the physical organs.
5. To know, as a result of volition, to dissociate the attributes of physical objects; for example in a bucket of wood, see only its geometric shape, separating it from colour, wood type, etc.

The exercises of this group help to delimit in the man the conscious pentagram that, in the future, will be separated.

Second group of exercises:

1. Imagine events that, according to our logic, are unfolding far from us in the time or space.
2. To imagine in detail the events of which we are aware by a sensory perception. We see, for example, people in the distance who are chopping down trees; imagine the arm movements, axe lifting, etc. which we cannot clearly see by far.
3. Meditate upon events which are purely imaginary. It is best to practice imaginary travel meditation; think over these trips in detail, especially in

the sphere of application of our body's resources (movement of arms, legs, eyeing objects, etc.).

4. To evoke another kind of existence, lost by us, and in which we were not limited by time or space. The easiest medium for this meditation is this: sitting next to a window, or better still, lying on your back in the late afternoon of a fine summer day, in a field or garden, looking at the sky, thinking about time and space, taking a turn of attitude, both in relation to them and to their own body. Such a state of relaxation prevents reactions that could lead us away from this meditation.

The exercises of the second group aim at the elaboration, in the human being, of a "being beyond " in relation to the three-dimensional plane In the first two exercises of the second group, we seek to overcome sensory experiences; in the third, to overcome the notion of space; the room, the time.

Third group of exercises:

1. Exercising in telepathy, that is, trying to transmit to a distant person geometric forms, moods and even ideas. From telepathic exercises we will speak in detail in the Arcanum XV. Here, we will confine ourselves to saying that telepathy is an astral contact, and therefore, it is already a particular case of the exteriorisation of certain astral ganglia.

2. To practice a monoidic concentration in relation to the desire to see in a dream something well-determined. "Monoideism" is a state of constantly returning to a chosen subject, and clearly defined, during the meditation of the day, afternoon or night, temporarily giving the importance to all other interests. In our exercise, the person, several times a day, should concentrate, for example, upon a subject for which, in the dream, we wish to receive a reply; in some process that seeks to understand or an entity you want to find.

3. Practicing self-suggestion - by one of the methods given by us in Arcanum V - of the ability to be externalised.

4. Do some elemental theurgic work, e.g. a simple sincere and ardent prayer, to become capable of externalising.

5. Call on the help of a powerful egrégore.

6. Try to enter into a cataleptic state. If the person has prepared adequately for the practice of meditation, this may, beginning at the feet, provoke in itself a progressive cataleptic state. Arriving in the region of the heart, its exteriorisation will become possible. Many people come into a cataleptic state by the simple method of convincing themselves that it is gradually the astral of the legs, then the astral of the abdominal

region. When you pass the solar plexus, the phenomenon can, in fact, take place.

7. Use some narcotic to cause a semi-lethargic state. The least damaging is the inspiration of sulphuric ether vapors or the ingestion of an aqueous or alcohol dilution of droplets of ether. Naturally, these means, like other similar ones, are contraindicated in certain organisms and, in general, not advisable. They are not part of the means indicated by the Great Arcanum of Magic.

8. Recreating, through meditation, a picture that in the past had already caused an involuntary exteriorisation. In other words, to favor the custom of externalising in certain astral conditions

9. Recreating on the physical plane the environment and the circumstances that in the past have already unconsciously exteriorised or helped a conscious exteriorisation, that is, to try to get used to the physical body in releasing the astral under certain physical conditions. If someone, exhausted by a long walk, then accidentally exteriorised yourself during your sleep. You may try to overdo it again with the same exercise and focus on the desire to exteriorise when going to bed after that.

10. Turning to another person with a request to inspire you to hypnotically or magnetically exteriorise.

11. Take part in a gathering of people who form a magical current. This method is adapted to mediumistic individuals who have already been externalised under the influence of the same chain.

The success of the exercises of the third group, as we can deduce, depends on the previous training, that is, the practice of the 1st and 2nd groups.

We will not speak separately of the traditional exteriorisation provoked by certain mantras, since the use of setrans is part of the means of exteriorisation mentioned in items 4 and 8, and the use of items 4 and 5 of the last enumeration.

The person who correctly practices the exercises presented by us will voluntarily externalise, at the moment chosen by her, or an involuntary one, perhaps at the moment in which you least expect it. During its exteriorisation, if the person developed in himself an active attention in relation to what is happening to it, the separation process will be clearly of the body's astrosome. You will see, or at least, discern by the sixth sense the presence of your physical body, as something external that is not part of your "I". Then you will notice or feel the "umbilical cord" that unites the energy entity externalised with the element, also energetic, but connected to the vital functions of the body. This last energy element has already been called by us the "astral placenta".

Those who have learned to externalise, and who, after having returned to their body, translate the language of visual perceptions the impressions received during the exteriorisation, affirm having seen the "umbilical cord", uniting them to the body, entering this body, not by the Brahma "as in the case of death, but in the vicinity of the solar plexus, in detail the "thickness" of the cord. We deduce that the "thickness" greatly increases the higher is the astral sub-plane reached in exteriorisation. A trained and attentive person, after noticing the position of his body and umbilical cord during externalisation, will notice the presence of the astrosomes of objects surrounding his body, and then of the elementals, whose shapes he found ugly and strange. This is the opinion of the "Ruach" element, observing the coarse and imperfect element "Nephesh". Then contact is established with the sub-plane of the elementals of the animals that work, as has already been said, in the improvement of their organs for future incarnations. This sphere no longer causes revulsion, but it does not attract either. We must understand that the perfection of the physical organs does not aim at astral harmony but its use in the physical world. Therefore, this region cannot attract the astrosome [and] is already superior to the physical plane.

Next, we encounter the powerful involutionary flux of the Earth's astrosome. To the person who is seriously prepared for the externalisation, the fight with this chain should not be very difficult. It is common, however, that someone has only partially overcome several aspects of their egoism. Often, a child of the Earth, although it has already become aware of its true nature, has not yet given up all the temptations of earthly life. Sometimes it's hard to break the attraction, even knowing how illusory its object is.

The one who fails to meet the Snake on the planet is left behind in the "dark cone" where are perceived their weaknesses, one by one, with awareness of their inability to overcome them totally. This experience is very depressing and causes, after the exteriorisation and for a long time, a fading of faith in the self. This can be expressed in misanthropy and melancholia which, may sometimes give way to malevolence, and may even lead to the desire to offer oneself consciously at the service of involution. In the latter case, it is often said that the person concluded a pact with the "dark cone".

If, on the contrary, the person beats the astral Serpent, it reaches the middle astral of our solar system. Here we study all the planetary fluxes and their various combinations. There occurs also the clear understanding of the harmony that must be realised within our being, what we are missing for this realisation, what is unilateral to us and what we totally lack. Then begins the planning of the conditions that, on the physical plane, will facilitate the future harmonisation.

As far as our possibilities of knowing, during the life, the astral plane and of learning more about postmortem experiences?

The Rosicrucian School teaches that an adept, who sincerely and unselfishly strives to unveil these mysteries, can reach, in his/her astral initiation, the threshold of the "second death." What is the "second death"?

To understand it, we need to analyse the human structure. Man is a being on three planes. According to the Law of Reflexes, each plane has its reflection - we could say "your representative "- in the other two planes, therefore, the human being is composed of 9 elements:

Mental plane:	Mental element in the own mental plane
	Reflection of the astral element in the mental plane
	Reflection of the physical element on the mental plane
Astral plane:	Reflection of the mental in the astral plane
	Astral element in its own plane
	Reflection of the physical on the astral plane
Physical plane:	Reflection of the mental on the physical plane
	Reflection of the astral in the physical plane
	Physical element in its own plane

This scheme allows us a priori logical analysis. However, in practice, even logic, we are not able to discern all nine elements. The imperfection of the sixth sense makes it difficult to discern between, for example, the reflection of the physical element in the astral, and that of the astral in the physical. In the same way it is difficult for us to separate the reflection from the physical in the mental and the reflection of the mental in the physical. The last difficulty is probably due to the imperfection of our mental health functions.

Thus, a trained adept practically discerns in the human being only seven elements:

1. Mental in the mind
2. Astral in the mental
3. Connection of the physical with the mental
4. Mental in the astral
5. Astral in the astral
6. Connection of the physical with the astral
7. The physical himself

In an embodied person, you must imagine these seven elements as interconnected. When the seventh element is worn out and is not able to serve as a reference point for the higher elements, the first death we are studying occurs. This is the breaking of our chain on the sixth element. The seventh element turns into a corpse, and the sixth, no longer serving as a link, becomes its phantom. The higher five elements study in the astral plane and again produce the sixth and seventh elements, i.e. reincarnate, die the first death again, etc. until the five human elements became so harmonious as to cease to obey the attraction of the funnels we mentioned (after all, a harmonious whole possesses complacency, like any androgynous one, and therefore does not lend itself to the downward attraction rod). For such an elementary element, the astral life is no longer reduced to the planning of the future physical, but to the refinement of the fifth element by influencing the fourth. But, making forms (the fifth element) more and more ideological (the fourth element), we will eventually bring them to a state that excludes the possibility of particularities of formal transitions to the physical. In the company of too thin the fourth and fifth elements, the third element cannot live. Once the elementary has ceased to prepare for physical life, the third element begins to erode in it. Having weathered, he naturally leads the elementary to a second death. The fifth element will be the corpse in the process of the second death, and the fourth element will be its phantom. To clearly imagine this process, draw an analogy of it in art history, where in some cases the corpse is a harmonic style, and its phantom is the guiding idea of this style.

The new, almost one-sided essence of the composition, the mental in the mental + astral in the astral, will be the pole of the future androgynous cell of the reintegrated Adam Protoplast. I say the "pole" of the cell, and not the "cell", because in order to make up the androgynous cell, our essence must wait for the second death of the sister soul, if the combination of these two polarities did not happen in the astral plane, which is the most common case. Many do not even allow the possibility of a single second death of a male or female soul. Indeed, the representation of the harmonic state of the fifth element is difficult to logically combine with the same-sex state of mind.

In this Arcanum we speak only of the perception on the astral plane, that is, of the receptivity (-) during the externalisations. Of the achievements, that is, of the activity (+) during the externalisations, we will speak in Arcanum XV.

It would be wrong to think that a good preparation for death consists in the practice of externalisations. It is more important that the person knows or believes deeply that certain experiences wait after death, on the way to a new existence. A deep faith can replace the experience.

Bringing in knowledge with the region of the elementals we discover our past bondage to the elements; knowledge of the region of organic improvement of animals and plants gives us the understanding of our future enslavement to the same elements during the next incarnations; the struggle with the Serpent is reduced to the consciousness of the need to break away sooner or later from the egoism dictated to us by the conditions of life on the planets; and contemplation of the cliché of the middle astral will come down to recognition of the need for harmonious self-improvement. He who believes this not in words but in the depths of his heart, he will always be able during the course of his earthly life to establish a strong connection with one of the powerful evolutionary egrégores, who will direct him through all the strata and pull him out of the arms of the Serpent. Believing and praying is a great help in preparing for dying.

Let us now speak of how a man, possessing faith and knowledge, can relieve others of the painful experiences of death. Help can be given in three ways: teaching, preparing, and sustaining.

If anyone has unlimited trust in us, then it will not be difficult to tell him what we are studying if this person meditates at length on what is reported, it will considerably [facilitate] guidance in the experiences of the hour of death. Possessing competence and time and consecrating it to the methodical development of the intuition of our inner sensitivity and ability to feel an individuality immortal, we will certainly have done for this our brother more than in the previous case, since we will have to discover for ourselves a part of what we are studying.

Suppose now that we wish to help, in the passage to the other world, someone who we were able to prepare in advance. We will then have the right and the duty (due to fraternal solidarity of all the cells of Adam Protoplasta) to help our brother, be it through magical acting on the body (if we possess the necessary knowledge) in order to sustain the activity of the astrosome, or by the theurgical performance, asking that the Light of Truth be lit before him.

The details of these procedures are part of a special Magic course, but here you can be given a brief general outline of the method of providing the aid referred to.

Let us not forget to have the process of death, from the hidden point of view, its beginning when medicine declares that the person has passed away. In order not to hinder and delay the process from birth to body should not be touched, pulled, disturbed or manipulated in any way, some for at least six hours after the death. In addition, it should be people whose fluids, in the life of the deceased, had not been sympathetic to him, since this could hamper the work of your astrosome. Do not talk about the body close to the body, material problems, since the conversations could be captured not only by the sixth sense of the "dead" but also by the subtle counterpart of his physical organs - his ghost.

During the second period, also of at least six hours (often more prolonged), the person who has set out to help the deceased should imagine himself accompanying him on the journey he is obliged to do for the other plan but for which he needs an affectionate "good-bye" from they who still have a foothold in the physical body. The "dead" who now understands his past dependence on the elementals, will be comforted knowing and feeling that one his brother, acting magically, rests on this same plane of elementals, to free him more quickly from that sphere.

During the later period and up to 40 days after the death, we would advise, due to the limitations of this course, there is only one thing: to pray for the dead, to feel solidarity with their needs but to avoid despair and distress. Even worse, and even almost criminal, would be to give up lamentations over the material damage done to us by the death of our neighbour. This could harm you during his fight with the Serpent.

In prayer and in magical acting, one must carefully tune in with the Evolutionary egrégores with which the "dead" felt in affinity.

When speaking of death as of the process of diminishing the number of planes that make up the being. It is also necessary to devote a few words to the reverse process: increasing the number of these planes, that is, the process known as the "incarnation of an elemental."

Suppose that the elemental has ended its stay in the middle astral of the solar system or even just in the dark cone; that the individualised currents of the biplane beings that govern involution, and which we call "Spiritus Directors" or "Archons", have already completed the redemptive experiences aimed at this elementary. In other words, its attraction for the lower astral is no longer mitigated by the study in the middle astral than it would be necessary for the next incarnation. He falls into the whirlwinds of the lower astral and, according to one who has learned and decided, is attracted and absorbed by a certain swirl-funnel, formed by the magic operation of "coitus" of their future land parents. Attraction is created by astral elements of the parents and by the zodiacal characteristics of their physical bodies. The choice of planetary influences is important so that the new human being can maintain, during his incarnation, the direction chosen by him at the time of his study in the middle astral. The zodiacal choice is important in determining the physical attributes - good or precarious - of the future body, according to the Karma of the determinate elemental. Attracted by the funnel, the elemental form, definitely his Nephesh which, in general lines, has already been delineated in the astral. The ease of forming the

Nephesh is conditioned by the already mentioned affinities with their future parents. In its turn, the formation of the physical body, ie the work of the Nephesh, is facilitated by the intrauterine life of the fetus, during which the struggle with adverse influences is limited to the minimum, due to the mother's astrosome energetic protection and the physical protection of her body, which supplies the fetus with appropriate elements.

The moment of birth, that is, the beginning of conflict with external influences, is very important for the human being, because the fact of the total inexperience of the newborn makes it, even for an instant, entirely receptive to planetary influences and zodiacal flows, which are more repelled by the astrosome of the mother. This is why astrology gives this moment a primordial importance.

After this analysis of the process of the death of a human being, one of the subjects belonging to the Arcanum XIII, we will move to the titles of the Arcanum. The first title, in common parlance, is "the Scythe"; in more erudite language - "the Death".

We have already observed that the idea of death, even in the presentation of the blade, is linked to the idea of Rebirth. In relation to the Archetype, this Arcanum tells us that the Archetype, triangle of Fabre d'Olivet corresponds to the present) never dies because it is continually reborn in its essence. Hence comes the title "Immortalitas in Essentia" or "Permanentia in Essentia "[38].

The adaptation of the Arcanum to the field of Man had already led us to the detailed analysis of the title "Mors et Reincarnatio"[39].

As for Nature, in her is always reborn, in a new form, everything that has disappeared. What will be this principle of constant rebirth which, despite the numerous transformations of forms, guards the collective value of your closed systems? This principle is energy. The third title of the Arcanum will therefore be "Transmutatio Energiae" or, in Helmholtz's terminology - "Transmutatio Virium. "It's interesting to notice that in the beginning the preservation of energy was formulated for the first time by a man whose profession obliged him to study the phases of illness and death (Dr. Meyer).

Let us turn now to the arithmetic analysis of the Arcanum.

13 = 1 + 12: A three-plane being (1) and the need for sacrifice on the physical plane (12) lead to the idea of death (13). This analysis alludes to the possibility of voluntary death, accepted as a sacrifice.

---

[38] Immortality in Essence or Permanence in Essence
[39] Death and Reincarnation

13 = 12 + 1: Here it is not a tri-plane entity that voluntarily renounces the third plane but, on the contrary, the zodiacal life (12) causes death, depriving the entity (1) of this third plane.

13 = 2 + 11: The polarity of good and evil (2), using force (11) can cause death (13). This is the formula of violent death.

13 = 11 + 2: The fully engaged force (11) must choose one of the two poles (2). This is Kadosh's formula: "If you have strength, be warm or cold."

13 = 3 + 10: The knowledge of the creative metaphysics of Hermes (3), together with the understanding of the higher purposes of the Mill of the World (10) leads to a complete reconciliation with the death (13). This is the formula of a natural death as development process.

13 = 10 + 3: This is again a natural death formula but seen from a point diametrically opposed and purely empirical. The Wheel of the Sphinx (10) turned and this movement created (3) a new state (13).

13 = 4 + 9: The power of authority (4) in Initiation (9) is due to knowledge of the mysteries of death (13).

13 = 9 + 4: Galvanising the degrees of Initiation (9) deprives of value any authority (4) of terrestrial character, because it reveals that this authority is subject to impermanence and death (13).

13 = 5 + 8: The pentagram (5) that dominates the impermanent laws (8) needs a large field of activity and, therefore, should change its plan (13). Or, it can also be: The religious sense (5), possessing primacy over the civic sense (8) denotes the presence of the awareness of death (13).

13 = 8 + 5: The primacy given to legality (8) oppresses the pentagram, depriving it (13) of point of support.

13 = 6 + 7: The problem of good and evil (6) leading to the victory of the subtle on the dense (7), contains in itself the germ of appreciation of the perennial values of the future life (13).

13 = 7 + 6: A winner (7) who, despite his victory, still evokes the question of good and evil (6), does it to emphasise the analogy of the subtle with the astral life and of the dense one with the physical life, that is, he preserves the consciousness of death (13).

We advise students, as an exercise, to do an arithmetic analysis of the Arcanum, not only in the field of Man as we have just done, but also in the two other fields or at least less in the third - that of Nature. For this, an elementary knowledge of physics and chemistry. We would like to add that many people consider the arithmetical Arcanum XIII corresponding to the various types of death, that is, several manifestations of Karma. We will therefore give them these correspondences so that each one, by himself, can check if the index is complete. The tone of each match is given by the last component of the formula.

13 = 1 + 12. Voluntary sacrifice of life for an ideal.

13 = 2 + 11. Death inflicted.

13 = 3 + 10. Natural death.

13 = 4 + 9. Adept death due to cord rupture during exteriorisation.

13 = 5 + 8. Death by force of law (eg execution of the condemned).

13 = 6 + 7. Death in struggle, bringing victory of the ideal.

13 = 7 + 6. Death in an unequal fight.

13 = 8 + 5. Death as an expression of the will of the pentagram, that is, suicide.

13 = 9 + 4. Premature death due to inadequate living conditions.

13 = 10 + 3. Death during childbirth.

13 = 11 + 2. Death due to the awareness of a tragic double situation.

13 = 12 + 1. The passage from the Adept to the other plane, due to the completion of his task on Earth. The instructor who will sustain the Egrégore in the astral plane. In France it is said that the person "is left to die. "

With this we end the study of the Arcanum XIII

Notes on the thirteenth Arcanum

The number thirteen has especially mystical properties in kabbalah and Judaism. It is the number of Unity/Oneness and Love – Echad and Ahava - and the number of the Mercies of God. The person of the Master Jesus, the personification of Love, is at Unified and at One with His 12 disciples.

The author Linda Goodman has written in her teachings on the kabbalah that the number 13 symbolises regeneration and: "The ancients claimed that 'he who understands how to use the number '13' will be given power and dominion."

I also recall here that most beautiful of New Testament verses, Corinthians 13:

1. I speak in the tongues of men and of angels, but have not love, I am only a resounding gong or a clanging cymbal.
2. If I have the gift of prophecy and can fathom all mysteries and all knowledge, and if I have a faith that can move mountains, but have not love, I am nothing.
3. If I give all I possess to the poor and surrender my body to the flames, but have not love, I gain nothing.
4. Love is patient, love is kind. It does not envy, it does not boast, it is not proud.

5. It is not rude, it is not self-seeking, it is not easily angered, it keeps no record of wrongs.
6. Love does not delight in evil but rejoices with the truth.
7. It always protects, always trusts, always hopes, always perseveres.
8. Love never fails. But where there are prophecies, they will cease; where there are tongues, they will be stilled; where there is knowledge, it will pass away.
9. For we know in part and we prophesy in part,
10. but when perfection comes, the imperfect disappears.
11. When I was a child, I talked like a child, I thought like a child, I reasoned like a child. When I became a man, I put childish ways behind me.
12. Now we see but a poor reflection as in a mirror; then we shall see face to face. Now I know in part; then I shall know fully, even as I am fully known.
13. And now these three remain: faith, hope and love. But the greatest of these is love.

It is in this Arcanum that Tomberg draws a clear analogy between sleeping, forgetting and death, contrasting it with the opposite state, whereby one remembers, awakens and is born.
It is not just the mind which forgets or remembers, but the soul and will may also participate. Similarly, just as there is a physical death, there may also be a psychic or a moral death.
Whilst forgetting is an aspect of death, remembrance is a magical operation of living which enables us to evoke an image or essence from the past. He speaks of four different sorts of memory: the mechanical or automatic, the logical, the moral and (a higher extension of this latter) the vertical, or revelatory memory. This latter is what "links the plane of ordinary consciousness to planes or states higher than that of ordinary consciousness." (MotT, Letter XIII, p346).
The ability of the higher self to engage this revelatory memory is largely dependent upon the discipline of the lower self in its fealty to the spiritual vows of poverty, chastity and obedience.
The moment when Jesus recalls Lazarus to life is presented as an ultimate act of divine remembrance. Thus is absolute recall analogous to Resurrection.
We might be said to forget the gravitational pull from below when we are recalled to reunion with God in heaven above. "It is through the mastery over forgetfulness, sleep and death that one arrived in the past, that one arrives today, and that one will arrive in the future, at the

mystical experience of the soul united with God, and therefore at the absolute certainty of immortality". (MotT, Letter XIII p367).
Herein is a glimpse inside the Mystery of the Mother Letter, Mem, which along with Aleph and Shin contains an Aeon of divine teaching, theurgical and psychological, astral and emotional, physical, mental and a word for the Soul to digest.

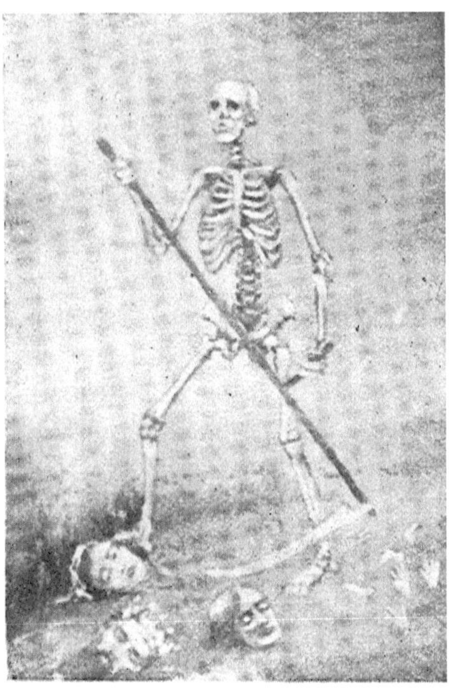

Arcanum XIV

ג

TEMPERANCE

The Pathway from Netzach to Tiphareth

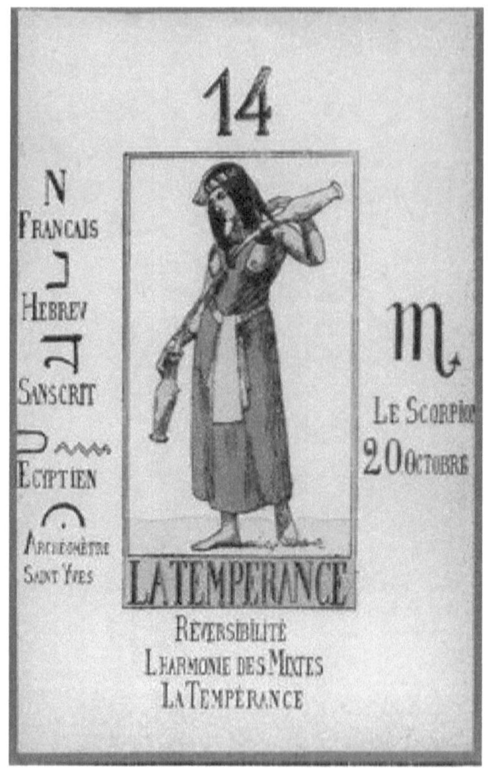

The Guardian Angel has the *Remedy*

Pass alternately from the triangle to the circle, and from the circle to the triangle

Levi

THE SOLAR SPIRIT: Initiative

N--50 expresses in the divine world the perpetual movement of life

Paul Christian

In great awe I understood that I was near the ultimate mysteries from which there is no return. I looked upon the angel, upon his symbols, his cups, the rainbow stream between the cups,--and my human heart trembled with fear and my human mind shrank with anguish and lack of understanding.

Ouspensky

The sign of the alphabet corresponding to this Arcanum is נ (Nun), whose numeric value is 50, its astrological correspondence: sign of Scorpio. The hieroglyph of the Arcanum is the fruit, that is, that which matures in the belly of the Woman of the Arcanum XIII.

The idea of the immortality of the Archetype has the fruit of the gift of the ability of a priori judgments, which would not exist if we decided to recognise the metaphysical principles as unstable in essence. The fruit of the idea of death and reincarnation is the consciousness of the need for a hermetic harmony of active and passive elements filtered by the human person. The fruit of a detailed study of energy transformations are theories in which the first question is the reversibility or irreversibility of processes. Here are three headlines for the Fourteenth Arcanum: Deductio, Harmonia Mixtorum, Reversibilitas.

The picture of the Fourteenth Arcanum shows us the image of the Solar Genius in clothes shining white, crowned with a gold band, girded with a gold belt, behind which a white plate is plugged, and carefully, without losing a single drop, pouring liquid from a golden vessel into a silver one.

What does this picture tell us, entitled in the scientific language "Ingenium Solare", and in the vulgar "la Temperance"?

This is the Solar Genius; the influence of the sun is synthetic; therefore, the fruit, symbolised by this Arcanum, should ultimately lead us to synthesis. So, deduction, often assuming an analytical character at the beginning of the study of an object, has the ultimate goal of its powerful synthesis. Pursuit of the harmony of the astral composition of the Personality, being satisfied at certain stages between incarnations with the equilibrium of a group of planetary influences, selects as the ultimate goal the Solar synthesis of these influences. Energy, studying the reversibility of particular processes of energy transfer, seeks to complete its system with a synthetic study of the entropy of closed systems.

The golden band and the golden belt of the figure, together with the white clothes and the board, are the simple attributes of the Solar Genius; they have nothing to give a special explanation. A continuous stream of liquid between the gold and silver vessels hints at equalising the liquid level in these vessels.

The purpose of deduction is to equalise a priori the validity of the existence of all objects of our judgments, to establish a complete system of associations that excludes any longing for the search for individual causal relationships.

The goal of harmonising the astrosome is to equalise all manifestations of our ability to perceive and generate volitional impulses, and thereby create a complete inner world in the heart of the androgynous personality.

The purpose of the modern formulation of the doctrine of entropy is the general layout of the future picture of calming the sum of energies in an ensemble of irreversible phases.

After this introduction, I can allow myself to proceed to the arithmetic analysis of the lasso, an idea of which is often conveyed by the term "Temperance".

14 = 1 + 13: Hermes Trismegistus (1), possessor of the principle of immortality (13) presents a grand scheme of deduction (14). A three-dimensional human being (1), wisely using his incarnations (13), ends up performing hermetic harmony (14).

The study of Nature as "Natura Naturans" (1) and the synthesis of studies in the physical plane of transformation of energy (13) give a correct understanding of reversible energy transformations (14) within a closed system.

We note that the inversion of the order of numerical values in Arithmetic changes the picture; changes only the order of appearance of the components. Analysing an Arcanum as synthetic as the XIV, we will limit ourselves to a single order of components.

14 = 2 + 12: The polarity (2) in the human being and the laws of mercy towards his fellows (12) are the keys to hermetic harmony (14). Let us remember that Geburah and Chesed give birth to Tiphareth.

14 = 3 + 11: The creativity (3) and the force of the egrégores (11) transmit the harmony (14) to the organs separated from Protoplast.

14 = 4 + 10: The intuitive capacity of one who represents authority (4) and initiation to Kabbalah (10) open the way to hermetic harmony (14).

14 = 5 + 9: The formation of the Pentagram (5) and its Initiation (9) lead to hermetic harmony (14).

14 = 6 + 8: Free will (6), together with respect for the Law (8) lead to hermetic harmony (14).

14 = 7 + 7: Hermetic harmony (14) is achieved by balancing the victory of activity (7) with victory of intuition (7). If our receptivity has been enriched with something new, we should also broaden the scope of our activity. In physics, reversibility (14) can be seen as two phases (7) of the same cycle.

As we see, the action of the Arcanum resembles it to the activity of the Solar Genius. It's relatively easy [to observe] their influence and realise their indispensability but it is extremely difficult to discover the details of their performance. In order to discover them one must be rich in fluids, as is the Solar Genius. For us these fluids consist of metaphysical understanding, ethical experience on the physical plane.

Complement to Arcanum XIV

Energy can take the form of matter and it is again transformed into energy. These are reversible processes reversible from subtle to dense and vice versa, represented on the slide by the flow which passes from the jar of gold to the jar of silver, and again returns to that of gold. Something similar happens with the human being. In this sense, the Arcanum XIV can be considered as a continuation of the XIII, because the subtle and dense states - disembodied and incarnate - are followed in the existence of being until it reaches Reintegration.

The further study of Arcanum XIV covers the teaching concerning the Monad, the androgyny, to the three basic types of souls and, finally, to differentiate septenary, planetary. From the latter depend the characteristics of the incarnated personality ie the pentagram immersed in matter. Because of this, the Arcanum XIV is often called the Arcanum of personality. It is a reflection of the Arcanum V. Its numeric value (14 = 5) and its correspondence to the Hebrew letter נ (value 50) confirm it. The title of the Arcanum in the plane of Man - "Harmony mixtorum" - indicates his harmonising action, both in the collectivities - by the integration and completely mutual of their members - as in the human personality which, too, is a set of diverse components. The fullness of the personality is acquired by the multiplication and polishing of all its facets, by the transmutation of its lower planetary attributes into superiors and by the development of the androgyny, by cultivating the qualities of the opposite polarity of each planet, especially the dominant one. Harmonization encompasses the three planes: the mental, the astral, and the physical. Only the realisation of a complete and perfect synthesis allows the personality to surpass its own plan - that of personality - and attain that of immortal individuality.

There is yet another aspect of Arcanum XIV, purely mystical, in which the silver jar symbolises the human soul, receiving the divine flow from the golden jar.

Notes on the fourteenth Arcanum

Being devoted to our own guardian angel and the Archangels Michael, Gabriel, Raphael, Uriel and Phanuel, we had been especially looking forward to G.O.M.'s teaching on the XIV Arcanum. As such, we were disappointed to find that it was the shortest chapter by far of the Tarot Majors.

This is in great contrast with the treatment of the same Arcanum in Meditations on the Tarot, which provides the most beautiful teachings on the Guardian Angel – the 'faithful ally' - that I have ever read. It is notable, here, that the author of MotT encourages his own readers to study this Arcanum in more depth, pointing out that what he terms 'angelology' is one of the most fruitful courses of further study [following completion of the Tarot Arcana exercises] that he can recommend. He positively encourages keen students to do so.
The Guardian Angel

...takes care that there is a connection between the great 'yesterday, today and tomorrow' of the human soul....[and who, if it is necessary] awakens recollections of the soul's previous earthly lives, in order to establish continuity of endeavour. (MotT, p376).

As the natural defender of his/her human being, the Guardian Angel can either participate or not participate in human affairs, depending upon what is required. On those occasions when he/she is required to take a more active role in human affairs – an action that must not only be permitted but actually called for – the Guardian Angel

...descends from the point of his ordinary post into the domain of human activity. He then visits the human being.

Such a 'visit' is of course the primary aim of so much magical work and we are put in mind of the 'Knowledge and Conversation of the Holy Guardian Angel', made famous by the English occultist, Aleister Crowley. This may have been an idea Crowley picked up from The Book of the Sacred Magic of Abra Melin the Mage written by 15th Century German Kabbalist, Abraham of Worms and translated by Samuel Liddell MacGregor Mathers, founder of the British order, Hermetic Order of the Golden Dawn.
The early teachings of Crowley are (for once, broadly speaking!) in alignment with Tomberg's in viewing the Guardian Angel as a representative of the 'higher self' of the human being, or the human being in their primordial 'pre-Fall' state. It is this Angel in Crowley's Thelema system who is to lead his/her human charge across the abyss, a sphere that may be represented by the Sephira Daath. We are not convinced this is something which can (or should) be achieved via artificial means, beyond the natural karmic and proper initiatory path of the individual, but it is testament to the magnetic appeal of the Guardian Angel that so much effort has been devoted to 'bringing him/her down' to Earth to guide lost human souls.

In later life and writing in his book, Magick without Tears, Crowley revises his view of the Angel as an aspect of the self, instead seeing the Guardian as an independent and discrete being. He goes so far as to say that to simply view the Angel as part of the self is an actual heresy, though heresy against which religion we are not sure. Magick without Tears is an interesting book which amply displays Crowley's infamously sharp intellect, also providing an interesting contrast with Tomberg's reference to the Gift of Tears in Letter II, The High Priestess of MotT:

An advanced pupil of yoga or Vedanta will for ever have dry eyes, whilst the masters of Cabbala, according to the Zohar, cry much and often. Christian mysticism speaks also of the "gift of tears" - as a precious gift of divine grace. (MotT, p36).

He returns to this theme in the fourteenth Arcanum, where he explains that the

"gift of tears" was always considered by the masters of Christian spirituality as a grace from the Holy Spirit, for it is thanks to this gift that the soul surpasses itself and ascends to a degree of intensity of life which is certainly above that to which it is accustomed. (MotT, p388).

Every revelation given in the Zohar is accompanied by the weeping of whomsover received and then shared this revelation. In this context we are also put in mind of the Wailing Wall in Jerusalem.

Blessed are those who mourn, for they shall be comforted (Matthew V).

Such subtle but vital variations of teaching can provide much food for thought to students who are trying to find their way amongst the rich forest of ideas and teachings which have been bequeathed to us by the masters of different occult schools.

We have not consciously performed the Abramelin procedure and it is not something we can personally recommend. We would rather suggest one simply prays to one's Angel – and indeed the Archangels – and speaks to him/her through the heart, as one would to an absolutely faithful friend and champion.

The proper place of our Angel is to stand above us, shielding us from the unbearable direct gaze of God with wings of perfect love, constituting our first direct link with the upward vertical hierarchy of divine beings consisting of: Angels, Archangels, Principalities, Powers (Exousia), Virtues (Dynamis), Dominions (Kyriotes), Thrones, Cherubim and Serpahim.

Tomberg recommends the study of angels as being particularly suitable for anyone wishing to advance The Work. Did he also feel that G.O.M. had underdone what for many occultists is the most ardently longed for attainment: The knowledge and conversation of the Holy Guardian Angels?
Whatever the answer might be, a pathwalker can be absolutely confident and sure that their Guardian Angel is with them every step of the way.

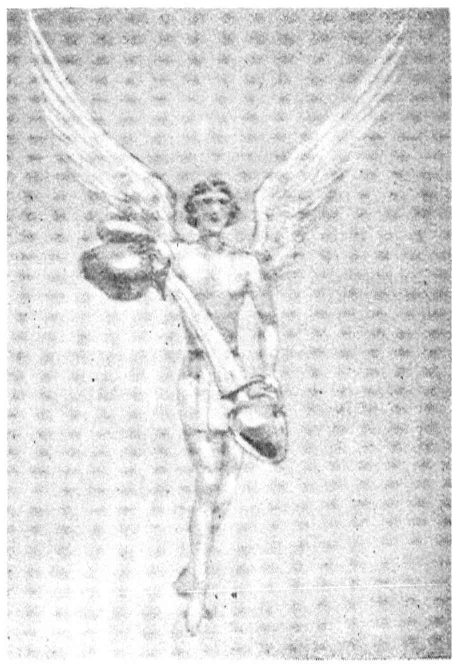

Arcanum XV

THE DEVIL

The Pathway from Tiphareth to Hod

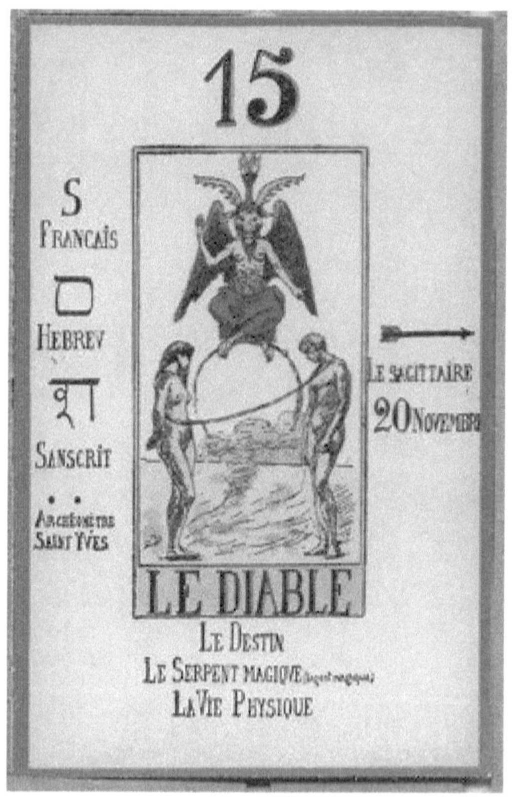

The Devil governs *Black Magic*

If you help the blind, you may be served by him; if you let the blind lead, you are lost

Levi

TYPHON: Fate

Paul Christian

"They forgot that It is a key to the gate of the magic world, the torch which lights the higher Path. They forgot that Love is real and immortal and they subjugated it to the unreal and temporary. And they each made love a tool for submitting the other to himself.

"Then love became dissension and fettered them with iron chains to the black cube of matter, on which sits deceit".

Ouspensky

The letter of the alphabet, corresponding to the Arcanum XV, is ס (Samekh). Its numerical value, 60, the astrological correspondence, Sagittarius.

The hieroglyph of the Arcanum is an arrow skirting the surface of a circle. It is no longer the arrow of Arcanum VII that followed a straight line and could eventually hurt us. The meeting with the arrow of Arcanum XV is inevitable and awaits us as we seek to go beyond the boundary of the circle. However, this encounter provides two possibilities: either we will be hit by the arrow ourselves, or we will have to use it against others. It's the constant whirlwind, out of which there is no life, there is no movement in any of the planes.

In the plane of the Archetype, the whirlpool represents the unchanging logic to govern all metaphysical conceptions, until reaching and including the transcendent region of the second family sephiroth. The transcendental region is not subject to its influence. Hence comes the first title of the Arcanum: "Logic".

In the field of Humanity, the whirlwind is manifested by the intense attractions that, according to inexorable laws from the astral plane, awaken and instigate desires. The source of these desires is the collective Nephesh that humanity itself has created since its fall. The powerful whirlwind, becomes a weapon in a man's hand - a weapon that he must use against others - or, imperceptibly, he makes of the man a slave of other pentagrams who knew how to put themselves in the upper levels and can observe and use their strength there.

The field of whirlwind activity is Universal Humanity. On every planet, in the uppermost levels of whirlwind, there is a genius working for the evolution of mankind on this planet. The lower planes of the same whirlwind are the sphere of the Serpent's influence of planetary involution which seeks to attract souls to the "dark cone". In the case of Earth, this influence is manifested in shape of the circular whirlwind of which we speak in Arcanum XIII.

The general denomination of this universal factor is Nahash, and this name will be the second title of the Arcanum XV. He is the serpent that seduced Eve.

The field of Nature is also subject to relentless whirlwinds governing all its manifestations, from the minor ones. Its general name is "Fatum", that will be the third title of the Arcanum. The essence of these eddies is no different from the essence of Nahash.

The influence of the Arcanum XV is involutive, for its swirls begin in the higher planes and descend to the lower ones. This is why the Arcanum has received negatively polarised names: the scholar, "Typhon" and the common, "Devil."

Let us now study the card of the Arcanum. Its upper part is occupied by the traditional Baphomet of the Templars, which is sitting on a cube, firmly implanted in a globe. Before the Baphomet, standing on the globe, there are two figures: on the right a man; left, a woman, both completely naked and chained to one another. The chain is wound around the neck of the man and, passing to the woman, wraps itself around her hip.

So, the traditional Baphomet with the world of its realisations (the cube standing on the globe) disconnected the polarities of the Human Androgyne. A simple, but amazingly empirically correct picture of the fall of אדם – הוה (Adam – Eve). An involutive nature of contemplation (הוה) was the beginning of the fall; the desire for involutive realisation (אדם Adam) completed it; intuition and activity were ultimately disconnected in life by the very element of the materialisation of life (globe). But the disconnected אדם and הוה are connected by a common chain of slavery to Baphomet. This slavery laid a yoke on the neck of activity, restricting its impulses, interfering with its movements (time, space). It also embraced the noblest parts of receptivity, those of her organs that allow her to harbor intuitive perceptions and give birth to harmonious pictures. If אדם (Adam) is constrained in freedom of movement, then Eve is constrained in freedom of imagination.

But how can they free themselves from this slavery? How do they reunite in the primary, powerful Androgyne? The picture gives a clear answer to this question. It is necessary, having thinned the matter of the globe, to penetrate through it towards each other, to take possession of Baphomet, to draw it to itself, to penetrate into it, boldly penetrating into its organic life, to get to its horns, to dematerialise them and to rush upwards, burning your personality in an ascending unitary flame, crowning the astral god. This is the way of Reintegration of those who are heavy in the chains of the lower part of the picture and who are not afraid to take on themselves the image of a winged androgynous monster. This is the Templar path, the path of people taking the sky by storm to break out of the tight yolk of the Earth.

The need to study the composition of Baphomet himself is clearly visible.

We already know that the person who wants to master it must subtlise the matter of the globe, located between his activity and receptivity, i.e. he must realise the illusions of the physical world, learn to despise the obstacles that he poses on the path to improvement.

Let this globe be already refined, let it become so transparent that it allows activity to see intuition and vice versa. What's next? Next - the Great Adaptation Cube - the ability to apply oneself to the environment in which you operate, when the non-essential comes into play, and the power to adapt the environment to itself, when essential issues come into play. Never forget that the "adaptation cube" is at the same time the "authority cube".

Moving on. On the cube sits the Great Androgyne himself, the bearer of the Signs of the Four Elements, and, consequently, the owner of the four "hermetic virtues." Earth globe under the legs of Androgyne; fish scales, symbolising water, covers his stomach; wings of air - behind him, and the flame of "fire" rises to the sky from a three-pointed torch, affirmed on his head. So, then comes the area of hermetic virtues, and the area of Fire is characteristically subordinate to the Great Metaphysical Ternary. Thus, we can see that the world of Baphomet; in its higher plane, is governed by the ternary principle, and on the lower plane, by the quaternary of the scheme of the Great Arcanum. However,

It is the medium plane - the binary - which is especially accentuated. The left arm is male; on it is written the word "solve" (dissolve). This arm points to a clear crescent moon sickle. The right arm is female and on it we see the word "coagulates" (densifies). He points to a dark scythe of waning moon.

It is important to note that the waning moon is at the lower level of the figure, and the crescent moon at the upper level, so that the male arm is raised and the female is lowered. The figure has female breasts. From the groin, a twin-convoluted Caduceus rises. The heads of snakes lean against the sphere located at the level of the solar plexus of the figure. It would be difficult to gather more indications of the bipolarity of the astral of the field of its influence.

Note that the number of the Arcanum is 15, and that the sum of its numbers is 6; this Arcanum, must therefore be mysteriously linked (as is the central part of the Great Arcanum) to the problem of Good and Evil, a problem of the two ways. If the sphere of the Caduceus, being in the Baphomet solar plexus height, alludes to the Tree of Life (Sephira Tiphareth), then there must also be allusions to the Tree of Knowledge of Good and Evil.

Let us look closely at the astral deity. Its horns, ears and beard outline an inverted pentagram, that is, involutive. This is the aspect of Evil that we find in the figure. However, the ternary of the triple torch dominates over the horns, forming with them a pentagram in the straight, evolutionary position. Many people do not perceive it and because of this, for the sake of clarity, in the forehead of the figure there is usually another, evolving, additional pentagram.

The figure has goat feet resting on the globe. Why? Those who composed the Tarot wanted to underline that, having declined, we subjected ourselves to the influence of the inverted pentagram, involutive, or the goat, and now we need the terrestrial globe as a point of support for evolution.

Why are the feet crossed so that the right hull is on the left side of the globe, and the left hull - on the right side? This is an allusion to the inverted sense in which we perceive the astral, for we perceive it as our image reflected in the mirror. People who are not sufficiently trained in the transmission, to the physical language, of their astral perceptions, reverse them. The clairvoyants and sleepwalkers who see from a distance, say they have always seen left, which is actually on the right, and vice versa.

The prophet Ezekiel who, during an exteriorisation, contemplated the cliché of one of the hermetic quaternaries, presented it as its reflection in the mirror and not in its actual placement. The same can be said of the Fourth Apostle of St. John. Only those who are trained in the astral clichés, acquire the ability to interpret them in their correct sense in relation to the physical plane.

Everything that has just been said proves to us that the figure of Arcanum XV is a complete representation of the great astral whirlwind, including its superior influence (the triple flame of the metaphysical ternary), and the inverted mode of transmission of the astral clichés to the physical plane (the feet crusaders).

The Arcanum XV received the sinister name of "Typhon" because, in the scheme of the three septenaries, in which the Tarot Major Arcana are classified according to the degree of density, the influence of this - the XV - was considered more obscuring than illuminating.

Interpreting the figure of the blade, we allowed ourselves to use the term templar "Baphomet". This obliges us to explain it.

The word "Baphomet", once read right to the left gives us "Temohpab". It's the Notarikon of the phrase: "Templi omnium hominum pacis abbas" which, translated from the Latin, means: "the abbot of the temple of peace for all men ".

With this term the Templars designated the personification of the astral swirl, general, that, well directed, can lead humanity through the path of peace and self-improvement. Let us not forget that the Templar Order dreamed of establishing on Earth the realm of peace and unity between all peoples, and in order to realise it, he used the powerful swirls of his astral chain.

The description of the image of Baphomet was made by us, not according to the templar representations (these were completely destroyed by the agents of the Inquisition of Pope Clement V and of them nothing remained), but according to Kunrath's engraving "The Great Androgyne" which, by his symbolic composition, corresponds to Baphomet.

In order that the astral god may be better imagined, we consider it useful to transcribe the description of its characteristics in the Emerald Verses. This description immediately follows the verses transcribed by us in the study of Arcanum VI;

"Pater ejus est Sol, mater ejus Luna; portavit illud Ventus in ventre suo; nutrix ejus Terra est Pater omnis Telesmi totius mundi est hic. Vis ejus integra est, si versa fuerit in Terram. Separabis terram ab igne, subtile a spisso, suaviter, cum magno ingenio. Ascendit a terra in coelum, iterumque descended in terram, et recipit vim superiorum et inferiorum".

What, in the literal translation, is:

"His father is the Sun, his mother is the Moon; the Wind carried him in his womb; His land is the nurse. It is the source of all Expediency in the whole universe. His strength is fully exhausted if it is turned into the earth. You will separate the earth from the fire, subtle from the dense, smoothly, with great skill. He ascends from earth to heaven and returns to earth again, being charged with the power of higher and lower (principles)."

This can be commented on as follows:

Baphomet is born, according to the great Gnostic Law, of an active " י" and a passive "He", to which this י corresponds; vampirises the global environment and establishes its point of support in clots more dense. The volitional entities, born of any beings of the Universe, are entirely formed of its substance. As much as it is involved in the crust of physical clots, their substance become more concrete. You will need to discern which are the active elements and which are the liabilities of each action. He (the Baphomet) is a double whirlwind, whose upward movement receives the energy of the point of support in the coagulates, and the descendant - of its point of suspension in the higher metaphysical principles.

This is the subject matter for meditation on Arcanum XV. At first glance, this Arcanum does not seem to be adding new elements to the ones we already had. But if we meditate well on the whole presented by the image of the great astral deity, we will find answers to many mysteries of realisation.

Let us try, by arithmetical analysis, to familiarise ourselves with the general character of the adaptations of Arcanum XV.

15 = 1 + 14: This is the formula of the Divine Essence (1) that governs the logical deduction (14) of the man of three planes (1) that harmonise its astrosome (14); of the active Nature (1) that takes its entropy (14) to a given numerical value. In other words, it is the formula of the Arcanum Samekh when ruled from above, acting upon the noblest organs of his ganglion system.

This image is so complete, so satisfying in its universality, that many find their way there. One seeks their happiness and perfection simply by contemplating it (contemplatives schools of union with Nature); others - penetrating into the universal whirlwind, as a of their passive cells (certain Hindu schools); still others seek to introduce the government of a elite to improve - by the same formula 1 + 14 - the social and political status of the people. This is the of the Synarchists of China, India and the West. We will make a quick appreciation of these possibilities for progress.

If a human being goes deep into the passive contemplation of the powerful picture symbolised by formula 15 = 1 + 14, imperceptibly and by the very fact of being in this field magnetising in an analogous way, acquiring harmony and internal peace and realising in itself even the supremacy of the subtle over the dense. In other words, the practice of this contemplation will lead the contemplative into the domain of Arcanum VII, and this without the strenuous efforts that usually accompany the victory of the "three" over the "four" in the experience of Arcanum VII himself.

However, initiation in Arcanum VII completes only the first step, that of "apprentice" in the Masonic initiation. For a cell of the great Adam Protoplast it is not enough to tune in only with the evolutionary note. It is also necessary for her to have an exact knowledge of the work of other cells of the same organism, in order to establish an appropriate relationship with them. Certain schools, therefore, seek to carry out the second step by teaching their followers that, both in metaphysical meditation and in astral exercises and in activity on the physical plane, experience every hour, every minute, every moment, the motto "I am united with everyone and everything; that which is in accord with the great evolutionary whirlwind of humanity; I want to follow only that which represents the metaphysics of the Ascending Triangle; I want to do only what propitiates the designs of the Karma of Nature. I clearly understand that my task is to be a gear that correctly and efficiently transmits the movement of the Universal Mechanism; in this transmission I do not want to provoke friction with my personal fantasies."

This, so to speak, is the School of Evolutionary Naturalism. But besides this Masonic He, which constitutes the Partnership's task, there is also the Initiation into the Masters, striving to create a ו, born of a correctly-magnetised Father and fed by a correctly-naturalised Mother. The implementation of this ו in the field of world politics is the cherished dream of the so-called. Synarchists. He dreams of the United States of all cultural nationalities regulated in the internal governance of the Three Great Chambers - Spiritual, Legal and Economic. The Spiritual Chamber will, so to speak, generate the logic of collective deduction and scientific aspirations. Representatives of cults, philosophical movements and Orthodox Freemasonry will find a place in it. The Law Chamber, managing the Nahash of national and personal aspirations, will develop legal norms that harmonise these aspirations, ensure lasting peace on the planet and prevent any crime. The Economic Chamber will regulate the fortune of individuals and nationalities in such a way as to maintain the welfare of Mankind at the level of the best possible expression of Fatum of this era. The way to operate this Chamber will be a comprehensive understanding of the principle of reversibility of values.

It might be objected that in logic the first premise is often chosen; also, that in the unification of different desires, there is a choice between different combinations, and that the theory of probability applied to the reversibility of values also allows a choice between possibilities.

The synarchists reply that: "Yes, everybody needs a strong-willed monad to choose a solution in cases of hesitation, and therefore the Patriarch will be at the head of the Spiritual Chamber, the Monarch at the head of the Legal Chamber, and the General-Economy at the head of the Economic."

The other details about the synarchic system, the method of constitution of parliaments, appointment of the hierarchs etc, do not enter our present study. We speak of synarchy only to give a general example of the influence of the Contemplative - Naturist line on the minds attracted by politics. Those interested in the subject can find more material in the works of St. Yves d'Alveydre.

$15 = 14 + 1$: logical deduction (14) limited by the influences of a given epoch drowns in the human being the Divine Essence (1). This is the formula of the pitiful framework of atheism based on pseudo-scientific conclusions, in fashion in the eighteenth century. We will not talk much about this current. It has many representatives, but fortunately it no longer includes most minds.

A false harmony of desires (14), based on conventionalism, stifles the high impulses, intelligence and practical of individuals (1), who voluntarily submit to the relaxed morality of the time. This influence gives birth to the deplorable currents of literature, pornographic works and anti-aesthetics that flood the bookstores and whose authors are often talented but always of weak will.

The processes of transforming energy (14) in Nature serve as a measure for its creative resources (1). This is the formula of determinism in the field of physical phenomena, and this, when more pronounced, leads to complete fatalism. Fatalism may help certain people to live a few years more, due to the reduced wear of vital fluids in volitional activity; however, the history shows us that the fatalism restricts the lives of peoples and makes them lose their capacities as individuals.

15 = 2 + 13: Knowing the mystery of Divine Substance (2), accepting it as the basis and, in the spirit of the mystery of immortality (13) of metaphysical principles, is to master the logic of the world of Aziluth (15). To know the mystery of human receptivity (2) and the reincarnation of souls (13) means to rule the mighty serpent Nahash, in the field of his influence upon men (15).

15 = 13 + 2: To seek the permanent metaphysical principles (13) and to become sensitive to the substance (2) is to master the logic of the Second Family. To arrive, through many incarnations (13), to feel the subtle (2), means to begin in Nahash (15), that is, to understand the details of their mode of action.

15 = 3 + 12 and 15 = 12 + 3: Understand the great words of the Emerald Verses that affirm that Baphomet (15) descends: From the metaphysically creative heaven (3), to the zodiacally materialised Earth (12); of knowledge of the Gnostic Law of creativity (3) to the understanding of the principle of sacrifice (12); of the divine Nature (3) to the mystery of the Incarnation of the Word (12), and do not forget, therefore, that the same powerful whirlwind rises in the opposite direction – from Earth for the Sky, means get knowledge of one of the aspects of Arcanum XV. It is necessary to understand that if, on the one hand, God gave the Testament to Abraham, on the other hand, the sincere metaphysical quest of Abraham magnetically attracted this gift.

15 = 4 + 11 and 15 = 11 + 4: The union of Form (4) and the invincible force (11) of the Metaphysical Triangle, determine our logic (15). The authority (4) attached to the resources of the chain (11), covers everything we have created in the field of usefulness and of the rational (15). The adaptation to the environment (4), joining the mysterious principles, called Forces of Nature (11) determines the manifestations of the "Fatum" (15).

15 = 5 + 10 and 15 = 10 + 5: The science of Good and Evil (5) and the knowledge of the Testament (10) create the framework of Absolute Logic (15). The formation of the pentagram (5) and the knowledge of the Kabbalah (10) reveal the mystery of Baphomet (15). Religion (5) - memory of the past Nature - and the relentless Mill of the World (10) determine the "Fatum" of the phenomenal world. Let us dwell on the last formulas.

We have already spoken in Arcanum V of the formation of the
Pentagram, and in Arcanum X, of the understanding of the Universe
through the Kabbalah. We would like to add a few words about the role
of the "+" element that joins the two components of one of the terms of
the equation. This "+" in the last formulas plays the role of neutralising
element between the two movements of the whirlwind - the ascendant
and the descending - uniting them in totality. Thus, the element "+" has
an androgynous character we shall call the "pentagrammatic-cosmic" or
"cosmic-pentagrammatic."
The mystery of this "+" is that Kabbalah (10) must in part be created by
the pentagram (5) but, on the other hand, the pentagram (5) must have
been formed in a kabbalistic way (10), not just any way.
The magic of the Templars had, as a point of support, a logic common to
all mankind and used in its operations the active power of the Nahash
Serpent. They took advantage of all the favourable circumstances of the
"Fatum", that is, carefully planned its activity, utlising the power of
human desires and availing themselves immediately of favorable
situations. Such magic is possible only when a pentagram is nourished
by the Kabbalah and this is, in turn, marked by the will of the same
pentagram. Here, it is indispensable that there be a "Sabbath" for the
"Son of Man" and that, at the same time, the "Son of Man" is the master
of the "Sabbath".
If we put ourselves at the disposal of a human being, in particular, or of
a chain of human beings, all the manuscripts relating to the metaphysics
of the ancient and modern schools, all the magical writings, and if that
person or this chain, does not add their own understanding to them, their
individual participation, their own intelligent use of the received
material, all this will remain sterile and no magic operation can be
performed by that person or chain. If we have a food, we do not just look
at it or hold it to increase the supply of our food, organic energy; it is
necessary to ingest and assimilate it, and for this, it is usually necessary
to prepare it and cook it in advance. This basic truth is often ignored by
so-called "profane". Only self-understanding and the right job can
achieve positive results. The mere possession of materials produced by
others is insufficient.
In order to establish harmony, in any system, through the use of the
mantram אמש (Emesh), we must have realised in ourselves the three
types of equilibrium: the metaphysical, the hermetic, and the submission
to Karma. If we have performed them incompletely or unilaterally, then
the effects of our operation will be either incomplete or unilateral. If, in
order to manifest dynamically our will, choose the Great Name יהוה
then the effects of our performance would be to prove clearly, to what
extent we apply in our private life, the great principle of the gnostic

formula. Suppose someone lives plagiarising; in this case, the mantra instead of producing the effects expected by it, may lead to different manifestations due to of other pentagrams of the surrounding environment. If somebody superficially adopts ideas without digesting them and assimilating, the manifestation will be partial or unfinished. Let us suppose that the element " ו" of the person is weak, that is, that it does not implement the ideas theoretically accepted; then the whirlwind will form but will remain without force. Suppose, finally, that the "second He" of the person is not formed, that is, that he has not yet synthesised everything he has acquired, has not yet made it an appropriate instrument of realisation; here the manifestation may outwardly be very beautiful, but it will not be the basis of any serious realisation. It will be like a firework that soon goes out without a trace. No one should try to exteriorise himself, without first having the conviction that he is an independent entity regardless of his physical enclosure. One must be well aware that exteriorisation is of the self itself and not something alien to it.

We should not try to act upon others if we are not convinced that it is our own influence, not some external influence.

We should not attempt a theurgical performance if prayer is for us only a banal repetition according to a mold established by others, if we speak these words only with our lips, if we have not yet learned to pray in our hearts, if we have not yet condensed our individual resonances, that is, if we have not yet heard the voice of our "Hermetic Lion."

We should not use other people's pantaculos if we do not feel our own worldview in them; if the kabbalistic signs do not seem to us to be organs of our own astral being, if the limits of these pantaculos are not felt by us as outlines formed by our own active fluids.

I also repeat that an imperfect Kabbalah but authentically ours is better than a perfect but alien system that is not lived by us, not studied by us deeply. It is better to use a phrase without sense that for some reason we interpret in our own way and which we consider as a mantram, than to use the wisest set of kabbalistic elements that do not even make sense to us and we have not even bothered to meditate upon.

Here is the wisdom we can deduce from the unfolding of Arcanum XV in 5 and 10.

$15 = 6 + 9$ and $15 = 9 + 6$: The Law of Analogy (6) and the Superior Protection (9) in the choice of support points for this Law, guarantee the purity of absolute logic (15). Free will (6) and traditional initiation (9) condition the control of our passions and use of the passions of others (15).

Knowledge of the environment (6) and prudence (9) ensure the choice of a karmically propitious moment (15). These deep but simple truths almost dispense with comment.

15 = 7 + 8 and 15 = 8 + 7: The victory (7) of the idea about the form and knowledge of the law of equilibrium in the world (8) guarantee the logic of thought (15).

The victory (7) about oneself and the knowledge of conditioning laws (8) allow to explore the passions of others (15). The understanding of property rights (7) and the law of retribution (8) explains the performance of "Fatum" (15).

This is the theoretical part of Arcanum analysis. Let us turn to its practical application, dividing it into two aspects: the active and the passive.

The passive states obtained by the understanding of the Arcanum XV consist in the tuning of the whirlwind which normally govern the ganglion system of the human astrosome, with the vibrations of whirlwinds of considerably greater magnitude.

Let us try to imagine the astral plane as something alive, that is, to consider everything that happens in it as modifications within a single organism, vast and uniplanic. This organism is the "Baphomet" of the Templars, that is the astrosome of the Macrocosm, plus the sum of the astrosomes of all entities evolutionary pentagrammatic, involutive and neutral that do not belong to Malkuth. On the other hand, clearly imagine our own astrosome, as being an astral microcosm governed by our mind, and already possessing the domain of the Arcanum of Adaptation. It's up to us to tune it in with one or another chosen macrocosmic vibration. In the evolutionary sense, this choice is unlimited.

Of course, however, in order to tune into a very high vibration, we need to raise also our own vibrations through prolonged training, which sometimes leads to many incarnations.

As for vibrations less than ours, it is very easy to tune in with them. However, instead of the ascent, the descent is limited, because the condensation of the fluids does not go beyond a certain point.

Contacting one of the organs of Baphomet means tuning our resonator, or rather, our system of astral resonators to the pitch of the certain organ of Baphomet. This body can be highly elevated (such as, for example, the subtle astral of the Egrégore of the Reintegrated Cross + Rose) or a medium level (e.g., the synthesis of clichés of a certain chain, for example, the synthesis of the misleading clichés of some of the currents called "satanists"). Of course, the tuning of our resonators with certain vibrations, in general requires prolonged work and is a task, necessary for the realisation of some general, broader plan. If the target is achieved, our astrosome integrates and strengthens the symphony of organ vibrations corresponding to Baphomet. It is said, in this case, that our astrosome united with a determined Egrégore. From Baphomet's point of view, one can also say that the Egrégore astrally vampirised our astrosome.

Let us now ask what it means if we have to carry out the task described above, whether in a particular scale, or in a general plan. To be exact, we will say that there is only one way: monoideism. If, from two ideas, we consider one more important than the other, the creation of forms that correspond to you will be easier than the creation of forms corresponding to the other. If, in the entire field of activity of our mens, we give primacy to a certain idea, we will create forms that correspond to this idea more easily, than to any others. People who have attained the "Templar" degree of Masonic initiation, can see for themselves to what extent our power to create astral forms corresponding to ideas given privilege by us is immense.

It is useful to mention – though this is more in reference to the Arcanum XXI than the XV – whereas to apply the same system of primacy, not to ideas but to forms, then everything that was said above about the creation of forms will refer to manifestation on the physical plane; however, there will already be a certain force limitation. The rules of this limitation are given by certain theses of initiatory freemasonry.

What concerns us now, are not the manifestations in the physical plane, but the creation of forms; however, not from external forms, but from the astral forms of our own microcosm.

The method of monoideism consists in having and placing first a target (or targets) determined, until the moment of its realisation in one or another plane. This is the essence of monoideism; as to its substance, we know only what has already been said in Arcanum XI concerning the formation of collective units. The astral, that is, the "monoform" of a certain idea must be formed of "cells" of our own astrosome. We use the word "cells" in the figurative sense, because it is really elemental swirls with the addition of astral elements of alien organisms that we have managed to vampire, and sometimes even without the help of such an addition.

We can say that the nature of monoideism resembles the nature of Baphomet (see our citation of the Emerald Verses). Thus, the swirl of the monoform, descends from the plane of the monoidéia to its point of support in the physical plane and, by impulse of return, it rises again to the plane of the idea, sustaining it and being at the same time vivified by it.

Now we can better understand the role of breathing exercises, linked to a mental ideation and formal ability to acquire some ability or perform some state (see Arcanum V). The same law governs the creation of thoughts-forces.

The self-suggestion sephirotic method (Arcanum V) is just a more detailed way of passing the mono-idea through various subplanes of its existence.

It should be added here that, since the nature of the monoform is analogous to the Baphomet, it has the same tendency to fill any gaps in its construction. Due to this tendency, self-suggestion can be performed even when it is not clearly outlined. Moreover, it is not indispensable for the operator to maintain monoidia in mind, without interruption. Of course, he should go back to it often, especially if he does not have much practice in magic, to sustain the vitality of this idea. Here comes into play the degree of dominance of Arcanum VIII and other considerations; I repeat, however, that the monoform lives and develops on its own. We may not even believe in the success of our self-suggestion, and yet it will be realised on the condition, however, that we do not consciously create counter-forms.

Everything hitherto quoted, concerning the passive application of the Arcanum XV, is quite important in the elementary exercises of the passive form of telepathy and psychometry. It will be even more important in cases where we consciously allow ourselves to be magnetised by an operator for any other purpose, e.g. therapy.

The passive form of telepathy consists of the receptive state of perceptions and sensations that can be luminous (e.g. figures), auditory (e.g. phrases), olfactory (smell), taste (taste) or tactile, or even psychic states such as sadness, joy, surprise, fear, etc. or a particular desire like, for example, making a move or receiving advice from an operator who may be in a very distant place. The most noble and valuable purpose of cultivating telepathic receptivity at a distance is becoming able to receive teachings (receptivity to ideas) or to heal from a physical or moral weakness (receptivity to the transfer of psychic and nervous force). This wireless "telegraphy" process requires a great attunement of the patient's astrosome with that of the operator, so that all the vibrations emitted by the latter are fully and correctly captured. This can be achieved by means of a monoideaic contact between the two, at fixed times. Sometimes a monoidea of this contact is strengthened by the monoform. The patient imagines, for example, they are connected to the operator by a pipe or wire, or that the operator is visiting it. Many people, to receive a telepathic cliché, are limited to a simple passive concentration, submitting to the operator his astral apparatus and leaving him the initiative and the task of loading its influence. Of course, the more frequent the astral contact between two people - regardless of the type of the contact - the easier the tuning. If one side always cultivates the passive form (discipleship, submission), it will develop in him the receptivity in relation to the other.

Psychometry, as we know, consists of a contact with the astrosome of a given object, with the purpose of capturing the astral clichés of the influences that impregnated it. Therefore, the success of the psychometric experiments depends on the existence of resonances in the recipient of vibrations of certain clichés. That is why, generally, better results in psychometrics are achieved with people who have a wide field of interest than people with a limited field of interest.

The possibility of sensitising an astrosome to external influences was empirically proven by clinical experiences pertinent to the submission of the will of one being to that of another. Several degrees of this submission were studied. The experiments made by Dr. Charcot, with very good faith but rather superficial, allowed to distinguish three phases:

1. Lethargy. The external symptoms are the flexibility of the patient's body, lack of control of the patient over your body and a regular deep breathing. It is a state that resembles a deep physical sleep.
2. Catalepsy, whose physical symptoms consist of extreme muscular tension, absence of flexibility of the extremities, trunk and neck, the ability of the whole body to remain in an artificially imposed posture, the fixation of the gaze on a single point (which can be the operator) and the inability to listen to a conversation (even high). This is a picture of the patient's total isolation and totalisation from the external physical world.
3. Sleepwalking with clairvoyance. In this state the patient answers the questions, talks about motorcycles but does not know where it is. He often thinks he is somewhere else and sees what is happening there. He often transfers his conscience, as the operator. In general, obey it, execute its orders, not only during the state but also after this, at moments previously determined by the operator. In these latter cases, by executing the orders, the patient stays for a certain time as if unconscious, acting in a purely automatic way, losing in the meantime the sensitivity and the sense of real circumstances. He not only does everything that has been commanded him, but he even sees and hears anything that is suggested by the operator. A person who does not exist will be considered if this was the order, and will act according to this exchange of personality. However, it should be noted that in cases of orders extremely strange to the usual circumstances or in the criminal suggestions, one observes, in general, a fight of the pentagram with the suggestion, a fight that can result in not compliance with the order. Actions made under the influence of suggestion, as well as impressions

received, are or are not forgotten, according to the operator's instructions.

As we have said, Charcot's[40] researches were incomplete. The Colonel of Rochas[41], through clinical experiments, increased to thirteen the number of the suggestion phases. Here's a brief list of them.

1. Patient confidence in relation to the operator. At this stage the operator, for a simple conversation, can persuade the patient of something that, until then, nobody has been able to do. This state is, in general, is equivalent to that of a student in relation to a beloved teacher.
2. Lethargy - just as it was characterised by Charcot.
3. Catalepsy - similar to that already described. De Rochas adds the observation of the patient to automatically mimic the operator's movements.
4. Lethargy - similar to that of item 2 but presenting already a less deep sleep aspect.
5. Sleepwalking - similar to that described by Charcot, with its characteristic symptoms.
6. Lethargy - presenting a state of sleep lighter than in item 4, already similar to sleep, normal and healthy.
7. The so-called "state of rapport" ("état de rapport"), characterised by the affinity typical of the astrosome of the patient with the astrosome of the operator. This stage has two phases: first, the patient is sensitive to receptions coming from other sources, besides the person of the operator, but evaluates them as unpleasant. So when playing, p. eg another person, affirms that the constitution of this one is different from his and, therefore, it is repulsive to him. In the second phase, the patient completely loses his receptivity to everything that is not connected to some manifestation of the operator. Do not hear, for example, the sound of a piano, played by another person; However, as soon as the operator puts his or her hand in the patient's ear, the patient begins to hear the piano. In general, the patient needs to take advantage of the operator's view, even to see the objects existing around him. The cutaneous reaction caused by objects brought into contact with the operator are generally pleasing to the patient. The same touch, but of

---

[40] Jean-Martin Charcot (29 November 1825 – 16 August 1893) was a French neurologist and professor of anatomical pathology, who is most well-known for his work on hypnosis and hysteria. He is also known as "the founder of modern neurology" and his name has been associated with at least 15 medical eponyms, including Charcot disease.
[41] Eugène Auguste Albert de Rochas d'Aiglun (20 May 1837 – 2 September 1914) was a prominent French parapsychologist, historian, writer and military engineer. He had to resign a position at the École Polytechnique but had to resign due to his involvement in paranormal research activities.

objects not connected to the operator, makes the patient completely insensitive, and may even cause him / her an intense pain. These two phases of the "relationship state" are also characterised by patient contentment and his desire to continue in the same situation. In this state many patients are able to evaluate the intensity and polarisation of the magnetiser operator fluids, discerning the colors of the positive and negative fluids.

8. Bland lethargy, with weakened pulsations and decreased elasticity of the muscular system.

9. State of sympathy for contact ("sympathie au contact"). The patient feels in contact only with the operator and with the people it touches. If one of the people feels pain or discomfort, the patient feels the same, without, however, relating it to the functions of his body.

10. Lethargy that's still bland.

11. State of lucidity - The patient acquires the gift of seeing the internal organs of the people with which, through the operator, has been brought into contact, and makes a very reasonable diagnosis of the diseases and abnormalities of various organs, by comparing these organs with their own. At this stage, in addition, the patient demonstrates psychometric capabilities, indicating, unequivocally, the person, among those with whom he is in contact, who touched a certain object.

12. Lethargy.

13. Sympathies at distance. Manifestations similar to those state of lucidity but without the operator having to touch the patient.

The ability to be receptive to suggestions emerges at the beginning, in stage 1, intensifies and reaches the maximum point in phase 3 (catalepsy) and then slowly decreases, disappearing at all in step 7. These are the results of the clinical researches regarding the astrosome tuning process of the patient with that of the operator.

It is interesting to note that this attunement which, as we will see later, in most cases, is the result of the effort of the operator's will, weakens the attachment of the patient's astrosome to his own physical body as well as his mental. The progressive weakening of the connection with the body manifests itself in the patient by the loss of awareness of the conditions and environment of his normal life, daily. Difficulties in this sense already appear in the stage 7 (state of relationship) and increase greatly in stage 9 (sympathy for contact). We can say that the present incarnation loses to the patient its real sense; he even forgets his name and profession. The weakening of the connection between the astrosome and the mental state of the patient is a consequence of the limitation from the "mens" of the patient to the field of contacts. However, this latter weakening is not as the first, because the patient's logical faculties remain after the empirical knowledge acquired during his life disappears. He does not remember anymore the multiplication table but intelligently compares its organs with those of people with which it contacts.

Let us turn to the active application of the mysteries of the Arcanum XV. Each microcosm has the possibility of enriching the field of their vibrations, making their, power, one might say, more persistent. With this persistence, the microcosm-operator not only attracts of their own influence the astrosomes that have the same type of vibrations (although less pronounced) but also causes the attunement to its own vibration of the vibrations of other people. The broader the vibrational scale of the microcosm operator, so much greater will be the number of the Baphomet organs on which potentially the vampirism of this microcosm will extend, for the said organs have the faculty to adapt to the tones of others, similar to yours. In addition, the more vigorous the vibration of the microcosm, so far (in the figurative sense) it had penetrated and thus again attracted alien organisms into its own field. In both cases, the operator will increase its energy supply and, consequently, its resources. Here is fully confirmed the "Parable of the Talents. "In the work, which we call" passive ", we are united with the Egrégores, in work that is "active," one might say, we create an egrégore for ourselves.

Let us now examine this "active" part of the application of Arcanum XV in the operations of which we speak.

In telepathic suggestion, the operator, that is the active side, intensifies its vibrations in a certain field (eg clearly picture a picture, a psychic state, etc.). In addition, it attracts the appropriate entities from the astral, remagnetising them so that they vibrate in unison with him, thus forming with them a current, governed by the egregious monoform of suggestion. Using the energy of its own vibrations and that of the current formed, it tunes in a suitable way the astrosome of the patient, making him receptive to the desired suggestion. Meanwhile, the Baphomet descends, and it rises again (we already know the sephirotic scheme of the double diabatic process of suggestion).

As physical support of the operation can serve material representations, such as images, geometric figures, photographs, etc. by the operator, or gestures corresponding to certain psychic states that the operator seeks to transmit, etc.

In psychometrics, it is important to increase the resonance capacity of several types of clichés, eventually found in the aura of the object being psychometrised. Exactly because of the fortuitous nature of these clichés, it is recommended to become as sensitive as possible to any kind of vibration. It would be like adapting a good microphone to your telephone. This is the purpose of active concentration that precedes psychometric contact with objects.

In the case of the application of so-called "magnetism" (odic forces and radiations), the preparation process consists not only of the desire to succeed in minutely all the possibilities that can arise in the descent and ascent of the astral whirlwind. As we have already said, we can count on the help of Baphomet, due to its nature of filling the gaps and make the formation of whirlwinds uninterrupted. However, we also need to attend duly to our own strength; we cannot expect too strong an impulse beyond certain limits.

The more powerful and trained the operator's astrosome, the less the need to delineate the details of the suggestion scheme. From all that has just been said, it follows that it would be a very useful detailed study of all the elements of the sephirotic construction of the so-called "volitional entity" of the suggestion. It would also be useful to study the astral process of emanations of the operator. As for your mind, we assume that its functioning is according to the general laws of deductive logic. Let us turn to the study of the astrosome of the operator.

In Arcanum V a pentagrammatic scheme of fluid distribution was given to humans (fig. 20 a and 21) and in Arcanum X this scheme was expanded in a decimal - the sephirotic scheme. Figure 51 which is the inverse side of the Great Seal of Solomon (on the front side we have already spoken in Arcanum VI, fig. 22) gives us the complete picture of this distribution of fluids in the human being.

The Sephira Keter corresponds to a specific region of the forehead, above the base of the nose (type "n", that is, neutral); Sephira Chokmah - to the right eye (subtle, active, "+" type emanations); Binah - to the left eye (subtle, passive, "-" type emanations); Chesed or Gedulah – the right hand, male (dense "+" type fluids); Pechad or Geburah - on the left hand (even degree of density but of type "-"); Tiphareth corresponds to the solar plexus, neutral fluids (type "n"); Netzach corresponds to the negative fluid reserve of the right foot (type "-"); we use the expression "reserve" because it is rare to consciously use the emanations of the feet, usually protecting them for transference to the other centres, through the androgynous ganglia of the central part of the sephirotic scheme. This is the reason why in Figure 51 the ends of the lower crossbar are facing upwards, thus differing from the upper bar which is straight and corresponds to the eye emanation centres; Hod corresponds to the reserve of the positive fluids of the left foot of the male asthmus (+); Yesod - to the emanations of the sexual organs which, theoretically, are androgynous, but in which, in practice, both active and passive fluids predominate. The name of the Sephira Malkuth is not in the pantáculo because this Sephira corresponds to the physical points of support, constituting a small world, in general very passive (inertia of matter) in comparison with other Sephiroth. However, its internal construction is androgynous, complete and capable of producing manifestations. In figure 51 this small world is represented by the envelopes of the pantáculo and that contains, as symbol of the human fall, the alphabet of 22 Arcana.

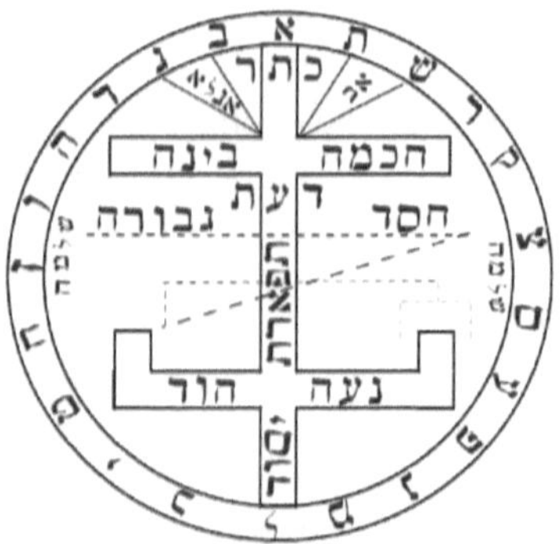

Figure 51

Commenting on the pantáculo, we also highlight the following particularities:

1. At the cross there is no special bar for Gedulah and Geburah, this being great for mobility of the hands during magnetic therapy, contrasting with the poor mobility of the other support of the centres of odic emanations.
2. An angle, as if it were a wedge, penetrates the pantaculo on either side of Keter. The one on the right has an inscription "Ab", the one of the left - "Agla". This means that Keter, polarising himself in Chokmah-Binah, is illuminated by an intuitive double apprehension: that of the high origin and union of differentiating human beings into only three basic types, or the "Aleph", "Ghimel" and "Lamed" types, all three having the same task of reunification. The two penetrating angles play the role of "talismans" that must protect Chokmah and Binah against involutive actions.
3. Just below the upper crossbar we see the word "Daath" - the global name of the falling middle Sephira. It is a warning that caution is needed as we move from the use of subtle emanations from the higher Sephiras to the use of denser emanations, centered at and below the solar plexus..
4. On each side of the marsh is an inscription "Shlomoh" - the name of King Solomon. It would be interesting for students to cabbalistically explore this name.

5. Above the Netzach end we see what might be called a small stirrup, suspended in a horizontal line that leads the fluids from Netzach to the left. There, the line descends a little, by a vertical line, to ascend, diagonally to the right, passing through Tiphareth until Gedulah and from there, horizontally, to Geburah, where it ends. So that the trace of this line is understandable, it should be noted that, in general, transmission of active (+) environment causes a partial and temporary loss of positive (+) fluids in the operator. As regards negative fluids, this corresponds to vampirism, whether of the environment, or of a particular entity, causing a weakening or impairment of its normal functions, this is, damaging them. The zigzag line is nothing more than a very old scheme of what nowadays is called "throwing of astral balls" to the adversary, in order to harm his health or to paralyse its activity. Solomon's zigzag teaches you to do it this way: concentrate the negative fluids in the astral of the right foot (as if seen in a mirror); to add to them all the negative fluids that can be provided by the secondary ganglia of the left part of the body and the solar plexus that is androgynous. At the same time, try to concentrate in the hands the maximum of fluids normally polarised. Then, converge to the left hand all the negative fluids of the body, and cast them on the enemy, through the fingers and the palm of the left hand. Of course, fluids will be of dense type and the attack will make it difficult for the enemy to perform a bottom level operation. This procedure was practiced already in the remote past to make, for example, stop an attacking animal or to stop the hand of a man who stood against his fellow man. Today, this action has been taken even further by the use of Binah's negative emanations. In this the left eye and the left temple are taken as the point of support for the release. These "modern balls" produce more durable results, and often cause head or any other nervous disorder.

We will conclude the description of the pantaculo of Solomon indicating the colours that compose it. The background colour, as well as the central part - blue; the whole cross and the sacred upper angles – golden (activity); the circle (Malkuth) - silver, or pink or green (Venus), but with contours of silver (passivity). The inscriptions, for convenience, are in black; the silver of the zigzag line is conducting negative, passive fluids.

In therapeutics by magnetism, negative emanations are used in cases where it is necessary to moderate the activity or the faculty of absorption of some centre. The positive emanations, instead, they are used when a centre has to be activated.

We shall confine ourselves to this brief information on magnetism therapy. Those interested in it can find more information on Kramer's work (Therapeutic Magnetism) or in the book of Brandler-Pracht "The Occultism"[42].

We will now mention some requirements in the physical plane that can assure the operator a better distribution of astral resources between the body's ganglia. Moderation is recommended in feeding and using stimulants; if possible, continence in sex life; frequent exercises of odic irradiation, even if it is about objects, in case there are no patients; sufficient hours of sleep and an environment that does not provoke nervousness and discontent.

Let us now turn to the subject of environmental vampirisation. This is done by tuning the number of environment elements to the operator's fork. The whirlwind itself must be tuned to the vibration of the operator, but to have vitality and power to penetrate the organism's astral body, must be formed according to the scheme proper to Baphomet, and resemble it.

Undoubtedly, there was no selfish purpose on the part of the Mental Principles which, condensed into the periphery, gave birth to the astral, universal whirlwind - the Baphomet. Therefore, the same principle should govern the formation of the little whirlwind of the volitional entity, that is, the ideals and impulses of the operator must be the highest and disinterested. It may be objected that this is not so easy, for an individual whirlwind can hardly be exempt from personal desire, due to the volitional character of the whirlwind. In fact, this is so, and so the whirlwinds created by us, are generally short-lived. However, this duration increases in proportion to the level of its purpose rises and the personal character decreases A purely mystical base will create very enduring astral manifestation.; a scientific purpose will cause less lasting results; philanthropic altruism will have an even shorter durability, and patriotism - still less. Based in family egoism, the astral manifestation, even when achieved, will be very fleeting, and as to personal, material selfishness, it is extremely rare that any result can be obtained. All this explains us why people seeking to use magic to improve their situation not only fail but also lose their reputation as serious occultists.

We repeat: the Aziluth world was reflected in the Briah world, not because [it was] "wanted for itself" but for the need to establish the phases of the diabetic process. A magical act can be attempted only

---

[42] It seems likely that the highly regarded Karl Brandler-Pracht was an important source for G.O.M. If we look at Brandler-Pracht's Manual for Magical Development (first published in 1906), we discover such chapter headings as 'Breathing Exercises' (including Prana and Psychic Breathing), Telepathy, Psychometry, The Astral Body the Healing Power of Magnetism and The Magnetic Gaze, which as we have seen are both topics explored in depth by G.O.M. in this denouement of the Tarot Majors. We are not 100 per cent certain which book of Brandler-Pracht is meant by "The Occultism" but it is possibly "How to Develop your Occult Powers".

when indicated by the conscience and not when it is expected for some benefit to favour the operator or their family members. The future may reveal that this operation has involved many benefits to the operator or other people, but this is a separate issue. What is important is that the impulse is pure and disinterested.

The lower the plan of a magical procedure, the less necessary are our warnings, but both lesser, too, will be your life force. Reading, for money, the cards from the deck, can bring some satisfactory benefit. The treatment by magnetism already requires a lack of interest of deeper [aspects of] the patient's disorder, the more important are his fees for the magnetiser. To teach, for money, the practice of magic, is from the occult point of view, true recklessness.

All we have just said refers to the mental aspect, called "sky" of a whirlwind. Let's go now to its mid-level. Here it would be difficult to comprehend in words all the ways of acting. Usually these are dictated by the intuition of the operator. The main instrument is your imagination. The plasticity of thought conditions the plasticity of formation; the clarity and stability of the rational and useful quality of training. There are, of course, reserved techniques, concerning the formation of the middle part of an astral swirl, both within us and externally. These techniques, as well as the physical elements that support them, cannot be revealed here. They are part of the second degree of Templar initiation. However, each human being who follows the path of self-initiation will, in time, through the sixth sense and logical deduction, [arrive at] the knowledge of this occult part. These are not secrets but arcana.

Let us now turn to the physical points of support for astral operations, points on which we can speak without restriction.

We have already listed the 13 phases found by de Rochas. These 13 phases arise as a result of the transmission of positive fluids from the operator to the patient, at least as it was carried out by de Rochas. He was able to move the most sensitive patients from one phase to the next, deeper phase by imposing his right hand on the patient's forehead or upper skull. To obtain the reverse passage, that is from a more pronounced phase to not so deep, de Rochas used his left hand. In addition, de Rochas has imposed the left hand on subjects in a normal waking state, and thus obtained three negative phases: the excitation phase, the edema phase of the limbs and the phase of a general paralysis. That provoked so depressing an impression on the operator that he did not want to continue the experiments.

It is very important to note the following: the imposition of the right hand on the patient's head is not the the only means of transmitting positive fluids. The same result can be achieved by:

1. Participation of the patient in a group of people in a circle and whose bodies touch each other, forming thus a current.
2. Patient subjection to operator fluid circulation. This can be done in several ways: a central look; an energetic concentration of the look on the patient's Chokmah (fixation of right eyelash); the patient's left hand in the operator's right hand and, simultaneously, the right hand in the left hand of the operator; there is also a variant: hold with the left hand the thumb of the patient's right hand and, with the right hand, the thumb of the left hand of the patient; the use of normal passes from top to bottom along the anterior side of the patient's body (starting at the head and descending at least at the level of the abdomen) or passes crossed by hands crossed along the posterior side of the body, beginning at the nape of the neck and passing through the patient's back; holding both of the patient's thumbs in the operator's left hand, the operator's right hand while simultaneously swiping from the top to the front of the patient's body; other combinations of the procedures enumerated in this topic.
3. A direct suggestion from the operator to the patient, done from near or far, to receive the patient their positive fluids.
4. Providing the patient with a more direct contact with the Baphomet universal fluids, for partial weakening of the connection between the mental and the astral or between the astral and the physical of the patient. The first is obtained by deep meditation of the patient on mystical or very abstract philosophical subjects; the second, by a series of procedures called purely hypnotic, differing from magnetic or mixed. The findings that we have just presented allow us to conclude that a patient, placed within the fluid circulation range of both the universal swirl and the swirl of a particular stream (for example, that of a Spiritist session, where the psychic-sensitives gradually passes from phase 1 to that of 6, inclusive) or in the field of fluid circulation of a given operator, is by its nature more capable of absorbing positive rather than negative fluids. In other words, it will evolve more easily toward the positive phases listed by Rocks, than to the negatives he obtained. The latter states resemble the lack of desire, on the part of the patient, to accept the general laws of life.

The human tendency to assimilate positive rather than negative fluids more easily could be called the instinct of astral self-preservation or, better still, instinct to imitate something healthy, built on a normal dynamic cycle, without introducing anarchy into its own astrosome.

It would be helpful to meditate on this tendency, innate in the human being.

Having spoken of the influence of the longitudinal passes, that is, made along the body, it is necessary to also mention transverse passes (made at the level of the chest). These have a contrary action. If the action of the former resembles that of the right hand of the operator, the latter influence of the left hand. Let us turn now to the "purely hypnotic" procedures that purpose of increasing contact of the patient's astrosome with the universal astral, through weakening of the connection between the physical and the astral body of the patient. Let's enumerate these procedures:

1. A bright spot. The patient fixes his gaze on a bright object (eg, a diamond on a black background, a nickel-plated button, a small mirror, etc.) placed before the centre of your forehead.
2. A rotating mirror. The mirror is placed at a distance of half a meter in front of the level of your eyes. The patient remains seated in an armchair, the neck comfortably supported.
3. A gong beat. The patient, resting comfortably in an armchair, listens suddenly and unexpectedly a loud noise (beating of a gong, a loud cry, etc.) and enters one of the phases listed by Charcot.
These methods are based on the unusual methods of stimulation of the patient's nervous system, which, by making the astrosome's work in relation to the body too specific, violates the norm of astrosome communication with the body.
Hypnotic techniques, however, will have to include all gestures and views, which usually serve as a reference point for magnetic methods of influence, if they are used by the hypnotist purely mechanically, without a certain voluntary concentration, but only if they wish to conscientiously perform the external side of the operation. In this case, the operator's astrosome plays the role of only a healthy organism of Nature, facilitating the patient's communication with the latter; The eyes, the hands, the words of the operator replace the mirror or gong. Individualisation of the operation has no place here. The eyes, hands, words of the operator in this case play the role of a mirror, a gong, etc. The fastest methods of purely hypnotic techniques are sound. Gong banging or loud shouting give almost instant results. The monotonous repetition of the same sounds euthanises the patient for 10-15 minutes. Of the optical techniques, the brilliant point gives the fastest results (from 3 to 10 minutes). A rotating mirror euthanises the patient for about half an hour.
In general the magnetic performance gives faster results than the hypnotic one.
Approximately 40 per cent of men and 64 per cent of women are susceptible to hypnotism. We will not speak here of the methods to test in advance the sensitivity of people to hypnosis. These are just details. We prefer instead to say a few words with respect to the means of

transferring the patient from the phase of first lethargy to that of the first catalepsy, and sleepwalking.

In order to pass the patient from lethargy (stage 2) to catalepsy (stage 3), the operator usually opens the patient's eyes with his fingers. The passage of catalepsy (stage 3) directly to the

Sleepwalking (stage 5) is often obtained by a breath in the patient's eyes or by a slight rub of his forehead. These actuating means are less gentle than the longitudinal passes or the imposition of the right hand. We can prove it by the fact of the passage (3) to somnambulism (stage 5), without going through the stage of lethargy (stage 4).

Let us go on to the methods of awakening the patient that is found in any of the states analysed.

1. Order of awakening. For the patient who is in the stage of somnambulism is given an order to wake up within a set time or after the combined operation, utter a phrase or word, count to a certain number, clap hands, etc. In general, greater security requires that the patient, after having received the order, promises to execute it. This procedure can also be applied to a patient who is in the stage of lethargy (stage 1), but in this case your action will be less rapid.

2. Blow between the eyes. Applies to all phases.

3. Passes. These are especially applied in the deep stages. Apply long passes, with the right hand only, or with both hands (in the latter case, going from the centre of the body towards the sides). The passes are started at the level of the chest and then at the level of the forehead. This is the most suitable method for awakening, although it is the slowest method.

4. Look. The patient's "Keter" is magnetically focused by the "central gaze", suggesting the wake up, without saying anything. It is applied in cases where it is difficult to wake up.

5. Combination of the methods listed. To the patient who is in the phase of somnambulism, it is suggested verbally that he will awake when he receives a breath between his eyes. When it is necessary the operator blows in the indicated place, simultaneously making rapid passes on the forehead (with both hands) going from the center towards the temples. When the patient is already waking up, once again blow heavily on his face.

In clinical practice, difficulties sometimes arise in awakening a patient immersed in one of the deep phases of lethargy. These phases almost exclude receptivity to suggestion; therefore, to awaken a patient in such a state, it is first sought to make him go on to catalepsy or of sleepwalking, only to wake him up by the above methods.

This information regarding hypnotism is not given in order to stimulate the desire for you to try it out. On the contrary, we are committed to advising those sensitive to hypnosis, using their psychic forces to suggest to themselves the immunity that would protect them against a possible intrusion on the orientation of his life.

So far, speaking of the active applications of the Arcanum XV, we take into account only the predominance of the will of one human being relative to that of another, predominance almost always due to a vibratory amplitude superiority. We have not touched on the subject of the influence of an individual human being on a chain of men, or organ of Nature. In both cases, the energy power and the vibratory amplitude of the receiving entity may be greater than those of the operator.

The influence of an individual on a collective still remains scarcely studied in the Western Schools. Even in the field of psychology, the lesser known branch is the psychology of the masses. In that regard, we have only confused knowledge. Greater still is our ignorance of the psicurgia of the masses[43].

We know that in the chain formed in a common spiritist circle, its most active participant can use the fluids of those present to act on one of them. We also know that a speaker who addresses the mass of people who have formed a circle around it, quickly takes it to the "state of confidence. "These, however, are sparse items of a knowledge that is not yet a science. In the initiatory centres of India the study of mass psychology is much more advanced.

As for the relationship of a human being with Nature, there are two main paths:

1. To learn to depend as little as possible on the illusory resources of the Macrocosm, to allow you not to be a slave anymore, but to put yourself at your own level.

2. To learn to act on certain organs of the Macrocosm, suddenly and surprisingly, when they are engaged in some task that acts upon their plexuses, they find themselves weakened, and take advantage of this situation to compel them to the manifestations we desire.

We have already talked about the first method, and we will return to it. From the second method we will turn to the study of Arcanum XVI.

---

[43] By the term 'psicurgia' we assume G.O.M. is referring to a collective form of theurgy. It stands to reason that this – mass theurgy, that is - be related to the generation of socio-political egrégores by harnessing the huge quantity of energy, astrosome, physical, mental, spiritual etc, available in large and determined groups. Communism and Nazism would be good examples, both of which are referenced by the author of MotT in his own writing on egrégores.

Analysing Arcanum XV, we can verify that the human being sometimes needs to adapt to the conditions, and sometimes adapt those conditions to their will. We will also note how artificial seems to be the line separating astral work "IMO" ("י" in the very being) from astral work "OBITO" ("He" in itself). The terms "Imo" and "Obito" were explained to us during the study of the Paracelsus Trident in Arcanum IV.

We will see, finally, that neither the "Father" nor the "Mother" manifest visibly in Arcanum XV, but the androgynous "Gentleman", and so, only through his "Jack".

One of the most interesting and most real manifestations of the domain of the Arcanum XV and perhaps the only one which can be called truly magical - the manifestation of energy at a distance - is only achieved by performing the complete androgyny of the two abilities, or be it "Imo" and "Obito". In order for the exteriorisation of our astrosome to be useful, we need not only know how to guide us in the astral, but also how to exert our influence there.

The ability to orient oneself in the astral is in close dependence on the capacity to know clearly, in life, what one wants; is, one could say a capacity that is acquired by the well-founded knowledge of a particular sub-sector.

In the astral world, world of forms of energetic manifestations, world where clichés are the knowledge gained in some sector is invariably power in the same area. In the astral there are no entities that, with perfect knowledge in a given field, have no power and authority in it. These contradictions are only in the physical world.

We have previously said that the physical plane is the world of facts, the astral - the world of laws, and the mental - the world of principles. Therefore, it is logical that in the world of laws, laws are never infringed; in the world of forms, rules the form. Dealing with the astral, with bi-plane life, we have to submit to laws and form.

It may happen that something interests us very much and we want to find in the astral the corresponding cliché. This is not so easy, because, in addition to several other difficulties, accustomed to the physical plane, in which everything is segregated by time and space of three dimensions, we have to look for the desired cliché in a multidimensional world where everything interpenetrates.

One can also inquire whether it is easy to exteriorise in a predetermined sub-plane. For we must overcome our preference for a plane that is lower or higher than that which we want to achieve. At the same time, there must be full manifestation of our own individuality in all sub-planes of existence in which it manifests. If we lose consciousness of the manifestation of our individuality in the inferior sub-planes, we will lose our point of support and, along with it, our power (active aspect) and the memory of our experiences (passive aspect). If we escape the consciousness of manifestation of our individuality in the higher sub-planes, we will lack the understanding of what we are experimenting, and in this case, neither our pentagrammatic power nor our memory. We can finally ask ourselves what the "Knave" of our "Gentleman" consists of. It consists in an accurate and rigorous system in everything we undertake. The value of such a system may be best enjoyed in the mornings with external factors, a subject we will study in the Next arcanum - the sixteenth.

Notes on the fifteenth Arcanum

As we began to study this Arcanum e wondered whether G.O.M. had been racing through the Guardian Angel teaching in keen anticipation of the Baphomet of Arcanum XV, which clearly holds great fascination for him. We could not help but contrast this enthusiasm with the warnings of in MotT to not fully engage with the work of The Devil – Fools rush in where Angels fear to tread, we might say.
Tomberg warns this Arcanum is not to be deeply *contemplated* in the manner of the other Arcana – and certainly not communed with - though it must still be seen and understood. We can only grasp intuitively what we love and evil is void of love. Evil cannot and should not be known, but only observed. To preoccupy ourselves with evil is to risk losing the precious gift of creative elan which inspires all spiritual work.

The world of the hierarchies of evil appears like a luxuriant jungle, where you can certainly, if necessary, distinguish hundreds and thousands of particular plants, but where you can never attain to a clear view of the totality. (MotT, p403).

This is where we see quite some contrast between his attitude to certain things and that of G.O.M. For Tomberg, The Devil represents "electrical fire" – the opposite of sacred tears - and is the basis for all counter-inspiration or evil initiations. Not only does he point to those (G.O.M. included?) who sought to penetrate equally the mysteries of good and evil, he also warns that many Anthoposophists have been seduced into communion with this Arcana via an unhealthy preoccupation with the twofold evil of Ahriman and Lucifer. Threefold, even, if Adzura is also taken into account.

The result is a lame wisdom without wings, deprived of creative elan, which only repeats and comments to satiety what the master, Dr Rudolf

*Steiner, said. And yet Rudolf Steiner has certainly said things of a nature
to awaken the greatest creative elan! (MotT, p402).*

Whilst he can be highly critical of Anthroposphists in general – and no
wonder given his treatment by this group following the death of its
master – it should be acknowledged that Tomberg is both respectful and
affectionate in his remembrance of Rudolf Steiner himself.

Tomberg compares the humility of a human being endowed with Christ
consciousness with the egoic madness of the 'Superman', who believes
him (or her) self is able to fulfill the grandiose 'Privileges and Powers of
a Magus described by Eliphas Lévi in connection with the Hebrew
alphabet. The Seven Grand Privileges include, under the sign of Aleph,
the ability to see God and commune with the Seven Genii around the
Throne, whilst the first of the Seven Major Powers involves the making
of the Philosopher's Stone. The first of the Seven Minor Powers falls
under the sign of Samekh, as in the Fifteenth Arcanum, and involves the
ability *"to know in a moment the hidden thoughts of any man or
woman."*

Suffice to say that whilst G.O.M. may have approved of Eliphas Lévi's
amazing list, in concord with the aims of any really serious and/or
accomplished wizard, Tomberg guides us away from focusing directly
on practical magical attainments, filing them away into the hazardous
Fifteenth Arcanum, whilst Eliphas Lévi had them listed under the
Twentieth. We must always bear in mind that in the realm of magic our
task – as in all other realms – is to seek the divine. If charisms and sidhis
are meant to be bestowed upon us, then so they shall be given. If they
are to be renounced, then so be it.

Robert Powell asserts that, drawing upon the prophetic vision of Russian
philosopher, Vladimir, Solovyov, *"Tomberg describes the encounter
with the Antichrist as the greatest trial facing modern humanity"*. He
describes a personality of utmost deceptiveness, a figure whose outward
life seems irreproachable, *"an outstanding figure in the realm of thought
and whose works, read with enthusiasm by all, proclaim universal
peace."*

The weird goal of this entity is *"to produce a new human being: a
human being whose thinking reflects, not heaven, but the interior of the
earth"* and many are those who *"yearn to be possessed"* by him. Hitler
and Stalin are referenced as ultimate examples of this demonic
possession via the interior of the earth. Was he thinking of the
Shambhala with which so many of his fellow Russian occultists and
other interested parties became preoccupied, just as alliances with Tibet
were sought by contending political powers on Earth?

The stark choice faced by human beings is thus between enlightenment and possession, which is why we must approach, with the utmost caution, the symbol of The Devil in the 22 Arcana, notwithstanding the cult of Baphomet which constitutes a grey area for present day occult students and Hermetic practitioners, and is an astral icon for a great many Freemasons.

In his essay, Secret Motto of Bolshevism, Tomberg examines the inversion of the human being's thought process, a phenomenon just as relevant to modern Western society as it was to Soviet Russia. Any such inversion must surely fall under the banner of 'anti-Christ', which can be seen to be symbolised in the image of the Fifteenth Arcanum, unpopular though this interpretation may be amongst non-Christian occultists.

It is interesting to pause here and consider the somewhat grander and much better known career of Tomberg's older contemporary, Nicholas Roerich, who reputedly participated in the Martinist groups of St Petersburg with Alexander Barchenko around 1909. The story of 'Red Shambhala' which ensued has already been extremely well told[44] so I shall suffice to note that whilst it wasn't always easy to tell which side of the revolution Roerich supported, the clearly White Russian Tomberg warns in MotT that the realm of the Anti-Christ is the centre of the Earth.

This is a region that legend has it is associated with Shambhala and pondering this highly complex – and still deeply occult – matter, is likely to yield more questions than answers. Tomberg further alludes to it in his description of two entirely different conceptions of eternity, which the would-be adept should be conscious of before walking too far along a certain path.

It is notable how the work of The Devil is so occupied with political maneuvering. The intricacies of esoteric and exoteric politics in Bolshevik Russia – also Czarist Russia before it and modern Russia since then – constitute a titanic field of study which is complicated by the inaccessibility of records and literature associated with the period. So much has been lost and as much of what remains is still hidden, especially from the eyes of curious westeners! We have not attempted to do more than touch upon this field, but nonetheless consider it to be something that's essential to bear in mind when studying the work of both G.O.M. and Tomberg. It is similarly relevant to a fuller

---

[44] See especially Red Shambhala: Magic, Prophesy, and Geopolitics in the Heart of Asia, Andrei Znamenski, 2011, which explores links between Bolshevik revolutionaries and their attempt to influence Vajrayana Buddhism in Mongolia and Tibet, as well as indigenous shamanic elements in the Russian Far East.

understanding of Roerich, Gurdjieff, the great mothership of contemporary occultism, Helena Blavatsky (HPB) and others besides. With regard to G.O.M.'s references to synarchy in the Fifteenth Arcanum, it is perhaps notable that as we write, the United Kingdom has made a decision to leave the European Union. The EU is perhaps the clearest manifestation – even the supreme example - of the 'synarchic dream' envisaged by Saint Yves d'Alveydre.

The problem with this dream, which is certainly not without merit, are apparent when we consider the first of the 'major parliaments' described by G.O.M., which is the spiritual. Whilst the legal and economic bases for the EU are readily apparent, the spiritual underpinnings – if they exist at all - are by now obscured, except as appeals for fraternal love between all European nations, which is in itself a good and noble thing. More, however, is needed, for the 'spiritual parliament' sets the moral and ethical foundation for the rest. This is something we must contemplate deeply in the context of all global politics of the modern age.

Finally - warnings against contemplation of The Devil accepted - for those (and there are likely many) who find themselves consciously or unconsciously stuck in the vortex of the Fifteenth Arcanum, G.O.M.'s guidance might well turn out to be of primary importance and to justify the attention shown it at the expense of the wholly benign Guardian Angel.

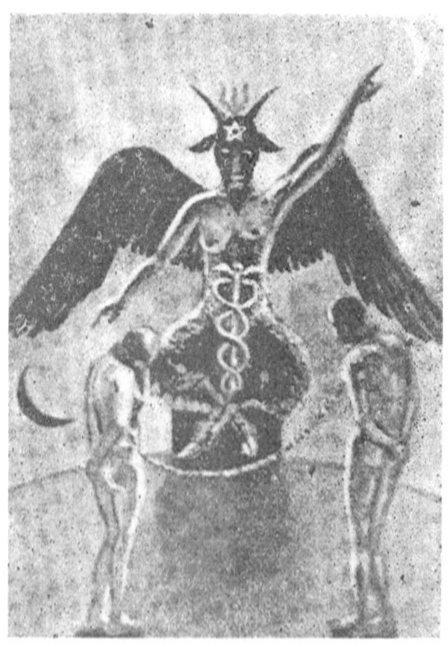

Arcanum XVI

THE TOWER

Pathway between Netzach and Hod

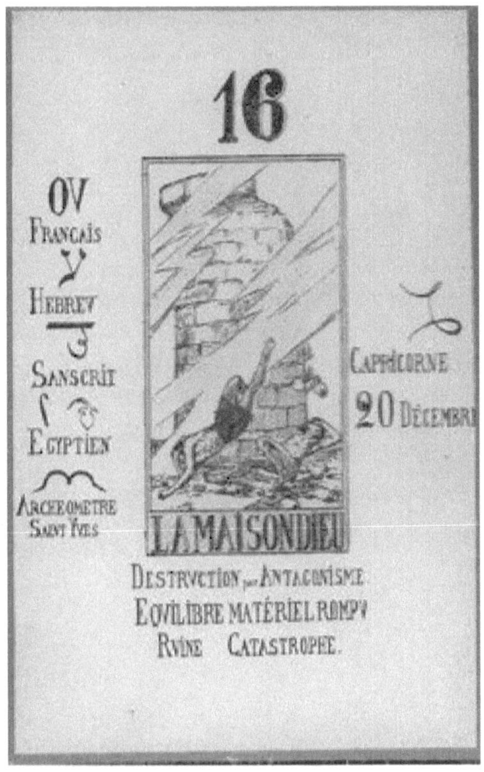

The Tower is struck by a *Lightning Flash*

These events have been necessary because the Great Arcanum of the Knowledge of Good and of Evil has been revealed.

Levi

THE LIGHTNING-STRUCK TOWER: Ruin

O--70 expresses in the divine world the punishment of pride

Paul Christian

And the voice said:--

"The building of the tower was begun by the disciples of the great Master in order to have a constant reminder of the Master's teaching that the true tower must be built in one's own soul, that in the tower built by hands there can be no mysteries, that no one can ascend to Heaven by treading stone steps.

"The tower should warn the people not to believe in it

Ouspensky

The sign of the alphabet corresponding to the Arcanum XVI is ע (Ayin), whose numeric value is 70. The hieroglyph of the Arcanum is an already existing connection that materialises and is even in a "state of tension the sense used in mechanics. This connection always causes a reaction. The reaction, which in itself is not a force, in certain cases can be used as such. In general, this happens when other forces exist simultaneously. This is the case of the Arcanum XVI which can only act in the presence of the Arcanum XV. The Arcanum XVI is the "jack" of the family whose mother is the Arcanum XIV, and the androgynous son, the Arcanum XV (see Figure 43). In other words, the mother - the deduction - convinced of the indispensability of logic, applies it to the demonstration of theses. However, the thesis is usually demonstrated by the logical exclusion of other possibilities. This exclusion is conditioned by the metaphysical reactions of the basic laws of thought, which "connection in a state of tension".

In the same way, the need for astral harmony felt by a pentagram, that is, its desire to balance activity with intuition, leads one to create a whirlwind of the Nahash type. This whirlwind, taking advantage of the astral connections and the "state of tension" in which it finds itself, acts for astral constraint, activating the vitality of one of the forms, at the expense of the vitality of others.

The complicated process of energy transformations in the Universe sets in motion the agent called "FATUM" which, by means of the physical reactions of the connections in a "state of tension", surpasses one at the expense of another, which often seemed to have the same potential to manifest

Now we will better understand the three titles of the Arcanum: "logical Elimination", "astral Constriction" and "physical Destruction". In erudite language, the Arcanum is called "Tower of Destruction" or "Tower struck by lightning "in the common language," House of God. "

The astrological correspondence of the Arcanum is the sign of Capricorn. Its blade features a tower which collapses, struck by lightning. Along with the wreckage of the tower, two men: one crowned; another without a crown. The arms and legs of one of them were arranged so as to form the letter Ayin. The blade illustrates the third title of the Arcanum which, by the law of analogy, makes us remember the two others. The physical destruction is very visible: the tower is crumbling. But beyond two men who wanted to remain on the heights fell from it and who, without no regard to any land authority (one of them is crowned) are precipitated down by an energetic manifestation (electric discharge).

This is the image of an astral constraint, ruled by a superior force, who does not care for worldly privilege.

This image may also help us to better understand what logical elimination is. Let us turn to arithmetic analysis to be able, through the particular characteristics of the Arcanum, discover its general meaning.

16 = 1 + 15 and 16 = 15 + 1: The individual (1) applies the Arcanum XV and this, in turn, transfers the action to another individual. It is a clear indication that the Arcanum XVI may come into play only when there is the "operator" and the "patient". These two words should be understood in the widest possible sense.

16 = 2 + 14 and 16 = 14 + 2: The metaphysical substance (2) and the deduction (14) determine the logical elimination (16). Of course, without the necessary substance, nothing can be done. The polarity of human nature (2) and the aspiration to harmonise it (14) lead to the use of astral constraint (16). In general, we felt the need to act in order to manifest that which penetrated us, thanks to our receptivity.

16 = 3 + 13 and 16 = 13 + 3: The powerful creativity (3) of the metaphysical world and the permanence (13) of the values of it, together, justify the theses of elimination (16). Birth (3) and the inevitability of death (13) lead us to use the period between the two, or physical existence, as a point of support for astral constraints (16). The creativity of Nature (3) and the transformations of energy (13), together, result in frequent destruction (16).

16 = 4 + 12 and 16 = 12 + 4: The inevitability of the existence of form (4) in thought and faith in the possibility of incarnation of the Superior Principles (12) condition the correction of logical deductions (16) in the field of philosophy. Authority (4) along with mercy (12) are a powerful stimulus to the constraints astral (16). The adaptability (4) and the existence of several facets of the Zodiacal Life (12) make it inevitable destruction of achievements (16).

16 = 5 + 11 and 16 = 11 + 5: Universal magnetism (5) together with the force of metaphysical principles (11), in themselves create theses (16). The pentagram (5) resting on the Egrégores of the chains (11) constricts astrally (16). Religion (5) and conformation to the forces of Nature (11) make one accept the inevitability of physical destruction

16 = 6 + 10 and 16 = 10 + 6: The Law of Analogy (6) and Revelation (10) are enough to determine the set of theses (16) of a normal philosophy. Free will (6) and knowledge of Kabbalah (10) give the power of astral constraints (16). The Laws of Life of a certain environment (6) and the implacability of the Mill of the World (10) determine physical destruction (16).

16-7 + 9 and 16 = 9 + 7: If in us the spirit predominates (7) over form, and we are not deprived of Superior Protection (9), then we will construct a complex of philosophical theses (16). If we are winners (7)

in the proof of the two paths and attain initiation (9), we will be given the power of astral constraints (16).

16 = 8 + 8: The comparison of one thesis (8), compared to another (8), the conditional predominance of a situation (8) opposite to the conditional predominance of another situation (8), an individual karma (8) opposed to another individual karma (8), all this must lead to the application of Arcanum XVI in the field of the Theosophical Ternary. This brief arithmetic analysis clearly indicates the presence of the fighting element in the Arcanum analysed and - importantly - an intelligent struggle, with full evaluation of both the forces, and at the right time, taking into account the Superior Influences, as well as the conditioning of the shape element and the role of the support, physicists. We will not, in our present study, deal with the logical elimination of metaphysical theses, nor of physical destruction. We shall confine ourselves to matters of astral constraint.

In Arcanum XV, we speak little of the struggle with Nature. Now, we will give this fight the first place, for the meaning of Arcanum XVI is best revealed by the examination of the resources of what is called "Ceremonial Magic".

Through this, the operator, alone or assisted by a current, having chosen the moment and the conditions, obliges a certain body of Baphomet to the desired manifestations.

An operation in Ceremonial Magic can be likened to an attack by an expert in "Jiu-Jitsu" against an astral entity that would have easily defeated him, and there were no attacker.

In order to perform a Magic Ceremony one usually needs a suitable operator, of instruments, magicians, of the panacea, of a certain contribution of mediumistic energy, of the help of mantrans or setrans and, as we have just mentioned, the place and time conducive to action. These main and other secondary factors are very well described in what is called "the operation. "Everything that is necessary for the operation, which we have just enumerated, has its correspondence in such a pantaculo.

The scales of astral operations are generally circular in shape. The circle is drawn, or by a magic sword not isolated from the hand, or by a consecrated charcoal or chalk. An experienced operator can draw it also with the astral hand, that is, doing it in his imagination, of a very firm way, with all the necessary details and joining it to an act of will, which causes fluid emanation. The presence of these fluids is important, and because of this, when the circle is drawn by the physical hand, metal is used (which is a good conductor of fluids) or some absorbent material, such as charcoal or chalk.

What does the circle mean?

The circle symbolically represents the field within which the operator feels fully fit, and therefore, fully protected. In this field, belonging to the operator, no enemy can penetrate. Within the circle can only manifest their own influences, those of the entities that help him or those that are totally and permanently subordinate to him, and also the influences of the Chains or Protectors that authorised him to carry out this operation by means of a corresponding initiation, a blessing, an order or a permission. The circumference plays the role of a subtle barrier to isolating the operator from extraneous influences. The senses perceive, in the darkness, this circumference as a fence of fire.

Let us now look at the field where the operator feels "at home". This field should be part of the permanent metaphysical worldview of the operative himself. Your monad must be aware of the source of its existence (which corresponds to the Alpha sign) and its purpose (Omega sign). If the operator has in mind, for example, The Fall and the Plane of Human Reintegration, he had drawn upon the face of this circle, that which, as we shall see, shall be the internal, a great cross of equal arms, symbolising the Hermetic Quaternary. The centre point will be reserved for the operator. At the eastern end of the cross is the letter Alpha; on the west end, Omega.

But in addition to the general world view, which never leaves him, the operator must be mentally focused on any confidence and intentions that make up the mental starting point of the operation, if one attaches to them the solid and complete consciousness of Freedom of the pentagram will of the operator. Accordingly, at a certain distance from the first circle, concentric to it, a second circle of a larger diameter will pass, limiting the symbolically mental layout of the operation by the actor.

But how to characterise the kabbalistic composition of the operation? Of course, by God's Names as Sephirotic Manifestations of the activity of the pentagram in the pre-selected phases of the World Diabatic Process. There are eleven of all Names to choose from (Ehieh, Iah, Iave, El, Elohim, Eloha, Sabbaoth, Shaddai, Adonai, Ab and Agla) or twelve, if you allow the use of the Name Elhai; four of them are chosen, which are placed in quarters of the ring defined by the continuation of the Hermetic Cross of the inner circle, sometimes separating them from each other with small crosses. The choice of Names for the operation is determined, of course, by a rigorous analysis of the Names themselves (using Notarikon and Gematria methods). It should be noted that the arrangement of the Names along the quarters of the ring, as well as the selection of the fourth Name to the three already selected, are far from arbitrary, but subject to two laws, which I allow myself to speak about in lectures of a special cycle of Magic Initiation, but which it would be very inappropriate to formulate in an elementary encyclopedic course.

The first law makes the arrangement of Names in quarters of the ring dependent on the objectives of the Operation; the second law determines the selection of the fourth Name to the first three so that the ring kabbalistically formulates the principle of Pentagrammatic Freedom of the operator. In the attached drawing, the pantaculo refers to the call of entities constantly operating in the astral plane, so that we can say about the operation that it uses the existing ready-made elements of the astral plane.

But in addition to orientation in the mental part of the operation, one must also be oriented in the astral; one must know, so to speak, what are the most important egrégore of the Macrocosm affected by the operation. The Kabbalistic symbolisation of these egrégores will find their place in the next circular ring formed by the addition of a third circle, which plays the role of protection against harmful astral influences. If, when drawing the first two circles, we focused on the mental knowledge of ourselves and the operation, then when drawing the third, we must strictly take into account the role of Secondary Causations in ourselves and in the operation. This concentration is kabbalistically fixed by writing in the ring the names of the Angels of the Planets, which play a role in the operation. In the attached drawing (Figure 52) the name Shebtaiel is written, which belongs to the Angel of Saturn.

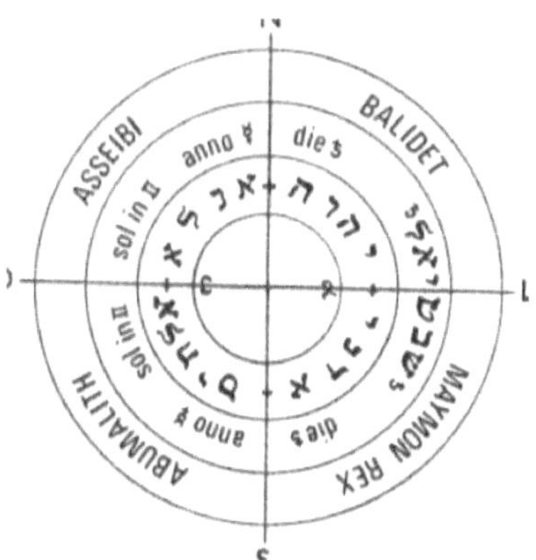

Figure 52

The mention of Secondary Causes gives us an idea of the need to select the moment of operation, in the sense of choosing a planetary day and planetary hour. This remark is so important that it is customary to put in the astral ring, in addition to the names of the Angels, the planetary designation of the hour (in our drawing is written "hora Saturn") and day (in our drawing is written "die Saturn"). To complete the idea of a moment in time, we can mention the year (we have Anno Mercury) and the magic month (we have Sol in Gemini). Many mention the moon phase. We have not done this. The Pantacle we bring is designed to challenge the Cause of Saturn in its astrosome on Saturday, May 26, 1912 (old style) at the hour of Saturn.

In operations of Ceremonial Magic, generally speaking, one seeks not only communication with the sixth sense with evoked entities, but also manifestations of the latter, accessible to the five physical senses. In other words, one wishes to materialise entities. This materialisation depends on the complex process of lower vampirism, in the mechanics of which the elementals play a prominent role. Under ordinary conditions of a call, the most important thing is the activity of sylphs or elementary chains in general, which are close to this group. That's why the operator draws a fourth circle, which serves as a fence from the harmful effects of semi-materialised elements of the outer region and outlines a circle, inside of which the operator considers himself to be expediently disposing of semi-material resources favorable to him. In the new, last ring, it is customary to place the names of the leaders of the sylphs on four sides of the horizon for a given planetary day, with the senior leader controlling the region of the ring between south and east. For completeness, I give two tables. The first contains the names of the Planetary Angels, written in Hebrew; the second is the names of the leaders of the sylphs on the quarters of the horizon for different days of the week. The name of the senior leader is accompanied by the word Rex (king). These last names are usually written in Latin, because for many centuries they were so distorted in their pronunciation that it is not possible to restore their Jewish, Chaldean or Syriac spelling.

In the outer circle (in Figure 52) were placed the names of the rulers of the sylphs, in an order suitable for the Sabbath and the hour of the ceremony.

Saturn	Cassiel or Shebtaiel
Jupiter	Sachiel or Zadkiel (Zedekiel)
Mars	Kemael
Sun	Michael
Venus	Haniel
Mercury	Raphael
Moon	Gabriel

Between	East & North	North & West	West & South	South & East
Sunday	Cynabal	Andas	Thus	Varcan Rex
Monday	Abuzaha	Mistabu	Bilet	Arcan Rex
Tuesday	Paffran	Ismoli	Carmax	Sammy Rex
Wednesday	Aercus	Sallales	Suquinos	Modiath Rex
Thursday	Zebul	Gutriz	Maguth	Guth Rex
Friday	Flaef	Abalidoth	Amabiel	Sarabotes Rex
Saturday	Balidet	Asseibi	Abumalith	Maymon Rex

In the accompanying drawing, the Sabbath overlords of the sylphs are marked in the outer ring, according to the time of the ceremonies.

Here is our pantaculo and is characterised in general terms. Now let's get the operation elements out of it.

An operator (or operators) should fit in the inner circle. The tradition allows one operator, three operators and nine operators. In the last two cases, one speaks, although others can operate the instruments. If the main operator is a virgin or hermaphrodite, or a child, then there can only be two faces in a circle, instead of three. One or more persons can be replaced by animals tied inside the circle or trained not to leave it. Here are the requirements of the tradition for the so-called. "Great Operation." "Small operations" are allowed, which can be performed by an operator who does not leave the circle and an assistant who has the right to enter and exit the circle. There are also "androgynous operations" performed either by the hermaphrodite in the singular, or by a man and a woman who have been in mental and astral communication and physical matrimony for quite some time before the operation.

It is assumed that the operator or operators have been initiated into the hermetic quaternary (the Cross and the theme of the Fall and Reintegration of man (the "alpha" and the "omega" in the pantaculo). All this makes mystical preparation obligatory for them by preliminary theurgic operations for 3-40 days (depending on the importance of the operation), and for the animals that are with them, a mystical ceremony of cleansing prayers and sprinkling with holy water.

The first ring enclosing the circle gives us an indication of the monoideistic preparation of the operators for the operation with lengthy meditation and their consciousness of their pentagram freedom. Next comes the astral ring, indicating the need to prepare the astral (correcting planetary defects in the work of the imagination with astral fasting -

silence and silence - and efforts to extinguish in oneself at least temporarily planetary influences, which are simply unsuitable for operation). In the astral ring, however, we can find a continuation of the four ends of the inner cross, which will remind us of the four main tools of the magician: a wand (for coagulating dispersed fluids); the chalice, to concentrate the pure image, previously created and that would support the imagination; swords (to disperse inappropriate coagulated elements) and pentagrams (to remind the operator of their own freedom). A sword is absolutely necessary; the pentagram is very necessary (or instead of it - the flip side of the Great Pantaculo of Solomon, also reminding of Freedom with its fluid distribution scheme). A chalice and a staff are rarely needed. The outer ring of elementals will remind the operator of the need for systematic preparation by the regime of the physical plane for the operation (fasting, preliminary washing and fumigation of the body, preserving physical health by the day of the operation, developing auto-mediumism, etc.). This is the general scheme of the operator's preparation. I should add to this that it is important for the latter to protect himself from the interference of people hostile to him or other entities in the external course of the operation. And here it is in the corners of the pantaculo, i.e. against the midpoints of the quarters of the outer circle, on the outside, it draws four pentagrams (three points outward, two inwards), as if to reflect unexpected interventions. These are his advanced sentinels outside the fortress. It is equally important at any ceremony to know which side the coagulates will appear, the impression of which can be perceived by physical vision. And so, the operator pre-forces the region of phenomena, drawing an equilateral triangle outside the circle in the east with its apex outward and inscribing the Great Name ה ו ה י inside this triangle, which belongs to the region of the oldest of the involutive (and therefore coagulating) Sephira.
We have been doing so far the operator himself and what he needs, regardless of the specific nature of the operation. Now let's take care of the interests of the entity called by the operator.
We have already noted the timing and astrological conditions in general. But in the energy world, one should also pay attention to the other correspondences of Secondary Causes. It is necessary to properly choose the color of the clothes for the operator, the metals and stones that are with him, the content of mantrams and sets that he uses, the aroma of those herbs and extracts that will be burned or evaporated in a smoking room, placed in a special small pantacle on the south side of the circle, outside the last; finally, the color of the beam that will be directed from the magic lantern into the region of space above the ה ו ה י triangle (the lantern itself is placed in the South-West, outside the circle).

All this prompted the followers of Occultism to generate numerous manuscripts and printed Grimoires, giving details of the ritual of one or another ceremony. It is useful to disassemble these grimoires in order to be aware of their understanding of the goals and composition of the operations themselves. It is impossible to consider them legislative manifestations, because there is no operation equally understood by two operators who did not prepare together.

Ceremonial Magic operations extend not only to two-planes, but also to incarnated entities. One can call and force something (of course, under favorable conditions) by an astrosome of a living person, an egrégore of a chain having embodied representatives; etc., I will say more, those methods of magical operations that we do not call ceremonial, nevertheless carry within themselves the underdeveloped embryos of ceremonics or the equivalents of developed ceremonies. Everywhere there is reliance on the physical plane, everywhere special formulas of influence, methods of delivering or borrowing medium elements, focusing on mental and astral features of operations, and finally, methods of protecting the operator himself from chance and from return blows.

The preparation and setting of a Spiritist session can serve as an example of ceremonial magic. In a Spiritist session, the magic circles are replaced by the circulation of fluids in the chain formed by the people hand in hand. The danger of rupture of the circulation of these fluids sufficiently characterises the current as a protective circle of the participants. The role of the rod that condenses the fluids is played by the table. Sometimes there is also a sword and a smoker. The sung formulas of the ceremonies are replaced by some musical instrument, to facilitate the transmission of energy and to at a certain point, the form of this transmission. Often, conjurations are used and in this case, a single operator speaks. In general, these sessions lack adequate preparation of participants. This fact and its result - the absence of unification of participants' wishes, aggravated by the impressions that they may have received immediately prior to the meeting – cause usually a certain disorder in phenomena, during the session.

Finishing the study of Arcanum XVI, we will add that, if the Arcanum XV mobilised an astral swirl, the XVI gives the possibility of using it, to act on other beings. Arcanum XVIII צ (Tzadik), in turn, will lead us to the field of misuse of the ability to create astral whirlwinds. The Arcana XVI and XVIII are separated by a very important Arcanum - the XVII - that makes it easier for us to understand all the manifestations of life, and thereby reduces both the danger to become victims of bad intentions, as letting us be carried away by our own proud presumption in discovering our astral power.

Notes on the sixteenth Arcanum

What first comes to mind when we reflect upon this Arcanum is the lightning flash, which we have understood to be a force applied to the crown chakra from above or, in kabbalistic terms, is applied from the Ein Soph region to the crown of the Tree of Life, which is Keter.
The limitless power of this force is such that it cannot be contained by any of the sephirotic spheres and thus emanates downwards through the Tree. The light cascades downwards through Chokmah, Binah and the occulted sphere, Daath – which together constitute the upper Trinity of the Tree of Life – its Godhead – until it reaches to Chesed, the Sphere of Mercy and henceforth moves into Geburah on the Pillar of Severity. An aspect of Geburah is strength and its associated planet is Mars.
In a sign of the omnipotence of the Absolute, it is in the vessel of Geburah that a crack appears, and it is understood that this is, therefore, the sphere where the 'shattering of the vessels' occurs, though we also recognise G.O.M.'s teachings on the 'fallen sphere Daath' given in the Eleventh Arcanum:

The Sephira Daath intended to create an illusion of independence for itself; for this it needed Freedom, without which there can be no independent life. But the desire for freedom was tantamount to a refusal of food transmitted by the Higher Influx. This refusal was processed and what happened is called the fall of the Six Sephira — and is what led these Sephira to the Kabbalistic Death.
Not fed by Higher Currents, the very subtle shell of these Sephira coagulated into what we now call the lower astral. The sephirotic organism is fragmented, its polarities appear as unresolved binaries. The Sephira Tiphereth has ceased to emanate its Light. The differentiation of the cells that made up Daath went to extremes, and its name became legion. Here is the so-called Fall of the Angels, which revealed to the Universe the Mystery of Death.

The Fall of Angels is attended by the Fall of Man and in Letter XVI of MotT the author applies himself to the problem of evil in man, whose inner seed of soul rebellion is what gives fertile ground for the higher forces of evil to act upon and work through humankind. Whilst he exposes latent evil in the human soul, Tomberg is also keen to advocate for the innocence of the human body and to contrast negative forms of asceticism with a more positive expression, aiming at reunification with God rather than mortification of the body for earthly reasons.

The doctrine that the pre-existent soul, in having sinned, took into itself the seed of evil in the pre-terrestrial sphere, has as a practical consequence - positive asceticism - the soul's atonement and reunion with God...Positive asceticism does not struggle against the body but rather against the seed of evil in the soul. (MotT, p435)

The original sin, meanwhile, is detailed in Kore Kosmou. Here the seed of human evil lies is said to be not so much the result of primordial ignorance but the *"sin of knowledge at one's own instigation instead of that through God."* (p436). It is an act of disobedience towards God.

The great hermetic text, Kore Kosmou, is quoted:

*But the souls, my son, thinking that they had now done something great, began to arrange themselves in presumptuous audacity and transgress God's commands; for they sought to vie with the gods in heaven, claiming nobility equal to theirs, in that the souls themselves had been made by the same Maker. And so they now began to overstep teh bounds of their own divisions of the atmosphere; for they would not any longer abide in one place, but were ever on the move, and thought it death to stay in one abode..*Isis speaking to Horus, Kore Kosmou 24

The philosophical conviction expressed in this teaching is set beside the magical account of the expulsion from Paradise given in Genesis, the aim of which is to awaken in humanity a soul memory of The Fall, memories from what Jung would call, the collective unconscious.
We are told that the mission of humankind is to cultivate the "garden" which constitutes the "world in a state of equilibrium and cooperation between Spirit and Nature!" and this is given as a "seed statement" which, if properly planted will result in appropriate actions being taken upon the ground in which it is sown.
Thus do we attempt to cultivate and maintain *"culture and tradition...To will and to dare...to know and to be silent"*, a key hermetic maxim.
Thereby do the memories awakened in our soul of our primordial state of living in Paradise motivate humanity's eternal mission, which is to return to this place.
The 'lightning flash' which destroys the Tower – analogous to the Tower of Babel described in Genesis – may be seen as a manifestation of divine wisdom, which according to St John of the Cross in his seminal teaching on The Dark Night of the Soul, *"is so high that it transcends the capacity of the soul, and therefore is, in that respect, darkness"*.

So it is that the human soul that has been struck by this lightning, is inevitably plunged into his or her own 'dark night' and made to cross the abyss contained within the fallen sphere of Daath. The difficulty of this crossing is dependent upon the relative purity of the soul which has been struck.

According to this law, it is written in the Gospel of St Luke (xiv, 11):

Everyone who exalts himself will be abased, and he who humbles himself will be exalted.

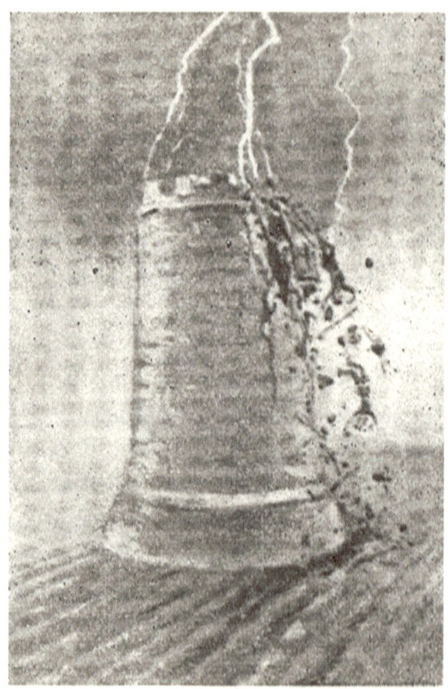

Arcanum XVII

Pathway between Hod and Yesod

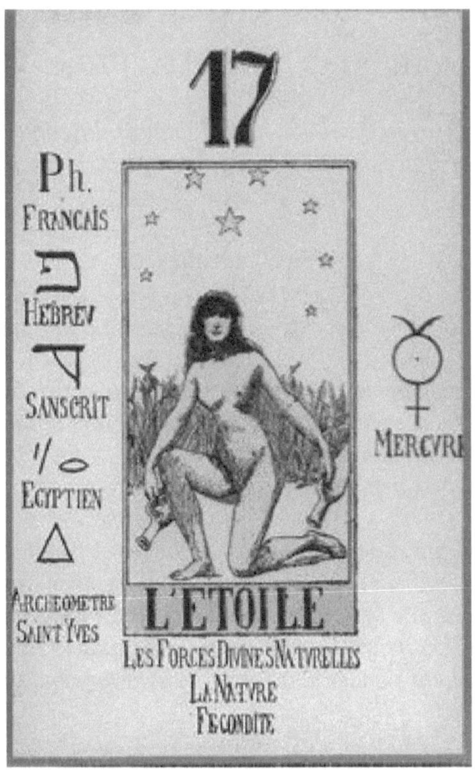

The Star is *Youthful*

You must discover the particular hours and in what sign the Psyche of the World pours forth from her two goblets the waters of life like two rivers.

Levi

THE STAR OF THE MAGI: Hope

F, P--80 expresses in the divine world Immortality: in the intellectual world the Inner Light that illuminates the Spirit: in the physical world Hope.

Paul Christian

I discovered unexpected correlations in things which hitherto I had thought foreign to each other. Objects distant and different from one another appeared near and similar. The facts of the world arranged themselves before my eyes according to a new pattern

And beneath the radiant stars beside the blue river I saw a naked maiden, young and beautiful. She stooped on one knee and poured water from two vessels, one of gold and one of silver. A little bird in a nearby bush lifted its wings and was poised ready to fly away.
For a moment I understood that I beheld the Soul of Nature.

Ouspensky

The sign of the alphabet corresponding to the Arcanum XVII is פ (Peh); its numerical value, 80. The Arcanum's astrological correspondence is the planet Mercury and its hieroglyph is a mouth with tongue, that is, **a** mouth that speaks.

What expresses the language of the Archetype? In what form does the voice reach us, even when everything around us breathes silence or coercion? The language of the Archetype is Hope, inherently belonging to everyone who hears the voice of the Archetype. Hope is a great gift from heaven.

But even Humanity, thanks to its own abilities, can navigate in the maze of compelling vortices and foresee astral dangers. Human Intuition is a great talent that it is a sin to lose and which seems to us to be a precious gift made to ourselves at that time when we, having lost it, began to recover it again by our own efforts.

But Nature also has a living language, which was better comprehended by the ancients during periods of the primitive simplicity of life than is now understood by us. But nevertheless, we are also striving energetically for the Natural Divination, realising the frankness of nature's speech addressed to those who know how to hear them.

This Arcanum, which wears, according to what has just been said, the headings of Spes (Hope), Intuitio (Intuition), Divinatio naturalis (Natural Divination), is called by its scientists and laypeople "Stella Magorum" (star of the Magi) by the properties of the picture.

Indeed, in the upper part of the picture we see a large eight-pointed star surrounded by the same, but small. Under these stars on earth, we see a completely naked girl, watering dry soil from two vessels, gold and silver. In the background, a butterfly sits on a rose.

In the midst of aridity and desolation, when there is no rain, there is a comforter – Hope - forever young, forever virgin, to pour the moisture of both Gnostic polarities to the earth. In a metaphysical drought, the outlook of discouraged people will be helped by the beneficent Hope, who will always renew us with the fresh moisture of waiting for Higher Influx (a silver vessel, a passive pole) and self-confidence (a gold vessel, an active pole). Hope comes from the same source as the Consciousness, and it shows us everything without veils.

If we wish to develop our own intuition, to regain the gift that our ancestors possessed to a great degree, then we will know how to discern, the rose from the weeds, as do the wings of a butterfly.

If we do not close our eyes to the spectacle of Nature, and trouble ourselves to delve into it in order to discover its secrets, then we will see the stars in the sky, astrologically showing us those laws (the stars have eight points), which are dictated by balance, conventions and Karma and which are similarly written not only in the starry sky, not only in the grandiose organism of the Solar system but, by the Law of Analogy, also in any organism of the smallest amplitudes of manifestation, in any organ of this organism, in any of its cells.

Thus, the card proclaims that Hope (symbolised by the apex of the triangle of Fabre d'Olivet) never leaves us; that we can avoid the distancing of Intuition (the right point of this triangle) and that karma (the left point) reveals to us at every moment its mystery through the sky (Phrenology), the face (Physiognomy), the hand (palmistry), each of our movements or our activities (Graphology, cartomancy, etc.) of the reactions of sensory effects of our nervous system (divination by water, coffee grounds, crystals, etc.) in everything and everything, on than we want to focus on.

Let us turn to the arithmetic analysis of the Arcanum:

17 = 1 + 16: The Divine Essence (1) together with the logical exclusion (16) of Evil, in order to make the Good triumph in the metaphysical field, give rise to Hope (17).

The tri-planar man (1) who knows how to exclude (16) unnecessary astral forms, to examine better those that interest him, develop the Intuition (17). The active nature (1) and the destruction of forms (16) leave marks that allow us to decipher (17) the mysteries of Destiny.

17 = 16 + 1: The prayer for the Good excludes (16) metaphysically the Evil and approaches the one (1), giving birth to the Hope (17).

The procedures of astral constraint (16), applied to a human being (1), may compel him not to mislead our Intuition (17) and tell the truth, when we evoke its astrosome.

17 = 2 + 15 and 17 = 15 + 2: The Metaphysical Substance (2) and pure logic (15) give Hope (17), indicating the triumph of the subtle in that they show us the power of pervasive deduction.

The mystery of the relation of the sexes (2), related to the understanding of the formation of a Tourbillon (15), gives the Higher Intuition (17) of Universal Love, to which we ascend through many steps, of which the first is a feeling of unity in matrimony.

The world of achievements (2) and Karma (15) of these achievements leave decipherable traits (17).

17 = 3 + 14 and 17 = 14 + 3: Understanding the gnostic nature of the Archetype (3) and the ability to use deduction (14) will firmly establish in a person Hope (17) for a favorable tonality of the lower manifestations of the Archetype. The principle of multiplication (reproduction) (3) of human individuals in the physical plane and the desire of reincarnating souls for inner harmony (14) develop intuition in individuals (17), which becomes at least equal to activity.

The principle of production (3) and the nature of the change in entropy (14) are sufficient to outline the picture in which we read (17) the Karma of Nature.

17 = 4 + 13 and 17 = 13 + 4: The existence of form (4) in the manifestations of the Archetype and its permanence (13) lead to the Hope (17). The aspiration to acquire authority (4) and the consciousness of inevitable death (13) lead man to develop intuition itself (17). The laws of adaptability (4) and the principle of the transformation of energy (13) create the world of Nature (17) as we see it.

17 = 5 + 12 and 17 = 12 + 5: The science of Good and Evil (5) and the expectation of the Messiah (12) are equivalent to Hope (17). The pentagram (5), which fully admits the duty of sacrifice (12), has the Intuition (17). The natural religion (5), applied to the zodiacal cycle (12), reveals the mysteries of Astrology (17).

17 = 6 + 11 and 17 = 11 + 6: The Law of Analogy (6), together with the conviction of the existence of the Higher Forces (11), give Hope (17). Free will (6), along with the power of egregorial currents (11), lead to Intuition (17).

17 = 7 + 10 and 17 = 10 + 7: The victory of the spirit over form (7) and acceptance of the Testament (10) give Hope (17). The victory in the test of the two paths (7) and the knowledge of Kabbalah (10) prove the full intuition (17) of the adept.

17 = 8 + 9 and 17 = 9 + 8: Whoever knows that the pointer of the great metaphysical scale can lean as far to the right as to the left (8) and who, at the same time, has faith in the Superior Protection (9), will have Hope (17) to go to the right. Whoever knows the conditional law (8) and is initiated into the unconditional (9), has the Intuition (17).

Several branches of study are part of Arcanum XVII.

Hope is taught to us by conscience (in the sense used in religion). Intuition can be developed by personal efforts. We learn to Read in Nature for the knowledge of empirical data and knowledge of the traditional data of the Initiatory Revelations.

Let us examine some of the ways of divination, beginning with Astrology which, for many centuries, has so penetrated all branches of the occult that even as a beginner disciple you need to know something about these methods.

"When it comes to the advanced initiatory stages, a harmonious synthesis of all astral influences would be desirable; for people who wish to become instructors of esotericism - strong Saturn, Mercury and Venus are indispensable. The presence of the Sun and, sometimes, of Mars, are desirable. For the higher degrees of Freemasonry and an efficient activity in this sector: Jupiter, Venus and Mars; for a magician: Saturn, Mercury and Mars; for a theurgist: Sun and Venus; for a theoretical cabalist and an astrologer: Saturn and Mercury; for clairvoyance, psychometry, cartomancy, etc., the influence of the Moon is fundamental.

In mediumistic, sensory experiences, etc. it is recommended to choose people who have a strong influence of Venus and Moon, without adding other influences. If you cannot find them, then it serves a pure Venusian type. Such people are very receptive to subtle influences.

In the initiation centres, among the students, there are always many young people with a predominant Lunar influence. These students, in the beginning, progress well, obeying their instructors but usually, in a short time they move away from the current because due to the action of the Moon, they are very much subject to external factors. The spiritual branch most suited to a solar type is to be a priest, but excluding teaching.

For a Jupiterian, one should look at the history of esotericism.

Of course, almost no pure types exist. In the choice of branch it is necessary to consider the set of influences on the human being.

The rest of G.O.M.'s long discourse on astrology and other divinatory arts has been included in the Appendix to the present volume.

Notes on the seventeenth Arcanum

In Letter XVII of MotT we catch a fascinating biographic glimpse of the author's early occult studies, possibly with representatives of the St Petersburg school, which offers and a deeper comprehension of the importance of the divine name as a vital thread uniting initiates of the Martinist tradition and kabbalists alike:

Thus it was in 1919/20 that I was for the first time occupied with the Major Arcana of the Tarot under the four aspects comprising the divine name (ה ו ה י),

Tomberg came to see in this divine name the *"unity of mysticism, gnosis and sacred magic in Hermeticism"* and reflected upon the growth of tradition within the mysterious spiral of time and space

Following the trials of The Devil and The Tower of Destruction – and before we are beholden to contemplate the serious business of The Moon – workers of the Arcana are given some respite via The Star, which is abundant with the virtue of Hope.

The mechanical construction of the Tower of Babel is contrasted with the spiritual agency of growth represented by The Star.

the righteous flourish like a palm tree…they are ever full of sap and green. (Psalm 92)

There is a great analogy here with the mysteries of nature, marveled upon by any gardener, where a diverse array of plants miraculously shoot out from small, hard seeds.
Whilst all the Arcana have the greatest of significance when viewed in the light of present-day problems of humanity, the wounded state of Mother Earth – of nature – is of utmost concern for the present generation. The Star encourages us to incline towards natural and organic growth – spiritual, psychological, emotional and physical life – and away from the artificial building blocks which society has constructed for itself over the equally artificial construct of time.
Sacred Magic, as described in the Third Arcanum, utilises this divine agent of growth and thereby works miracles, whereas practical magic enlists the dry electrical force epitomised by The Devil.

Continuous transformation is the essential manifestation of the agent of growth, just as creative lightning is that of the magical agent. (MotT, p465).

Like the stream-carrying Guardian Angel who illumines the Arcanum of Temperance, The Star is of a watery essence, whilst the two preceding it are both of fire:

…a down cast spirit dries up the bones… (Proverbs xvii, 22).

And yet, as any occultist well knows, there is a place for both fire and water, two essential elements of the magical quarternary which is completed with Earth and Air. It is the great occult attainment of 'fiery water' which is derived from the harmonious reconciliation of these two opposites; the resolution of elemental binaries, which is symbolised by the Seal of Solomon and an integral attribute of the Tree of Life. The fire which purifies the pathways makes clear the way for Holy Water and the two together are unified in the Sephirot Tiphareth.
In addition to many years of reflection upon this mystery, the work we have found most useful in helping to explain it is Sefer Yetzirah Magic by the Australian Qabbalist, Patrick Mulcahy. In Mulcahy's revelatory exposition of the Kabbalistic masterpiece that is the Sefer Yetzirah, Tiphareth is presented as the Holy Temple of the Tree of Life. At the heart of this Holy Temple the centrally connecting vertical pathways of Shin and Mem (fire and water) merge into what might be regarded as the fabled fiery water (the *Esh Mayim* described in the Sefer Bahir). This

then moves upwards into the divine consciousness of Daath and onto the pathway of Air (or Breath) via the third Mother letter, Aleph.

The mystical interplay between fire and water is fundamental to any interpretation of the Tree of Life and is what vivifies the entire 'octahedron' of the lower section. A key to the secret of the 'fiery water' maybe found in verse 59 of the Sefer Bahir:

'Why is heaven called Shamayim? This teaches that God kneaded fire and water and combined them together. From this He made the "beginning of His word." It is thus written (Psalm 119:160), "The beginning of your word is truth." It is therefore called Shamayim - Sham Mayim (there is water) - Esh Mayim (fire water). He said to them: This is the meaning of the verse (Job 25:2), "He makes peace in His heights." He placed peace and love between them. May He also place peace and love among us'.

Mulcahy explains that it is the merging of the paths of fire and water in the middle of the Tree that is delineated by the 'Shem Pillar', extending vertically through the middle of the Tree of Life along the pathways of the Mother letters. "All human-beings eventually undergo this high initiation, called the ShM Initiation (or 'Name' Initiation)", which saw the name of Israel bestowed upon the Patriarch Jacob *following the struggle with his angel.* This initiation empowers Jacob/Israel to consciously participate in the divine work of Formation (Yetzirah).

Just as the three pathways of the Middle Pillar running through the Tree of Life via Keter, Da'at, Tipharethh and Yesod are assigned (successively from top to bottom) to Aleph, Mem and Shin, so are the Sefira of the upper 'trinity' connected to the Mother letters: Keter to Aleph, Chockmah to Mem and Binah to Shin.

Here we must point out that Mulcahy's seminal denouement of the structure of the Tree of Life, based on precise instructions given in the Sefer Yetzirah, diverges from traditional Kabbalistic interpretations and images of the Tree of Life. For example, in most other systems the Aleph, Mem and Shin pathways are placed horizontally, between Chokmah-Binah, Chesed- Geburah and Netzach-Hod. It would be simpler for you to read his book than for me to explain these differences. Returning to The Star, Tomberg cites the German philosopher, Leibnitz, as a prime example of one who displays good continuity of thinking, in accord with the natural agent of growth, which enables him to avoid the conflict of ideas and gulfs between more artificially formulated beliefs. In the cooperative transformations of thought shown by Leibnitz, Tomberg sees a "rainbow of peace".

He also pays tribute to the engineer Schmakov and declares that he shall "rescue from oblivion" his great work, The Sacred Book of Thoth[45] – The Major Arcana of the Tarot, published in 1916/17 in Russia.

Likewise is Henri Bergson lauded as "a great spirit, a star in the heaven of the perennial philosophy…a hermeticist by the grace of God alone, without any external affiliations with initiation orders or societies."

This serves as a prelude to Tomberg's equally heartfelt warning against the formation of occult societies and closed magical groups, which are strongly contrasted with the living spiral represented by Christianity, the door to which is Jesus Christ. Students are asked to not form groups or schools with Tomberg at their centre. His is a living and transformative expression of spirituality and esotericism, which flows like the water of life, and he clearly wishes to dissociate from the electrical charge of such closed circles as he witnessed on the long course of his journey through the esoteric fields.

The image of the Seventeenth Arcanum shows a woman pouring water from both her right and left hand into the same stream. Herein lies the difficulty, for such a blend means that whilst all that is good, pure, beautiful, holy and true is enabled to flow, so is that which is "infectious, vile, blasphemous and diabolical."

This stark contrast is all too clearly visible in the physical world, where the life carried by our rivers and streams is becoming ever-more polluted. Hope is renewed by the fact that whilst the present state may appear dire as a result of such malign influences – pollutants – in the future this is resolved by a return to the perfect state through rectification. As such we need not fall into a dualist position when contemplating this paradox.

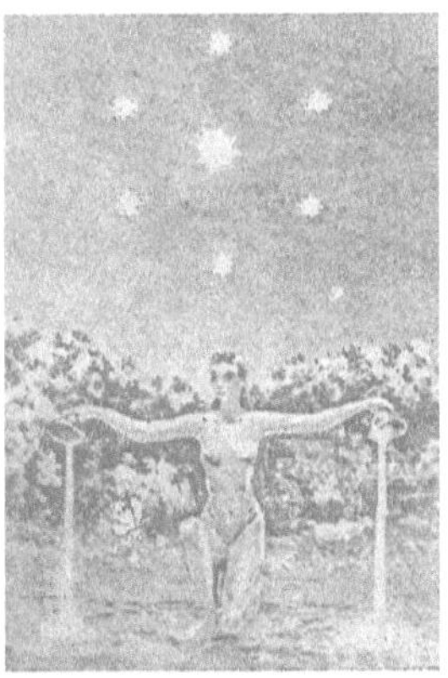

---

[45] It seems likely, therefore, that this great work by Schmakov was a key foundation stone for Meditations on the Tarot itself

Arcanum XVIII

Pathway between Yesod and Netzach

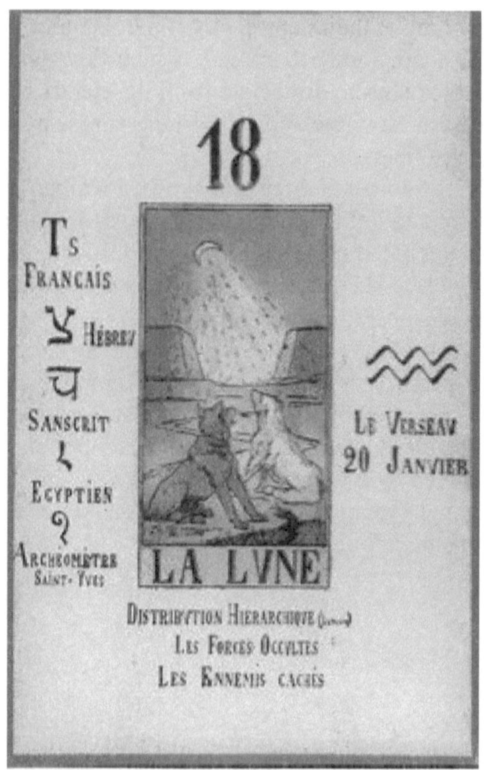

The Moon is *Mysterious*

examine carefully the effects of the influences of the Moon in her several phases

Levi

TWILIGHT: Deceptions

TS--90 expresses in the divine world the abysses of the Infinite

Paul Christian

Dread fell upon me. I sensed the presence of a mysterious world, a world of hostile spirits, of corpses rising from graves, of wailing ghosts. In this pale moonlight I seemed to feel the presence of apparitions; someone watched me from behind the towers - and I knew it was dangerous to look back.

Ouspensky

The letter of the alphabet corresponding to the Arcanum XVIII is צ (Tzadik); its numerical value, 90; astrological correspondence: the sign of Aquarius.

The hieroglyph of the Arcanum is a cover, but not in the sense of protection against weathering, but a cover that closes over us like a trapdoor, something. who oppresses us, deprives us of the free air, limits our freedom and our horizon. Wanting to lift us, we hit our heads against this obstacle; as soon as some joy appears, immediately comes his threat; we only start something, we feel its oppression.

The picture, mysteriously explaining this Arcanum to us, is called by the scientist Crepusculum (The Twilight); its common name is The Moon. At the very top of the picture, the Moon pours its quiet light, hopelessly mathematically, directing its cone of rays in a strict system, but moonlight is reflected light. "Where is the Source of Light?" You exclaim; "we want to receive the Light directly from it." The picture answers you: "You are subordinate to the Hierarchical Law; you do not have the right to light from the Source; it is released to you by the nearest hierarchical authority; be satisfied with your portion of light, you who voluntarily plunged yourself into the illusionary plan of reproduction of binaries by falling."

The only light accessible to us is transmitted to each of us by the nearest hierarchical nucleus. Shall we be content with what we have received, not forgetting that because of the fall, we are voluntarily immersed in the illusory world of the multiplication of binaries. This explains the first title of the Arcanum that is "Occult Hierarchy".

You peer at dusk and in the background you see the Binary of Towers, or the Binary of the Pyramids. Between these towers there passes a winding path of your being, as if only for that it is strewn with light sand to make visible the stains of blood with which it abounds. You, having just understood the first headline of the Arcana (Hierarchia Occulta), are thinking about the strange impression this blood made on you. Someone was losing vitality, and this strikes us with the consciousness of the weakness that makes us cherish the gross resources of life condensed to the extreme. On the one hand, these resources seem to be ours, and on the other hand, the very rudeness of these resources puts them at the disposal of everyone who wants to take their belonging to us as a reference point for hostile implementations. On our blood, we can evolve us. This is terrible! But who can evolve us? The answer is ready in the foreground of the picture. There is a wolf (mirrored) to the left, who has always openly declared himself our enemy. On the right we see a dog that recently flattered us and imposed itself on our friend. Now we understand who is driving us: declared enemies and false friends. Are they completely free in their terrible deeds? No, something is not good for them - they howl at the moon: they are constrained by the nearest hierarchical authority, which gives us light. So if they are constrained, why should we be so afraid of them? Because we are like Cancer the crab that just comes out of its puddle and quickly returns to it. This tendency to retreat – to backtrack - is that it makes us subject to bewitchment.

Realising the second title of the picture (Hostes Occulti – secret enemies), we ask – are there the same dangers in Nature? Yes, there is still physical danger from natural conditions, which is sometimes as hidden from backward Cancer as astral threats: Pericula Occulta (hidden dangers) - this is the third heading of the Arcanum.

We proceed to the arithmetic analysis of the Arcanum.

18 = 1 + 17 and 18 = 17 + 1: The Divine Essence (1) and Hope (17), coming from the metaphysical plane, are sufficient to determine the existence of the Hierarchical Law (18). The One Active Principle (nothing could be expected of an inactive principle) creates the organs for its activity, according to hierarchical rank and according to their progressive departure from the Primordial Source.

The triplane man (1), with intuition (17), clearly perceives the astral dangers that threaten (18). Active nature (1), when we read its warnings (17), reveals to us the imminence of its dangers (18), which remain hidden from the ignorant.

18 = 2 + 16 and 18 = 16 + 2: The metaphysical substance (2) and the method of logical exclusion (16) determine the constitution of the Hierarchy (18) in the world of ideas. The principle of polarisation (2) and the possibility of astral constraint (16) reveal the mystery of enchantment (18). The latter is possible only when the subject is passive, and the operator is active. The possibility of the physical destruction (16) of the forms created by Nature (2) constitutes the called "danger" (18).

18 = 3 + 15 and 18 = 15 + 3: The triplicity of the one Principle (3) and the logic of the metaphysical construction (15) of the Second Family, determine the Hierarchical Laws (18) for our world. The formulation of these Laws is linked to the mystery of the Trinity and the logical application of this mystery.

The mysteries of birth (3) and the features of the Nahash element (15) are components of the process of bewitchment (18). The creativity of Nature (3) and the Law to Karma (15), influencing this creativity, constitute the totality of physical hazards (18).

18 = 4 + 14 and 18 = 14 + 4: The processes of formation (4) and deduction (14) determine the constitution of Hierarchy (18).

The principle of authority (4) and the ability to balance its activity and its passivity (14), cause one man to become an opponent of another (18).

18 = 5 + 13 and 18 = 13 + 5: The knowledge of Good and Evil (5), together with the permanence of the Superior Principles (13), suffice for the establishment of the Hierarchy (18). The pentagrammatic character of the human being (5) and its subjection to the laws of death (13) bewitching (18).

18 = 6 + 12 and 18 = 12 + 6: The understanding of the Law of Analogy (6) and the expectation of the Messiah (12) compel man, even superficial, to admit Hierarchical Law (18). The primacy given to freedom (6) in relation to mercy (12) can lead man to practice bewitching (18). However, the primacy given to mercy (12), in relation to the freedom (6) of the human will (for example, pray for enemies), undo all the traps of opponents (18).

18 = 7 + 11 and 18 = 11 + 7: The essence of Hierarchy (18) is that in it the subtle governs the dense (7) and possesses the power (11) to permeate it. The possibility of astral aggression (18) is that the man who has already won victory (7) on himself, uses both his own strength and that of the current (11) in promoting its ends.

We consider as a danger (18) the possibility of losing what we intend to possess as property (7) and whose destruction by the forces of Nature (11) is normal.

18 = 8 + 10 and 18 = 10 + 8: The Libration of the World Scale (8), together with the Great Testament (10), give the key to the Hierarchical Law (18). The conditions of the ethical life of man (8) and the knowledge of Kabbalah (10) make it possible for the use of bewitching (18).

18 = 9 + 9: The hierarchical graduation (18) is the consequence of the meeting between two protectors (9 + 9), one less and another higher. The least protects the interests of any particular organ; the highest, the interests of the general organism, tracing, for this, to his subordinate, directives which may not be advantageous to the organ under the care of the first protector. The Hierarchy Law gives priority to general interests in relation to individuals and thus determines the triumph of one 9 over another 9.

A human being initiated (9) only in self-protection can easily be bewitched (18) by another, initiated (9) in the mysteries of Baphomet. A particular organism saves its physical resources, using probability calculation (9). Nature, which has the knowledge of all the data, calculates the certainties (9). The second "9" wins the first "9", and this is called "danger on the physical plane" (18).

This analysis gives us some points of support for a better understanding of the Arcanum. We will not deal with the physical dangers. We shall confine ourselves to the Hierarchical Law and the process of bewitching.

The Hierarchical Law

The unitary worldview of the Spiritual Schools has the following main thesis: The principles are clothed in Laws; Laws work with facts. Clothing without a carrier is not capable of life; they may serve as a scarecrow for some time for sparrows, but even those in the end will recognise its powerlessness.

Materialistic Schools say differently: they think that a complex of facts gives rise to a law, that a complex of laws gives rise to a principle. In other words, they think that the strong-willed monad of the Chain is an illusion created by a series of facts that are within this chain. For them, a cell is more real than an organ; an organ is more real than an organism. According to the unitary spiritualist schools, life is hidden behind its visible manifestations and, sometimes even independent of these. Materialists assert that life comes from matter, from the inanimate.

"I am the God of Abraham, Isaac, and Jacob; not the God of the dead, but the God of the living." Here is the guiding text of living unitarianism. Proponents of this direction, of course, will conduct the Hierarchy, based on a priori recognition of the existence of its starting point: there is an Archetype, and therefore there are both Man and Nature. There is a boss, and he has subordinates; there is a leader conducting certain volitional impulses, and there are people gathered around this leader who are ready to formally and really defend the conduct of these impulses; there is a Teacher - and the School appears; there is a Mental Monad, it formed itself an astrosome, and the latter made itself a physical body.

Materialists proclaim that a human being represents only the synthesis of their cells. If we imagine everything existing for only one moment, then it will be equally possible for us to carry out one or another system. The materialist will tell you: "Show me a person who is not a synthesis of your cells; you tell me that the astrosome of the fetus vampirises the elements of subplanes of the physical environment; so you yourself admit that apart from the existence of this environment, incarnation could not take place; who forbids me to think that individual consciousness "here is a direct consequence of the state of convergence of the elements of the environment; who forbids me to think that every crowd has a boss because of the very functions of the collective existence of the crowd?"

Now, instead of talking about a particular life - a phenomenon of only ephemeral duration - let's talk about a longer period: eg an entire epoch Studying the history of the human masses and the history of the hierarchical collectivities, it is verified that the predominance of mass always leads to divergences, to the disintegration of the collectivity, to death. The hierarchical system, on the other hand, leads to the consolidation of collectivity, unity, the search for a common target. Disorganised waves flow through the mass; in hierarchical collectivities circulate the ordered currents of the Telesma[46]. In a parliament whose members are chosen by oppositions appearing from the outset and, during the existence of the parliament, not only the parties fight among themselves, but also the fractions of these parties. No parliament in the world gives real powers to its president. It only instructs you to ensure certain regulations and even these are soon infringed by the parliamentarians themselves. Compare these anarchic manifestations with the life of a normal and healthy family or of a community based in the patriarchal principle, that is, organised according to the Hierarchical Law, and in which each member is ready to sacrifice something of himself for the sake of his community. It is said that even a fox whose leg or tail has been caught in a trap, will cut it with its own teeth to save what is really important: life.

It could be said that the two philosophies - that of the spiritualists and that of the materialists - form a great binary. In the history of mankind we may even find attempts to neutralise it.

Spiritualists say that everything comes from on high; that everything was created by the Ascending Triangle; that the Sun is the Father of everything. The materialists claim that everything comes from Baixo, from the Triangle Descending, created through adaptation; that the Moon is the Mother of all.

In this discussion the pantheists enter, saying: "the solution lies in the centre of the Star of Solomon, in the Stau-ros, this symbol of the gnostic law, of the fertilisation of the passive by the active. Both Triangles existed before us. We already find them as instruments for our use. The key of our power is in the Stauros; depends on how we will act with Telesma, this substance transmitting both the constructiveness of the Active and the reaction of the Passive. Both opponents have reason, for the Baphomet's Father is the Sun, and the Mother, the Moon; but it is the wind that carries him in his bosom, this same wind that allows us to breathe and thanks to which all can live. We do not seek the principle of all principles, we do not intend to decide which is the beginning and the end. Do we not care about the origin, with the parents. We live and need to learn to live in the field of action of the androgynous son. "

---

[46]Telesma (from the Greek word "Telos"), the primordial substance from which all was made and which, according to Hermes Trimegistos is, at the same time, the "heaven" and the earth, "that is, the subtle and the dense.

Which of the three currents must we unite? Spiritualist, materialistic or pantheistic?

We will follow the example of the Egyptian schools. We will bow before Hermes Trismegistus, this we will adopt the synthesis of the three philosophical currents. We will be materialists, supporting ourselves firmly on the physical plane. For the magician, the physical plane is a valuable point of support to allow him to create Facts from other Facts. We will be pantheistic when we want the Forms to create the other forms when we want to affirm our Pentagram rights, not as slaves of Nature but as free children of God. However, as soon as we feel that our self is extinguished before Something Greater manifesting as soon as we overtake our attraction to the Form and are drawn to the world of ideas, we will become audaciously spiritualists, for then we will belong to the kingdom of the Father, the "Sun", the "☉."

We can ask ourselves which of these three planes man belongs to, according to the essence of his nature. What, essentially, is man? The body, the personality? Or his aspiration to the High, that High where man seems to dissolve into the Universal and Infinite?

We cannot answer that question. We can offer only words, and these are not capable to give such an answer. Each one has to look for it for himself. As for us, we can only say that the body is more impermanent and has less power than personality; that personalities are united on the basis of common ideas and that sometimes, for the sake of these ideas a human being voluntarily performs the fox or tail role of the aforementioned fox.

In relation to these problems, it would be good, and even necessary to meditate on what was said in the Arcanum XI concerning the fall of souls.

We will further add that a pure spiritualist will undoubtedly be an absolutist in his conception of Hierarchy; to a pantheist, the idea of the kingdom of the spiritual monad, the eastern kingdom limited by the reaction of matter; according to a materialist, finally, every essential subject of the Universe-and everything that happens in time and space, results from "voting" the respective cells.

The external rules concerning the achievements of the Spiritual Hierarchy have already been formulated in the study of the Arcanum III.

Bewitching

If one wanted to characterise the three symbolic degrees of Masonic initiation, exclusively from the point of view of the ability to influence another being, I would say that the degree of "apprentice" teaches one to be strong within oneself, that is, to fight against one's own weaknesses, gradually overcoming them. This degree aims to develop the active side in one's self. I would say that the degree of "companion" teaches how to discover and learn to exploit others' weaknesses (when we already learn to overcome our own); teaches to know how to profit from the ignorance, and inertia of others. I would say, finally, that the of "master" teaches that only operations in which our knowledge and active power oppose, in the same field, the ignorance and inertia of the adversary. In other words, if we are intellectually capable and possess the necessary knowledge, we will choose the confrontation with our adversary in the intellectual field, knowing that he is there, weaker, and consequently we will carry it wherever we want. However, we will avoid physical struggle with it, because its muscles may be stronger than ours. If we know well the technique of some procedure, it will be in this determined field that we will try to face our adversary, thus avoiding any possible disputes.

These general principles are especially important in the processes we will define as exploitation by the force of astral and physical resources of an incarnated human being by another incarnate human being. Imagine, on the one hand, someone who neglects their own; possessions, leaving them unsupervised, or an empire that, having colonies on various continents, leaves them without any organisation or protection. Imagine, on the other hand, someone to guard and take good care of your properties, or a country to perfectly administer its colonies, being in contact with them continuously and always prepared to protect them against any aggression. Let us assume that the second man or the second country, wants to take advantage of the situation of the first. Clearly he could do it easily. Even though both sides are equally passive and disorganised, if one of them becomes active for a while or assaults the other, he will gain advantage. It is true that the other may also awaken from its inertia and repel the attack, but by then it has already suffered losses.

This is the whole secret of a bewitching success.

Bewitching always attaches to the physical plane or lower astral sub-planes. Bewitchments for awakening a passion, causing illness or death, a material or other ruin, or hamper useful work, etc. Since these activities are linked to the lower Universe, the very term "bewitching" already sounds bad. It is always a very despicable operation and dense, to demand a solid point of support.

The process is as follows: a volitive entity is created according to the sephirotic scheme. The world Aziluth of this entity belongs in its entirety to the operator. The influence of this world must penetrate into the worlds Briah, Yetzirah and Assiah of the victim. However, the operator's Aziluth world is connected to its three other worlds.

Therefore, the operator must be able to connect his Briah, Yezirah and Assiah with the corresponding worlds of the victim, taking advantage of this transient inertia of the Aziluth world. Thus, the victim's three lower worlds will be like temporary organs of a new entity, composed of the operator and the victim.

After that, the task of the operator is a certain auto-suggestion. The operator suggests, for example, an "ethical disease" to that part of the new compound Briah which, previously, belonged to the Briah independent of the victim; a disease of form, to that part of ordinary Yetzirah - who formerly comprised the independent Yetzirah of the victim and a physical disease to the corresponding part to Aziah.

We might ask whether it is possible to seize the whole of the three alien worlds. We will say that getting hold of the whole is not necessary. It suffices for the operator to subjugate only a small part and contagious with an illness, letting it spread to other organs, previously belonging to the victim, while at the same time protecting the organs that now also enter in the composition of the entity common. It is known that an ethical transgression, caused by some particular reason, can destroy harmony in the soul of a weak individual; that a small defect can ruin the whole of a shape and that a microbe, upon penetrating in a cell, can infect the entire organism.

From all of the above, it can be deduced that the matter, held by the operator, intentionally infected must possess in itself, for the occurrence of the contagion, some important elementary aspects of the victim or of one of its main organs, functionally related to the phenomena that the operator wants to trigger. In other words, to bewitch on the ethical plane, p. e.g., for a proud man, it is important to seize the elements connected with your self-love. For bewitching, on the plane of form, someone whose main characteristic is aesthetic sensibility, it is important to introduce into your world Yetzirah, the element of deformity. To provoke passion or cause illness or death, bewitching the victim's Aziah world, some of his red blood cells give more result than something more superficial, such as, e.g., an epithelium fragment.

It is also important that these elements, in themselves insignificant but coming from the person involved, are artificially linked to the whole organism, even by means of an operation on a plane different from that to which the elements in the operator's possession belong. Like this, having some hair from the victim, the operator makes a wax doll, representing it, and sets the hair on the doll's head. The material of the Assiah world, by itself insufficient, is completed through the world Yetzirah.

Suppose that the operator, for some reason, wants to suggest to the patient a sensation of permanent fear; However, he does not know what the patient is afraid of, yet he knows what scares him. Then the operator prepares the whole composite entity - his and the victim's - to feel the fright and, as far as it is possible, causes fear in himself. It will also penetrate the body of the victim. When fear has pervaded the person well, the operator is free from both fear and fright. He will do so on the condition that he is not himself, sensitive to fright. Otherwise, she will be inoculated with the fear that had been associated with the ease of being frightened.

The so-called "return coup", in the process of bewitching, results from an attempt to inoculate in someone a weakness to which the operator himself is more sensitive than the victim. In this case, everything will fall on itself. A man who fears for his own safety will receive the "return stroke" if he attempts to bewitch another to some disgrace on the physical plane. A man who easily falls in love, enticing another to provoke love, will fall in love madly and without any hope of reciprocity, etc.

The operator secures himself against the return stroke by placing a second victim in the scheme of bewitching (we've already mentioned that). However, the choice of this second victim should be very suitable for its astral and physical characteristics, since, as we have already explained, it must be, in the lower three worlds of the sephrototic system, more likely to receive the charge of the bewitching than the operator himself.

Now we can understand better why the sorcerer needs a few drops of blood, a tooth, a nail, sweat, semen, etc. of the person who wishes to bewitch. These elements are introduced into the composition of the physical support point of the operation. Often the elements that belonged to the victim are mixed with corresponding elements of the operator. In certain cases the operator uses a doll, a photograph or some other representation of the victim, introducing in it some cells actually coming from the organism of this. In other cases, the operator prefers to use a living organism (eg, a frog), trying to link it to the victim, giving it the same name or using some other procedure. In the case of a purely energy, such as making someone fall on the street, the operator follows the victim step-by-step, imitating his way of walking. Stumbles voluntarily, trying to convey to the victim his or her own loss of balance, but containing himself, at the last moment, not to fall.

All the procedures of sorcerers, macumbeiros, black magicians, etc. are based on the same principles, and all create very heavy karma to their promoters or executors. The very easy operation itself is profoundly abject and disgusting, and its key is always in the active power on one side and the passivity of the other.

The means to be immune to aggression, whatever your plan, is always the same: to be active, not to remain half-asleep, to be busy concentrating on something. A watchful man inside at home, soon realises that a thief wants to penetrate it.

You have to be active on the mental plane. You must pray, especially pray for your enemies. Who now for his enemies, does not form plans of revenge, and who does not form plans of revenge, loses the habit of assigning such plans to their fellow men. Whoever does not attribute bad thoughts to others, he is not subject to fear. Such a person will hardly be bewitched.

It is necessary to be active in the astral plane, concentrated in certain forms, chosen or created by ourselves. Thus, the forms created by others cannot be imposed on us. It's necessary to know clearly what we want, so that in our confusion are not implanted the desires others. If we sincerely love a being chosen by our heart, a deceptive simulation of love cannot be imposed on us. If we join an Egrégore that fully corresponds to our spiritual aspirations, we will not be impelled to another, more strange, that perhaps would to be harmful to us.

To be active in the physical plane is to train our body to produce a quality and quantity of life force for certain purposes, and for our bodies to monofunctional mode. In this way, they will oppose any bewitchment. Let us remember, once and for all, that an inactive and amorphous human being, a being who dissipates all planes of existence, is more likely to be bewitched than any other. A worker in the field of ideas, in the field of form, or in the field of effort, his body is protected by a solid armor against any aggression. In it, the world of Aziluth permeates the three others; it is individualised, it resembles a closed system. To the external world it is always an "ɔ". He becomes "He" only when, according to his will, he is receptive to the Higher Influx.

In life one cannot act like the crab that retreats to its puddle. If we know, if we are active, then we will fear neither the wolf nor the dog, and on the way we will not spill a drop of our blood that someone could use against us. We will limit our submission only to the binary of the pyramids and we will submit, consciously and voluntarily, to the Hierarchy of two Lunar rays. Knowing the source of this reflected light, we will learn to venerate, through it, the Primordial Source.

This is what Tradition and the occult experience teach us. Let us see what profane science tells us.

From the year 1891, Colonel de Rochas dedicated himself to the research on what was called "exteriorisation of the sensibility" of the people immersed in the state of deep hypnosis.

It is easy to note that the first stage of the process of bewitchment tends to establish, in between the operator, and the victim, something to remember the "state of contact" observed by Colonel de Rochas (see Arcanum XV).

The colonel of Rochas, by a magnetic action, directed especially to the region of the visual centres of the patient and consisting of short passes along the forehead, or circular on the forehead or near the eyes, reached the following results: the surface of the patient's skin became insensitive; The sensitivity, as the passes continued, gradually transported around the patient's body, and 5 to 6 centimeters apart. The first level, this is closest to the patient, at a distance of 3 cm. of your skin. In the intervals between two levels, the patient showed no sensitivity. The number of sensitive layers increased as the magnetisation work proceeded, so that the last layer was found within a few meters of the patient. The prick with a pin on the level of sensitivity caused pain in the patient. A glass of water placed on the level system produced what Rochas called the "odic shadow", that is, behind the glass the sensitivity of some previously sensitive levels disappeared, as if, in that place, it was dissolved by the Water. In addition, the water seemed to absorb the sensitivity, as taking the glass away from the patient and "chopping" the water, it caused him pain; it cooled, a shiver ran through her.

Approximately the same results were obtained by placing, instead of water, at the sensitive, a wax doll. However, the "bites" in the water, while it was at the sensitivity, caused pain in that place of the body of the patient situated nearer the water, while, putting the doll in the same place where there was water, and stinging it in the part the pain was felt in the upper body of the patient. Chopping the bottom of the puppet, the pain reverberated in the lower part of the patient's body.

The experiments with the glass of water and the doll gave only positive results when his distance from the patient did not exceed a certain limit. However, this limit extended well beyond the distance between the patient's body and the last sensitive level.

The clairvoyants present at the scene of the experiments saw that the levels of sensitivity were luminous, for them, the skin of a man whose is externalised.

The results of these experiments were published in 1892.

Attempts were made to take photographs of these experiences by placing the negative, in the first case, close to the skin of a non-hypnotised patient and, in the second case, at the level of externalised sensitivity, of a hypnotised patient. In the first case the attempts to reach the patient through photography, did not produce any result, which is explained by the more positive condition of a non-hypnotised subject and by the absence of the "state of contact". In the second case, touching the photograph was felt by the patient, and the scratches on the negative caused stigmas in the form of a reddish-coloured skin.

These experiments were performed in the presence of two physicians and a mathematician and confirm the existence of a real base in bewitching.

Notes on the eighteenth Arcanum

So much occultism, natural and practical magic is associated with the moon that it can be disconcerting to see it is presented within the Tarot course as a negatively charged body of woe.

We recall that Rosicrucian training exercises aiming for the stimulation of active imagination were designed specifically to overcome what was seen as an overriding lunar influence upon the human psyche, and in particular somnambulic, trance and hypnotic states. In the Moon we are made to see the force of the unconscious over the conscious, of forgetfulness over remembering and sleep over waking. By actively reinforcing memory and consciously directing the imagination – to the point of controlling one's own dreams and astral travels – the individual brings him or herself under more solar than lunar influences.

The eighteenth Arcanum also draws our attention to "the problem of inversion…of retrograde movement" (MotT, p493), of slipping backwards rather moving in a continuous progression, of moving in a way that is "contrary to that of life" (sic). Whilst the sun and stars are considered to be creative and revealed luminaries respectively, the moon is only reflective – it sends back an image of this true light from its dead and dusty surface.

The horror of 'back-sliding' is well-known in orthodox religions but it can also be difficult to avoid, for example, during periods of great stress, trauma, sickness, upheaval, grief or boredom, when the impulse to "slide back" is likely to affect us most strongly. In this backwards motion, The Moon, with its sense of hopelessness and tragedy, is shown to be the antithesis of The Star.

The friend of The Moon and its backwards inclination is materialism in all its expression, just as the opposing force is composed of spiritual consciousness and intuitive thought. Whilst the sun represents creative consciousness and the star is an expression of revelation, shining through the darkness, the moon is inorganic intelligence and together with the Earth forms an 'inseparable couple'.

The Arcanum of The Moon teaches us to strive beyond the limits of materialistic intelligence and make a leap from its hypnotic sphere into that of the following Arcanum, which is The Sun. Henri Bergson is quoted to effect on p506 of MotT:

You may speculate as intelligently as you will on the mechanism of intelligence; you will never, by this method, succeed in getting beyond it. You may get something more complex, but not something higher nor even something different. You must take things by storm: you must thrust intelligence outside itself by an act of will.[47]

This action described by Bergson is analogous to the kabbalistic idea of Kavana, a form of meditation which probes "the dark depths which surround it". It is the action whereby wisdom (Chokmah) is wedded to intelligent understanding (Binah) in the generation of the occult Sephirot, Daath, which Tomberg equates with intuition.
The development of strong intuition is an express goal of Hermetic study, although it is also fair to say that some people are naturally born with this gift of the Spirit.

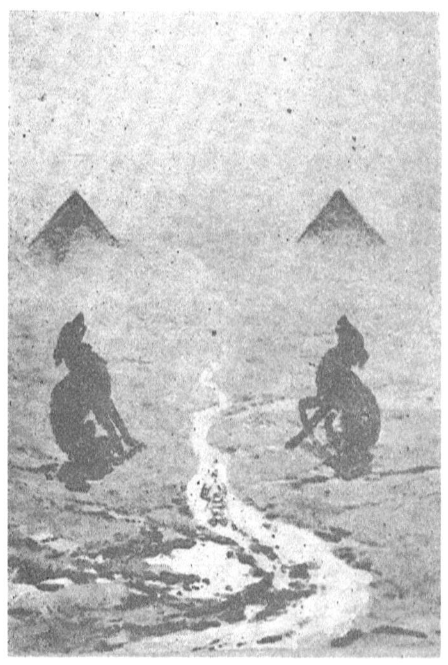

---

[47] Henri Bergson, Creative Evolution, trsl. A. Mitchell, London, 1964, pp202-204

Arcanum XIX

Pathway between Tiphareth and Yesod

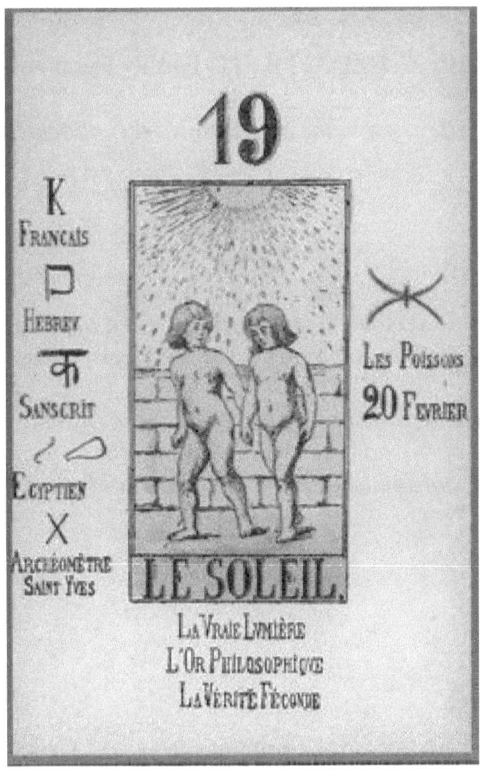

The Sun radiates *Truth*

The Sun is the sanctuary of spiritual beings who have been loosed from the ties of earth life, and there is the blazing tabernacle in which resides the Soul of the Messiah

Levi

THE BLAZING LIGHT: Earthly Happiness

Q--100 expresses in the divine world the supreme Heaven

Paul Christian

I shut my eyes for a moment and when I opened them again I saw that each ray of the Sun is the sceptre of the Emperor and bears life.

And I saw how under the concentration of these rays the mystic flowers of the waters open and receive the rays into themselves and how all Nature is constantly born from the union of two principles.

Ouspensky

The sign of the alphabet corresponding to the Arcanum XIX is ק (Qoph); its numerical value, 100. Astrological correspondence: sign of Pisces.

The hieroglyph of the Arcanum is an axe, tool to make an opening in the roof of the Previous Arcanum, giving access to light.

The erudite title of the blade is "Lux Resplendens" (Resplendent Light); its common name, "The Sun".

The card of the Arcanum features two children playing in a space surrounded by a wall of stones and illuminated by strong rays of light that transform, near the earth, in a shower of gold.

The three titles of this Arcanum: "Veritas fecunda", "Virtus humana" and "Aurum Philosophale", have already been sufficiently explained in Arcanum X.

Let us turn to arithmetic deconstruction.

19 = 1 + 18 and 19 = 18 + 1: The essence of One (1) and the mysteries of Hierarchy (18) together are the ladder leading to Truth. Creator (19). The triplanar man (1), knowing the mysteries of en-sorcery (18) protects himself against enemies, cultivating in themselves true virtue (19).

19 = 2 + 17 and 19 = 17 + 2: Divine Substance (2) and Hope (17) lead to Truth (19). The polarity of human nature (2), together with Intuition (17) create Virtue (19). This is: if we understand (the receptive pole) the value of the Good and we are active (another pole), we will practice the Good.

19 = 3 + 16 and 19 = 16 + 3: The triplicity of metaphysical nature (3) together with the method of logical exclusion (16) leads to Virtue (19). Understanding the mystery of birth (3) and the mystery of astral constraint (16) leads to Fruitful Truths (19). The Gnostic understanding of the principle of creativity (3) and the necessity of physical destruction (16) determines the basic phases of the alchemical process (19), that is, the phase of the "crow head". First, rotting; then rebirth.

19 = 4 + 15 and 19 = 15 + 4: Form (4) together with logic (15) leads to fruitful truths (19). Authority (4) and knowledge of Baphomet (15) make Virtue triumph (19), (even though procedures such as those of Clement V and Philip IV).

19 = 5 + 14 and 19 = 14 + 5: The knowledge of Good and Evil (5) leads, by (14), to fruitful Truths (19). The Pentagram (5) which performed the harmony (14) itself becomes virtuous (19).

19 = 6 + 13 and 19 = 13 + 6: To realise the permanence of the Superior Principles (13) applying the Law of Analogy (6) leads to fruitful truths (19). The knowledge of the environment (6) and energetic transformations (13), gives the key to alchemy (19).

19 = 7 + 12 and 19 = 12 + 7: If we believe in the Messiah (12) and give more value to the spirit than to form (7), then we will possess fruitful

truths (19). If we overcome ourselves (7) by severity, and are merciful toward others (12), then we will be virtuous (19).

19 = 8 + 11 and 19 = 11 + 8: If we observe the metaphysical libration (8) of the Great Scale and admit to the force (11) of Superior Influx's, then we will possess fruitful truths (19). If we address the moral force (11) of humanity to the fulfillment of the Laws (8), we will be virtuous (19).

19 = 9 + 10 and 19 = 10 + 9: A Kabbalistic initiate (9) is undoubtedly virtuous (19). The Divine Testament (10) and the Guardians (9) protect us from errors and lead to truths fruit trees (19). These are the general indications as to the field of action of the Arcanum. Now, we will try to characterise, only briefly and superficially, the three mysterious processes, namely: reaching the truths fruit, which corresponds to the "Great Work" in the field of ideas; to acquire the Hermetic Virtues (the "Great Work" of ethical hermeticism); the realisation of the Philosopher's Stone (the "Great Work" of alchemy).

Hermetic Philosophy

The excerpts from the "Emerald Verses," quoted in Arcanum VI and XV, have already clarified much. Let us study some more of these verses, for they are directly related to the Arcanum XIX.

"Sic habebis gloriam totius mundi, fugitive idea omnis obscuritas Hic est totius fortitudinis fortitudo fortis: wanted vincet omnem rem subtilem omnemque solidam penetrabit. Sic mundus creatus est. Hinc erunt adaptations mirabiles, quarum modus est hic. Itaque vocatus sum Hermes Trismegistus, you have three parts philosophiae totius mundi. Completum est quod dixi de operatione Solis ".

Translated:

"In this way you will take possession of the glory of the whole world, and all darkness will be removed from you. This is the powerful power of all power; for it will conquer all that is subtle and penetrate into all that is dense. The world is created in the same way. Wonderful achievements flow from here, the mechanism of which is the same. That is why I am called Hermes Trismegistus, who owns the three parts of world philosophy. What I said about Solar Work is completed. "

Let us examine these words from the point of view of the title of our Arcanum, that is, metaphysically fruitful truths.

The verses just quoted are those that directly follow the characteristic of Baphomet. In this characteristic one is advised to look for the elements of World Glory and all enlightenment. In other words, the mysteries of the Star of Solomon and the Gnostic worldview are the key of metaphysical omniscience.

How to understand this? In the nineteenth chapter of the Dogma of Higher Magic, Eliphas Lévi says that in the metaphysical plane the Philosopher's Stone has the shape of a cube. In this cube, he invites you to consider three pairs of mutually opposite faces: on the first pair of faces are written - the name of Solomon (שלמה) and the name of God; on the second pair of faces are the names אדם (Adam) and הוה (Heva); on the third pair are the names AZOTH and INRI.

He wants to say by this that the key to the Fruitful Truth is given by the three degrees of the Templar Initiation; that the first degree - the degree of the Kabbalistic Cycle - reveals the Secret of the relationship between the Archetype and the Initiated Man (שלמה - Shlomoh, Solomon); The name of God with intent is not indicated: why - the Initiates know this; the second degree - that of the Magic Cycle - reveals the Secret of the influence of the Active on the Passive; the third degree - the degree of the Hermetic Cycle - reveals the Secrets of the Universal Solvent (AZOTH) and Universal Renewal (INRI).

That is all we can and have the license to say about this aspect of the Arcanum XIX.

Ethical Hermeticism

We already know the task of Ethical Hermeticism. Each human being is composed of a substance whose disposition and fixation in proper order make one become virtuous. The "father" of the virtue is the activity (the Sun) of the subject; his "mother", the passivity (the Moon). During the embryonic period, this virtue is "carried by the Wind," that is, the astral environment. It is nourished by the "mother" - the Earth - because it will have to manifest itself in the world of sacrifice – the zodiacal world. However, causing the process of gestation, birth and only the Telesma that is the envelope of the Will. In other words, it is the Pentagram itself that creates its virtue.

In the same way that, in order to form convictions in the field of Hermetic Philosophy, first to separate faith from knowledge, and then to synthesise them in a harmoniousness, thus, in Ethical Hermeticism one would have to be aware which impulses are of the Higher Triangle and which ones are of the Lower Triangle. A conscious receptivity to the principles from above and a capacity to evaluate dense manifestations of the lower must be developed within them. From the High comes to us the precept "love your neighbour". But how, and What to love in him? What do you do for him? The answer is "to love as yourself." However, we can only fully understand "loving oneself" in the plane of involution, in the plane of the Lower Triangle.

Thus, we need to know the high ideals and the aspiration to Reintegration and, in parallel, observe and study our own low selfishness so that we can then link them to the great laws of ethics. It is absolutely necessary to know how to rise from Earth to Heaven, and to return, again, from Heaven to the Earth, seeking the principles in its sources, in the High, and in its manifestation, in the Low.

Then our virtue will acquire its full strength and any darkness will disappear from the heart. Able to assimilate everything that is subtle, we will become more virtuous. Through the chains that we will form and, through them, this Virtue will penetrate into all that is dense, will overcome inertia, the selfishness of the masses, and even against their will, instill in them ethical principles.

In the purely mental plane of Hermeticism, the intellect oscillates between Heaven (principles) and Earth (facts) that is, practice deduction and induction. The same must be done by the heart.

On the mental plane, the reward is the understanding of Causes. On the plane of feelings – a complete peace in the heart itself, a full harmony of the astrosome that will actively manifest itself as mercy and justice, as man perceives the desires and needs of his fellow man. In the first field, the mind learns to solve abstract problems, that is, to "overcome the subtle "and also" to penetrate the dense, "that is, to explain the world of facts participating in the formation of the Fraternity of Virtue, influences and elevates the ethical society.

In both camps we will find "wonders", closely linked with the cosmogony ("thus the world was created"). In both, there are the three main principles: the "Sulphur" (active) of the aspiration to the Heights; the "Mercury" (passive) of the knowledge of the plains, and the "Salt" (neutral), harmonisation of the two preceding elements.

Both there and there are four Elements: in metaphysics – (1) the desire to find the Truth and (2) the desire to convey it; the desire to perceive and assimilate it (3) and the desire to synthesise the perceived into the system (4). The first two elements are the י and the ו; the second two are ה; in Ethical Hermeticism י corresponds to evolutionary activity, ו to the involutive; the first ה to positive emotions and the second ה to negative passivity. In the field of mind as well as in the heart there is a fifth active element in the role of the operator in the center of the Quaternary; in metaphysics the fifth element corresponds to the mind of the fallen אדם (Adam), who knew the Good and Evil of the Great Scale which maintains the balance of the world; in Ethical Hermeticism the fifth element is the quintessence, that is, the Will which governs the Hermetic

Cross. In both there is the Monad, able to achieve universal glory ("sic habebis gloriam totius mundi"[48]).

Alchemy

The final sentences of the text of the "Emerald Table" state that:

- the power of Hermes extends through all three planes;
- the Solar Work was concluded, that is, it was realised not only in the two higher planes, but also on the physical plane.

We will not speak here of the historical confirmation of the alchemical work. Those interested in the subject can look for the book of Papus, "The Philosopher's Stone". We will only sketch a general picture of alchemy, in which the stages of the transformation correspond to the upper stages of the hermetic transformation of the human being. This will help us to better understand the classical works of alchemy. Each verse of the Emerald Board will contribute to this.

The first verse proclaims the Law of Analogy, which allows us to make an analogy between the higher phases of Hermeticism and alchemy.

The second verse proclaims the oneness of the universal substance and, consequently, the uniqueness of the physical matter.

The third verse clearly indicates the participation of "Gold" (Sun) and "Silver" (Moon) in "Work Magna." The same verse underscores the importance of the environment in which the Work proceeds, as well as of the material support point (the Earth).

The fourth verse alludes to the influence of the magnetism of the operator in the "Work" process. The modern alchemists assumed that this astral agent could be replaced by a natural electric Kabir.

The fifth verse deals with the solid state of the Philosopher's Stone, that is, of the Powder.

The sixth verse clearly points to one of the basic teachings of alchemy, stating that all metals can be classified, in the sense of their bipolarity, on a progressive scale. One of the poles of perfection corresponds to silver (or platinum); the other to gold. In these two metals two principles are more perfectly connected: "sulphur" and "mercury". The call, existing in silver, allows the more perfect manifestation of "mercurian" qualities; and, in gold, of sulphur. Other metals are considered as not having achieved the perfection of silver, in regard to the negative qualities, or the perfection of gold, as to the positive qualities.

---

[48] sic habebis gloriam totius mundi

It follows logically that each metal (and even every single body) is a "sulphur" alloy with "Mercury"; yet this alloy is hermetically perfect only in gold and silver.

To transmute some metal into silver or gold, you would first have to undo the imperfect bond existing in that metal, that is, to separate the subtle ("sulphur" or "fire") from the dense ("mercury" or "water"). Only after that can a new and perfect connection be made, either of the type liabilities or assets, depending on which of the metals nobles are looking to transmute the non-noble. It is this separation from the subtle and dense that the "Emerald Tablet" speaks to us.

The principles "sulphur" and "mercury" (respectively, active and passive) are neutralised by the third, the "salt" (neutral), with the three forming together the "azoth of the sages".

In practice "salt" is always the agent of the manifestation of bodies and the "azoth of the wise" - the agent of the liberation of the principles bound by "salt".

The seventh verse of the Emerald Table underscores the importance of the transformation of matter itself, of the work, of its subtler state - the "fire" - for a denser - the "earth." That refers to the distillation of the compound.

The eighth verse simply animates the alchemist to continue the work. The ninth verse affirms the basic oneness of any and all matter obtained by the alchemical process.

The "son" - the result - is always the son, although he possesses, in his various stages of transmutation, different attributes. The method of preparing a powder which will ennoble an alloy non-noble transmuting it into silver, or a powder that transmutes it into gold, weighing 10 or even 1000 times the weight of the powder used, it is always the same. The quality and quantity of powder obtained depends only on the time it takes to "work" and not on the difference of methods. The essence of the "Stone" is always the same, it varies only the stage of its maturation.

The tenth verse tells us about the existence of gold and silver on earth. It says that Nature, by its own resources, took various chemical combinations to varying degrees of perfection. In nature there is gold and silver, that is, metals that have reached the poles of perfection; why not take imperfect metals and try to bring them to perfection? Why not imitate the Creator, separating two principles, making them go back to the previous state and reunite them, in a perfect way? To stimulate the alchemist, the verse adds: "There are wonderful adaptations of the same work". This brings traditional frameworks: rejuvenation through the internal use of the Philosopher's Stone, the Elixir of Life, stimulation of rapid growth of plants, etc.

Verses eleven and twelve we have already addressed.

Knowing that in the alchemical work there are also three principles ("sulphur", "salt" and "mercury") and four states of matter (radiant, gaseous, liquid and dense), we can approach the dynamic cycle of "Great Work" which contains four phases.

1st Stage: Preparation of the "Work"

This phase consists of the preparation of the "Mercury of the Philosophers" also called "azoth of the sages" or "universal solvent". It is the astral light that comes from the condensation of the bipolarised swirls. To obtain this agent, a particular mineral is used, called "magnesium of the wise" or "marcasite of the wise". The "azoth" is obtained from this "magncsium" by mcans of a mysterious application of electricity or personal magnetism, which gave rise to the expression "steel of the philosophers" or "Magnet of the philosophers."

2nd Stage: the "Work"

The common metallic gold and silver are subjected to the "azoth of the sages" to free them the "living sun" ("sulphur") and the "living moon" ("mercury") in maximum quantities. It is also possible to operate on non-noble metals or only on gold, but in these cases the work unfolding would be slower.

Principles released in the form of two yeasts are enclosed in a glass vessel called "egg" and subjected to slow heating in low flame of an oil lamp, in an apparatus called "athanor".

Time and heat cause, within the "egg", a series of physical and chemical phenomena. In the first weeks of carabinisation, matter takes on indefinite tonalities. This period calls "kingdom of mercury". Later, the mass called "Rebis" becomes greenish and, finally, black. At first, the color black is observed only on the surface. And the "head of Crow". Then the whole mass becomes black. The "kingdom of Saturn" begins. The mass dies to be reborn, similar to the Mason, in the ritual of initiation in the degree of master. The colour black, after quite a prolonged period, passes to the brown tonalities, often with blueish reflections. It can be observed the formation of vapor that falls again in the form of rain. This is the "kingdom of Jupiter. "Next comes the" kingdom of Diana, characterised by a dazzling white colour of the mass. If the desired result is a powder for white transmutation, i.e. in silver, the second stage of the operation will be completed. If, on the contrary, a red transmutation is sought - in gold - it is necessary to continue to heat without paying attention to the passage of the mass ("Rebis") from liquid to solid states and vice versa. The mass becomes green, blue and red dark. All of this is the "kingdom of Venus." Then the mass takes on an orange hue and, then it is coloured like a peacock's tail, that is, it takes all the colours simultaneously of the rainbow. It is the "kingdom of Mars." Finally, crimson vapours appear in the egg above the mass; they condense, the mass dries and becomes incandescent. When the eggs are cooled, it is fixed in the form of small grains of a shade of poppy color. This is the end of the last period called the "Kingdom of Apollo." When the "egg" cools, small red grains form. Then the egg is broken and a very heavy crystalline powder of bright red color with the smell of charred sea salt is found in it. This powder has the property, after two hours of boiling, to convert mercury or molten lead into gold in an amount equal to ten times the weight of the powder itself.

3rd Stage: Multiplication of power gives the "Stone"

The "stone", or is again subjected to the action of the "azoth of the wise" or, what is simpler, placed and enclosed within the "egg", along with an amount of gold whose weight is 100 times greater than the weight of the stone itself. The "egg" is subjected once more to the action of fire. Colours begin to change in the same order, but much more quickly. The new "red stone" weighs much more than the mixture placed in the "egg", that is, the previous" stone "and the gold melted that was added to it. Its transmutation power is 10 times greater than that of first stone. A new operation increases the coefficient up to 100 times in relation to the first intervention. Generally, the multiplication is done three times, so that the stone thus obtained can mercury or molten lead, the weight of which is 10,000 times your own.

4th Stage: The "Projection" of the Stone, its use

Liquid mercury, or lead, or molten tin, is taken in a quantity corresponding to the power of the "stone". If a large quantity of the stone is available, only one part is used at a time. The "stone" crystals are crushed and thin powder. Small amounts of this powder are carefully placed inside wax tablets which, in turn, are placed in an appropriate vessel containing a non-noble metal. It boils all. In the case of "red" powder - to obtain gold - the mixture is boiled for two hours or two hours and a half. In the case of white powder - to get silver - just boil for a quarter of an hour.
The ancient "immortal fireplace" or "athanor", is composed of three parts. In the lower part was placed an oil lamp. From the start of the operation, up to the "crow head" stage, a four-wire wick was used. Then a wick of fourteen wires, and finally, already in the phase of "Diana", a

24-wire. The part centre of the "athanor" had protrusions that supported a kind of frying pan or saucer. In this the sand was placed in the vessel, into which the "egg" was inserted up to a third of its diameter. The level of "rebis" mass, inside the "egg", reached only a quarter of the height of the diameter of the same.

The upper part of the "athanor" consisted of a glass dome reflecting the heat into the appliance.

We also repeat that in the second phase of the "work" it is not indispensable to use gold and silver. Many people only submitted gold to the action of "sages azoth" and obtained a "rebis" satisfactory.

For persons intending to read essays on Alchemy, I must add that in our terminology, Sulphur is the Father; Mercury is the Mother, and Salt is the Androgynous Child. If you read somewhere that Salt is Mother, Mercury is an Androgynous child, this will mean that Mercury is not understood as the Principle, but Mercury-Solvent (Azoth of the Wise), extracted from Magnesia (finished matter - therefore, something such that both principles are balanced in a living form; but only Salt can balance them; it means that living salt dominates in the Magnesium of the Wise, like a child is extracted from a mother. Now we understand the picture of the Arcanum. The Active Sun pours out Light, materialising up to the state of golden rain. Two boys are holding hands in the picture (or a boy with a girl: Rebis can be prepared in many ways). These children are cheerful; they are renewed by the Light falling upon them. And all this is limited by a stone wall that defines the limit of condensation interpreted by the picture of the Gift of Heaven.

So the Qoph axe cut through the window; It remains for us to enjoy this access with wisdom, renewing ourselves and supporting our work for solid achievements that will enable us to the triumph of the passage to the world of the Minor Arcana

Arcana. From the renewal of ourselves we will consider the Arcanum XX; the establishment of support points, Arcanum XXI and the knowledge to guide in our own triumph, the Arcanum XXII.

Notes on the nineteenth Arcanum

According to Paul Christian, herein lies The Blazing Light of earthly happiness.

In his own reflections upon this, the star of hermeticists, Tomberg urges:

May those who follow the star do so completely and without reserve!

This faithfulness to the "star" confers the strength to resist the impatience and "weakness of revolt" and enables us to develop real intuition, which is "the cooperation of human intelligence with superhuman wisdom", thus creating a link between that which is absolute and that which is only relative, "between the supernatural and the natural, between faith and reason." Such a gift, he says, "is reserved for believing thinkers" and is beyond the reach of the unbelieving, belief being essential to the attainment of "transcendental things that intuition alone can give."

The Sun is, indeed, the Arcanum of intuition, of knowing how to raise creative and reflective intelligence and unite it with wisdom. This is an essential facet of the work of Reintegration, enabling us to re-establish unity between the diminished light of human intellect and the absolute light of divine wisdom. This is accomplished not through a suppression of intelligence but "its intensification" to the point of transcendent creativity or, alternatively, via a "sunstroke": "namely, the annihilation of intelligence by the brilliance of wisdom", which is a theme explored in the Twenty First Arcanum.

We are also reminded via the symbol of Isis that "intelligence united to wisdom in intuition still does not signify the [full] achievement of the work of the reintegration of consciousness, if it is not crowned with a third element which corresponds to the "stars", just as intelligence corresponds to the "moon" and wisdom to the "sun" In order to reach the ONE God, we must try to elevate ourselves through the successive degrees of consciousness of the nine spiritual hierarchies and the Holy Trinity. Here Tomberg points out the inherent error inherent in Vedanta, where the transcendental self is identified wholly with the One God, where the image and likeness of God is confused with God Absolute.

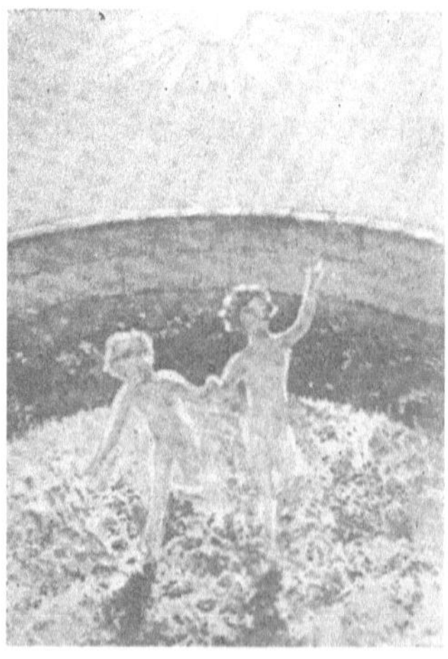

Arcanum XX

Pathway between Yesod and Malkulth

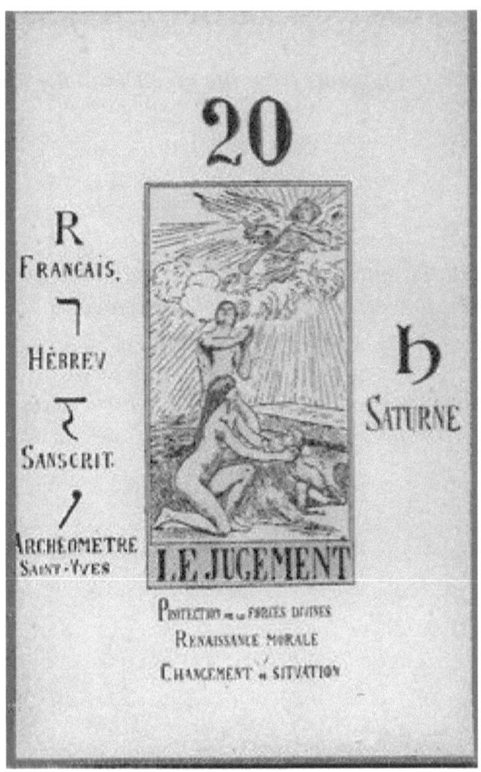

The Judgement is the gateway to *Resurrection*

He understands the reasons for the Present, the Past, and the Future

Levi

THE AWAKENING OF THE DEAD: Renewal

R--200 represents the passage from life on earth to the life of the future.

Paul Christian

in its tones I felt the smile of the Empress and in the opening graves I saw the opening flowers whose fragrance seemed to be wafted by the outstretched arms.

Then I understood the mystery of birth in death.

Ouspensky

The sign of the alphabet corresponding to the 20th Arcanum is ר (Resh). The numerical value of this sign = 200; astrological correspondence the planet Saturn. The hieroglyph of the Arcanum is the head of a person who understands the benefits of the axe handed to him in the previous Arcanum, looking out of the window he has cut through and guiding the person during conscious transitions from one phase of life to another. The scientific name for this Arcanum is Resurrectio mortuum (resurrection of the dead). its common name: "The judgement".

On the card we see an angel trumpeting in the sky. The sound of its trumpet symbolises the attractive power from the call of the Archetype to the evolution. The Arcanum XX represents the mystery of the attraction it exerts on human life (He) the Divine Love (י). Hence the first title of the Arcanum: "Divine Attraction". Below we see a man, a woman and a child, transformed by aspiration and reborn to a new life. This explains the second title of the Arcanum: "Astral Transformation." Here we have the two poles of Humanity (י and He) and the neutralising link (ו) - the child. At the work of astral self-improvement, as we know, activity and intuition should be involved. This work is evaluated, both by ourselves and by our fellow men, according to the androgyny of androgyny that it entails. The evolution of one's own personality also subtle his impulses and his volitional achievements. That is why, along with the father and the mother we see the son.

The three figures left the tomb. Witness this to the turned tombstone and the open pit. For these creatures there was a complete change in the conditions of existence. Hence the third title: "Mutations in tempore "(Transformations in time).

Every effort to free itself from the Tzadik arrest of the Arcanum XVIII, causes, first of all, internal changes, but it does not bring liberation, this comes only later.

The bird locked in a cage, begins by arguing against the bars until it is convinced entirely of the impossibility of escaping. So it is with us.

For many incarnations we look for the most enjoyable way to play our part in life. If something is not as we wanted, we expect the new body, new cells, to realise then that this new body is a prison, similar to the previous one. We are looking for new conditions and new places on the physical plane, but, nevertheless, we remain slaves of the Zodiacal Plane. Finally, we find that we – as being like trapped birds - must change ourselves so we can escape slavery. We begin our astral self-transformation. Turning, we simultaneously subtilise Nature. We hear better the trumpet sound of the Archetype. Not shaking world, driven by the Wheel of Fortune, we could not hear this voice, except in the rare moments of the complete silence of our passions. Now this sound becomes more and more audible.

This is what life herself instructs us in continuously, in turn. But we need it consciously and evolutionarily. It is. should be our goal. When on the horizon we noticed some rise, it's needed to advance horizontally, waiting until she rises. Sometimes it is necessary to descend, if we are firmly convinced that there we will find a steep climb. Such is the way of him who seeks.

Let us now examine some arithmetic decompositions of the Arcanum.

$20 = 1 + 19$ and $20 = 19 + 1$: The metaphysical essence (1) and the creative of their truths (19) draw powerfully upward (20). The tri-plane man (1) who performs the task of Ethical Hermeticism (19) becomes astrally (20). The active nature (1), transmuting the minerals (19), causes transformations in the earth's crust (20).

$20 = 2 + 18$ and $20 = 18 + 2$: The only Hierarchy (18) of Substance One (2) attracts us powerfully to the Primordial Source (20). The mystery of polarities (2) and the existence of enemies in the astral (18) compel us to defend ourselves by means of the transformation (20).

$20 = 3 + 17$ and $20 = 17 + 3$: The understanding of the great Ternary of the Divine Nature (3), along with Hope (17), explain the attraction to the High (20). The understanding of the utility of the multiplication of the incarnates (3) and the human intuition (17) are stimulations to astral transformation (20). The understanding of the Gnostic principle of creativity (3) and the ability to read Nature (17) of time transformations (20).

$20 = 4 + 16$ and $20 = 16 + 4$: The coating of ideas into forms (4) and logical exclusion (16) in certain ways, determine the metaphysical attraction (20) to the remaining forms. The empire over itself (4) and the self-suggestion mechanism (16) determine the transformation astral (20). Adaptation (4) and destruction (16) are elements of transformation in Nature.

$20 = 5 + 15$ and $20 = 15 + 5$: The logical application (15) of the knowledge of Good and Evil (5) causes attraction to the High (20). The pentagram (5) that dominates the mysteries of Baphomet (15) transforms the astrosome (20). The natural religion (5) and the understanding of Karma (15) make accept the changes in Nature (20).

$20 = 6 + 14$ and $20 = 14 + 6$: The application of the Law of Analogy (6) and the deduction (14) prove the existence of the attraction to the High (20). The consciousness of free will (6) and internal harmony (14), proves the astral transformation (20).

$20 = 7 + 13$ and $20 = 13 + 7$: The recognition of the permanence of the Archetype (13) and the primacy given to the spirit on the form (7) ensure the attraction to the High (20). The victory (7) about oneself at the end of the incarnation (13) is a guarantee of perfecting the astrosome (20).

20 = 8 + 12 and 20 = 12 + 8: The understanding of the libration of the Universal Scale (8) and faith in the Redeemer (12) are stimuli to attract to the High (20). The observance of the Law (8) and the practice of compassion (12) prove the astral transformation of the person (20). The Karma (8) of the Zodiacal Plan (12) condemns the human being to continuous transformations (20).

20 = 9 + 11 and 20 = 11 + 9: The recognition of Superior Protection (9) and its power (11), determine the attraction to the High (20). The moral force (11) and Initiation (9) transform the astrosome (20).

20 = 10 + 10: The seriousness of the promises made by Humanity to the Archetype (10) and the perfection of the Testament (10) determine the power of attraction to the High (20). An internal and rigorous Kabbalah (10), in response to external Kabbalah (10), transforms the astrosome (20).

Summarising what has been said, we can affirm that it is not without reason that Saturn rules astrologically this Arcanum. We perceive the passage of time by the changes that occur in the clusters of phenomena; but, on the other hand, we put them back into time.

Notes on the twentieth Arcanum

In his reflections upon The Judgement, the author of MotT speaks much of memory, with reference made to the mysterious "Akasha chronicle" about which Rudolf Steiner spoke so much and pointing to its frequently *"decisive role in the unfolding of universal history."* There follows in Letter XX an incredible denouement of the Akasha which is of revelatory quality and resolves certain difficulties posed by earlier incomplete teachings on this subject.

As far as individuals are concerned, it is the 'moral memory' – "the travelled way of the past" – that is of primary importance to the present study. Just as individuals bear within their psyche an "automatic memory" of basic facts and a "logical memory" wherein "one is led more and more to replace the semi-photographic tableau of memory of the past the by the tableau of facts relating to the logical relationship between them", in addition to the "moral memory" afforded by older age and greater wisdom, so is the macrocosmic memory encompassed in the threefold Akashic chronicle.

With his definition of a threefold Akashic chronicle Tomberg departs from the regular course of occult literature, which makes a case only for one, as a "kind of cinematographic film of the world's past" which unfolds before the seer's eye. We are rather to consider a macrocosmic memory where there is a higher chronicle composed of typological symbolic facts and a lower chronicle consisting of the jumbled mass of other facts which are of no value to the higher universal record. In this respect the two records might be considered as the qualitative and quantitative of macrocosmic memory.

The higher chronicle is the "book of truth" that as well as being seen may also be swallowed (as described in the foreword of the present volume), that is assimilated by the seer. Should you ingest this book it will become part of the fabric of your being and which "will be bitter to your stomach, but sweet as honey in your mouth". (Revelation X). The lower chronicle, Tomberg explains, is more like an archive, cannot be similarly "swallowed" and nor does it play any part in initiation.

This brings us then to the third part of the threefold Akashic chronicle, which we are told is the "book of life" itself, analogous to the moral memory of individuals and composed solely of what is of eternal value, that is *that which is worthy of living eternally – that which is worthy of resurrection.*" (MotT, p565). This book contains information about the past which is of significance to the future firstly and ultimately is of eternal significance.

"The book of life, therefore, is the moral memory of the world". It is constantly being updated and rewritten to account for sins which have been forgiven and atoned for and may therefore be struck from the record as 'paid in full'. A similar process occurs within the memories of individuals, which are adjusted as wrongs are written off, personal digressions made good and henceforth are forgotten. As such, the book of life is the essence of karma and under the dominion of Jesus Christ. This is in stark contrast with the lower chronicle described above – the "book of facts" – from which "entities of the hierarchies of the left, ie, those of strict justice, draw evidence for their accusations" and forms the "archives of the cosmic prosecution."

The second Akashic chronicle forms the logical balance between these two and the contents of the debate between them, providing equilibrium over time.

Whilst the conscious 'reading' of the third Akashic chronicle will produce joyful optimism – even seemingly against all odds – in the seer, knowledge of the second can appear to have the opposite effect. "for it is characteristic that the intuitive experience of the second Akasha chronicle comprises a state of psychic depression due to the gravity of its contents, but that this depression is transformed into joy as soon as the intuitive experience is understood and grasped by the intelligence, ie, when it becomes articulated word. Then it becomes sweet as honey in the mouth."

It is said that no human being can bear to take in the Akashic chronicle in its entirety – nobody can swallow it whole – and it may only be ingested in parts. Therefore, even the most exalted of saints, mystics or occult teachers can only achieve a partial perspective of what is written therein, let alone transmit it to others who may lack the same ability to see or comprehend the content of those fragments. We are given a subtle reminder – even warning – that no matter how distinguished the seer, even someone of Rudolf Steiner's immense stature cannot be infallible with respect to their readings and recordings of the Akashic records, all of whom relied on their own intellectual or artistic efforts to 'fill in the gaps' between fragments seen, intuited or grasped in moments of high inspiration. Such writings as they have left us should not be seen as pure 'Gospel truth', but more as indications of what the cosmic Akasha holds. "Thus, the situation of esoteric historicism is at present such that one cannot swear by any particular work; here, also, collective work is necessary from generation to generation – ie, a living tradition, where each continues the work of his predecessors, by confirming the truth, filling in the gaps, and correcting errors of interpretation or vision." By the same token, no esotericist working within this tradition is required to start everything over anew, and nor is it advisable to do so. We are not striving for "isolated flashes of genius, but rather of a continuous collective endeavour" to slowly grow the seed of light that Tomberg believes was sown by Fabre d'Olivet, despite his acknowledged flaws and errors.

It is then that Tomberg makes two quite serious requests of his readers. The first is that they should undertake of their own volition to grow this aforementioned light of the tradition (and is the reason we are here to fulfill our part of the mission), and the second is that they will not found any sort of organisation, society or other group in order to do so, in order to not fallen into the trap of a 'closed circle', as previously described. *"For the tradition lives not thanks to organisations but rather in spite of them"*. (MotT, p569).

Hermetic though he undoubtedly was, Tomberg inspired love and devotion from friends and would-be students, some of whom were quite persistent in trying to make of him their own occult master. It is notable that he consistently shunned such attentions and even to those who made it to his front door was known to have suggested simply that they pray and not put him up on a pedestal.

He had good reason to dislike societies and circles, having experienced many a bitter blow from the anthroposophical society in the wake of Rudolf Steiner's death and, of course, carrying with him the memory of the horrors which befell his countrymen and women in St Petersburg between the two World Wars. Anyone who's joined an occult group of any kind will be aware that 'flame throwing' is quite often in evidence, which is anathema to any truly Christian endeavour, wherein cooperation in the spirit of fraternal love is to be cultivated as electrical polemics and polarising arguments are to be avoided at all costs.

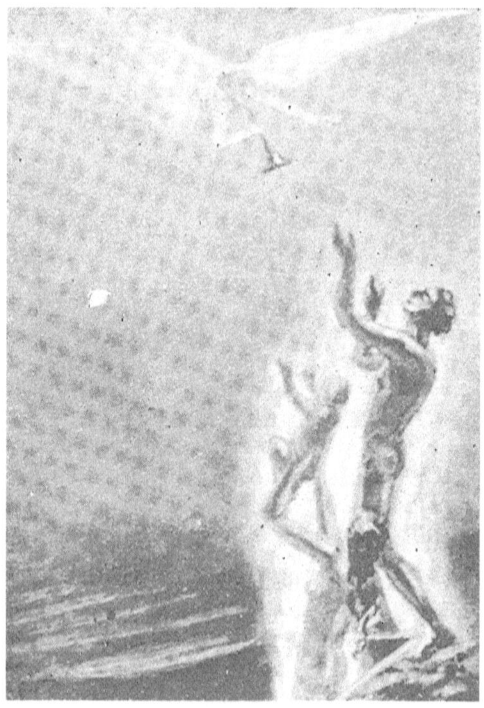

Arcanum XXI

Pathway between Malkulth and Netzach

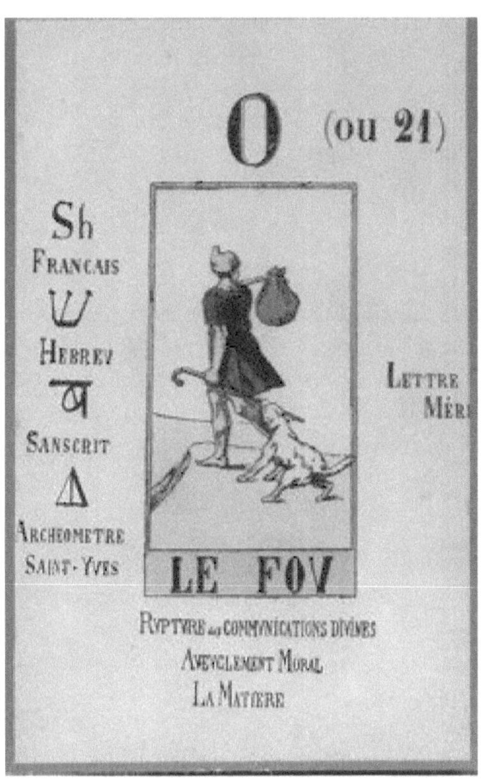

The Fool is *Prophetic*

Such has been the mode of conduct of all the great Masters of Magic, and in such an attitude there is wisdom

Levi

THE CROCODILE: Expiation

S--300 represents the punishment following every error.

Paul Christian

"What has he in the bag?" I inquired, not knowing why I asked. And after a long silence the voice replied: "The four magic symbols, the sceptre, the cup, the sword and the pentacle. The fool always carries them, although he has long since forgotten what they mean. Nevertheless they belong to him, even though he does not know their use. The symbols have not lost their power, they retain it in themselves.

Ouspensky

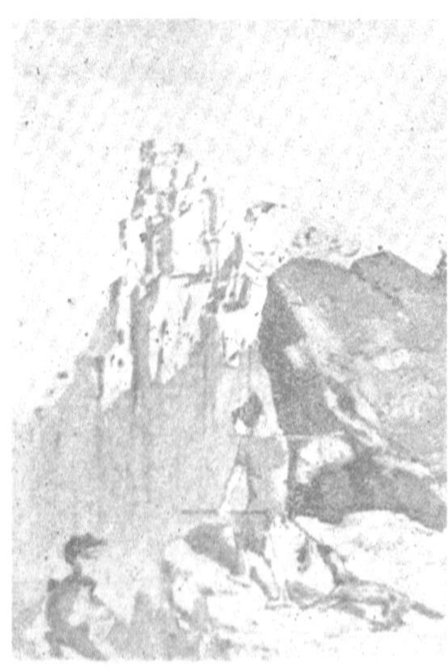

In the Hebrew alphabet, the sign of this Arcanum is ש (Shin). The numerical value of the Shin arcanum is 300. There are no astrological correspondences for the arcana. The hieroglyph is an arrow in an oscillatory motion.

This symbol leads us to the idea of something ultimate, elusive without a preliminary study of the unsound, more general phases of the movement of the same arrow, which was found in the 7th and 15th Arcana.

In the seventh Arcana, an arrow flies straightforwardly according to laws that are metaphysically necessary and scientifically understandable. In the fifteenth Arcana, it moves around the circumference of a circle or, better, along a spiral line that defines the nodal points of the astral vortex.

Here, in the twenty-first and most mysterious of the Arcana, this movement has turned into an oscillatory one. The oscillatory movement can be conditionally included in the types of movement along a closed circuit, considering it as a very particular case of this movement. This does not prevent this particularity from attaching great importance to the practical field of manifestations.

The erudite name of the Arcanum - Furca (forked) - gives only a hint of the shape of the letter itself; the common name – The Fool - refers only to the picture.

Let us look at the card for the true explanation of the Arcanum, or at least some of its meaning.

Approaching the rock, a human figure goes quickly towards a precipice. The head is covered by a hood. The man does not look at himself, but he looks at a point in the sky, where nothing is seen. He does not notice the open-mouthed monster waiting for him behind a cliff. Dressed in rags, he does not care about the appearance of his clothes, which are being torn apart even more by a dog. In hand the foolish pilgrim has a solid staff that neither uses nor defense against the dog. With the right hand, the "madman" holds a long stick against the tip on his shoulder and brings, on the other end, a bulky and heavy bundle. Who would this pilgrim be?

The human figure serves as an indication of the individualisation of the forces affected by the Arcanum. But how are these forces used?

The corporeal man, apparently, was created for life in the physical plane, and in the picture he goes to the abyss, where, moreover, the crocodile's mouth awaits him.

The purpose of clothes is to cover and protect the body. Here, clothes do not fulfill their purpose, nor does the wanderer's staff. He is in a hurry, but at the same time he is not aware that by dropping his burden and driving away the dog he could advance more easily. In a word - he behaves surprisingly, unexpectedly for the viewer.

His behaviour seems to suggest that he is expecting a miraculous intervention and that, for this to be better demonstrated, the pilgrim renounced using the resources at his disposal that would be useful to him. There is an effect, but it is produced by some contrasts, the desire to neglect the normal logic of actions.

We complement the impression with an arithmetic analysis of the number of the Arcanum.

But what to take for the number – 0 or 21?

The zero number should be understood as a hint at the exceptional position of the Arcanum in relation to the others. The number 21 is more fruitful.

$21 = 1 + 20$: The balanced element, capable of manifesting itself (1), introduces new conditions in the world, modifies the existing state of affairs (20).

Here are examples: The Archetype emanates a mental category; an idea takes shape through a process beyond our comprehension; a manifestation causes, mysteriously, certain facts on the physical plane. According to this decomposition, we will establish the titles of the Arcanum in the fields of Theosophical Ternary.

In the field of manifestations of the Archetype, the Arcanum ש reflects the highly mysterious process of the emanation of the Aziluth World. The purely spiritual Principle manifests itself through something radiant - the 10 primordial Sephira - whose radiations, however, are already mental, that is, dense to a high degree once confronted with the Essence of the Archetype. This process is entitled "Radiation" (radiation). In the field of Humanity, the Arcanum ש reflects the process no less mysterious than the transformation of the purely mental manifestations of Humanity into something that could be called a "sign" or "astral signaling." Under this term we mean the capacity, inherent in the human being, to acquire formal knowledge of something that exists in another human being, by means of the "sixth sense" or astral receptivity. The impressions thus received are expressed by a more accessible language, either as a particular colour, geometric figure or impression acoustic, olfactory or tactile. For the moment, we do not care how the "astral sign" manifests itself perception, but rather the very mystery of the emergence of the sign, as the envelope of the idea. Thus, the second title of the Arcanum is: "Sign".

As for the Nature plane, from the beginning of the course we were interested in the subject of transformation of astral energy concentrated in attributes of physical matter. The mystery of the transformation of a determined amount of kinetic energy in attribute of hardness; the mystery of being able to movement in the patient through the use of the imaginative energy of which we have already spoken several times and which are part of the manifestation of the Arcanum 𝐰 in the plane of Nature.

The existence of this great illusion which we call the "material world" - the 𝐰 enigma in Nature - gives us the third title of the Arcanum: "The Matter".

The inverse order of the same decomposition (21 = 20 + 1), presents the scheme of the situation of a personality (1) balanced, capable of constructive achievements but that is hampered by the performance of the Arcanum XX, that is, by the process of rebirth. The purpose of his life has changed and the person has not yet ordered his new tasks, very different from the old ones. He walks, but does not look where he goes, though he has eyes to see; does not rest on the staff of the initiation, does not even use it to guard against aggressions and externalities, allowing them to make progress. He abandoned logic and imagined himself to be protected by some nonexistent privileges. He is considered dressed, but the inadequate dress does not ensure either heat or decency. Carefully carried on the back, hanging on the end of a long stick, a heavy burden of old superstitions, prejudices and constraints that no longer harmonise with their maturation and with their task of astral transformation.

As we see, the card presents precisely this negative side of the Arcanum, symbolised by the order inversion of the first arithmetic decomposition. Arcanum XXI covers the greatest and most dangerous initiatory mysteries. It would be too risky to indicate, even only symbolically, the mechanism of action of this Arcanum. However, he integrates a series of initiatory studies and some explanation must be given. Thus, instructors have decided to represent on the card what should not be done, so that the serious student, thanks to his own efforts, can find out what needs to be done.

How, then, to guide our meditation to begin with the positive aspect of this Arcanum?

A kabbalist will begin by studying other arithmetic decompositions of number 21 in order of positive appearance of Shin. Let us strive to do the same by carefully examining the following breakdowns:

21 = 2 + 19: The Shin mystery (21) is based on knowledge of the Law of Analogy, Law of Opposites (2) and mystery of the Magna Work (19).

21 = 3 + 18: Knowledge of the Shin mystery (21) requires a complete metaphysical culture (3), knowledge of the absolute power of the Hierarchy, of the power of the occult forces, and of their possibilities of adverse effects on the physical plane as a result of their actin (18).

21 = 4 + 17 To master the Arcanum 𝐰 (21) requires a thorough study of both the physical and chemical (4) and of the astral influences in Nature and of the mental bases of them (17).

21 = 5 + 16: Wanting to apply the Arcanum Shin (21) it is essential to be aware of the immeasurable freedom of the power of one's own will (5), and to remember that the same freedom can cause the fall and disintegration, an inevitable consequence of materialisation (16).

21 = 6 + 15: Let us know that everywhere there are two paths (6) and that everywhere we can become the lord or the slave of the great Baphomet (15).

21 = 7 + 14: When we consider ourselves winners (7) we must moderate and harmonise (14) the manifestations of our strength.

21 = 8 + 13: If we work in the established legality field (8), let us know and remember that the final target of our work is the preparation for the change of the plane of existence (13). If we are able to plan our lives, we should choose as a purpose a dignified preparation for death, that is, for birth to the astral life. When looking after a pregnant woman, we need to choose the feeding and living arrangements during the relatively short period of pregnancy, preparing his future child for the long life that awaits him. Caring for a child, we should not forget that one day she will need instruction; giving him the instruction, we must remember that the student of today will become an active member of Humanity tomorrow. It is also important to remember the reverse, that is, by contacting an elemental (a disincarnate), remember that he has already been incarnated; finding an adult man, take into account previous influences (school, family, etc.) who acted upon it.

21 = 9 + 12: Whoever wants to master the great mystery w (21) must begin (9) in the corresponding planes and be ready for sacrifice (12).

21 = 10 + 11: He who dominates the w mystery (21) relies, on the one hand, on the automatic functioning of the Mill of the World (10), and on the other hand, in the resources of the powerful currents (11) of the related planes.

This is the general outline of the meditations of the occultist desirous of overthrowing the mystery and applications of Arcanum w.

The number corresponding to w is 300, that is, a three, but an enlarged three, a three that penetrated into the complex world of the tenth Sephira in its tenth manifestation.

We would like to add a few words about this mysterious Arcanum of the mechanisms of evolution and involution.

It is important not to go by your own will to the cliff where lies the open throat of the monster; It is important to shed both time and the burden itself, to push the dog away, to lean on the staff, provide yourself with decent clothes, throw off the hood, and look in front of you. Then we will not be subject to the involuntary action of the invincible w. On the contrary, when we need to act on sub-planes lower than ours, we will know how to put the cap on the heads of those who start the evolutionary work.

It is also useful to note that the card intentionally presents the negative aspect of the Arcanum שׁ, not just so that the occultist does not let others put a cap on his head, not only so that he himself learns to decorate with this cap the head of those who deserve it, but also so that he can use himself, when necessary, this garment on his own head, imitating the figure of the card[49].

An evolved being is always aware of the illusory character of values and pleasures, usually so appreciated on Earth. He feels the weight of his physical wrapping, but in spite of this he has no right to get rid of it before a set time. Karma outlines a program of trials and sacrifices during his incarnation and he must tread this path in its full extent.

In certain difficult moments it is useful to know how to close your eyes to the impermanence of the physical plane, to know and awaken in itself the interest for the joys of life, instill in itself an illusion of happiness which, effectively is in the world.

Would such an imitation of the fool be a complete and voluntary oblivion of what was absorbed in the Initiation? No. It would be just a momentary rest in the difficult road of life.

It is certain that the Pilgrim must learn to progress resolutely and intimately; but must, also, know how to predict and reasonably share the moments of rest for the restoration of their forces. We will say even more: who never ceases to be wise, who completely forgot the selfish pleasures, will no longer appreciate the small sacrifices you make to one another in life, he will know how to bring pleasure to his fellow men. It has been said that we should love the like as ourselves, and that is to say, also, to give him what we ourselves would appreciate if we forgot our wisdom.

As mentioned, the "mechanism" of involution is analogous to that of the inverse process, that is, of rebirth. However, the fall is metaphysically fast and the rebirth metaphysically slow. Add the word "metaphysically" purposely, for it is not physical time, but rather from the fact that the process of rebirth is carried out in general, according to several planned and consecutive phases, while in the fall tell only the causes and their consequences. Because of this, the attempts of a kabbalistic analysis of the human fall give the impression of there being complications, while the scheme of the rebirth of man through Ethical Hermeticsm is easily understood and acceptable. The profane understand and study the Gospel without fear but are stunned trying to analyse the Old Testament.

---

[49] Meditations on the Tarot presents the other side of Shin more fully – the esoteric name of The Fool is AMOR.

We can see that ש is a terrible Arcanum. To apply it ineptly or not in time is to delay the course of World Evolution. That is why its mark frightens so many, even the Initiates. Meanwhile, the Highest, Most Powerful, Synthetic Pentagram of the Astral י ה ש ו ה, precisely by its sign ש, provides itself with the possibility of incarnation, this reference point of the Atonement of human collectivities, and, consequently, the Reintegration of the Primary Perfect Man.

We will not be afraid of realisations, but we will emphasise in our prayers for Initiation our desire to know the twenty-first Arcanum not by a trick, not by a thieves method, not by the price of a pact with the lower astral, but hermetically honestly, after systematic penetration into the previous twenty Arcana.

Then he will lead us not to fatal errors, not to stains on Karma, but to the conscious Triumph of the Rosicrucian Reintegration by the process of the full Threefold application of the Great Arcanum of Magic.

Complement to Arcanum XXI

One of the important aspects of this Arcanum is the problem of the real and the illusory, the appearance of many deceptive times under which both the real and the illusory can manifest themselves, and also of the relativity of the two, depending on the point of view of which they are being perceived.

For each human being, the concept of the "real" and the "illusory" depends on the plane in which is the centre of their consciousness. The three titles of the Arcanum - "Radiatio", "Signum" and "Matter" correspond to the three degrees of densification of the Single Substance, from its Source to the dense state. The intermediate plane – that of the symbols or the astral - is sometimes called the "universal mirror", because it reflects the emanations ("Radiatio") and form everything ("Signum") that will manifest in the dense plane ("Matter"). However, descending, Reality loses a part of its strength and its purity, and this loss will be all the greater the lower the plane of its manifestation.

The symbol is more real than its dense manifestation, for it exists on the astral plane before it appears in the physical and will still exist in the astral after the disappearance of its manifestation in the physical plane. THE Astral form is the "sine qua non" condition of any appearance on the physical plane, and therefore it is more real than the dense form. From this we can deduce that the lower the manifestation, the more ephemeral it will be.

It is very important to understand that the concept of the "real" and the "illusory" has a meaning only in confrontation with the various planes. It is a relative rather than an absolute concept. He changes progressively, as far as the ascent or descent on the ladder of Jacob.

Of course, the divine world, being the highest, is absolutely real; however, each plane, seen within its own limits, seems to be the only real one. This "reality" must be taken into account as long as we live in a certain plane, without forgetting, however, its ephemeral character comparatively to the higher planes.

It is not the circumstances of earthly life that can negatively influence the soul, but the importance that it can attribute to them, considering them as the only reality. In such a case, the graduation becomes inverted, and it is the higher planes that seem to be illusory. In such conditions, the whole effort of life is directed towards the acquisition of terrestrial values. Among these, occupying the first position are material goods and the women. The slightly more subtle aspect of terrestrial values is the desire for fame, for social success and also for family happiness. As man evolves, his goals become higher. However, as long as the search is not directed to the plane of the Higher Self, there will always be something illusory about it.

The deeper one goes into the study of the Arcanum XXI, the more aspects he will discover that are totally new and unexpected. The card has only one negative aspect of Arcanum XXI; however, even in this presentation we can also discern two facets: "the real" and "the illusory." Common humanity will see a "fool" or "madman" who, following something illusory, creates his own perdition. This is the "reality" for human society. For the "fool", subjectively, the real is diametrically opposite. He no longer gives value to what men in general appreciate so much, for he perceives something "real", invisible to others. He advances resolutely and neither the cliff nor the monster can stop it or push it back. Perhaps there is no other way for him to approach his "real", and he is ready to take risks and, if need be, to sacrifice everything. Meditate a little on how much the words of the Gospel:

Whoever wants to keep his life (or his "soul" in certain Gospels) loses it; who, however, loses his life (or "soul") because of Me, finds it. (Matthew xx, 25 and also Matthew X, 39).

It is also possible that the precipice and the monster no longer have power over the pilgrim, if he already knows they are only delusional. The "fool" does not care about his own appearance, does not bother to be considered silly, does not reject the hood, even if it were easy to do so. Their possessions are tiny in quantity and in value. His environment, his friends, and public opinion bitterly criticise him - it is the dog that he attacks - judging by his own measure. For them, he has no judgment, since he does not seek to "live well". The pilgrim, if he wished, could defend himself and even punish them; has the means to do it, has a staff - the power - but does not want to use it for that purpose. Such is your will. The "real" of ordinary humanity is despicable and "illusory" for the pilgrim. The real", of the pilgrim is inconceivable and ignored by mankind who, in the conduct of the only madness.

We also add that the Eastern teaching concerning the "Maya" of the physical world belongs totally to the field of Arcanum XXI.

Hermeticism, however, emphasises the difference between the concept of the "illusory nature" of the physical world and the "non-existence" of this world, considering the last concept as being a deformation of the Truth, which can lead to contempt of life and to the denial of the value of any work in the physical world.

Notes on the twenty first Arcanum

Like G.O.M., Paul Christian hears a strong warning in this Arcanum, seeing it as denoting the punishment for errors meted out by the fearsome Crocodile.

It is the second interpretation – G.O.M.'s 'Complement to the Twenty First Arcanum - which sees the divinely ordained Fool free from fear of either "precipice" or "monster" which Tomberg expands upon in MotT. For him The Fool is guided by love – he is, quite literally, the one who *falls in love* - and whose esoteric name is AMOR. The development of this softer approach to the Twenty First Arcanum – governed, as it is, by the fiery Mother Letter, Shin – provides welcome relief for other wandering Fools who might have found themselves in a (seemingly unavoidable) difficult position.

Here we recall the teachings of another Occult Master, Peter Deunov, who warned that humanity had entered the 'belt of lies', 'zone of delusion' or, indeed the 'realm of Maya' which G.O.M. introduces a glimpse of at the end of his teaching on the Tarot Majors. Tomberg's response to the hazardous reality of our passage through this zone is to advise that only by wearing the 'Mantle of the Virgin', which in the present context is analogous to the blindfold of the novice during initiation, or eyes-closed attitude of The Fool, might we safely pass through this zone. As such, his opus is dedicated to Our Lady of Chartres, as this volume is to Our Lady of Guadalupe.

We will recall that in MotT it is explained that devotion to sacred magic and avoidance of both personal magic and sorcery (into which category we can include the practical aspects of Kabbalah) can help us to avoid such pitfalls of the path as spiritual inflation and the Zone of Delusion.

Similarly do the sacred vows of Poverty, Chastity and Obedience support us on the path, helping walkers to maintain the Mantle of the Virgin about their own shoulders.

The practising occultist, esotericist or Hermeticist…experiences the higher forces which work beyond his consciousness and which make their entrance there. At what price?…Either at the price of worshipping on his knees - or otherwise at the price of the identification of self with these higher forces, which results in megalomania. (MotT, p162).

It is also in the Twenty First Arcanum that Tomberg pays poignant homage to past masters of the schools of Paris and St Petersburg, as given in the 'In Memoriam' dedication at the start of the present volume. His words inspired in us a burning curiosity to find out more of the fascinating individuals to whom he refers. 'Burning' is said quite deliberately, not only for the books that were lost, but for the Hebrew Letter Shin, Mother of Fire, which is the hallmark of The Fool and the pivot of this Great Work.

We are not alone amongst occultists in wanting to solve mysteries; you might even say that our world revolves around them to some degree. So when, in the midst of an incredible of occult history in the Eleventh Arcanum, we see that "The publication of the Shin element was not authorised by Master G.O. Mebes" it only made us want to know more. Throughout this work on the Tarot Majors, G.O.M continually refers to the individual Hebrew letters which are associated with various Arcana and clearly allocates a letter to each card, but the same cannot be said of Valentin Tomberg in MotT. Apart from his association of the first four Arcana – Magician, High Priestess, Empress and Emperor – with the letters of the Tetragrammaton, יהוה (as does G.O.M. before him), Tomberg does not pay over-much attention to specific letters. Except for Shin[50].

Other letters are mentioned – for example, the pivotal 'He' of Arcanum V, The Pope - but they are not given nearly the same emphasis as Shin. The sudden insistence on silence by G.O.M. with respect to Shin – a letter he references constantly throughout the work in other contexts – coupled with the startling emphasis placed upon this one letter by Tomberg, were easily enough to convince us that any advancement of the Opus would require further penetration of this fiery mystery. Indeed, for many years of our study of the Great Work, before developing an

---

[50] The placement of Shin with respect to Tarot has for long been controversial amongst various occult schools. For further exploration of this interesting topic see our Commentary to Arcanum I, The Magician.

interesting in G.O.M., we meditated upon Shin alone amongst the letters, knowing next to nothing about Kabbalah but primed by the subtle Tomberg to focus on the key of these mysteries with the fullest attention. The first thing which occurred to us when we read the ruling of G.O.M. during the course of this translation, was that the deep secret of Shin, too precious to risk revealing to any but the fully initiated, was an esoteric teaching of the Master Jesus and therefore of the highest order. Something which must be kept hidden from the profane and held safe in the Holy of Holies. It is a matter for the soul and spirit combined. Further penetration of this aspect of the Mystery might be discovered through contemplation of the esoteric four-pronged (white letter[51]) Shin, sometimes called the 23rd letter of the Hebrew alphabet.

Whilst the three prongs of the black shin - ‫ש‬ - are attributed to Abraham, Isaac and Jacob, the four prongs of 'white shin' are attributed to Sarah, Rebekah, Leah and Rachel, all of which names, in Hebrew, are composed of 13 letters. The two Shins represent the male and female energies created by Hashem (God). The Tetragrammaton – ‫יהוה‬ has the numerical value of 26, which we now see represents the unity of the fathers and mothers (two 13s), the masculine and feminine principles.

---

[51] An occult property revealed when we switch from meditating upon black letters on a white background to the 'negative' image of white letters on a black background. In this respect we see that the white 'negative' of Shin has four rather than three prongs and vice versa. The White Shin is said in the Zohar to have been hidden by HaShem because of the sin of the golden calf and will be revealed again at the time of the second coming.

The contemporary spiritual teacher, Tau Malachi, has said the four-pronged Shin "is the letter associated with the Holy Shekinah – this Fiery Light, the Divine Presence and Power of God. The three-pronged Shin may be said to correspond with Iod-He-Vau, the metaphysical matrix behind creation and the four pronged Shin may be said to correspond to Iod-He-Vau-He, the actual manifestation of creation… the two represent Yahweh and Elohim, respectively – Elohim being the Name of God in the action of Creation, and Yahweh being the Force within and behind…. One cannot help but contemplate in Holy Shin the Union of the Groom and Bride in the Bridal Chamber, and the mystery of the outpouring of the Pentecostal Fire that comes from this Sacred Marriage – the mystery of Hieros Gamos".

In classical Jewish Kabbalah, the three and four-pronged Shin letters can also represent the unified material and spiritual worlds. In this system, the three upper Sephiroth of Keter, Chockmah and Binah signify the three prongs of the letter and the divine names, Eheieh, Yahweh and Elohim respectively. In the four-pronged letter 'Adonay' is added to the scheme as the name associated with the tenth Sephirah, Malkuth, the Kingdom. The Divine triad united to the material world is achieved when the Shekinah comes to rest on Earth.

In the Sephir Yetzirah Shin is associated with the Thirty First path, described as "Continuous Consciousness", which determines the path of the sun and moon.

Four plus three also adds up to seven, another magically charged number, whilst three multiplied by four gives us 12. Thus do the united three and four-pronged Shin letters produce the number of Double and Simple Letters of the Alphabet.

In Don Quixote and the Brilliant Name of Fire: Qabalah, Tarot and Shakespeare, Michael Buhagiar explains that Shin corresponds to the quintessence, to Spirit, which 16th Century Christian Kabbalists believed could be assimilated into the Tetragrammaton to form the name Yeheshua.

Another factor to be born in mind is that the fullness of Shin knowledge was considered by G.O.M. to be a grave potential danger if abused by practitioners of black magic. And yet, it is an unusual aspect to the initiatory school of G.O.M. that within it were given both 'light and dark initiations'. The reason for the initiation of light hardly needs further explanation, but that of the dark gave me pause; surely the so-called 'counter-initiation' was something to be feared, shunned and avoided at all costs?

Given the controversy surrounding the position of this Arcanum it is helpful to refer to the early Inspired by Eliphas Lévi, for whom the Letter Shin represented the fatality and blindness of The Fool in an almost entirely negative interpretation. In this we see both the influence of Eliphas Lévi upon G.O.M., who adopted a similar stance with respect to the poor Fool, and the departure in MotT from this aspect of the teaching and towards the Second Coming seen by Sophianic occultists. Eliphas Lévi also points out that this Arcanum was originally called 'Furca', a Latin word denoting a two-pronged fork, which might have been used as an "instrument of punishment, a frame in the form of a fork, which was placed on a culprit's neck, while his hands were fastened to the two ends; yoke[52]."

Suddenly more becomes clear, as we recall the playful – and yet, "most serious!" – exhortation given at the very beginning of MotT in Letter I, The Magician, where the author strongly counsels that the yoke should be easy and the burden light.

Whilst our White Russian mages reveal great touches of humour and wit, as one might expect of any great Adept, Tomberg applied himself to the matter of Universal Salvation and did not speak in quite the same way about the dreadful pitfalls in the way of G.O.M.'s Fool, who seems doomed to never return if ever he chances to fall into the abyss. And who amongst esoteric students has managed to avoid the abyss?!

---

[52] The Kabalistic and Occult Tarot of Eliphas Lévi, A Study Guide, Daath Gnostic Publishing, p. 120

Not for Tomberg the horror of closed circles of electrical force, no matter what the order of the magus, for truly divine magic is open like a living spiral; we are always shown the way out and given a reference point of safety in a particular spiritual exercise within the magical arcana. His profoundly Christological focus offers further protection to the Wandering Fool, who without the benefit of expert individual tuition from G.O.M. himself, might otherwise get stuck on the Arcane Wheel ad infinitum, or even broken upon it.

All of this is a major bone of contention for PFC – whose BOTA is one of the most highly regarded occult schools - who confirms in The Tarot, A Key to the Wisdom of the Ages, that: "The attribution of the major Trumps to the Hebrew alphabet is the crux in Tarot study." According to him, Eliphas Lévi received the correct attributions from a secret order and was inhibited by oaths from revealing the accurate scheme. "He did, however, announce the fact that the major trumps correspond to the Hebrew letters, and then proceeded to give an attribution so patently absurd that one wonders how it ever gained credence."

With respect to the correct placement of The Fool. " Eliphas Lévi evidently chose this position for the Zero Key", PFC claims, "because the latter was thereby assigned to the only Hebrew letter (besides the one to which it rightly belongs) which is a symbol of Spirit."

Known as the "Holy Letter" by Kabbalists, Shin has a numerical value of 300 which corresponds to the Hebrew term, Ruach Elohim. This may be translated as the Breath of God or Spirit of God. In the eyes of PFC, therefore, it was a form of absurd blasphemy to assign this exalted Mother Letter, symbol of the Holy Spirit, to The Fool of the Tarot. PFC prefers to associate The Fool in its zero position with "another letter in the alphabet which is also a symbol of Spirit, or Life-Breath, and this is Aleph".

Whilst we admire PFC and think there is very much to value in his teaching, as one might expect, the friends and followers of Eliphas Lévi – or in our case, Tomberg, and before him, G.O.M. - have not let his somewhat scathing assessment be the final word on the Hebrew letters and Tarot associations. Further denouement is necessary.

A helpful elucidation of the Eliphas Lévi scheme is given in a study guide to The Kabalistic and Occult Tarot of Eliphas Lévi by Daath Gnostic Publishing, where it is acknowledged from the first sentence that: "The associations that Eliphas Lévi gives to the Tarot have been questioned by many English readers, some even saying that he does not give the correct attributes in his books".

Hebrew letters are, as is well known, associated in a fixed and very specific way with numbers, as are the Tarot keys. Eliphas Lévi's scheme is based quite simply on the alphabetical order of the Hebrew letters, wherein ש is in 21st position and ת the 22nd. As soon as we start shifting ש into the zero position to accommodate The Fool which may have wandered there, it has a disruptive knock-on effect which moves ת down from 22nd to 21st place.

As the editors of aforementioned publication explain, the matter of correspondences is generally confused:

...because of the last two Tarot cards (although plenty of other deviations are also perpetuated). The value of these last two Tarot cards has been altered to conceal a mystery related to the symbolism of the Hebrew letter Shin. Eliphas Lévi has explained this mystery (the mystery of the Great Arcanum) in his books and it is summarised with the statement given in Ch. 10 of Dogma of High Magic for Shin: "Where the mortals who lack a brake descend in herds".

Careful study of the symbolism associated with Shin will explain why 0 might make sense for this letter individually, although this value causes confusion with Tau and therefore becomes problematic when used along with other letters."[53]

---

[53] In the classic occult novel, The Zelator, by Mark Hedsel, the Master of the story speaks to his pupil about The Fool Arcanum, telling him that the three-pronged cap is representative of the letter shin: "The early Hebraic scholars used what they called the "three flames" of shin to represent the highermost trinity in the Sephirotic Tree. This meant that the triple shin sat on top of the tree, just as the human head sits on top of the spine.... The Fool of esotericism recognises the value of the Spiritual, and will sacrifice anything to obtain ingress to its upper realms, guarded so well by the three flames of shin. This is the reason why he elects to wear the cap. It is a sign that he is prepared to suffer the three flames, which echo the three wounds of Christ. In truth, this shin is symbol of a way of a path, the path of suffering. You see, then, young Mark - pain is also a Way. It is sometimes called the Triple Way".

Arcanum XXII

Pathway between Hod and Malkulth

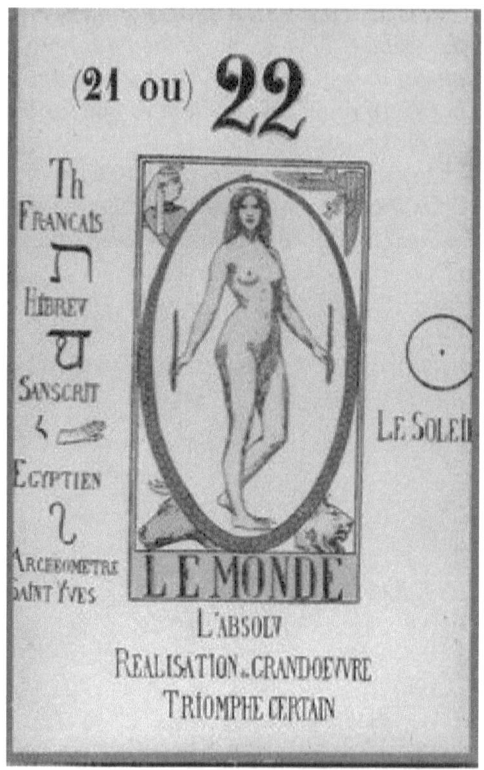

The World is *Truth*

Do you now understand the Enigma of the Sphynx?

Levi

THE CROWN OF THE MAGI: The Reward

THIS, the supreme Arcanum of Magism... is the sign with which the Magus decorates himself when he has reached the highest degree of initiation

Paul Christian

"It is the image of the world," the voice said, "but it can be understood only after the Temple has been entered. This is a vision of the world in the circle of Time, amidst the four principles. But thou seest differently because thou seest the world outside thyself. Learn to see it in thyself and thou wilt understand the infinite essence, hidden in all illusory forms."

Ouspensky

The sign corresponding to Arcanum XXII is ת; its numerical value, 400. Its hieroglyph is the chest, in a sense close to the term bosom; something synthetic, containing everything in itself; a necessary summary of previous arcana.

The astrological correspondence of the Arcanum is the Sun, the Centre and the Synthesis of astral manifestations of the Solar System.

As you can see, everything here indicates the need for a vault into a single whole, the need for gluing, cementing – unifying - already acquired information and skills.

Let's start by analysing the picture of the Arcanum, called Corona Magica (Magical Crown) in the learned language and Mundus (The World) in common language.

In the center of the picture, a naked woman is triumphantly dancing, slightly touching the ground with one foot. This is in metaphysics - the Synthesis of Absolute Truths, no longer in need of coverings, with which you cannot deceive the one who got to them. This is the highest manifestation of the Archetype available to our mentality; hence the first headline of the Arcanum – The Absolute.

I repeat - these are not fragments of absolutely fair theses; it's not a clue on the difficult path of ascending to the Secret of the Great Metaphysical Arcana — it is the Arcana itself, like the Synthesis of the Metaphysical Foundations of World Life. In short - this is the Upper Triangle of the ה י Matrimony in the scheme we presented when studying the fourth Arcanum.

But this Synthesis does not remain dead, even if completed, by the acquisition in the Higher planes, it is still alive and always fruitful: a female figure, and a woman can bear, can give birth. This acquisition mysteriously spills a life-giving stream into the lower subplanes. Look at the figure - in her hands is a wand; both sticks are on the same level; she holds them parallel to each other; this symbolises the mastery of binaries and freely operates in the astral region, symbolised by the Great Serpent, the Oroboros, entwining a figure and biting its own tail.

The ancient, symbol of the astral plane - tamed, obeys the will of the girl and forms a perfect ellipse around the figure. It operates with the compensation binary, dominates the powerful and fearsome astral plane, creator of forms, and rests, with one foot, on the physical plane. The power of the girl comes from higher: from the mental; extends through the entire astral and has a foothold in the achievements already achieved on the physical plane. This is the scheme shown on the card.

The astral manifestation of the figure corresponds, for humanity, to the total of what it has already accomplished of the Great Work. The central part of the composite symbol, introduced in the Arcanum IV, is the hexagon, the ו. It is the ability to utilise your Hermetic Victory. Hence the second title of the Arcanum: "Adaptatio Operis Magni" (Adaptation of the Master Work).

But let's get back to the card. At each of its angles we see one of the four sacred animals. It's the quaternary of the Sphinx, ie the motto known: to dare, to know, to will, to be silent. They are, once again, the same four elements, presented in such different ways, according to different degrees of the Hermetic School.

Its oldest and most common names are: Air, Water, Earth and Fire. These elements, in their manifold manifestations, constitute what we call the Nature. "To those who dominate them, Laws from nature become instruments for the achievements desired. Failure cannot, because he will never want something contrary to these Laws, something foreign to the absolute metaphysical, astral or physical legality. Your being vibrates in absolute unison with the note of nature, and therefore he is omnipotent because he wants everything that comes through universal evolutionary chain, and that alone. Thus, the third title of the Arcanum is "Omnipotentia Naturalis" the same name given to the above-mentioned universal current.

The numeric value of the Arcanum is 400. Its affinity with the number of elements - 4 - confirms the symbolism of the card angles.

Let us see what would give us a brief arithmetic analysis of the Arcanum and what it would add to the summary, with which it would be natural to complete the cycle of 22 phases of receptivity to the Universe, accessible to fallen humanity.

22 = 1 + 21: The א (1), complete and harmonious, dominates the ש achievement (21). This is exactly the analysis made in the presentation of the blade of Arcanum XXII.

22 = 21 + 1: The same א (1) voluntarily undergoes exploitation by the Arcanum ש (21), by itself or due to the influence of other entities. All who have suffered in life because of their own prejudices, recklessness, voluntary blindness, etc., they know perfectly well how important it is not to fall into a similar exploitation on the part of another.

The students should meditate seriously on the subject: would it be advisable, at times, that an occultist voluntarily take charge of the burden of superstitions and not use the prudence, closing his eyes and letting himself be carried away in sweet abandonment? When and in which circumstances? A supporter of esotericism, even highly evolved, will always be an unhappy face of the Earth if it has not satisfactorily resolved this matter. No doubt, it is necessary to see, but, sometimes it's better to close the eyes. It is good to be prudent, even though a recklessness may not be bad. It is certain that an instructor must not have attachments, conditions, superstitions or prejudices, however it is distractions make life, at times, more enjoyable. Let us go on to the other decompositions:

22 = 2 + 20: Science (2) and exact knowledge of the value of regeneration (20) make it possible to master the Great Arcanum and make man a true Rosicrucian. It is not easy to acquire, in all its fullness, the first component, nor keep the faith and the pure heart of the second component. More difficult, yet, will be to unite these two.

22 = 20 + 2: The reverse, that is, to acquire science (2) when the principle of regeneration reigns in the heart (20) perhaps, an even more difficult process than the first.

22 = 3 + 19: Productivity (3) governs the Magna Work (19).

22 = 19 + 3: An hermetic regeneration (19) results in productivity (3). From history we know examples of these two Adept schemes. Pythagoras can serve as an example of the first; Orpheus, of the latter.

22 = 4 + 18: The authority (4) combined with the occult power (18) becomes the general scheme of the formation of a White Wizard.

22 = 18 + 4: The occult power (18) propitiating authority (4), is the scheme of the formation of a Mason Director. There are in history numerous examples of the scabrous path of such militants, (eg, the Lutheran and Calvin reforms) or in the political field (eg, the struggle for independence in the United States of North America).

22 = 5 + 17: The self-knowledge acquired in the work of elaboration within oneself, of the quintessence (quintessence) (5), together with initiations in the Laws of Nature (17) lead to Adepthood, because they realise the harmony between the microcosm and the macrocosm.

22 = 17 + 5: This order of the same decomposition resembles a bit to naturalism. This, carried out in all its fullness, leads to the same results as the preceding order.

22 = 6 + 16: To know the existence of the two paths and base the choice of the right (6) in the knowledge of the laws of the Fall (16), seems to be a better method to reach the Adepthood than that of the inverse order, that is:

22 = 16 + 6: In which the choice of the right path (6) results from the experience of falls (16) in the present life and in the previous incarnations.

22 = 7 + 15: The primacy of spirit over form (7) in the static field, together with the knowledge of the dynamic processes (15) which, however, occupy the second place, lead to the Enlightenment Adept.

22 = 15 + 7: A personality who began his career by the practical contact with the astral (15), and who perhaps underwent many difficult trials, but through self-analysis and with help of Superior Protection, arrives at Victory (7). Of this person it can be said that Magic Black took her to White Magic. The end result is the same; but in this way, the person

finds, at the beginning, some personal satisfactions, but in the final phase it goes through terrible sufferings and painful trials knowing that only through tremendous sacrifices can it reach the Light.

22 = 8 + 14: The legality (8), predominating over moderation (14), - the "*Fiat justitia, pereat mundus*" - is the path of the severe Geburah, in relation to himself and others. It is the way of Moses.

22 = 14 + 8: Here moderation (14) in manifestations dominates legality (8). It is the way of the instructors who, little by little and with care, compensate for weaknesses in themselves and in others, if they allow a short rest; which admit, outside the stages of undeniable progress, intermediate periods of relative human improvement. This is the way of good Christian-Masons; the way of Ashmole, of Willarmooz, of the kind theurgist, Claude de St. Martin.

22 = 9 + 13: The initiation (9) causes the plane (13) to change.

22 = 13 + 9: The change of plane (13) leads to Initiation (9). These two formulas are understandable to all. The choosing between the two orders does not always depend on our will.

22 = 10 + 12: The implacable activity of the Mill of the World (10) gives rise to the idea of the Sacrifice in us (12).

22 = 12 + 10: The aspiration to sacrifice (12) in a soul that seeks God the Holy Spirit causes that before it the mysteries of the Closed Systems are revealed (10). It does not matter if Kabbalah (10) leads to Sacrifice (12), or Sacrifice to Kabbalah, the result is the same, that is, Adepthood.

22 = 11 + 11: Let us confront a force (11) with another force (11); ours and the others; that of a current with another; that of a conviction with that of another conviction. Doing so always and in relation to everything, we will find ourselves, without realizing it, in the situation of the figure holding the two wands (22). However, in our "dance", let us not forget to support ourselves, at least with one foot, on the Earth. Then the Astral Serpent will no longer be a danger to us, but will obediently form in our surroundings a regular ellipse.

Analysing deeply our life, we will perceive the role played in our evolution by the four sacred animals. Then we will no longer fear being naked, that is, showing us such as we are in reality, because we will have nothing to hide.

Advantages acquired by the Master of the 22 Arcana

Let us suppose that a profane person asks us what advantages are gained by the dominion of the 22 Arcana. The medieval literature of the Kabbalistic School responds to this question by enumerating, enigmatic, the 22 Advantages of the Magician over a Common Man. We will seek them in a more accessible language.

1. א advantage: the wizard sees god face-to-face, being still in life and speaking, naturally, with the seven planetary genii. How to understand this text? It means that: On the mental plane, despite the perfect contact with the Flow of Oneness, the Initiate retains his own kind of soul, while that is possible. It is understood under the expression "soul type" the characteristic mental state of the Monad whether it be of the א type, that is, a soul in the metaphysical field, whether it be of the ג type - a welcoming soul that gathers and protects, or even a soul of the type ל, that is, servant, aspiring to the sacrifice; on the astral plane, the same Initiate contemplating the all-encompassing cliché י ה ו ש ה and transmitting down the performance of this cliché, offers itself in order to maintain until a certain time your personality and remain under planetary influences; on the physical plane, the same Initiate, though fully aware of the illusion of terrestrial life, does not voluntarily destroy either his body nor the conditions in which this body is found.

2. ב advantage: the magic remains beyond all the sadness and all the fears. This means that: - on the mental plane, he is not disturbed by obstacles of a metaphysical or logical order; - on the astral plane, does not become discouraged by the separation of his soul mate, nor by the slowness with which his disciples progress; - on the physical plane, he does not fear suffering and death, neither for himself nor for others.

3. ג advantage: the wizard reinforces with the forces of heaven; hell or serve. This means that: - on the mental plane, he participates in the work of evolutionary flows, as Theurgist; - in the astral plane is a Magician, in the strict sense of that word; leads the Whirlwinds of Baphomet, from the "sky" (their mental origins) to "hell" (the astral coagulations of the lower sub-planes); - on the physical plane, he is a Masonic Initiate, using the weaknesses, blindness and other ש of the men to direct them to the virtues.

4. ד advantage: the magician revokes his life and his health and, also, the life and health of others. This means that: - on the mental plane, he governs the philosophical flows of his time; - on the astral plane, it improves its planetary characteristics and those of its Chain, influencing

the evolutionary trends and the art of his time; - on the physical plane, you can use your animal magnetism to heal yourself and others.

5. ה advantage: destiny cannot take surprise the adopt, the infortúnio cannot abide it or the enemies win me. This means that you know: - reactions of the basic laws of logic (metaphysical destiny); - human paralogisms (metaphysical misfortunes); - human sufferings (metaphysical enemies). This also means that he knows the karma of his incarnation, the laws of evolution of his own astral and the mysteries of action counteraction. This means that he does not fear the alternatives of existence on the physical plane, and the destruction of what it knows to be ephemeral.

6. ו advantage: the adept knows the "ratio" of the past, of the present and of the future. This means that his intuition, encompassing the three planes, possesses the knowledge of the causes, in the metaphysical plane, of the Gnostic Law, in the astral and of the theory of probability, in the physical plane.

7. ז advantage: The Magus knows the mystery of the resurrection of the dead and has the key to immortality. This means that, metaphysically, he can live the life of unfallen humanity (resuscitation), without changing the theories enunciated (key of immortality); it also means that establishes new astral formulas and clichés (based on the elemental composition of the ancients) thus resurrecting the latter, and fixes the astrally created forms by its Stream; means even though, by relying on Tradition, it continually resurrects the elements of the symbolism of this Tradition, carried out in the physical plane, establishing solid operational support points of the type of Immortal Phoenix.

The seven advantages of the Magus enumerated above are called GREAT by the Kabbalists. Then come seven medium advantages[54].

1. ח advantage: the adept masters the mystery of the philosophical stone. In our language, this means that it dominates the Arcanum XIX in the three fields of the Theosophical Ternary.

2. ט advantage. the adept has the power of universal therapeutics. This means that it has the capacity for absolute criticism on the mental plane,

---

[54] It seems that the danger for inflation begins in earnest with the volatile sevens?

the ability to undo the bewitchment on the astral plane and the ability to heal by magnetism on the physical plane.

3.ׁ advantage: the adept makes the "perpetu a mobile and the quadrature of the circle, which, in our language, means the power to create bipolar swirls and spinning the Elementary Wheel.

4. כ advantage: The adept makes gold not only from metals, but any refuse. This means that in metaphysics, to the Absolute Truth we are led not only by truths but also the errors of others; which, on the astral plane, may not only overturn the incomplete forms, but also has the power to use the wrongly reflected ones; that in the activity Freemasonry, it not only ends the properly started, but also has the power to use the wrongly begun. This thesis involves a literal sense in the field of alchemy.

5. ל advantage: The wizard has power over animals. Beyond literal sense, this also refers to the domain over the elementals, to the power to expel the larvae, etc.

6. מ advantage: The adept masters the art of notarikon that it reveal all mysteries. In other words, it dominates the Kabbalah.

7. ו advantage: The adept has the gift of speaking with wisdom and conviction on all themes, without preparation. It is a direct reference to which Lulle calls "Ars Magna" (see in Arcanum X the multiplication of the Arcana, etc.).

The following advantages are called small. They are:

1. ס advantage: The mage evaluates a human being at a glance (intuition, divination).
2. ע advantage: The mage has power about nature (Ceremonial Magic and natural Sciences).
3. פ advantage: The mage predicts the events that depend on the destiny.
4. צ advantage: The mage can console everyone and with respect to everything, and how to give good advice in all cases in life.
5. כ advantage: The mage has the capacity to overcome all the difficulties.
6. ר advantage: The mage controls in you love and anger.
7. ש advantage: The mage knows the mystery of wealth; knows how to be its master, never its slave. one can even choose poverty without ever jumping into insignificance.

There are attempts, out of circles outside the Kabbalists, to summarise all the above advantages of the Adept, in the following advantage "Tau", of the Arcanum XXII.

Advantage ת. the mage impresses all the profane by his power to dominate the elements, cure the sick, resurrect the dead, etc.

This concludes our encyclopedic course. Some students will only allow themselves to know the content and methodology of various traditional branches of wisdom, which for a long time attracted the interest of Humanity. Other people will try, perhaps, to introduce into their life something of what has been learned, without changing, however, its basic course. There may also be some which will give a new character to their work and life, introducing something apparently uncomfortable but developing the willpower and the ability to deepen the material initiation, as well as helping in internal transformation.

This third group will understand that everything presented in this course can only serve as an alphabet, it is necessary to learn the language whose literature is so rich and vast that its study requires not only one, but several incarnations.

Notes on the twenty second Arcanum

In Letter VII, The Chariot, of MotT, Tomberg cites the same perceived 'advantages' – as highlighted by the above quotes taken from Eliphas Lévi's Transcendental Magic, its Doctrine and Ritual - as symptoms of madness and megalomania.

Is it a matter here of a programme or of actual experience? If it is experience, it is one of inflation pushed very far. If it is a programme, he who takes its realisation seriously cannot fail to fall prey to inflation, be it positive (superiority complex) or negative (inferiority complex). (MotT, p159)

In the 16th Century Hebrew manuscript which Eliphas Lévi used as his source for the 'programme' of advantages, Tomberg sees a remarkable similarity to the experience of John Custance, described in his book Wisdom, Madness and Folly: The Philosophy of Lunatic.

I feel so close to God, so inspired by His Spirit that in a sense I am God. I see the future, plan the Universe, save mankind; I am utterly and completely immortal; I am even male and female. (MotT, p160)

Custance charted his experience of mental illness over several years, describing in detail his fluctuating states of despair and "the gradual building of an individual philosophy of reality" . In good moments he felt "part of the universe- of all-embracing good fellowship" and lost his sense of self during the "universe of bliss" periods. These were in stark contrast with "the opposing abyss of isolation, suspicion, terror." Parallels are also seen with the Yin and Yang symbol, Nietzschean, Dionysian and Apollonian states"[55].

Whilst and interest in the occult and fragile mental states often go hand in glove and will not be surprising, Tomberg goes further by drawing an analogy between such spiritual megalomania and the 'superman' aims and characteristics described in some eastern philosophies.

He who has found and awakened to the Soul that has entered this conglomerate whole – he is the maker of everything, for he is the creator of all; the world is his: indeed, he is the world itself. (Brhadaranyaka Upanishad 4.4.13, trsl. R.E. Hume, The Thirteen Principal Upanishads, Oxford, 1962, p142).

He then goes onto warn that "Spiritual megalomania is as old as the world. Its origin is found well beyond the terrestrial world, according to the millennial-old tradition concerning the fall of Lucifer" and quotes a beautiful passage from the Book of Ezekiel:

You were the signet of perfection, you were full of wisdom, and perfect in beauty. You were in Eden, the garden of God; You were covered with every kind of precious stone: Sardonyx, topaz, and diamond, chrysolite, onyx and jasper, sapphire, carbuncle, emerald, and gold, with which you were adorned, and which were prepared for you on the day that you were created. You were a guardian Cherubim, with outspread wings; I placed you, and you were, on the holy mountain of God; You walked in the midst of stones of fire... Your heart was proud because of your beauty, You corrupted your wisdom for the sake of your splendour. I cast you to the ground, I exposed you before kings, to feast their eyes on you. (Ezekiel, xxviii, 12-17)

As a refugee escaping the Red Terror who went on to become the focal point for a serious division in the Anthroposphical Society following the death of Rudolf Steiner, Tomberg had ample opportunity to witness the consequences of this inflationary spiritual megalomania, or 'ego trips',

---

[55] Kirkus review

as it were. He was, after all, the witness of many Magicians or would-be magicians in action. We can only imagine the characters he encountered along the way, starting with the city of the Czar -the real Unknown Superior' of the Martinists - which attracted almost every occult character of note during the highpoint of his reign. Tomberg viewed such inflation as the greatest danger facing pathwalkers and it is interesting to consider the full Arcana – especially the seventh - in light of this warning.

inflation is always simultaneously sublime and absurd.

In this context it is intriguing to note the following snippet published in The Occult Digest of February 1929, entitled Soviet Secret Socities, written from Warsaw:

Investigations made by the political detective forces of the Soviet have revealed that there still exist in Russia secret societies that are a continuation of the "Rasputin circles," so common when that sinister monk held sway over the court of the Czar.
At many of these secret "circles" there are weird rites and ceremonies and some of the leaders claim to be reincarnated great ones of the past.
One is an author named Otto Mebes, who seriously claims that he is the reincarnation of one of the favourite lovers of the infamous Catharine the Great of Russia.
The head of another society makes the modest assertion that he is Louis XVI of France.
All the circles are said to be pervaded by a sort of "mysticism" and perverted eroticism.

Whilst it seems almost certain that the Otto Mebes in question here is identical with our own G.O.M., we have not been able to confirm this in any other source. It is a fascinating detail, nonetheless, though we should also bear in mind that the Bolshevik regime was actively involved in discrediting such groups which had clear White Russian sympathies. This note was published a couple of years after the elderly G.O.M. had been sent to a gulag.
It is also worth reminding ourselves that a belief in reincarnation and attempts to identify past lives were – and still are - standard fare in many occult schools, as shown by the later work of Rudolf Steiner in Karmic Relations.
Valentin Tomberg, who could not be called inflationary by any stretch of the imagination, has also been attributed with a possible past life in the form of William of Gellone (William of Orange), that is the Medieval

second Duke of Toulouse and founder of the Abbey of Gellone, who is syncretised in occult lore with Kyot, master of the Grail Mysteries, Lord of St Guilhelm le Desert. This is not something he wrote about or publicly claimed, but part of an oral tradition that has been preserved by teachers and students of anthroposophy.

Towards the end of MotT, in Letter XXII, The World, Tomberg returns to the starting point - the Tetragrammaton - within a Christian Hermetic description of the four sacred animals (Lion, Bull, Eagle and Man/Angel and signs of the zodiac.

But it is not the constellations of the zodiac which manifest the principle of the quarternary of the "cosmic elements" or "basic instincts". This principle is found 'tested in the ineffable name of God - the Tetragrammaton (ה ו ה י) - the imprint of which on a cosmic scale constitutes the quarternary in question. (MotT, p648)

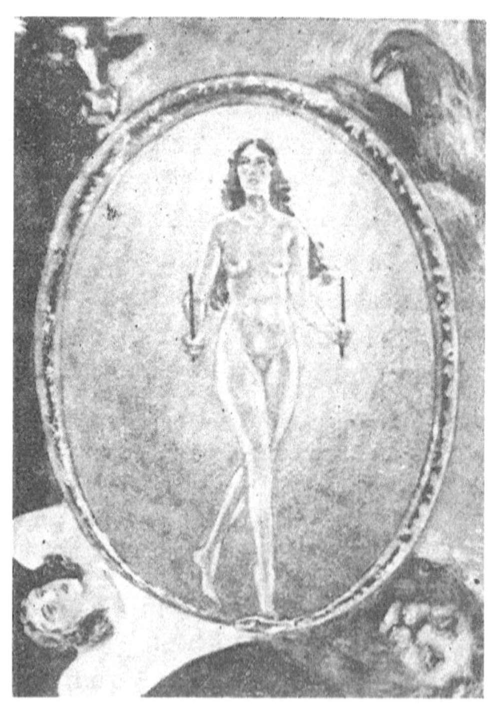

Appendix

The Arcanum XXII closes the cycle, becoming an א of the upper cycle
and thus forming a scroll of the spiral. The spiral characterises, in
general, all evolutionary movement. The experience of each Arcanum,
experienced again, may seem a repetition; however, it is different
because it is of a higher level or in another aspect.
In the Initiatory Schools, the study of the Arcana is done in separate
groups, that is, the teaching is given according to the evolutionary grade
of the students. As far as their development is concerned, the study is
resumed, each time in a deeper and more esoteric aspect. The Initiatory
Schools in general, give a threefold study of each Arcanum.
The text of the present book corresponds to basic, general studies. We
are allowed to add to two Arcana - the XIV (Temperance) and the XXI
(The Fool) - some words, spoken in other Circles: For Arcanum XIV -
very brief in the present book – this is to outline the role of the Guardian
Angel with a little more clarity; for The Fool, it is in order to allow the
reader to glimpse and meditate upon different aspects of this Arcanum to
those presented in the main body of this book.

Appendix to Arcanum XVII

The interests of the triplane universe, as well as those of any organism, are the synthesis of interests of all its organs. In the Karma of Nature we can see the outlines of manifestation of the Archetype and the traces left by the performance of the human will.

The destiny of the human being, whether in the series of his incarnations or within the limits of only one, is clearly influenced by the agreements concluded with the Archetype and karmic phenomena from nature. The same can be said of the fate of an incarnate egrégore artificially created organism and even a set of phenomena of a given time. In the Universe, everything is strictly connected and intertwined.

Wanting to predict the future of a group of manifestations, we must find and follow the threads linking these manifestations to the complex of phenomena accessible to our knowledge. The more core thread we find, the safer our prognosis. However, such a prediction requires a penetrating mind, capable of synthesising, capable of immersing itself in the essence of the subject, finding specific methods to study it, that is, mind that knows how to adapt to the subject. However, our minds, in general, are lazy; preferring, as mathematicians say "the analytical solution of the problem"; want to create, once for all, a general alphabet, applicable in all cases. They prefer a partial response but given methods already established and that they consider well elaborated. Do not accept that all the notes of the problem, contending with a known octave.

Let's talk a bit, therefore, of this "octave" well known in Astrology.

The relatively important bodies of the Universe, that is, the luminaries – stars - naturally exert an influence upon our world. By "stars" we mean a complex of Secondary Causes, having material points of support, that is, physical bodies whose positions and movements are studied by astronomy and whose composition, by astrophysics. Astrology limits the influences they exert on life on Earth, the seven planetary egrégores and the additional sounds, given by the so-called "fixed stars" and especially those belonging to the zodiacal region.

The great Law of Analogy can serve as justification for astrological claims. If the illumination of sites in the physical world, has a direct relation to the angular coordinates of the bodies of light relative to the horizon, then why not think that purely astral influences in general are to some extent the functions of these corner elements? If the bodies of what we conventionally call the seven planets have relatively large visible diameters for observation on the earth's surface, then why not allow the predominance of the action of astral egrégores based on these bodies? If, moreover, the orbits of these bodies (visible or true) are far removed from the ecliptic plane, then why not pay special attention to those overtones whose developers rely on bodies placed next to the same plane? After all, the intrusion of every new element into the sphere of astral influences begs for accounting all the more so as it is more about changing the assessment of already well-considered influences.

A good astrologer, in general, is interested in all the stars of the zodiacal band of the celestial vault, but in what area does he want to extend his divination? Of course, not the Archetype, the judgments about which are just as difficult to justify on the analysis of the illusory facts of the physical plane, as the judgements about the picture are fifteen times photographed by imperfect cliché apparatuses. The general unitary nature of the manifestations of the Archetype and their harmonic grandeur are reflected, of course, in every blade of grass. But the sephirotic details of his mental emanatory activity are too general and distracted to be measured with a pair of compasses in a bad photograph. Of course, the Archetype's plan is beyond that. As for man, he often scarcely uses his innate privilege, free will, and thus enslaves himself to Secondary Causes. Then the consequences to some extent become predictable. However, it is also necessary to consider the theory of probability.

Destiny is often called the "blind" because its manifestations give the impression that it cannot be changed in advance and, as it were, not subject to cancellation by themselves, that is, without the other two vertices of the two remaining triangle points of Fabre d'Olivet. (see Arcanum III). Astrology, clinging to the tip of the destiny (or Karma) risks making predictions. If they refer, for example, to the time of volcanic eruptions or other phenomena of nature, accuracy will cause people to subserviently bow to the omniscience of astrologers.

If they relate to human actions, then in countries where fatalism predominates, the predictions will be very successful, and people will say: "everything was written in the stars." But if you fall into the circle of people involved in the development of the Will, then in response to your praise of astrology, they proudly raise their heads and say: "Astra inclinant non necessitant (the stars incline they do not compel).[56]"

If, finally, you find yourself a hermit who is not looking for disciples and, therefore, not taking into account planetary temperaments, or even looking for those, but directing them not to the path of Rosicrucianism,

---

[56] This beautifully instructive and poignant phrase of Origen is also quoted in Meditations on the Tarot and has, in turn become one of the phrases quoted most frequently by the present author. We tend to recognise these words of wisdom in tandem with another – equally poignant – reference to the influence of the stars to be found in MotT, this time by Justinian: "When were children, under compulsion from the stars".

but to the path of the Beggars of the Spirit, he will calmly answer you: "What do I care about your dark Destiny? What do I care about the planetary shades of the manifestations of your faith? I look at the top point of the Triangle - there the Eternal Light shines, the Lamp of Conscience, giving sufficient lighting to distinguish the right path from the left; my will always leads me to the right path, and no matter how your planets are located, I always know that all seven Secondary Causes favour me in my evolution. Your Saturn will always provide an opportunity to submit to the blows of fate; your Jupiter will always support my voice in the authority of Good; your Mars gives me courage and strength to patiently endure suffering and accept martyrdom; your Sun will always supply me with something that I will be able to deny in favor of my neighbour; your Venus will always pull me to the place where the neighbour needs comfort and fellowship with a hopeful heart; your Mercury will give me the Gifts of the Holy Spirit, allowing me to speak in a language understood by the students; your moon will give me the power of non-resistance. Leave your predictions, because they are insignificant in comparison with those that are dictated to me by both my higher self and your luminaries - we all reintegrate." For him, the predictions of the astrologer are of no use.

In order to give an idea of astrology and at the same time not to scatter the listeners' attention to the extreme, we will choose its private area, which is engaged in compiling horoscopes of the incarnation of individual human beings. In this particular matter, we are dealing with three realisations: 1) more or less accurate determination of the position of the planets in the zodiac; 2) the distribution of the planets in relation to the so-called. horoscopic homes; 3) reading a horoscope, i.e. interpretation of the contents of the horoscope in ordinary language. We will first deal with the first part:

Determining the position of the planets on the ecliptic or, more precisely, the determination of the geocentric longitudes of the planets. In most questions of horoscopy, planetary latitudes can be neglected, taking them into consideration only in the question of the exact angular distance of the centre of the Sun and the centre of the planet at a time when this distance is insignificant. That is why I entitled this part of the definition of geocentric longitudes. The longitude of the Planets, as well as the "ascending and descending lunar nodes" (otherwise called the Head and Tail of the Dragon) is determined for a given moment using various astronomical tables. Equally suitable for this purpose are Nautical Almanacs, Connaissance des temps and Raphael Ephemeride. In addition to these manuals, the methods of use of which are explained in the preface to the corresponding tables, graphical methods are also conveniently used when using the manual E.C. Ephemerides

Perpetuelles (Paris, 1906). All these manuals relate the corresponding Ephemeris of planets and lunar nodes to a certain point in average astronomical time; therefore, to determine the longitude of the planets at some point, given by the civil calendar time of a certain place, it is necessary first of all to switch from the average civil time to the average astronomical time for the same place. Finally, this average time should be transferred to Greenwich or Paris, looking at the observatory for which the calendar was compiled. So, if we were interested in the longitudes of the planets for a point in time, which in St. Petersburg is defined as 9 hours. 30 min. On the morning of March 25, 1887 civil time, we must first notice that this time on the St. Petersburg astronomical calendar reads like 21 hours 30 minutes. average astronomical time on March 24 of the same year. Or, taking into account that the eastern longitude of St. Petersburg in relation to Paris is 1 hour 52 minutes 52 seconds, we will define our moment as 19 hour 37 minutes 8 sec Parisian astronomical average time on March 24, 1887. At this point, 19:00. 37 minutes 8 sec we must select planetary longitudes in the corresponding astronomical calendar or in the tables for the graphic determination of ephemeris.

Tables M. C (after appropriate amendments):

Longitude of the Moon, 12° 02 ', i.e. 12° 02' Aries
Longitude ad Moon Node, 145° 52 ', i.e., 25° 52' Leo
Longitude nish. Moon Node, 325° 52 ', i.e. 25° 52' Aquarius
Longitude of the Sun, 3° 10 ', i.e. 3 ° 10' Aries
Longitude of Mercury, 21° 40 ', i.e., 21° 40' Aries
Longitude of Venus, 29° 40 ', i.e., 29° 40' Aries
Longitude of Mars, 10° 40 ', i.e., 10° 40' Aries
Jupiter longitude, 211° 10 ', i.e. 1° 10' Scorpio
Saturn Longitude, 104° 40 ', i.e., 14° 40' Cancer

These values of longitudes are, of course, approximate, but the degree of accuracy of their determination, generally speaking, satisfies the requirements of ordinary horoscopy.
The first column shows the geocentric longitudes of the planets, and the second shows their angular distances from the radii, i.e. starting points of those Signs (or Zodiac Houses) in which they are located. The second recording scheme among astrologers is more preferable than the first. The location of the planets in the ecliptic or, more precisely, the location of the orthogonal projections of the visible places of the planets on the ecliptic, considered geocentrically, will determine the attitude of the Planets to the Signs and the relationship of the Planets themselves.

According to astrological data, the Zodiac Sign refers to the Planet, abiding in it, like a body to a soul. In other words, the sign in which not a single planet is located should manifest astrally no more intensely than the body manifests itself in the physical plane, whose astrosome has exteriorised more or less far, or even completely retreated.

You remember what was said in the Twelfth lesson about planetary houses. A planet in its zodiacal house behaves astrologically, like a soul in a suitable body, like a master in its house. A planet in a strange house feels more or less good, depending on its "friendship" or "unfriendliness" with the planet to which this sign belongs as a house. In addition to this (and sometimes in connection with this), the planet feels especially bad in the Zodiac Signs, diametrically opposed to its homes. So, for example, Mars will feel unwell in Libra and Taurus, just because it feels good in Aries and Scorpio. Saturn will be weakened in Cancer and Leo, because it is strong in Capricorn and in Aquarius. The planet's own house is called "Domicilium" in astrology; the sector opposite the home defines the Detrimentum (loss of strength) for the planet. Finding a planet in Domicilium is estimated in arithmological astrology by adding five points to it; being in Detrimentum is the same deduction.

We just mentioned the friendship and unfriendliness of the planets. In addition to the magical evaluation of friendship, already indicated by us in the seventh Arcanum, it is also necessary to remember the traditional table of the so-called astrological friendship and antagonism. Here is the contents of this table. Saturn is especially friendly with Mars and unfriendly with the Sun; Jupiter is friendly with the Moon and unfriendly with Mars; Mars is friendly with the Sun and unfriendly with Jupiter; The Sun is on friendly terms with Mars and unfriendly with Saturn; Venus is friendly with Jupiter and unfriendly with Mercury; Mercury applies to all planets; The moon is friendly with Jupiter and unfriendly with Mars.

You can see from the table that by the term "friendship" is understood something else than in Magic, namely the general nature of the applicability of the planet's house to alien planets. In addition to the planet's sympathy for certain signs that it is convenient for her to clothe herself with for astral work, Astrology distinguishes between the exaltation of the planet (exaltatio), i.e. a flash of its influence in certain degrees, and the opposite of this exaltation is the fall (casus) of the planet. So, for example, Saturn is exalted at 21° Libra and falls at 21° Aries. Exaltation and decline are evaluated by changes of four points. Each zodiacal sign contains 30°, distributed between five planets so that some degrees are favourable to one and the other to the other. These areas (terminus) strengthen the corresponding planets, arithmologically giving them two points.

Each Zodiac Sign is divided into three decans of 10°. Decans (facies) are also distributed between the planets and in some cases give them one point.

Ecliptic degrees are considered partly male, partly female, and partly neutral. The male planet in the male degree, the female in the female, and the Mercury in the male or female receive 1 point each; Mercury in a neutral degree gets two points.

From Arcanum XII you already know the distribution of signs between the four elements. Each element has three signs, so to speak, the entire triplicitas signs, and each triplicitas has three planets as overlords. The first overlord (Senior) is called diurnus; the second - at night (nocturnus); and the third has the title of "participant" (participants). Triplicitas of Fire is ruled by the Sun, Jupiter and Saturn; triplicitas of the Earth by Venus, the Moon and Mars; triplicitas of Air by Saturn, Mercury and Jupiter, triplicitas of Water - by Venus, Mars and the Moon. Finding a planet in one of the signs of its own triplicitas gives the planet three points. The planet in its own triplicitas feels as comfortable as an official in the company of colleagues in common with them. In addition to the dependence of the astral action of the planet on the Sign and the Degree in which it is located, one should take into account the relative position of the planets themselves.

Of significant importance in astrology are only the following phases of the mutual positions of two planets, which according to tradition is called the 'aspect' of the planets (aspectum), i.e. as if by the glances of one planet to another:

If the difference in the longitudes of the two planets is ± 60°, then they say that the planets are in sextile; if this difference is ± 120°, then they say that the planets are in a trine; if the difference in the longitudes of the planets is ± 90°, then the planets are squared; if the mentioned difference is ± 180°, then the planets are in opposition; if this difference = 0, then they say that the planets are in conjunction.

Trine is considered a good aspect; sextile - moderately good; opposition as evil; square - moderately bad; conjunction modifies the influence of two planets; conjunction with a good planet strengthens the good influences of this planet and weakens the bad; conunction with a bad planet weakens the good and strengthens the bad. Of the two planets, the influence of the one in which the longitude changes faster is dominant.

The aspects of the planets are calculated in two ways: They distinguish the exact aspect (aspectum particulare), i.e. approximated to 1° of the arc, and aspect aspect (aspectum elementare), i.e. aspect approaching half the sum - the so-called. orb (orbis) planets looking at each other. The orbits of Saturn and Jupiter are calculated at 9°; the orbs of Venus and Mercury - at 7°; the orbit of Mars - at 8°; the orbit of the Moon at

12°, and the orbit of the Sun at 15°. The approximate (or elementary) aspects of the planets are usually calculated by a simple combination of signs separating the planets, with an additional estimate of the orbs in case of doubt.

If the centre of the planet is less than 16 minutes from the centre of the Sun in the arc of a large circle (i.e., the shortest distance), then they say that the planet in Cazimi[57] and that the rays of the Sun exacerbate its influence, bringing it to the Earth. If the centre of the planet is more than 16' arcs from the centre of the Sun, but less than 12° of the arc, then they say that the planet is burned by the Sun, i.e. that her influence is paralysed by the sun.

At a great distance from the Sun, the planet follows the general laws of conjunction with it. The planet can be burned not only by the influence of the Sun, but also by the fact of being in longitude between 13 Libra and 9 Scorpio (this part of the ecliptic is called Via combusta).

When taking into account the forces of planetary action, a whole series of circumstances are taken into account, which we cannot talk about without expanding the overly extensive article on astrology. You will find all these details in the purest from the point of view of tradition from Fludd'a (De Astrologia - is in the French translation of Piobb, Paris 1907).

I will now turn to the description of the actual horoscopy, which I will headline:

Methods for determining the radii of horoscopic houses on the ecliptic arc

As we have already said, horoscopic predictions relate to a specific point in time, for which they determine, again according to the foregoing, the longitudes of the planets. The arrangement of the latter characterises, so to speak, the general picture of their astral influences on earthly life at the horoscopic moment. But horoscopes are made to predict the course of a particular process, for example, the course of a certain incarnation of a certain personality. Since we have chosen this particular example, we will stick to the interpretation of it alone. Having spread the circle of your interest in astrology by reading special essays on this subject, you can easily imagine by analogy all other applications of horoscope construction methods, such as the horoscope of the legal process, the

---

[57] Cazimi is an Arabian astronomical term applied to the centre of the Solar disc and used to describe a planet located within an arc of seventeen minutes (17') of the Sun's longitude or, according to other authorities, within half a degree of the Sun's centre. It is then said to be "in the heart of the Sun."

reign horoscope, the meteorological horoscope of a given day or month, the horoscope of the egregoric chain or of a historical era, etc.

The horoscope of human life is usually attributed to the time of birth. There are several reasons for this: 1) the difficulty in determining the moment of conception and the doubtfulness of the methods proposed by various astrologers to determine its moment by the horoscope of birth that has already been drawn up; 2) the importance of the very moment of birth, which determines the susceptibility of the born to living conditions in the elements from which he was previously protected by maternal influence (after all, the course of phenomena in the elements from the moment of birth of a person is closely connected with horoscopic data corresponding to this moment); 3) the difficulty of schematising, according to the duodener, the events of a complex process of two lives - the uterine and the external, about the relationship of which we know too little.

So, it's decided - we are focusing on the moment of birth. Besides the question of the moment, however, which determines the general picture of astral influences, the question of the difference in the complex of these influences for different points of the earth's surface should also be raised. The energetic effects of the light rays of the bodies on different sites will vary depending on the position of the bodies relative to the horizons of these sites. The same will be by analogy with all other rays. The ancients mainly took into account in the horoscopes the geographical longitude of the place of birth, almost neglecting the geographical latitude. This happened, probably because their life was spent on a relatively narrow strip of the globe, which did not allow the empirical determination of the shortcomings of the accepted methods. Nowadays, with the expansion of the surface, for the points of which astrological data are taken into account, one cannot be content with the so-called direct astrological sphere of the ancients with twelve horoscopic houses of 30° each. After all, the task of the horoscope is to lay down the duodener of the phases of life of the zodiac, i.e. physical plane for an individual person on the duodener of the phases of life of the whole Earth on which he embodied, i.e. simply on a geocentrically constructed ecliptic with planets positioned upon it. The duodener of human life according to the Great Law of Analogies is also depicted in a full circle of 360°. From the point of view of the interests of man himself, all twelve sectors of this circle can be considered equal to each other, just as the sectors of the Zodiac Signs are equal for the whole Earth.

This accepted, from the point of view of common earthly life we might ask whether there will also be such equal sectors of a person's private life and vice versa? That is the question. The ancients answer: "Yes, this is approximately true, but, of course, the branches of the stages of life of an individual do not coincide with the branches of life of the entire planet. The radii separating the twelve private sectors do not coincide with the radii defining the Zodiac Signs." We are more exacting than this and therefore say: "Of course, one system of borders does not coincide with another; but, in addition, there is no reason to admit in advance that the stages of the life of an individual are equal between themselves in terms of the overall life of the planet and vice versa; and therefore: if we consider the Signs of the Zodiac as 30°, then the horoscopic houses that control the phases of the life of an individual must be considered unequal to each other and some condition must be set which makes it possible to determine by calculation the position of their dividing lines in a less stereotypical fashion than was done by the Ancients[58]. "

So I have to build two spheres for the same horoscope, one straight line, according to the ancient system, the other oblique, according to the Montereggio scheme, which is now preferred by the rest.

The direct sphere is constructed as follows: calling M.S. (Medium Coeli) the intersection point of the ecliptic with the meridian of this place, take this point for the radii of the tenth house. The radii of the remaining houses are marked further 30 degrees from one another in the normal sequence of houses of the 11th, 12th, 1st, 2nd, 3rd, etc.

The radii of the first house is called Ascendens; 4th Custodian - Fundus Coeli (F.C.); 7th Custodian - Occidens. We will not give a drawing in this case - everyone will easily build it himself.

To establish a direct horoscopic sphere, it is enough to know the position of the Middle Sky (MS) on the ecliptic. But the longitude of the Mid-Sky can be easily determined if you know the right ascension of the Mid-Sky (longitude will be the hypotenuse of a spherical right triangle, in which the leg = right ascension, and the angle adjacent to the leg, = 23 ° 27'30' '). Right ascension of Mid-Sky = right ascension of the meridional plane = star time of a given place. In the horoscope example for 9 o'clock. 30 min. On the morning of March 13-25, 1887, this stellar time is calculated as follows:

---

[58] Translator's note: We wonder if it may be worth considering that very traditional societies which maintain (to a greater degree) strict boundaries which determine in some way the lives of its members, might possibly point to greater congruence between the fixed zodiacal points.

Star time at midday on January 1, 1887 = 18 hours 43 minutes
Counting of stellar time on + 24th March com years = + 5 hours. 23 minutes
21 hours 30 minutes average time pass into 21 hours 33 minutes 35 sec
45 hours 39 minutes 35 sec
- 24 hours
21 hours 39 minutes 35 sec.,

which, when converted to an arc measure, gives a numerical value of
323° 08'20' 'for a direct ascent of the Middle Sky, and approximately
326° 45' for the longitude of the Middle Sky.

So, the point of MC falls to the 27th degree of the Sign of Aquarius, the
custodian of the XIth house to the 27th degree of Pisces, the custodian of
the 12th house to the 27th degree of Aries, Ascendens to the 27th degree of
Taurus, etc.

That's how simple the so-called construction is. direct sphere.

Now I turn to the sphere of Montereggio:

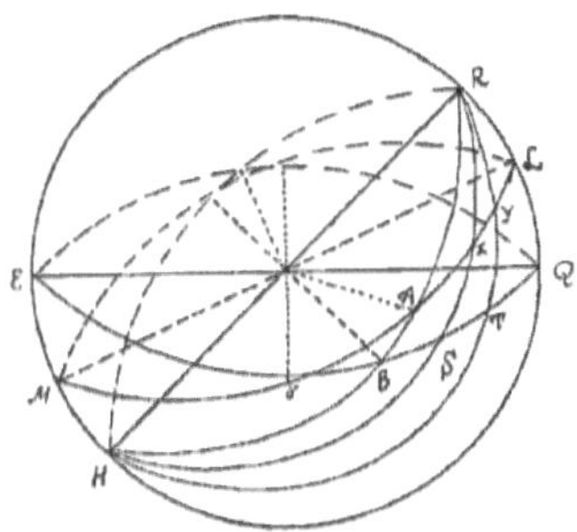

Figure 53

Let EQ be the celestial equator and ML the ecliptic; then A will be the
vernal equinox. Imagine the HR horizon of this place. Point A is one of
the points of its intersection with the ecliptic, and point B is one of the
points of its intersection with the equator. If the QLR arc belongs to the
meridian of this place, then L will be Mid-Sky, M.S. (or the Custodian
of the Xth house). Point A will be taken as Ascendants of the horoscope.
The radii of the Xth and XIIth houses are determined by the following
construction: the BQ arc is divided into three equal parts at points S and
T and then two large circles HSR and HTR are drawn. The points X and
Y of the intersection of these arcs with the ecliptic arc will be the radii of
the 12th and 11th houses.

The diametrically opposite points of the sphere will be the branches of
the 6th and 5th houses. The division of the EB arc into three equal parts
and the corresponding drawing of large circles through R, H and the

433

division points will determine the radii of the II and III houses on the ecliptic, and the points diametrically opposite to these radii will serve as the radii of the VIII and IX houses. With this construction of the astrological sphere, horoscopic houses come out not only unequal to each other, but do not even regularly alternate their radii with the radii of the zodiac houses. Two horoscopic radii can fall on one zodiac house, or two zodiac radii on one horoscopic house.

Determining the position of points X, Y, etc. comes down to either solving spherical triangles, or to applying special techniques to approximate the longitudes of these points. A rather convenient method of such approximate calculus is given by Piobb in the preface to his translation of Fludd's Astrology. By the way, we note that such approximate calculus can in particular cases lead to errors of one and a half degrees or even 2° in the position of the radius on the ecliptic. In most cases, this distorts the interpretation of the horoscope; but with dubious combinations it is better to resort to exact methods. In the horoscope, which I will analyse, the places of the radii are determined approximately. Raphael's ephemeris relieves the labour of calculating the longitudes of the radii extensions, giving them ready in special tables, embracing, unfortunately, only a region of mid-latitudes and therefore not applicable to northern Russia.

The horoscope that I will bring to your attention is calculated approximately for St. Petersburg (longitude 27° 58' from Paris; latitude 59° 46') for 9 hours. 30 min. on the morning of March 25, 1887. The radii of the houses of this horoscope are given by the following table of their longitudes:

Custodian of the Xth house, 326° 45' (or 26° 45') of Aquarius
Custodian of the XI-th house, 1° 45' (or 1° 45') Aries
Custodian of the XIIth house, 42° 45' (or 12° 45') Taurus
Custodian of the 1st house, 79° 30' (or 19° 30') Gemini
Custodian of the 2nd house, 101° 10' (or 11° 10') Cancer
Custodian of the 3rd house, 125° (or 5°) of Leo
Custod of IV house, 146° 45' (or 26° 45') Leo
Custodian of the Vth house, 181° 45' (or 1° 45') of Libra
Custodian of VI house, 222° 45' (or 12° 45') Scorpio
Custodian of the VII house, 259° 30 '(or 19° 30') Sagittarius
Custodian of the VIII-th house, 281° 10 '(or 11° 10') Capricorn
Custodian of IX house, 305° (or 5°) of Aquarius

For the convenience of recording horoscopic data, resort to one of the following two schemes; or (Fig. 9) depict horoscopic houses in equal sectors, inscribing on their radii a degree count from the radii of the corresponding Zodiac Signs, with the designation of the names of the Signs themselves and marking in the sectors the name of the planets that are located in longitude, with exact degree designations of places of the same planets in the Zodiac Signs, not forgetting to note, in sectors embracing more than one Sign, the names of the Signs lying entirely within the sector; or (damn. 10) making exactly the same notes on the squares of twelve triangles, the complex of which gives a figure called the "plan of the New Jerusalem".

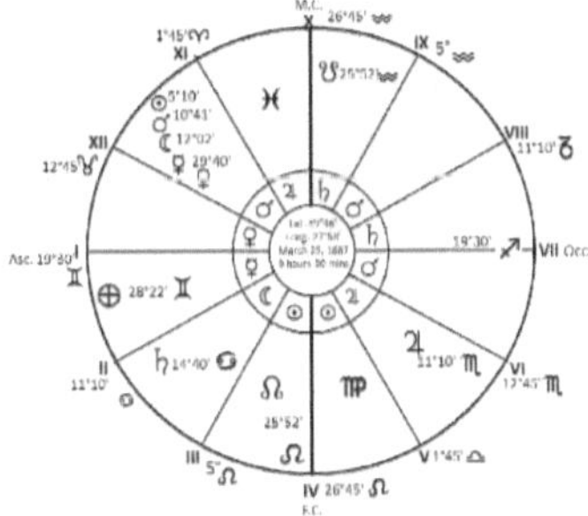

Figures 54[59] and 55

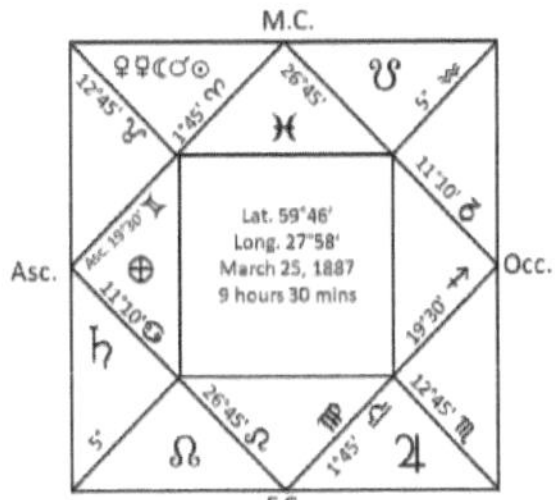

By applying one of the two schemes to the horoscope, they begin to compile a table of the aspects of the planets among themselves, as well as aspects of the planets with the most important radii of horoscopic houses. Most often, in the preliminary aspect, the radii are limited to Ascendants and the Middle of the Sky, leaving the labour of defining the remaining aspects of the planets to the radii at the times when they arise.

---

[59] Some of the figures on the original diagram were so tiny we were unable to decipher them and therefore omitted the middle circle in our version.

	♄	♃	♂	☉	♀	☿	☽	☊	☋	⊕	Asc.	M.C.	meaning
♄	–		□	□		□	□	✶	△				☌ Conjunction
♃		–			☍	☍	✶	△	△	(△)	△	△	☍ Opposition
♂	□		–	☌			☌						△ Trine
☉	□		☌	–			☌			□	□		✶ Sextile
♀		☍			–	(☌)		△	✶	✶	(✶)	✶	□ Square
☿	□	☍			(☌)	–	☌	△	✶	✶	✶	△	
☽	□	✶	☌	☌		☌	–				✶		⊕ Part of Fortune
☊	✶	△			△	△		–	☍	✶		☍	☊ North Node
☋	△	△			✶	✶		☍	–	△		☌	☋ South Node
⊕		△		□	✶	✶		✶	△	–		△	
Asc.		(△)		□	(✶)	✶	✶				–		
M.C.		△			✶	△		☍	☌	△		–	

Then, in the table of aspects, in addition to the planets is the so-called "Pars Fortunae", Part of Fortune. This is a geometric point on the ecliptic, traditionally managing the principle of luck to the owner of the horoscope. It is calculated according to the following scheme.

Ascendens longitude minus the longitude of the Pars Fortunae = longitude of the Sun minus the longitude of the Moon.

In other words, the longitude of the Pars Fortunae is obtained by adding the longitude of Ascendens to the longitude of the Moon and subtracting from the sum of the longitude of the Sun. Of course, if the difference is more than 360°, then you should throw off 360°, and if the difference is negative, then add 360°.

In our example, Ascendens longitude = 79° 30'; Longitude of the Moon = 12° 02'; and the longitude of the Sun is 3° 10'. For the longitude of the Pars Fortunae point, we have the value 88° 22', which corresponds to 28° 22' in the Sign of Gemini. By compiling a complete table of aspects (by the way, the aspects of the planets on the radii are calculated accurate to the half-orbits of the corresponding planet; the same applies to the aspects of Pars Fortunae on the planets, as well as to the aspects of the Moon Nodes), we should proceed to assess the absolute dignity of the planets in the horoscope. To do this, they are armed first with tables of the Zodiac houses of the planets, sectors of planets opposite to them, extinctions and falls, triples, terms, deans, male and female degrees, and some other other differences that we will not talk about, and take into account all these tabular data for seven planets.

In our example, Saturn has a detrimentum (- 5 points), a male degree (+ 1 point), an honorary degree (+ 1 point), which gives Saturn a total of tabular merits (- 3) points.

In the same way, Jupiter will receive 1 point for the male degree, and a small censure for the shadow degree, which as a result of the table Signs will give him slightly less than one point.

Mars table gives 5 points for Domicilium; To the Sun - 3 points for Triplicitas; Venus will receive (- 5) points for the Detrimentum, (+ 1) point for the dean, another 1 point for the female degree and praise for being close to the Taurus radius, which in general will give her more than (- 3) points of tabular advantages; The table gives nothing to Mercury; The moon will receive 2 points for the term.

To the points received by the planets for absolute dignity according to the table of degrees, more points for staying in certain houses (horoscopic) will be added. Houses 1, 4, 7 and 10 are called main (Domus cardinales); houses 2, 5, 8 and 11 are called minor (Domus succedentes); finally, houses 3, 6, 9 and 12 are tertiary (Domus cadentes). For being in the 10th or 1st house, the planet is given 5 points; for an 7, 4 or 11 house, 4 points; for the 2nd and 5th to 3 points; for being in the 12th house, the planet is reduced by 3 points; for staying in the 8th or 6th houses, considered to be especially weakening of the planet, a penalty of 4 points is due. Taking this into consideration, we will calculate 3 points for Saturn and Jupiter, and 4 points for the other five planets.

Having estimated the planets with points for dignity and for houses, it remains to take into account their strength in aspects with other planets. For connecting with the Sun, Mars and the Moon are entitled to 5 points.

For a sextile or trigon with another planet and for a quadrature with a good planet, the planets are rewarded with 3 points. For squaring or confrontation with the Sun, a deduction of 3 points would be relied on, for "distance" - a deduction of 5 points.

Now let's take into account the position of the planets on the ecliptic. Two quarters of the ecliptic adjacent to the vernal equinox are called the "rising quarters" of the ecliptic; two quarters adjacent to the summer solstice are called the "northern quarters" of the ecliptic. If a horoscope is compiled for a place in the northern hemisphere of the Earth, then the planet's location on one of the ascending quarters or on one of the northern quarters gives the planet 3 points. In our case, Mars, the Sun, the Moon, Venus and Mercury lie in the first quarter of the ecliptic, which is both ascending and northern; therefore, the aforementioned planets gain 6 more points. Saturn lies already in the second quarter of the ecliptic, northern, but not ascending; he is only entitled to 3 points. If we refuse to take into account the more subtle circumstances for the planets (direct and reverse motion, the so-called "west" and "east", etc.), then the planets in our horoscope will have the following number of points: Mars - 20 points; Moon - 17 points; The sun - 13 points; Mercury - 10 points; Jupiter - less than 4 points; Saturn - 3 points.

The owner of the entire horoscope, we can proclaim the planet Mars. The influence of the moon also greatly affects it.

Now we have to determine the so-called. "owners" (Arabic "Almuten") of individual houses of the horoscope. To do this, you must first determine to which triplicitas of the Zodiac Signs the house's radius grower belongs: to the same triplicitas it is customary to attribute the whole house. So, for example, the first house of our horoscope belongs to triplicitas Air, because its radius is in the sign of Gemini. The senior custodian of our triplicitas are Saturn, Mercury, Jupiter. They will be called the designators of the house (significant). Of these signifiers, the first (Mercury) has a domicilium in the sign of Gemini, which gives it 5 points in this house. Another signifier, Jupiter, will receive (–5) points in this house for detrimentum and at least 1 positive point for almost looking at the house's radius with an inferior trigon. Saturn has 0 points. Mercury is all the stronger in the house, still looking at him with a sextile from a strong eleventh house. If any planet were available in the very first house, it could still argue with Mercury for the primacy in the house, but with an empty house, Mercury remains its master, being included in it along with that second signifier. We will deal in the same way with the Vth house, also related to triplicitas Air (the house radius in Libra). Signifiers again Saturn, Mercury and Jupiter. But here Saturn gets 4 points for exaltation, Mercury does not get anything in the house, and Jupiter gets 4 points for being in the sign of his triplicitas, and another 5 points for being in the house itself. Venus, having the domicilium in Libra, is not even in aspect with the house, and therefore Jupiter remains the owner of the house, being at the same time listed as its third signifier.

In drawing 9 of the horoscope, in the first of the small inner circles, I have marked the signifiers of the houses (counterclockwise order), and in the smallest ring - the house owners, fluently determined by considerations similar to those just given.

Now we turn to the third part of the presentation, which we will head:

Horoscope Interpretation

In interpreting this, one must firmly remember: The values of the houses themselves in general and their signifiers in particular (sometimes the value of the signifier seems to go a little beyond their sphere of common competence at home).

To end this question, I give a complete table of the meaning of the houses, which were already mentioned in the XIIth Arcanum.

1. The first house - Vita - determines the general direction of life, a complex of astral features, an ethical worldview, a physical type. The 1st signifier controls these elements in the first third of life; the 2nd signifier controls them in the second third of life and the 3rd signifier in the third third.

2. The second house - Lucrum - determines the wealth of property, and the beginning, middle and end of life are distributed among the signifiers in the same way as in the first house.

3. The third house - Fratres - defines the attitude towards brothers and peers, with the first signifier related to the relationship to the older brothers and the fate of these brothers, the second signifier to the younger brothers, and the third corresponds to the usual movements near the permanent residence imposed on us by fate along with brothers and sisters .

4. The fourth house - Genitor - characterises parents. The first signifier of this house concerns the father, the second - the family property of the family, the third - the so-called finis rerum, i.e. end of things (understand how you want).

5. The fifth house – Nati - characterises the children and their fate, with the first signifier specifically for children, the second for the areas of affection of the owner of the horoscope, and the third for the areas of his missions.

6. The sixth house - Valetudo - deals with the health of the owner of the horoscope and its servants. Moreover, the first signifier is assigned diseases, the second - servants, the third - small pets.

7. The seventh house - Uxor - manages matrimony and some elements that are almost as inevitable as matrimony. The first signifier is dedicated to the spouse, the second to processes, the third to enemies.

8. The eighth house, Mors, manages death and what is associated with the idea of death. The first signifier is dedicated to the death conditions of the owner of the horoscope; the second is the question of traditions and relics; the third is about inheritance.

9. The ninth house - Pietas - is a rather mixed content, in which the issue of religious worldview is preferred. The first signifier is assigned to travel; the second is the field of religion; the third is the dream area.

10. Tenth House - Regnum - positions, profession, honors, etc. The first signifier is dedicated to the profession; the second to honors; the third - to the influence and fate of the mother of the owner of the horoscope.

11. The eleventh house - Benefacta - all that will be acquired by the owner of the horoscope. The first signifier is dedicated specifically to the field of acquired trust; the second to the nature of labour; the third - to the results of labour.

12. The twelfth house - Carcer - is dedicated to secret enemies, deprivation or restriction of liberty, grief and all kinds of constraints and damages. The first signifier refers to the intrigues of enemies; the second - to sorrows, overwork and imprisonment; the third - to the harm that large animals can do to the owner of the horoscope.

In addition to the meaning of houses, when interpreting a horoscope, one must also firmly remember that every planet can play two roles in a horoscope: Firstly, it is taken into account as an acting factor and secondly, it can serve as a chip that takes on the influence of other planets and radii extensions.

When taking into account the active influence of the nature of the planet as a Second Causality plays a role; the zodiac sign in which the planet is located (an instrument used by the planet); the horoscopic house in which the planet is located; the horoscopic house in which she rules as the owner.

These last two circumstances determine the sphere of life from which the influence of the planet comes; strength or weakness of the planet in the horoscope; the importance of the house in which it is located;

proximity to the middle of the sky; if the active influence of the planet is not reduced to being in the house, but to an aspect on another planet or on the house (i.e. on its radius), then the aspect is still good or bad; aspects of planets or geometric points (nodes of the Moon, Pars Fortunae) falling on our planet.

The passive role of the planet as receiving other people's influences is inherent in it when it is considered by us as the owner of a certain house or as a signifier of a certain area of this house. In this case, the nature of the planet is not taken into account. If the host planet or the planet-signifier of the house is visible in the house itself, then it plays a double role in relation to it - it is both active and passive, and then, of course, its nature is taken into account.

In the case of passivity of the planet, all the influences of planets, radii extensions and moving geometric points on it are accepted falling on the area of the house, which it is the owner, or on the area of the subdivision, to which it serves as a signifier. How to take into account the active influence of planets and points is explained above.

According to the aforesaid, let us imagine that the Sun serves as a token of the children's home (5th) or, even better, the signifier of the child's question in the woman's horoscope. Let the Moon in quadrature with the Sun look at it from the first house, and Mars and Saturn look at the Moon with trigons, and Saturn in conjunction with Mercury. Then I will say that this woman's question about children is invariably connected with difficulties in childbirth (squaring the moon, head of motherhood), depending on the characteristics of her health (the moon in the 1st house), but that she will always come out of these difficulties safely (Saturn's trigon), thanks to the ingenuity (conjunction with Mercury) of doctors, which suddenly (Mars) prompts them with convenient tricks.

If someone had the Moon served as a token of marriage and was in the Regnum house in the trigon with Jupiter, and the latter would be the master in the Lucrum house, then it could be said that the owner of the horoscope will marry a rich (favourable influence of Jupiter from the Lucrum house) bride in a business setting (Regnum houses); I would even venture to say that he embraces the boss (Jupiter).

If Mars had connected with someone to Saturn in the Mors house, and the Sun had an aspect on this house, then one could expect violent or sudden death (Mars) in a crowded assembly (Sun), fatally (Saturn) by something prepared or lite, etc.

Let us attach our general remarks to the interpretation of the 1st and 5th houses of the horoscope we cited, and confine ourselves to conclusions from general positions, without resorting to the traditional empirical, and sometimes arbitrarily set signs that overwhelmed astrology textbooks printed over the past two centuries.

First House

The owner of the house (Mercury) looks at the house with a sextile (moderately favorable aspect) from the Eleventh house (house acquired). From this (taking into consideration the nature of Mercury) I conclude: Scientific speculation is moderately favorable for the development of mental abilities (mental plane). The use of medicine in cases of health disorders is quite appropriate (astral plane). Speculation in matters of the physical plane is appropriate (material plane).

The owner of the horoscope (Mars) does not look at the owner of the house. Fate is little dependent on health and innate abilities and inclinations.

A house without planets. So, we must take into account the influence of the Sign of Gemini, in which there is a housekeeper. This sign with its motionless stars has a person in the astral plane to understand the subtleties in forms, love of arts and, in particular, music, inconsistency in tastes, ability for logical reasoning and ability to gain the respect of others; and in terms of the physical, to proportional body composition, face symmetry, stiffness and good development of the muscles of the hands in the absence of fullness and elasticity of the remaining muscles.

Pars Fortunae casts a moderately favorable aspect on the landlord. Fate is moderately favourable to the general conditions of development.

Saturn is looking at the owner of the Ist with a quadrature from the 2nd house. Poor financial circumstances can fatally affect health and well-being.

Jupiter in the 5th house and in confrontation with the owner of the 1st indicates that illegitimate children are a problem.

Venus in the 11th house in conjunction with the owner of the 1st. Cases of shared love sometimes make you feel good.

The moon in the 11th house in conjunction with the owner of the 1st. The property acquired by the mother contributes to the proper development of well-being abilities.

The good aspects of the nodes and the presence of Pars Fortunae in the house itself increase the likelihood of good influences.

Now consider the effects that fall on the signifiers of three-thirds of life.

First Signifier (Saturn) in square with Mars signifies the connections and worked out beliefs of the parents slowed down something in childhood; in square with the Sun: then the official position of the father badly influenced; in square with Mercury: childhood is far from the happiest third; in square with the moon: the position of the mother in the family and in the world did not help in childhood.

Second Signifier (Mercury) is at the same time the master of the whole house, and therefore the second third of life is characteristic; to it can be attributed all that is said about the whole house.

Third Signifier (Jupiter) is in confrontation with Venus: love can be a little embarrassing in connection with career issues and attitudes towards people, but it does not bring anything fatal, and everything works out well; in confrontation with Mercury: the general nature of inclinations and state of health moderately spoil this third of life. (Probably the consequences of fatigue and improper youth regimes.)

Fifth House

The owner of the house (Jupiter) is in the house. The happiness of the children themselves and the happiness that they bring to their father depends on the rights transferred to them and the concerns addressed to them. Now let's deal with the signifiers.

First Signifier (Saturn, children) receives four aspects, therefore that there are chances for four children; in a quadrature with Mercury, looking from the 11th house: with the first child troubles and expenses; in quadrature with the Moon: from the 2nd child, unpleasant impressions, depending on the nature of his mother; in quadrature with Mars (the owner of the horoscope): the fate of the father adversely affects the development of the 3rd child; element of the struggle in the issue of education; in quadrature with the Sun: the 4th child causes trouble on the issue of gossip and officialities.

Second Signifier (Mercury, affection): In confrontation with Jupiter, which is in the 5th house in one of the attachments, formal difficulties on the children's issue; quadrature with Saturn, located in the 2nd house: the chances of a fatal connection, bringing financial troubles; poor connection with Venus in the 11th house: the chances of love by misunderstanding; conjunction with the Moon in the 11th house: the chances of attachment in an environment suitable for the subject and, moreover, with the approval of the mother.

Third Signifier (Jupiter, missions) at the same time can be attributed to the whole house: There is in the house: the results of the mission depend on the degree of authority of the person himself; in confrontation with Venus (which is in the 11th house): missions are somewhat ruined in material terms, if an element of love is mixed with their fulfillment; in confrontation with Mercury (11th house): material calculations deviate from the desire to receive missions.

In the form of a curious contradiction to the above, it is necessary to note the favorable aspect of the Pars Fortunae point on the just dismantled house.

The essay on astrology was for the sole purpose of acquainting you with astrological terminology that has so penetrated for centuries in all branches of occultism that even a novice student cannot do without it.

Physiognomonics

The physiognomic type, meaning by this expression not only facial features, but also the impression caused by the general structure of the body and the nature of certain movements from an astrological point of view, is determined by the following circumstances, which I cite in the order of their meaning:

1. Presence in the 1st house of certain planets;
2. Kind of owner of the 1st house;
3. Natures of planets casting aspects on Ascendant;
4. Nature of the Zodiac Sign, which accounts for Ascendant;
5. Kind of Master of the entire horoscope;
6. Other horoscopic data.

In this brief essay of physiognomy, we have no opportunity to deal with the influence of the zodiac signs. We will only talk about those features (anatomical, physiological, and partly astral and mental) that are determined by planetary influences listed under numbers 1, 2, 3, and 5. These influences are always (or almost always) mixed; to talk about them, they artificially imagine seven pure planetary types, theoretically corresponding to the influence of only one planet on the subject. This is how Tradition characterises these "Planetary Types".

Saturn Type: Characteristic features of this type are: high growth; excellent development of the skeleton; pallor of the face, often taking earthy shades; dryness and roughness of the skin; black thick hair, falling out partly in adulthood, without leaving, however, bald spots and bald patches. Saturnians usually bend their knees when walking; they move slowly, lowering their gaze to the ground. The heads are elongated, with sunken cheeks, long ears, thin pointed noses and a large mouth bordered by thin lips, of which the lower one protrudes markedly. Saturnian teeth are white and short-lived; the gums are pale; the beard is black, sparse. The lower jaw is very massive and protrudes forward; Adam's apple is very developed. The chest is covered with hair; shoulders are high; hands are narrow and bony. Leg tendons and veins are very noticeable.

Saturnians are prone to movement fatigue; they are decrepit early. Of the unpleasant accidents, they are peculiar: falling with a broken bone and all sorts of dislocations. Of the diseases they are characterised by: nervous diseases, paralysis, rheumatism, diseases of the legs, teeth, ears and hemorrhoids. Saturnians are distrustful in everything; independence of judgment, with some, however, inclination towards superstition. Of the professions that suit them: classes in mathematics, law, agriculture, mining. They like black in clothes; are stingy; seek solitude and are prone to melancholy.

Jupiter Type: People of medium height with fresh, pinkish skin tone, with a good complexion, moderately full; they have large cheerful eyes, wide arched eyebrows, chestnut-colored hair, a straight nose of moderate size, a rather large mouth, fleshy lips (the upper covers the lower), large teeth (especially the incisors protrude), full cheeks, an elongated chin with a dimple, tightly fitting to the head ears, graceful and powerful neck. They are distinguished by a clear voice, a tendency to early baldness. Sweat easily (especially the forehead). They show arrogance, love for festivities, formalities, noisy feasts and conversations. Big grocery stores and drink connoisseurs; hunters before official appearances; proud and love to patronise others; when working, they always count on remuneration in one form or another. Differ in lively temperament; sometimes quick-tempered, sometimes conceited, but, in general, show kindness; value religious and family traditions, always friendly and easily make and keep friends. Typical Jupiterian diseases: A rush of blood to the brain and apoplexy strokes. Good administrators, convincing Masters of Ceremonies and good chairmen of large gatherings come out of Jupiter.

Mars Type: Martians have a height above average, a strong physique, a small wide head, a high forehead, round rosy cheeks with a dark complexion; red hair growing with a brush; large sparkling, often bloodshot eyes; whiskers darker than hair on the head; a large mouth with thin lips and a wide lower jaw; small broad teeth of a yellowish tint; strongly prominent chin, covered with a short and stiff beard; a coracoid, curved nose, small protruding ears and a very broad and prominent chest. Often have a red spot on the rise of the right leg. Their voice is commanding; cutting movements; walk in big steps; love to dress in red; characterised by fearlessness; big lovers of all weapons and all noise and din; wasteful; willingly lead a tavern life; love meat and spirits; easily offended; very annoyed; able to become furious and prone to violent acts.

Of the professions, Martians are suitable for military service, theatrical and decorative work, surgery, and fire-fighting.

Diseases inherent in them are: all kinds of inflammatory processes (most of all pneumonia; blood diseases; diseases of the cervical vessels). Due to their natural inclinations, Martians are more than other types at risk of getting wounds, concussions, etc. We have a parody of the pure type of Mars in the figure of the traditional open door.

Sun Type: People of the Solar type have a beautiful appearance, medium height, yellowish-dark complexion, lush beard, long thin, most often blond with a golden tint, hair; a low but convex forehead; large beautiful eyes with a damp sheen, expressing either the softness of character, or extreme severity; fleshy cheeks, a thin straight nose, long arched eyebrows, a medium-sized mouth, moderate lips, not quite white teeth, a round prominent chin, medium-sized ears and a long muscular neck. They are broad shoulders and distinguished by the grace of elongated limbs, in particular, very graceful thin feet. Their voice is very clear; in a gait through nobility, often along with clumsiness. The sunny type greatly appreciates the respect of others, is prone to short temper, which, however, easily dies; they seems very nice to everyone, but does not know how to make reliable friends. Men of the Solar type are often deceived by their own wives and abandoned by their own children. They love walking and reading and are religious, gullible, proud and inclined to conceit, dress is original but elegant and they like jewellery. Very prone to Occultism. By profession, they are most often inventors in the field of technology, good commentators and industrialists, and even more often - artists. Of the diseases characteristic of this type are heart disease, eye disease and heavy bleeding.

Venus Type: People of this type are very similar to Jupiterian, differing from them in their great beauty and tenderness. They typically possess whitish-pinkish transparent skin and are small in stature; distinguished by a beautiful small plump face, full cheeks with a dimple on one of them and a beautiful, albeit small, round forehead. Have magnificent eyebrows; wonderful hair of black or chestnut color, a graceful nose with a rounded tip and dilated nostrils, large, cheerful dark-colored eyes, a thick pink mouth with swelling on the right half of the lower lip, well-colored gums and white, regular-shaped teeth. Their chin is round, fat, with a dimple; ears are small and fleshy. The neck is mostly full and white. Venusians stoop, including the Venusian woman, which does not prevent them from possessing some meatiness of the breasts with their typical saggy appearance, so elegantly appearing on the ancient statues of Venus. Small legs complete the ensemble of the type that loves bright colors in clothes, preliminaries in love, etc., which does not prevent them from sometimes impeccable behaviour and even naivete. They are judged and invented by Venus best at first impression. They adore flowers and perfumes, they are lovers of fine gastronomy, in music they prefer the melody over harmony, they hate quarrels and abuse, they are distinguished by courtesy and affability; gullible to the extreme and to the extreme are compassionate and merciful. Of the diseases, venereal and female problems are assigned to this type.

Mercury Type: This type is characterised by smallness with proportional addition, something childlike in appearance, elongated with a pretty pale, slightly yellowish face, moreover, easily blushing, rich dark curly hair, soft skin, high forehead, short typical chin, covered with sparse dark vegetation, narrow long intergrowths eyebrows, sunken, restless, but penetrating eyes, a long straight nose with a rounded tip, thin lips (the upper one is thicker than the lower one and protrudes forward), miniature teeth, a mighty neck, broad shoulders, well-formed chest and a strong, but flexible spine. The bones of the arms and legs are very thin, but elegantly shaped. The voice is weak. They differ from nature by liveliness, agility, dexterity and sharpness. In circulation, the Mercury are soft; in trade, inventive of all kinds of speculation; prone to rivalry. Merry disposition; They love jokes, are distinguished by domesticity and love of lovers. By profession - speakers, professors, doctors, astrologers. Prone to doing magic. Skillfully engaged in trade. They manage well the affairs of others, but do not deserve unlimited trust. Women of this type are unlikely. They are distinguished by coquetry, precocity, cunning and a tendency to betrayal and deception. Of the pathological phenomena this type is characterised by liver and gall bladder diseases and some disorders of the nervous system.

Lunar type: This type is characterised by high growth, round, too broad in the cheekbones, head, white matte (rarely reddish) complexion, sagging muscular system. Lunar-type people, long-haired, most often blond, short-nosed, have a small mouth, thick lips, long, wide, slightly irregular yellowish teeth, pale high gums, large round transparent convex, slightly watery eyes of greenish-bluish tones, hardly noticeable, but with converging blond eyebrows, a wide fat chin, ears tightly fitting to the head, a rather long beautiful white neck, broad shoulders. The chest in men is fleshy; in women, breasts are very poorly developed. The lunar type is also characterised by a swollen belly and thin legs with knotted knees. Representatives and representatives of this type are very unstable, easily give in to moods, frivolous, are egoistic, cold, lazy, prone to melancholy, lack of love for family life and thirst for travel, mainly sea. The picture is completed by their love for drugs, constant concern for their own health, love for the fantastic in art, commitment to reading romantic literature, easy inspiration; propensity for mysticism, ability for clairvoyance, prophetic dreams; love for the use of animal magnetism and the constant search for a society of mature and experienced people. The lunar type gives many poets, many occultists of the lower degrees of Initiation, many travelers and adventurers. Meet among the representatives of high mystics. Lunar-type diseases are: dropsy, visual apparatus disorders, up to blindness; kidney and bladder disorders (of course, and the whole class of gouty diseases) and all kinds of uterine diseases.

Of course, it is rare to meet a person who fits exactly one of the types described. We almost always encounter a mixture of types but with the predominance of certain planets, the nature of which we must take into account. When deciding on the subject's abilities, on his choice of profession, etc. The occultist is most interested in knowing how the types of ability to separate branches of esotericism and a tendency to one or another of its practical applications are distributed.

At the high steps of the circle of initiates it is naturally advisable to deal with a synthetic type that has absorbed the influxes of all seven Secondary Causes and distributed them harmoniously in itself. This does not prevent us from making a few specific instructions.

Esoteric teachers need Saturn, Mercury, and Venus. Presence of the Sun is desirable: Mars is sometimes appropriate; for senior figures in Freemasonry, Jupiter, Venus and Mars are important; the magician needs Saturn, Mercury and Mars; theurgy needs the Sun and Venus; the Kabbalist theorist, as well as the cabinet astrologer, needs Saturn and Mercury; clairvoyants, psychometers, fortunetellers, etc. always have a solid moon.

For experiments with mediums, tantrums, sensitivities, etc. it is most advisable to deal with patients such as a pure mixture of Venus with the Moon, and for lack of such, a pure type of Venus. The latter are very pliable for all kinds of suggestions.

In Initiation Chains, among the representatives of the lower degrees of Initiation, there is always an abundance of young people with a predominant Lunar influence. At first they obediently obey the Teachers, make good progress, but almost always subsequently fight off the Initiation Chains due to the inherent lunar type of compliance with extraneous influences.

Regarding the pure or almost pure Solar type, I will say that Priestly studies are very suitable for him without complicating those of the Teacher.

Pure Jupiter is very suitable for studying the history of Esotericism.

Palmistry

Deus in manu omnium signa posuit, it noverint singuli opera sua

Book of Job, ch. XXXVII, v. 7

There was much debate about the translation of this text; we write "sua" from small s, which is tantamount to wanting to translate the text as follows: "God put signs on everyone's hand so that individuals can judge their own affairs." "About one's own affairs", or rather, about one's own inclinations towards affairs of a certain kind. Palmistry has the same citizenship right as other divinational methods. It developed in ancient times on a purely aristocratic basis, passed through the school in the Middle Ages, sometimes illiterate, fortunetellers and fortunetellers completely unfamiliar with astrology, who brought into it the fruits of personal intuition and popular observation; it was recognised in the 15th, 16th and 17th, centuries as Initiative Centres, which tried to carefully clean it of the crusts of superstitious arbitrariness adhering to it, without damaging its living parts; then it was somewhat abandoned by the proud metaphysicians of the 18th century, and in the second half of the 19th century it flourished again, brilliantly supplementing its composition with the fruits of the meditation of the witty Desbarolles and the scientific empiricism of the workers of the Charite hospital - Dr. Papus and Ch.I. von Chinsky.

If you do not forget that in the 60s the empirical research of captain d'Arpentigny on the so-called joined her area. chiognomony, i.e. characterisation of the general inclinations of the subject in the form of his fingers, it will be necessary to recognise the modern code of palmistry theses as a solid and noteworthy system.

Due to the history of palmistry itself, we are forced to distinguish the following parts in it:

1. Chirosophia, or the deductive part of palmistry, closely associated with the astrological and Kabbalistic worldviews and often referred to colloquially as Analytical Palmistry.
2. The traditional data, presented in the form of a bunch of separate private theses, of which the Debaroll School tried to mold a code known as Synthetic Palmistry.
3. A compilation of the latest empirical data obtained clinically and mainly related to the accurate determination of the patient's age, to which this or that event of his life should be attributed.
4. The already mentioned Chirohomonia d'Arpentigny.

In today's short essay, I only set out to characterise the content of these parts, sending listeners eager to get a detailed look at the subject to the works of Desbarolles, Papus, as well as to the excellent German Chinsky pamphlet published in Dresden and becoming a bibliographic rarity ("Das Deuten der Vergangenheit, Gegenwart und Zukunft aus den Linien der Hand ", from which we borrowed a lot from the presentation of the current XVIIth Arcanum).

Chirosophia teaches us that the horoscope of every subject is written on the palms of his hands, and the clichés of the future and the present should be read on both hands, and the cliché of the past is predominantly on the left. To characterise the subject, use both palms. We will characterise palmistically only planetary influences, leaving aside the zodiac. The effects of the planets, which we have just connected with physiognomic data, and, therefore, specially related to the 1st house, I allow myself to be called static in relation to palmistry. The rest of the planetary influences in the horoscope I will call dynamic. After that, I allow myself to say that the static in Chirosophia is determined by the so-called. "planetary hills," and dynamics — planetary lines. The bulge (very broad and fleshy), corresponding to the thumb, will be the hill of Venus. Under the index finger you will find the hill of Jupiter; under the middle finger is usually a subtle hill of Saturn; beneath the nameless finger the hill of Apollo; under the little finger is the hill of Mercury. The further bulge of the arm from the hill of Mercury down is called the hill of Mars; even lower is the hill of the moon.

If the hill is very convex, then a good planetary influence on the Ascendant of the horoscope is ensured and sufficiently isolated from impurities; if the size of the hill is much smaller than normal, then this is reflected in the lack of appropriate planetary influence; if the hill is shaded in one direction, this indicates a desire to scatter planetary influence and its abuse, which some call the "evil influence" of the planet; if the hill is shaded into a cell, then the planet is as if in captivity, and for the manifestation of its properties, the subject needs serious volitional efforts; if a planetary hill is shifted in relation to the corresponding finger, then this is taken as an indication of the official position of the shifted hill in relation to the planet of the finger to which it is moved, as well as the coloring of the work of the second planet (to which the hill is shifted) by the tone of the shifted planet: for example, Mercury, shifted to Apollo, can be understood as "science in the service of art" and as "art colored by scientific methodology"; the fusion of the hills corresponds to a combination of static planetary influences. So, for example, the merger of the hill of Jupiter with the hill of Saturn would characterise in the subject an idea of fate, inextricably linked with the idea of a successful career.

Every planetary hill has a planetary line. The line of Jupiter usually begins under the hill of Mercury, runs horizontally through the palm of your hand and most often ascends the hill of Jupiter; the Saturn line most often leaves the gap between the hill of the Moon and the hill of Venus, ascending vertically to the hill of Saturn; the Apollo line begins, generally speaking, in the same area as the Saturn line, tending almost vertically to the hill of Apollo; the line of Mercury rises on its hill parallel to the line of Apollo; line of Venus, starting at the foot of the hill of Jupiter, arcuately covers the hill of Venus; the line of Mars, starting on its hill and crossing the palm, is approaching the beginning of the line of Venus; The lunar line (or lunar lines) are outlined in short lines on Lunar Hill.

The line of Venus is otherwise called the line of life (vitalis); the line of Jupiter - the line of the heart (naturalis); the line of Mars - the line of the head (mentalis); the line of the Sun (Apollo) is called - solaris; the line of Saturn is often called the line of Fate (fatalis); line of Mercury is given the name of the hepatic or gall line (hepatica).

I have already said that these lines characterise the game of Secondary Causes in all houses of the horoscope. The Venus line is associated with the area of health and judgment on the supply of vitality; with the line of Saturn - questions of fate; with the line of Jupiter - the area of feelings, affections, etc .; with the line of Mars - the area of thinking and other functions of the central nervous system; with the Apollo line - judgments about material wealth, about productivity in art and about the height of ideals; with the line of Mercury - judgments about speculative abilities and the state of the digestive organs; Lunar lines relate to the presence of Lunar influences in general.

I will not talk about what the absence of one or more lines means. That goes without saying. I will say in passing that a doubling of the line is a direct sign of the strength of the influence, that interruptions in the lines mean sharp changes in the nature of a certain influence, or at least its situation; that islands on the line mean a bifurcation of the corresponding influences (for example, an island on the heart line - split affection; an island on the line of Mars - hysterical phenomena or frequent paralysis; an island on the line of Venus - most often headaches and neurasthenic phenomena, sometimes local anemia; an island on the line of Saturn - false, ambiguous provisions, etc.); that the points on the lines mean sudden jolts in the corresponding influences (for example, a point on the line of the heart - a sharp or sudden grief; a point on the line of Saturn is an incident that strikes with unexpectedness in the course of fate, etc.). But if the lines characterise the dynamic influences of the planets, then it is desirable to have an element that chirosophically corresponds to the idea of the aspects of the planets among themselves. Aspects on the chips of the 1st house correspond to the passage of the line along other people's hills and dashes from the line to the hills; other aspects - dashes from lines to lines.

In order to complete the general picture of chirosophic constructions, I need to say that the static influence of Venus, besides Venus hill, also belongs to the so-called "Venus ring", covering the upper hills of Saturn and Apollo in an arc. People who possess this ring are especially vividly focusing mentally on the areas they study, even if this study did not appeal to them in itself, but was a random element in their activity; in the astral region, the same people are especially passionate about all the forms in which for one reason or another their ideas are clothed; finally, physically, the possessors of the ring of Venus show finesse in the manifestations of voluptuousness.

Static Mars, in addition to Mars Hill, which determines the elements of patience in the broadest sense of the word as the so-called "passive Mars", also has the "Martian Field", the greater or lesser bulge of which characterises "Mars activity" or courage and enthusiasm. "Field of Mars" is called the middle of the palm; generally, the head line, the Apollo line and the Saturn line run along its middle parts.

It is difficult to familiarise yourself with Traditional Data in a cursory presentation. I think that you will imagine at least a distant way the structure of synthetic palmistry, if I tell you that, noting the general character of the icons found on the hand, it connects with these icons certain conclusions about the character, or an omen about the facts. Well, let's say - the cross at the beginning of the line delays its manifestations; the cross is a bad sign on a good line and a good sign on a badly formed line. The cross at the end of the line is a hint of mystical influence; a cross in the middle of the line is a temporary obstacle; a cross on a hill is a protectorate sign in the area of this hill (for example, a cross on a hill of Jupiter is a happy marriage). A star has the same meaning as a cross, but here the manifestations will be more sudden and intense (for example, a star on the hill of Apollo - the subject will suddenly get rich). Let us also say that the square in general is a sign of protection, but, in particular, the square near the line of Saturn in the Field of Mars may portend some deprivation of freedom.

The Mars line, separated from the life line and, as it were, sewn to it with small crosses, traditionally means either an eye disease or extreme recklessness in actions.

The latest empirical data obtained by clinical practice relate mainly to the so-called. the age of the lines. The fact is that on each line, depending on the general structure of the hand, determined by the intersection of the lines, it is possible to outline points corresponding to certain ages of the subject, which will allow for prediction to attribute the interpretation of planetary aspects and traditional icons to a certain age.

Say, I know that along the Saturn line the twenty-year age corresponds to the point of intersection of this line with the line of Mars, and the forty-year-old age corresponds to the point of intersection with the line of Jupiter, and at the same time I observe in my hand a break of the Saturn line with a jump to the left (to Jupiter hill) on two-thirds of the segment of the Saturn line between the two points. This gives me the right to tell the subject: "you will have an improvement in your career at the 34th year of life." For another I see a point on the line of Jupiter, exactly at the place where it intersects the Apollo line, and I predict, accordingly, heart affliction at the age of 25. The attached drawing gives a diagram of the distribution of ages along three lines, according to the teachings of the newest Paris school. The drawing is borrowed from the palmistry of Papus (figure 56).

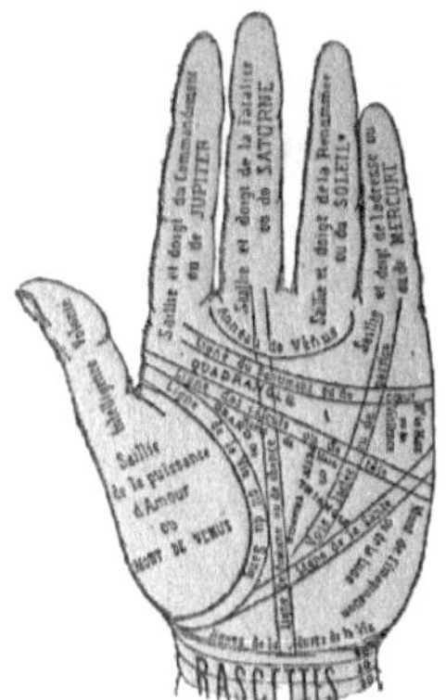

Figure 56

The Paris School judges the probable duration of human life by the arithmetic mean of the readings of three lines (Saturn, Jupiter and Mars), taking into account the age corresponding to its endpoint on each line. The ancients did otherwise. They counted the ages only along the line of Venus and gave the readings of this line decisive, but the line of Venus represents a great variety of curvature in different subjects and this makes it difficult to establish constant points. In addition, her testimony, on average, strongly contradicts empirical data, while the predictions of the Paris School are justified in 70 percent of cases.

Chirohomonomy d'Arpentigny takes as reference points for the existence of three types of finger endings: pointed type, square type and extended type; and in addition, two types of nodes found on the fingers (node on the upper joint and node on the lower joint). Combining these elements and characterizing them by the presence or absence (nodes) of various inclinations, d'Arpentigny builds a strict system, and Desbarolles expands it with chirosophical considerations. This system is very appropriate in determining the ability of children to master one or another group of knowledge.

It should be noted that the use of palmistry first of all requires that the palmist be aware of the general interests that dominate the life of the subject. If this plan is defined correctly, then all chirosophic and traditional judgments acquire amazing vitality and authenticity. That is why most prominent palmists are not limited to examining hands, but use physiognomic data and random general signs that characterise the scope of activity and the sphere of interests of the person who came to the consultation.

I will not bore the audience with reviews of phrenology, graphology, and similar systems, because I think the 17th Arcanum is sufficiently characterised by what I managed to say. Special human reading classes in nature are dedicated to whole human incarnations. Our goal is an understanding of the terminology of these special industries and a clear idea of the sources from which professionals draw their information.

END

The Symbolic Degrees Of Masonry

Journal "Isis", December 1910 and January 1911

B.M.Pryamin-Morozov

Frequent misunderstandings arising on the history of Freemasonry depend mainly on a different understanding of the word Freemasonry. Some use this word as the common name of all Secret Societies of Initiation; others understand only certain Orders that have appropriated this name to themselves by virtue of their using one or another symbolic ritual; still others advocate the restrictive use of this word to name only those associations that have kept sufficiently clean a certain number of traditional symbols handed to them by the dominant schools of the occult of one century or another.

On this basis, there are well-known debates about whether Freemasonry arose under אדם (Adam), or whether it dates back to the first century after R.H., or from the 6th of 11th or, finally, from the 17th century AD. Our article does not at all aim to embrace all these interpretations. This would require a complete overview of the history of Traditions.

We set a more modest goal to outline the emergence of those Masonic movements that owe their origin to the activities of Christian Illuminism in the 17th century.

At this time, the famous Brotherhood of the Rosicrucians was the main and central repository of dogmatic and practical esotericism in Europe. The members of this Brotherhood possessed numerous secrets in the field of Kabbalah, were diligently engaged in both speculative and practical development of these secrets, and at the same time, there was no stranger to the desire to increase their power and power in all the plans of the Universe due to the knowledge they acquired.

They considered themselves, as it were, the spirit of mankind, and their activity - the highest active manifestation of such and were right from a philosophical point of view.

Consciousness of their spiritual superiority could not completely satisfy them. It is characteristic of the spirit to manifest itself by the principle of energy that creates forms, and these forms, in turn, must manifest themselves in the material, physical world.

The Templar Order at one time suffered severely for trying to independently prove themselves in the physical world.

Taught by his bitter experience, the Rosicrucians showed themselves more cautious and, in order to realise their aspirations, resorted to creating a special association in which their formative energy should manifest itself and which, in turn, should influence the world of profane, giving rise to one or another current in it .

At the beginning of the second half of the 17th century, the Brotherhood of the Rosicrucians entrusted several of their members (of which Ashmole and Fludd are most prominent with their activities) with the creation of the Order, which has the following tasks:

Firstly, to strengthen and, if possible, widely disseminate in Mankind confidence in the Esoteric Teaching and its representatives, respect for its symbols and moral and spiritual preparation, without which it is impossible to master the foundations of Kabbalah; secondly, to ensure the storage and transfer of the elements of Symbolism in due cleanliness and integrity and thirdly, to create an environment that has been developed morally and spiritually in order to use it as a reservoir of energy to influence the Society, and in part to borrow from it future adherents of Christian Illuminism.

To create the mentioned Order, its founders resorted to the transformation of the already well-formed and having a centuries-old history of the association of the so-called free masons.

In the Middle Ages, the workshops of builders of buildings in the Gothic style were united by a common charter, legalisation, customs and hierarchy. These unifying principles later penetrated into England and spread to builders in general.

During Ashmole and Fludd, the associations of free masons consisted partly of active workers in the respective workshops, partly of workers in the field of mental and spiritual activity, likened to masons by the strength of the results and the methodical nature of their work. These workers of thought played the role of an evolutionary element in the Association.

The predominance of this element in associations was so significant that the founders of the New Order took advantage of their organisation plan, i.e. they simply created an Association consisting exclusively of masons of spirit and thought, preserving the traditional terminology of former partnerships, and introduced the majority of their symbols and customs into the ritual of the Order. Of course, all of this was given a higher, broad interpretation, moreover, different at different degrees of initiation. The new Order received the name of the Masonic.

Let us consider briefly the degrees originally created by him, explaining their Symbolism as it is possible and permissible.

There were three degrees in the English associations of free masons: apprentice, comrade, and fellow master. The transition to the senior degree from the youngest was determined by the knowledge, performance and good behavior of the mason.

The founders of Freemasonry preserved the general plan of these divisions, establishing the initial three degrees of Freemasonry - the Apprentice, Comrade and the Master - later named symbolic.

These degrees were confined to the expression of the main ideas of the so-called Gnostic teachings, reduced to the following abbreviated wording:

Nothing is going on; everything is produced (in all planes). In the process of production, an active (male, impregnating) principle (symbolism of the 1st degree), passive (female, impregnated) principle (symbolism of the 2nd degree) is involved.

The result of the production process, the idea of its product, so to speak, will form the basis of the symbolism of the 3rd degree of Freemasonry, completing the characterisation of the process.

The most ritual symbolism was chosen by the founders of the degrees so that it easily led to a number of interpretations of a more private nature than the above. Thus, people at different stages of their mental and spiritual development could interpret Masonic symbols differently, gradually approaching the worldview of their Masters.

Before considering the ritual of symbolic degrees, we give some examples of such interpretations.

You can see in three degrees the idea of dividing a sunny day into morning (student), midday (comrade) and evening with night-time (master). It is possible to see in the same degrees a hint of a periodic change of seasons: the student is spring; comrade - summer; master - autumn and winter.

It is possible to establish a correspondence between the most important phases of a plant's life and the same degrees: a student - growing grain, a friend - the flowering period, a master - growing the fruit and dropping it in order to create a further process of insemination of the soil.

Nothing impedes the alchemical interpretation of degrees: the student degree is the preparation of materials and devices for producing the philosopher's stone, the comradely degree is the control of fire, the master's degree is the process of producing the philosopher's stone.

For people familiar with the language of Hermeticism, let's say that the student's degree can be likened to completing the first quarter of a circle, a friend's degree to the second quarter, and a workshop to passing the remaining two quarters and getting acquainted with the center.

Interpretations directly imparted to those who were ordained to Freemasonry were different from those given and tended mainly to establish a correspondence between the Masonic degrees and the phases of the moral life of a person striving for self-improvement.

We proceed to consider these phases in connection with the symbolism of degrees.

The degree of the student (1646), both by the preparatory teachings and the initiation ceremony, was supposed to arouse in the initiate a mood conducive to the work of self-correction. To this extent, the freemason was supposed to feel his darkness, vices and learn to work, obey, and be silent. The initiate was led to a bed with his eyes closed (darkness); he had to step cautiously, dodging to the sides (delusions). He entered the box through blows that reminded him of the vigilant vigil, diligence, the search for truth by his own experiences. He was given, as a sign of his degree, an unpolished spatula, which he must polish (figuratively) with his own work. His task was characterised as the preparation of stone, i.e. preparing oneself for the role of a worthy and suitable leader (i.e., an active principle in the above Gnostic formulation).

The degree of a comrade (1648) introduces a freemason into the field of application of the good qualities he acquired. He is considered already to some extent ready for the well-known category of exercises, why the symbol of the Partnership is an equally trimmed stone.

The subject of his work (i.e., as it were, the passive beginning of the Gnostic formulation) is the refinement of the power of the mind, its purification from prejudice, thought, scientific pride, its accustoming to the contemplation of the Almighty. From the point of view of Occultism in general and Gnosticism in particular, this stage of the development of the Freemason with his symbolism gives hints of the existence of the astral plane[60] and the possibility of operating in it provided that sufficient activity is possessed. The area of operations itself (i.e., the passive beginning) should seem to the operator to be extremely attractive both with its novelty and with the results of work. That is why the ritual of the second degree is imprinted with joy and fun. The comrade enters the box - connected with the rest of the members by a chain of friendship. The introduction itself takes place to the sound of fun music.

The Master's degree (1649), firstly, contains symbolic indications of the product of fertilization of the Gnostic passive glow active, i.e. on the idea of life and death, and secondly, gives the key to understanding the relationship of all three degrees. This key is taught to the initiate in the form of the famous legend of Hiram and his three murderers, which we will give with sufficient completeness due to its close connection with the initiation ritual itself in the degree of the Master.

---

[60] His Masonic symbol is a flaming star.

The legend of Hiram

Solomon entrusts the construction of the Temple to Hiram, the leader of the chosen people in the amount of 30,000, managed by 300 craftsmen. Hiram divides the workers into three categories: manufacturers of metal objects, masons and carpenters. In each category there are students, comrades and craftsmen who receive different salaries.

Pupils receive their bribes from the Jachim column, comrades from the Boas column, and the masters in the middle space (i.e. between the columns).

In order to avoid fraudulent assignment by lower ranks of higher wages to three degrees, special signs, touches and words are communicated. The disciple word is Jachim, the comradely one is Boas, and the third Kabbalistic name of God, depicted by the 4 letters ה ו ה י, full of comprehensive, deepest symbolic and realization meaning, serves as the student word.

Three comrades Jubelas, Jubelos, Jubelum (conditional names and in different versions of the legend are replaced by others) are planning to master the masterful word for appropriating an improper bribe. To do this, they wait for Hiram at the three gates of the Temple at the time of his evening tour. At the South Gate of the Great Master, he meets Jubelas and demands that he reveal the masterful word under the threat of death. Hiram replies with dignity that the knowledge of this word is possible only to someone who can earn the appropriate degree with his diligence and experience in work. Jubelas strikes him with a heavy iron ruler, 24 inches long. The blow falls on the neck, Hiram retreats to the Western Gate, but there stands Jubelos, repeating the request of a friend. The architect responds with silence and receives a punch against the heart with a square.

He has the strength to reach the East Gate, where his adversary is Jubelum, killing him with a hammer blow on his forehead. The killers hide the body in the temple under a stone mass, and later, under cover of night, take it to the nearest forest, where they bury it, marking the grave with a green branch of acacia.

Solomon, worried about the disappearance of the Temple Architect, sends on the wanted list first 3 Masters, and then 9 Masters. Hiram is sought first in the Temple, then outside it. On the seventh day, his grave is marked, marked by the branch of Acacia (in some versions of the legend, the grave is recognised by the special radiance emanating from it, and the branch of Acacia relies on it by the Masters who found it). To extract the body from the grave, the king sends 15 masters and at the same time instructs them to change the master word (for fear that it was plucked from Hiram by his killers). For a new word, they should take the first of those that they will pronounce when removing the body from the grave. Having dug up the body, the masters try to touch the index and middle fingers of his hand. In this case, due to decomposition, the flesh is separated from the bones, which prompts the masters to exclaim *Mak benach* (which gives the phrase in italics in the translation; sometimes they translate - the body decays).

In most versions, this is followed by a description of Hiram's burial in the Temple in the presence of all the Masters, adorned with their cufflinks and other attributes, including white mittens indicating the innocence of the masters in the crime that happened. According to the Czar's command, a silver triangular plaque with the image of the old masterful word is laid on the coffin as a token of gratitude to the deceased for his firmness in keeping the secret.

The main killer is found thanks to the dog issuing his shelter (a cave near the source) and is killed, the other two criminals commit suicide by plunging into a quarry, over which they found refuge and the heads of the killers are delivered to Solomon. For completeness, we add that in many versions of the legend the names of the temple gates are changed, in which Hiram is hit, and, however, a mortal blow is always struck at the East Gate.

There are variations in other details of the story, which, however, does not respond to the essence of its symbolic interpretations.

Let us now say a few words about the interpretation of the legend itself. There are several of them, and the question of the ascent from gross interpretations to more subtle, is directly dependent on the individual development of the person to whom the legend is conveyed.

The simplest interpretation is social. At the very beginning of the legend, we see an explicit indication of the ideal of the social system, created by categorising the builders of the Temple.

Two ideas dominate here: 1) The social role of a person should be determined by his natural abilities (persons who process metals, masons, carpenters). 2) The hierarchical level of the employee should be determined by his knowledge and merits in the field of his specialty (students, comrades, masters).

Immediately there is an indication of the need for extreme caution when communicating to figures information revealing the general nature of their activities at the appropriate levels (passwords, signs, touches).

The dangers arising for society due to the moral imperfection of many of its leaders are indicated (conspiracy of three comrades, due to their selfish motives), as well as means to combat those (Hiram's unshakable selfless stamina and firmness).

There is a clear indication of the architect on a path that is saving for those tormented by a thirst for goods or honors (Hiram tells Jubelas at the South Gate that these benefits are achieved only through work and knowledge).

Finally, the legend tells that outraged egoism can only temporarily triumph over the deep idea that virtue in the end triumphs, and vice is always punished, and often personally carries out its punishment.

The astronomical interpretation of the legend is also not particularly difficult. It is easy to guess that we are talking about the annual cycle of the Sun, which is already in danger at the summer solstice (south gate): days (the 24-inch line symbolises the day) will begin to decrease, but the solar path can still be used wisely (the above words of Hiram to the first killer) . The autumnal equinox (West Gate) already entails numbness of nature (Hiram is silent), leading first to autumn, and then to winter. Only in the spring (East Gate) was the dead sun (struck by Hiram) reborn for a new life.

In the moral interpretation, special attention should be paid to the struggle of the spiritual light (Hiram) with its three killers (thirst for power, lies and ignorance), to nine masters symbolising the main Masonic virtues, and to the green branch of Acacia, which serves as a symbol of hope, as a connection of the visible world with the invisible (the sixth Arcanum of Tarot, corresponding to the sign ו of the Hebrew alphabet)

One cannot but mention a higher hermetic interpretation of the legend. Here, of course, the understanding of its meaning entirely depends on the degree of initiation of the person who knows her.

In any case, when trying to build such an interpretation, one should not lose sight of the fact that the Hiram legend summarises for the initiate the Great Mystery of Rota, illustrated by the circulation of a circle in the quaternary of double contrast.

We pass to the ritual of initiation into symbolic degrees. There is no need to talk much about the student and comradely degree. The general nature of their symbolism has already been elucidated at the very beginning of this article and, moreover, with the mention of some details.

We note the predominance of the number 3 (the composition of the human being) in the ritual of the student's box and the number 5 (astral operations) in the comradely (the number of steps in front of the columns, the number of lamps in the box, the number of hammer blows when tapping, the number of steps in a conditional walk corresponding to the degree, number years in the symbolic age of a Mason). We mention the cufflinks (in the student, the upper part of the cuff covers the chest; in the comrade, it is omitted; both cuffs are white).

The traditional passwords of the first two steps were Tubalcain and Schibboleth, and the traditional sacred words were Jachim and Boas.

Conventional signs were: for a student - draw along the throat with an edge of the right palm, holding the thumb at right angles to the rest; horizontally take your hand to the level of the right shoulder and then drop it along the body; for a comrade - with the fingers of his right hand make a gesture, as if ejecting a heart from his chest, and then take away and drop his hand as described above; in some boxes, the open palm of the left hand was still raised flush with the head, and then the left hand fell down along the body.

Masonic touches were performed as follows: the student, holding out his brother's hand, touched the first joint of his index finger with his fingernail, and the comrade touched the first joint of the middle finger (see Hiram's legend - lifting the body).

The interpretation of conventional signs is unlikely to complicate anyone.

Once again, recall the cash in the comradely box of the so-called A flaming star (a symbol of astral light), which is not present in the setting of the student box, and this concludes our brief comparative essay of the first two degrees.

Turning to the master's degree ritual, we begin with the decoration of the box. The whole bed is upholstered in black cloth; the platform or floor is covered with a black blanket (carpet) strewn with golden tears. In the middle of the carpet is a black coffin (foot to the east, head to the west). At the feet on the coffin lid is a dead head (skull with 2 crossbones); in their heads - a branch of acacia and a silver plaque, which was mentioned in the Legend of Hiram. The rest of the decoration of the workshop box undergoes various changes: in any case, black with gold embroideries (tears, dead heads) predominates. Three triple candlesticks at the coffin are supported by skeletons sitting on cubic stones.

The altar (in the eastern part of the box) is covered in black with tears embroidered with gold and a dead head, with silver festoons. On the altar there are three triple candlesticks in the form of dead heads.

Black paintings hang in the middle of the south and north walls of the lodge (images of a dead head with the inscription Memento mori - remember death). Between the coffin and the western wall (i.e., in the heads of the coffin) is an open compass. At the feet of the coffin (to the east) is a square (sometimes crossed compasses and a square rely on the coffin cover at his feet).

The preparation of the Comrade for admission to the Master takes place in a dark temple. Brother Ritoron visits the Companion who has retired in her twice. On his first visit, he asked the latter about the subject of his thoughts and received, "I think of death", approves the choice of this topic, and then subjects the comrade to the exam in the first two degrees of Freemasonry, accompanying the answers with his extensive and explanatory interpretations.

Ritor ends the first visit by reminding Comrade that no one knows the hour of his death and that he, perhaps, will immediately end his earthly existence. A second visit to Ritor again entails an invitation to deepen the thought into a gloomy but salvific view of death. Then the question arises as to whether only a person was born, then to disappear without a trace, or should he leave a mark on himself. Hence the transition to a reminder of the promise to follow virtues and run away from vices and to the invitation to sincerely repent.

After a long pause - the demand for a cordial confession in Hiram's murder and again an invitation to repent, after which Ritor leaves.

After a while, the introducer brother appears, sent from the Lodge, previously opened in three degrees (in the third degree, the bed opens with 9 strokes).

Returning to the Lodge, the administrator reports that the comrade has served his time, that the Masters are happy with his work, and that there are guarantors for him. To the question of the Grand Master - about the consent of the Lodge to the adoption of a new member - the masters respond with their arms extended over the sign of the Workshop.

Then the brother-introducer introduces the newcomer with his back (Hiram, entering the temple, could not foresee the danger that threatened him; this is the case with us in life).

From this moment, for the candidate for the Master, the full experience of the Legend of Hiram begins, for the greater assimilation of it.

After tapping and a second interrogation about the Comrade's readiness for admission to the Master, the Grand Master invites him to travel around the Studio Lodge.

During the trip, the brothers are standing nearby and near the tomb itself, and in the coffin under the bloodied shroud lies one of the younger masters. The second overseer orders it to be acceptable to take the end of his sword with his left hand, and he, taking his right hand, begins to travel with him (Masters travel from East to West to spread the rays of light), and when he leads him to a dead head written in the South, then stops and asks to remember death. Same thing in the North. The Great Master, with each passing passage of the initiate, says: *Remember death.*

At the end of three journeys, the seeker is placed facing the east and (by exchanging conventional signs, bows and questioning the brothers) are brought to the altar in three steps through the coffin (three directions in which Hiram wanted to leave the Temple).

In this case, the neophyte receives three blows from the brothers with paper rolled into a tube. After that, the younger master, who was lying under the shroud, quietly and whenever possible imperceptibly rises from the coffin and leaves. Meanwhile, the Grand Master, having once again reminded the initiate of the sorrows of life and the meaning of death, leads him to the oath (the right hand of the kneeling initiate touches the Gospel and the sword of the Grand Master, and the left puts the compasses on his chest). The oath concerns the secrets of Freemasonry and the promise to help the Masters against the rebellious Companions.

The initiate is lifted and taken away. The Great Master becomes between him and the altar, and with three blows of a hammer in the brow he takes him into the Master, saying: At the first stroke: "By the power given to me by power and power through my superiors, from those who rule over life and death "; at the second: "By the power of the will of all the brethren of Masters present here"; with the third: "I accept you into the Masters of this most respectable assembly."

The overseers plunge the new Master with their backs in the coffin and cover them with a shroud. There is a great silence. The Great Master strikes the hilt of the sword. Overseers respond in the same way. The brothers grab their hands crosswise and say each other the Master Word (Mak Benach) in each ear in half, and the overseers finally accept it and let the Old Master word back from them.

Following is the reading of the Legend of Hiram by Brother Secretary. At the mention in the story of touching Hiram's index finger, the 2nd overseer takes the index finger lying in the coffin and says: Jachim. At the mention of touching the middle finger, the 1st overseer does the same and says: Boas. At the mention of Hiram's rise by the hand, the Grand Master takes the candidate by the hand, accepts with a Master touch and says "Mak Benach"; at the end of the reading, the Ceremonial Brother brings the new Master to the altar (on the South side), where the Grand Master presents him with signs of dignity:

1. White leather zapon is a reward to the venerable Order rendered.
2. A blue ribbon with an ivory key (free entry into the boxes).
3. Golden shovel on a blue ribbon.
4. White mittens (purity of conscience and innocence in the killing of Hiram).
5. White female mittens - are intended for that woman to whom the Mason has the highest respect.

The symbolism of female mittens is directness, honesty and detachment in all acts of influencing the active (male) principle on the passive (attractive, female) in any plans.

Then the master of ceremonies brings the newcomer to the Altar and teaches signs, touches and words of his degree. The reader reads an explanation of the symbolism of the carpet and the box, after which the meeting closes in the reverse order of opening. The passing word in the Workshop box is Giblim; the sacred word, as you know, is Mak Benach. Of the signs, the following should be noted.

Ordinary (at a meeting) - the right hand with outstretched fingers (thumb at the level of the gastric cavity), as it were, sawing the stomach.

Then both hands are lifted behind the head with palms turned out, then fall down on the lock, as if in a sign of amazement.

The so-called Signe de detresse, which plays the role of a prayer for help addressed to the Brothers in a moment of danger: Both hands are lifted behind the head, as in the previous case, the legs are set at right angles (left to right) and an exclamation is made: *A moi, les enfants de la veuve de naphthalie!*

The touch of the custom of free masons (attouchement maconnique), not constituting the exclusive affiliation of the Master's degree, but common to all symbolic degrees. It has already been mentioned about the Student and Fellow degree.

The masters touch each other as if they are going to scratch the interlocutor's palm with their fingers.

This sign in the catechism of M. degree is also mentioned among 5 special workshop signs, which we will mention only briefly, noting in parentheses the lowest level of symbolism produced by the said catechism:

- Leg against leg (willingness to help brothers).
- Knee versus knee (duty to kneelfully ask for the brother of God's Mercy).
- Breast against breast (sincerity and fidelity of the heart, by which all brothers are obliged to each other).
- The right hand in the right hand (friendship and unity in Freemasonry).
- The left hand on the shoulder (or behind the back) of the interlocutor (the duty of a true freemason to prevent the brother from falling).

We also note the age of the Master (seven past years - sept ans et plus), master tapping (three times three hits - only nine hits), master gait (with the right foot as if stepping over the coffin, with the left foot in the same way, and again with the right foot to bring the feet closer).

A Mason, having reached the Master's degree, is considered to be already a full member of the Order and is called Gibaon, in memory of the city in which the Ark of the Covenant stood for a long time.

The sons of the Masters are named Lufton (the name of the device used to raise stones to a height during the construction of the Temple) and enjoy special privileges when entering the Masonic Lodges.
The French terms Louveton or even Louveteau (literally - a wolf cub) are distortions of this name and apply to the children of Masons and Portholes, who enjoy the right to be consecrated at the age of 17, whereas usually only adults are ordained.

Dear Unknown Friends

*I have been unable to arrest the current of the river of thought which
bears me towards mysteries*[61]

The decision to publish a new English-language translation of the Tarot
Majors course taught by Gregory Ottonovich Mebes (G.O.M.) was, like
so many things, born of both love and selfish desire – binaries I hoped to
resolve in the course of my own Great Work.
Inspired by Meditations on the Tarot (MotT), I was irresistibly drawn to
help unveil the work of the earlier Russian Master. The editor of the
Portuguese edition of G.O.M.'s work, Sociedade das Ciencias Antigas,
perhaps sums it up best:

*I am here because an unbroken stream of initiates shone a light upon the
primordial tradition and have bequeathed an extraordinary legacy I
believe is worth continuation.*

All at once a Master Mason, Magus and Mathematician (yes, there is a
key and a secret to the mother letter, 'M', as I have come to realise),
G.O.M. established an initiatory school of elite students in the volatile
environment of St Petersburg in the years preceding the Bolshevik
Revolution. It was from this fertile ground of intellectual and spiritual
striving that G.O.M. and his second wife, Maria Nesterova, taught the
secrets of Kabbalah, Rosicrucianism, Freemasonry and Occult History.
As I digested the incredible material shared in G.O.M.'s teaching on the
eleventh Arcanum, which details such momentous subjects as the Fall of
Angels and Humanity, I can only imagine the impression this might
have had on his teenaged pupils and other students of the esoteric who
gathered around G.O.M. in those days. It put me in mind of Letter XX of
MotT, where the author describes the second Akashic Chronicle as the
"Book the Soul Ate", sweet in the mouth but bitter to the stomach, with
contents so grave they are bound to leave an indelible impression upon
those who ingest them.
Both G.O.M. and MotT author, Valentin Tomberg, experienced the most
profound suffering during the course of their respective lives, between
them witnessing the brutal murder of loved ones as they lived – and in
the case of G.O.M., died - through the dark days of the Red Terror. And

---

[61] Meditations on the Tarot, Letter X, The Wheel of Fortune

yet the thoughts and words they have left for us are infused with warmth, wit and a perpetual ode to joy.

The joy which results from truth and the belief which results from joy – here is the key which opens the door to understanding the Arcanum of the world as a work of art. (MotT, p626).

In 1912 G.O.M. agreed that his disciples could publish his lecture series on the 22 Major Arcana of the Tarot as The Course of Encyclopedia of Occultism, which was largely based on instructions given by Papus, who in 1888 had founded the Rosicrucian Kabbalistic Order of the Rose Croix, the inner circle of the Martinist order, with Saint Yves d'Aldeyvre, Stanislas De Guaita and Josephin Péladan.
Encausse visited Russia three times - 1901, 1905, and 1906 – in the service of Czar Nicholas II and Czarina Alexandra, as a doctor and occult consultant, also introducing them to his countryman and fellow occultist, Maitre Philippe de Lyon (Anthelme Nizier Philippe). The Czar was then President of Russia's 'Unknown Superiors' who ran the Martinist lodges in St Petersburg[62].
G.O.M.'s knowledge of kabbalah came to far exceed that of Papus but was not necessarily fully congruent with traditional Jewish kabbalah. Nevertheless, in Kabbalah and Modernity: Interpretation, Transformations, Adaptations, editors Bo'az Hus, Marco Pasi and Kocku Von Stuckrad conclude that:

One can say without exaggeration that Mebes not only knew Hebrew well enough but was also its propagator in occultist circles.

G.O.M. viewed Hebrew as a sacred language and kabbalah formed the basis of all his occult teachings. He also believed the Russian language, with its 33 letters, to be sacred in its own right and particularly suited to esoteric work. To this arcane linguistic knowledge he introduced "elements considered Templar, and emphasised occultist suppositions about the 'bodies', claiming that 'the astral and mental bodies comprise an 'astrosome'"[63] capable of moving independently of the physical being.
The success of G.O.M.'s lecture series and publication, which quickly sold out and achieved cult status, came at a high price and in 1917 his school was forced underground by the new Soviet regime. Whilst its

---

[62] Aleister Crowley also sought an appointment at his court in 1897.

[63] The History of Occult Tarot, Ronald Decker and Michael Dummett, Duckworth Publishers, 2013

founding father would be arrested within ten years and sent to the gulag where he eventually died, the legacy of his St Petersburg school was destined to survive the Red Terror, leaving a faint but definite thread for us to follow.

I was tantalised by stories of his devoted pupils, Nina Rudnikoff and Catarina Sreznewska-Zelenzeff, escaping Russia with one of the only surviving manuscripts of the Major Arcana course and its companion study, the Minor Arcana. Created from notes made during G.O.M.'s secretive lectures and faithfully reproduced for posterity by friends who were determined to save them, the Portuguese edition became a beacon for his occult school whose light, though veiled to the English-speaking world, was undiminished.

The other esotericist who escaped from the Terror – though not before witnessing the assassination of both his parents by Soviet troops in Estonia – was of course Valentin Tomberg, whose Meditations on the Tarot was originally written in French with the date of May 21 1967 given by the author. It was translated into English by Robert Powell and published posthumously and anonymously in 1980. For more than half of my life I have been fascinated by this book, not only for the myriad esoteric and exoteric spiritual influences it so masterfully synthesises, but also for the history behind its creation and the journey taken by its author as he walked the Path of Return.

Both G.O.M and Tomberg emphasise that the Tarot Arcana constitute a complex series of spiritual exercises. More than merely books, these are plans for both active spiritual work necessitating praxis and passive work whose students must be receptive to higher subtle forces. The passive – active binaries are of course encountered many times throughout the Tarot Majors course.

Whilst both Roman Catholic and Anthroposophical readers of Meditations on the Tarot have claimed Tomberg as one of their sworn brethren, a recourse to the earlier work of G.O.M. can answer them both. The powerful influence of the St Petersburg school becomes very clear when we study the text of the G.O.M's Tarot Majors alongside Meditations on the Tarot and the two works shed crucial light upon each other.

The bright light of Tomberg's hermetic lamp, when shone directly upon G.O.M.'s study course – devised for the cream of Russia's intelligensia - can help us to properly consume and digest this challenging material.

In the final letter of MotT, The World, he reveals what readers might already have discovered from the present book, which is that G.O.M. believed the Tarot Minors actually constitute the greater of the Arcana, over and above the Majors. This strikes me as an instinctive preference for the mathematics professor, but is one which Tomberg did not share, having discovered a deeper profundity within the Majors over the course of 45 years of "effort and study":

There was a school (that of St Petersburg in the first quarter of this century) where it was taught that the so-called "Minor" Arcana of the Tarot are in reality Major Arcana in the sense that they signify a more elevated degree of knowledge and experience than that corresponding to the so-called "Major" Arcana of the Tarot.

He further explains that G.O.M. makes of the 22 Majors a "framework for an encyclopaedic teaching concerning the Cabbala, magic, astrology and alchemy", a useful means by which to teach a coherent programme of traditional occult sciences "whilst the [higher] role of the psychurgical practice was reserved for the Minor Arcana".

In Tomberg's view this is a misapplication of the Majors, which are "rather a school of meditation aiming at awakening consciousness to laws and forces". The Minor Arcana, he says, are really a systematic summary of experiences that can be gained during serious meditation upon the Majors, and in particular upon the final Arcanum, The World, as it extends across the four kabbalistic worlds of Atziluth, Briah, Yetzirah and Assiah. The 56 Minor Arcana are therefore a kabbalistic and mathematical development of the final Major Arcanum[64].

We should not therefore suppose that study of the Major Arcana has no direct theurgical potential, for *surely it does*.

---

[64] We have found it very helpful to study the Minor Arcana from the perspective of the Pythagorean Tarot developed by John Opsopaus, for its lucid numerical formulation which provides a very useful framework for grasping the overall scheme.

Index